The Complete Guide to

Sales Force Incentive Compensation

How to Design and Implement Plans That Work

**Andris A. Zoltners,
Prabhakant Sinha,
and Sally E. Lorimer**

American Management Association

New York • Atlanta • Brussels • Chicago • Mexico City • San Francisco
Shanghai • Tokyo • Toronto • Washington, D.C.

Special discounts on bulk quantities of AMACOM books are available to corporations, professional associations, and other organizations. For details, contact Special Sales Department, AMACOM, a division of American Management Association, 1601 Broadway, New York, NY 10019.
Tel.: 212-903-8316. Fax: 212-903-8083.
Website: www.amacombooks.org

This publication is designed to provide accurate and authoritative information in regard to the subject matter covered. It is sold with the understanding that the publisher is not engaged in rendering legal, accounting, or other professional service. If legal advice or other expert assistance is required, the services of a competent professional person should be sought.

Library of Congress Cataloging-in-Publication Data

Zoltners, Andris A.
    The complete guide to sales force incentive compensation : how to design and implement plans that work / Andris A. Zoltners, Prabhakant Sinha, and Sally E. Lorimer.
        p.   cm.
    Includes index.
    ISBN-10: 0-8144-7324-5
    ISBN-13: 978-0-8144-7324-5
    1. Sales personnel—Salaries, etc.   2. Incentives in industry.
3. Compensation management.   I. Sinha, Prabhakant.   II. Lorimer, Sally E.   III. Title.

HF5439.7.Z65   2006
658.3′2—dc22

                                                                                        2006012201

Printing number

10   9   8   7   6   5   4

*To Linda, Sally, and Prabha, who make writing
books easy and enjoyable.*
—AZ

*To Joe Balintfy, my teacher and mentor,
who taught me to always keep learning.*
—PS

*To my husband, Al Cotrone, and our children,
Jamie and Jack, with love.*
—SL

Contents

Preface   viii

Acknowledgments   xi

Chapter 1   Sales Force Incentive Compensation and the Successful Sales Organization

Introduction   2

The Drivers of Sales Force Compensation Change   12

The Sales Force Compensation Challenge   17

The Sales Management System   19

The Role of Incentive Compensation Within the Sales Management System   23

Diagnosing Sales Force Issues   29

How This Book Is Organized   32

Chapter 2   Reviewing a Current Incentive Compensation Plan and Setting Objectives for a New Plan

Introduction   40

Is It Really an Incentive Compensation Plan Problem?   41

An Overview of a Sales Incentive Plan Assessment Process   44

Assessment of Current Sales Compensation Plan Consequences   45

Assessment of Current Sales Compensation Plan Consistency and Compatibility   76

Developing New Plan Objectives   83

Chapter 3   Plan Design Fundamentals

Introduction   93
Sales Compensation Plan Design Terminology   94

Chapter 4   Plan Design Part 1: Determining the Correct Pay Level

Is Your Sales Force Pay Level Correct?   108
The Range of Sales Force Pay Levels   112
How to Determine the Right Sales Force Pay Level   115
Conclusion   137

Chapter 5   Plan Design Part 2: Finding the Best Salary–Incentive Mix

Introduction   141
Do You Have the Right Pay Mix?   143
The Range of Salary–Incentive Mix   151
How to Determine the Right Salary–Incentive Mix   160
A Pay Mix Scorecard   179

Chapter 6   Plan Design Part 3: Selecting Performance Measures

Are You Using the Most Appropriate Performance Measures to
   Determine Your Incentive Plan Payout?   184
Types of Measures   187
How to Determine the Most Appropriate Sales Incentive
   Measures: An Advisory   192
How to Determine the Most Appropriate Sales Incentive
   Measures: Specifics   198

Chapter 7   Plan Design Part 4: Determining the Right Performance–Payout Relationship

Introduction   226
Is the Most Appropriate Performance—Payout Relationship
   Used for Determining the Incentive Plan Payout?   227
Representing Performance—Payout Relationships   228
Decision 1: Bonus Plan or Commission Plan?   231
Decision 2: Progressive or Regressive Plan?   237
Decision 3: Caps or No Caps?   243
Decision 4: Pay from the First Dollar or from Goal or a Fraction
   of Goal?   245
Decision 5: Single Measure or Multiple Measures?   251
Concluding Insights   261

Chapter 8   Evaluating Proposed Sales Incentive Compensation Plan Alternatives and Selecting a New Plan

Introduction   265
An Overview of Candidate Sales Compensation Plan Assessment   267

Quantitative Assessment of a Candidate Sales Compensation Plan   271
Qualitative Assessment of a Candidate Sales Compensation Plan   295
Future-Proofing Assessment of a Candidate Sales Compensation
    Plan   306
Conclusion: From Objectives to Reality   308

Chapter 9   Setting Effective Goals and Objectives
Introduction   313
Are Your Sales Force Goals Appropriate?   314
Types of Goals   327
How to Set Effective Sales Force Goals: a Five Step Process   330
Tracking Performance Against Goals   369
Goal-Setting Recommendations   372
Concluding Insights   375

**Chapter 10   Increasing Sales Force Motivation Through Sales
    Contests, SPIFFs, and Recognition Programs**
Introduction   378
Sales Contests and SPIFFS   380
Recognition Programs   403
Insights   407

**Chapter 11   Making an Effective Transition with a Major
    Incentive Compensation Plan Change**
Introduction   410
Sales Incentive Compensation Plan Change and the Sales
    Management System   415
Challenging Sales Incentive Compensation Plan Transitions   421
A Sales Force Change Process Framework   435

Chapter 12   Incentive Compensation Plan Administration
Introduction   454
Is the Incentive Compensation Plan Administered Well?   458
IC Plan Administration Systems and Processes   461
How to Design an Effective IC Plan Administration System   476
Summary   489

Index   491
About the Authors   000

Preface

The use of incentives for effective sales force management is a two-edged sword. On the one side, the right incentive plan can inspire and energize a sales force to work hard to achieve challenging goals. Incentives provide salespeople, who often face rejection, with the motivation to keep going and to perform the difficult work of finding new accounts and closing sales. They also set expectations for salespeople of what is important to the company. Incentives help to hold salespeople, who often work alone and unsupervised, accountable for results. They are a powerful recognition of a sales force's efforts. Incentives are an important means through which many firms reinforce a sales-oriented culture and attract high-performing achievers to the sales job. Paying for performance helps a company hire and retain salespeople who are highly motivated to do what it takes to drive company results.

On the other side, incentives also create many sales force management challenges. Incentives can inspire mercenary, greedy sales force behaviors that create short-term sales, but conflict with long-term company success. Incentives can actually reduce motivation and lead to turnover among salespeople who feel that they are not getting as much incentive money as they deserve or who feel that others who are performing worse are making more money. Incentives also limit sales force flexibility and reduce management's ability to control the sales force through means other than money. Sales strategy changes (such as changes in customer responsibilities, product emphasis, or selling activity focus) that are in the company's best interest may meet resistance from salespeople, if they feel that the changes will reduce their personal income. Other company employees may feel that sales force incentives are excessive, thereby hindering teamwork among departments and compromising customer relationships. Finally, sales incentive programs can be costly to manage, requiring considerable investment in internal support systems and people and/or substantial fees paid to consultants.

The Complete Guide to Sales Force Incentive Compensation: How to Design and Implement Plans That Work was written to help firms harvest the positive aspects and eliminate or mitigate the negative consequences of using incentive compensation as a means of motivating salespeople. The right incentive plan, when implemented effectively, can help a firm attract and retain the best salespeople and can motivate the sales force to engage in activities and behaviors that drive sales success. On the other hand, the wrong plan or a good plan that is implemented poorly has the potential to do considerable harm. Salespeople may feel discouraged and let down. The best sales candidates may not join the company, good salespeople may leave, the sales force may not be motivated to work hard or spend time effectively, relationships with customers may suffer, and sales performance may fail to reach company expectations. With an ineffective incentive plan, the considerable money spent on incentives generates very low incremental sales.

Our goal in writing *The Complete Guide to Sales Force Incentive Compensation: How to Design and Implement Plans That Work* is to create a comprehensive and highly practical book that is unique within the compensation literature. Kash Rangan, Malcolm McNair Professor of Marketing at the Harvard Business School, sums up the book's contribution when he writes:

> "This third book in the remarkable series on sales force management provides a strategic overview as well as an in-depth guide to the subject of incentive compensation for the sales force. The book is brilliantly architected along three important dimensions for the reader. First is the strategic overview for top management provided by a compelling 3-Cs framework, which serves as the platform within which each of the twelve chapters fits. Second is the in-depth treatment of the design issues in the first half of the book. Each chapter is illustrated with problems faced by managers in a wide range of industries. The examples are crisp and the accompanying figures and descriptions make the problems come alive. The proposed solutions are nuanced and rich in detail, reflecting the deep expertise of the authors on the topic. Finally, in the last several chapters, the authors provide many practical tips and a wealth of advice on implementation issues. If your firm has significant sales force activity, this book is not just a 'must read,' it is a 'must act upon' if you want to improve your bottom line."

The book is designed as a sourcebook for sales, marketing, finance, and human resource managers and executives—anyone who is responsible for designing, implementing, and/or administering a sales incentive compensation plan. We draw on our extensive experience consulting with companies on a wide range of strategic and tactical sales force issues to position sales compensation effectively as one component of a successful sales management system and advising how to avoid the common trap of using changes in the incentive plan to fix problems that originate elsewhere within the sales management system. We use hundreds of examples and illustrations to transform complex and elusive concepts into easy-to-understand and practical ideas. We present concepts in considerable detail so that new ideas can be immediately applied by compensation plan designers. We describe numerous innovative approaches and metrics for measuring how effective the current sales compensation program has been and how effective alternative new incentive plans are likely to be if they are implemented. We emphasize implementation by sharing practical ideas for successfully making the transition to a new incentive compensation plan, for establishing efficient and effective incentive compensation plan management systems and processes, and for setting effective territory-level goals.

The Complete Guide to Sales Force Incentive Compensation: How to Design and Implement Plans That Work is part of a series of sales management reference books. The first book in the series, entitled *The Complete Guide to Accelerating Sales Force Performance* (AMACOM Books, American Management Association, 2001), presents innovative, yet practical ideas for improving sales force productivity in all areas of sales management, including sales force assessment, sizing, structuring, territory design, recruiting, training, first-line management, motivation, compensation, goal setting, precision selling, customer relationship management, performance management, and culture. Subsequent books in the series explore specific areas of sales management in greater detail. The second book, entitled *Sales Force Design for Strategic Advantage* (Palgrave/Macmillan, 2004), focuses on strategic issues of sales force planning and management, including sales strategy, go-to-market strategy, sales force structure and roles, sales force size, sales territory alignment, and sales force assessment and implementation. This third book in the series, entitled *The Complete Guide to Sales Force Incentive Compensation: How to Design and Implement Plans That Work* (AMACOM Books, American Management Association, 2006), focuses on sales force incentive compensation.

How the Book Is Organized

The Complete Guide to Sales Force Incentive Compensation: How to Design and Implement Plans That Work emphasizes four main themes:

- The *role of incentives* within the context of the sales management system (Chapter 1)
- Techniques and analytical methods for effective incentive compensation plan *assessment* (Chapters 2 and 8)
- Frameworks and approaches that enable successful incentive compensation *plan design* (Chapters 3, 4, 5, 6, 7, 9 and 10)
- Approaches for successful incentive plan *implementation* (Chapters 11 and 12)

A road map illustrating these themes is provided in Figure 1-10 at the end of Chapter 1.

Acknowledgments

As academic researchers and consultants, we have worked personally with executives, sales managers, and salespeople at hundreds of companies all over the world. Our thanks go to all the people at these fine companies who have helped us to discover and develop the material presented in this book. Because of confidentiality, many of the people and companies must remain nameless, but we owe a great deal of gratitude to all the clients who have worked with us to improve the productivity of their sales forces.

We would like to thank Northwestern University's Kellogg School of Management for providing a fertile environment for ideas to flourish. We owe our gratitude to thousands of executives and midlevel managers who have participated in the Executive Education and MBA programs at Kellogg. Our classroom interactions with these individuals have been invaluable for transforming our theories and frameworks into practical sales force management tools. We are grateful to all our colleagues at Northwestern and elsewhere who have supported us, both academically and as friends.

We would also like to thank the people of ZS Associates, the consulting firm that we founded in 1983. ZS Associates today has grown to more than 650 employees, with offices in eight countries. ZS employs some of the finest consultants and businesspeople in the world, and those people have contributed to the book immensely through their creativity as well as through their evaluation of our concepts. Special contributions came from the following people: Chad Albrecht, Chris Arzt, Vibhooti Ashar, Jaideep Bajaj, Adrian Cook, Tony Ehrbar, Ammar Feroz, Scott Fink, Jeff Gold, Kevin Josephson, Jude Konzelmann, Songjun Luo, Yogesh Madaan, Sharif Omar, Marissa Paine, Stephen Redden, Scott Shimamoto,

Nancy Smith, Marshall Solem, Joel Stevenson, Subbu Thekenkattil, Neeraj Vashisht, and Jim Wartinbee.

Thank you to our Incentive Compensation Advisory Board. This board was created for the purpose of writing this book to share best practices in the sales incentive compensation area and to brainstorm solutions to difficult compensation issues. The board members brought experience, creativity, judgment, and interesting examples of good and inappropriate incentive compensation practices. Their input and guidance strengthened the book significantly. Corporate board members include Mark Bate (MBCI/HomeCrest Cabinetry), Steve Broas (Ft. Wayne Newspaper, Inc.), John Early (Harley Davidson Financial Services), Cassandra Faurote (Roche Diagnostics), Jeff Foland (United Airlines), Peggy Forssell (Novartis Ophthalmics), Stephen Grimaldi (GE Consumer Finance), Thomas Kenney (Abbott Laboratories), Lilia Kiselev (Abbott Laboratories), Bill Kotcher (UGI/AmeriGas Propane), and Joseph Strasinger (GE Energy). Board members from ZS Associates include Chad Albrecht, Stephen Redden, Scott Shimamoto, and Marshall Solem.

We owe very special thanks to several research and editorial assistants whose work has improved the quality of the book substantially. Mary Henske (ZS Associates) carefully reviewed every chapter for clarity and content, suggesting revisions based on her extensive sales force knowledge and expertise. Linda Kluver (ZS Associates) developed many of the book's illustrations, and her careful attention to detail improved the consistency and clarity of the more than 250 figures in the book. Ramya Balasubramanian applied her outstanding research skills to discover many of the examples used throughout the book. Greg Zoltners researched and developed content as a coauthor of one of our earlier books, providing a strong foundation upon which to build the ideas for this book. Without the help of these fine collaborators, this book would not be in your hands today.

Sales Force Incentive Compensation and the Successful Sales Organization

How This Chapter Is Organized

Introduction   2

Examples of Some Common Sales Incentive Plan Design Successes
and Failures   4

    Can Incentives Encourage Effective Cross-Selling?   4

    Will Incentives Enhance the Success of a New Product
Introduction?   5

    Can Sales Contests and SPIFFs (Special Performance
Incentives for Field Force) Promote Attainment of Company
Goals?   6

    Will an Incentive Plan That Works Today Still Be Effective
Tomorrow?   6

    Is the Incentive Compensation Plan Too Complex?   7

    Does Paying Incentives on Sales Force Activity Drive the
Desired Results?   7

    Can Sales Force Pay Levels Be Reduced Successfully?   8

    Can the Impact of a New Incentive Plan Be Predicted?   9

    Is the Sales Compensation Plan Consistent with the New Sales
Strategy?   10

Why Companies Use Sales Incentives   11

    Salespeople Drive the Company's Top Line   11

    The Output of Salespeople Is Usually Measurable   11

Variable Pay Helps Ensure That Salespeople (Who Are Largely Unsupervised) Produce Results	12
Variable Pay Acknowledges a Salesperson's Success	12
The Drivers of Sales Force Compensation Change	12
The Need to Adapt	12
The Desire to Improve	15
The Sales Force Compensation Challenge	17
The Sales Management System	19
The Role of Incentive Compensation Within the Sales Management System	23
Consistency: An Upstream View	23
Compatibility: Alignment with Other Sales Force Effectiveness Drivers	24
Consequences: A Downstream View	25
How the Sales Incentive Compensation Plan Affects Salespeople	26
How the Sales Incentive Plan Affects Sales Force Activities	26
How the Sales Incentive Plan Affects Customer Results	28
How the Sales Incentive Plan Affects Company Results	28
Diagnosing Sales Force Issues	29
How This Book Is Organized	32

Introduction

Variable sales force compensation—or incentive compensation—represents a major investment for many firms. In the United States alone, companies spend $200 billion each year on variable sales force compensation—approximately as much as they spend on advertising. Almost all companies use some form of variable compensation for their sales force, including cash bonuses, commissions, trips, or other awards that are tied to the achievement of performance outcomes. The average salesperson in the United States earns approximately 40 percent of his total cash compensation through performance-based incentives. At one end of the spectrum, approximately 15 percent of salespeople do not earn any salary at all—100 percent of their income comes from variable pay that is tied to performance. A small percentage of U.S. companies pay their salespeople 100 percent salary with no incentive opportunity.

The impact of a sales force incentive program goes well beyond cost. The sales force compensation plan is an important driver of sales success. A well-designed plan that is implemented effectively helps a company attract and retain the best salespeople. It energizes salespeople, who often work alone, face frequent customer rejection, and consequently seek positive reinforcement for success. It motivates salespeople to engage in activities and behaviors that will drive high levels of customer satisfaction and good company results. An effective incentive plan can be a considerable source of sales force enthusiasm and inspiration. On the other hand, an ineffective plan can cause salespeople to feel discouraged and disengaged. If the incentive plan is not right, the best salespeople may not come to work for the company, and above-average salespeople may leave for better opportunities. Salespeople may not be motivated to work hard or may focus on the wrong customers, products, or selling activities. Even worse, salespeople may spend their time looking for ways to game the incentive plan to maximize their personal earnings, rather than acting in the company's and their customers' best interests. Relationships with customers may suffer. Sales, growth, market share, or profits may fail to reach company expectations. An inappropriate sales incentive plan, or the poor implementation of a good plan, has the potential to do considerable harm to a firm.

Lack of an Incentive Plan Hurts Retention at a Courier Company; Introducing a Plan Turns Performance Around

A small local courier service set a company objective to "grow revenues by positioning the company as the fastest, most reliable, most competitively priced courier service in the local area." Unfortunately, the sales compensation plan did not align well with this business objective. Salespeople were paid a straight salary, and good salespeople would demand raises whenever they grew their business. Many of them left the firm for competitors who offered higher pay for top performance by paying salespeople an attractive commission. Revenue growth was severely hampered by the high sales force turnover. In addition, the sales force sold too much unprofitable business, acquiring customers who were so distant from the home office that drivers were left stranded, too far away to be dispatched to another job quickly.

In an effort to fuel sales growth and improve profitability, the company changed its incentive plan. A new commission-based plan was implemented. Salespeople earned 5 percent commission on business generated within a defined geographic area close to the home office. Commission rates rose to 7 percent at $75,000 in sales and to 10 percent at $100,000 in sales. Sales jumped 130 percent after the new pay plan was instituted.

FedEx Revamps Compensation Plan to Address Sales Force and Management Concerns

In 2002, executives at shipping and logistics giant FedEx realized that they needed a new compensation plan. Both salespeople and top management had voiced significant concerns about the current pay plan. Field salespeople complained excessively to management about how confusing and unpredictable the plan was. The plan had been adjusted so many times that it had become overly complex and was no longer motivating to the sales force. At the same time, as the FedEx product line was becoming more diverse, top management felt that the current plan was not encouraging salespeople to spend their time on the right mix of products.

FedEx developed a new compensation plan to address these concerns. Salespeople were given quotas for each of the three major FedEx product lines, and certain bonuses and commissions could be earned only if the quota were achieved for all three. This made it clear to the sales force that all product lines were important, since the highest payout levels could be attained only by salespeople who did well in selling all three product lines. The new plan was supported with a comprehensive communication program that educated salespeople about the new plan and provided constant feedback on performance.

Authors' note: Tying significant payouts to achievement of multiple goals is not always a positive feature. If salespeople have unrealistic goals for even one of the product lines, the incentive plan can become demotivating. Does the company believe, for example, that for every salesperson, achieving 120 percent of goal on two product lines and 95 percent on one is worse than being at 100 percent on all three product lines?

In addition, incentive plans need to adapt to new situations over time. Plans that worked well yesterday in one environment can fail in tomorrow's context. Sales incentive compensation has high salience for sales leaders, since sales incentives have a high cost, high impact, considerable opportunity for misdirection, and the need to evolve. Designing and managing an effective sales incentive program is a complex and difficult sales management challenge.

Examples of Some Common Sales Incentive Plan Design Successes and Failures

Successful incentive compensation plan design requires a complex mixture of experience-based wisdom and analytics. Without both of these, serious mistakes are easy to make and are in fact very common. Experience enables a management team to foresee the consequences of plan features and to design a plan with longevity. Analytics provide insights regarding the likely impact of future events on sales force motivation and plan costs. Here are some examples of incentive plan design successes and mistakes that have resulted from the presence or lack of experience and analytical rigor in the incentive plan design process.

Can Incentives Encourage Effective Cross-Selling? A bank wants to encourage its tellers to upsell customers when they come into a branch location to deposit money. Tellers are offered $10 for every customer who opens an account with the bank's investment division as a result of teller referral to one of the bank's investment advisers. This incentive has almost no impact on teller behavior; the vast majority of the tellers feel that the prospect of earning a $10 reward is not worth the effort and the possible humiliation of appearing to be "pushy." In addition, the tellers do not know the investment advisers and therefore do not trust them to necessarily act in the customers' best interest.

In addition to incentives, successful implementation of cross-selling initiatives usually involves adjustments to other sales force effectiveness drivers. For example, management at Iowa-based Brenton Banks wanted to encourage successful cross-selling of banking and brokerage products and services. The banking division, which sold deposits, loans, and trust services, operated totally independently from the brokerage division, which sold investment products. A strong referral culture between the two divisions did not exist, and bankers and brokers preferred to keep their customers to themselves. Brenton's management recognized that incentives alone would not be enough to change this culture. To start, management redrew the organization chart, creating a single Brenton sales force. Bankers and brokers were given a single net income goal that was not broken down according to the old banking and brokerage divisions. Bankers and brokers met twice a week, at first to discuss their plans for the week, and later to share their best client names. Joint sales calls crossing the traditional banking and brokerage boundaries were encouraged. A training company was hired to provide training across the sales force on the full range of product offerings. In addition, the incentive plan was revamped so that bankers could receive commissions for broker product sales and brokers could receive commissions for bank product sales. The new approach, incorporating multiple sales force effectiveness driver changes, encouraged the entire sales force to be much more sales-oriented and proactive about developing leads and cross-selling.

Will Incentives Enhance the Success of a New Product Introduction? A company that currently sells one major product is launching a new product. The sales force uses a quarterly bonus plan that begins payouts at 95 percent of territory goal achievement. Historically, the vast majority of salespeople have achieved at least 95 percent of their goal each quarter. When the company adds the new product to the incentive plan, it uses the same payout schedule for the new product as for the existing product. Within two months, it is clear that the company's sales expectations for the new product are too high, with sales tracking at only 70 percent of goal. Not a single salesperson is expected to hit the 95 percent threshold. The sales force is so demotivated that it spends much less time than planned on the new product, making the problem of low sales even worse.

It is usually a mistake to treat a new product like an existing product in an incentive plan. For example, in the following year, the same company launches another new product, and this time a more appropriate incentive plan is adopted. The company realizes that the national forecast for the new product is likely to be wrong (either way too low or way too high), and the design of the new incentive plan takes this uncertainty into account. In the first quarter following launch, salespeople are paid a commission on new product sales. This rewards the sales force for early success, ensures that every salesperson is engaged, and protects the sales force and the company in the likely event of a national goal-setting error. In the second through fourth quarters following launch, commissions are paid for sales growth, thus encouraging the sales force to continue to build sales momentum and drive product success. By the second year following launch, the firm has gained considerable experience in the market, and sales become more predictable. At that point, the product is incorporated into the firm's regular quarterly quota bonus plan.

Can Sales Contests and SPIFFs (Special Performance Incentives for Field Force) Promote Attainment of Company Goals? A sales force sells two strategically important products that account for the vast majority of company sales and profits and 90 percent of the incentive plan focus. A small product that accounts for just 10 percent of target incentive pay is also sold. The small product is being largely ignored by the sales force, and so its product manager launches a sales contest for a three-month period to stimulate sales. Any salesperson who grows sales to 105 percent or more of goal during the contest period will receive a 42-inch plasma television set. The contest is a huge success for the small product, with over half of the sales force exceeding 105 percent goal attainment. However, the contest causes a significant loss of sales focus for the two strategic products. Neither core product achieves goal. Company sales and profits suffer measurably.

Effective sales contests and SPIFFs are aligned with the firm's strategic priorities. For example, a sales force that sells computer servers to medium-sized businesses becomes demotivated when it becomes clear that most salespeople will not make their territory sales goal and therefore will not make any incentive money because the firm's management has set an overly aggressive national goal for a new server line. Sales leaders do not want the sales force to abandon this strategically important new server line, and so they establish a supplemental incentive program to encourage the sales force to continue to support it. Salespeople receive a supplemental bonus of $200 to $500 per server sold (depending on the model) during the last five months of the year. The program encourages the sales force to continue selling the new product, thus strengthening the company's competitive position and enhancing the new server line's chance for future success.

Will an Incentive Plan That Works Today Still Be Effective Tomorrow? A manufacturing company has maintained the same sales compensation plan for over 30 years. The plan targets 80 percent incentives and 20 percent salary. Incentives are paid as a commission on total revenues from the first dollar, with an accelerated rate for revenues beyond goal. With this plan design, the firm's veteran salespeople earn generous commissions on the book of business they have built over the years. Management has been reluctant to change the plan, for fear of angering the salespeople who control the majority of the business. However, lately it has become increasingly difficult to recruit and hire new salespeople at the low guaranteed salary level that the firm offers. In addition, many veteran salespeople seem complacent, content to live off their earnings from existing customers and unwilling to work hard to grow sales in an increasingly competitive market. Management wonders if perhaps the time has come to revamp the sales incentive plan. Yet it fears that veteran salespeople might leave for competitors (and take accounts with them) if an incentive plan change were to reduce sales force earning power.

Effective sales incentive plans have built-in flexibility that makes them "future-proof." For example, a company launches a revolutionary new product and pays its sales force a commission on all sales. The plan rewards salespeople appropriately for their hard work to establish the product and increase sales during the first year. As the product's success grows, management can foresee that in the future, repeat sales are likely to increase substantially, and the sales job will evolve from one of driving new sales to one of retaining and servicing established customers. The company does not want its sales force to feel entitled to receive high commissions indefinitely, particularly as the sales job evolves. To encourage future management flexibility, the company establishes a hybrid plan in which bonuses are tied to goal achievement, and commissions are paid on all sales above 90 percent of goal. That way, territory goals can be adjusted appropriately as circumstances change. In addition, by changing the plan after just one year, a precedent for change is established, and future changes are likely to be accepted more readily by the sales force.

Is the Incentive Compensation Plan Too Complex? A medical equipment manufacturer has a complex sales incentive plan. The plan includes a monthly guarantee plus various commissions and bonuses. There are dozens of different commission schedules covering hundreds of products. In addition, there are bonuses for goal achievement on certain products, and numerous special bonuses and accelerators that kick in when various combinations of goals are achieved. Every salesperson has a binder of information detailing all the rules. Yet despite extensive training and documentation, most salespeople can't remember the key elements of the plan and don't seem to be responding to its numerous nuances and features. Too often, they cannot explain how their bonus was calculated.

The company decides to simplify the plan to increase sales force understanding and focus and to encourage the attainment of strategic goals. Dozens of commission schedules are condensed down to a single table:

	To Goal	Above Goal
Instruments	5%	11%
Disposables	1%	6%

In addition, there is one bonus opportunity: $50 for every competitive instrument displacement.

The new plan is summarized on a business card that fits in a salesperson's wallet.

Does Paying Incentives on Sales Force Activity Drive the Desired Results? A seller of hair care products wants to motivate greater sales force activity to drive sales results. A reward program is implemented that recognizes two salespeople each month for "touching the most customers" (including teaching customer classes, making cold calls, setting appointments, and visiting customers and prospects). At first, the program energizes the sales team and produces greater sales force activity levels, resulting in higher sales. However, several months later, sales force energy seems to have faded. Although the quantity of activities being reported is still high, sales are lagging. Management suspects that while the program has sparked an increase in the *quantity* of desirable activities, it has also triggered a decrease in the *quality* of the activity.

Paying incentives on activities, though usually not recommended, can be effective when it is used for a short period of time to encourage specific sales force behaviors. For example, experienced salespeople at a small executive-search firm are paid exclusively on commission, but new salespeople who are just learning the business earn a salary plus about 20 percent of their compensation based on achievement of activity goals. The firm's best salespeople are used as the benchmark for determining the activities that lead to sales success. Three important activities are identified and are tracked weekly: daily calls to potential job candidates, company visits, and "balls in the air," or leads that could be converted to sales. A new salesperson who meets all three of her activity goals earns $400 a month in bonuses on top of her salary. The program gives sales training more focus and new salespeople more confidence. It allows new salespeople to make a decent living while encouraging them to establish a network that will generate the referrals they will need if they are to succeed in the future. Once a new salesperson learns the business and establishes a referral network, she transitions to the firm's traditional commission plan.

Can Sales Force Pay Levels Be Reduced Successfully? A financial services firm that sells investment products to high-net-worth individuals pays its salespeople a commission on the investments they sell. Veteran salespeople who have established relationships and built their book of business earn a lot of money; about a third of them make well over $1 million a year while working a relatively low 30 to 40 hours a week. A new management team at the company feels that the sales force is overpaid. It introduces a new team-based incentive compensation plan designed to reduce the customer power of salespeople. It also cuts commission rates in half. The sales force is extremely angry. Over a two-year period, over half of the salespeople quit, taking business representing over 60 percent of the firm's assets with them.

Reducing sales force pay is always challenging and needs to be managed carefully. For example, another large financial services company has acquired a smaller brokerage firm whose sales force is paid significantly more than what salespeople at the acquiring company are making. This is due in part to the brokerage firm's rapid growth and entrepreneurial spirit. Corporate management at the acquiring company wants the compensation of the brokerage salespeople to be brought down quickly to a level more consistent with that of the rest of the company. However, the company's astute and experienced sales incentive design team advises against this strategy. A drastic pay cut would be likely to incite a large exodus of salespeople from the acquired company who control key customer relationships. If these salespeople were to leave the firm and go to work for competitors, they would certainly take many of their customers with them. The company decides to keep the brokerage incentive plan intact in the short term. Meanwhile, management focuses on learning the brokerage business and establishing additional links (besides the brokerage salespeople) between the company and key customers. Once the necessary market knowledge and customer relationships have been established, the pay reduction is implemented, with some short-term earnings protection built into the plan. Even though this prompts some brokerage salespeople to leave the firm, the company retains most of the customers, and the integration is considered a success.

Can the Impact of a New Incentive Plan Be Predicted? A sales force has a quarterly quota bonus plan for its core product lines. When a new product is launched, rather than incorporating the new product into the core incentive plan, the company develops a separate plan that pays the sales force a commission on all sales of the new product. The new product is extremely successful, and the sales force earns a lot of money selling it. In fact, commissions on the new product are so lucrative that the sales force all but abandons the firm's core products, devoting almost all its time to the new product. Core product sales suffer, along with company profits. The sales force makes too much money—people get a windfall. Finance is concerned about plan costs. Company leaders are concerned that unrealistic sales force income expectations have been established.

Thorough analytic testing of a new sales incentive plan prior to its implementation can help a firm anticipate and avoid problems like this one. Testing reveals the financial consequences of a plan under different future scenarios, allowing the firm to select a plan that consistently produces the desired results. For example, a paper company is changing its selling process to become more consultative in several important market segments. A new incentive plan is designed to accommodate the change in the selling process. There is considerable uncertainty about the motivational impact of the new plan and how much it will cost the company. The company analyzes past data to predict:

- The total cost of the new plan if the company forecast is achieved
- The total cost of the new plan if the company forecast is too high or too low
- The payout distribution across the sales force
- Which salespeople will earn more money and which ones will earn less money under the new plan
- Whether the plan pays for performance

Given the considerable uncertainty as to how well the new plan will perform, these analytics provide a significant enhancement to the wisdom of sales leaders and allow the firm to launch the new incentive plan with confidence.

Is the Sales Compensation Plan Consistent with the New Sales Strategy? In 1993, computer giant IBM redefined its sales processes and restructured its worldwide sales organization to better meet the needs of large multinational customers. The sales force, which had traditionally been structured to sell mainframes and other IBM product lines, was reorganized around customers. Senior managers became account executives for major clients in their region and could utilize a pool of regional product specialists and service reps to help them meet customer needs. Salespeople were encouraged to sell total solutions, not just products. For the largest global clients, salespeople were encouraged to develop highly customized solutions by drawing on ideas and resources from multiple countries.

Unfortunately, sales compensation was not initially included in IBM's global strategy. Incentive compensation had become a serious problem by the mid-1990s. For example, the global account manager (GAM) for Ford Motor Company closed a $7 million networking system sale to Ford's European operations. When the Ford GAM (located in Dearborn, Michigan) asked the IBM service reps in Germany (the project's headquarters) to install the system throughout Europe, he encountered resistance. Service reps earned incentives only for installations within their own country, and since 80 percent of the scheduled work was elsewhere in Europe, they were less than enthusiastic about helping out. The service reps spent three weeks negotiating with management about how they should be compensated for the work done outside Germany, instead of focusing their energy on the customer.

In 1995, IBM took on the massive project of revamping its sales incentive compensation plan to better align with the firm's global strategy. Three key priority areas were identified:

1. The existing incentive plans encouraged salespeople to think regionally, not globally; as a result, when salespeople from different countries came together to service a global client, their priorities—which were influenced by the sales incentive plan—often clashed.

2. The existing incentive plans suffered from "incentive plan obesity"—the plans were overly complex and required salespeople to worry about as many as 20 different performance measures, thus taking focus away from customers.

3. The existing incentive plans discouraged sales through partners, such as remarketers, distributors, and VARs (value-added resellers). IBM salespeople received credit for the full list price when they sold to a customer directly, but received credit for only 85 percent of list price on partner sales. Thus IBM salespeople often competed with partners selling the same IBM products.

A new worldwide sales incentive compensation solution was developed to address these issues. The new plan included a balance of worldwide consistency, with an element of local control. Some specific features of the plan included:

- Local countries could determine the frequency of incentive payouts and the split between base salary and incentive pay.

- All plans followed a worldwide framework of performance measures and were limited to a total of 10 measures to reduce plan complexity.

- In all counties, 20 percent of incentive pay was based on team performance, 60 percent was based on individual performance, and 20 percent came from challenges and contests that were set locally. The substantial team component encouraged greater cooperation across country lines.

- Salespeople received equal compensation for direct and partner sales, and the more challenging quotas required salespeople to cooperate with and encourage sales through channel partners in order to achieve quota.

Why Companies Use Sales Incentives

There are multiple characteristics of sales jobs that make it desirable to incorporate variable pay into a salesperson's total income.

Salespeople Drive the Company's Top Line. At many companies, the sales force drives the top line: A highly motivated sales force creates more sales than a less motivated one. This is especially true in selling environments with high sales force causality—where the skill, knowledge, motivation, and effort of the sales force are a significant determinant of sales. For example, in competitive markets, such as insurance sales, stock brokering, real estate, and office products, sales success depends primarily on the effectiveness of the salesperson. For many salespeople in these industries, their income is entirely variable pay. Variable pay is also used in environments with lower sales force causality, but usually as a supplement to salary. For example, in the retail health and beauty aids industry, marketing instruments such as brand name, pricing, and advertising have a larger impact on sales than the sales force does. Most salespeople in this industry receive the majority of their earnings through salary, but also earn a small variable-pay component. Variable pay is used to reward accomplishment and is very motivating when salespeople feel they can affect the outcome. When sufficient sales force causality exists, variable pay can inspire a sales force to work hard to achieve aggressive sales, growth, profit, and market share goals.

The Output of Salespeople Is Usually Measurable. Variable pay for sales forces is possible because a salesperson's output is usually measurable and comparable. Most companies track sales, costs, and other company performance metrics at the sales territory level. Territory results can be benchmarked against last year's results, territory market potential, territory goals, or national or regional averages, and sometimes even against the competition. This benchmarking allows management to measure each salesperson's performance objectively, identify those who are doing well, and assess the value that each salesperson contributes to the company.

As sales organizations become more complex, with shared responsibilities for outcomes and blurred causality across multiple members of a sales team, the role of variable pay has to evolve as well. This is a transition that firms need to manage well.

Variable Pay Helps Ensure that Salespeople (Who Are Largely Unsupervised) Produce Results. Incentive pay also helps with control and risk management. Salespeople often work alone and unsupervised. Many of them spend the vast majority of their time "on the road" visiting customers. As a result, management cannot possibly know exactly how salespeople are spending their time every day. A manager cannot look over a salesperson's shoulder and provide guidance or tell him to "get back to work." By paying for results, management gives the sales force a strong economic incentive to work hard to accomplish what is expected.

Variable Pay Acknowledges a Salesperson's Success. Many sales jobs are devoid of the supportive social interaction that comes from working with supervisors and peers on a daily basis. A salesperson's primary social contacts are with her customers. The sales job also involves considerable rejection, and in some environments, customers perceive the salesperson as intrusive. An incentive payout provides both a reward for and a measure of a salesperson's success. Incentives provide the motivation to go forth and get the next sale. The sales job attracts people who are excited by the possibility of earning high returns through incentives. Many sales jobs in the United States would not attract people with the right skills, capabilities, and instincts if compensation consisted of salary alone.

The Drivers of Sales Force Compensation Change

As markets and company strategies evolve, successful firms adapt their sales incentive compensation plans in order to ensure that sales force energy stays aligned appropriately. Most companies fine-tune their incentive compensation plans at least every year and make major changes to those plans at least every two to three years. The decision to change a sales incentive compensation plan is never taken lightly, as it can have a significant impact on customers, salespeople, and company performance.

The Need to Adapt

Constant change is both an opportunity and a threat for a sales force. On the one hand, opportunities arise when new customers emerge, helpful technologies appear, competitors go out of business, or there is innovation in the company's products and sales processes. On the other hand, threats emerge when sales strategies become dated as customers change their buying approaches, the number of competitors increases and/or existing competitors become more aggressive, radical unanticipated technologies appear, and salespeople's skills and knowledge plateau. These changes can have a significant impact on the sales force. The scope of this impact often extends beyond the sales compensation plan and can include other aspects of sales management that define the sales job and influence the salesperson.

Major events that drive sales force compensation change can be either external or internal to the company. External events include evolving customer needs, a changing competitive landscape, and environmental changes such as advancing technology, economic swings, or new government regulations. Internal events that lead to incentive plan change include the launch of new products, entry into new markets, and mergers and acquisitions. Often, major events like these require significant changes to the sales job itself. New go-to-market strategies may be needed. Sales force design may be required to change, with a new organizational structure, different sales roles, or changes in sales force size and territory alignment. The incentive compensation plan will need to adapt to all of these changes. Even in situations where the influence of major internal and external events on the sales force does not lead to significant adjustments in sales and go-to-market strategies and sales force design, the sales incentive plan may still need to evolve in order to encourage sales force behaviors that are more appropriate for new market and company conditions.

External Change Prompts an Incentive Plan Revamping at Circuit City

Prior to 2003, Circuit City had long embraced its commissioned sales force as a key point of differentiation between it and its main competitor, Best Buy. The in-store commissioned salespeople at Circuit City provided customers with service and advice regarding complex technology purchases. However, as more and more consumers began to rely on outside sources of information about technology, such as Internet research, the value added by commissioned salespeople diminished substantially. Customers no longer wanted or needed advice from a salesperson. Instead, they wanted low prices, the opportunity to browse on their own, and the chance to ask additional questions and to purchase or sign up for services. In response, Circuit City eliminated all of its 3,900 commissioned sales positions, replacing them with 2,100 new in-store associates who were paid an hourly wage. The move was projected to save the firm approximately $130 million per year.

Internal Changes at Compaq Lead to Sales Strategy Changes That Prompt an Incentive Plan Revamping

Compaq's acquisitions of Tandem Computers and Digital Equipment Corporation in 1997 and 1998, respectively, gave the Compaq sales force many new products and services to sell. This increased the complexity of the selling process and required successful salespeople to become well-rounded business advisers. As a result, Compaq revised its compensation system. In addition to receiving variable pay based on revenue growth and profitability, Compaq salespeople began to receive 20 to 40 percent of their variable pay based on the accomplishment of focused sales objectives (FSOs). The FSOs rewarded salespeople for strategic, nonrevenue accomplishments, such as engaging with a new business partner to develop a customer proposal, improving customer satisfaction, or increasing sales on a specific product line.

Reasons for Reassessing Your Sales Force Incentive Plan That Reflect the Need to Adapt to Change

When we asked this question of sales and HR managers attending our executive education course on sales force compensation at Northwestern University, we got many responses focusing on the need to adapt to change. For example:

- *"We are moving into new markets with different sales cycle times."* (Software)

- *"Our sales force has restructured due to customer consolidation and increasing demands, as well as revised stakeholder expectations."* (Chemicals)

- *"A competitor has become very aggressive. We want to elevate the importance of design wins (market share) versus revenues in our incentive plan."* (Semiconductors)

- *"The market has matured and competition has increased."* (Pharmaceuticals)

- *"Our competitors are changing their compensation plans (for salespeople). We need a plan that helps us stay in line with plans used by other sales forces."* (Food)

- *"The industry has become more competitive after deregulation."* (Petroleum)

- *"New technology—electronic inventory management—is affecting our business."* (Chemicals)

- *"Distribution channels are changing. An increase in business at large national chains, as well as through the Internet and mail order, means that more business is spanning across territory lines."* (Musical instruments)

- *"Our product portfolio and strategic focus are changing."* (Health care)

- *"We want to align our compensation plan with product marketing programs for new products."* (Telecommunications)

- *"We just merged two companies, and the new plan has not been accepted well."* (Human resource recruiting)

- *"We want to encourage cross-selling."* (Office equipment)

- *"Our plan encourages transactional selling, and we want to emphasize solution selling."* (Office products)

- *"We just started measuring profitability at the territory level. Should we pay on this instead of on revenue?"* (Transportation)

- *"We are working with an outside firm that is helping us measure customer satisfaction. Should we pay salespeople on customer satisfaction?"* (High-tech)

The Desire to Improve

Best-in-class sales forces do not wait until major market and company changes necessitate incentive plan adjustments. Successful companies are constantly looking for ways to improve, particularly in areas like incentive compensation that are closely linked to sales success.

The sales incentive plan influences the firm's ability to attract and retain good salespeople. A plan that is not competitive will not draw the best salespeople to the firm. In addition, the wrong plan may cause rainmakers to leave, while average performers stay with the company too long. Management may also improve the firm's ability to motivate and direct the activities of salespeople through the incentive plan. For example, management may feel that veteran salespeople have become complacent and are not motivated to pursue new accounts, since they can live comfortably on the high commissions they make from repeat business. Or it may feel that the sales incentive plan no longer sends a message that is consistent with company objectives. To illustrate, if the company wants to emphasize long-term relationships and customer service, but pays salespeople for short-term results, a change in the incentive plan may help the firm better achieve its goals. Sometimes management feels that a sales force compensation plan has become too complex to be motivational. One sales manager at a leading technology firm advised a new salesperson during training, "Don't worry about the compensation plan—it's so complex that it's nearly impossible to understand it. Just do your job."

Carpet Manufacturer Changes the Sales Incentive Program to Improve Profitability

When a manufacturer of residential carpeting that is sold through retailers faced declining margins, management looked to the sales incentive plan to help boost profits. Like its competitors, the company had historically paid salespeople a draw against a commission on sales. The gross margins on different carpet brands and styles ranged from 25 to 45 percent, but salespeople had little incentive to emphasize the more profitable carpets because they were paid based on sales volume alone. Management needed a plan that would encourage salespeople to emphasize the more profitable product lines, while at the same time continuing to build volume and maintain high levels of customer service.

Before changing the incentive plan, management saw that some adjustments to the firm's sales strategy were required. Greater sales force emphasis needed to be directed toward the best prospects for the higher-margin products: upscale retailers and medium-sized dealers. The sales force was trained on how to execute this new sales strategy. Next, a new sales incentive plan was designed and implemented. The new plan paid salespeople 60 percent salary plus 40 percent variable pay. The variable portion of pay included two components: a bonus for making a sales volume quota, plus a 3 percent commission on sales of "emphasis products"— the high-margin styles that management wanted to sell. The "emphasis" group was reviewed and adjusted twice a year, in alignment with the firm's existing selling seasons.

One year into the program, management proclaimed the new plan a success. Although sales volume had risen just 1 percent, sales of "emphasis" products were up 3 percent and gross margins had jumped 12 percent. In addition, sales force turnover, never high to begin with, actually declined after the new program was introduced.

Authors' note: What about doing what is best for the customer? One challenge to the long-term success of a plan that encourages salespeople to spend time on high-profit-margin products is to ensure that salespeople also continue to focus on meeting the needs of customers.

Reasons for Reassessing Your Sales Force Incentive Plan That Reflect the Desire to Improve

When we asked this question of sales and HR managers attending our executive education course on sales compensation at Northwestern University, we got many responses focusing on the desire to improve. For example:

- *"We need to better align our incentive plan with the firm's strategic initiatives."* (Not-for-profit)

- *"Too many salespeople have become comfortable with the income they earn from sales to current clients."* (Insurance)

- *"We want to eliminate loopholes and be fair and equitable to everyone in the sales force."* (Computer maintenance)

- *"We want to achieve greater differentiation between high and low performers."* (Pharmaceuticals)

- *"Our current plan focuses on financial targets, not strategic activities."* (Telecommunications)

- *"Our plan is too hard for the sales force to understand."* (Mortgage banking)

- *"Many customers are unhappy because the sales force is not meeting all their important service needs, particularly for those products that are not part of the incentive plan."* (Tools manufacturing)

- *"Too many of our best salespeople are being lured to the competition."* (Health care)

- *"Our top performers 'max out' and quit, while low performers stay too long."* (Building products)

- *"We need a plan that ties our labor costs more directly to sales."* (Medical instruments)

- *"We want to make our plan more aggressive."* (Educational testing)

- *"We want to make the plan more consistent with our corporate culture."* (Software)

The Sales Force Compensation Challenge

Designing and implementing an effective sales incentive compensation plan is a sizable management challenge. The impact of the sales incentive plan can be significant, and the forces at work can be subtle. Sales force compensation dynamics can be understood through the framework shown in Figure 1-1.

Three major constituents are affected by the compensation plan: the company, the sales force, and the customer. These three constituents make decisions and see results. The *company* decides upon a compensation plan. The *sales force* decides how it will spend its time. Although numerous factors affect the salesperson's choice of activities, the compensation plan has a significant influence. The *customer* decides if she wants to buy the company's products or services. Although many factors influence customer purchase decisions, the sales compensation plan affects the relationship between salespeople and customers and therefore affects customer satisfaction and purchasing.

It is important to note that the company can decide upon only the plan. The other two decisions, sales force activities and customer purchasing, are not under its direct control, although they are influenced by the compensation plan selected.

Since each stakeholder has a different perspective, each one looks for different results. Customers want their needs to be met. They want a good product at a fair price along with the appropriate mixture of advice, service, and support through an effective working relationship with the selling company. Salespeople want good

Figure 1-1. A compensation framework.

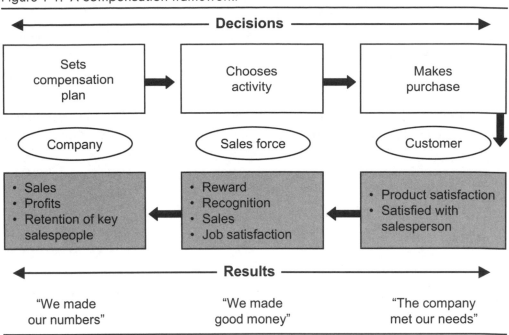

pay, recognition, and job satisfaction. The company wants to make its numbers, which may include goals for sales, profits, growth, or market share.

Anticipated results shape the decisions of the three constituents. Customers make their purchase decision based on the degree to which they expect their needs to be met. Salespeople make their time allocation decision based on how well they believe that different activities will create the results they desire. The company makes its incentive plan decision based on a plan's projected impact on important company metrics. A thorough assessment of this impact requires an understanding of how the incentive plan affects the decisions of both customers and salespeople.

It is a challenge to create an incentive plan that meets the needs of all three constituents concurrently. To be effective, incentive plans need to be simple. But in an increasingly complex world, it becomes harder and harder for a company to distill the key messages that it wants to send to the sales force into a simple incentive plan. The best incentive plan from the customers' perspective is one that encourages salespeople to engage in behaviors that meet customer needs. Customers also want a plan that allows the firm to offer reasonable prices. The best plan from a salesperson's perspective is one that is easy to understand, is fair, and pays good money for reasonable work. The best plan from a company standpoint is one that produces the desired results, retains good salespeople, and helps the firm accomplish its corporate objectives. An effective compensation plan successfully balances these sometimes competing objectives to meet the needs of customers, salespeople, and the company simultaneously.

Balancing Customer, Employee, and Company Objectives at US West

When workers at communications giant US West went on strike in August of 1998, the firm's pay-for-performance incentive plan was one of the major issues in contention. Customer service representatives at US West earned variable pay for selling extra services to customers, as well as for servicing customers quickly. Workers argued that this plan was simply a way to speed them up, and was designed more to enhance company revenues than to improve customer service. While revenues generated and speed of service are easily tracked and measured, they are not necessarily integral to providing the type of service that customers really need. Management argued that speedy service was, in fact, one of several things that customers value. The union was not very successful in its quest to eliminate the incentive program. Management did agree to make the plan voluntary for some workers, and also gave the union more say in the plan's design and implementation.

The Sales Management System

Sales compensation is just one component of an effective sales management system. It is not possible to successfully diagnose sales compensation problems and develop effective solutions without understanding the entire sales management system and the role of the incentive compensation plan within this system. Often, companies blame their problems on the compensation plan when, in fact, the true source of the problems lies elsewhere within the sales management system.

Figure 1-2 shows a framework that includes the five major components of the sales management system. The framework is a causal model in that the components affect one another in a sequential fashion. For example, *sales force activities* affect *customer results*, and *customer results* have an impact on *company results*. Meanwhile, the skills, capabilities, values, and motivation of the *salespeople* drive their behavior and activities. Finally, every selling organization needs to make a

Figure 1-2. A sales management system framework.

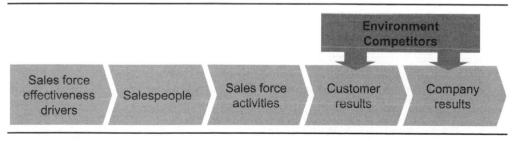

set of fundamental decisions that affect the salespeople, and in turn the sales force activities, customer results, and company results. These fundamental decisions are called the *sales force effectiveness drivers*. Sales compensation is just one of these drivers.

Each of the five components of the sales management system is described here, moving from right to left in the framework.

Company results, such as sales, profits, and market share, are outputs of the system. These are the metrics that the company uses to evaluate its performance. A well-honed selling organization helps the company achieve its financial objectives. Company results can be measured in terms of absolute levels, percent of goal attainment, or growth over last year. It is useful to evaluate these statistics from both a short-term and a long-term perspective, because sales force decisions affect both time frames.

Customer results drive company results. Customers buy consistently from companies that they trust. Sales forces that have high customer satisfaction ratings, high customer retention, and high repeat rates will usually have higher sales, profits, and market share.

It should be noted that the sales force is not the only variable that affects customer and company results. Other parts of a company, such as the marketing department, research and development, and finance, may also touch customers and affect sales. Environmental factors and competitive activity also affect customer and company results.

Sales force activities create customer results. Salespeople bring life to the sales process by executing activities such as lead generation, needs analysis, solution development, proposal presentation, negotiation, installation, customer service, and account maintenance and expansion.

Salespeople determine sales force activities. Competent, motivated people working in a "success" culture demonstrate the right behaviors and engage in the right activities.

Sales force effectiveness drivers are at the root of the causal model. They are the basic decisions that sales leaders make and the processes they use that directly determine the composition of the sales job and the personality and behavior of the selling team. Sales compensation is one of these decisions. Sales force effectiveness driver decisions ultimately affect all subsequent components of the sales management system. The sales force effectiveness drivers are developed in Figure 1-3.

The sales force effectiveness drivers can be organized into five main categories. The *Definers* include all of the decisions that define the sales job. Three major types of decisions are included in this category:

- *Sales strategy:* specification of a customer segmentation (whom will we sell to?), a customer offering (what will we sell?), and a sales process (how will we sell?)

- *Go-to-market strategy:* definition of the marketing channels, including the sales force, that will be used to carry out the sales strategy

Figure 1-3. A sales management system framework: the sales force effectiveness drivers.

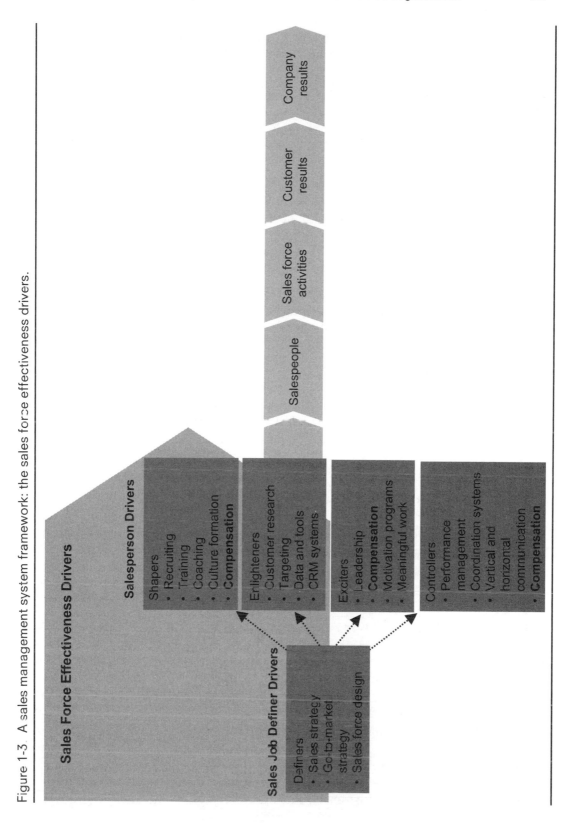

- *Sales force design:* development of organization structure, sales roles, sales force size, and sales territory alignment

Our 2004 book, *Sales Force Design for Strategic Advantage,* focuses exclusively on the sales force definers.

The remaining four categories of sales force effectiveness drivers contain the decisions that influence the salesperson. The categories are:

- *Shapers.* The processes that shape the skills, capabilities, and values of the sales team, including strategies for culture formation; processes for hiring, training, and coaching salespeople; and processes for hiring and developing the management team. Sales compensation plays an indirect role in shaping the sales force, as it influences what type of person is attracted to the sales job and helps to shape the sales force culture.

- *Enlighteners.* The processes that provide the sales force with customer insight, enabling salespeople to understand the marketplace, prioritize opportunities, solve customer problems, and use their time more effectively. Customer research, targeting, product prioritization, sales process design, CRM, and account planning are programs that fall into this category.

- *Exciters.* The decisions and programs that affect the selling organization's inspiration and motivation, including how sales leaders inspire, the fulfilling nature of the work, and motivational programs. The sales compensation plan has a major influence within the exciter category of drivers.

- *Controllers.* The systems that manage performance by defining success, setting expectations, and tracking performance. Sales compensation can also play a role in controlling the sales force. For example, by paying a higher commission rate on sales of the most profitable product lines or by paying a bonus for sales to strategically important customers, the company encourages sales force behaviors that are aligned with firm objectives.

The drivers are presented here in categories with clean lines of causality, but in reality the influence of each driver may cut across categories. For example, coaching has been placed in the shaper category, but it also has an element of control. Similarly, communication has been placed in the controller category, but it also can enlighten a salesperson. Compensation is the only driver that has been placed in multiple categories within the framework, since it is the focus of this book.

All of the sales force effectiveness drivers have consequences for the downstream components of the sales management system: salespeople, sales force activities, customer results, and company results. If the driver decisions are made correctly, the sales force is much more likely to be successful. Salespeople will be of top quality and will work within a success culture. The sales force will perform the right activities to satisfy customers. The firm's strategic and financial objectives are much more likely to be achieved when a management team makes smart sales force driver decisions and implements them well.

The Role of Incentive Compensation Within the Sales Management System

As a salesperson driver, compensation falls in the middle of the causal stream of the sales management system (see Figure 1-3). Effective sales compensation decisions are aligned appropriately with the upstream (sales job definer drivers) and downstream (salespeople, activities, customer results, and company results) components of this system. The "3 Cs" approach illustrated in Figure 1-4 shows the importance of this alignment:

- *Consistency.* The incentive compensation plan should be *consistent* with corporate and marketing strategies and with the firm's upstream decisions (sales strategy, go-to-market strategy, and sales force design) that define the sales job.

- *Compatibility:* The incentive compensation plan should be *compatible* with other salesperson-focused effectiveness drivers (such as hiring and training programs, performance management systems, sales force motivators, and the sales force culture).

- *Consequences:* The incentive compensation plan, jointly with the other sales force effectiveness drivers, should produce the desired *consequences* for the downstream components of the system (salespeople, sales force activities, and customer and company results).

Further insights regarding the consistency, compatibility, and consequences of sales incentive compensation decisions are provided here.

Consistency: An Upstream View

The sales force effectiveness driver decisions follow a natural sequence. Decisions about the leftmost category of sales force effectiveness drivers (see Figure 1-3),

Figure 1-4. The 3 Cs approach to understanding the role of sales incentive compensation.

definers, such as sales strategy, go-to-market strategy, and sales force design, pre-cede decisions about the other sales force effectiveness drivers, including the sales compensation plan. Good sales compensation choices are consistent with and therefore reinforce the definer decisions.

The definer decisions and all subsequent driver decisions should also be con-sistent with the firm's overall corporate and marketing strategies. These strategies are typically cascaded down to the sales force. Effective sales compensation deci-sions help to reinforce corporate and marketing strategies.

Sales Roles Must Be Defined Before Compensation Decisions Can Be Made

In 1999, MathWorks, a Massachusetts-based software company, set out to redesign its sales compensation plan in order to be more competitive with software industry leaders. Management quickly realized that the rea-son it had been struggling to figure out what to pay people was that the firm's sales jobs were poorly defined. There were six different job levels for 35 people, yet all had similar responsibilities. Everyone was paid 50 percent salary and 50 percent variable pay for duties that ranged from calling on large corporate purchasing departments to following up on leads that would amount to just one or two users.

Working with a consultant, the firm spent three months analyzing ex-actly what salespeople did. Through this analysis, two distinct sales roles emerged. One role was an inside sales role involving telephone lead gener-ation and selling to single users. The second role was an outside sales role involving the use of established contacts to sell to entire departments or companies.

Once the new sales roles were defined, the company was able to rede-sign its compensation plan in a matter of days. The new pay plan reflected the responsibilities and impact of each sales role. Both sales roles received variable pay for new product revenues. For outside salespeople, 35 percent of total pay was variable, while for inside salespeople, just 20 percent of total pay was variable.

Compatibility: Alignment with Other Sales Force Effectiveness Drivers

In a successful sales management system, sales compensation decisions align not only with corporate and marketing strategies and with the definer decisions, but also with all the other sales force effectiveness driver decisions. Consider several examples that demonstrate the importance of this compatibility.

- If the sales force hiring profile calls for experienced and aggressive risk takers, then a compensation plan that is 100 percent salary and pays at the industry median will not attract desirable candidates. A highly leveraged plan offering high risk with high rewards will be more effective.

- If the company has sales territories that vary greatly in terms of market potential, then a 100 percent commission plan that ties rewards to total sales volume will be perceived as unfair, and sales force morale will suffer. A plan that is goal based may be more appropriate.

- If the company's data that measure territory market share are not uniformly accurate across all territories, then a plan that bases rewards on this measure will fail. Until the accuracy of the data is improved, alternative measures are more appropriate for determining variable pay.

Compensation Must Be Compatible with Other Sales Force Effectiveness Drivers

The success of a maker of preprinted business forms in an intensely competitive and fragmented industry had been driven historically by an aggressive "eat what you kill" sales culture. During the mid-1990s, the industry experienced a transformation as electronic forms that customers could design and modify themselves began to dominate the market, and the demand for preprinted paper forms shrank rapidly. In order to be successful in the new environment, the company needed a sales approach that was more customer-focused and encouraged salespeople to "do the right thing." As a first step toward implementing this cultural transformation, the company eliminated its sales incentive plan. Salespeople who had once earned a significant portion of their income through variable pay began to be paid salary exclusively. The sales force was not happy about this change. Most of the firm's salespeople were aggressive risk takers who had thrived in the high-risk, high-return environment. The firm's sales force culture was totally incompatible with a salaried sales environment. In the long term, it is likely that the firm's people and culture would need to change in order for the firm to continue its success. However, the dramatic change in pay structure was too sudden, and its incompatibility with the firm's people and culture hurt financial results.

Authors' note: In our experience, changing a pay plan from mostly salary to a significant incentive component or eliminating a large incentive component is almost impossible to pull off while keeping the same salespeople. Incentive cultures and salary cultures are different, and the people that can succeed in the two cultures are also different.

Consequences: A Downstream View

The sales force incentive compensation decision has an impact on salespeople, sales force activities, customer results, and company results. In its role as a sales force exciter, the right incentive plan inspires and energizes a sales force to work hard to achieve challenging goals. In its role as a sales force controller, the incentive plan sets expectations that define what is important and directs sales force energy to the products, markets, and selling activities that are of the greatest strategic importance to the company. In its role as a sales force shaper, the incentive plan helps to define the sales force culture and influences the type of person that is attracted to the sales job.

The consequences of the sales compensation decision for salespeople, sales force activities, customer results, and company results are described further here. In each section, the relevant component is highlighted within the framework, and an example is provided showing how that component is affected by the compensation plan.

How the Sales Incentive Compensation Plan Affects Salespeople.

The compensation plan influences the type of person who is attracted to the company. Consider the two plans shown in Figure 1-5. What type of salesperson might each plan attract to the company?

Plan A is a highly aggressive plan. In a selling environment with high sales force causality, it could be very attractive to salespeople who are risk takers and who desire the opportunity to earn a high income as a reward for hard work and sales success. Plan B might be appropriate in a selling environment with lower sales force causality, where sales force loyalty, professional development, customer satisfaction, and steady sales and profit growth are valued by the firm. The two plans will attract very different types of salespeople.

How the Sales Incentive Plan Affects Sales Force Activities.

An effective sales incentive compensation plan motivates the sales force to work hard to achieve results. Thus, incentive compensation plans have a significant impact on how much energy salespeople will give to their jobs. For example, consider the two plans shown in Figure 1-6. Which one would encourage a salesperson to work harder?

Figure 1-5. A comparison of two incentive plans. What type of salesperson would each plan attract?

Plan A	Plan B
• 100% commission from dollar one • No cap • No draw • On-the-job training	• 100% salary reviewed annually • Company car • Generous health and insurance benefits • Promotions into marketing and sales management are encouraged • Professional development is valued

Figure 1-6. A comparison of two incentive plans. Which one would encourage salespeople to work harder?

Plan C		Plan D	
Quota Attainment	Commission Rate		Commission Rate
Sales up to quota	2.0%	All sales	2.0%
Sales from quota to 120% of quota	3.0%		
Sales over 120% of quota	4.0%		

For many salespeople, particularly those for whom money is a strong motivator, Plan C will result in greater amounts of energy being devoted to selling, provided that the territory quotas are realistic and accurate. The higher commission rates that kick in at quota and 120 percent of quota will inspire many to work harder in order to make more money. However, not all salespeople are strongly motivated by money. For some, Plan C will actually result in less work than Plan D because Plan C enables the salesperson to reach an income level that he finds sufficient sooner. Once that level has been achieved, the salesperson may feel that it is acceptable to work less and enjoy more leisure time.

The sales incentive plan also affects how a salesperson will allocate her time to different products, customers, and selling activities. For example, consider the two plans shown in Figure 1-7. How would a salesperson allocate her time to different product groups with each plan?

Figure 1-7. A comparison of two incentive plans. How would each plan direct sales force energy to different product lines?

Plan E		Plan F	
Product Group	Commission Rate	Product Group	Commission Rate
Strategic	6.0%	All products	4.0%
Growth	4.0%		
Core	2.0%		

Plan E directs sales force energy away from core products and toward strategic products. It sends a powerful message to the sales force about which products are most important to the company. Plan F does not differentiate among product categories. It encourages salespeople to sell whichever products they are comfortable selling and fit best with customer needs.

How the Sales Incentive Plan Affects Customer Results.

How a sales force is paid affects its relationships with customers. For example, consider the two plans shown in Figure 1-8. What kind of relationship might a salesperson paid under each of these plans have with customers?

Figure 1-8. A comparison of two incentive plans. How would each affect customers?

Plan G	Plan H

• 2.5% commission on all sales up to last year's sales
 	
 • 7.5% commission on sales exceeding last year's sales
	• Salary plus a 20% bonus opportunity
	 • Bonus is paid in the following proportions:
	   – Customer satisfaction—20%
	   – Profitability—60%
	   – Educational and service objectives—20%

Plan H encourages salespeople to cultivate long-term relationships with their customers. A salesperson who is paid under this plan is more likely to "do the right thing" for a customer, even if it means sacrificing short-term sales. Plan G encourages a different relationship between salespeople and their customers. It encourages salespeople to "do what it takes to make a sale" and then move on. Often, companies with pay plans like Plan G have separate service organizations to meet the ongoing needs of customers. That way, the sales force can focus all of its energy on selling.

How the Sales Incentive Plan Affects Company Results.

The sales force directly affects both the top line (sales or revenues) and the bottom line (profits) and has a major impact on the attainment of company results goals. Consider the two plans shown in Figure 1-9. How would each plan affect the firm's ability to achieve its market share and profit objectives?

Figure 1-9. A comparison of two incentive plans. How would each affect the firm's achievement of market share and profit goals?

Plan I	Plan J
• 6% commission on sales exceeding last year's sales • Bonus for wins versus a major competitor	• 2.5% commission on product margin

Plan I encourages salespeople to do what it takes to make a sale, even if that means cutting price. It can help a firm achieve aggressive sales growth and market share gains in competitive markets, but possibly at the expense of company profitability. Plan J encourages salespeople to pay close attention to the bottom line. It can help a company remain profitable, although it may sacrifice sales growth or market share.

Diagnosing Sales Force Issues

Companies often misattribute the cause of their problems to the compensation plan when the true source of the problem lies elsewhere within the sales management system. We have been asked by managers at hundreds of companies, both through our teaching and through our consulting, "How do I fix the sales compensation plan in order to solve the following problem that our organization faces?" The problem might be any one of a number of sales management challenges, including:

- "We are not attracting and retaining the best salespeople, and our turnover is too high."
- "We are not servicing current customers adequately."
- "We are not spending enough time on strategically important products."
- "Sales are not growing as fast as expected."
- "The sales force is not developing enough new business."

Consider the last challenge mentioned, one that is faced by many sales organizations: The sales force is not developing enough new business. This problem is frequently diagnosed by sales leaders as a compensation issue. Management believes that salespeople are comfortable with their earnings on easy sales to repeat buyers, and are not motivated to go out and prospect for harder-to-get new business. It therefore reasons that a change in the compensation plan to provide greater variable pay for sales to new customers will motivate salespeople to engage in more new business development activities.

While adjusting the compensation plan may be an effective way to stimulate new business development in some situations, there can be many other reasons why new business development is below expectations. Very rarely is the compensation plan alone to blame for this important sales management challenge. For example, consider the following other reasonable explanations:

- The sales force *size* is too small. Salespeople are so busy managing the business from repeat customers that they do not have enough time for new business development.

- The sales force is not *structured* appropriately. Generating new business requires very different sales skills from generating repeat business, and it is not always possible to have a single sales force that does both well. A sales force specializing in new business development is needed.

- The company is not *hiring* the right people for the sales force. The current salespeople are good at maintaining relationships and servicing customers, but they do not have the right personality to aggressively pursue business from new customers.

- The company is not *training* salespeople adequately. Salespeople need guidance on the sales process for hunting new business successfully.

- The sales force does not have the *data and tools* that it needs for successful new business generation. Better targeting lists and tools are needed to help salespeople identify good prospects in their territory.

Clearly, changing the incentive compensation plan will solve some sales management problems. However, about half of the time, when we are asked to solve a sales force challenge or concern by redesigning the sales compensation plan, the primary source of the problem turns out to be some other aspect of the sales management system.

Consider another example. Companies frequently misdiagnose territory alignment inequities as an incentive compensation plan problem. When market potential is not allocated equitably across sales territories, compensation may be perceived as unfair, especially if rewards are tied to total sales. Market potential is often a better predictor of territory sales than any characteristic related to the salesperson, including experience, ability, motivation, or effort. Thus, territories with high market potential often have high sales, regardless of sales force effort. A sales force compensation plan that ties rewards to total territory sales needs to be especially careful that market potential is equitably distributed across salespeople. Otherwise, salespeople in territories with high potential will have an unfair advantage over those in territories with low potential. If it is not possible or practical to distribute potential equitably across salespeople, then the company should consider adopting a sales incentive plan that acknowledges territory differences, such as one that ties rewards to the attainment of territory-specific goals rather than to total sales.

What Needs to Change—the Compensation Plan or the Territory Alignment?

The management at a medical devices company thought that something was wrong with the sales force compensation plan. The extremely wide range of variable incentive payouts across the sales force did not accurately reflect true performance differences. The "best" salesperson in the sales force received over six times as much variable pay as the "worst" salesperson in the sales force. The top ten salespeople (who averaged $116,000 in variable pay) earned four times as much variable pay as the bottom ten salespeople (who averaged $28,500 in variable pay). Our analysis revealed that it was not necessary to change the current compensation plan. Poor territory alignment was the major cause of the significant variation in variable payout for this sales force. Many salespeople who were making a large amount of incentive money had territories with huge market potential, while those making little incentive money had territories with very low market potential. The company realigned sales territories so that market potential was distributed more equitably across salespeople, and the variable pay distribution improved substantially.

Authors' note: It can be quite challenging to realign sales territories in commission environments where the size of the territory is tied to the pay of salespeople. Any realignment moves potential earnings among salespeople, and there are bound to be winners and losers. See Chapter 11 for a discussion on how to make such transitions.

Companies also frequently misattribute the cause of excessive sales force turnover to the compensation plan when in fact numerous influences within the sales management system often contribute to this problem. A pay level that is not competitive is just one reason why good salespeople leave a firm. Salespeople have many explanations for why they leave their jobs, including lack of home office support, poor-quality products, unfavorable work environment, weak field management, poor coaching and training, and a lack of defined career paths.

Sales leaders are often too quick to assume that changing the compensation plan will solve their sales management issues. The compensation plan should be viewed as just one important component of a successful sales management system. The incentive compensation program influences, but does not by itself determine, sales success.

Sales Incentive Program Helps to Drive Culture Change at Compass Bank

Top management at Massachusetts-based Compass Bank wanted to build a stronger sales and service culture. In 1997, it began an initiative to transform tellers and other retail customer–facing bank employees from mere order takers to proactive sellers of the bank's products and services. Top management was anxious to put a sales incentive program in place quickly to jump-start the effort. However, an assessment of the bank's current sales climate revealed that several other sales force effectiveness drivers needed to be upgraded first. Job descriptions were enhanced to make it clear to employees that selling was an expected part of their job. A sales training program was implemented to teach employees how to spot sales opportunities and sell effectively. A PC-based sales tracking and measurement system was put in place. Back-office processes were improved, making it possible for salespeople to deliver effectively on their promises to customers. Branch managers hired assistants so that they would have enough time to both oversee the sales effort and manage the day-to-day business operations.

After considerable preparation, the bank implemented a new sales incentive compensation plan. Every branch was assigned a quota to meet for deposits and deposit-related services. Incentive money began to accumulate in a branch incentive pool once the branch passed its historical level of sales for these products. An additional kicker was added to the pool once the branch passed its quota. The pool provided payouts for tellers, sales employees, and branch managers. Additional incentive money was given to the branch that came in first among all the branches. Based on the success of the scheme, the bank extended the incentive program to loan products and services.

How This Book Is Organized

This book is designed to help answer two major questions:

1. What is the best design for the sales force incentive compensation plan?
2. How does a sales organization effectively make the transition to a new incentive compensation plan?

As shown in the organizational overview of the book in Figure 1-10, four main themes are emphasized:

1. The *role of incentives* within the context of the sales management system (Chapter 1)
2. Techniques and analytical methods for effective incentive compensation plan *assessment* (Chapters 2 and 8)
3. Frameworks and approaches that enable successful incentive compensation *plan design* (Chapters 3, 4, 5, 6, 7, 9 and 10)

Figure 1-10. Organizational overview of *The Complete Guide to Sales Force Incentive Compensation: How to Design and Implement Plans That Work.*

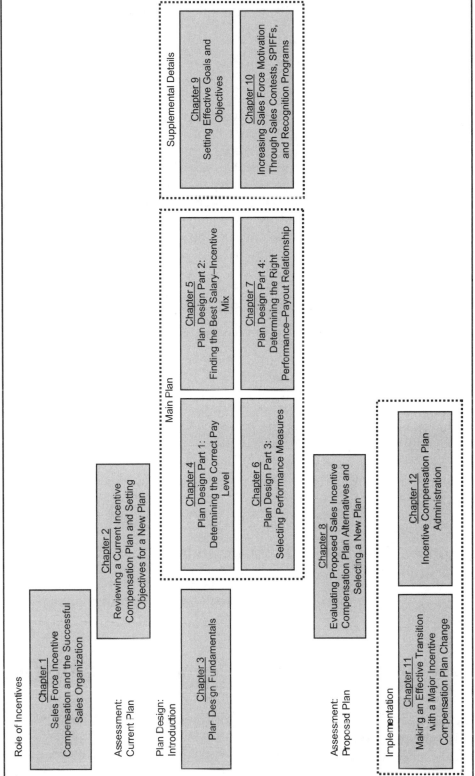

4. Approaches for successful incentive plan *implementation* (Chapters 11 and 12)

A summary of each chapter is provided here.

Chapter 1: Sales Force Incentive Compensation and the Successful Sales Organization

As markets and company strategies evolve, successful companies adapt their sales incentive compensation plans to ensure that sales force energy stays appropriately aligned. Sales force compensation decisions are never taken lightly, as they have a significant impact on customers, salespeople, and company performance. This chapter presents a framework for understanding the important role that a sales force compensation plan plays within the sales management system.

Chapter 2: Reviewing a Current Incentive Compensation Plan and Setting Objectives for a New Plan

Does your company's sales incentive compensation plan attract and retain the right salespeople? Does it motivate the sales force to perform the activities that support the firm's business strategy? Does it help to create satisfied customers? Is it producing the business results that the firm desires? This chapter presents a framework for assessing the effectiveness of an existing sales incentive compensation plan and for identifying how the plan may need to be adapted as company strategies and market conditions evolve. Specific metrics and diagnostic tools are provided to help you identify potential problems and areas for improvement and change.

Chapter 3: Plan Design Fundamentals

This chapter organizes the sales compensation plan design process by introducing some important terminology and summarizing four key sales compensation plan design decisions.

Chapter 4: Plan Design Part 1: Determining the Correct Pay Level

This chapter focuses on how to determine the level of total pay (target pay) that is appropriate for the sales force, including both salary and incentive (or variable pay) components. The chapter also shares insights on how pay level should vary with performance; for example, how much should a top performer earn relative to an average performer? A variety of external and internal factors influence the sales force pay level and variation. From an external market perspective, the right pay level allows the firm to attract and retain good salespeople who can implement the firm's selling process effectively. From an internal company perspective, the sales force pay level is commensurate with the value that a sales role creates and is consistent with the firm's culture.

Chapter 5: Plan Design Part 2: Finding the Best Salary–Incentive Mix

What proportion of sales force compensation should be salary and what proportion should be incentive? The answer to this question varies greatly across industries, companies, and sales roles. This chapter describes a range of diverse compensation environments—from 100 percent salary to 100 percent incentive—and explores how the firm's sales process and ability to measure results accurately drive pay mix decisions. In addition, industry norms and company history, culture, and management philosophy influence the salary–incentive mix.

Chapter 6: Plan Design Part 3: Selecting Performance Measures

This chapter explores how to select the performance measures used to determine the incentive plan payout. For example, should salespeople be paid for their results or for their activities? Should they be paid for absolute performance or for performance relative to a goal or quota? Which products, customers, or sales channels should be included? What timing and frequency of performance measurement is most effective? The best incentive plans are based on no more than three or four performance metrics that are important for the business and compatible with the firm's strategy, can be affected by sales force activity, and are objective, fair, and measurable.

Chapter 7: Plan Design Part 4: Determining the Right Performance–Payout Relationship

This chapter focuses on how the performance–payout relationship in an incentive plan affects the firm's ability to achieve important objectives, such as rewarding top performers, increasing sales force motivation, and controlling incentive plan costs. The chapter addresses numerous incentive plan design issues, such as whether to include bonuses, commissions, or both; when to begin incentive payment (for example, from the first dollar, from goal, or from some fraction of goal); under what conditions to make payout curves progressive or regressive (including when to use payout caps); and how to incorporate multiple performance measures.

Chapter 8: Evaluating Proposed Sales Incentive Compensation Plan Alternatives and Selecting a New Plan

No single incentive plan can solve every sales management problem. A compensation plan that has many advantages will at the same time encourage some sales force behavior that is undesirable, and this must be planned for and managed. The prudent firm will test any proposed new incentive before it is launched. This chapter explains how to evaluate and compare proposed sales incentive compensation plans, both quantitatively and qualitatively, in order to select the best plan for a specific selling environment.

Chapter 9: Setting Effective Goals and Objectives

Organizations and individuals that are goal-focused are typically more successful in the long run than those that do not set goals for themselves. Over 85 percent of companies incorporate goals into their sales force incentive plans. Yet when goals are too difficult, too easy, or not assigned fairly across the sales force, there are adverse consequences for sales force motivation, morale, costs, and expectations. This chapter describes effective formulas and processes that companies can use to set territory-level goals that are fair, realistic, and motivational.

Chapter 10: Increasing Sales Force Motivation Through Sales Contests, SPIFFs, and Recognition Programs

Sales contests, SPIFFs (Special Performance Incentives for Field Force), and recognition programs are a powerful and relatively inexpensive way to enhance a sales force incentive program. When used appropriately, such add-on incentives can effectively focus sales force attention on specific short-term goals, improve morale and team effort, and recognize the extraordinary efforts of top-performing salespeople. Yet contests, SPIFFs, and recognition programs harbor some dangers. Too many add-on plans can confuse salespeople, or can divert sales force attention away from strategically important products or customers. This chapter provides advice on how to create and manage fair and effective sales contests, SPIFFs, and recognition programs that support the firm's strategic goals.

Chapter 11: Making an Effective Transition with a Major Incentive Compensation Plan Change

Implementing a new sales incentive compensation plan successfully is often more challenging than designing the plan itself. This chapter describes a framework for understanding sales force change and provides insight on how to successfully make the transition to a new sales compensation philosophy. It addresses how to implement a major change in the pay mix effectively, how to deal with incentive plan changes that significantly redistribute money among salespeople, how to implement a pay cut, and how to deal with incentives during territory realignments. The chapter suggests work steps and best practices for managing a successful implementation, including how to effectively communicate plan features and benefits to the field.

Chapter 12: Incentive Compensation Plan Administration

Creating an efficient and effective process for ongoing compensation plan administration is a challenge. A high-quality administration system enh ır ces sales force motivation by producing accurate and timely payments and by communicating information that lets salespeople know how they are doing and how they can improve. In addition, an effective administration system produces plan health check reports that allow sales leaders to assess plan quality and take mid-course corrective steps as needed. This chapter shares many insights for developing a flexible and cost-effective compensation administration system that supports the long-term success of a sales incentive plan.

Reviewing a Current Incentive Compensation Plan and Setting Objectives for a New Plan

How This Chapter Is Organized

Introduction   40

Is It Really an Incentive Compensation Plan Problem?   41

An Overview of a Sales Incentive Plan Assessment Process   44

Assessment of Current Sales Compensation Plan Consequences   45

    Introduction to the MRG Company Case Study   48

    Consequences for Salespeople   48

        Quantitative Tests of Consequences for Salespeople   50

            Test A: Sales Force Attraction and Retention Statistics: Does the Current Plan Attract and Retain the Best Salespeople?   50

            Test B: External and Internal Benchmarking: Is the Current Plan Competitive?   52

            Test C: Plan Traction, Engagement, and Excitement: Is the Current Plan Motivating?   53

            Test D: Performance Distribution Analysis: Is the Payout Variation Appropriate?   57

            Test E: Bias Check: Is the Current Incentive Plan Fair?   59

            Test F: Analysis of the Relationship Between Incentive Pay and Performance Evaluation Ratings: Does the Current Plan Reward Performance?   62

Qualititative Test of Consequences for Salespeople 65

Test G: Sales Force Input: How Does the Sales Force Like the Current Plan? 65

Consequences for Sales Force Activities 65

Quantitative Tests of Consequences for Sales Force Activities 66

Test H: Sales Tracking Analysis: Does the Current Plan Motivate a Sufficient Quantity of Sales Force Activity? 66

Test I: Time Allocation Analysis: Does the Current Plan Direct Effort Appropriately? 67

Test J: Engagement and Excitement Decomposition: Does the Current Plan Direct Effort Appropriately? 67

Qualititative Test of Consequences for Sales Force Activities 69

Test K: Evaluation of Plan Complexity: Does the Sales Force Understand the Current Plan? 69

Consequences for Customer Results 70

Qualitative Test of Consequences for Customer Results 70

Test L: Customer Input: How Does the Current Plan Affect Customer Results? 70

Consequences for Company Results 72

Quantitative Test of Consequences for Company Results 72

Test M: Cost Analysis: Does the Current Plan Cost Too Much? 72

Qualititative Test of Consequences for Company Results 74

Test N: Qualitative Diagnosis: What Is the Role of the Incentive Plan in Delivering Company Results? 74

Assessment of Current Sales Compensation Plan Consistency and Compatibility 76

Consistency with Strategies and Sales Job Definers 76

Qualititative Tests of Consistency 77

Test O: Check for Consistency with Corporate Strategies 77

Test P: Check for Consistency with Sales Job Definer Decisions 79

Compatibility with Other Sales Force Effectiveness Drivers 81

Qualititative Test of Compatibility 82

Test Q: Check for Compatibility with Culture and Other Sales Force Effectiveness Drivers 82

Developing New Plan Objectives 83

Example of a Comprehensive Plan Review and Setting New Plan Objectives 84

Introduction

A sales executive at an insurance company recently asked, "How do I know if the multimillions of dollars my company spends on sales incentive compensation are really driving the sales force behaviors we desire and are supporting our business strategy effectively?" This is an important question, but finding an answer is not always easy. A sales incentive plan can have a significant impact on sales force behavior and on sales results, yet that impact is often subtle and nonobservable. A successful review of a company's current sales force compensation plan is an important first step for any management team that wants to determine if a change in the compensation plan can improve sales effectiveness. Such a review needs to go beyond simplistic observations such as "We made our numbers; the plan worked great" or "The company is 7 percent below target; the plan needs to be fixed."

Some parts of the sales compensation plan review are very simple—for example, "What did the incentive plan cost the firm versus the budgeted amount?" Other parts of the review are more complex—for example, "Are salespeople motivated by the plan, and does the plan encourage salespeople to succeed?" Reviews can include both quantitative and qualitative evaluations. Quantitative analysis might include a financial breakdown of the plan's cost, while a qualitative evaluation might include a survey of the firm's sales force to determine how salespeople feel about the plan. In addition, a review of the sales compensation plan can include views that are both short-term and long-term. A short-term view might look at the plan's impact on sales this quarter or this year. A longer-term view might look at a sales trend over multiple years or at data on the attraction and retention of high-performing salespeople.

All companies reevaluate their sales incentive compensation plans periodically, and many make changes with some regularity. Incentive plan change tends to be driven by two forces, as shown in Figure 2-1. First, there is the need to look ahead and adapt the plan to take into account external forces and company strategy changes. For example, evolving customer needs, changing competition, advancing technology, a shifting economy, and company plans to launch new products or enter new markets are just some of the forces that can require adjustments in the sales incentive plan in order to keep sales force effort aligned with company objectives. The need to adapt all of the sales force effectiveness drivers, including the sales compensation plan, to the various customer, competitive, environmental, and company forces that influence a sales force is discussed in Chapter 1.

Second, successful companies are constantly examining their past performance to find ways in which they can improve, particularly in areas that are closely linked to sales success, such as incentive compensation. A historical review of the current incentive plan may reveal that the incentive plan is not driving the activity or the results that the company desires. By understanding what elements of the compensation plan have and have not worked well in the past, a management team learns from its mistakes, fixes problems, and evolves to become better. This chapter

Figure 2-1. Sales compensation plan assessment: determinants of plan strategy and objectives.

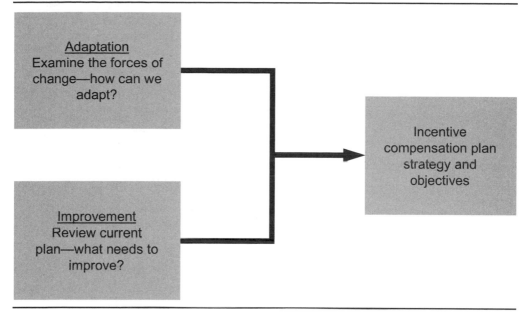

focuses on how a review of an incentive plan's historical impact can reveal improvement opportunities and contribute to the development of a new incentive plan strategy and objectives that will enhance future firm success.

Is It Really an Incentive Compensation Plan Problem?

Sales compensation is just one of many sales force effectiveness drivers. A successful sales compensation plan review requires an understanding of the impact of the sales compensation plan within the context of the entire sales management system. Figure 2-2 shows the sales management system framework that was introduced in Chapter 1. Compensation is a salesperson effectiveness driver; it plays an important role as a *shaper*, an *exciter*, and a *controller* of salespeople.

As discussed in Chapter 1, firms frequently assume that a problem can be fixed with incentives when in fact the source of the problem may lie exclusively elsewhere within the sales management system or can be addressed only by changing both the incentive plan *and* some other performance drivers. The sales incentive plan is just one of many drivers that can increase sales force effectiveness.

It is very common for problems to be attributed to the sales incentive plan that should really be attributed to other sales force effectiveness drivers. For example:

- Problems with unfairness in compensation are often due to a poor territory alignment that does not provide equal opportunity for all salespeople.

Figure 2-2. A sales management system framework.

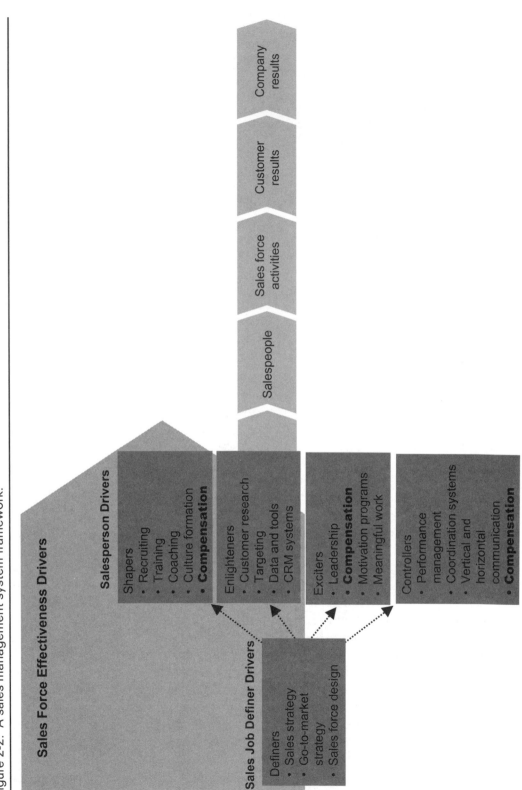

- Problems with misdirection, such as the sales force not spending enough time on a particular product or a certain selling activity, may be due to a lack of proper sales force training on that product or activity.

- Problems with retention of good salespeople may be caused by weak sales managers or an unhealthy sales force culture, rather than by the compensation plan.

- Problems of inadequate new account development may be due to too few salespeople, a lack of specialization, or poor training.

Before starting a major project to review and fix a sales compensation plan, be sure to consider all the sales force effectiveness drivers that may contribute to the problem. Very rarely is a redesign of the compensation plan a complete solution by itself.

Even when the cause of a problem does originate within the compensation system, the problem is frequently not with the design of the main incentive plan itself. For example:

- With goal-based sales incentive plans, poor goal setting is a common cause of inadequate sales force motivation, low morale, and high turnover. Goals that are not reasonable or fair can cause a good incentive plan to fail. Goal setting is discussed further in Chapter 9.

- Many firms run ad hoc SPIFFs and sales contests that are not part of the firm's main incentive plan. When such programs are not centrally coordinated and strategically aligned, they can divert sales force attention away from the most important strategic priorities and dilute the impact of the main incentive plan. SPIFFs and sales contests are discussed further in Chapter 10.

- Poor implementation of a transition to a new sales incentive plan can cause a good plan to fail. Common implementation errors include insufficient communication with the sales force, a lack of key stakeholder buy-in, and ineffective or nonexistent transition strategies for top-performing salespeople. Effective strategies for implementing a new incentive compensation plan are discussed further in Chapter 11.

- Poor incentive compensation plan administration can lead to decreased sales force effectiveness. Common plan administration errors include reports that are late in getting out to the field or that contain inaccurate data and calculation errors, inflexible systems that cannot adapt to ad hoc or medium-term needs, and inadequate or nonexistent feedback systems that provide too little or confusing information to the field and management about incentive plan performance. Incentive plan administration is discussed further in Chapter 12.

Before assuming that the compensation plan needs to be redesigned, consider the possibility that the firm's goal-setting method, ad hoc SPIFFs and sales contests, plan implementation process, and/or ongoing plan administration processes and systems could be undermining an otherwise effective incentive compensation plan design.

An Overview of a Sales Incentive Plan Assessment Process

There can be many signs that a sales compensation plan is not working well. The 3 Cs framework shown in Figure 2-3 provides a logical way to think about a current sales compensation plan and to look for signs that the plan needs to be reviewed and most likely changed.

A plan can be tested for its effectiveness within each of the categories of the 3 Cs framework. The incentive plan assessment process includes a number of quantitative and qualitative tests. As summarized in Figure 2-4, quantitative and qualitative assessments usually focus on different components within the framework. Quantitative approaches are most useful for understanding salespeople consequences (such as income distribution and incentive plan engagement and excitement), sales force activities consequences (such as allocation of effort to products, customers, and activities), and company results consequences (such as incentive plan costs). These are factors that tend to be of high concern to most sales leaders. Qualitative assessment further enriches the quantitative assessment of salespeople and sales force activity consequences, as well as being useful for judging the compatibility of the plan with company sales and marketing strategies, and the consistency of the plan with other sales force effectiveness drivers.

Organized around the 3 Cs framework, the remainder of this chapter discusses quantitative and qualitative tests for assessing the consistency, compatibility, and consequences of a current sales compensation plan. Typically, firms will want to perform a number of these assessments and tests when reviewing their sales compensation plan. The results of the various assessments and tests can be organized into a Sales Incentive Compensation Plan Assessment Scorecard, such as the example shown in Figure 2-5. Scorecards like this one can also be used to evaluate proposed new compensation plans (see Chapter 8), to allow easy comparison of the relative strengths and weaknesses of alternative plans.

Regular Plan Health Reports Can Provide Timely Plan Assessment Data

Some firms produce periodic Plan Health Reports as part of their ongoing sales incentive compensation plan administration (see Chapter 12). These reports are produced in each incentive period and report on many of the evaluation criteria listed on the scorecard in Figure 2-5. The Plan Health Reports provide management with timely feedback for assessing whether the plan is doing what it was designed to do while checking for undesirable side effects such as unfair payouts.

Figure 2-3. Some signs that the current compensation plan needs to be reviewed and most likely changed.

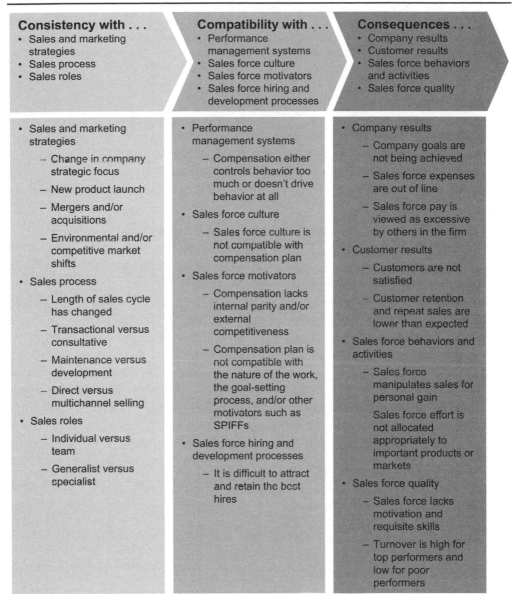

Consistency with . . .	Compatibility with . . .	Consequences . . .
• Sales and marketing strategies • Sales process • Sales roles	• Performance management systems • Sales force culture • Sales force motivators • Sales force hiring and development processes	• Company results • Customer results • Sales force behaviors and activities • Sales force quality

• Sales and marketing strategies
  – Change in company strategic focus
  – New product launch
  – Mergers and/or acquisitions
  – Environmental and/or competitive market shifts
• Sales process
  – Length of sales cycle has changed
  – Transactional versus consultative
  – Maintenance versus development
  – Direct versus multichannel selling
• Sales roles
  – Individual versus team
  – Generalist versus specialist
	• Performance management systems
	  – Compensation either controls behavior too much or doesn't drive behavior at all
	• Sales force culture
	  – Sales force culture is not compatible with compensation plan
	• Sales force motivators
	  – Compensation lacks internal parity and/or external competitiveness
	  – Compensation plan is not compatible with the nature of the work, the goal-setting process, and/or other motivators such as SPIFFs
	• Sales force hiring and development processes
	  – It is difficult to attract and retain the best hires
		• Company results
		  – Company goals are not being achieved
		  – Sales force expenses are out of line
		  – Sales force pay is viewed as excessive by others in the firm
		• Customer results
		  – Customers are not satisfied
		  – Customer retention and repeat sales are lower than expected
		• Sales force behaviors and activities
		  – Sales force manipulates sales for personal gain
		    Sales force effort is not allocated appropriately to important products or markets
		• Sales force quality
		  – Sales force lacks motivation and requisite skills
		  – Turnover is high for top performers and low for poor performers

Assessment of Current Sales Compensation Plan Consequences

As a sales force effectiveness driver, the sales compensation decision has consequences for all the downstream components of the sales management system. Compensation influences the skills, capabilities, values, and motivation of *salespeople*, which drive their behavior and *activities*. Sales force activities affect *customer results,* and customer results in turn affect *company results*. A thorough

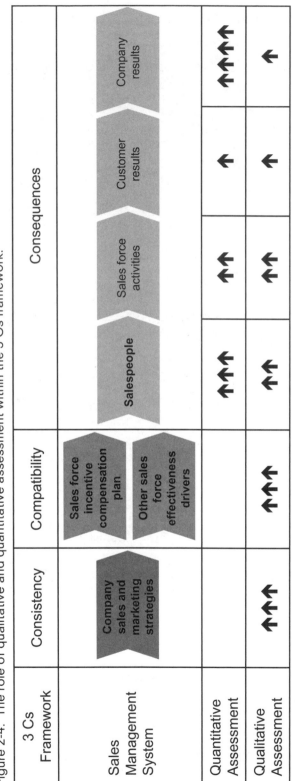

Figure 2-4. The role of qualitative and quantitative assessment within the 3 Cs framework.

Figure 2-5 An example of a Sales Incentive Compensation Plan Assessment Scorecard.

Use the assessment techniques described in Chapter 2 of *The Complete Guide to Sales Force Incentive Compensation: How to Design and Implement Plans That Work* to rate incentive compensation plan effectiveness in the following areas using the following rating scale: 5 = Excellent; 4 = Very good; 3 = Good; 2 = Fair; 1 = Poor

Compensation Plan Design—Evaluation Criteria	Rating (1–5)
Consequences for Salespeople	
Quantitative Tests	
Test A: Sales force attraction and retention statistics: Does the current plan attract and retain the best salespeople?	
Test B: External and internal benchmarking: Is the current plan competitive?	
Test C: Plan traction, engagement, and excitement: Is the current plan motivating?	
Test D: Performance distribution analysis: Is the payout variation appropriate?	
Test E: Bias check: Is the current incentive plan fair?	
Test F: Analysis of the relationship between incentive pay and performance evaluation ratings: Does the current plan reward performance?	
Qualitative Test	
Test G: Sales force input: How does the sales force like the current plan?	
Consequences for Sales Force Activities	
Quantitative Tests	
Test H: Sales tracking analysis: Does the current plan motivate a sufficient quantity of sales force activity?	
Test I: Time allocation analysis: Does the current plan direct effort appropriately?	
Test J: Engagement and excitement decomposition: Does the current plan direct effort appropriately?	
Qualitative Test	
Test K: Evaluation of plan complexity: Does the sales force understand the current plan?	
Consequences for Customer Results	
Qualitative Test	
Test L: Customer input: How does the current plan affect customer results?	
Consequences for Company Results	
Quantitative Test	
Test M: Cost analysis: Does the current plan cost too much?	
Qualitative Test	
Test N: Qualitative diagnosis: What is the role of the incentive plan in delivering company results?	

Consistency with Company Strategies

Qualitative Tests

Test O: Check for consistency with corporate strategies

Test P: Check for consistency with sales and go-to-market strategies and sales force design

Compatibility with Other Sales Force Effectiveness Drivers

Qualitative Test

Test Q: Check for compatibility with culture and other sales force effectiveness drivers

Note: This scorecard is an example that highlights some commonly used evaluation criteria for sales compensation plan assessment. Depending upon the particular circumstances, some evaluation areas may merit a more detailed breakdown, while other areas may be less relevant. The scorecard is most effective when the list of evaluation criteria is tailored to specific sales force issues.

compensation plan review looks at the consequences of sales compensation for each of the downstream components of the sales management system.

Introduction to the MRG Company Case Study

A discussion of the assessment of incentive plan consequences is enriched through examples from the MRG Company, a firm that is facing several sales incentive compensation challenges. MRG Company examples are also used extensively in Chapter 8 to enhance the discussion on assessing a proposed new sales compensation plan. MRG's current incentive compensation plan is a bonus–commission plan that begins its incentive payout once territory goal is achieved. The plan is depicted in Figure 2-6 along with the last 12 months' payout distribution. Over 60 percent of the salespeople did not achieve their territory goal and hence did not receive any incentive compensation. The company is very disappointed with the 96 percent achievement of the overall company sales goal. MRG's leadership team theorizes that the sales force incentive compensation plan misfired, leading to low morale and sales force underperformance.

The MRG sales leadership team hopes that an assessment of the current sales compensation plan can reveal improvement opportunities that will contribute to the development of a new incentive plan that will improve sales force morale and performance.

Consequences for Salespeople

- *"Our top performers 'max out' and quit, while low performers stay too long,"* says a vice president of sales for a building products manufacturer.

Figure 2-6. The current MRG plan and the incentive payout distribution for the last 12 months.

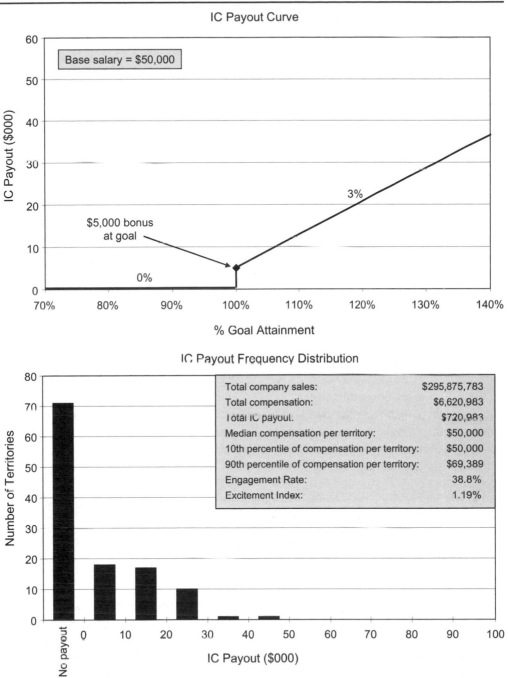

- *"We want to improve our ability to recruit top salespeople,"* states a manager at a software firm.

- *"Too many of our best salespeople are being lured to the competition. We need to pay more if we hope to be the 'employer of choice' within the industry,"* says a human resource director at a health-care firm.

- *"Too many salespeople have become comfortable with the income they earn from sales to current customers,"* says the director of field support for an insurance company.

- *"We want to eliminate loopholes and be fair and equitable to everyone in the sales force,"* says the director of sales operations at a computer maintenance company.

- *"We want to achieve greater differentiation between high and low performers,"* says the director of sales incentives and compensation for a pharmaceutical firm.

The sales compensation decision affects the type of salespeople that are attracted to the firm. It also affects sales force motivation and the extent to which the firm pays for performance. The following quantitative and qualitative tests help sales leaders assess the impact that a current compensation plan has on their salespeople.

Quantitative Tests of Consequences for Salespeople. Test A: Sales Force Attraction and Retention Statistics: Does the Current Plan Attract and Retain the Best Salespeople? The sales compensation plan has a very important long-term impact on the firm—it can be one of the key influences on a firm's ability to attract and retain good salespeople. Management can look at several different human resources statistics to help determine whether the current plan is attracting and retaining the right salespeople. For example:

- What is the firm's retention rate for salespeople who are currently or are expected to be strong performers long-term?

- Does the sales force see adequate turnover of nonperformers?

- How successful has the firm been at attracting top candidates?

Direct Marketing Firm Reduces New Salesperson Turnover by Establishing New Pay Metrics for First-Line Sales Managers

Analysis of turnover statistics for a direct marketing company revealed that many new salespeople left the firm within the first six months. Through exit interviews, the company learned that lack of training and attention from first-line district sales managers was the leading cause of this turnover. First-line district sales managers' primary responsibility was to train and guide new salespeople, but these managers also retained some selling responsibility, and a substantial portion of their incentive pay was based on their own individual sales performance. Thus, the sales managers' pay did not align well with their expected job responsibilities. The company responded by implementing a new district sales manager compensation program that placed less emphasis on individual sales and more on new performance metrics reflecting other important sales manager responsibilities. For example, metrics such as achievement of sales goals by new employees and year-to-year district revenue growth were added to the managers' incentive pay formula. This change dramatically reduced new salesperson turnover and ultimately helped drive sales growth.

Figure 2-7 illustrates goal achievement levels for salespeople who left and those who stayed at three different companies. At Company A, those who stayed have significantly higher goal achievement than those who left. In fact, the leavers achieved only 72 percent of goal, while those who stayed averaged 107 percent. In contrast, those who stayed and those who left have similar performance at Company B. Company C is losing its high-performing salespeople.

Figure 2-8 illustrates a deeper turnover analysis for one company's sales force. In this example, "respectful treatment," "recognition," and "pay" are the three top reasons that salespeople voluntarily left the firm. Of the 20 percent mentioning pay, 73 percent are in the lower half of the performance ratings. If the higher performers were leaving for more pay, this would point to a potential pay prob-

Figure 2-7. Comparison of goal achievement for salespeople who left and those who stayed.

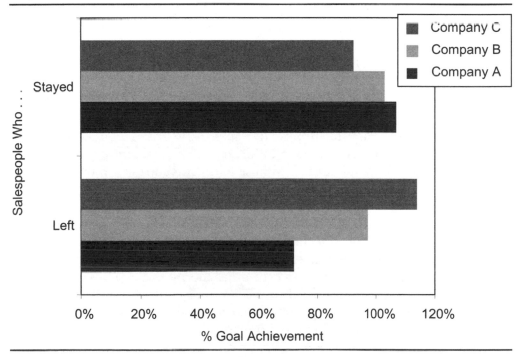

Figure 2-8. Analysis of turnover showing stated reasons for departure.

Primary Reason for Departure	% of Sales Force	% of Salespeople in Upper Half of Ratings	% of Salespeople in Lower Half of Ratings
Respectful treatment	23%	52%	48%
Recognition	21%	26%	74%
Pay	20%	27%	73%
Advancement opportunities	13%	70%	30%
Interesting and challenging work	10%	45%	55%
Quality of life	9%	40%	60%
Other	4%	50%	50%
Overall	100%	42%	58%

lem. Although some high performers are leaving for higher pay, a substantial number mention "respectful treatment" as their reason for leaving. (Other surveys directly identify the first line manager as a predominant cause of salesperson turnover.)

As this example illustrates, looking only at the reasons why salespeople leave a firm (the first two columns of Figure 2-8) is usually not enough. Important insights are gained from examining why high performers leave versus low performers. In this example, the departures are skewed toward low performers—58 percent of those leaving are in the bottom half of the ratings. A potential shortcoming of such analyses is that it can be difficult to unearth the true reasons for people departing, particularly if exit interviews are conducted by the firm's own personnel.

Test B: External and Internal Benchmarking: Is the Current Plan Competitive? Available industry surveys can help sales leaders assess whether or not the firm's pay level and mix are competitive with those of other companies in their industry or those of other industries from which they want to recruit salespeople (see Chapter 4, Figure 4-6, for a partial list of survey sources). In addition, information obtained through exit interviews with people leaving the firm and interviews with candidates who receive job offers from the firm can provide useful benchmarks for comparison. Figures 2-9 and 2-10 show scorecards used by one company to benchmark key pay statistics against peer firms and internally across sales roles. Benchmarks for top performers (such as the 90th percentile pay level) are particularly useful; every company wants the pay for its highest-performing salespeople to be competitive with that of high performers in the industry. Even though the company in Figure 2-9 targets its 90th percentile performers to be above the

Figure 2-9. Scorecard for benchmarking key pay statistics against industry norms.

Statistic	Actual	Target	Industry Benchmark
Median compensation	$73,500	$75,000	$75,000
10th percentile	$60,200	$54,000	$59,200
90th percentile	$89,389	$100,000	$95,000
Pay mix (variable pay % of total comp)	21%	25%	25%

Note: Table includes only salespeople who were in the job for the full year.

Figure 2-10. Scorecard for internal benchmarking of key pay statistics.

Statistic	Account Managers	Senior Account Managers	Field Managers
Median compensation	$55,500	$82,000	$97,000
10th percentile	$43,200	$61,900	$79,200
90th percentile	$71,389	$107,000	$108,000
Pay mix (variable pay % of total comp)	16%	31%	20%

Note: Table includes only salespeople and managers who were in the job for the full year.

industry benchmark, and median compensation to be at the industry benchmark, the actual pay fell short of target, particularly for top performers.

Benchmarks can take other forms as well. For example, some companies examine the evolution of total pay by tenure within the company to ensure that pay follows a desired pattern. Others also look at how pay and sales per salesperson compare across companies in the industry.

It is also useful to track a company's pay evolution over time for the same position. Figure 2-11 illustrates this analysis for a high-tech firm. Sales and pay are escalating rapidly. This situation has all the markings of a "runaway plan." If the trend continues, pay will exceed the value of the salesperson at some point, and it will become necessary for the company to cut pay, a move that is likely to be very traumatic for the organization. The opposite dynamic can also be discovered from such an analysis—pay for salespeople or for top performers that is not keeping pace with the value that they are adding.

Test C: Plan Traction, Engagement, and Excitement: Is the Current Plan Motivating? The incentive plan is closely linked to sales force motivation and morale. Incentive plan traction measures the degree to which a plan motivates the sales force. Traction can be measured through two important metrics:

Figure 2-11. Comparison of pay over time.

	2002		2003		2004		2005 Estimated		2006 Plan	
	Amount	Growth	Amount	Growth	Amount	Growth	Amount	Growth	Amount	Growth
Sales ($000,000)	$129	42%	$255	98%	$398	56%	$570	43%	$946	66%
No. of account executives	43	20%	50	16%	57	14%	63	11%	80	27%
Sales per account executive ($000)	$3,000	18%	$5,121	71%	$7,007	37%	$9,027	29%	$11,800	31%
Total comp high	$143,098		$215,063	50%	$274,566	28%	$303,029	10%		
75th percentile	$121,098		$181,059	50%	$209,844	16%	$240,317	15%		
50th percentile	$101,656		$163,940	61%	$188,133	15%	$221,934	18%		
25th percentile	$81,741		$103,915	27%	$124,508	20%	$137,530	10%		
Total comp low	$61,099		$73,983	21%	$91,359	23%	$104,576	14%		

- The Engagement Rate measures what percentage of a sales force receives incentive pay with a plan. Sales forces that use commission plans where the whole sales force earns incentive money often look at a Meaningful Engagement Rate when evaluating a plan's motivational strength. The Meaningful Engagement Rate measures the percentage of the sales force that earns an amount of incentive money that is large enough to be noticed by the salesperson.

- The Excitement Index measures the rate at which salespeople earn their last incremental incentive dollar. A plan that pays at a higher rate creates more excitement than one that pays at a lower rate.

Figure 2-12 shows the current plan and the performance distribution for the last incentive period for the MRG sales force. Figure 2-13 shows the payout distribution and some traction statistics. The Engagement Rate (ER) is just 38.8 percent, since less than half the sales force attained at least 100 percent of goal. The Excitement Index (EI) measures the average incremental reward for the last percentage of goal attained. In this example, the 38.8 percent of the people "engaged" all had an incentive compensation rate of 3 percent, and so the calculated Excitement Index for the whole sales force is (38.8 percent) × (3 percent) + (61.2 percent) × (0 percent) = 1.16 percent. MRG sales leaders feel that the low plan Engagement Rate and Excitement Index are hurting sales force motivation and causing poor sales force morale and underperformance.

Figure 2-12. Example of an IC plan and performance distribution.

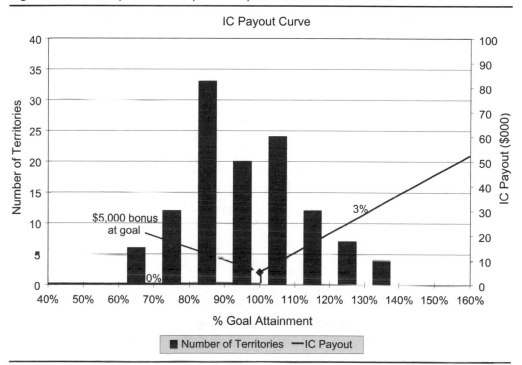

Figure 2-13. Distribution of incentive payout and traction calculations.

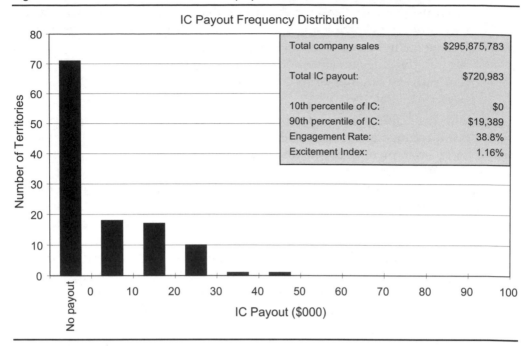

By benchmarking the Engagement Rate and Excitement Index against prior years, management gains insights concerning the degree to which the incentive plan is motivating the sales force. The ideal Engagement Rate and Excitement Index vary, depending upon the incentive plan design, the company's strategy, and the culture of the sales force.

If the incentive budget is fixed, incentive design has to trade off engagement and excitement. High engagement distributes money across the performance spectrum. High excitement rewards those who are engaged at a high rate of payout. An incentive plan signals success as much as it rewards salespeople. Many sales forces strive for an Engagement Rate that allows every salesperson who works a reasonable amount to earn some incentive money. Typically, this means that for a moderate pay mix plan (about 30 percent of cash compensation as variable pay), at least 70 percent of the sales force is engaged in the incentive plan. If a company feels that it cannot engage at least 70 percent of its salespeople, then it needs to change more than its incentive compensation plan. At the same time, sales forces often attempt to create an Excitement Index that is high for those salespeople who are willing to work harder than what is expected, so that star performers are rewarded for exceptional effort.

A Third Dimension of Plan Traction: Sales Force Understanding

Sales incentive plan traction, as measured by the Meaningful Engagement Rate and Excitement Index, is a reflection of the degree to which a plan motivates the sales force. However, this assumes that the sales-people understand the plan and use it to influence their activity. Some firms have plans that are so complex that salespeople are unwilling to invest the time required to understand them. When a plan is overly complex, salespeople may continue to do their job and ignore the plan. The Engagement Rate and Excitement Index may be high, and salespeople may appreciate the rewards that the plan provides, yet the plan is not truly motivating sales force behavior. (See "Test K: Evaluation of Plan Complexity: Does the Sales Force Understand the Current Plan?" later in this chapter.)

Test D: Performance Distribution Analysis: Is the Payout Variation Appropriate? Companies can conduct analyses to determine whether the sales incentive pay has enough variation. It is useful to study the distribution of plan payout, and then compare this distribution with what is known about performance variation within the sales force. For example at MRG, sales leaders feel that the payout distribution (see Figure 2-13) is unfair; more than 38.8 percent of the sales force deserves to earn incentive money. The low Engagement Rate is the primary symptom of plan ineffectiveness.

Payout distributions can reveal other problems as well. An appropriate payout distribution accurately reflects differences in value contribution across salespeople.

For example, evaluate the two sales force incentive payout distributions that are compared in Figure 2-14. For Sales Force A, sales leaders are comfortable with the payout distribution. The median payout for the sales force is approximately $8,400 per quarter (target incentive pay is $8,250), and 100 percent of sales-people earned at least 73 percent of target pay. The distribution is fairly tight; 90 percent of the sales force earned between 73 percent and 127 percent of target pay. The top salesperson earned about 179 percent of target. This is an unusually tight distribution, yet sales leaders feel that it accurately reflects differences in value contribution and performance across the sales force.

For Sales Force B, sales leaders are unhappy with the payout distribution. They are pleased that there is 80 percent engagement in the incentive plan, yet the performance distribution reveals two problems. First, only 37 percent of the sales force achieved the target incentive pay level. This is the result of sales goals for one of the firm's major products that are too aggressive. Second, while the average salesperson earned just over $5,200 in incentive pay, there is too wide a distribution in incentive earnings around that average. Sales leaders feel that this wide payout distribution does not accurately reflect true performance differences. Further analysis reveals that unequal territory potential is not effectively accounted for in this firm's goal-setting process, and this contributes significantly to the payout variation.

A sales force that is very heterogeneous in terms of the value contribution of each salesperson should have a wide variation in incentive pay across salespeople,

Figure 2-14. Distribution of incentive payout for two sales forces.

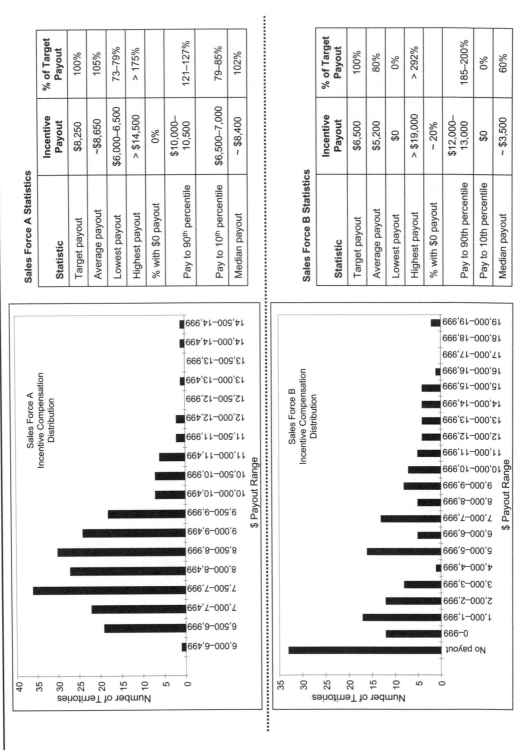

Sales Force A Statistics

Statistic	Incentive Payout	% of Target Payout
Target payout	$8,250	100%
Average payout	~$8,650	105%
Lowest payout	$6,000–6,500	73–79%
Highest payout	> $14,500	> 175%
% with $0 payout	0%	
Pay to 90th percentile	$10,000–10,500	121–127%
Pay to 10th percentile	$6,500–7,000	79–85%
Median payout	~ $8,400	102%

Sales Force B Statistics

Statistic	Incentive Payout	% of Target Payout
Target payout	$6,500	100%
Average payout	$5,200	80%
Lowest payout	$0	0%
Highest payout	> $19,000	> 292%
% with $0 payout	~ 20%	
Pay to 90th percentile	$12,000–13,000	185–200%
Pay to 10th percentile	$0	0%
Median payout	~ $3,500	60%

while a sales force in which salespeople are more equal in value contribution should have less variation.

Test E: Bias Check: Is the Current Incentive Plan Fair?

Our Sense of Fairness Demands a Relationship Between Work and Pay

It is innately human to care about fairness and to feel that rewards should be linked rationally to accomplishments. A 2003 study by primatologists Sarah F. Brosnan and Frans B. M. de Waal showed that this innate desire for fairness extends to the animal world as well. Pairs of monkeys were trained to give a scientist pebbles in exchange for slices of cucumber. One day the scientists changed the reward for just one of the monkeys in each pair to a delicious grape, while the other partner continued to receive the less appetizing cucumber. The monkeys given the cucumbers began to exhibit behaviors showing their severe unhappiness about the unfairness. They often refused to eat; 40 percent of the time, they stopped trading altogether. Things got worse when the lucky monkey in each pair was given a grape for doing nothing at all. The other monkeys then tossed away their pebbles and refused to trade 80 percent of the time. The cucumber-rewarded monkeys were willing to give up their reward simply to express their extreme displeasure at their partners' undeserved better reward. The monkeys seemed to believe that there should be a clear connection between work and pay.

Sources of Unfairness in Sales Forces

All employees expect to be treated fairly by management; perceived unfairness can be extremely disruptive in any organization. In a sales force, incentive compensation plans often accentuate any unfairness that exists. Eliminating unfairness can be very difficult, as there are so many potential sources of unfairness that affect the sales force:

- *Sales territory potential.* For example, territories in the southeast region have significant growth potential, while those in the northeast are stagnant.

- *Sales territory difficulty.* For example, the main competitor's top salesperson has been working the Chicago market aggressively, while the competitor's Minneapolis territory has been vacant for several months.

- *Product assignment.* For example, one sales team sells the high-growth products with easy goals, while another sells older products with challenging goals.

- *Acts of nature.* For example, a Category 4 hurricane season gives the Florida sales district an unfair advantage in a sales force that sells power tools.
- *Goal setting.* For example, the firm's top performer last year is rewarded with an even higher goal this year, while last year's average performers get easy goals.

Effective compensation plans do not have an inadvertent bias toward or against salespeople or territories with predictable characteristics.

Statistical analysis can be used to discover incentive plan biases. Figure 2-15 shows several examples of bias testing for an incentive plan. The analysis demonstrates tests for three possible biases: geographic, market share, and market size. The territories displayed in Figure 2-15 have been clustered into five groups based on geography, market share (low to high), and territory market potential (low to high). The median payout and payout range are shown for each cluster on each dimension. Even though each dimension has five clusters, the clusters are composed of different territories across the three analyses.

The first test (top) compares the payout range for each of five regions of the country. Payouts for the South are lower than those for the other regions. The second test (middle) groups territories based on historical market share, which ranges from about 0.5 percent to 2 percent. The analysis reveals a serious problem—territories with higher historical market share have lower payout. The third test (bottom) groups territories based on historical market sales, which range from $150 million up to $325 million. This analysis shows no clear pattern of payouts being biased by the size of the market in a salesperson's territory. Looking into the situation more deeply reveals that the geographic problem (the South getting lower pay) and the market share problem (high-share territories getting lower pay) is mostly the same issue—market share tends to be higher in the South, and the goal-setting process penalizes high-market-share territories.

Figure 2-16 shows another example of bias testing. This case shows how territory level analysis reveals biases in the sales incentive plan of a company where national account contracting influences territory sales. The company's sales force sells to local customers and "pulls through" sales in local outlets of national accounts. As can be seen from Figure 2-16, sales success is strongly influenced by the contract status. The average incentive payout is considerably higher for salespeople in territories where the contracts are favorable.

Incentive plan and quota-setting deficiencies are likely whenever there is a significant correlation between incentive payout and an independent territory variable that does not reflect a salesperson's effort or skill. Analyses like the ones just given can reveal incentive plan biases based on variables such as territory size, geographic region, served market segments, market potential, past sales level, market share, and quota increase.

What Types of Biases Are Tolerated?

It is practically impossible to eliminate all biases from an incentive plan. Companies tend to tolerate biases that can be justified in some way. For

Figure 2-15. Examples of bias tests for a quota–bonus plan.

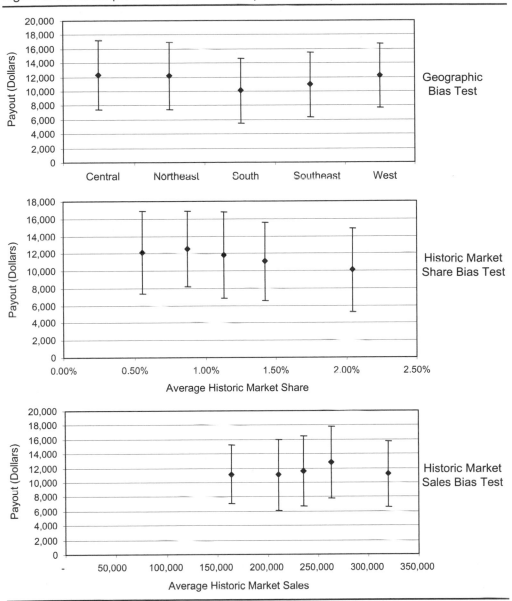

example, a quota-based plan that is biased toward salespeople with higher sales volume, higher quotas, higher market share, or higher growth is likely to be accepted, since it can be argued that these salespeople have responsibility for a greater amount of business. On the other hand, a plan that is biased in the other direction—toward salespeople with lower sales, lower quotas, lower market share, or lower growth—is demotivating and not financially responsible. Nevertheless, this type of bias is not uncommon. For example, many sales forces set every salesperson's quota by applying a

Figure 2-16. Incentive plan bias based on national account contract status.

National Account Contract Status	Average Payout
Very unfavorable	$13,982
Unfavorable	$14,439
Neutral	$15,142
Favorable	$16,104
Very favorable	$16,918

constant percent growth over the previous year (for example, if national sales are expected to grow by 5 percent, then every salesperson is asked to grow her sales by 5 percent). Such plans are usually biased against salespeople with high sales and market share.

Another example of an incentive plan bias that is often tolerated occurs in commission plans that pay from the first dollar. Such plans are biased toward territories with greater potential. Salespeople in high-potential territories make more money largely because they have more opportunity; their high earnings are due to their attractive territory and not necessarily to their performance. However, companies often accept this bias, particularly when the large, lucrative territories belong to veteran salespeople who have built them through years of service. This acceptance can lead to considerable loss of sales force power, as salespeople in high-potential territories may become complacent, content to live off their earnings from easy-to-sell-to existing customers.

Test F: Analysis of the Relationship Between Incentive Pay and Performance Evaluation Ratings: Does the Current Plan Reward Performance? It is particularly important to ensure that a current plan is not biased against high-performing salespeople. One effective way to identify high performers is to examine performance ratings from the sales force performance evaluation system. Figure 2-17 plots recent performance evaluation ratings of salespeople at one company against their incentive earnings for the last period. The performance ratings consider long-term success measures such as capability, motivation, and mentoring, in addition to sales results. By studying the relationship between the performance ratings and the incentive plan payout, the company gains insight into the extent to which the firm's "winners" are being rewarded by the current compensation plan. Those in the "high pay relative to ratings" quadrant received above-average earnings de-

Figure 2-17. A metric for evaluating the extent to which an incentive plan pays for performance.

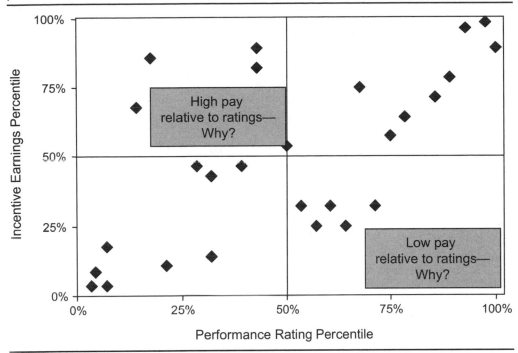

spite below-average performance ratings. Similarly, those in the "low pay relative to ratings" quadrant received below-average earnings despite above-average performance ratings. It is expected that a few salespeople will fall into the "high pay" and "low pay" quadrants temporarily as a result of explainable factors, such as unexpected market dynamics, poor goal setting, or characteristics of the salespeople themselves. However, having a large number of salespeople in these quadrants is often an indication of an incentive compensation problem.

Data analysis correlating key performance measures, such as market share or sales growth, with incentive earnings can also provide insight into whether there is a payout bias. For example, Figure 2-18 looks at the relationship between sales growth and incentive earnings within the same year. The analysis reveals a negative correlation between the two measures. Salespeople in high-growth territories are making less money. The interpretation of this analysis depends on the type of incentive plan that is in use.

For a sales force that is paid a percentage of revenues from the first dollar of sales, there are two plausible explanations:

1. Many high-growth territories have a low sales base (and therefore low incentive earnings). It is actually easier to get stellar growth rates in such territories. If this explanation proves to be true, then the relationship revealed by the analysis is not problematic.

Figure 2-18. Testing pay for performance for a commission sales force.

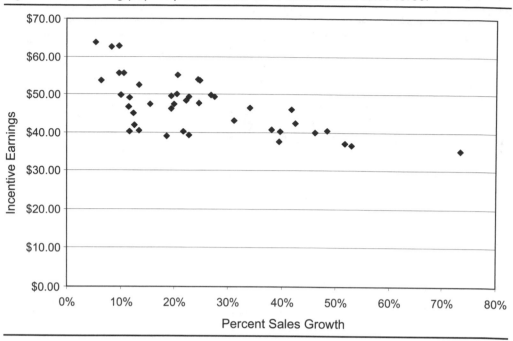

2. Some salespeople may have plateaued and are content to live off the book of business that they have built or inherited. These salespeople are earning considerable incentive money on carryover sales and are not motivated to work hard to drive sales growth. If this explanation proves to be true, then the relationship revealed by the analysis is a symptom of a potentially serious incentive plan problem.

In a sales force that earns incentives in the form of bonuses tied to goal attainment, the analysis in Figure 2-18 may point to problems with the goal-setting process. Presumably, high goal achievement means high performance. However, goals can be biased against certain types of territories, such as those with a large sales base or those where the goal increase is the highest. A common bias is that a salesperson with high achievement one year is saddled with an even larger goal the following year, creating a consistent pattern of high achievement one year followed by low achievement the next.

The validity of analyses like the one in Figure 2-18 rests on the quality of the performance measure or measures chosen (for example, sales growth or market share) and the appropriateness of the measures to the specific context and sales situation.

Pay for Performance Philosophy Sets the Right Sales Force Expectations

A compensation plan that consistently pays for performance is important for managing salespeople's long-term expectations. A pay plan that time and again pays out good money regardless of how hard the sales force works creates unrealistic sales force income expectations. A vice president of sales for a fireplace manufacturer observed, "The salespeople have come to expect high incentive pay whether they earn it or not." Companies in this situation can find it extremely difficult to change their incentive plan without adversely affecting sales force morale.

Qualitative Test of Consequences for Salespeople. Test G: Sales Force Input: How Does the Sales Force Like the Current Plan? Insights can be gained by asking the salespeople what they like and dislike about the current sales compensation plan, though the meaning of such input needs to be interpreted with caution. The successful gathering of qualitative sales force input requires that any feedback shared with management be anonymous, so that those participating feel free to share candid views. For this reason, many companies use outside consultants to moderate the feedback process, but home-office staff can perform this role as well. Some techniques that can be effective for gathering sales force input about the compensation plan include:

- Periodic surveys of the entire sales force (often administered through the firm's intranet), asking specific, open-ended questions such as: What is confusing about the current plan? How would you improve the current plan?
- One-on-one interviews of salespeople and sales managers
- Focus groups that include a cross section of salespeople and managers
- Focus groups that include a selected group of salespeople or managers (for example, groups consisting of just the top performers, just the low performers, just veterans, or just new salespeople)

When interpreting the results of qualitative input processes, be aware that salespeople and managers will selectively share the information that they believe will benefit them personally. Don't be surprised if most participants report, "Our goals are too high," "Our pay is too low," or "I recently received a better employment offer." Sales force qualitative input should always be checked against input from other more analytical and unbiased sources.

Consequences for Sales Force Activities

- *"We want to drive behavior to achieve and exceed sales goals,"* reports the director of sales operations for a telecommunications firm.

- *"Our current plan focuses on financial targets and not strategic activities,"* reports the director of sales for a telecommunications company.

- *"We want to provide increased incentive to sell services,"* says a principal at a high-tech consulting firm.

- *"Our plan does not motivate the right sales force behaviors because the plan is too hard for the sales force to understand,"* reports the vice president of compensation and benefits for a mortgage bank.

The sales incentive plan affects sales force activity. A plan can influence both how hard the sales force works and how salespeople divide their time among different products, customers, and selling activities. Quantitative and qualitative analysis can help a firm assess the impact of a current compensation plan on sales force activities.

Quantitative Tests of Consequences for Sales Force Activities. Test H: Sales Tracking Analysis: Does the Current Plan Motivate a Sufficient Quantity of Sales Force Activity? An ineffective incentive plan can adversely affect sales force motivation, leading to decreased sales force activity levels and ultimately poor results. Figure 2-19 shows sales data for a salesperson who has become demotivated as a result of a goal-based incentive plan with overly aggressive stretch goals. After several months of hard work, the salesperson realizes that the goal is unattainable and that he is not going to earn any incentive money. The salesperson gives up and stops working so hard, and the gap between the goal and actual performance becomes increasingly large over time. When this effect is summed across an entire sales force, the results can be disastrous for national goal attainment.

Figure 2-19. A salesperson's sales trail off when the goal seems unattainable.

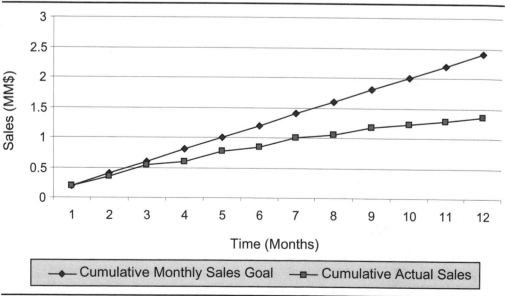

Test I: Time Allocation Analysis: Does the Current Plan Direct Effort Appropriately? Through the incentive plan, management can help to direct sales force effort toward those products, markets, and selling activities that have the greatest strategic importance and/or the largest impact on overall sales results. An analysis of how salespeople spend their time can provide insight into whether the sales incentive plan is directing sales force energy appropriately. Figure 2-20 contrasts how a sales force spends its time with various market segments versus how management wants the sales force to spend its time. Too little time is being spent with some critical market segments—specifically, large customers and prospects. One way that management can increase the amount of time devoted to these markets is through the incentive plan. For example, incentive pay could be adjusted so that salespeople earn more money for sales to large or new customers and less for sales to small customers. Notice also that the sales force in this example may be undersized or the salespeople may be working fewer hours than expected, since total ideal hours sum to more than total actual hours worked.

Test J: Engagement and Excitement Decomposition: Does the Current Plan Direct Effort Appropriately? An additional analysis that is useful for evaluating an incentive plan's impact on sales force effort allocation involves comparing an incentive plan's Engagement Rate and Excitement Index across different products or customer segments. Figure 2-21 shows a product-based analysis for a computer in-

Figure 2-20. Ideal versus actual sales force hours spent by market segment.

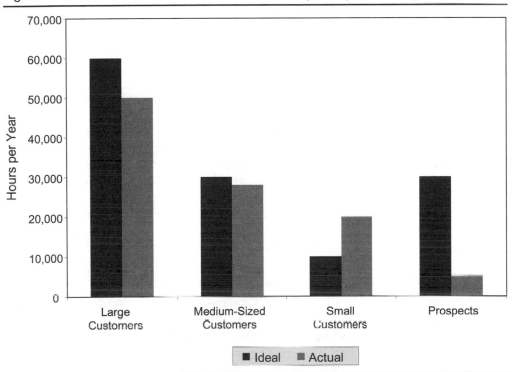

Figure 2-21. Example analysis of Engagement Rate and Excitement Index by product line for a computer sales force.

	Software	Servers	PCs	Services
Engagement Index	89%	43%	60%	100%
Excitement Index*	4.2	1.5	2.0	7.9

*Excitement Index is expressed as the average commission rate.

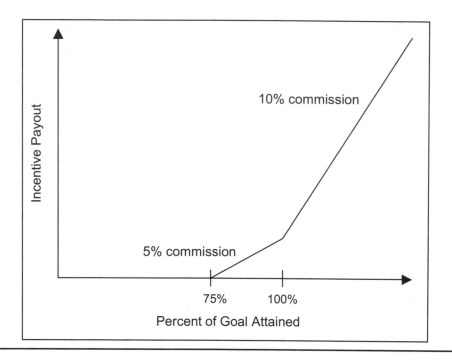

dustry sales force that sells four major product lines. Each salesperson is given a sales goal for each product line and is paid a 5 percent commission on sales beginning at 75 percent of goal and a 10 percent commission on sales above goal. The Engagement Rate and Excitement Index are drastically different across the four product lines. Every salesperson is making money on services, and the Excitement Index is high. However, on servers, fewer than half of the salespeople are making money, and the Excitement Index is quite low. This discrepancy in the Engagement Rate and Excitement Index across the different product lines was the result of poor goal setting. Servers were a new product line for the firm, and sales were difficult to predict. The server sales goals were too aggressive, and since the majority of the salespeople felt that their server goal was unattainable, they stopped selling the product. Instead, they spent their time on products with more achievable goals (such as services) so that they could begin earning commissions at the accelerated rate sooner. This hurt the firm's initial entry into the server market.

Qualitative Test of Consequences for Sales Force Activities. Test K: Evaluation of Plan Complexity: Does the Sales Force Understand the Current Plan? A review of the current plan's influence on sales force effort allocation should include an evaluation of how well the sales force understands the plan. Managers often report that their compensation plans do not direct effort appropriately because they are too complicated.

Six Months to Figure Out an Incentive Plan

New salespeople in a technology company's printer division were told, "Don't worry about the sales incentive plan. It will take you six months to understand it. Just do your job in the meantime."

What Is This For?

A number of salespeople at a large pharmaceutical company recently received cash rewards but were totally unaware of why they received the bonuses. The incentive plan was just too complex.

As the complexity of an incentive plan increases, it becomes more likely that the sales force will ignore it. Often complex plans are rewarding but not motivating to salespeople. If too much energy is required to understand the plan, salespeople either will pay no attention to the plan or may misinterpret its intent. In either case, the result can be that sales effort gets allocated inappropriately. Most evaluations of incentive plan complexity are qualitative. Interviews with salespeople and sales managers will usually reveal complexity issues if they exist. In addition, a few heuristic tests for evaluating plan complexity can be useful:

- *The elevator ride test.* The average elevator ride lasts under one minute. If a plan cannot be explained to a salesperson in an elevator ride, it needs to be simplified.
- *The four-measures test.* If the plan is tied to more than four key metrics, it needs to be simplified.
- *The business card test.* If the plan cannot be summarized on a business card that fits into a salesperson's wallet, it needs to be simplified.

Complexity Hinders Pay Plan's Influence on Allocation of Sales Effort at Phoenix Technologies

Software company Phoenix Technologies started out each year with an incentive plan consisting of three relatively simple components: a base salary, a quota-based commission structure, and an annual bonus. Yet the plan's complexity would grow significantly throughout the year. Whenever volume was down or there was a need to boost sales of a specific product line, management looked to the compensation plan for a quick fix. For example, the product groups often competed for the time and attention of the sales force by adding special incentives to the pay plan. By the end of the fiscal year, the plan might have as many as 20 special incentives for six different product groups. The plan became so bulky and without a singular purpose that the value of any single metric included in the plan was lost on the sales force. Like an overdone Christmas tree, excessive "decoration" detracted from the plan's main purpose.

Consequences for Customer Results

- *"Many customers are unhappy because the sales force is not meeting all their important service needs, particularly for those products that are not part of the incentive plan,"* a director at a tool manufacturing company reports.

The sales incentive plan influences the relationship that salespeople have with their customers. Qualitative assessment can help a firm determine the impact of a current compensation plan on customer results.

Qualitative Test of Consequences for Customer Results. *Test L: Customer Input: How Does the Current Plan Affect Customer Results?* To determine whether the sales incentive plan has the desired impact on customer results, survey or speak with customers to get their perspective on how the sales incentive plan affects their relationship with the firm. Does the plan seem to encourage sales force behaviors that meet customer needs? Or does the plan encourage salespeople to engage in behaviors that are undesirable from the customer's perspective, such as:

- Overselling
- Ignoring the customer
- Overlooking servicing or other important steps of the sales process
- Creating distrust
- Selling products that do not meet customer needs
- Selling to the wrong customers

Many companies use survey-based customer satisfaction measures to assess customer results. The advantages and disadvantages of basing incentives on such measures are discussed in Chapter 6.

Insurance Industry Under Scrutiny for Paying Broker Commissions That Encourage Deception of Customers

In October 2004, the world's largest insurance broker, Marsh Inc. (a unit of the Marsh & McLennan Cos.), faced a New York State investigation for an incentive scheme that allegedly cheated customers out of the best deals for insurance. Customers ranging from major corporations to small businesses hire insurance brokers like Marsh to find the proper insurance coverage at the best possible price. Brokers receive commissions from customers for arranging the coverage. The controversy stems from the fact that brokers also collect commissions from the other side of the deal, the insurers. Insurance companies often pay brokers a commission for steering business to their company or for arranging a particularly profitable form of coverage. These payments, investigators claimed, enticed Marsh to choose insurers for customers based on the size of the fees that the insurance companies paid Marsh, not on the price and value of the policies offered to the customers. Marsh and the insurers were even accused of deceiving customers into believing that several bids for their business were being competitively submitted, when in fact Marsh had determined in advance which company would get the sale based on the size of the commission it would receive. As a result of these allegations, some insurance industry brokers stopped accepting commissions from insurance companies. Other industry reforms are likely, in order to make sure that brokers' financial interests do not conflict with those of their customers.

Sears Modifies Pay Plan to Create Customer Focus

In the early 1990s, 3,500 employees of Sears Auto Center, the retail giant's very profitable automotive repair division, were paid straight commission on the parts and services they sold to customers who brought their cars in for repair. Not surprisingly, the company discovered that as a result of this incentive scheme, some employees were charging customers for work that was unnecessary. In 1992, the company faced several lawsuits that were tied directly to its incentive pay plan. Sears had to pay out millions of dollars to consumers who felt that they had been enticed into authorizing and paying for needless repairs. In the wake of the scandal, Sears abolished commissions and sales goals in its automotive division, making customer satisfaction its number one priority. The company continued to use at-risk, performance-based pay in many of its other divisions. The overall compensation philosophy at Sears is to design pay plans that align with management and shareholder interests, reinforce and motivate a customer-focused culture and work force, and attract good employees.

Consequences for Company Results

- *"We need a plan that ties our labor costs more directly to sales,"* reports a manager at a medical instruments manufacturer.

- *"Our sales compensation plan has become too expensive relative to profits,"* states a director of compensation and benefits for a seller of recreation products.

- *"We are getting poor results with our current plan,"* says the president of a hydraulics company.

- *"We need a plan that ensures that we hit our goals,"* says a sales manager at a newspaper syndication company.

- *"We want to drive sales earlier in the quarter rather than at the end,"* says the sales operations manager for a maintenance, repair, and operating supplies (MRO) company.

The sales force directly affects both the top line and the bottom line and has a major impact on the attainment of company financial goals. The following quantitative and qualitative approaches can help a firm assess the impact of a current compensation plan on company results.

Quantitative Test of Consequences for Company Results. Test M: Cost Analysis: Does the Current Plan Cost Too Much? Often, excessive cost is cited as the driving force behind the need to change an incentive plan. Plan costs should be evaluated relative to firm sales and profits. It is easy for firms to overlook the fact that the cost of most incentive plans depends to a large extent upon the level of sales generated. If the sales force sells more than expected, plan costs will be higher than budgeted. Similarly, if sales are below expectation, plan costs should be lower. Sometimes, firms will try to spend their entire incentive budget by finding ways to give the money to the sales force, even if sales come in below budget. This is a mistake. Any evaluation of incentive plan cost should not only compare that cost to the budgeted amount, but also consider the cost of the plan relative to what sales were actually achieved. Figure 2-22 shows an example of this analysis

Figure 2-22. Budgeted results and plan cost versus actual results and plan cost.

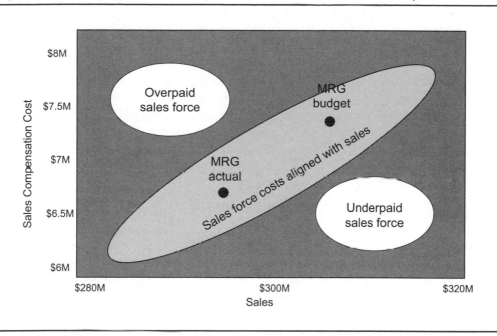

for MRG (the company introduced earlier in the chapter). The dot labeled "MRG Budget" shows the level of sales and incentive plan cost that were assumed in the company's budget. The actual outcome of sales results and plan cost has also been plotted and can be compared to this budgeted amount. When the actual outcome falls within the diagonal shaded area labeled "sales force costs aligned with sales," it is reasonable; costs as a percentage of sales are consistent with the budget. However, outcomes outside of this range are problematic. Outcomes in the "overpaid sales force" area indicate that somehow costs have gotten out of control despite lackluster performance. Outcomes in the "underpaid sales force" area indicate that the plan is not paying out enough for strong performance; the sales force delivered, but it was not rewarded to the extent that management had planned.

Many firms track sales force costs as a percentage of sales and compare this ratio to company historical and industry norms.

An Incentive Cost Breakdown by Product Enlightens Management at a Pharmaceutical Firm

Incentive cost breakdowns by product can also provide valuable insights concerning the cost-effectiveness of an incentive plan. For example, a pharmaceutical sales force sold two drugs—one for ulcers and another for high blood pressure. The blood pressure drug generated the majority of the firm's profits, so the company encouraged salespeople to spend most of their time selling that product. Incentive payout was tied to goal attainment on each product, and the more profitable product had a higher payout rate. Unfortunately, the company did a poor job of goal setting. Sales goals for the more profitable blood pressure drug were set too high, while goals for the ulcer drug were set too low. When it became evident to salespeople that the goals on the higher-profit product could not be attained and they could not make any incentive money selling that product, they began spending a disproportionately large amount of time selling the lower-profit ulcer medicine. At the end of the year, the total cost of the incentive plan was within budget. However, too much money had been spent for sales of the lower-profit ulcer drug, and too little had been spent for sales of the more important blood pressure drug.

While the major cost component of most sales incentive plans is the actual payout to salespeople, plan costs also include the expenses associated with administering the plan. For example, a vice president of sales for a semiconductor firm reports a need to reevaluate a sales incentive plan in order to "simplify our plan and eliminate administrative overhead." At some firms, the cost of administering the incentive plan is quite significant. Efficient yet accurate processes for tracking performance, calculating payouts, and distributing performance feedback to the field are essential in order to keep administrative costs to a reasonable level. As plan complexity increases, the additional cost of administering each new plan feature should be evaluated relative to the benefit of offering that feature.

Plan Complexity Affects Administrative Costs

A large pharmaceutical company had an incentive plan that was so complex that a consultant was hired to administer the plan. Plan administration cost the firm over $6 million annually, including both internal costs and consulting fees. Simplification of the plan eliminated the need for the consultant and resulted in a savings of approximately $4 million per year in administrative overhead.

Qualitative Test of Consequences for Company Results. Test N: Qualitative Diagnosis: What Is the Role of the Incentive Plan in Delivering Company Results? Poor company results can signal the need to change an incentive plan, but poor results can also be an indication that other sales effectiveness drivers need adjustment as well. The causality depicted within the sales management system framework can be traced upstream to the drivers of sales force effectiveness in order to diagnose the cause of many sales force problems. Compensation plan change is typically only part of the solution to most problems (see "Is It Really an Incentive Compensation Plan Problem?" on page 41.

Cutler-Hammer Sales Force Fails to Produce Desired Results

In the early 1990s, sales management at the Cutler-Hammer division of Eaton Corporation faced some serious challenges. The division's broad and complex product line, which consisted of industrial controls, circuit break-ers, motor starters, and other electrical distribution equipment, was grow-ing and changing rapidly. Customers, including heavy manufacturers such as automobile companies as well as contractors, were demanding solutions that required salespeople to have considerable technical expertise in many different product areas. Keeping salespeople up-to-date with the latest product specifications was almost impossible. Competitors such as Square D, Allen-Bradley, and General Electric had responded by establishing sales teams for major customers, made up of multiple product and technical sales specialists. Yet Cutler-Hammer sales management was skeptical that team selling could work, given the firm's strong culture of individual achievement. Management tried offering a pooled component of incentive compensation to encourage teamwork, but this was an insufficient solution. Despite the incentive plan changes, salespeople were still not operating effectively as a team, the sales force was not meeting the demands of customers, and too many opportunities were being lost to competitors.

The successful transition to team selling at Cutler-Hammer took con-siderable time and hard work, and it became even more difficult when, in early 1994, the division merged with the Distribution and Control Business Unit of Westinghouse. Ultimately, changes to several sales force effective-ness drivers contributed to the success of team selling at Cutler-Hammer:

- *Sales roles and team structure.* Within each sales district, salespeople were divided into three- and four-person groups called pods, based on geography and market concentration. Each salesperson within each pod became responsible for expertise in a subset of the products—12 to 15 products. Approximately 30 to 40 percent of sales calls were conducted as a team, with a pod product specialist helping her col-leagues explain technical product features or close an important deal. Pod members met weekly to discuss team strategy and share customer information.

- *Recruiting.* The old Cutler-Hammer and Westinghouse sales forces had many "lone rangers" who were used to working alone and did not have the skills and personality to be successful team players. Hence, the change to team selling required some tough personnel decisions. Sev-eral salespeople left the company or were demoted as a result of their inability to adapt successfully to the new team sales environment. Teamwork became part of the hiring profile.

- *Training.* The sales training process was rebuilt and was updated regu-larly. Each salesperson was required to complete 80 hours of training annually, with a good deal of the instruction being conducted peer-to-peer during pod meetings.

- *Performance management.* Evaluating team performance was an im-portant part of each pod's weekly meeting agenda. Team members

commended top sellers and offered help to colleagues who were running into hurdles.

- *Sales compensation.* While the majority of a Cutler-Hammer salesperson's pay was salary, incentives were designed to drive team selling.
All pod members would benefit financially by working together as a
team. Commissions were distributed according to each team's overall
performance, with payout based on salary grade. If, for instance, the
team reached 100 percent of its sales objective, a junior salesperson
might receive a payout equal to 15 percent of his monthly salary. Someone with five to eight years of experience might receive a 20 percent
payout. For a senior salesperson, the payout could be as high as 25
percent.

- *Leadership.* In the past, Cutler-Hammer management had said that it
was committed to team selling, but it hadn't put sufficient resources
behind the effort. This time, top management developed and communicated a clear vision to inspire the sales force, and backed up that vision
with the resources to make it happen.

Assessment of Current Sales Compensation Plan Consistency and Compatibility

In order to produce appropriate consequences, a compensation plan must be *consistent* with corporate and marketing strategies, sales and go-to-market strategies,
and sales force design. In addition, an effective plan is *compatible* with other
salesperson-focused effectiveness drivers, such as hiring and training programs,
performance management systems, sales force motivators, and the sales force culture.

Consistency with Strategies and Sales Job Definers

- *"Our current plan is not consistent with company goals,"* reports a regional
sales manager for a medical sales company.

- *"We need to better align our incentive plan with the firm's strategic initiatives,"* says a director of business operations for a not-for-profit firm.

- *"We need to direct sales force effort to better match channel strategies and expectations,"* states a director at a tools manufacturer.

- *"Our incentive plan encourages transactional selling, but we want to emphasize solution selling,"* reports a compensation director for a seller of office equipment.

As discussed in Chapter 1 and illustrated in Figure 2-2, sales force effectiveness driver decisions follow a natural sequence. The sales compensation decision is one of several sales force effectiveness drivers that influence a salesperson. Several decisions called the definer drivers precede the sales compensation decision. These definer decisions characterize the sales job and include choices in three major areas:

1. *Sales strategy.* Customer segmentation (whom will we sell to?), customer offering (what will we sell?), and sales process (how will we sell?)

2. *Go-to-market strategy.* How different marketing channels, including the sales force, will be used to carry out the sales strategy

3. *Sales force design.* Sales force size, organization structure, roles, and territory alignment

Sales compensation choices should always be made after the definer decisions and should reinforce and be consistent with those decisions.

Looking further upstream, the definer decisions and all subsequent driver decisions should align with the firm's overall corporate strategies. These strategies are typically handed down to the sales force from top management. A thorough compensation plan review traces the sales management system all the way upstream to ensure that sales compensation decisions are consistent with the firm's sales strategy, go-to-market strategy, and sales force design, as well as with corporate strategies.

Qualitative Tests of Consistency. *Test O: Check for Consistency with Corporate Strategies.* A review of the current sales incentive plan should include a comparison of the company's strategic corporate plan with the sales incentive plan. The comparison should look for inconsistencies in the messages sent by the two plans. Figure 2-23 looks at some disconnects between a firm's statements of corporate strategy and a sales incentive plan that pays out solely based on total sales revenue.

Food Company Experiences Misalignment Between Marketing Strategy and Sales Incentives

A company in the food industry invested heavily in plant and equipment and wanted a sales incentive plan that would encourage aggressive sales effort in order to cover its overhead costs quickly. An incentive plan was established that paid salespeople a commission based on total tonnage

Figure 2-23. Examples of inconsistencies between corporate strategy and a sales incentive plan that pays only on sales revenue.

Corporate Strategy Says . . .	While the Incentive Plan That Pays on Total Sales Revenue Says . . .
Build long-term customer relationships by providing excellent customer service.	The only incentive to provide customer service is to the extent that it affects this year's sales.
Stress profitability.	The only incentive to maximize price or to sell more profitable product lines is to the extent that it creates greater sales revenue.
Successfully introduce a new product.	The only incentive to sell the new product is to the extent that new product sales increase total sales revenue.
Generate more new customers.	The only incentive to sell to new customers is to the extent that new customer sales increase total sales revenue.

sold. Over time, the company developed more specialty food lines, and marketing wanted to emphasize these more profitable products. However, the company kept its old sales incentive compensation plan too long, and salespeople continued to push the lower-profit commodity products because they could sell greater tonnage and make more incentive money.

Inconsistencies between corporate strategies and sales incentive plans can arise when firms fail to adapt their sales incentive approach as new products are introduced and other products mature. Figure 2-24 shows how sales and marketing goals and challenges change over a product's life cycle and how the design of the sales compensation plan may need to evolve in response to these issues.

The Cost of Not Adapting the Pay Plan Between the Launch and Growth Stages of a Product's Life Cycle

A footwear company hired a sales force and paid 100 percent on commission to launch a new line of golf shoes that would be sold at golf shops. The incentive plan attracted experienced "go-getters" to the sales force, and the pay structure encouraged aggressive sales effort to get customers to try the product and to drive rapid sales growth. Customers liked the quality and value of the product line, and over time, significant repeat business was generated. Salespeople who had built strong customer bases during the product launch phase were making good money without having to work very hard. At the same time, chain shoe stores began to play a more important role in the golf shoe market. Salespeople found that they could generate high sales with relatively less effort at large chain stores. Many of the firm's salespeople became quite comfortable with the income they were

Figure 2-24. Life-cycle effects and sales compensation.

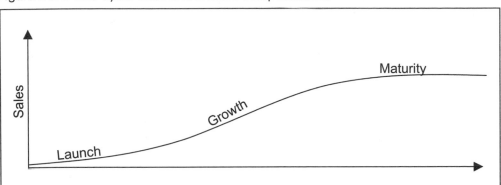

	Launch	Growth	Maturity
Goals and Challenges	• Build awareness and generate trial • Forecasting accuracy • Fairness	• Build momentum • Grow sales	• Sustain sales • Protect strengths
Measures and Plans	• Reward early sales • Commission and relative plans	• Sales growth and share growth • Commission and quota-bonus plans	• Goal achievement • Profitability • Goal-based plans

earning from easy sales to current customers, particularly the large chains. Salespeople were not motivated to go out and aggressively pursue more difficult sales to new customers. Sales growth was not what it used to be.

The Cost of Not Adapting the Pay Plan Between the Growth and Maturity Stages of a Product's Life Cycle

A diagnostics imaging company paid its salespeople a commission on sales growth over the prior year. This worked well during the first few years after the product's launch. But over time, the company did not update and improve its products, competitors began to catch up with and surpass the firm's technology, and sales growth slowed dramatically. The sales force could not grow sales despite its hard work, and salespeople could not make any money. Eventually, the pay plan was adjusted to pay on sales retention rather than sales growth.

Test P: Check for Consistency with Sales Job Definer Decisions. A compensation plan that does not align well with the firm's sales job definer decisions, including sales strategy, go-to-market strategy, and sales force design, sends mixed signals to salespeople and may not encourage the right sales force activities.

It is important to look for inconsistencies in the messages that the sales job definer drivers and the sales compensation plan send to the sales force. Some examples of common inconsistencies are listed in Figure 2-25.

Lack of Alignment Between the Go-to-Market Strategy and Other Sales Effectiveness Drivers Hurts a Computer Firm

A seller of computer data storage hardware, software, and consulting services historically sold its products and services directly to customers, while most of the firm's competitors utilized indirect channel partners, particularly to reach small and medium-sized customers. The use of channel partners allowed the competitors to reach a wider audience and offer better prices through reduced cost of sales. Management realized that in order to take market share away from its competitors, the firm would need to partner more effectively with channel members.

Management issued a corporate directive to the sales force: "Utilize partners more often." However, the directive was not supported by the programs needed to make it work. The compensation plan penalized salespeople for indirect channel sales. To reflect the commission paid to the partner, a salesperson's revenue was reduced by 5 to 10 percent for sales

Figure 2-25. Examples of inconsistencies between sales force definers and a sales incentive plan.

Sales Force Job Definers	Current Incentive Plan Incompatibility
Sales strategy calls for significant focus on servicing customers and nurturing long-term relationships.	The compensation plan has a large variable component based on sales volume; salespeople who focus on short-term selling earn more.
Sales strategy calls for cross-selling of the products and services of other company divisions.	Salespeople get variable pay only for sales of their own division's products and services; salespeople who cross-sell earn nothing for their efforts.
Go-to-market strategy encourages Internet sales.	Salespeople get no commission when their customers purchase from the company's web site and therefore discourage their customers from using the Web.
The sales force design encourages team selling.	Salespeople are paid for individual results only and therefore have no incentive to work as a team.
The sales force design assigns each salesperson to an exclusive territory; several territories make up a sales region.	Salespeople are paid for region-level results over which they have no control.
The sales force design includes sales territories with unequal market potential or opportunity.	The compensation plan rewards salespeople for territory sales results; salespeople in high-potential territories have an unfair advantage.

involving partners. The firm also did not provide training to salespeople on how to work effectively with partners. Since these important sales force effectiveness drivers did not align with the corporate directive, the directive had very little impact on sales force behavior.

Sales Compensation Realigned to Match Channel Strategy at Cisco

The vast majority of enterprise and commercial revenue at Cisco comes through the 40,000 channel partners (such as value-added resellers, systems integrators, and network consultants) who sell Cisco networking equipment. When the Internet bubble burst in the early 2000s, these channel partners were hit hard and voiced concerns to Cisco about the challenges of commoditized equipment prices, reduced profits, higher customer expectations, and increasingly complex technologies. Cisco management realized that in this new, more challenging environment, a stronger relationship between the firm and its channel partners could provide a strategic advantage. A plan was implemented to encourage a closer working relationship between Cisco and its channel partners. The plan included a variety of channel partner programs, many of which involved incentives. For example, Cisco offered a rebate to partners who sold Cisco IP telephony and security networking technologies. In addition, a new program compensated channel partners for acting as sales agents. Also, a change to the company's sales force compensation program allowed Cisco salespeople to receive equal compensation, regardless of whether sales went through the channel or direct to the customer. Many other programs besides incentives were also implemented to support channel partners. For example, several Web-based systems were established, including online training for channel partners, a portal for channel application data, and an online service contract center. All of these programs helped Cisco create stronger partnerships with channel members and contributed significantly to company revenue growth and cost savings.

Compatibility with Other Sales Force Effectiveness Drivers

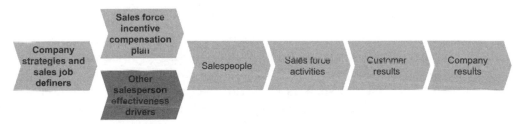

- *"We want a plan that helps drive our corporate culture,"* says the CEO at a software company.

- *"We are sending mixed signals to the sales force,"* says a vice president of sales for a fireplace manufacturer.

- *"Our recruiting process breaks down when we tell our candidates about our incentive plan, or lack of incentive plan,"* says a manager at a consumer packaged goods company.

Thus far, the sales compensation plan assessment has included a view downstream in the sales management system to assess the consequences of a plan for salespeople, sales force activities, and customer and company results, as well as a view upstream to assess the plan's consistency with the sales force definer drivers and corporate strategies. One additional view is required in order to complete a review: a look at compatibility across all the salesperson effectiveness drivers. In a successful sales management system, the incentive compensation program works together with sales force hiring and training programs, performance management systems, sales information systems, sales force culture, and other sales force motivation programs. Together, these effectiveness drivers align to reinforce sales and marketing strategies and accomplish company goals.

Qualitative Test of Compatibility. Test Q: Check for Compatibility with Culture and Other Sales Force Effectiveness Drivers. It is useful for a firm to make a list of all the major sales force effectiveness drivers and to look for inconsistencies in the messages that the different drivers deliver to the sales force. Figure 2-26 shows some examples of common incompatibilities between the sales compensation plan and other sales force effectiveness drivers.

Sales Incentive Plan and Other Sales Force Effectiveness Drivers Align to Support a Unique Culture at W. L. Gore

Newark, Delaware–based industrial products company W. L. Gore, the maker of Gore-Tex lining for weatherproof jackets, has a unique culture built around innovation, empowerment, and teamwork. All of the company's sales force effectiveness drivers align to encourage this culture. The sales force is organized into what Gore calls a lattice structure, in which there are no titles and no official lines of reporting. Every salesperson has a sponsor, who functions as a mentor, not a boss. Sales leaders function like coaches. Salespeople work together in teams to meet the needs of their customers. Compensation is determined by a ranking from one's own team members, as well as by the recommendations of a compensation committee that looks at each individual's overall long-term contribution to the firm. This includes factors such as long-term growth, customer retention, and time devoted to sponsoring less-experienced salespeople or helping on accounts that aren't the salesperson's direct responsibility. Salespeople also participate in company stock ownership and profit-sharing plans. At W. L.

Gore, all of the sales force effectiveness drivers align with one another and help to perpetuate the entrepreneurial culture of the company.

Figure 2-26. Examples of incompatibilities between the sales compensation plan and other salesperson-focused sales force effectiveness drivers.

The Shaper Drivers (Recruiting, Training, Coaching, and Culture)

- The hiring profile calls for experienced, assertive, highly motivated salespeople, but the compensation plan is straight salary and pays at the industry median.

- The company says that training is important, but it pays 100 percent on commission, so that salespeople are not willing to take time off from selling to attend company sponsored classes and workshops.

- The culture calls for cooperation and teamwork, yet salespeople are stack ranked and rewarded for where they rank.

The Enlightener Drivers (Customer Research, Targeting, Data and Tools, and CRM)

- The compensation plan pays for business with new customers, but the company does not provide the sales force with accurate data on good prospects.

- The compensation plan is tied to territory sales, yet the territory sales data that are disseminated to the field are routinely late and inaccurate.

The Controller Drivers (Performance Management, Coordination Systems, and Vertical and Horizontal Communication)

- Sales management encourages salespeople to focus on a particular hard-to-sell but very profitable product line. The sales force is rewarded for sales of all product lines, so it focuses on those that are easiest to sell.

- The performance management system encourages consultative selling and the development of long-term customer relationships. The compensation plan is highly leveraged and pays for short-term results.

- Top management wants first-line district sales managers to spend most of their time in the field coaching and developing the skills of the salespeople who report to them. The sales managers' incentives are based solely on short-term district results.

Developing New Plan Objectives

A review using the 3 Cs approach for examining downstream consequences, upstream consistency, and compatibility with other sales force effectiveness drivers provides insights into ways in which a sales incentive plan may need to be changed to enhance sales force performance or to adapt to changing conditions. These insights help the sales leadership team formulate specific new plan objectives. Effective compensation plan objectives are usually tied to company strategies, such as:

- "Encourage a successful new product introduction."
- "Increase sales growth in key customer segment."
- "Limit sales force costs to a percentage of sales no higher than the industry average."

The creation of specific sales compensation plan objectives is a critical first step in a successful new plan design process. Objectives define what is important to the firm and thus provide important criteria against which all proposed compensation plan design changes can be judged. Figure 2-27 shows the incentive plan objectives or guiding principles developed by a biotechnology company. The company was looking to simplify its plan and increase sales force motivation in order to drive continued revenue growth in the face of increasing competition. The guiding principles resulted from a review of the current plan that included both quantitative analysis and qualitative input. Sources of qualitative input included executive interviews, a field survey, and small focus group workshops.

The 3 Cs framework provides a convenient way to organize incentive plan objectives. Objectives can be formulated for upstream consistency, downstream consequences, and compatibility with other sales force effectiveness drivers. For example, consider the objectives used by the company in Figure 2-28.

Example of a Comprehensive Plan Review and Setting New Plan Objectives

The remainder of this chapter uses an example to illustrate how a comprehensive review of the current compensation plan leads to the development of objectives for a new plan. The example is for the sales force for MNP Inc., a computer

Figure 2-27. Example of guiding principles for incentive plan redesign.

New Incentive Plan Guiding Principles

Understanding
- Limit complexity
- Enhance communication and provide timely communication of plan details

Motivation
- Pay for performance
- Maintain uncapped (but self-funding) payouts
- Provide tangible goals
- Provide for accountability toward individual goals

Fairness
- Consider differences in growth opportunities across territories in plan design
- Improve accountability and measurement of territory performance
- Gain field-level acceptance of goals

Budget
- Have a fiscally responsible budget
- Develop goals tied to corporate objectives

Figure 2-28. Incentive plan objectives using the 3 Cs framework for a key account manager (KAM) organization that coordinates its activities with geographic salespeople.

Sales Management System Component	Plan Objectives
Consistency upstream • Corporate and marketing strategies • Sales job definer decisions	• Encourage key account managers (KAMs) to support company's marketing strategy. • Maintain consistency of incentive plan design elements across business units.
Compatibility with other sales force effectiveness drivers • Hiring and training programs • Performance management • Sales force motivators • Sales force culture	• Enable KAMs to monitor their own performance. • Metrics are as objective and measurable as possible. • Provide motivation for high performance through goals that are challenging, yet attainable. • Encourage KAMs and salespeople in the same region to collaborate appropriately.
Consequences downstream	
Salespeople	• Compensate KAMs fairly and equitably for the value they provide to the company. • Accurately credit the KAMs for business that they generate.
Sales activities	• Reward KAMs for closing formal contracts. • Encourage KAMs to consider sales impact beyond the key accounts. • Account for regional differences.
Customer results	• Allow focus on new products that improve customer productivity.
Company results	• Meet financial requirements.

equipment manufacturing company. MNP manufactures computers, peripherals, and related equipment targeted at two major customer segments: businesses and government entities. MNP takes pride in its value-added product offering. In an increasingly price-driven market, MNP's products are priced higher than competitors' products because of the value that MNP believes it brings to customers through targeted solutions (tools and add-on products and services that meet specific customer needs) and after-sale support.

MNP's product offering for the business segment is broadly categorized as enterprise hardware solutions (EHS) and software solutions (SS). EHS includes servers and peripherals, while SS includes customized software products that are sold by MNP as a value-added reseller. The product offering for the government segment is aimed primarily at educational institutions, including public universities, colleges, and schools. The products targeting this segment are called innovative educational solutions (IES) and include a combination of hardware and software. MNP management is particularly concerned about the IES product line, since a major competitor is about to launch a new product targeted at the educational market segment.

Figure 2-29 shows the components of MNP's current sales incentive compensation plan and a typical payout calculation. Each salesperson has a quarterly goal for each of the three main product groups. At the end of the quarter, the payout is calculated as target payout times the percent of goal achievement, as long as the salesperson achieves at least 50 percent of her sales goal.

MNP conducted a comprehensive review of the current incentive plan, using many of the quantitative and qualitative tests described in this chapter. A summary of the review results is shown in Figure 2-30. Figures 2-31, 2-32, and 2-33 provide further detail for three of the quantitative tests.

Based on the review of MNP's current incentive plan, sales leaders establish the objectives shown in Figure 2-34 for a new incentive plan to be implemented next quarter. These objectives become the criteria against which all proposed incentive plan design changes are judged.

Figure 2-29. Components of the MNP plan.

Metrics, Weights and Target Payout

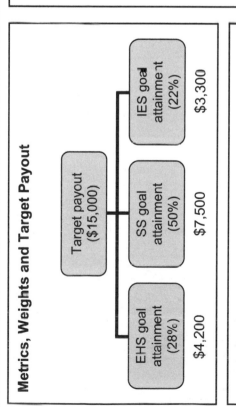

Target payout ($15,000)

EHS goal attainment (28%) — $4,200

SS goal attainment (50%) — $7,500

IES goal attainment (22%) — $3,300

Eligibility Criteria
- Salespeople have to attain 50% of goal on a metric to be eligible for payout on that metric.

Time Periods
- Payout frequency will be quarterly.
- Goal attainment will be calculated based on quarterly performance (not year to date).
- Next quarter goals will be communicated at end of previous quarter.

Payout Calculation
- For each metric, for eligible salespeople a goal attainment % will be calculated by comparing sales in the quarter to a quarterly goal.
- Eligible salespeople's payout for each metric = metric target payout X metric % goal attainment.
- Total payout for each salesperson = sum of payouts across metrics.

Calculation Example

Product	Territory Attainment %	Eligibility >50%	Target Payout	Actual Payout
EHS	40%	No	$4,200	—
SS	85%	Yes	$7,500	$6,375
IES	125%	Yes	$3,300	$4,125
Total				$10,500

Figure 2-30. Review of the MNP current plan: A summary scorecard.

MNP sales leaders conducted a subset of the qualitative and quantitative tests from this chapter that were appropriate given their specific sales force issues. The results of these tests are summarized in the following scorecard. Detailed results for three of the tests are included as separate figures.

Compensation Plan Design—Evaluation Criteria	Comments
Consequences for Salespeople	
Quantitative Tests	
Test C: Plan traction, engagement, and excitement	Overall engagement is at 100 percent. All salespeople are earning at least some incentive money.
Test D: Performance distribution analysis	Quarterly payout distribution is shown in Figure 2-31. Sales leaders believe that there is not enough variation in pay across the sales force.
Test E: Bias check	No correlation is found between market size and payout. A slight geographic bias exists—a few regions of the country have more favorable payouts.
Test F: Pay-for-performance check	Figure 2-32 shows the relationship between performance score and payout. Sales leaders are pleased that performance ratings and pay are positively correlated. However, they are concerned that the lowest-rated salespeople make about half as much money as the highest-paid people. They feel that outstanding performers should make much more and poor performers should make less.
Consequences for Salespeople	
Qualitative Test	
Test G: Qualitative sales force input	No formal surveys have been done, but there have been complaints from top performers that the plan is too "socialistic."
Consequences for Sales Force Activities	
Quantitative Tests	
Test I: Time allocation analysis	Sales force effort allocation appears consistent with past strategy.
Test J: Engagement and excitement decomposition	Product Engagement Rates (the percentage of salespeople making incentive money on each product, or those above 50 percent of goal) are high for all products: EHS, 86 percent; SS, 100 percent; IES, 100 percent.
Consequences for Sales Force Activites	
Qualitative Test	
Test K: Evaluation of plan complexity	Salespeople are well versed in the plan and routinely see past payouts and forecast future payouts using a Web-based tool.
Consequences for Customers	
Qualitative Test	
Test L: Customer input	Not gathered.

Consequences for Company Results

Quantitative Test

Test M: Cost analysis

Figure 2-33 compares the planned and actual incentive costs by product. Although actual costs vary from planned costs, these differences are explained by variation in goal achievement and therefore do not adversely affect profitability.

Consistency with Company Strategies

Qualitative Test

Test O: Check for consistency with corporate strategies

Product weights and effort allocation reflect past marketing strategy.

Compatibility with Other Sales Force Drivers

Qualitative Test

Test Q: Check for compatibility with culture and other sales force effectiveness drivers

The message sent by the incentive plan differs from the message sent by sales managers. Sales managers view 80 percent goal attainment as failure (and coach their salespeople accordingly), yet salespeople who make just 80 percent of goal still make 80 percent of target pay.

Figure 2-31. Test D: Performance distribution analysis for the MNP sales force.

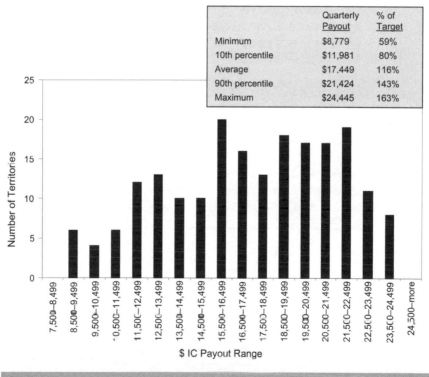

	Quarterly Payout	% of Target
Minimum	$8,779	59%
10th percentile	$11,981	80%
Average	$17,449	116%
90th percentile	$21,424	143%
Maximum	$24,445	163%

Sales leaders believe that there is too little variation in pay across the sales force. They feel that top salespeople deserve to earn more than 143 percent of target pay, and low performers deserve less than 59 percent of target.

Figure 2-32. Test F: Pay for performance check.

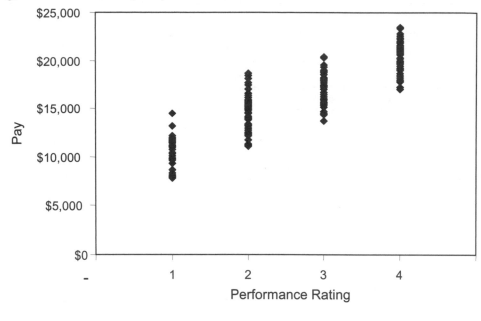

Performance Rating

Performance Rating Scale
1 = Unacceptable performance (on probation)
2 = Consistently acceptable performance
3 = Consistently good performance
4 = Consistently outstanding performance

Sales leaders are pleased that performance ratings and pay are positively correlated. On average, 4-rated performers earn more than 3-rated performers, who in turn earn more than 2-rated performers, who earn more than 1-rated performers. However, there is concern that there is not enough differentiation in pay between the groups. The lowest-rated salespeople make about half as much money as the highest-rated people. This is perceived to be a very serious problem. Sales leaders feel that the highest-rated performers should earn much more, and the lowest-rated performers should earn less.

Figure 2-33. Test M: Cost analysis (by product line).

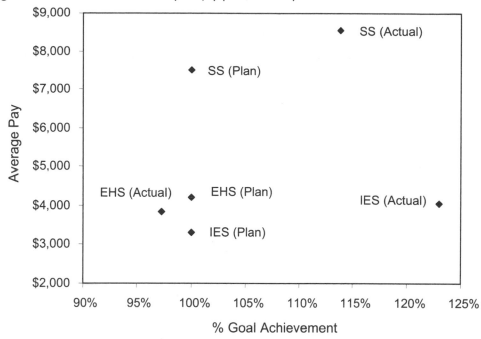

Actual costs are higher than planned for the SS and IES product lines, while actual costs are lower than planned for EHS. These cost differences are explained by variation in goal achievement for the different product lines and therefore do not adversely affect profitability. The design of MNP's incentive plan, which ties payout directly to goal attainment, keeps incentive costs in line with company sales.

Figure 2-34. New MNP incentive plan objectives.

Sales Management System Component	Plan Objectives
Consistency upstream • Corporate and marketing strategies • Sales job definer decisions	Encourage salespeople to allocate effort consistent with marketing strategy. Product weights should be modified based on company goals for the next period. Specifically, more effort should be allocated to the IES product line to thwart the competitive launch.
Compatibility with other sales force effectiveness drivers • Hiring and training programs • Performance management • Sales force motivators • Sales force culture	Make the success message of the incentive plan consistent with that of the performance management system by increasing the threshold at which incentive payout begins.
Consequences downstream	
Salespeople	Pay for performance; significantly increase pay variation across the sales force.
Sales activities	Encourage salespeople to allocate effort consistently with marketing strategy by adjusting product weights appropriately.
Customer results	Ensure that costs continue to stay aligned with revenues.
IC program management	Keep the plan easy to communicate and administer.

Plan Design Fundamentals

How This Chapter Is Organized

Introduction   93
Sales Compensation Plan Design Terminology   94
   Total Pay Components, Mix, and Leverage   94
   Risk   96
   Total Sales Components   97
      Sales Force Causality and Prominence: Free Sales and
      Salesperson Sales   97
      The Effect of Market Volatility: Random Sales   101
Four Key Incentive Compensation Plan Design Decisions   103
   Pay Level   103
   Salary–Incentive Mix   104
   Performance Measures   104
   Performance–Payout Relationships   105
   Plan Design Choices: A Summary   105

Introduction

Designing or revamping a sales incentive compensation plan can be a challenging task. Any plan designer who is given this responsibility struggles over when and how to tackle such an important project. In the words of one IBM executive who participated in a major redesign of the firm's worldwide sales incentive plan, "These projects can take on a life of their own." Even with a small sales force, the task of redesigning the sales compensation plan can be complex, and the impact of making a mistake significant.

This chapter organizes the sales compensation plan design process by introducing some important terminology and summarizing four key sales compensation plan design decisions. Chapters 4 through 7 of the book are organized around these four key decisions, and will use the concepts introduced here. Plan designers can refer back to the definitions presented in this chapter throughout the compensation plan design process.

Sales Compensation Plan Design Terminology

The world of sales compensation plan design has its own language. Terms such as *target incentive, target pay, pay mix, variable pay, leverage*, and *at-risk pay* are used frequently, but often inconsistently. Here, we define the way these terms are used throughout this book.

Total Pay Components, Mix, and Leverage

Figure 3-1 defines some terms that are commonly used when discussing sales force pay. The figure shows three example compensation plans (called low, medium, and high) and breaks down *total pay* into three components within each plan. *Base salary* is the fixed amount of compensation that salespeople receive, regardless of how much they sell or how well they perform in the short term. *Target incentive* is the amount of money the firm expects salespeople to earn in variable pay (or incentive pay), including bonuses and/or commissions. The actual amount of variable pay that each salesperson earns depends upon how well she performs; target incentive is based on the firm's prediction of what that performance should be. Base salary plus target incentive is often referred to as *target pay*.

Target pay mix refers to the proportion of total target pay that is base salary versus target incentive. Pay mix is often expressed as the percentage of salary relative to the percentage of target incentive. For example, Figure 3-1 includes plans with an 85/15 target pay mix, a 75/25 target pay mix, and a 50/50 target pay mix.

It is important to note that target pay mix can be different from *actual pay mix*. The firm's compensation plan specifies the target pay mix. Actual pay mix, however, depends upon how well the sales force performs relative to expectations. For example, suppose a company expects its sales force to average $1 million in sales per salesperson. Each salesperson receives a base salary of $50,000 plus a 5 percent commission on sales. Target incentive is thus $50,000 ($1 million × 5

Figure 3-1. Components of total pay.

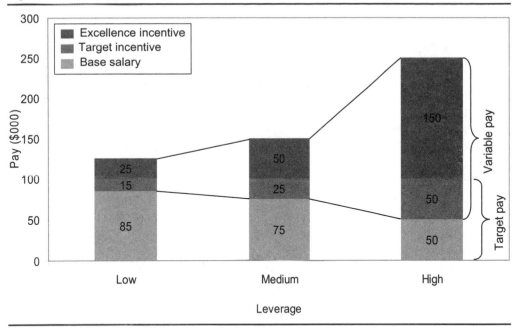

percent), and total target pay is $100,000 ($50,000 base salary plus $50,000 target incentive). Target pay mix is 50/50. Now suppose the firm's estimate of $1 million in sales per salesperson turns out to be incorrect and the sales force actually sells $1.2 million per salesperson. The sales above expectation could be the result of a number of factors, including an extraordinary sales force effort, an unexpected market change, or a poor initial sales forecast. In this example, actual incentive is $60,000 ($1.2 million × 5 percent), and actual pay is $110,000 ($50,000 base salary plus $60,000 incentive). Actual pay mix is approximately 45/55. Similarly, if sales force performance is below the $1 million per salesperson expectation, salespeople will earn less than the target incentive amount and the actual pay mix will contain more than 50 percent salary and less than 50 percent incentive.

It is also important to note that the concepts of target pay and target pay mix are averages across all salespeople. Those salespeople who perform well will earn more than the target pay level, while those who do poorly will earn less than the target level. *Excellence incentive* is the amount of incentive pay beyond the target incentive that the firm's very best salespeople (for example, those in the top 5 to 10 percent of the sales force) are expected to earn. Excellence incentive is $25,000 for the low plan, $50,000 for the medium plan, and $150,000 for the high plan. Excellence incentive plus target incentive is the potential *variable pay* that a salesperson can earn. Variable pay is another term for *incentive pay*; it includes all sales force bonuses and/or commissions that vary with performance.

Pay mix is a statistic showing how much variable pay the firm desires to provide its sales force. Another useful statistic, the *leverage multiple*, provides a measure of how much incentive the firm is willing to provide its top performers. The leverage multiple is defined as the sum of excellence incentive plus target incentive divided by target incentive. Using this definition for the plans in Figure 3-1, Figure 3-2 shows that the high-leverage plan has a leverage multiple of 4 [($150 + $50)/$50], the medium-leverage plan has a leverage multiple of 3 [($50 + $25)/$25], and the low-leverage plan has a leverage multiple of 2.7 [($25 + $15)/$15]. *High-leverage* plans combine a high variable pay mix with a high leverage multiple. They have significant upside variable-pay opportunity. A plan with *low leverage* has a small variable-pay opportunity; this happens when a substantial portion of the target pay mix is salary and the excellence incentive is small.

Notice that all three pay plans in Figure 3-1 have the same total target pay of $100,000. The three plans differ greatly, however, in the amount of potential variable pay and the amount of leverage. Notice that there is a positive relationship between leverage and total pay opportunity. A salesperson with outstanding performance earns just $125,000 with the low-leverage pay plan. Yet he is guaranteed to earn at least $85,000, regardless of performance. On the other hand, a salesperson who achieves outstanding results under the high-leverage pay plan has a much greater upside—with incentive earnings, she can earn up to $250,000, or five times her base salary. Yet, she could earn as little as $50,000 if her territory performance is poor. Usually, a pay plan with a large variable component will have greater upside opportunity but lower guaranteed earnings, while a plan with a smaller variable component will have less upside earnings potential but a greater earnings guarantee.

Risk

Pay mix and leverage contribute to the level of inherent risk for the salesperson, but they are not the only factors that determine risk. Risk in a pay plan depends upon the likelihood that salespeople will earn at least the target level of income, regardless of how that money is paid (salary or incentive). Consider the following two situations:

1. A sales force is compensated using the high-leverage plan in Figure 3-1 with a 50/50 pay mix. Incentives are paid as a commission on total sales

Figure 3-2. Examples of leverage multiple calculation.

Measure	Formula	Leverage Examples		
		Low	Medium	High
[S] Salary		$85,000	$75,000	$50,000
[I] Target incentive		$15,000	$25,000	$50,000
[P] Target pay	[P] = [S] + [I]	$100,000	$100,000	$100,000
[E] Excellence incentive		$25,000	$50,000	$150,000
[L] Leverage multiple	[L] = { [I] + [E] } / [I]	2.7	3.0	4.0

from the first dollar sold. Since most sales are repeat purchases from existing customers who have predictable usage and buying patterns, the firm can project sales results at the territory level with great accuracy. Commission rates are set and territories are aligned such that each salesperson earns very close to the target incentive. For the vast majority of salespeople, actual pay varies from total target pay by less than 10 percent.

2. A sales force is compensated using the medium-leverage plan in Figure 3-1 with a 75/25 pay mix. Incentives are paid as a commission on sales above a territory goal. Territory goals are challenging "stretch" goals, designed to motivate the sales force to achieve peak performance. Over half of the salespeople do not make goal and thus earn only the base salary of $75,000, which is 25 percent below the total target pay. Only those who make the stretch goal can earn the target pay level or above.

Even though the first pay plan is more highly leveraged (i.e., has a greater proportion of variable pay and greater upside opportunity) than the second pay plan, the first pay plan has less risk for the salesperson. A good portion of the variable pay in the first plan is actually a "hidden salary." Salespeople earn many of their commissions on repeat sales that will probably occur regardless of what they do. This pay is not truly at risk. Compensation plan designers sometimes refer to the variable incentive portion of a pay plan as the "at-risk" component. These two examples show that high leverage does not always imply high risk. *At-risk pay* should be defined as that portion of variable pay that will be realized only because of a salesperson's skills, capabilities, motivation, and effort. We prefer to use the term *performance pay* for this concept. Performance pay is thus defined as the portion of variable pay that will be earned because of a salesperson's skills, competencies, motivation, and energy. In selling situations where a large proportion of sales is realized regardless of what the sales force does, performance pay is often significantly smaller than variable pay.

Total Sales Components

Effective sales incentive compensation plan design requires understanding the various factors that contribute to total sales, including the importance of the sales force in the sales creation process. The sales force is just one influencer of sales. Product features and quality, brand name, pricing, and distribution are also important factors. Other forms of promotion, such as advertising, direct mail, and web sites, also have an impact. Environmental influences such as the economy and competitors' moves are another important consideration. Understanding the importance of the sales force in creating sales and the nature of salespeople's impact helps an incentive plan designer create a plan that is appropriate for a specific selling situation.

Sales Force Causality and Prominence: Free Sales and Salesperson Sales. The ability of a sales force to affect total sales results is often called *sales force causality* or *sales force prominence*. There is considerable sales force causality and the sales force has high prominence in sales environments where the sales force plays a primary role in creating sales. There is less sales force causality and the sales force has lower prominence in sales environments where other influences besides the sales force have considerable sales impact. Sales force causality and prominence can be both short term and long term. In environments with high short-term causality, sales are primarily determined by the skill, motivation, and efforts of salespeople *in the current incentive period*. Other environments have high long-term causality: Sales force effort today has an impact in future periods. Figure 3-3 shows some examples of selling situations with high and low sales force causality, and with causality that is short term and long term. The extent of sales force causality and the time frame of that causality are important considerations when designing an incentive plan.

To further illustrate the concept of sales force causality and prominence, Figure 3-4 decomposes total annual sales for two firms into three components that identify how those sales were created. The two companies in the figure—an automobile dealership and a medical diagnostic instruments company—were selected because salespeople at these companies have fairly high prominence and causality, but the timing of their sales impact (short-term versus long-term) varies considerably as a result of differences in their roles and selling processes.

- Salespeople at the automobile dealership sell cars to consumers who come into the showroom. Occasionally salespeople sell to repeat or referred cus-

Figure 3-3. Sales force causality and prominence in some example selling situations.

	Short-Term Impact	Long-Term Impact
High Sales Force Causality and Prominence	Office product sales • Products are commodities; purchases are small and frequent. • There are few buying decision makers. • Sales success requires persistence and strong transactional selling skills. • Sales force effort drives short-term results.	Computer system sales • Products are complex and customized; purchases are large and infrequent. • There are many buying decision makers. • Sales success requires problem solving and strong consultative selling skills. • Sales effort today builds customer relationships that will create sales in the future.
Low Sales Force Causality and Prominence	Health and beauty aids merchandising • Salespeople visit individual retail store locations to stock shelves, conduct inventories, and set up merchandise displays. • While this function is important, it has less direct sales impact than other sales drivers, such as brand name, pricing, advertising, trade promotions, and national account selling.	

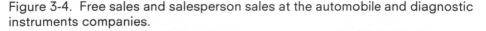

Figure 3-4. Free sales and salesperson sales at the automobile and diagnostic instruments companies.

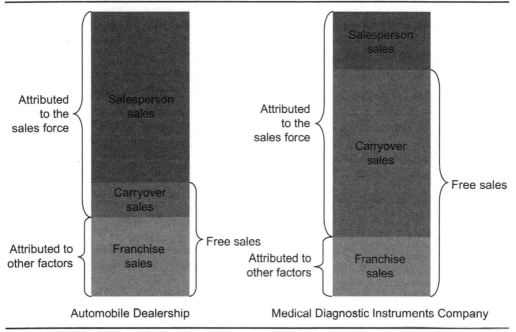

tomers, but the vast majority of sales are to people who have no prior knowledge of the salesperson. Salespeople's earnings depend mostly on commissions, which are typically a percentage of net profits on the cars the salespeople sell. Since other dealerships sell the same makes and models of cars, the marketplace is very competitive and price competition is fierce. Salespeople begin each day at sea level, not knowing how much they will sell or earn.

- Salespeople at the medical diagnostic instruments company call on hospitals and large reference laboratories, selling a family of well-known and highly differentiated products. The firm earns a modest profit when an instrument is placed, but the majority of its sales and profits come from the ongoing sales of the chemical reagents necessary to perform tests using the instruments. Salespeople strive to sell units at competitive prices, knowing that if they continue to provide good service to the account, the reagent orders arising from the instrument placement can help them earn an attractive bonus to supplement their competitive salary.

As a result of the different sales environments at these two companies, the proportion of total sales coming from each of the three components shown in Figure 3-4 varies. The three components, which together explain sales force causality and prominence, are as follows:

- *Franchise sales* is the portion of this year's sales that can be attributed to non-sales force factors, such as dominant products, effective branding, competitive pricing, and effective advertising. Both the automobile sales-people and the diagnostic instruments salespeople realize a moderate amount of franchise sales. The automobile manufacturer spends large amounts of money advertising to consumers. In addition, the dealership runs local television, radio, and newspaper ads and has a well-known name and reputation. The medical diagnostic instruments company sells brand-name products that are differentiated from those of competitors and are backed by industrial advertising, trade shows, and other non-sales force marketing support. Franchise sales do not depend on the sales force.

- *Carryover sales* is the portion of this year's sales that results from prior years' sales force effort. These sales are attributed to the relationships that salespeople have built with customers in the past; they are a consequence of long-term sales force causality. The medical diagnostic instruments sales force has high carryover sales. Customers have high switching costs, and each instrument placed creates future demand for reagents. As a result, a diagnostic instruments salesperson's impact is long term; the relationships she develops today will pay off significantly in future years. Salespeople at the automobile dealership have low carryover sales. Customers will shop around with multiple dealers in order to get the best price, often using the Internet to find deals well outside of their local area. Repeat customers are a small percentage of a car salesperson's total business.

- *Salesperson sales* is sales resulting from the skill, knowledge, motivation, and effort of the sales force in the current incentive period. Salesperson sales is a consequence of short-term sales force causality. Most of the sales attributed to the sales force at the automobile dealership are salesperson sales. They result from an assertive, persuasive sales approach in which a salesperson quickly closes a deal before the consumer leaves the showroom to go to another dealership. The medical diagnostic instruments sales-people, on the other hand, generate a smaller level of salesperson sales. They spend the majority of their time servicing customers and nurturing relationships, activities that may not result in immediate salesperson sales but that pay off over the long term in the form of carryover sales.

Note that both the diagnostic instruments company and the automobile deal-ership have considerable sales force causality and prominence; the proportion of total sales attributed to the sales force is large. A primary difference between the two selling environments, however, is the time frame of the causality. At the auto-mobile dealership, causality is primarily short term. Sales effort this year results in considerable sales this year (large salesperson sales) and only very minor sales in future years (small carryover sales). At the diagnostic instruments company, cau-sality is primarily long term. Sales effort this year creates modest sales this year (small salesperson sales) but substantial sales in future years (large carryover sales).

Carryover sales (which are created by past sales force effort) and franchise sales (which are created by non-sales force factors) together equal *free sales*. Free sales will be realized regardless of what the sales force does this year. This is an important concept in incentive plan design. An accurate estimation of the proportion of total sales that is free sales and the proportion that is salesperson sales in a given selling situation has important implications for an incentive plan. These implications are explored in future chapters.

The Effect of Market Volatility: Random Sales. Many environmental factors that are outside of a company's and a salesperson's control also influence sales. For example, a seller of emergency home power generators sees dramatic sales increases when a major power outage affects customers in his territory. A business service company loses sales when an important customer is acquired by another firm that uses a competitor's service. Environmental volatility and uncertainty make it difficult for firms to predict their sales accurately.

Market volatility varies considerably across sales environments. Some events that can contribute significantly to market volatility include:

- Customer volatility
- The launch of a new product or a major competitive launch
- Changes in the channel structure or regulatory environment
- Technological advances
- Economic trends
- Unexpected events, such as major stock market swings or acts of nature

Windfall gains and losses that occur with very little sales force effort are another example of market volatility. Sometimes a salesperson gets a "bluebird." For example, a salesperson at a newspaper company sells advertising space to companies. She plays a very prominent role in creating most of her sales, so that ordinarily her free sales are very low. However, one day she happens to be in the office when the phone rings. She picks it up. A marketing executive for a global electronics firm is at the other end. The firm wants to place 30 pages of advertising to launch a new product. The order makes the salesperson's year. How much did she have to do to generate the sale? Hardly anything—she gets a windfall gain. Windfall gains are a result of market volatility.

The effect of market volatility on sales is called *random sales* and is illustrated for the automobile dealership and the medical diagnostic instruments company in Figure 3-5. Random sales are sales that come in unexpectedly and require very minimal sales force effort relative to their value. Random sales can be high in one year and low in the next. Random sales can also be negative, such as when sales are lost as a result of customer consolidation or a successful competitive launch. Like free sales, random sales will be realized regardless of what the sales force does.

Notice that random sales are larger at the automobile dealership than at the

Figure 3-5. Market volatility and random sales.

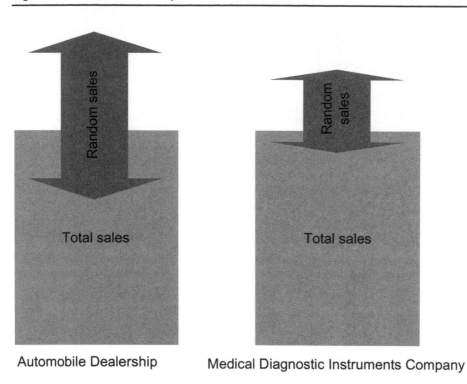

diagnostic instruments company. Automobile sales can be influenced significantly by numerous events that are outside the dealership's control, including the economy, manufacturer-offered rebates and financing deals, information from consumer advocate groups, gasoline prices, and competitors' moves. All of these factors create volatility in the automobile market. The diagnostic instruments company is affected by random sales as well, but to a lesser extent than the automobile dealership. Examples of random sales for the diagnostic instruments company include sales lost as a result of consolidation in the customer base and sales increases as a result of an unsolicited endorsement by a leading diagnostic physician.

Random sales sometimes vary across market segments or product lines within the same company. For example, the advertising sales department for the *New York Times* works in teams that are organized by market. Some teams work in more stable markets, where revenue is easier to predict, while others (particularly many of the smaller teams) work in volatile markets, where accurate prediction is very difficult. Each team has its own incentive plan that recognizes and accounts for the level of volatility in the team's assigned market (see Chapter 7 for more on this story).

Random sales are very difficult to predict. Since they are not affected by the salesperson, they threaten short-term sales force causality and are therefore an important consideration for effective sales compensation plan design. The effect of random sales on incentive planning (as well as that of free sales and salesperson sales) will be explored in future chapters.

Four Key Incentive Compensation Plan Design Decisions

The next four chapters of this book are dedicated to the specifics of plan design, with each chapter focusing on one of four key incentive compensation plan design decisions. These decisions are shown in Figure 3-6.

Chapters 4 through 7 provide thinking frameworks, practical advice, and examples that will help you make the best sales incentive plan design choices in each of these four areas. Each of the chapters is organized around two major themes:

1. *Assessment of a current plan.* Does an existing plan have the right pay level, pay mix, performance measures, or performance–payout relationship?

2. *Designing a new plan.* How do you determine the right pay level, pay mix, performance measures, or performance–payout relationship?

Pay Level

A first important sales incentive compensation plan design decision is how much salespeople should be paid in total. There are two parts to this decision: the average target pay for each sales job, and how total pay should vary across salespeople (payout distribution) within each job. There are wide differences in sales force pay levels across industries. There are even differences in pay levels within the same industry. Several factors influence a company's pay level and payout distribution decisions, including:

- The level of sales force causality and prominence
- Labor market value
- Company job value assessment, pay level history, and budget
- Variation in performance, tenure, and levels across the sales force
- Firm culture

Some firms choose to lead the industry in total pay in order to attract the best possible candidates. Others choose a level of total pay that is competitive within the industry and use alternative strategies for attracting top talent, such as providing a favorable working environment, collegial colleagues, an effective manage-

Figure 3-6. Four key sales incentive compensation plan design decisions.

Chapter	Decision	Description
4	Pay level	How much should salespeople be paid?
5	Salary–incentive mix	What proportion of sales force compensation should be variable pay and what proportion should be salary?
6	Performance measures	What measures should be used to determine the incentive component of sales force compensation?
7	Performance–payout relationships	How should the incentive payment vary with measured performance?

ment team, professional development, significant opportunity for advancement, and/or an appealing culture. The design issues surrounding the decision on total pay level and payout distribution are discussed in detail in Chapter 4.

Salary–Incentive Mix

A second important sales incentive compensation plan design decision is what proportion of a salesperson's pay should be salary and what proportion should be variable performance-based incentive pay. As with total pay, significant variation in the salary–incentive mix exists across industries. Differences also exist within the same industry as a result of varying management philosophies and cultures. Several factors influence the pay mix decision, including:

- The firm's selling process and the role of the sales force
- The level of sales force causality and prominence
- The measurability of company and customer results
- Industry norms
- Company history, culture, and management philosophy

The pay mix decision has a significant impact on the sales force culture and influences the degree to which management uses incentives, rather than other sales force effectiveness drivers (for example, nonmonetary motivation programs and performance management systems), to motivate and control the sales force. The design issues surrounding the salary–incentive mix decision are discussed in detail in Chapter 5.

Performance Measures

A third important sales incentive compensation plan design decision is what measures should be used to determine the variable component (and to a lesser degree the salary component) of sales compensation. Most firms link incentive pay to sales revenues, but other metrics can also be used as incentive pay determinants. Determining the best performance measure to use requires examining issues such as:

- Should incentive pay be determined by results metrics (such as sales revenues, units, gross margin, market share, and customer satisfaction) or by activity metrics (such as the number of calls, proposals, or demonstrations)?

- Should payout be determined by the absolute level of performance, by growth over last year, by percent of goal achieved, or by ranking versus peers?

- Should the metrics used for incentives be broken down by market segment, product, or channel?

- What proportion of sales force pay should be based on team performance versus individual performance?

- How often should incentives be paid?

The design issues surrounding the performance measure decision are discussed in detail in Chapter 6.

Performance–Payout Relationships

A fourth important sales incentive compensation plan design decision is determining how sales force incentive payout should vary with measured performance. Some important performance–payout relationship decisions include:

- Should the firm adopt a commission plan (where the salesperson earns a specified percentage of every sale) or a bonus plan (where a bonus is earned only if a certain level of sales or some other goal is achieved)?

- Should plan payout accelerate as performance increases, or should earnings decelerate once a goal or other threshold has been achieved?

- Should the incentive plan be capped?

- Should the plan pay out from the first dollar or from goal or some fraction of goal?

- Should plan payout be based on a single measure or multiple measures?

The design issues surrounding the decision on performance–payout relationships are discussed in detail in Chapter 7.

Plan Design Choices: A Summary

There are many drivers of incentive plan design. Industry practice, the company's financial situation, product marketing strategies, the firm's selling process, sales force causality, data availability and accuracy, and the firm's culture and management philosophy are all important factors to be considered by plan designers. The specific influence of these factors on each of the four key incentive plan design decisions is explored further in the next four chapters.

A Holistic View of Plan Design Decisions

This book organizes the compensation plan design decision into four parts—pay level, pay mix, performance measures, and performance–payout relationships—and these four parts are presented sequentially in the following four chapters. Even though the decisions are discussed in separate chapters, they are highly interdependent. For example:

- The pay level decision and the pay mix decision are closely linked. A compensation plan that pays a high fixed salary with only a small variable component tied to performance is risky for a firm. Salaries must be paid regardless of performance. Thus, pay levels must be kept reasonable so that sales force costs are managed in case performance is below expectation. On the other hand, a compensation plan that pays a small salary and a large variable component tied to performance is to a great extent self-funding. The firm can afford to pay more because a substantial portion of the cost is realized only if the desired results are achieved.

- The pay mix decision is linked to the performance measures decision. Accurate territory-level company and customer results measurement is essential for a pay plan with a large variable-pay component. If it is not possible to measure performance accurately, then it is impossible to pay fairly based on that performance. When salespeople perceive performance measures to be unfair, the desired motivational impact of the variable-pay plan is lost, and the sales force may spend its time arguing about the unfairness of the measures instead of selling. When results measurability is poor, a plan with mostly salary is usually the best option.

- The performance measures and performance–payout relationship decisions are interdependent. An effective bonus plan requires that accurate territory-level goal setting be possible. A successful commission plan requires frequent and accurate measurement of territory results, so that payments are timely and correct. A volatile market in which it is difficult to set accurate territory-level goals may necessitate income caps or decelerators, so that salespeople do not receive undeserved windfalls.

Although the decisions on pay level, pay mix, performance measures, and performance–payout relationships are presented as separate and sequential decisions in this book, these decisions cannot be made independently of one another. A holistic view of sales compensation plan design ensures the best possible plan result.

Plan Design Part 1: Determining the Correct Pay Level

How This Chapter Is Organized

Is Your Sales Force Pay Level Correct?	108
Consequences: A Downstream View	108
Consistency: An Upstream View	110
Compatibility: Alignment with Other Sales Force Effectiveness Drivers	110
Summary of Symptoms of Sales Forces That Are Over- and Underpaid	112
The Range of Sales Force Pay Levels	112
Target Pay Level	114
Pay Variation	114
How to Determine the Right Sales Force Pay Level	115
Primary Drivers of Sales Force Pay Level and Variation	117
Sales Force Role in Demand Creation	117
Labor Market Value	119
Company Influences on Pay Levels	125
Job Value Assessment	125
Historical Company Pay Levels	126
Company Budget	127
Company Culture and Philosophy	129
Company Influences on Pay Variation	132
Differences in Individual Performance	132

Variation in Salesperson Tenure and Number of Job Levels   135

Sales Force Culture and Values   137

Conclusion   137

Is Your Sales Force Pay Level Correct?

Determining the pay level for each sales position is an important sales management decision that has two components: determining the average target pay for the position, and determining the pay variation across different performance levels and tenures. Paying too little implies that the firm will not be able to attract salespeople with the skills, knowledge, and/or motivation required to do the job effectively. Strong performers will leave the firm for more lucrative opportunities, resulting in low sales force productivity, lost customers, and the need to constantly recruit and train new salespeople. Yet paying the sales force too much creates problems as well. The firm sacrifices profitability and creates a sense of high-pay entitlement across the sales force. Overpaid salespeople may become complacent and not be motivated to work harder to earn more money. Poor performers will not leave the company voluntarily, as they will not be able to find another job that pays as well. While it is relatively easy to increase pay, it is very difficult to rein in pay once it is out of control.

Although the term *pay level* implies that there is a single number (target sales force pay), there is really a distribution around target pay. Some salespeople will earn more than target pay, while others will earn less, based on tenure and/or performance. Some firms set their target pay level appropriately, but get into trouble because their distribution around target pay is inappropriate and demotivating. A common problem is that low performers are paid too much and top performers are paid too little. This leads to excessive turnover among the firm's best salespeople—the ones the firm does not want to lose. At the same time, poor performers stay on too long. The opposite situation is also possible: The variation between low and high performers can be too great. For example, in some situations, new salespeople make so little money before they are able to build a "book of business" that few survive for more than a few months.

There can be many signs that the current sales force pay level is not working well. The symptoms fall into clear categories within the sales management system framework introduced in Chapter 1.

Consequences: A Downstream View

Sales compensation is a key salesperson-focused effectiveness driver; it plays an important role in shaping, exciting, and controlling salespeople. How much salespeople are paid affects all the downstream components of the sales management system. Pay level affects which *salespeople* are initially attracted to the firm, as well as who stays and who leaves. In addition, pay level influences the motivation of salespeople. Attraction, retention, and motivation affect *sales force activities*, which in turn affect *customer results* and ultimately *company results.*

The Consequences of Paying the Sales Force Too Much

A large, diversified manufacturer of industrial and commercial fuel-handling products has a compensation plan where salespeople on average earn $120,000 per year in salary plus 50 percent additional as a target bonus. Many salespeople make well over $200,000 per year—more than many vice presidents at this company. No other sales force in the industry is paid so well, and as a result no salesperson has left the company in over five years. Even though the company is the market leader, management feels that many of the salespeople are too complacent, living off their existing customer base, and not putting in the extra energy to go after new opportunities.

The Consequences of Paying the Sales Force Too Little

Salespeople for a small financial consulting firm are paid an average salary of $50,000, plus a 1.5 percent commission on sales that is equivalent to $33,000 for salespeople who achieve their sales goal. Thus, average target pay is $83,000. Commission rates accelerate beyond goal. However, recent goals have been too aggressive, and last year only 20 percent of the sales force made goal. Average pay in the industry is $115,000, and many of the firm's best salespeople have left for more lucrative competitive offers. In fact, the firm lost more than one-third of the sales force last year, making the average sales force tenure just two years. Since it takes two years to fully train a salesperson to be effective in this market, sales leadership feels that it has too many inexperienced salespeople attempting to sell complex products, missing sales opportunities, damaging client relationships, and harming the company's reputation.

The Consequences of Paying Top Performers Too Little and Low Performers Too Much

Target pay for a building materials sales force is $60,000, earned 85 percent through salary and 15 percent through a quarterly bonus based on territory revenue and revenue growth relative to goal. Pay ranges from $50,000 for the lowest-paid salespeople up to $90,000 for the highest-paid salespeople. Management has observed that top performers often "max out" and quit, while low performers seem to stay too long. This excessive turnover of good salespeople has begun to hurt the firm's relationships with its customers and is adversely affecting company sales and profits.

Consistency: An Upstream View

Effective pay level decisions are compatible with all of the upstream sales force effectiveness driver decisions, including sales strategy, go-to-market strategy, and sales force design. A clear definition of sales roles (part of the sales force design decision) is an important prerequisite to the pay level decision. A firm will need to pay more to attract salespeople for roles that are difficult, require great skill and knowledge, and have high customer impact, while lower pay may be adequate for roles that are easier, require less skill and knowledge, and have moderate customer impact.

Sales force restructuring often necessitates changes in sales force pay levels. As sales roles are redefined, hiring profiles change. The appropriate pay level for salespeople with the new hiring profile may be different from the appropriate pay level for salespeople with the old profile. Pay level issues can be particularly challenging in merger situations when two merging partners have very different sales force pay scales.

Pay Level Conflicts Following a Sales Force Merger

A large financing company acquired a small mortgage company whose sales force compensation was way out of line with the acquiring company's compensation practices. Salespeople at the mortgage company were making a lot of money, in part because of the company's rapid growth and entrepreneurial spirit. The mortgage company had grown extremely fast, yet had never adjusted its original commission scale. Corporate management at the acquiring company strongly suggested that the generous compensation for these salespeople be brought down to a more palatable level. Sales management wondered how to address this request while avoiding a morale issue within the acquired sales force. "The last thing we need is for the new division to think that we are changing everything—we can't afford to lose folks who are critical to the company's ongoing success."

Compatibility: Alignment with Other Sales Force Effectiveness Drivers

Pay level decisions must also align well with the other sales force effectiveness drivers. A salesperson values:

- The work content—how interesting, fulfilling, and satisfying it is
- The work environment—how supportive and enjoyable it is
- The skills gained on the job—how "employable" the salesperson becomes (some companies, such as Johnson & Johnson and General Electric, are well-known "training" companies in their industries)

- The company itself—its reputation and career progression opportunities
- The pay the job provides
- The benefits that go with the job

If a job is very attractive on other dimensions, the pay does not have to be the highest competitively for the package to become dominant. On the other hand, in companies that are weak on some of these nonpay dimensions, salespeople will demand "combat pay" to compensate for the deficiencies and make the job competitive in the marketplace.

Procter & Gamble Gives Employees Two Days Off

In 2004, Procter & Gamble gave employees an unexpected gift—two extra vacation days—as a reward for outstanding stock performance over the previous four years. P&G employees also had the option of taking two days' pay instead of the time off. Companies have used various forms of paid time off to reward employees, including flextime core hours, shared positions, extended lunches, and "hour off" passes. Rewarding employees with paid time off shows that the company truly values its workers and believes that employees with a balanced life are happier and more productive.

What Attracts and Motivates Younger Producers in the Insurance Industry?

Attracting young people to sales positions is a constant challenge for insurance companies. According to *National Underwriter Life & Health* magazine, monetary compensation is not the most important motivator for insurance agents in their late twenties to mid-thirties. Workers in this age group value nonmonetary benefits, such as support of work-life balance; extra time off; continuing education benefits; in-house mentoring by experienced salespeople; stock options; perks such as paid vacations, club memberships, or box seats at sporting events; the opportunity to travel and attend conferences; and a positive work environment that provides professional recognition, a sense of being needed, and opportunity for growth and advancement within the company.

Career Stage Influences Which Job Aspects Are Valued

Research shows that the importance of various job dimensions changes throughout a salesperson's career. Early in their career, salespeople place greater value on intrinsic rewards, such as feelings of worthwhile accomplishment, personal success, and respect from coworkers. Later in their career, the importance of these dimensions decreases and greater value is placed on extrinsic rewards, such as pay increases and formal recognition for achievement.

Recruiting, training, and performance management processes need to be aligned with the type of people that will be attracted by the proposed pay level. For example:

- The recruiting applicant pool is affected by the established pay level. Higher pay creates a larger, more attractive applicant pool, making recruiting easier. If pay levels are below industry norms, hiring profiles may need to be adjusted in order to attract candidates.

- Training programs may need to change if applicant experience levels are either above or below expectation.

- Sales managers will need to work differently with their direct reports, depending upon whether the reports feel that they are paid appropriately or not.

Summary of Symptoms of Sales Forces That Are Over- and Underpaid

Figures 4-1 and 4-2 summarize some common symptoms of sales forces that are overpaid and underpaid.

The Range of Sales Force Pay Levels

The sales force pay level decision has two parts:

1. The first part of the decision is setting the target pay level. In other words, how much should a salesperson who meets the company's expectations earn? Actual earnings will depend upon the extent to which these expectations are missed, met, or exceeded.

2. The second part of the sales force pay level decision is determining how much variation in pay should exist across the sales force. For example, how much more than the target pay level should a top performer earn, and how much less than the target should a salesperson who fails to meet expectations receive? How much should an experienced salesperson who makes his goal earn compared to a new person who makes her goal?

Sales force pay level and pay variation are important sales force incentive design decisions.

Figure 4-1. Some signs that the sales force *may* be overpaid.

Consistency with . . .	Compatibility with . . .	Consequences . . .
• Sales and marketing strategies • Sales process • Sales roles	• Performance management systems • Sales force culture • Sales force motivators • Sales force hiring and development processes	• Company results • Customer results • Sales force behaviors and activities • Sales force quality
• Some sales process steps can be moved to sales assistants and/or cheaper and more efficient channels. • As the company's product has become a commodity, the associated sales process has evolved from being complex and adding significant customer value to being simple and adding modest value, but sales force pay levels remain high.	• The company relies heavily on pay and incentives to manage the sales force, having an inadequate sales force performance management system and a weak or inconsistent culture. • People are making much less money at other companies or within other parts of the company for jobs requiring similar skills and capabilities. • Company leadership overvalues the sales force. • The job offers interesting work and great growth opportunities, and the environment is supportive, making the high pay levels unnecessary. • The job offers many attractive forms of noncash compensation, such as benefits, retirement program, generous vacation policy, trips to conferences, and recognition programs.	• Sales goals are being achieved, but profit goals are not. • The sales force expense-to-sales ratio is too high. • Sales force compensation is viewed as excessive by other employees within the company. • Customers complain that the sales force is complacent. • Sales leadership feels that the sales force is not motivated; high-performing salespeople are not interested in working harder to make more money. • There is hardly any sales force turnover of poor performers, who rarely leave the firm without being asked.

Target Income Ranges

While companies often specify a target income level for the sales force, an *income range* may be a more useful concept. Instead of a single number, the income range specifies what people should earn depending on both their performance and the company's performance. For example, rather than designating an average target income of $100,000 for a salesperson, a firm might specify target income ranges for different levels of performance. For example, an average performer might expect to earn $80,000 to $90,000, a better performer might expect $95,000 to $105,000, and the top 25 percent of performers might expect $120,000 to $130,000, depend-

Figure 4-2. Some signs that the sales force *may* be underpaid.

Consistency with . . .	Compatibility with . . .	Consequences . . .
• Sales and marketing strategies • Sales process • Sales roles	• Performance management systems • Sales force culture • Sales force motivators • Sales force hiring and development processes	• Company results • Customer results • Sales force behaviors and activities • Sales force quality
• The sales process has evolved from one requiring focus on the product to one requiring complex solution design, but sales force pay levels remain low. • The sales force structure has evolved into specialized roles that are quite different in terms of skills required and value to the customers. The pay has not increased for specialized sales roles requiring a high degree of skill.	• Company leadership thinks that the sales force adds little value and that products can sell themselves. • Company leadership is cost focused, which drives it to pay the sales force below-market rates. • Training instructors complain that the new class presents a significant challenge. ("You can't send ducks to eagle school.") • Sales managers and the HR department find it difficult to attract and retain quality people.	• The sales force is not achieving sales goals. • Salespeople lack the motivation to produce the quantity and quality of sales effort desired. • Difficult selling tasks are not getting done effectively. • Customers complain that there is too much sales force turnover or that salespeople lack customer and product knowledge or important skills and capabilities. • The best salespeople are leaving the firm. The average sales force tenure is low.

ing upon the overall sales force performance, and hence company performance. Notice that the income range concept captures both the pay level and pay variation aspects of the decision.

Target Pay Level

Target pay levels for full-time salespeople vary significantly. When we surveyed managers of 110 sales forces, of varying sizes and in various industries, who attended our sales compensation executive education programs at Northwestern University between 2000 and 2004 (the Sales Incentive Executive Education Survey), target sales force pay ranged from $27,000 up to $265,000. Figure 4-3 shows the range and variation across the 110 sales forces. The pay level for companies in selected industries is also shown.

Pay Variation

There is also significant variation in the total pay that top performers earn relative to average performers in the same role at the same company. Some firms pay top

Figure 4-3. Distribution of target pay level in the Sales Incentive Executive Education Survey.

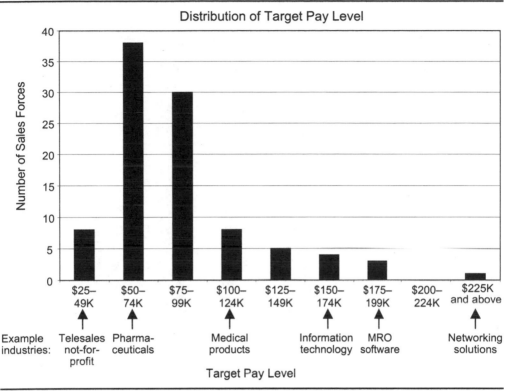

performers multiples of what average performers earn. In other cases, the difference is much less. In the Sales Incentive Executive Education Survey, the median values show that the lowest-paid salespeople in a sales force earn 67 percent of what average performers earn, while the highest-paid salespeople earn 163 percent of what average performers earn. The distribution of low and high earnings as a percentage of average earnings across all the sales forces in the survey is shown in Figure 4-4.

How to Determine the Right Sales Force Pay Level

As shown in Figure 4-5, there are two primary drivers of sales force pay level and variation:

1. The sales force role in demand creation for the company's products and/or services

2. The labor market value for this type of position

The sales force role in demand creation defines the value that the salesperson brings to the customer and the company, and the degree to which the salesperson

Figure 4-4. Distribution of total earnings for the lowest- and highest-paid salespeople compared to average earnings in the Sales Incentive Executive Education Survey.

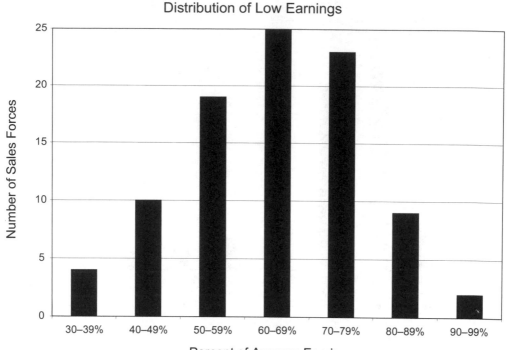

Distribution of Low Earnings

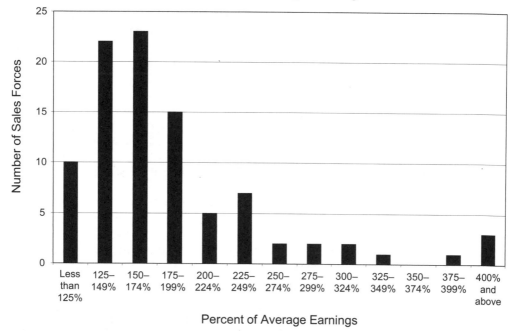

Distribution of High Earnings

Figure 4-5. Sales force pay level and variation: drivers and influences.

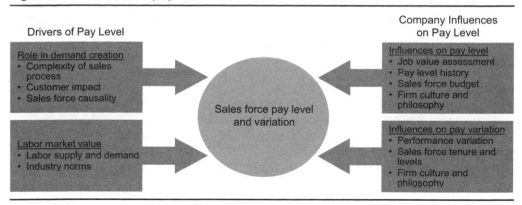

controls the customer relationship. It also depends on the complexity of the sales process, since more complex processes will need salespeople with more skill and experience. The sales force role determines what type of person can be successful at executing the required sales process. Supply and demand in the labor market and industry norms determine what a firm needs to pay in order to attract and retain salespeople who possess the skills, traits, expertise, and capabilities required to execute the role successfully.

In addition to the primary drivers, there are several company influences on the pay level and variation decisions. Job value assessment, pay level history, and company budgets influence what pay levels are feasible. Performance variations across the sales force, as well as variation in sales force tenure and the number of job levels within the sales force, influence what variation in pay level is appropriate. The firm's culture also has an important influence on both the pay level decision and the variation decision. Determining the right pay level and variation involves a thorough assessment of the drivers, followed by a check of the company influences to ensure compatibility and feasibility of implementation. Each of these assessments and checks is discussed further here.

Primary Drivers of Sales Force Pay Level and Variation

Sales Force Role in Demand Creation. Within a company, a field salesperson who handles key accounts and has an average territory of $20 million is likely to earn more than a field salesperson who controls a $1.5 million territory. The field salesperson who controls the $1.5 million territory will, in turn, make more than a telesales person who produces $360,000 in a year. Among the determinants of total pay are the degree of impact the salesperson has in producing results for a company and the control the salesperson has over the customer. Salespeople who have significant customer impact and control are likely to be paid more than those with less customer impact and control. The salesperson's role in demand creation is sometimes referred to as the *prominence* of the sales role. Prominence reflects the ability of an individual salesperson to affect results and control the customer relationship. The salesperson *is* the company to the customer in a high-prominence environment. In high-prominence environments, sales are primarily determined by the skill, motivation, and efforts of individual salespeople. In low-prominence environments, other factors besides the sales force have a significant impact on sales. These include non-individual salesperson factors such as brand name, pricing, advertising, the economy, competitors' moves, and the sales effort of other members of a sales team. Sales force pay levels tend to be higher and the variation between high and low performers larger in selling environments with high sales force prominence.

All other things being equal, salespeople who perform complex sales processes that require considerable knowledge and skill are likely to be paid more than those who perform simpler sales processes. For example, a salesperson who sells highly customized high-tech networking solutions needs to orchestrate the design of a beneficial solution with a technical team from his own company, while understanding how the products will fit into the customer's business, and perhaps even coexist with products of co-suppliers or other vendors. The sales process requires creative customization of the offering in order to meet each customer's needs and strong knowledge of the customer's business and the company's own products, services, and capabilities. High pay levels are required to attract salespeople with the knowledge, skills, and capabilities required to do this job effectively. On the other hand, a consumer products merchandiser performs sales tasks that are more straightforward (such as setting up store displays, stocking store shelves, and checking product inventory) and works with customers (retail store managers) whose needs are more predictable and clearly defined. Merchandisers can acquire the skill and knowledge needed to do their job in a relatively short period of time, and a great deal of experience is not necessary in order to be effective at executing the necessary selling tasks. Thus, the firm does not need to pay as much to attract salespeople who fit the profile of a successful merchandiser. The right pay level attracts and retains salespeople with the skill, knowledge, and capabilities necessary to fill a sales role successfully, yet does not overpay and waste the firm's money.

Sales Force Pay Should Align with the Sales Role

Sales force pay levels can vary significantly within a single company if there are salespeople in different sales roles. For example, a distributor of plastic components pays outside field salespeople an average of $90,000 per year, but pays inside salespeople (telesales) an average of just $50,000 per year. This is because the selling tasks assigned to outside salespeople require greater skill and have higher customer impact than the tasks assigned to inside salespeople. In another example, "hunter" salespeople, who focus on lead generation, prospecting, and new customer development, usually make more money than "farmer" salespeople, who are responsible for servicing, stocking, and customer maintenance. Customer assignments can also influence pay levels. Salespeople who are responsible for national or other major accounts usually make more money than those responsible for accounts in a local area. For instance, at a telecommunications company, national account salespeople average $112,000 per year, large account salespeople average $91,000 per year, and salespeople who cover small accounts in geographic territories average $54,000 per year.

Labor Market Value. Labor Supply and Demand. The labor market affects most sales forces. There is major competition for salespeople in high-employment economies. In the United States during the late 1990s, workers had numerous job opportunities and diverse career choices. As a result, sales forces needed to pay more in order to attract and retain the best people. As the economy slowed down and unemployment increased in the early 2000s, the demand for salespeople decreased and the supply of potential workers increased, and as a result sales force pay levels moderated. The supply–demand balance often varies across industries as well as over time. Pay levels escalate when the supply of a particular type of salesperson is tight and demand for that type of salesperson is high. Demand usually exceeds supply in high-growth industries that need skilled salespeople. The medical device industry experienced this in the 1980s, the data communications industry experienced it in the 1990s, and the business-to-business e-commerce companies saw it in the early 2000s.

High-Growth Sales Force Employment Opportunities for 2005

In February 2005, *Sales and Marketing Management* magazine surveyed recruiters around the country and asked them which industries they believed to have the greatest potential for sales professionals in terms of job opportunities, compensation, and professional development. Five industries were identified:

1. *Health care and pharmaceuticals.* Despite recent drug scandals, the industry is booming, and sales departments within health-care and pharmaceutical firms can't hire salespeople fast enough.

2. *Office equipment.* As the digital world expands, corporate business needs for copiers, printers, and other equipment are growing dramatically as companies look for new ways to take advantage of available information.

3. *Business services.* More and more companies are cutting certain internal operations and outsourcing them to business service firms in an effort to keep budgets streamlined.

4. *Insurance.* The industry is thriving, particularly in areas such as benefits sales to companies. In addition, the industry is suffering from an immense talent drain, as the majority of agency owners are approaching retirement age.

5. *Technology.* A new wave of innovation and evolution is driving growth as companies look to technology firms to provide solutions in a more complicated world.

Should You Vary Pay Levels by Metropolitan Area?

There are substantial cost-of-living differences across U.S. urban areas. For example, the cost of living in New York City or San Francisco is more than double that in San Antonio or Oklahoma City. Some companies account for geographic cost-of-living differences explicitly by varying pay level according to the location of the salesperson. In our experience, most companies have a single national pay level range, but allow local market conditions to dictate specific pay levels within that range. Job candidates in New York City, for example, are likely to require pay at the high end of the range, while those in Oklahoma City may be willing to work for pay at the low end of the range.

Industry Norms. Sales force income differences across industries reflect variations in the complexity of selling and the involvement of the sales force in demand creation. Selling in some industries is difficult to do well, because of extensive or highly technical product lines and/or complex customer needs. Successful salespeople in these industries require deep levels of product knowledge and customer knowledge, which are often acquired only over several years of experience in the industry. On the other hand, selling in industries with simple product lines and easy-to-understand customer needs does not require the same investment in acquiring customer and product expertise. The skills, capabilities, education, and experience needed to be effective at selling in a particular industry help determine the sales force pay level that is appropriate.

Industry profitability, growth, and competitive intensity also affect sales force pay levels. Pay is usually higher in high-margin, high-growth industries, as well as in industries with considerable sales force prominence because of a lack of product differentiation and/or low customer switching costs. Pay is usually lower in low-margin, mature industries, as well as in industries with less sales force prominence because products are highly differentiated and/or customer switching costs are high. Sometimes the effects of these factors are in conflict with one another. For example, pay can be high if industry profitability is high and a salesperson has considerable prominence in the creation of a high level of territory profitability. But if the high profitability is due to a differentiated product and high intrinsic customer demand, rather than to the salesperson's efforts, pay can be low. When an industry leader sets a certain pay scale, followers and less competitive participants tend to emulate the leader's behavior. Over time, industry pay norms develop.

Sources of Information for Determining Market Pay Levels. Most firms use information gathered from external sources to determine industry sales force pay levels.

External assessment involves benchmarking sales force pay against the competition, analyzing market trends, and assessing the future labor supply–demand balance. External assessment helps a firm ensure that its pay level is competitive in the labor market and that the company will therefore be able to attract good salespeople. Market survey data, as well as information obtained through recruiting and exit interviews, can provide a firm with insights about market pay rates and trends.

Most companies benchmark externally once a year to see whether their sales force pay levels are competitive with the market. Many published market surveys are available for this purpose. There are surveys that:

- Focus exclusively on the sales function and include comparisons of pay for various sales positions across different industries.

- Focus on a particular industry and include comparisons across different functions and positions (including sales) within the industry.

- Include global data.

- Focus on a particular geographic market.

- Include breakdowns of pay by performance level (for example, how much do average, better, and best performers earn?).

External market benchmarks tell the firm what pay level is needed in order to be competitive with other firms for high-quality salespeople. Some sources of compensation survey data are listed in Figure 4-6.

With most of these surveys, a firm must agree to participate in future surveys in order to purchase the data. Some surveys will provide data to nonparticipants, but usually at a higher price than that for participants. Each survey has its own unique characteristics, and selecting the best survey depends upon a company's specific needs. It is common for different surveys to give a slightly different market rate for the same job. This is due to differences in the participating companies, the survey methodologies, and/or the judgments of the analysts providing the data as to how their organizations' sales roles map into the survey-defined roles.

> *"When a survey says we are paying below the market rate, our sales force enthusiastically believes the data. When a survey says we're paying above market rate, suddenly the sales force insists the data is all wrong."*
>
> A compensation manager at a large firm

Some key questions to consider when determining which survey is best for a particular firm include the following:

- What types of data are collected, and how are the data reported? Is the level of detail provided (for example, the breakdowns by industry, com-

Figure 4-6. Examples of published compensation surveys.

Note that it is necessary to participate in most surveys in order to access survey results.

Company	Survey Name	Contact Information
Alexander Group, Inc.	Sales Compensation Trends Survey	www.alexandergroupinc.com
Clark/Bardes Consulting	CHiPS Sales Plus Survey (IT industry)	www.clarkconsulting.com
Culpepper and Associates	High-Tech Sales Compensation Survey	www.culpepper.com
Hay Group	Industry-specific surveys	www.haygroup.com
Hewitt Associates	Sales Compensation Survey—U.S.	www.hewitt.com
McLagan Partners, Inc.	Compensation surveys—financial service industry	www.mclagan.com
MRA—The Management Association, Inc.	National Sales Compensation and Practices Survey	www.mranet.org
PPG	Pharmaceutical industry compensation survey	
Radford Division (Aon Consulting)	Radford Sales Survey	www.radford.com
Top Five Data Services, Inc.	Medic (Medical Device Industry) Sales Compensation Survey	www.top5.com
Towers Perrin	Compensation surveys	www.towersperrin.com
Watson Wyatt Data Services	Survey of Sales and Marketing Personnel Compensation	www.ecssurveys.com
Western Management Group, Inc.	High Technology Sales and Service Compensation Survey; Global Sales Remuneration Survey	www.wmgnet.com
Wm. H. Mercer Inc.	Sales Compensation Survey	www.imercer.com

pany size, sales role, geography, and/or performance ranking) sufficient for your needs?

- What is the sample size for the clusters that are relevant to your firm? Surveys have strengths and weaknesses in different areas; be sure that the data for your particular area of interest (industry, geography, company size, sales role, etc.) are sufficiently strong.

- Which companies participate in the survey? Are these the firms you consider to be your competition for salespeople? Some surveys will not disclose the survey participants; decide if this information is important for drawing conclusions about the data.

- How timely are the data? How frequently is the survey published? What is the time lag in reporting? Be sure the data are still relevant, given recent swings in business cycles in your industry.

- Is the survey well documented?

- What is the cost of the data?

- Are the delivery format choices compatible with your needs? Most surveys are available in multiple formats, such as hard copy, PDF, Excel spreadsheet, and online access.

Many companies find that the information obtained through published market surveys provides a reasonable benchmark for the majority of sales positions. However, some management teams are uncomfortable with published survey data because of the data's age or relevance to the firm's specific situation. For example, the results of a published survey may be too broad in terms of the types of companies or kinds of sales roles included in a single survey category. Many consulting firms are willing to design and conduct custom compensation surveys that provide a company with very timely, verifiable, and specifically relevant data. However, conducting a custom survey can be quite costly, time-consuming, and resource-intensive. An alternative between the extremes of purchasing a published survey and contracting for a custom survey is to work with a consulting firm that maintains a compensation database that includes many firms in the industry of interest. A selective extraction of companies from this database can provide a semicustomized benchmark at less cost and in less time than a custom survey conducted from scratch.

Information about competitive pay levels can also be gathered through recruiting and exit interviews. Job candidates who either accept or reject the firm's employment offer can share evidence of how they are valued by the market—particularly if they are choosing among multiple job offers. Recruiting firms can share labor market insights gathered from their direct experience with companies and potential recruits. New hires can provide information about the pay practices of their former employer. Similarly, exit interviews with salespeople leaving for other jobs can provide insight into how the firm's salespeople are valued externally. Exiting employees are often more candid in an exit interview with a third party who provides anonymous feedback to the company; they may be reluctant to taint their employment record by making unfavorable comments in an exit interview with the firm's human resource department.

Most firms use recruiting and exit interviews as a secondary source of pay level information to reinforce and verify more formally gathered benchmarking data. While recruiting and exit interviews can provide valuable insights, data gathered from these sources often lack the completeness and detail necessary for drawing definite conclusions.

Who Pays Below Industry Average?

We have yet to meet a sales management team that was willing to state that its company's goal is to pay the sales force below the industry average. Practically every company claims to have a pay level at least in the top half of its industry, with the vast majority of companies claiming to be in the top third of their industry. Of course, many of these claims are misleading. It is not easy for management to tell a sales force that the company's strategy is to pay in the lower half or lower quartile within the industry. Thus companies often select their peer group of companies carefully to create a benchmark to which their pay level compares favorably.

Perhaps this tendency to select a favorable peer group when comparing pay levels helps explain why CEO pay has escalated so dramatically in recent years. In 1992, CEOs were paid 82 times the average of blue-collar workers; in 2004, they were paid more than 400 times that average. A recent study at Stanford University found that CEO pay levels are unrelated to performance. Perhaps CEOs benchmark their pay against other CEOs who make more money than they do, and then use this information to demand greater pay.

Compare the Pay of the Company's Best Performers with That of the Best Performers in the Industry

A meaningful way to benchmark total pay level against the industry is to compare by performance level. For example, even if a firm pays below the industry average overall, its top performers can still be among the top earners in the industry. If poor performers earn only as much as the bottom quintile, they may be encouraged to look for a job elsewhere. Many firms that cannot afford to pay their entire sales force the market rate will still pay their star performers very well in order to attract and retain them.

A Biotechnology Firm's Hiring Strategy Influences Sales Force Pay Levels

When a biotechnology company was ready to launch its first product, the management team wanted to hire only the best pharmaceutical salespeople for its sales force quickly. The company's profile of an ideal candidate was a pharmaceutical salesperson with five or more years of experience, a life science degree, in-depth territory knowledge, and documented performance in his current position in the top 20 percent. Average target pay for a pharmaceutical salesperson was $60,000 to $70,000 a year in salary plus $25,000 to $40,000 in variable pay and limited stock options. In order to attract the best talent in the industry, new hires at the biotechnology firm were offered $100,000 a year in salary to start, $35,000 minimum variable pay with an uncapped maximum, and generous stock options.

Market Sales Force Pay Levels May Be Internally Inconsistent with Pay Levels in Other Company Departments

The need to offer salespeople a pay level that is competitive with the industry sometimes leads to internal parity problems. For example, an average salesperson may earn more than a product manager or sales manager at the same company. While not inherently a problem, this can lead to less desire for lateral career moves, which in turn leads to cultural isolation for the sales organization within the company.

Company Influences on Pay Levels

Information about external market pay levels should always be balanced with a view toward the company's internal compensation standards. An internal assessment of the value that the sales job creates for the firm helps in fine-tuning market pay rates. Additional internal influences on the pay level decision include historical company pay trends and budgets. These internal checks help to ensure that sales force pay levels are affordable, realistic, and appropriate. Internal checks also encourage fairness and consistency of pay levels across different sales roles within the firm.

Job Value Assessment. Job value assessment is based on the belief that pay should be linked to the total value that a job delivers to the organization. Job value assessment answers the question, "What is the sales job worth to the firm?"

There are many different job value assessment methodologies available. The Hay method, which was developed during the 1950s for valuing manufacturing jobs, is perhaps the best known of these techniques. The Hay method, like all job value assessment techniques, uses factors that measure a job's requirements for skill, effort, and responsibility. Job characteristics are organized into three clusters:

1. *Inputs,* or the knowledge, capabilities, and skills that a job requires
2. *Throughputs,* or the problem-solving competencies needed to be effective at the job
3. *Outputs,* or the results that the job produces

In addition, working conditions, such as the physical environment and hazards, physical effort required, and mental concentration demands, are taken into account. Analysis of all of these job characteristics leads to an assessment of the total value that the job creates for the organization, which is translated into an appropriate pay level.

Many companies use job value assessment to price different roles across various departments of the company—not just sales roles. This can help to ensure that sales force pay is fair and consistent with pay in other departments and with companywide values. This is particularly important if career progression involves movement between departments. For example, a salesperson with management aspirations might benefit from working in an internal position in the marketing department before getting promoted. Yet if salespeople are paid significantly more than marketing people at a comparable level, few salespeople will be willing to move to marketing and take a pay cut.

Job value assessment also helps to ensure that pay levels across different sales roles (for example, telesales, field sales, national account sales, and sales management) are fair and consistent. Salespeople will frequently make pay level comparisons with coworkers in other sales roles at the company, while comparisons with salespeople at other firms occur less frequently (for instance, when a salesperson is job shopping). Thus, perceived internal fairness can have a large impact on sales force morale.

Perceived Unfairness in Pay Across Roles Hurts Teamwork

At Prosoft, a provider of technical services and training to government agencies, the sales and engineering staff needed to work together to meet customer needs effectively. However, differences in the pay levels and pay structures for engineers and salespeople caused friction, which hindered cooperation between the two roles. Engineers were expected to help with sales presentations, yet they were paid a salary exclusively. They perceived the generous commissions earned by salespeople to be unfair. At the same time, salespeople, who felt a need to earn commission dollars, were reluctant to help engineers during the preparation of lengthy bid proposals or with critical after-sale support for customers. To promote better teamwork between salespeople and engineers, Prosoft realigned its pay structure and levels. Commissions for salespeople were eliminated, and salaries were raised to a level comparable to those of engineers. Following the change, repeat business and sales growth improved dramatically, and the firm made its first-ever contribution to the employee profit-sharing plan and paid all its employees a year-end bonus.

While eliminating sales force commissions was successful at Prosoft, drastic reductions in the incentive portion of sales force pay can be very hard to implement successfully. More information on how to implement such changes is provided in Chapter 11.

Job value assessment has helped many firms:

- Provide clarity to salespeople about how their role is valued and what criteria are important to the firm.

- Create a consistent, defendable compensation plan across varying sales roles within the company.

- Manage compensation costs by ensuring that increases in pay for a particular sales role are offset by increases in the value created by that role.

- Facilitate rational and objective decision making about sales force pay levels.

Historical Company Pay Levels. Sales force pay levels are often determined by what the firm has paid the sales force historically. Historical pay levels become the norm for corporate management, for financial planning, and for the salespeople. The pay history provides a benchmark for future pay. Companies try not to deviate significantly from the established norm: "It worked, didn't it?" A poor precedent can be established if variable pay or salary increases rapidly. The annual increase can become an expectation. A sales force that sees its pay escalate as the company and most of its salespeople exceed goal for several years in a row gets used to "being in the money." Such a sales force can become quite demotivated when growth slows or goals become more realistic and pay begins to moderate. Similarly, if the sales force has received a 5 percent pay increase in each of the last five years, there will be widespread disappointment if this year's increase is less than 5 percent. Very often companies get into trouble when historical pay increases become an expectation among salespeople. Many companies find that some random variation in pay increases can actually improve sales force motivation and diminish salespeople's feelings of entitlement.

Management at a Medical Device Firm Learns a Lesson: Think About Tomorrow When Setting Today's Pay Levels

A start-up firm developed a revolutionary new cardiac medical device in the early 1990s. The firm's 50 salespeople were paid a 4 percent commission on sales. In the first year after launch, salespeople made $100,000 to $150,000. As the use of the new device caught on across the medical community, sales grew dramatically. Five years after launch, salespeople were earning an average of $650,000. Since the company was incredibly profitable and didn't want to risk any decline in sales force morale, management decided that it should continue to "share the wealth" with the sales force. This caused some resentment among employees working in internal departments, such as marketing and research and development, who felt that it was unfair for the sales force to be rewarded so generously. In addition, competitors began to enter the market, cutting into company profits. It was clear that given the new market conditions, the company could no longer afford its high sales force costs, yet changing the compensation plan would be very disruptive and unpopular. The firm's salespeople were in high demand by competitors, and many jumped ship to seek the next big payoff. According to a top sales executive at the firm, "A few years ago, I was busy walking around with a big smile on my face." In 2004, the entire industry averaged $250,000 target pay for a salesperson, which is high, but well below the stratospheric levels of the mid-1990s.

Company Budget. Company profitability plays a role in determining sales force pay levels. In general, profitable companies that focus on growth are willing to pay more than unprofitable, stagnant, or cost-conscious companies. A company with weak products may need to pay less than the industry norm because it simply cannot afford to pay more. A firm with high sales per territory and high product margins can afford to pay more than a firm with low sales per territory and low product margins.

Most firms budget their sales force costs to ensure that company sales force expenditures are consistent with the achievement of corporate profit goals. The company budget dictates how much a firm can afford to pay its sales force. Top management typically takes a keen interest in the sales force budget because of its high cost. Many companies view their sales forces as an expensive way to connect with their customers. Consequently, they watch the sales expense line. Most of the costs associated with sales forces are listed in Figure 4-7. Sales compensation costs are typically the largest component of the total sales force expense.

Many companies manage sales force costs to a percentage of sales. The U.S. average is approximately 6.8 percent, although many industries spend 10 to 20 percent or more of sales on the sales force. Maintaining a sales force cost-to-sales ratio that is within historically established company and industry norms is often important to top financial management and shareholders, who want assurance that the firm's costs are under control. Industry benchmarks for sales force cost-to-sales ratios are available through some of the benchmarking data sources discussed earlier in this chapter.

Figure 4-7. Sales force costs.

Compensation costs. Salaries, commissions, bonuses, FICA/FUTA, state and miscellaneous taxes, insurance and retirement benefits, Medicare, benefit maintenance, reporting, and compliance

Recruiting and hiring costs. Advertisements, recruiting fees, testing, reference checking, background checks, interview time, interview travel, training, employee relocation expense, legal expense for contracts

Government requirement costs. State and local taxes and laws, workers' comp, licenses, required forms and filings

On-the-job costs. Travel and entertainment; auto expense; cell phone, laptop, and PDA expenses; customer promos; recurrent training; product training; accounting expense; dues and subscriptions; legal expense for HR responsibilities

Facilities costs. Rent, furniture and fixtures, computers and software, communications systems, administrative support, postage, office supplies, utilities, maintenance, business insurance

Marketing costs. Account forecasting, market share data, competitive awareness, sales meetings, product marketing materials

Account investment costs. Opening new markets and customers, new product development and introduction, routine distributor and customer training, interest on investment dollars

Sales support costs. Customer data, performance measurement, CRM systems

Source: Adapted from Manufacturers' Representatives Educational Research Foundation web site, www.mrerf.org.

A firm's total sales compensation costs are a function of both the size of the sales force and the pay level of each salesperson. Thus the pay level decision affects the number of salespeople a firm can afford. For example, a firm with a total sales compensation budget of $10 million can afford 100 salespeople making $100,000 each. Alternatively, if the firm pays $90,000 each, it can afford 11 additional salespeople. The decision to have a larger sales force with lower pay versus a smaller sales force with higher pay has significant implications for sales force recruiting. If the firm pays more, a larger pool of candidates will want the sales job, and the recruiting challenge will be to identify, attract, and retain the best of these candidates—candidates who are more talented and can generate higher sales than those in the pool at the $90,000 pay level. If the firm is successful in finding and retaining these more talented salespeople, the higher-pay strategy may pay off—a smaller but more talented sales force often can generate higher sales. If the firm is not successful in finding these best candidates, however, it may end up paying an extra $10,000 to salespeople who are no better than those willing to work for just $90,000. In this case, the firm is better off saving its money or spending the extra $10,000 per salesperson to hire additional salespeople, provided there is enough potential incremental business to support the additional people and a large enough pool of good potential salesperson candidates. The trade-off becomes one of quality versus coverage.

The Sales Force Is an Investment

Companies that focus excessively on cost containment and maintaining sales force cost-to-sales ratios tend to undersize and underpay their sales forces. While the sales force is a major expense, it is also a major producer of revenues. A larger, well-paid sales force creates more sales than a smaller, low-paid sales force. A motivated sales force creates more sales than an unmotivated one. Cost containment is not the same thing as profit maximization. A management team that views salespeople as a cost rather than an investment is likely to undersize and underpay its sales force.

Company Culture and Philosophy. Company culture and philosophy also play an important role in shaping sales force pay levels. Many firms have a stated corporate compensation philosophy that dictates how generously they will pay to attract and retain employees and top performers for all positions—for example, "we want to be in the top third of the industry" or "we will pay in the top quintile to attract and retain top performers." At the other end of the spectrum, "cheap" cultures can be found in sales forces run by frugal corporate leaders who are reluctant to part with their dollars.

Some firms will need to pay more than others in the industry in order to attract the best salespeople. Others can offer total pay that is competitive within the industry and attract top talent by providing other benefits, such as a favorable working environment or significant opportunity for advancement. Figure 4-8 illustrates many of the factors, in addition to pay, that often attract salespeople to a

Figure 4-8. Factors besides pay that attract salespeople to a job.

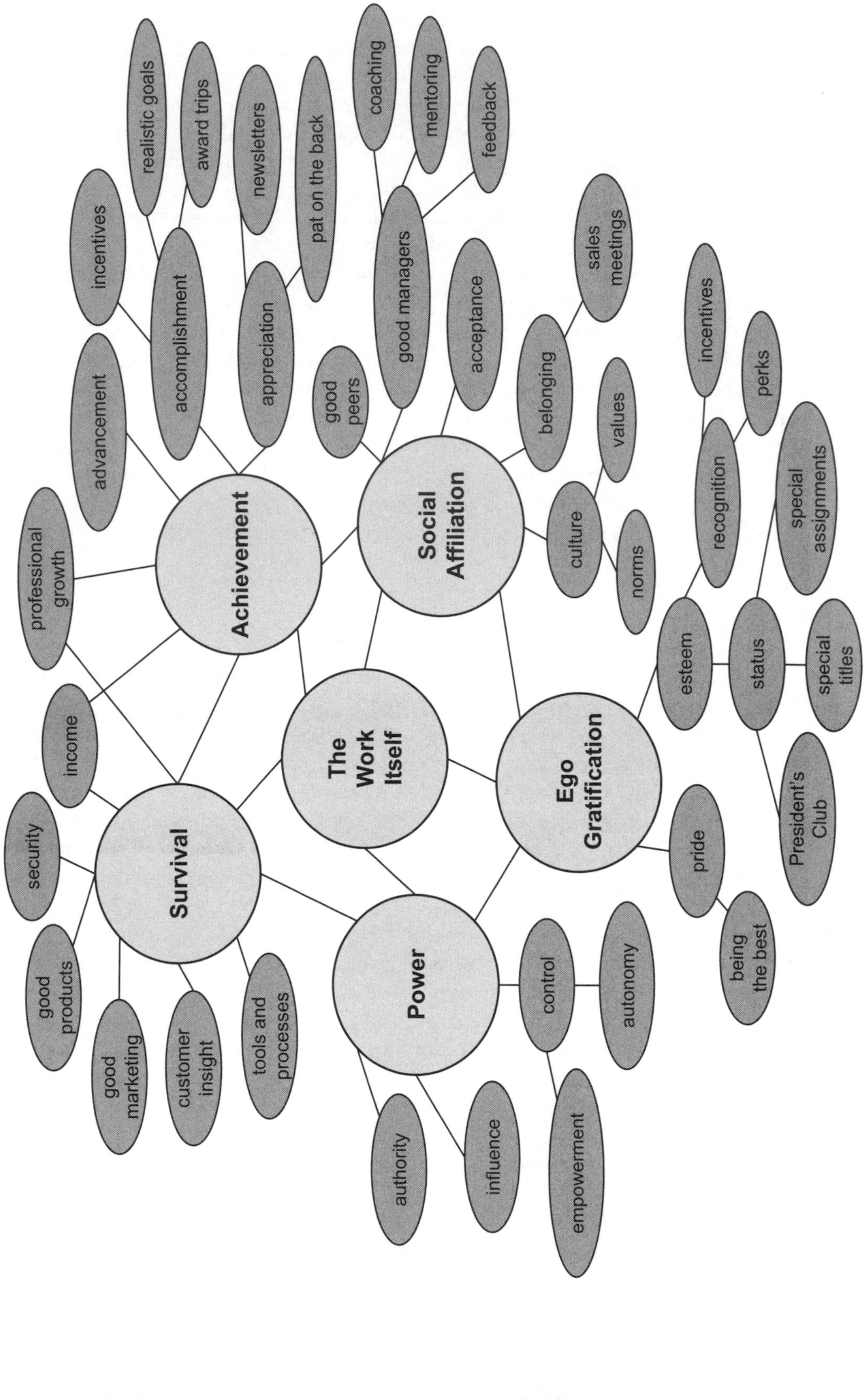

job. A company with a culture that does not emphasize many of these nonpay factors will need to pay more to attract top salespeople.

Sales Force Turnover Statistics and Pay Levels

Since salespeople stay in their jobs for many reasons besides money, pay level decisions are only one influence on the firm's ability to attract and retain talented salespeople. Sales force turnover statistics are an important input to the pay level decision. If turnover is at an acceptable level, then perhaps the current pay level is appropriate, even if it is below the market rate. Other elements that the company offers must be helping to retain people. If turnover is higher than desired, then possibly the pay level is too low, even if it is above the market rate. If undesired turnover of strong performers is high, then perhaps the top salespeople are not being paid enough. If desirable turnover of underperforming salespeople is less than planned, then possibly poor performers are being paid too much.

Desirable Companies Have Strong Positive Cultures

When *HR Magazine* compiled its 2004 list of the best small- and medium-sized companies to work for, competitive pay and benefits were only one consideration. Perhaps the most important element shared by all companies on the list was a strong positive culture. Some common attributes of such a culture include:

- Management is responsive to employee needs.
- Management maintains good communication with employees.
- Management values employee input.
- Management values employee training and development.
- Employees feel respected and appreciated, and are treated as equals.
- Employees are empowered to make decisions.
- Employees are encouraged to pursue their professional passions.
- Employees actively participate in the operation of the business.

PNCBank Uses Company Culture to Attract and Retain Good Employees

PNCBank (www.pncbank.com) considers its culture to be a source of competitive advantage for attracting highly effective employees. The firm has a web page devoted to the importance of attracting and retaining good staff that highlights the ingredients of its successful culture, including:

1. An effective initiation process for new employees, including recruitment and orientation. According to the web page, "Interviewers need to be able to simultaneously pick out prospective employees who will fit in with the company, and sell these individuals on the company." Once the candidate is hired, an effective orientation program allows new hires "to quickly determine that they 'fit in' and can make a contribution." The firm puts a premium on training, stating that "the right training program will help the new employee 'bond' with the company and colleagues."

2. Two-way, ongoing communication. Everyone in the company "should understand that they have the opportunity to speak out and that the company is talking back to them . . . there should be outlets in the form of company meetings, open-door approaches by top executives, and more formal techniques like newsletters."

3. An atmosphere of teamwork and appreciation. "Aside from obvious recognition like salary and benefits, companies need to focus on the less obvious attractions to employees," asserts PNC. These include incentives that inspire interdepartmental cooperation, recognition rewards, and sometimes "just a note or expression of thanks from the company president."

Company Influences on Pay Variation

Compensation experts occasionally suggest an ideal pay variation standard for all sales forces: Top performers should earn three times the target variable pay level. We disagree with the view that a standard variation is appropriate for all situations. External market factors drive the sales force pay variation decision to a large extent; there is a market price that a firm must pay if it hopes to be successful in attracting and retaining top performers. In addition to market drivers, several internal factors influence sales force pay variation. These internal factors include differences in individual performance across salespeople, variation in salesperson tenure, the number of job levels within the sales force, and sales force culture and values.

Differences in Individual Performance. Significant differences in pay across salespeople are most appropriate when these differences are warranted by large variations in performance. Sales leaders often desire a compensation plan that "pays for performance," one that rewards salespeople in proportion to the value they create. For example, Figure 4-9 illustrates pay variation across salespeople at two different firms. Total pay for salespeople at Firm A varies from $20,000 up to $80,000. The range of total pay for salespeople at Firm B is much smaller, ranging from $37,000 up to $64,000.

If Firm A's compensation plan truly pays for performance, then the top-performing salesperson creates four times the value and receives four times the

Figure 4-9. How much pay variation should exist across salespeople?

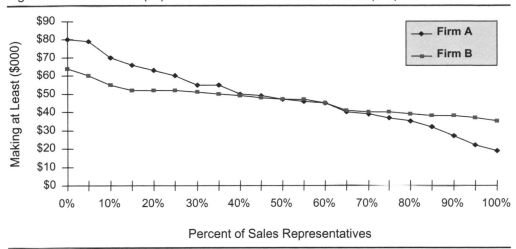

compensation of the poorest performer. At Firm B, on the other hand, if the compensation plan truly pays for performance, the variation in value created across salespeople, and therefore the disparity in compensation, is much less.

A pay-for-performance philosophy is intuitively attractive to most sales leaders. In theory, it is a highly effective way to allocate sales compensation dollars and motivate a sales force. However, in many selling situations, compensation plans that truly pay for performance are difficult to achieve because of low sales force prominence and weak causality. In a high-causality selling environment, sales are determined primarily by the skill, motivation, and efforts of salespeople. This allows management to successfully motivate salespeople to work hard to create more sales by tying variation in pay to differences in individual performance. However, in selling environments where causality is weak, the link between more work and higher sales may not be strong enough to motivate salespeople through pay-for-performance plans. Many factors besides current sales force effort drive sales. If sales force pay is strongly tied to results, some salespeople may earn a lot of money despite putting forth only minimal effort, while others may earn only a modest income even though they work very hard. Large variations in pay tied to performance tend to work best in situations with high sales force prominence and strong causality.

An Approach for Determining the Appropriate Level of Variation in Pay. Figures 4 10 and 4-11 show performance grids for two selling organizations. Each dot in each of the figures represents a salesperson. The dots representing salespeople are plotted with the market volume in their territory on the horizontal axis and this year's sales within their territory on the vertical axis. Market volume is the best measure of territory potential for these companies; companies that do not have accurate territory market volume data may use other territory characteristics, such as demographics or last year's sales, on the horizontal axis. A regression line is

Figure 4-10. Performance grid for a pharmaceutical company.

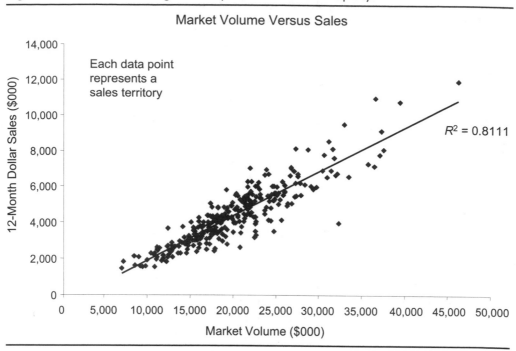

Figure 4-11. Performance grid for a medical diagnostics company.

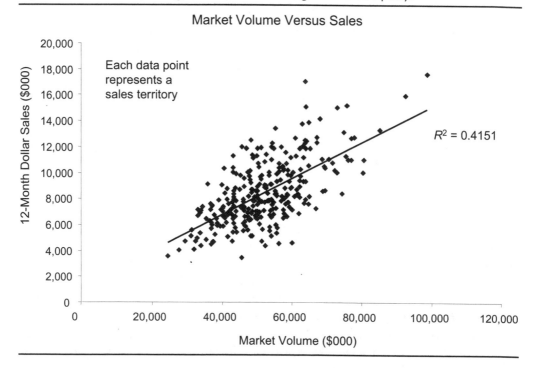

fit to the data. The regression line represents the average sales expectation (or performance) for every level of the chosen territory characteristic, in this case market volume. Salespeople whose dots are above the line are performing at a level above the average expectation captured by the regression line. Those salespeople whose dots are below the line are performing below expectation. The scatter in the plots represents the level of performance variation. Figure 4-10 represents a sales force that has more consistent performance across salespeople than does the sales force characterized in Figure 4-11. It is logical to expect the pay variation for the sales force in Figure 4-10 to be less than the pay variation for the sales force in Figure 4-11. Plots like these enable companies to determine good pay variation distributions.

Pay for Performance and the Salary–Incentive Mix. Usually, significant pay variation across people in the same sales role is achieved by having a larger incentive portion and a smaller salary portion of total pay. Highly leveraged plans (those with a large incentive component) tend to have higher variance in total salesperson income than plans that have a large salary component. For example, as shown in Figure 4-12:

- The low-leverage plan has a guaranteed income of $85,000 in salary, with a target incentive income opportunity of $15,000 (17.6 percent of salary). The best salespeople can make an additional $25,000 (an additional 29.4 percent of salary). Thus, sales force pay ranges from $85,000 up to $125,000; the highest-paid salesperson makes 47 percent more than the lowest-paid salesperson.

- The high-leverage plan has a guaranteed income of $50,000 in salary, with a target incentive income opportunity of $50,000 (100 percent of salary). The best salespeople can make an additional $150,000 (an additional 300 percent of salary). Thus, sales force pay ranges from $50,000 up to $250,000; the highest-paid salesperson makes five times what the lowest-paid salesperson makes.

- The medium-leverage plan falls between the low- and high-leverage plans, with the highest-paid salesperson making double what the lowest-paid salesperson makes.

See Chapter 5 for more information about determining the right salary–incentive mix for a sales force.

Variation in Salesperson Tenure and Number of Job Levels. Many firms place some value on seniority when compensating salespeople. Thus, variation in pay across salespeople is explained in part by disparities in tenure across the sales force. For example, Firm A in Figure 4-9 may have a sales force with a wider range of tenure than does Firm B.

The amount of pay variation within a sales role is also influenced by the num-

Figure 4-12. Higher variation can be achieved by having lower salary and higher incentive.

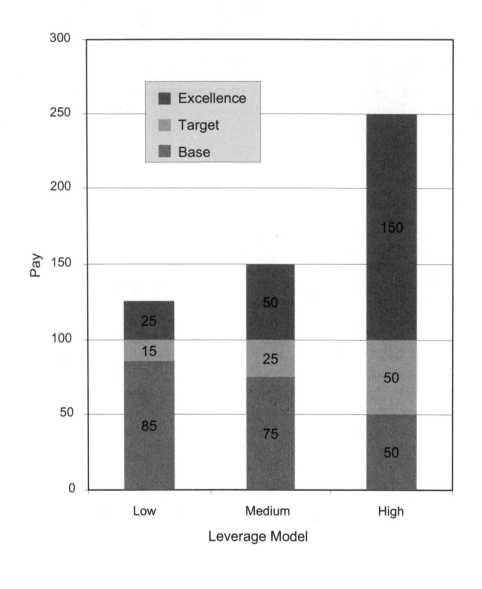

ber of different job levels and the significance of advancement to a higher level within the sales force. Some sales forces have many levels of salespeople (for example, sales rep level I, II, and III). Promotions to higher levels occur frequently, and there is less variation in pay within a particular level and greater variation across levels. Pay increases come primarily through promotions to the next level.

In other sales forces, there are fewer levels, and promotions occur less frequently. As a result, more variation is needed within each level.

Sales Force Culture and Values. Sales force culture and values also play a role in determining the degree of pay variation that is appropriate within a sales force. For instance:

- Sales forces composed of salespeople who are highly motivated by non-monetary factors such as career advancement, learning, or socialization tend to have less variation in pay across salespeople than those that consist of salespeople for whom money is a primary motivator.

- A sales force that encourages teamwork and cooperation among salespeople will want less variation in pay across salespeople than one that desires competition among salespeople to inspire individual success.

- A sales force that emphasizes personal development or encourages other nonselling activities will want less variation in total pay than one that emphasizes output and results.

- A management team with little tolerance for sales force turnover will want less variation in total pay than one that expects and manages turnover. All other things being equal, a greater variation in pay will result in higher turnover of both high and low performers. On the positive side, low performers will get the message that they are not succeeding, and they will leave the firm. On the negative side, however, the plan will attract high performers who are more motivated by money, and therefore will be constantly in search of new opportunities for earning more money, including moving to a competitor.

Conclusion

Figure 4-13 summarizes various sales force role drivers, market drivers, and company influences that help explain why some salespeople make more money than others.

Figure 4-14 summarizes the various sales role drivers, market drivers, and company influences that help explain the degree of pay variation across salespeople.

Figure 4-13. Summary of drivers of and influences on salesperson income levels.

← Low Income	High Income →
Sales Role Drivers	
• The salesperson executes a role that requires modest knowledge, skill, and capability and adds moderate value to the company and the customer.	• The salesperson executes a role that requires considerable knowledge, skill, and capability and adds significant value to the company and the customer.
• The salesperson is primarily a "farmer."	• The salesperson is primarily a "hunter."
• The salesperson controls a moderate amount of business.	• The salesperson controls a considerable amount of business.
• The salesperson is responsible for accounts in a local area.	• The salesperson is responsible for national or other major accounts.
• The customer has multiple links to the company; there is minimal risk of losing customers when a salesperson leaves.	• The customer's primary link to the company is through the salesperson; there is considerable risk of losing customers when a salesperson leaves.
• Sales force prominence is weak—sales are due primarily to a strong brand, advertising and promotion, or other non-sales force factors.	• Sales force prominence is strong—sales are due primarily to the skill, effort, and motivation of the individual salesperson.
Market Drivers	
• There is a surplus of good candidates for the sales job; the labor supply exceeds the demand for salespeople.	• It is hard to find good candidates for the sales job; the demand for salespeople exceeds the labor supply.
• Selling in the industry is straightforward: The selling process is easy to learn and execute, and selling is effort-based.	• Selling in the industry is difficult: The selling process requires high levels of competence to learn and execute, and selling is skill- and knowledge-based.
• The industry is low margin and declining.	• The industry is profitable and growing.
• The industry is only slightly competitive; products are highly differentiated, and customer switching costs are high.	• The industry is highly competitive; there is little product differentiation, and customer switching costs are low.
Company Influences	
• The sales job creates moderate value for the company, when compared to the value created by other company roles.	• The sales job creates considerable value for the company, when compared to the value created by other company roles.
• The company is not profitable and/or is focused on the need to control costs.	• The company is profitable and/or is focused on a desire to innovate and grow.
• The company has historically paid its sales force modestly.	• The company has historically paid its sales force well.
• The firm attracts people through a favorable culture, opportunity for advancement, or other nonpay factors.	• The firm attracts people by paying more than others in the industry.

- Management is not confident that the firm's recruiting process will successfully identify and attract better candidates if pay is higher.

- Management feels that sales force pay should be aligned with a common company culture and therefore should be comparable to pay in other company departments.

- Management is confident that the firm's recruiting process will identify and attract better candidates from a larger applicant pool if pay is higher.

- Management feels that the sales force is special; it has its own unique culture and therefore should have its own pay scale.

Figure 4-14. Summary of drivers of and influences on sales force pay variance.

← Low Pay Variance	High Pay Variance →
Sales Role Drivers	
• Sales force prominence is weak; therefore, sales are due primarily to a strong brand, advertising and promotion, or other non-sales force factors.	• Sales force prominence is strong; therefore, sales are due primarily to the skill, effort, and motivation of the individual salesperson.
• Salespeople work in teams—cooperation is sought.	• Salespeople work alone—competition motivates individuals to succeed.
Market Drivers	
• Top performers in the industry earn only slightly more than average performers.	• Top performers in the industry earn multiples of what average performers earn.
Company Influences	
• Salespeople have similar skills, experience, and motivation and thus produce similar results.	• Salespeople have a large range of skills, experience, and motivation and thus produce very different results.
• Salespeople care about job security, recognition, belonging, learning, and other nonpay factors more than they care about money.	• Salespeople are highly motivated by money.
• Personal development is valued.	• Results are valued.
• Low sales force turnover is desired.	• Sales force turnover is expected and managed.
• There is little variation in tenure across the sales force.	• There is wide variation in tenure across the sales force.
• There are many levels of salespeople; the pay range within each level is tight, and pay differences arise through promotion to the next level.	• There are few levels of salespeople; the pay range within each level is wide, and individual pay is based on performance.

CHAPTER 5

Plan Design Part 2
Finding the Best Salary–Incentive Mix

How This Chapter Is Organized

Introduction	141
Do You Have the Right Pay Mix?	143
Consequences: A Downstream View	143
The Pay Mix Can Be a Powerful Sales Force Shaper	143
Pay Mix as a Sales Force Exciter	146
Pay Mix as a Sales Force Controller	148
Consistency: An Upstream View	149
Compatibility: Alignment with Other Sales Force Drivers	150
The Range of Salary–Incentive Mix	151
The Sales Force with a Low Percent Incentive Pay Plan	154
The Sales Force with a High Percent Incentive Pay Plan	155
The Sales Force with a Moderate Percent Incentive Pay Plan	157
Pay Mix and Sales Force Management and Control	158
How to Determine the Right Salary–Incentive Mix	160
Assessing the Sales Process and the Role of the Salesperson	160
Pay Mix Should Encourage Desired Sales Force Behaviors	161
Pay Mix Should Acknowledge Sales Force Causality	165
Evaluating the Measurability of Company and Customer Results	170
The Consequences of a Pay Mix Decision That Does Not Acknowledge Causality and Measurability	171

Comparing to Industry Norms   173

Checking for Alignment with Company History, Culture, and
Management Philosophy   174

A Pay Mix Scorecard   179

Introduction

The use of incentives for effective sales force management is a two-edged sword.

Using Sales Force Incentives Can . . .	**But Incentives Can Also . . .**
Energize a salesperson to work hard and increase sales.	Lead to mercenary, greedy sales force behavior that creates short-term sales at the expense of long-term customer interest.
Communicate what is most important in terms of products or customers.	Limit the control of sales force activities, since salespeople are propelled to focus on those products and customers that make them the most money and to ignore the strategic interests of the company, which are not incorporated into the incentive plan.
Attract and retain performance-oriented people who will drive sales results.	Create a brittle relationship between salespeople and the company in which salespeople chase the next better job opportunity and have little company loyalty.
Reinforce a sales-oriented culture where rewards are tied to results.	Inhibit a service-oriented culture, hence sacrificing the long-term interests of the company and the customer.
Produce sales results.	Limit management's ability to make changes, such as sales force expansions, that disrupt the incentive program.
Drive an individualistic culture.	Constrain teamwork and cooperation among employees and departments.

The challenge when designing incentives is to harvest the positives and eliminate or mitigate the negatives.

The proportion of sales force pay that comes from salary versus incentives is often referred to as the *pay mix*. The salary portion is sometimes called fixed pay, and the incentive portion is often referred to as variable pay. Pay mix is typically expressed as the ratio of the percentage of cash compensation that comes from salary to the percentage that comes from incentives. For example, a sales force that receives 70 percent of its earnings through salary and 30 percent of its earnings through incentives at the expected or targeted performance level has a target pay mix of 70/30. The actual pay mix will deviate from the target pay mix if performance is above or below expectations. Pay mix varies greatly across industries, companies, and sales roles.

A Sales Environment Where Incentives Are a Large Proportion of the Pay Mix: Office Supplies

Joe sells office supplies to medium-sized businesses. Like many of his colleagues, he is a seasoned sales veteran and has developed a large customer base. His number one priority is to close sales. Leads are generated by the firm's telemarketing group, and qualified leads are passed on to Joe (or another salesperson) for follow-up. Since Joe is a proven closer, he gets many new leads assigned to him. Once an account is given to Joe, he "owns" the account, and no other salesperson can approach it. Joe visits potential customers with a sales kit and a needs assessment questionnaire. He presents the firm's products and services, describes the buying process, and provides a price estimate. He listens closely for closing signals and attempts to take an order. If an order is placed, he gives the customer a telephone number for a personal customer service representative who can take future orders and handle all ongoing service issues. Joe checks in on the customer from time to time to discuss promoted products and to make sure that the customer's needs are being met. All of Joe's earnings—100 percent—come from variable pay, based on a commission rate times the profit margin on his sales.

A Sales Environment Where Salary Is a Large Proportion of the Pay Mix: Animal Laboratory Systems

Mary sells computerized, automated watering systems to animal laboratories. These systems include many technical components, such as water purification and treatment processes, water distribution piping, and drinking valves that deliver water to animals automatically. The systems save customers time and labor and improve water quality. Solutions can be quite complex, are highly customized, and require a long sales process. Throughout this process, Mary works closely with animal laboratory managers (she is a former animal lab manager herself), and also with veterinarians to ensure that the system is designed to meet customer needs. Since many of her sales come from new laboratory construction, Mary also works with building contractors, often conducting the layout design of the watering

> system at no cost. Sales visits with customers involve many nonselling ac-
> tivities, such as addressing equipment problems and learning about new
> building plans. Maintaining good relationships with current customers is
> important to Mary, as most of her sales come through repeat business from
> end users and referrals from building contractors. Mary is paid 100 percent
> from salary.

The firm's selling process and the role of the sales force, combined with the measurability of company and customer results, drive the pay mix decision. In addition, pay mix is influenced by industry norms and by the company's history, culture, and management philosophy.

Do You Have the Right Pay Mix?

When diagnosing pay mix problems, sales leaders should look at the three views within the sales management system framework. First, the *downstream conse-quences* of pay mix decisions need to be checked. Is the current mix appealing to the salespeople the firm wants to attract and retain? Does the mix motivate the right activities that lead to appropriate treatment of customers and achievement of company financial results? Second, the *upstream consistency* of pay mix decisions needs to be assessed. Does the incentive mix reinforce the company's marketing strategy? Is it consistent with the firm's go-to-market strategy, sales processes, and sales force roles? Third, pay mix decisions should be *compatible* with salespeople's skills and capabilities, sales force culture, performance management systems, and nonmonetary sales force motivators.

Figures 5-1 and 5-2 provide a template for diagnosing whether the sales incentive plan has the appropriate pay mix. Figure 5-1 lists examples of signs that suggest that the variable portion of sales force pay may be too large, while Figure 5-2 lists examples of signs that suggest that the salary portion may be too large.

Consequences: A Downstream View

The pay mix decision affects which salespeople will be attracted to the firm, as well as the motivation of *salespeople*, who carry out the *sales force activities* that in turn affect *customer results* and ultimately influence *company results*. The downstream consequences of the pay mix decision can be understood by examining the role of pay mix as a shaper, exciter, and controller of the sales force.

The Pay Mix Can Be a Powerful Sales Force Shaper. "Our top performers 'max out' and quit, while our low performers stay too long," says the vice president of sales at a building materials firm. "Our best personnel are being lured away by the competition," says the director of human resources at a health-care company.

Figure 5-1. Some signs that the variable portion of sales force pay *may* be too large.

Consistency with . . .	Compatibility with . . .	Consequences . . .
• Sales and marketing strategies • Sales process • Sales roles	• Performance management systems • Sales force culture • Sales force motivators • Sales force hiring and development processes	• Company results • Customer results • Sales force behaviors and activities • Sales force quality
• The firm's product lines have matured. Marketing strategy has shifted from driving new sales and growth to retaining and servicing customers, but the variable-pay component remains high. • The firm has evolved to using a complex mixture of overlapping go-to-market vehicles, but the pay mix still reflects the old direct sales model. • The sales process has shifted from pressure and relationship selling of products to partnering and consultative selling of solutions, but the variable-pay component remains high. • Sales force roles have made a transition from individual selling to team selling, but the variable-pay component remains high.	• Management wants to control sales force activities through performance management systems, rather than with monetary incentives. • The incentive plan is incompatible with a sales force culture that is customer-centered, team-oriented, and focused on long-term success. • Management wants to excite the sales force in nonmonetary ways using extrinsic motivators such as effective leadership and recognition and intrinsic motivators such as meaningful work and empowerment. • The incentive portion is too high to attract service-oriented team players.	• The firm is falling behind on its accomplishment of long-term strategic objectives. • Other company employees feel that the sales force is excessively paid. • Customers complain that salespeople's actions do not align with customers' long-term interests. • The sales force engages in greedy or even unethical behaviors that create short-term sales, but conflict with long-term company success. • Salespeople resist sales strategy changes that are in the company's best interest because they feel that the changes will reduce their personal income. • Salespeople feel that the compensation plan is unfair. • Sales force loyalty to the company is low.

"Our 100 percent commission philosophy 'starves out' many competent new hires," laments the vice president of sales for an MRO (maintenance, repair, and operations) distributor. The salary versus incentive mix decision influences the type of person that is attracted to the sales job and helps shape the sales force culture. The right pay mix attracts and retains salespeople with the capabilities, work style, and values needed to successfully perform the selling activities that will drive customer and company results.

Pay Mix at Fusion Sales Partners Shapes a Results-Focused Sales Force Culture

Founded in 1988, Fusion Sales Partners is a high-end sales outsourcing company. Large companies such as GE and IBM hire Fusion Sales Partners

Figure 5-2. Some signs that the salary portion of sales force pay *may* be too large.

Consistency with . . .	Compatibility with . . .	Consequences . . .
• Sales and marketing strategies • Sales process • Sales roles	• Performance management systems • Sales force culture • Sales force motivators • Sales force hiring and development processes	• Company results • Customer results • Sales force behaviors and activities • Sales force quality
• The go-to-market strategy has shifted from selling to distributors to selling directly to customers, but the salary component of compensation remains high. • The industry has deregulated, leading to a more aggressive selling process, but the salary component of compensation remains high. • Sales roles have made a transition from retaining and servicing customers (farming) to driving new sales and growth (hunting), but the salary portion of compensation remains high.	• More accurate and timely measurability has enabled better tracking of individual performance. • The incentive plan is incompatible with a sales force culture that is sales-centered, competitive, and focused on short-term results. • Management thinks that money needs to become more important in exciting and controlling the sales force. • The new environment requires the company to attract individualistic risk takers.	• The company has missed its short-term financial goals. • The sales force expense-to-sales ratio is excessive. • Customers complain that the sales force is complacent. • Salespeople feel that they are not rewarded sufficiently for the high level of sales that they are generating through their skills, capabilities, and effort. • The sales force is not motivated to perform difficult selling activities. • Turnover of top performers is excessive, while low performers stay too long.

to sell their smaller product lines or to sell their large product lines into underserved markets. Fusion's salespeople are paid 100 percent commission. Salespeople must produce, or they do not get paid. Therefore, the company attracts self-directed, ambitious, results-oriented, and highly motivated individuals. In 2004, top performers made as much as $500,000 working for Fusion.

Pay Mix at Digital Equipment Corporation Shapes a Customer-Focused Culture

In the 1980s, almost all computer sales forces received a substantial portion of their earnings through incentive pay. For IBM reps, for instance, 30 to 40 percent of cash compensation was variable pay. Yet salespeople at Digital Equipment Corporation (DEC) were paid a straight salary. Ken Olsen, the founder of DEC and its president until 1992, felt that since the company's target customers were engineers, scientists, and educators who knew what they wanted, engineers and problem solvers, rather than aggressive salespeople, would meet customer needs most effectively.

(See more in the example "Pay Mix Reinforces Diverse Sales Strategies and Cultures at DEC and IBM," on p. 152.)

Pay Mix as a Sales Force Exciter. "We need a greater sense of urgency to prospect and close sales," says the vice president and general manager at a medical instruments firm. "We want to increase the incentive to grow our business," says a manager at a high-tech manufacturer. As an *exciter,* the salary–incentive mix decision influences the degree to which the compensation plan inspires and motivates the sales force. In the right selling environment, high incentives encourage a sales force to invest greater energy in the sales task in order to increase personal earnings

However, incentives will not create sales force excitement if the sales force perceives them to be unfair. "We need to make pay more reflective of performance; our sales force has no control over 30 to 40 percent of the accounts they are paid on," says a manager at an automotive company. "Our current system is demotivating—it disassociates sales and money earned," says a manager at a parts manufacturer. If salespeople feel that an incentive plan is unfair, the desired motivational impact of the incentive is lost, and the plan may backfire and actually decrease sales force excitement.

A highly leveraged and fair compensation plan can create considerable sales force excitement. A plan that pays mostly salary provides the sales force with security, but not excitement. In highly salaried sales forces, management must rely on other means besides compensation to create and sustain sales force excitement. The right pay mix decision is aligned with management's desire to use incentives as a means of creating sales force excitement and motivating salespeople to perform the activities needed to drive customer and company results.

RV Dealer Uses Sales Force Incentives to Jump-Start Sales

The salespeople at a local recreational-vehicle (RV) dealership were not performing up to management's expectations. A sale was closed for only one out of every 200 customers who walked onto the lot. To increase sales, management replaced the $250 weekly salary for salespeople with a sales incentive plan designed to promote more proactive selling. Salespeople could earn $10 for each customer whose information they captured (including name, address, and phone number). This information was used for follow-up calls and mailings. In addition, a $25 incentive was paid when a customer submitted a written offer for an RV. Total incentives that a salesperson could earn by capturing customer information and submitting offers were capped at $300 per week. However, on top of this, salespeople earned a generous 20 percent commission on net profits for every RV sold. The new incentive plan was a success. Follow-up calls increased and resulted in more than half of the dealership's RV sales, and the dealership's closing percentage improved from 0.5 to 10 percent in one year. Most salespeople reached the $300 cap each week, and sales-staff turnover decreased.

Authors' note: Incentive plans that tie earnings to specific salesperson activities are generally most effective when used for only a short period of time. If activity-based plans are left in place for too long, there is considerable risk that salespeople will focus excessively on generating high quantities of the desired activity at the expense of high-quality selling that produces good sales and profit results.

Much of Variable Pay Can Be Hidden Salary

Often, firms use the term *at-risk pay* to describe the incentive or variable component of total pay. However, this term is often misleading. High incentive pay does not always mean high risk to the salesperson and does not guarantee high levels of sales force excitement. In fact, managers from firms that pay their sales forces 100 percent through variable pay often state that the sales force is too complacent, content to live off income from current clients and unmotivated to seek out new accounts and drive growth. When motivation issues like this exist in sales forces that are paid largely through variable pay, the traditional definition of pay mix is often not an accurate reflection of the extent to which pay is tied to performance. Recall that territory sales have two components: *salesperson sales* and *free sales*. Salesperson sales are those sales that result from the skill, knowledge, motivation, and effort of the salesperson in the current year. Free sales will be realized regardless of what the sales force does; they can be the result of a strong brand identity, non-sales force marketing efforts, superior products, and/or carryover from prior years' sales efforts. True "pay-for-performance" plans link incentives to salesperson sales alone. Incentives on salesperson sales are called *performance pay,* since they are earned only if the sales force works for them. Since it is often difficult to isolate and measure salesperson sales, many pay plans tie incentives to *total sales*, which include both salesperson sales and free sales. The portion of incentives linked to free sales will be paid regardless of the salesperson's effort, and is therefore really a *hidden salary,* not performance pay.

When free sales are a large component of total sales and sales force incentives are tied to total sales, the traditional definition of pay mix (salary percentage/variable-pay percentage) is a misleading indicator of the extent to which pay is tied to performance. A more insightful definition of pay mix, called the *effective pay mix,* is the ratio of the total "salary" percentage (including both traditional salary *and* hidden salary) to the performance-pay percentage. For example, consider a sales force that is paid 100 percent through variable pay, but where 60 percent of total sales are free sales. While the traditional salary–incentive mix is 0/100, the effective mix is 60/40.

Pay Mix as a Sales Force Controller. "Our sales force pay has become too expensive relative to our profits," says a corporate director of compensation and benefits at a recreation products company. "The sales force needs to service all products—not just those they receive commission on," protests an e-business director at a tools manufacturing firm. The pay mix decision influences the degree to which the compensation plan is a *controller* of sales force costs as well as sales force activities.

A pay plan with a large variable-pay component helps management control the sales force expense-to-sales ratio because incentives are paid out only if the sales force earns them by generating sales. However, total sales force expenses will be harder to predict because compensation costs vary with performance. In a pay plan with a large salary component, the majority of sales force costs are fixed and do not depend on sales force performance, at least in the short term. Thus, a pay plan with a large salary component gives management more control over the total sales force expense, but less control over the sales force expense-to-sales ratio.

Salary and incentives also have an important role as *controllers* of sales force activity. The compensation plan helps to define success, set expectations, and encourage sales force behaviors that align with the firm's objectives. Most firms define a target pay amount or range for salespeople, which can include both salary and target incentive. The target incentive is based on the firm's prediction of what a salesperson's performance should be. Thus, there is an implicit (and sometimes explicit) message that success is defined as making and exceeding the target pay amount.

Figure 5-3 shows how salary and incentives act as levers of control for various components of the sales management system. Salary is usually the most appropriate lever of control for components near the beginning (left-hand side) of the sales management system. Salary rewards salespeople for accomplishments in the salespeople category (for example, enhancing product and market knowledge and developing selling skills) as well as for performance in the sales force activities category (for example, completing a number of calls to key customers and providing customer follow-up after closing a sale). These accomplishments have a long- to medium-term impact on the firm, and this impact is difficult to measure. Thus, salary is the preferred lever of control. Incentives, on the other hand, can be a very effective way to reward salespeople for accomplishments further downstream (right-hand side) in the sales management system. Incentives typically reward achievement of company results (for example, sales, sales growth, and market share). These accomplishments define the short-term success of the firm and are often accurately and objectively measurable. Incentives can also be used in part to reward salespeople for customer results (for example, customer satisfaction and

Figure 5-3. Controlling the sales force through salary and incentives.

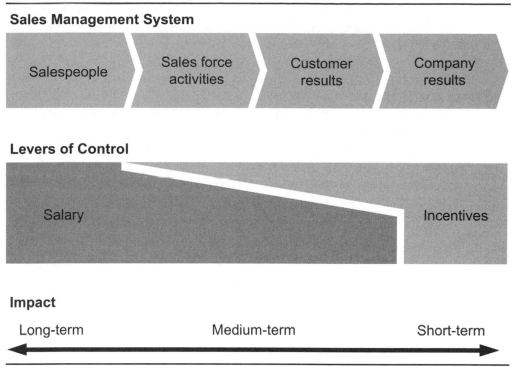

Sales Management System

Salespeople → Sales force activities → Customer results → Company results

Levers of Control

Salary — Incentives

Impact

Long-term ←——— Medium-term ———→ Short-term

retention), although salary usually plays a controlling role for these measures as well.

Consistency: An Upstream View

Effective pay mix decisions are consistent with all of the upstream sales force effectiveness driver decisions, including sales strategy, go-to-market strategy, and sales force design. A clear definition of sales roles (part of the sales force design decision) is an important prerequisite to the pay mix decision, as the pay mix should encourage the behaviors required for success in each sales role. Sales force restructuring often necessitates changes in the pay mix to ensure that sales force behaviors align appropriately with new sales role requirements.

Sales Force Structure Modifications Lead to Pay Mix Change for Enterprise Account Team

A high-tech networking equipment manufacturer paid its salespeople 30 percent salary and 70 percent incentive. Incentives were earned as a commission on sales beginning with the first dollar sold. In order to improve customer focus, the firm decided to restructure its single generalist sales force around customer segments. Three separate sales teams were established, one for the largest enterprise accounts, a second for medium to large corporate accounts, and a third for smaller accounts. Management decided to continue to use the existing sales incentive plan for all three sales teams, in order to avoid excessive disruption at a time when the sales force was adjusting to new sales roles and learning new customer assignments. However, the highly leveraged compensation plan was not appropriate for all of the sales teams, particularly the enterprise account team. Enterprise accounts were primarily long-standing, loyal customers that generated significant carryover sales. Since commissions were paid from the first dollar, enterprise salespeople earned many of their commissions on free sales. Approximately one year after implementing the new structure, the firm initiated a project to develop a new compensation plan with less variable pay and higher salary for the enterprise sales team.

Sales territory alignment is another upstream sales force effectiveness driver that can have a tricky effect on the outcome of an incentive plan. Often, the results a salesperson achieves are closely tied not only to the salesperson's own efforts, but also to sales territory opportunity. Incentive plans that pay on total sales favor territories with large opportunity (because there is more low-hanging fruit), while those that pay on market share favor territories with small opportunity (because the salesperson can spend more time penetrating each account). When sales territories have unequal potential, a highly variable compensation plan can reward the salesperson more for territory opportunity than for true performance. Incentive plan designers need to assess sales territory equity when designing incentive plans. An effective way to neutralize territory inequities is to have a goal-based plan with goals that account for differences in territory opportunity.

Compatibility: Alignment with Other Sales Force Drivers

An effective pay mix decision reinforces the desired sales force culture. For instance:

- A culture that is customer-centered, team-oriented, and focused on long-term success is compatible with a pay mix with a high proportion of salary.

- A culture that is sales-centered, competitive, and focused on short-term results is compatible with a pay mix having a high proportion of variable pay.

Pay mix decisions must also align well with the exciter and controller sales force effectiveness driver decisions. Compensation plans that have a considerable variable-pay component can be a powerful means of stimulating sales force excitement and controlling sales force activities and costs. Thus, nonmonetary sales force exciters and controllers are not as critical when the variable component of sales force pay is large. On the other hand, a management team that chooses a pay plan that is mostly salary has to rely heavily on nonmonetary sales force effectiveness drivers for creating excitement and maintaining control. In sales forces that are paid primarily salary, excitement is created through extrinsic motivators such as effective sales leadership, coaching, professional development, recognition, and trips for top performers and through intrinsic motivators such as meaningful work, achievement, and empowerment. Control is maintained through strong performance management and communication and control systems.

Companies Use Many Different Motivators to Create Sales Force Excitement

Motivators other than incentives can be very powerful. The following examples highlight companies that use intrinsic and extrinsic motivators to create sales force excitement:

- Management at an insurance company boosts sales force motivation by emphasizing to salespeople the value that life insurance creates for customers. Through training, the firm continuously reinforces the role of the insurance agent as an advocate for each customer's family members and business partners, who will benefit from the insurance when it is needed. When salespeople see their role as helpers of people, not peddlers of insurance, they feel more relevant, have an increased sense of purpose, and are more motivated in their jobs.

- Pharmaceutical giant Merck increases employee motivation by promoting a culture of empowerment. For example, in 1992 the firm implemented a sales force suggestion program called Improvement Driven by Employee Action (IDEA). Over 20 percent of the sales force submitted ideas for improving the productivity and profitability of the firm's sales and marketing efforts. Salespeople whose suggestions were implemented received merchandise, and winners were announced in Merck's daily newspaper.

- TruStar Solutions, a seller of Internet-based recruiting programs to corporations, increases the motivation of its top salespeople by asking them to help with recruiting and mentoring new salespeople. This shows top performers that the company values their input (and not just the sales they have brought in). The program has helped to improve retention of the firm's best salespeople.

The Range of Salary–Incentive Mix

When we surveyed managers at 110 sales forces, of varying sizes and in various industries, who attended our sales compensation executive education programs at Northwestern University between 2000 and 2004 (the Sales Incentive Executive

Education Survey), the percentage of salespeople's pay coming from incentives ranged from zero to 100 percent, with a median of 40 percent. Figure 5-4 shows the range and variation among the 110 sales forces. The percentage of pay coming from incentives for companies in selected industries is also shown.

Markets with comparable sales processes and environmental conditions can have pay plans that are quite different. Considerable differences can exist even within the same industry, if companies have different sales cultures and strategies.

Pay Mix Reinforces Diverse Sales Strategies and Cultures at DEC and IBM

Both IBM and Digital Equipment Corporation (DEC) were successful companies during the 1980s, despite paying their salespeople differently. DEC founder and president Ken Olsen wanted a sales culture that was focused on technical problem solving for customers; a pay mix that was 100 percent salary helped to promote this culture. IBM's sales culture was more sales-focused, and IBM salespeople earned 30 to 40 percent of their compensation as variable pay. (See the example "Pay Mix at Digital Equipment Corporation Shapes a Customer-Focused Culture," on p. 145.)

Just one year after the departure of Ken Olsen in 1992, DEC implemented a new sales compensation program that put virtually all of its formerly 100 percent salaried salespeople onto some form of variable-pay

Figure 5-4. Proportion of incentive pay among companies in the Sales Incentive Executive Education Survey.

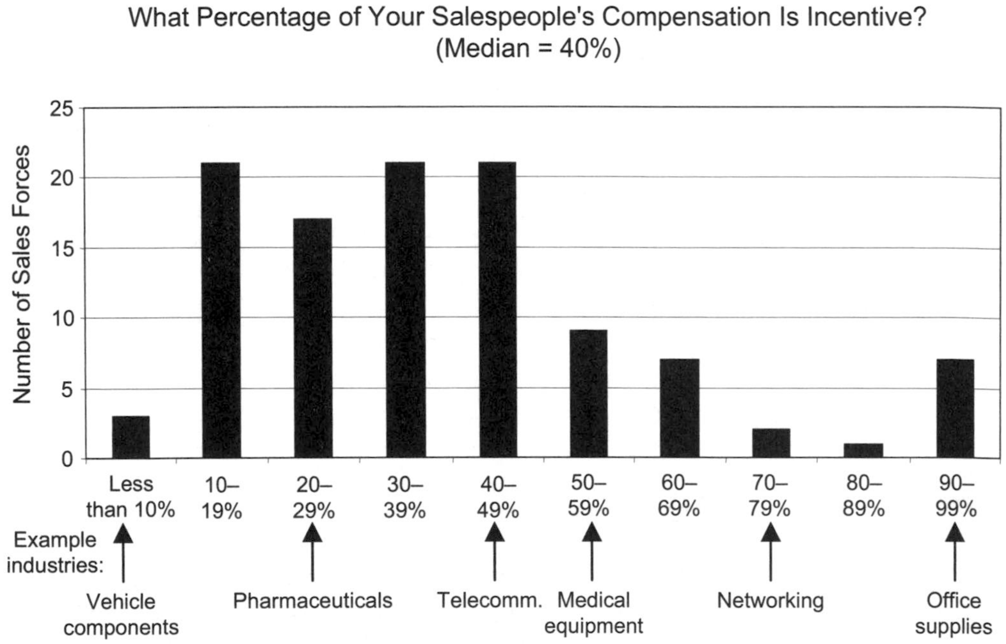

What Percentage of Your Salespeople's Compensation Is Incentive?
(Median = 40%)

plan. The new plan had 15 variations, ranging from 60 percent salary and 40 percent variable pay to 90 percent salary and 10 percent variable pay, depending upon the sales role. To ease the transition to the new plan, salespeople were offered a draw on future earnings for the first four months of the new program. Extensive training was provided to sales managers on how the plan would work and how to manage in an incentive environment. Salespeople were provided with an earnings simulation program on their PC so that they could see how their present sales would pay out under the new plan and what the upside potential was for exceeding quota. Sales force turnover rates did not increase when the new plan was put into place as a result of the extensive communication and training that was provided to the sales force during this transition.

In 1998, DEC was acquired by Compaq, which in 2002 was acquired by Hewlett-Packard.

There can be significant variation in the salary–incentive mix across different sales roles within the same company. A major accounts salesperson may have a different incentive opportunity from a geographic salesperson who covers smaller accounts. An inside salesperson may earn a different proportion of his income from incentives than an outside salesperson. Figure 5-5 shows some examples of how and why both total compensation and the salary–incentive mix vary across different sales positions.

Here we describe the characteristics of sales forces that have varying proportions of salary and incentive in their pay plans. Three distinctive categories are included:

- A low percent incentive pay plan: up to 15 percent of total pay is incentive.

- A high percent incentive pay plan: 50 percent or more of total pay is incentive.

- A moderate percent incentive pay plan: between 20 and 35 percent of total pay is incentive.

Pay plans with a percent incentive falling between the defined ranges will exhibit characteristics moderating those described in the categories on either end.

The Sales Force with a Low Percent Incentive Pay Plan

An Example of a Low Percent Incentive Compensation Plan: Engineering Sales

A maker of complex vehicle component systems pays its salespeople 100 percent salary. The firm sells to a limited number of customers (vehicle makers), and the sales force plays a critical role in maintaining strong ongo-

Figure 5-5. Examples of variation in pay mix across sales positions within a firm.

Industry	Sales Job	Average Total Compensation	Incentive Portion	Rationale
Telecommunications	National account salesperson	$112,000	20%	National account salespeople manage relationships with important major accounts with significant carryover. New sales are large and hard to forecast accurately. Geographic salespeople control less business and have greater short-term impact on sales.
	Large account salesperson	$91,000	35%	
	Geographic salesperson (small accounts)	$82,000	50%	
Rubber and plastics components distributor	Outside salesperson	$90,000	50%	Outside selling requires greater skill and has higher prominence than inside selling.
	Inside salesperson	$50,000	20%	
Oral health care	Professional salesperson (calls on dentists)	$54,000	25%	Professional salespeople influence dentists, who influence patients, but the sales impact of this influence is difficult to measure at the territory level. Retail salespeople have a higher and more measurable impact on sales.
	Retail salesperson (calls on retail store headquarters)	$100,000	35%	

ing relationships with those customers. Since each system is custom-designed for a particular vehicle, the sales process is long—typically 12 to 24 months. Salespeople serve as account managers and work in teams with engineers and R&D specialists, collaborating with the customer to create the best possible solutions. The salary-only sales position attracts engineers who want to move out of pure design work, are career-oriented, want predictable income, and prefer to be seen as problem solvers rather than high-pressure salespeople. The salary-only pay plan encourages salespeople to look after customer interests. It also allows management to successfully encourage salespeople to engage in activities that are of long-term strategic importance to the firm and its customers, such as attending training or promoting strategic products, because sales force income is not tied to short-term results.

Management sometimes wonders if perhaps the sales force has become too complacent, since sales force earnings are not linked to generating sales, at least not in the short term. Salespeople do receive merit increases in salary based on performance, but since salary is also a function of level and tenure, salary differences do not always differentiate performance substantially. An additional concern is that a new competitor is expected to enter the market next year. In order to attract the best salespeople, that competitor is likely to offer its sales force performance-based incentives. Management is concerned that the firm may lose some of its most ambitious, high-performing salespeople to the competitor.

Low percent incentive pay plans include those in which salespeople earn at least 85 percent of their income as salary and 15 percent or less as performance-based incentives. A decision to pay salespeople low incentives and high salary has advantages for salespeople, customers, and the firm. These advantages, along with the challenges of managing a sales force with a low percent incentive pay plan, are summarized in the middle column of Figure 5-6.

The Sales Force with a High Percent Incentive Pay Plan

An Example of a High Percent Incentive Compensation Plan: High-Tech Sales

A direct marketer of computers and technology products uses telesales account managers to reach small and medium-sized business customers. Account managers are paid entirely through commission on the gross profit they generate, with commission rates varying depending on the salesperson's gross profit per day performance ranking and on her tenure with the company. The pay plan reflects the firm's "pay-for-performance" philosophy; top salespeople earn multiples of what average performers earn. In addition, the pay plan communicates the company's primary objective of profitable growth very effectively to the sales force. The 100 percent variable-pay plan is attractive to salespeople with the right personality for the job—the sales force is tenacious, aggressive, and effective at creating sales in a competitive commodity market. In addition, since sales force pay is tied closely to gross profit results, sales force costs stay in line with company profits.

Management is concerned that many salespeople view their relationship with the company as purely financial; many salespeople act more like agents than like employees. The result is low sales force loyalty and fairly high turnover. At the same time, some veteran salespeople have developed very strong relationships with their customers, and as a result have built very lucrative, multimillion-dollar territories. Many of these veterans are content with the generous commissions they earn on easily obtained repeat business, and are not driven to penetrate new markets or promote aggressive growth with existing customers. As the market becomes more competitive and industry growth slows, it is becoming more difficult for newer account managers to build their book of business, and turnover of new sales talent is especially high. When the company tried to realign some accounts in order to balance account loads and provide better opportunity for new salespeople, several of the longer-tenure account managers refused to relinquish "ownership" of their accounts. Recently, the company was forced to abandon a plan to create vertical specialists for key markets

Figure 5-6. Advantages and challenges of pay plans with extreme pay mixes.

	High Percent Salary/ Low Percent Incentive	Low Percent Salary/ High Percent Incentive
Advantages for salespeople	• Provides predictable income. • Allows salespeople to do what's best for the customer without worrying about the pay impact. • Attracts career-oriented salespeople who are motivated by factors besides money.	• Provides significant upside earnings opportunity for strong performers. • Differentiates pay across high and low performers. • Attracts salespeople who are ambitious, hardworking, and results-oriented.
Advantages for customers	• Encourages salespeople to do what's best for the customer, not what's best for their paycheck.	• Encourages salespeople to put forth extraordinary effort for a customer to make a sale.
Advantages for the company	• Allows management to direct sales force activities through coaching, training, and other nonmonetary sales force effectiveness drivers. • Reduces jealousy of the sales force by nonsales employees. • Allows sales force costs to be predicted more precisely. • Is usually easier to administer.	• Motivates salespeople to put forth extra effort to create short-term results. • Is a powerful means of communicating company priorities and directing sales force effort. • Helps manage the bottom line by keeping sales force costs in line with sales.
Significant management challenges and possible solutions	• Keeping sales force motivation high through sales force effectiveness drivers other than monetary incentives, such as leadership, motivation programs, and meaningful work. • Directing and controlling the sales force through sales force effectiveness drivers other than monetary incentives, such as performance management systems and communication and coordination processes.	• Ensuring that sales force behaviors, which are influenced significantly by the incentive plan, are consistent with long-term customer and company success. • Connecting the salesperson to the company in nonfinancial ways to enhance sales force loyalty. • Creating multiple meaningful connections between customers and the company so that sales force customer power is limited.

because veteran salespeople did not want to give up their accounts, and the firm did not want to risk losing the salespeople who controlled the company's most important customer relationships. Management hopes to create additional meaningful connections between customers and the company in order to limit the power over the customer held by individual salespeople and to make it more difficult for veterans to take their accounts with them if they leave the firm.

High percent incentive pay plans include those in which salespeople earn at least half of their income as performance-based incentives. A decision to pay salespeople high incentives and low salary also has many advantages for salespeople, customers, and the firm. These advantages, along with the challenges of managing a sales force with a high percent incentive pay plan, are summarized in the right-hand column of Figure 5-6.

The Sales Force with a Moderate Percent Incentive Pay Plan

An Example of a Moderate Incentive Compensation Plan: Pharmaceutical Sales

A pharmaceutical manufacturer pays its salespeople 75 percent salary and 25 percent incentive. The incentive is significant enough to motivate the sales force and is implemented with a weighted goal-based plan that helps management direct effort to strategically important products and customer segments. Since salary is the largest component of total pay, management also guides sales force behavior with sales force drivers other than incentives, such as training, coaching, and culture. These other drivers are critical for ensuring that salespeople educate physicians about complex pharmaceutical products effectively with accurate sales messages that are within FDA guidelines. Paying salespeople primarily salary also gives the firm the flexibility to make frequent changes to its sales strategy. For example, last year the firm expanded its sales force, realigned sales territories, and introduced two new products, and all the changes were accepted by the sales force. Occasionally, the firm experiences undesired turnover of top producers, who leave the firm to go to biotechnology start-ups offering higher total pay or to medical equipment sellers with more highly leveraged compensation plans with significant upside potential.

Most companies attempt to balance the advantages and disadvantages of high and low percent incentive pay plans by establishing incentive schemes that are somewhere in the middle of the low and high extremes. Moderate percent incentive pay plans include those in which salespeople earn 20 to 35 percent of their income as performance-based incentives. A moderate percent incentive pay plan has many advantages, including the following:

- Salespeople have the security of a reasonable salary, yet simultaneously have upside earnings potential for high achievement.
- Customers see salespeople who are motivated to both sell and perform service activities that meet the customer's total needs.
- The firm maintains reasonable control of the sales force while providing salespeople with moderate incentive to deliver results.

These plans moderate the advantages and disadvantages described in Figure 5-6.

Pay Mix and Sales Force Management and Control

Figure 5-7 summarizes the range of possible choices for salary–incentive mix and shows the impact that the mix choice has on sales force management and control. The incentive plan's impact on sales force behavior becomes more significant as the proportion of total compensation that is variable performance pay increases. A low percent incentive plan helps to direct sales force effort to important products, customers, or activities; a moderate percent incentive plan does this and is also a considerable motivator of sales force effort; a high percent incentive plan does the same things and also helps the firm control sales force costs. At the same time, management's ability to use control mechanisms other than incentives, such as coaching and performance management, varies with the mix choice. Nonincentive control mechanisms have quite a large impact in low percent incentive plans, but this impact decreases considerably as the firm moves through the moderate percent incentive range into the high range. Management must determine the point

Figure 5-7. A range of salary–incentive mixes and their impact.

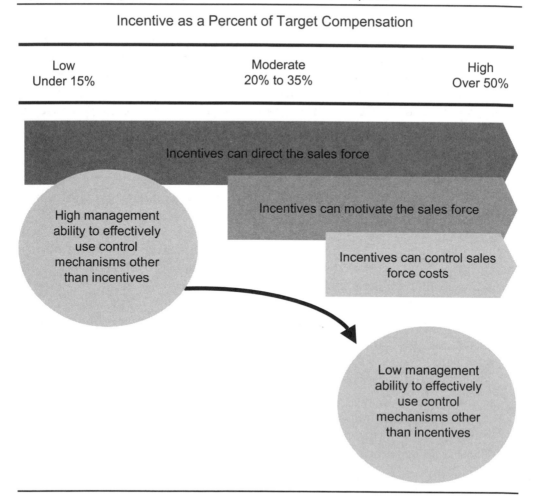

along the spectrum of possible performance-pay levels that is most desirable. Firms will choose different pay mix ideal points depending on how they want to use incentives and management directives in controlling the sales force.

The 30 Percent Rule of Sales Force Control

A power tools sales force is compensated with a 50/50 mix. Incentive earnings are a straight 2 percent commission on all sales. Product profit margins vary from 30 to 50 percent, depending on the product. In an effort to improve profitability, management encourages the sales force to focus on higher-margin products. However, since the higher-margin products are generally considered to be more complex and difficult to sell, the sales force continues to emphasize the lower-margin products, which are easier to promote. The sales force is controlled by the compensation plan and not by the directives that management communicates.

An important culture choice for any sales leadership team is how much control to exert over the sales force. In other words, to what degree should salespeople be empowered to make their own decisions? For example, should salespeople use activities and messages developed by marketing that have been proven to drive sales? Or should they be encouraged to exercise their own good judgment in serving customers? Should the company tell salespeople whom to call on? Or should salespeople decide for themselves who the best prospects are? Who decides which products to emphasize—management or the sales force? The compensation plan plays an important role in reinforcing a culture of control versus one of empowerment.

The 30 percent rule states that sales leadership's ability to influence sales force activity through means other than incentives diminishes as incentives grow beyond 30 percent of total compensation. A highly leveraged compensation plan may influence sales force behavior to such an extent that the plan itself becomes the control. For example, sales management's encouragement to the power tools sales force to sell high-margin products has diminished impact because salespeople believe that following this advice will result in lower personal earnings. Salespeople earn the same commission rate on sales of all products; therefore, it is in their personal best interest to sell the products that are easiest to sell, regardless of product margin. A management team that desires a culture of significant control over salespeople and their activities should adopt a compensation plan that is at least 70 percent salary. If the plan has a greater than 30 percent incentive component, management must accept that the plan will be a primary means of controlling sales force behavior. At the power tools company, telling salespeople to focus on high-margin products is not sufficient to change their behavior; the compensation plan needs to be changed as well, so that salespeople benefit personally from following management's advice. For example, a plan that pays on margins rather than on sales could encourage salespeople to spend more time on higher-margin products.

How to Determine the Right Salary–Incentive Mix

The mix of salary versus incentive in the sales compensation plan has a significant impact on the sales force culture and the degree to which management uses incentives to motivate and control the sales force. Determining the most effective sales force pay mix is an art; scientifically developed algorithms for formulating an optimal mix do not exist. However, through structured analysis of a firm's selling environment, a management team can learn which type of pay plan—a low percent incentive plan, a moderate percent incentive plan, or a high percent incentive plan—can best help the firm achieve its goals.

As shown in Figure 5-8, there are two primary pay mix drivers: (1) sales process and roles and (2) results measurability. These two factors together aid in determining the theoretically best sales force pay mix for a given selling environment. In addition to these drivers, two other influences on the mix decision need to be considered: industry norms and company history, culture, and philosophy. Determining the right pay mix involves a thorough assessment of the two pay mix drivers, followed by a check of the industry and company influences to ensure compatibility and feasibility of implementation. Each of these assessments and checks is discussed further here.

Assessing the Sales Process and the Role of the Salesperson

The sales process and the role of the salesperson in executing that process is a primary driver of the salary–incentive mix. The right pay mix encourages the sales force to engage in the behaviors needed to execute the appropriate selling process

Figure 5-8. The sales force pay mix decision: drivers and influences.

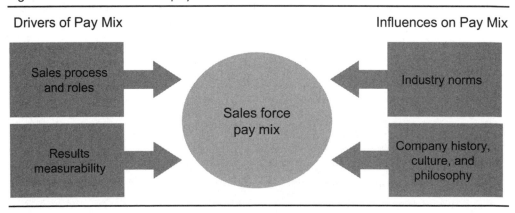

effectively. The right pay mix also acknowledges sales force causality, linking incentives only to outcomes that the sales force controls and management desires.

Pay Mix Should Encourage Desired Sales Force Behaviors. A mix that is heavily incentive-focused encourages different sales force behaviors from one that is heavily salary-focused. Consider the two selling environments described in the introduction to this chapter—office supplies and animal laboratory systems. The two environments have very dissimilar selling processes and very different roles and expectations for salespeople. As a result, the two environments have different philosophies regarding the salary–incentive mix. Recall that the office supply company pays its salespeople 100 percent through variable pay, while the animal laboratory systems company pays its salespeople 100 percent through salary.

Figure 5-9 compares and contrasts the role of the sales force in executing the sales process at the office supply and animal laboratory systems companies. At the animal laboratory systems company, salespeople are involved in all steps of the sales process—interest creation, prepurchase, purchase, immediate postpurchase, and ongoing postpurchase. At the office supply company, salespeople are involved in the prepurchase and purchase steps only; employees in other roles are responsible for the other steps.

The sales process and role for the office supply sales force favors high incentives. The sales process is short and straightforward. The salesperson's primary role is to execute the prepurchase and purchase steps of the sales process. These

Figure 5-9. A comparison of sales force responsibility at two companies.

Sales Process Step	Office Supply Company	Animal Laboratory Systems Company
Interest creation	<u>Telemarketing</u> generates leads for the sales force.	<u>Salesperson</u> develops relationships with building contractors who can pass on leads and networks to get other contacts.
Prepurchase	<u>Salesperson</u> learns customer needs and makes sales presentation and purchase recommendation.	<u>Salesperson</u> assesses customer needs and works with veterinarians, lab managers, and building contractors to propose a customized system design. This may involve creating detailed layout specifications.
Purchase	<u>Salesperson</u> finalizes terms, writes the order, and closes the sale.	<u>Salesperson</u> works with customer to finalize all details of system design and purchase, then closes the sale.
Postpurchase immediate	<u>Customer service</u> handles order placement and billing.	<u>Salesperson</u> assists with installation and training as needed.
Postpurchase ongoing	<u>Customer service</u> handles reorders and other ongoing customer needs. <u>Salesperson</u> checks in periodically to make sure that customer's needs are being met.	<u>Salesperson</u> helps troubleshoot system problems, suggests equipment modifications and upgrades, and maintains an ongoing relationship with customer.

are the steps that involve the direct pursuit of immediate sales. With a highly leveraged compensation plan, salespeople are motivated to focus on these specific activities. By doing so, they create more short-term sales for the firm and make more money for themselves. The nonselling support activities that are part of the firm's sales process and are necessary for maintaining ongoing relationships with customers are not handled by the sales force. These activities are performed by separate customer service and telemarketing departments. By paying the sales force 100 percent through variable pay, the office supply firm encourages salespeople to execute their role effectively and generate short-term results.

The sales process and role for the animal laboratory systems sales force, on the other hand, is not conducive to high incentives. The firm's selling cycle is long and complex—sales force actions today may not generate results for many months, or even until next year. Salespeople are involved in all stages of the selling process, which include many support activities in addition to selling. Excessive short-term incentives could drive salespeople to focus too heavily on short-term selling, at the expense of providing the support and partnership that are necessary to meet the customer's lasting needs and help the company achieve long-term success. By paying the sales force 100 percent through salary, the firm encourages salespeople to execute their role effectively and perform all the tasks necessary to maintain successful long-term customer relationships.

Psychological Theory Suggests that Incentive Levels Should Vary with the Nature of the Sales Role

Insights regarding the best salary–incentive mix can be gained by looking at the work of psychologists Robert M. Yerkes and John D. Dodson, who studied the relationship between arousal and performance in white mice. Mice were placed in a box that had several compartments and had to learn which compartment to enter. The mice were "encouraged" to learn with electric shocks that had three levels of intensity: low, medium, and high. It was discovered that medium-intensity shocks encouraged the fastest learning. Thus, the Yerkes-Dodson law, first published in 1908, predicts an inverted U-shaped relationship between arousal and performance. A certain amount of arousal motivates performance, yet too much creates stress, which hurts performance. Moderate levels of arousal produced the best results for the tasks to be performed by the mice in this experiment.

Of course, salespeople are not mice, and incentive pay (or lack of it) is not the same as electric shocks, but the Yerkes-Dodson law has been used to link stress and performance, which has some relevance in sales forces. When too little money is tied to performance, salespeople are not adequately motivated to perform. When too much money is tied to performance *and* salespeople feel stress about whether or not they can achieve their desired income level, the excessive stress leads to inferior results. The right stress level (or incentive level) depends upon the nature of the task to be performed. For example, the Yerkes-Dodson experiments revealed that the optimal level of arousal is lower for more difficult or intellectual tasks, as the learners need to concentrate on the material. On the other hand, the optimal level of arousal is higher for tasks requiring endurance and persistence, as the learners need more motivation. Thus, with sales jobs that require analytical and problem-solving skills, high incentives may distract the sales force and introduce stress that detracts from their ability to perform effectively. With sales jobs that require persistence, on the other hand, high incentives may be needed to provide the sales force with the motivation to keep going.

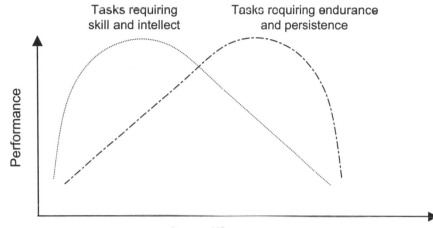

This finding is consistent with the salary–incentive mix philosophies used by the office supply and animal laboratory systems sales forces. Selling animal laboratory watering systems requires analytical and problem-solving skills—high incentives could distract the sales force and introduce stress that detracts from their ability to perform effectively. Selling office supplies, on the other hand, requires persistence—high incentives provide the sales force with the motivation to keep going.

Figure 5-10 summarizes some aspects (which are often related) of selling processes and sales roles that favor either salary or incentives.

Sales processes and roles often change as products mature. When products are new and sales are growing, a pay plan with a large incentive portion can motivate salespeople to work hard to generate trial among customers, seek new opportunities, build relationships, and create sales momentum. However, as the products mature, the role of the sales force changes. Instead of driving new sales and growth, salespeople must focus on customer retention and service. A pay plan with a greater proportion of salary and less incentive is often more compatible with this role.

Figure 5-10. Characteristics of selling processes and sales roles that favor salary or incentives.

Characteristic	Rationale
Selling cycle: Short sales cycles favor incentives, whereas long sales cycles favor salary.	High incentives create an environment where salespeople focus on closing the sale to produce their earnings. In order to sustain energy and encourage time-consuming creative thought in a long sales cycle, a larger salary component is preferred to avoid periods without sufficient income and sales force dissonance.
Number of transactions and sales predictability: When there are many small to moderate-sized sales to many different customers and territory sales volume can be forecast accurately, incentives are favored. Salary is favored when sales are very large, infrequent, and difficult to predict.	A few large, unpredictable transactions will create erratic earnings if the incentive component is large, which won't produce the baseline earnings stability that most people require.
Nature of customer interaction: Incentives are favored when the customer interaction is primarily transactional in nature and the relationship is focused on the product. Salary is favored when the customer partnerships focus on solutions that go beyond the product.	If incentives are too high in a solution-selling environment, a salesperson may be too focused on closing the sale at the expense of creating the best solution to the customer's problem. On the other hand, if transactional sales are paired with too high a salary component, a salesperson may not close sales rapidly enough.
Sources of salesperson satisfaction: When producing sales results is the primary source of satisfaction for a salesperson, incentives are more important. In such situations, selling requires persistence and effective salesmanship. Salary is favored when selling requires creativity, problem-solving skills, or extensive technical, product, and application knowledge. In such situations, a salesperson derives satisfaction and motivation by solving customer problems and creating customer solutions.	The salience of incentives is matched to what motivates a salesperson. If closing the sale is a key motivator, linking sales success to incentive pay is productive. However, if problem solving and creativity are strong motivators, and incentives are too high, the quality of the work will suffer, and this will lead to long-term demotivation.
Success measures: When sales is the primary measure of success, incentives are favored. When customer satisfaction and customer service are valued, salary is more important.	Results tend to suffer if incentives are too low in a sales-focused environment. If incentives are too high in a service-intensive environment, service suffers.
Sales process control: When the sales force is empowered to create sales messages that work with each customer, incentives can work. But if message control is important so that products are not misused, incentives need to be low.	When message control is important (such as in the pharmaceutical industry) and incentives are too high, the company will be unable to fully control salespeople.

Product Life-Cycle Effects and the Salary–Incentive Mix in the Television Industry

Fifty years ago, when television was in its infancy, a television network offered salespeople large commissions to generate advertising revenues with major national advertisers and agencies. Salespeople were pioneers in the industry and were absolutely critical for booking business, almost all of which came from new customers. Customers needed to be educated and convinced, and selling required salespeople with persistence and true entrepreneurial spirit. There was considerable risk of failure, and high commissions helped to motivate the sales force to do a difficult job. A successful salesperson earned a lot of money, typically 25 percent salary and 75 percent incentive, paid as a commission on revenues. This compensation plan helped the network accomplish its objective of making difficult new sales in order to build a strong base of business.

By the 1970s, the television network had become well established, and the role of the sales force in booking advertising sales had evolved. The sales job had become more service-oriented, as many customer purchasing decisions had become routine and most pricing decisions were predetermined. The salesperson's primary job was to develop and harvest known opportunities with long-time customers. The risk of failure was significantly less. Yet the same sales compensation plan remained in place, as the company was reluctant to change it for fear of disrupting the sales force and creating turnover. Salespeople continued to be paid very high variable pay even though they were no longer as prominent in creating sales as they had been in the early years. The high variable pay was really a hidden salary, since very little was truly at risk; a large fraction of territory sales were carried over from year to year through relationships and routines that had been established in the past.

Today, advertisers and agencies have many more media choices, including numerous electronic media options and cable television. Because of the competitive landscape, the sales force's role has once again become very prominent in creating sales, and most television networks offer high sales force incentives.

The Salary–Incentive Mix Can Vary with a Salesperson's Experience

A seller of automobile manufacturing components adjusts the salary–incentive mix based on the experience of the salesperson. New salespeople are paid 100 percent salary for their first year. From 12 to 18 months, salespeople are paid 50 percent salary and 50 percent commission. After 18 months, salespeople are paid 100 percent commission. Most companies that pay the sales force 100 percent variable pay, such as companies in the insurance industry, provide some form of safety net for new salespeople, allowing them to be compensated fairly while they are learning the job.

Pay Mix Should Acknowledge Sales Force Causality. Sales force causality is influenced by a firm's selling process and is an important consideration when deciding on the appropriate salary–incentive mix. Causality reflects the ability of individual salespeople to affect short-term results. In high-causality environments, salesperson sales are large: A considerable portion of total sales is determined by the skill, motivation, and efforts of salespeople in the current incentive period. In low-causality environments, free sales are large: Other factors besides current sales force effort have a large impact on sales. Factors that decrease sales force causality include the following:

- *Brand name.* Brands that are well known and differentiated from competitive products often have high sales, even in the absence of effective sales force support. These products sell themselves.

- *Non-sales force marketing instruments.* When pricing, advertising, tele-sales, and direct mail play a significant role in generating sales, sales force causality is typically less.

- *Team selling.* Several people working together to create a sale muddies the causal link between individual effort and results.

Selling environments with high sales force causality tend to favor incentives, while those with low causality usually favor salary. Incentives have a larger impact in high-causality environments. Salespeople like to feel that their effort will be rewarded. In a high-causality environment, work effort has high short-term sales impact. Immediate sales increases occur in such an environment when the sales force puts forth extra effort. Salespeople see sales rise and feel a sense of accomplishment. They receive commensurate financial reward when a high-variable-pay plan is adopted. The synergistic effects of high causality and high variable pay are very motivating.

Perceived Causality Motivates a High-Tech Sales Force

In order for incentives to be effective, salespeople must believe that their efforts lead to the rewarded results. The perception of causality—not actual causality—is what is important. Firms in rapidly growing markets can create incentive plans that are highly motivational—even in cases where actual causality is not high. For example, a networking equipment manufacturer sold through a complex distribution system and thus did not have sales data available at the territory level. Sales were growing rapidly, and management wanted to motivate the sales force by showing each salesperson how his effort led to territory success and then paying an appropriate incentive. The firm developed a complex formula for allocating sales through distributors to individual territories. The formula provided only an estimate—it was not possible to measure actual sales with a high degree of accuracy at the territory level. Nonetheless, the sales force was thrilled to see how quickly territory sales were growing. Salespeople concluded that their personal efforts had caused the growth estimated for their territory. As long as sales kept growing rapidly, incentives kept growing and everyone was happy. However, when sales growth slowed and stopped, salespeople began to look more deeply into the measurement of results and to challenge the allocation model. As more and more flaws in the model were discovered, the perception of causality disappeared, and the incentive plan had to be changed.

When high variable pay is used in a low-causality selling environment, salespeople may miss the connection between work effort and rewards. Plans that are not crafted well can be perceived as behaving like lotteries. Plans with high variable pay are effective only when the level of free sales is estimated accurately, so that incentives can be paid for salesperson sales alone. Often firms accomplish this by setting territory goals and paying incentives only upon goal attainment beyond free sales. Such plans can motivate the sales force to work to create salesperson sales and thus earn incentive pay, provided the goals are fair and accurate. When incentives are used to pay for free sales, the firm is actually paying a hidden salary. A good portion of variable pay does not depend on performance when incentives are paid for sales that will be realized regardless of what the sales force does. Incentives should reward accomplishment. They lose their emotional impact when a salesperson feels that her actions do not have a large effect on the outcome. Of course, companies that are designing a plan to pay incentives for salesperson sales will need to estimate the level of free sales for the sales force accurately and fairly. Otherwise, the sales force is likely to be dissatisfied with the compensation plan, particularly if the estimated level of free sales is too high, and as a result salespeople are underrewarded for their efforts.

Team selling is a common threat to causality. When several salespeople are in a position to influence the same customer, and each individual's sales are influenced significantly by the efforts of other team members, it is often difficult to determine each individual salesperson's contribution to company and customer results. Hence, environments that emphasize team selling typically favor higher salary, while those that emphasize individual selling are more likely to favor incentives. There are many different types of team-selling situations. Sometimes, a sales force has multiple salespeople calling on the same decision makers. Other times, a sales force has multiple salespeople calling on different decision makers who influence the same result. Team selling is common in sales forces with broad, complex product lines, where a single salesperson is unable to perform all the necessary selling tasks effectively. It is also common in sales forces that cover large national or global accounts with multiple locations.

Team-Selling Example: Multiple Salespeople Call on the Same Decision Maker

A firm that sells a broad line of software products to banks has a team sales structure. At large banks, an account manager (AM) represents the company's full product line. The AM is expected to understand the full spectrum of needs at the account and to act as a primary point of contact for the customer. Since the needs of large customers are complex and the firm's product line is broad, it is not possible for the AM to understand all the details required to sell each of the company's complex products. Thus, the AM relies on product specialists to provide technical details and consulting and to help close sales. Product specialists also provide customers with training and installation assistance. The AM coordinates the activities of the product specialists as needed. Since the AM and the product specialists work together as a team to create sales and meet customer needs, causality is attributed to the entire team, not to a specific sales role. Responsibility for results is shared, and, as a result, individual incentives are not effective.

Team-Selling Example: Multiple Salespeople Call on Different Decision Makers Who Influence the Same Result

Diabetics use blood glucose monitors to test their blood sugar daily. They purchase the monitor and testing strips in drugstores and health-care outlets. Since testing strips are not interchangeable between monitors, the patient's choice of monitor is a critical decision for the manufacturer. A monitor purchase generates many years of strip purchases.

Up to four different people often influence a patient's choice of monitor. First, the patient's treating physician may make a recommendation. Second, since the disease is diagnosed in a hospital, a hospital staff member may recommend a specific monitor. Third, most patients are referred to a diabetes nurse educator, who provides information about the disease, treatment options, and lifestyle implications. The diabetes nurse educator is in a position to recommend a product. Finally, when the patient visits a retail outlet to purchase a product, the pharmacist may provide advice about which monitor is best.

None of these buying influences can be ignored. Manufacturers usually ask their sales forces to call on all of them. Typically, multiple independent sales roles are used. For example, one salesperson calls on treating physicians, a second calls on hospital staff, a third calls on diabetes nurse educators, and a fourth calls on pharmacists. The impact of each sales role is impossible to measure—all of them influence the buying decision. The whole team shares the causality—salespeople in all roles contribute to the salesperson sales component. But since an individual salesperson's impact on the patient's final purchase decision is impossible to determine, individual incentives may not be very motivational for the sales force.

Team-Selling Example: Large National or Global Accounts Have Multiple Locations That Need Sales Force Coverage

The salespeople at a consumer packaged goods firm need to call on Wal-Mart headquarters, where companywide buying decisions are made. Selling at headquarters spans a wide range of activities, including promotion planning, category plan-o-grams, co-op advertising, packaging, and logistics. Experts from the consumer packaged goods firm participate in each of these along with Wal-Mart personnel. In addition, the firm needs to call on local stores to sell-in and pull through products and to provide merchandising services. Since people in different sales roles work together to provide the various kinds of coverage the customer needs, sales force causality gets blurred across the various sales positions. Individuals feel less personal control over results, and hence the motivational power of individual incentives is reduced.

While team-selling environments generally favor higher salary, many firms that sell through teams do use incentives successfully. Team-based incentive plans vary greatly in their design, depending upon the type of selling team, the types of sales roles, and the firm's culture. Team incentives are often paid into a pool based on the team's total results. This pool is then divided appropriately among team members based on the nature and content of each member's role and his perceived contribution to results. Alternatively, some firms double-count sales and give each salesperson on the team credit for the entire sale. Many firms with team-based incentive plans continue to pay a portion of incentives based on individual performance as well. Several examples of team-based incentive plans are provided in Chapter 6.

Market Volatility Can Threaten Sales Force Causality

Market volatility is another common threat to sales force causality. In volatile markets, sales are very hard to predict. Sales that require minimal sales force effort relative to their value—often referred to as "windfalls" or "bluebirds"—are booked unexpectedly and frequently. These *random sales* can be very high in one year and low in the next. Companies that develop highly leveraged compensation plans that ignore market volatility can incur two negative consequences. First, the sales force develops high income expectations subsequent to a successful year in which random sales are high and salespeople receive considerable windfall gains. The sales force takes credit for the success and feels entitled to a similar income level in the future. Then, sales force morale suffers the following year when random sales are low. Second, a perception of unfairness envelops the sales force when the windfalls are not uniform across all salespeople. Paying a higher salary and lower incentive in volatile markets is one way to ensure a more fair and predictable distribution of earnings. Another way is to try to measure and account for random sales. For example, some firms put a cap on earnings to limit the impact of windfall gains resulting from random sales. Other firms account for volatility by flattening the payout and spreading incentive payments across a wider performance range, so that random sales have less impact on the payout distribution. Chapter 7 provides more detail on performance–payout relationships that effectively account for market volatility.

In markets that are not excessively volatile, paying incentives on occasional bluebirds or windfalls can actually have a positive impact on sales force morale. A random, unexpected hit makes a salesperson feel good, and may inspire her to go out and work harder to create future sales. Others in the sales organization are motivated to await their turn at a bluebird. Thus, paying incentives for bluebirds can be a positive strategy, as long as these windfalls occur infrequently and are spread randomly across the sales force so that every salesperson feels that he can benefit over time.

Evaluating the Measurability of Company and Customer Results

Incentives cannot work if the measures on which they are based are unavailable or inaccurate. Thus, selling environments in which company and customer results are highly measurable at the territory level allow incentives, while those with poor measurability favor salary.

Measurement Inaccuracies Lead to Decreased Productivity at a Health-Care Firm

The management team at a health-care products manufacturer believed strongly in the concept of variable sales force pay and wanted to create a "pay-for-performance" culture. The firm's products were used in hospitals, although sales went through distributors. Salespeople spent the majority of their time influencing hospital-based decision makers in an assigned geographic territory, and these decision makers would then purchase the products from a distributor. Often the distributor was located geographically close to the hospital, but this was not always the case.

Unfortunately, sales could be tracked only to the distributor level, not to the hospital level. The firm based incentives on sales to distributors in each salesperson's geographic sales territory; it was assumed that these sales were eventually realized at the local hospitals that the salesperson called on. Salespeople knew that this logic was flawed; hospitals often purchased from distributors outside their local area. Salespeople challenged the method of sales crediting. To prove their point, they began to track down hospital invoices that confirmed that they should receive credit for sales to distributors that were not in their local territory. This activity was an incredible drain on sales force productivity; at one point, management estimated that the sales force was spending as much as one-third of its time tracking invoices, rather than selling.

The most effective sales incentive programs tie incentive pay to the achievement of company and customer results. Each salesperson's performance is assessed in terms of one or more performance criteria. For example, territory revenues, contribution, and market share are typical ways to measure a salesperson's contribution to company results. Customer satisfaction and retention are commonly used measures of customer results. (See Chapter 6 for a more detailed discussion of incentive plan measures.) Whatever measures are selected, incentive pay is tied to the salesperson's success on these performance criteria.

Accurate measurability of the selected criteria at the individual salesperson level is critical to the success of any incentive-based plan. If it is not possible to measure performance accurately, then it is impossible to pay fairly on that performance. The less accurate the measurement is, the less desirable its use to reward salespeople with incentive pay is. When salespeople perceive performance measurement to be unfair, the desired motivational impact of the incentive is lost. Salespeople will spend their time arguing about measures instead of focusing on customers. The entire incentive plan may backfire, causing low sales force morale, reduced productivity, and high turnover.

Measurability depends upon data availability, accuracy, and timeliness. At many companies, accurate performance data are simply not available at the territory level. Some sales tracking systems do not capture all of the sales transactions and thus cannot give a salesperson full credit for her results. In addition, many companies (such as the health-care products manufacturer described in the example above) have multitiered distribution systems and know how much they sell to distributors, but not how much those distributors sell to end users. As a result, the outcome of salespeople's work with end users cannot be determined. Often, distributors are willing to sell data to a manufacturer that tracks the distributor's sales to the end-user level. In many circumstances, the benefits of improved sales force measurement justify the cost of buying these data. In other situations, distributors view these data as a competitive advantage and are unwilling to share them with manufacturers. In such cases, manufacturers need to be more creative in devising performance metrics.

Data accuracy and timeliness are an important part of measurability and thus influence the degree to which a firm can use incentive-based sales compensation. In some cases, performance measures are estimated from a sample when a census is not available. Such estimates can have sampling errors, and few salespeople will be content to accept a sampling error that they feel adversely affects their compensation. Customer satisfaction surveys often have data accuracy issues, particularly when a salesperson can influence a customer inappropriately to provide good survey results. Data timeliness is also important for measurability. Data that are months late because of collection delays and data processing errors are not very motivational to a sales force.

The Consequences of a Pay Mix Decision That Does Not Acknowledge Causality and Measurability. A sales compensation plan that is incompatible with sales force causality and measurability creates dissonance within the sales organization.

Two possible types of misalignment are illustrated in Figure 5-11. The upper left-hand area of the figure represents companies that have low sales force causality and/or poor results measurability, yet have chosen compensation plans with a high variable-pay component. The effect of this choice is that the company will be paying salespeople for outcomes that they have not created. Salespeople may feel that the incentive plan is a lottery, and thus the motivational power of the plan is lost. In fact, the plan will be demotivating if the sales force perceives it to be unfair. The lower right-hand area of the figure represents a different incompatibility: A company with high sales force causality and good measurability chooses a compensation plan with high salary and a low variable-pay component. The danger in this choice is that the sales force may go to sleep. The salespeople can make good money regardless of how much they sell. The firm misses out on the power of monetary incentives to motivate the sales force to achieve high levels of sales. Management needs to rely on levers other than incentives, such as leadership, recognition, and fulfilling work, to create excitement for salespeople in this case.

The large middle oval represents situations in which causality and measurability are in alignment with variable pay. When causality and measurability are high, a compensation plan with a large incentive component works best. An individual salesperson's efforts are strongly tied to results, and individual results can be mea-

Figure 5-11. Misalignment of causality and/or measurability with pay mix.

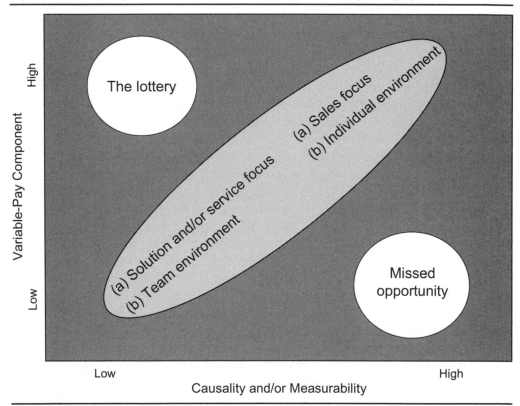

sured accurately. Therefore, having a larger portion of compensation at risk is motivational for the sales force. When causality and measurability are low, a compensation plan with a small incentive component works best. An individual salesperson's efforts are not strongly tied to results, and individual results cannot be measured accurately. In this situation, the sales force can work collaboratively and focus on meeting the long-term needs of customers, knowing that most of their compensation is predetermined.

Comparing to Industry Norms

Most companies look at industry norms when determining pay mix for two reasons. First, since companies in the same industry often have comparable selling processes and have access to similar performance measures, industry norms provide a good model of what pay mix has worked well for other companies in analogous situations. Second, awareness of industry norms is important for competitiveness in the market for salespeople. Particularly in industries where job hopping is common, companies that deviate unfavorably from the mix of salary and incentive offered by their competitors may experience excessive sales force turnover. The pay mix is particularly important to the extent that it affects the pay range for top performers. Plans with a greater incentive component typically have greater upside potential. If a firm's best performers feel that they can make more money at another firm with a more highly leveraged compensation plan, they will migrate to that opportunity (all other things being equal). A success strategy used by many companies is to ensure that top performers can earn as much money with them as anywhere else in the industry.

Many industry surveys, including those discussed in Chapter 4, provide information about the mix of salary versus incentive by industry, in addition to providing data on total pay for average and top performers.

Blue Cross Blue Shield Creates a More Aggressive Salary–Incentive Mix Based on Benchmarking Outside Its Industry

When management at Blue Cross Blue Shield (BCBS) of Massachusetts decided to revamp the company's sales compensation plan, it compared its plan not only with the plans of other managed-care companies, but also with those of successful service companies in industries such as banking and technology. Management had observed that many of the high-performing salespeople who had left BCBS had joined companies in other service industries. Thus, the firm's industry competitors were only a subset of its personnel competitors. After reviewing the benchmarking data, management felt that service firms with more aggressive incentive structures created hunger in the sales organization, while those offering larger base salaries fostered complacency. Thus, the firm reversed its compensation plan from 60 percent base salary and 40 percent incentive to a plan offering 40 percent base and 60 percent incentive.

Service Firm Adjusts Pay Mix to Attract the Right People

When new management took over at a small Chicago-based service firm, a complete makeover of the sales organization was a top priority. A new sales force hiring profile was developed, and since the majority of the current salespeople did not match this profile, two-thirds of the sales force was let go. Management wanted to attract experienced salespeople from organizations such as Dun & Bradstreet and RR Donnelley who were aggressive and motivated but also had the skill, poise, and charm to sell business services effectively. In order to attract people with the right attitude and aptitude, they discovered that a change in the salary–incentive mix was needed. The base salary was raised from $50,000 to $80,000, and commission rates were lowered.

When Should Industry Norms Be Ignored?

Industry norms may be irrelevant for a company that has a very different sales strategy or selling process from other firms in the same industry. In addition, industry pay mix norms occasionally get out of whack with industry sales strategies because pay plan changes often lag sales strategy changes. For example, in the early 2000s, most pharmaceutical salespeople earned approximately 20 to 25 percent of their cash compensation as variable pay. However, several recent trends in the industry have blurred causality at the individual salesperson level, suggesting that perhaps this variable-pay percentage is too high. These trends include the increased prevalence of team selling, the influence of managed care, the effect of direct-to-consumer advertising, and more rapid dissemination of medical news via the Internet. Despite these trends, most companies have been reluctant to deviate from industry norms by reducing the incentive pay component for fear of losing their top performers to competitors offering greater upside earnings potential. Today, industry leaders are just beginning to adjust pay plans to include a larger salary component, lagging several years behind the changes in the sales strategy and selling environment.

Checking for Alignment with Company History, Culture, and Management Philosophy

Company history, culture, and management philosophy play an important role in determining the appropriate mix of salary versus incentive. Salespeople base their expectations about how they will be paid in the future on how they have been paid in the past. Making major changes to the pay mix—for example, going from a high-salary environment to a high-incentive environment, or vice versa—can be very disruptive and challenging. Often, companies are reluctant to make such major changes, for fear of unsettling the sales force. Pay mix changes often have a considerable impact on the distribution of earnings across salespeople. This redistribution is particularly problematic for sales forces that are making the transition from a highly incentive-focused pay mix to a highly salary-focused mix. Pay plans with large salary components tend to have smaller variation in earnings across salespeople than plans with large incentive components. Thus, top performers typically make less money when the salary component is large and more when the incentive component is large. As a result, a move to a larger salary component runs the risk of disappointing top-performing salespeople and causing undesired sales force turnover.

Mix decisions also have a considerable impact on sales force culture. Figure 5-12 characterizes five attributes of sales force culture by describing diametrically opposed management philosophies that help to define the culture. The figure hypothesizes about how the salary–incentive mix decision helps to shape the culture by reinforcing the desired management philosophy. The figure also provides insight into the type of person that will be attracted to each incentive plan. Because of the considerable differences between cultures that favor incentives and those that favor salary, a substantial change to the salary–incentive mix in either direction often leads to significant sales force turnover. After the implementation of a significant mix change, it is common for over 50 percent of salespeople to leave a company within three years. Chapter 11 shares some strategies for implementing significant salary–incentive mix changes successfully.

Who Bears the Risk of Poor Company Results?

The salary–incentive mix decision makes a culture statement about the selling organization's risk-taking posture. It influences how much financial risk is assumed by the firm and how much by the sales force. This has a major effect on the type of salesperson that is attracted to the firm. With a highly leveraged compensation plan, the sales force assumes the risk of poor performance. Salespeople will not make much money in a bad year, even if the poor performance is the result of factors beyond the sales force's control, such as a bad economy or poor product quality. On the other hand, the salespeople benefit from higher upside potential in good years. The company may still be profitable in both good and bad years, since sales force costs are tied to sales. When salespeople are paid mostly salary, on the other hand, the company assumes the risk of poor performance. In a bad year, company profits will take a hit, since sales force costs are mostly fixed. However, salespeople will continue to earn good incomes despite the poor performance. Salespeople who are willing to risk income swings from year to year in exchange for higher upside earnings potential prefer high-

Figure 5-12. Sales force culture attributes and their impact on the salary–incentive mix.

◀━━━ Favor Incentives	Favor Salary ━━━▶
Empowerment • Salespeople "own" their accounts—in the eyes of customers, the salesperson is the firm. • Salespeople determine the sales activities that they deem appropriate with each customer.	**Control** • The firm "owns" the accounts—the salesperson is just one connection a customer has to the firm. • The firm directs and controls sales force activity.
Focus on results • The sales force is sales-centered and is tasked with doing whatever it takes to make a sale. • The sales force spends as much time as possible in the field selling.	**Focus on activities and behaviors** • The sales force is customer-centered, doing what is best for the customer. • The sales force enhances its skills by investing in professional development.
Short-term focus • Short-term results are important. Quick hits by the sales force help the firm make its goal. The sales force focuses on completing as many transactions as possible. • New business development is critical for sustained success. The sales force is encouraged to "hunt" by visiting prospects and creating new accounts. • The firm hires experienced talent into the sales force.	**Long-term focus** • Long-term results are important. As an example, the sales force invests significant time to penetrate large competitive accounts, even though the outcome is uncertain. The sales force focuses on building the business. • Business maintenance is vitally important. The sales force spends most of its time serving existing customers. • The firm develops the best talent from within.
Internally competitive environment • An individual orientation is favored. Competition motivates salespeople and is good for business. • The sales force is special—these important company ambassadors receive incentives if they produce results.	**Cooperative environment** • A team orientation is desired. Cooperation is vital for success with customers. • The sales force is important but should be treated like everyone else at the company.
Adaptive to individual customer needs • Each salesperson is encouraged to creatively adapt the selling process to meet the needs of each customer.	**Adaptive organization structure** • Management desires to change sales force size and structure, sales roles, and account assignments freely as markets evolve.

incentive environments. Those who prefer greater income stability with lower overall earnings potential prefer high-salary environments.

A sales compensation plan that is incompatible with the firm's culture and values creates dissonance within the sales organization. Two possible types of incompatibility are illustrated in Figure 5-13. Companies that fall in the upper left-hand area of the figure have a culture that embraces salary-friendly norms and

Figure 5-13. Incompatibility of sales force culture and pay mix.

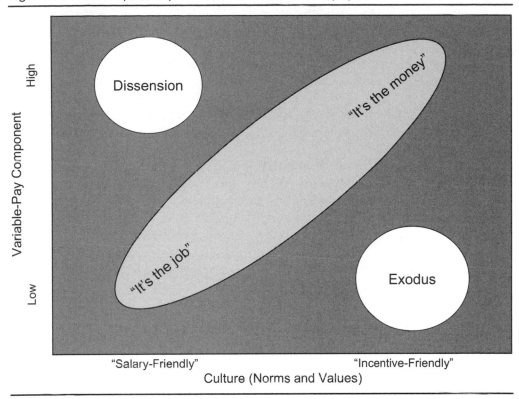

values (i.e., they favor the choices on the right-hand side of Figure 5-12), yet have chosen compensation plans with high performance pay. This misalignment creates dissension and a lack of consistency within the sales organization. Management says, "Be customer-centric," yet a salesperson who is sales-centric makes more money. Management says, "Professional development is important," yet salespeople who take time out of the field to attend training earn less money in the short term. Management says, "Focus on developing long-term relationships with customers," yet salespeople are paid for producing short-term results. The incompatibility between the behaviors that management says are important and the behaviors for which salespeople are paid creates uncertainty and diminishes productivity. This incompatibility can also cause the sales force culture to diverge from the company culture, creating animosity between the sales force and other company departments and reducing mobility between sales and other company jobs.

Outer Circle Eliminates Sales Incentive Pay to Support Company Culture

Outer Circle Products, a small privately held maker of lunch boxes and coolers, eliminated the sales incentive program for its 11 salespeople because management felt that the plan clashed with the company's all-for-one culture. The sales incentive plan motivated salespeople to manipulate numbers and make decisions that benefited their wallets, but not necessarily their customers. Under the new compensation plan, salespeople were paid straight salaries, just like everyone else in the firm. In addition, all employees (including salespeople) could participate in the firm's profit-sharing plan. Management recognized that the unique culture at Outer Circle was not right for everyone: A candidate who saw the salaried sales compensation plan as a negative was not right for the company.

Companies in the lower right-hand corner of Figure 5-13 have a different incompatibility: These companies embrace incentive-friendly norms and values that celebrate results and sales performance differences, yet they have chosen a compensation plan with high salary and low performance pay. This misalignment is likely to result in significant sales force turnover, as the lack of monetary incentives will make it difficult to retain and attract salespeople with the right success profile. The firm also misses out on the power of monetary incentives to motivate the sales force to achieve higher levels of sales.

Disney Offers Sales Force Incentives to Support Its Aggressive Marketing Campaign

In 1996, Disney Attractions wanted to attack the marketplace with a powerful sales message: Disney is much more than just a family destination. Disney launched a marketing campaign emphasizing the fact that many of its theme parks cater to adults as well as children, offering recreational activities such as golfing and water sports and educational courses at the Disney Institute. Disney's 100 salespeople were critical to the success of the campaign, as they had the power to influence travel agents and meeting planners who could persuade travelers to try a Disney vacation. To support the marketing effort, Disney expanded its sales force and added regional offices. To enhance sales force motivation, the firm revamped its sales compensation plan. Salespeople who had previously been paid a straight salary could now earn commissions for meeting and exceeding ambitious sales quotas.

Finally, the extent to which management desires to use incentives as a means of motivating and controlling salespeople is an important consideration in the pay mix decision. Some management teams have a strong pay-for-performance philosophy. They feel that "pay should be more reflective of performance," "there should be greater differentiation between high and low performers," and "labor costs should be tied more directly to sales." Other sales management teams have a more long-term customer-oriented view. They tell us, "We need to encourage closer customer relationships and improve customer satisfaction," "the compensation plan should be better aligned with long-term company goals," and "we want to focus sales effort on strategic activities, not just short-term sales targets." The pay mix decision should reflect and reinforce management's beliefs and philosophies.

A Pay Mix Scorecard

The discussion thus far on how to determine the right salary–incentive mix has examined the company and market conditions that favor sales compensation plans with either a high, moderate, or low percent incentive. These drivers and influences were discussed individually. A final mix decision requires that they be considered jointly. The pay mix scorecard provides a mechanism for integrating the various factors that lead to an appropriate salary–incentive mix decision. Using a scorecard, an incentive plan designer evaluates how the various drivers and influences affect the pay mix decision, based on the company's specific situation. The best scorecards are customized to the specific selling organization. Figure 5-14 presents a generic scorecard.

Each factor can be weighted to reflect its importance to the mix decision. It is possible that some factors will clearly dominate. For example, the firm may decide that it will modify an existing compensation plan only slightly. In this case, Company History is a dominant factor. Figures 5-15 and 5-16 illustrate pay mix scorecards for the office supply company and the animal laboratory systems company described earlier in the chapter.

The pay mix decision for both the office supply company and the animal laboratory systems company is reasonably clear, since the arrows on each company's pay mix scorecard are aligned fairly consistently. On occasion, companies face more difficult pay mix decisions. Figure 5-17 shows a pay mix scorecard for a newspaper company whose advertising sales force is paid primarily salary. The decision to have a mostly salaried sales force dates back to a time when the newspaper had a virtual monopoly on advertising in its local market and the sales force was selling to a captive audience. In recent years, the number of print media options has expanded, and electronic media and cable television have become viable alternatives to newspaper advertising. As a result, the newspaper's sales force has become much more prominent in creating advertising sales. Management needs to decide whether it should change its historical incentive system and move toward one that is more consistent with its market.

Figure 5-14. An example of a generic pay mix scorecard.

	Level of Incentives		
	Low	Moderate	High

Sales Process and Roles
- Selling cycle
- Number of transactions
- Nature of customer interaction
- Sources of salesperson satisfaction
- Success measures
- Sales process control

Sales Force Causality
- Brand name
- Other marketing instruments
- Team selling

Measurability
- Company results
- Customer results

Industry Norms

Company History

Culture
- Empowerment/control
- Results/activity
- Short-term/long-term
- Competitive/cooperative
- Adaptive/stable

Management Philosophy

Figure 5-15. Pay mix scorecard for an office supply company.

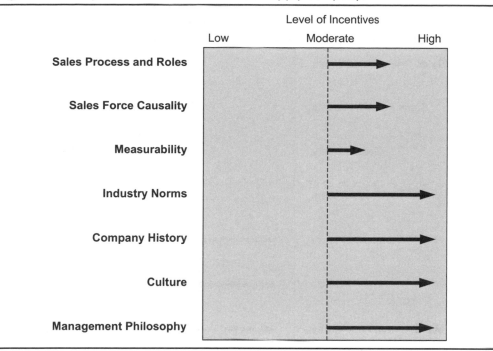

Figure 5-16. Pay mix scorecard for an animal laboratory systems company.

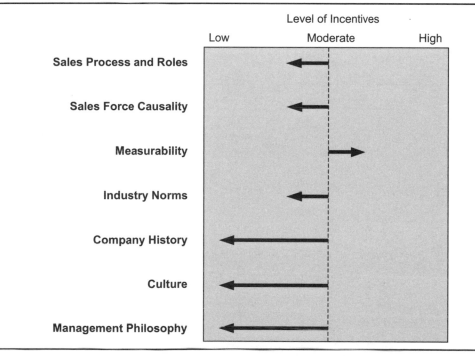

Figure 5-17. Pay mix scorecard for a newspaper company.

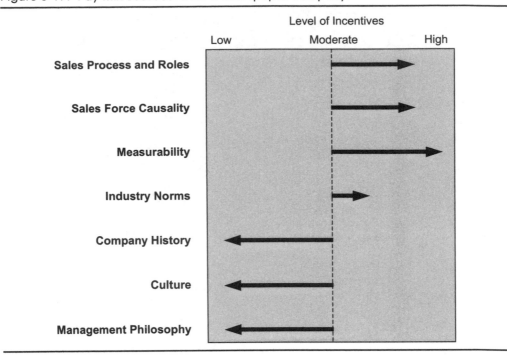

CHAPTER 6

Plan Design Part 3
Selecting Performance Measures

How This Chapter Is Organized

Are You Using the Most Appropriate Performance Measures to
Determine Your Incentive Plan Payout?   184
Types of Measures   187
The Role of Performance Management Versus Incentives   188
Who Should Take Accountability for the Performance Measures?   190
How to Determine the Most Appropriate Sales Incentive Measures:
An Advisory   191
Effective Incentive Plan Performance Measures Pass the 3 Cs Test   192
Effective Incentive Plan Performance Measures Are Objectively and
Accurately Measurable   192
Effective Incentive Plan Performance Measures Should Be Affected by
Sales Force Capability and Activity   193
Effective Incentive Plan Performance Measures Do Not Favor Any
Particular Group   194
Effective Incentive Plan Performance Measures Are Adaptive to
Business Strategy Change   195
Keep It Simple: Have No More than Three or Four Total Measures   196
How to Determine the Most Appropriate Sales Incentive Measures:
Specifics   198
Metrics   199
Company Results Metrics   200
Sales Revenue Metrics   201
Contribution Margin and Profit Metrics   201

Market Share Metrics	203
Customer Results Metrics	204
Activity Metrics	206
Salespeople Metrics	208
Data Views	209
Absolute-Level Metrics	209
Comparing to Past Performance	210
Comparing to a Goal	210
Ranking Relative to Peers	215
Focus	216
Market Segment Focus	216
Product Focus	216
Channel Focus	216
Organizational-Level Focus and Team Rewards	216
Timing	221
How Often Should Incentives Be Paid?	221
Should Incentives Be Paid When the Order Is Taken or When the Company Collects the Funds from the Customer?	223

Are You Using the Most Appropriate Performance Measures to Determine Your Incentive Plan Payout?

Incentives reward successful sales force performance. Performance cannot be judged without evaluative criteria. Selecting the performance measures that are used to determine incentive plan payout is a critical incentive plan design decision, and the impact of choosing the wrong measures is significant. Consider the following situations:

Paying on Sales Encourages Undesired Discounting

The sales force of an office equipment maker is paid a commission on sales volume; salespeople earn 2 percent of sales up to quota and 5 percent of sales above quota. The sales force books very few sales at list price, despite the fact that the firm's products are widely recognized to be superior to those of competitors. Salespeople have the authority to offer discounts of up to 20 percent, and further discounts are possible with approval from senior levels. On average, sales are booked at a 29 percent discount off list price. Salespeople typically start pricing discussions with the preauthorized 20 percent discount and then push their managers for deeper discounts. The compensation plan provides no incentive for salespeople to think in terms of margin. Salespeople are constantly looking for a low-risk way (by cutting prices to the bone) to build volume and get to the 5 percent commission level as quickly as possible.

Paying on Short-Term Sales Undermines Teamwork and Customer Relationships

A computer products and services company pays salespeople 25 percent base salary and 75 percent commission, based on quarterly sales goal achievement. The pay plan promotes a sales force culture that is hungry, aggressive, and focused on short-term results. This worked well in the firm's early years, when sales cycles were short and selling was straightforward. However, over the last decade, as the industry has evolved and the firm's product line has broadened, the sales process has become increasingly long, complex, and team-oriented. Today, sales success involves salespeople working together with systems engineers, service managers, technical consultants, and product specialists over a period of many months to reach multiple decision makers. The importance of developing and maintaining long-term customer relationships has increased considerably. Yet an intense quarter-to-quarter focus by management puts pressure on salespeople to deliver short-term results. This focus is beginning to hurt the firm; many customers have expressed doubt that the firm's salespeople are truly concerned with their interests.

Paying on Growth in a Stagnant Market Causes Excessive Sales Force Turnover

A diagnostics imaging company pays its salespeople a 1 percent commission on all sales up to the sales achieved in the same six-month period last year, and a 6 percent commission on sales growth over the base sales. Most of the salespeople's earnings come from the growth component. This plan worked well during the first few years after a major product launch, as sales grew smartly every year. However, as competitors launched similar products and the market became saturated, sales growth has slowed dramatically. Most salespeople are not making much incentive money, and there has been a steady exodus of the best salespeople, who have left to work for competitors and other medical device companies.

Paying on Sales That Salespeople Cannot Influence Creates Morale Problems

A distributor of tools and maintenance equipment for automobiles sells to automotive parts retailers, mobile tool dealers, and fleets. The company has a national accounts manager for major national accounts with centralized buying (for example, Advance Auto Parts), and local territory salespeople who may service the local stores of national accounts and also sell to independently owned accounts within their territory. Local salespeople earn commissions on all territory sales. This means that they sometimes receive commissions on sales to outlets of national accounts that require little or no effort on their part. As the sales to national accounts have increased, complaints of unfairness from salespeople who have few national account outlets in their territory have become more and more widespread across the sales force.

Paying on Multiple Measures Leads to Sales Force Confusion

A pharmaceutical firm's incentive plan uses three different metrics—goal attainment, market share, and market share change—to determine payout for four different products. Having multiple measures helps to reinforce the company's goals of achieving sales objectives and improving its competitive position for strategic products. Multiple measures also help to protect salespeople from data inaccuracies in any single metric. However, many salespeople are confused by the multiple measures in the incentive plan. "Hedging on three different metrics for four different products is too much for the field," reports an area vice president. "I'm not sure which metric is really driving my salespeople's compensation," said a district manager. Management realizes that the plan is not providing a clear focus for the sales force.

Paying on Margins That Cannot Be Measured Accurately Causes Frustration

One division of a medical device company sells infusion pumps and supplies to hospitals. Over time, the product line became wider, and additional products were added from another manufacturer. The incentive plan was changed from a commission plan based on sales to a commission plan based on product margins. It seemed like a good idea, but as the year progressed, it became clear that this was not a simple change. Trying to determine the margin on each item sold became a nightmare, with changing product costs, distribution costs, product rebates, and portfolio rebates. The plan was abandoned after the first quarter.

These examples illustrate how important it is to use the most appropriate measures for determining incentive plan payout. When the office equipment maker pays salespeople on sales rather than margins, the incentive plan drives sales force behaviors that hurt profitability and are inconsistent with the company's premium product image. When the seller of computer products and services emphasizes short-term sales measures, salespeople adopt a mind-set that undermines teamwork, hurts customer relationships, and ultimately decreases customer satisfaction. When the imaging company pays on growth in a stagnant and saturated market, too many salespeople get frustrated and leave the company. When the tools and maintenance equipment distributor bases incentive payouts on performance measures that salespeople do not control, a lottery culture is created, undermining sales force morale. When the pharmaceutical company selects a multitude of metrics, the result is sales force confusion and unpredictable salesperson behavior. When the medical device company pays on margins, but can't measure margins accurately and in a timely manner, the incentive plan itself becomes dysfunctional.

The diagnosis of performance measures begins by examining the three views within the sales management system framework:

- The downstream consequences of selected performance measures for salespeople, sales force activities, and customer and company results
- The upstream consistency of performance measures with marketing and go-to-market strategies, sales processes, and sales force roles
- The compatibility of measures with salespeople's skills and capabilities, sales force culture, performance management systems, and nonmonetary sales force motivators

Figure 6-1 provides a template for diagnosing whether the appropriate performance measures are being used in the sales incentive plan by illustrating possible signs of trouble.

Types of Measures

A variety of measures can be used to assess and manage performance, and some of these measures are appropriate for incentive plans. Figure 6-2 organizes the measure choices into the five components that make up the sales management system framework.

Companies employ two important and complementary sales force effectiveness drivers to influence sales force behavior and activity: sales incentives and sales performance management. Sales incentives affect a salesperson's variable pay, while performance management consists of the ongoing planning, coaching, measurement, communication, coordination, evaluation, and course-correction activities that ensure that success is achieved or corrective actions are taken. Figure 6-3 shows a typical performance management system. Performance reviews are often linked to salary changes.

The metrics in each of the last four columns of Figure 6-2 can be used for both incentives and performance management. This leads to the performance management versus incentives dilemma. Which metrics should be used for incentives, and which metrics should be used for performance management?

The Role of Performance Management Versus Incentives

Performance management processes and incentive compensation can employ all of the metrics listed in the last four columns of Figure 6-2. These metrics differ in the timing of their impact and their measurability. As one moves from left to right in the figure, the time frame of impact becomes shorter. The achievement of salespeople goals (for example, enhancing sales force product knowledge or improving selling skills) and sales activity goals (for example, completing detailed account plans, conducting customer demos, or submitting proposals) tends to have a longer-term impact; the results may not be fully realized until several incentive periods into the future. On the other hand, the achievement of customer and

Figure 6-1. Some signs that the incentive compensation plan measures *may* not be appropriate.

Consistency with . . .	Compatibility with . . .	Consequences . . .
• Sales and marketing strategies • Sales process • Sales roles	• Performance management systems • Sales force culture • Sales force motivators • Sales force hiring and development processes	• Company results • Customer results • Sales force behaviors and activities • Sales force quality
• What gets measured gets done. The sales force doesn't appear to be executing the company's marketing strategy. • Sales processes and roles have evolved, but the performance measures have not changed in years. • Sales success depends on effective teamwork, yet the performance metrics in the compensation system encourage a salesperson to hoard quality leads and withhold good ideas so that he can get all the credit. • Sales requires a team effort, but the compensation plan pays commission only to the lead salesperson on the account. • The sales territories are unbalanced in terms of market opportunity, creating unfairness in payout based on sales and/or market share.	• Measures that are best controlled through performance management, such as professional development and call activity, are carrying a heavy weight in the incentive plan. • Cultural statements like "we want to be customer-centric" collide with incentive metrics such as short-term sales. • Too many motivation programs and SPIFFs are emphasizing short-term performance metrics at the expense of developing long-term relationships with customers.	• Sales, profit, and/or market share goals are not being achieved because incentive plan measures encourage the wrong sales force behaviors. • Customer satisfaction is suffering because incentive plan measures focus on short-term results, not long-term customer needs. • Sales activities are inappropriate because salespeople are measured, for example, on number of calls, not call quality; on total sales, not business development; or on self-reported customer satisfaction scores, not repeat sales. • Salespeople are leaving because the metrics that are used in the incentive plan do not allow them to feel successful. For example, they are paid on sales growth in a declining market.

company results goals has a shorter-term impact; the results are realized in the current incentive period. Results metrics are often used in determining incentive pay, since most selling organizations have significant short-term pressure to drive results.

Metrics in the last four columns of Figure 6-2 also differ in the degree of difficulty of developing objective and accurate measures. As one moves from left to right in the figure, the ability to create objective and accurate measures increases. Salespeople's characteristics are frequently derived judgmentally. Activity metrics can also be derived judgmentally or can be self-reported by the salesperson. Customer and company results metrics, on the other hand, are typically more objective, developed by analyzing sales, margin, and customer satisfaction data.

Figure 6-2. Metrics for the five components of the sales management system framework.

Sales force effectiveness drivers	Salespeople	Sales force activities	Customer results	Company results
• Assessments and evaluations of the decisions and programs that define, shape, enlighten, excite, and control the sales force	• Knowledge • Competencies • Skills • Attitudes • Behaviors • Motivation • Success profile • Employee satisfaction • Turnover • Peer and subordinate reviews	• Account planning • Targeting • Calls • Reach • Frequency • Hours • Coverage index • Maintenance • Prospecting • Needs assessment • Demonstrations • Proposals • Evaluations • Solutions • Customer service	• Customer satisfaction • Customer retention • Customer loyalty • Repeat rate • Complaints about the sales force • Returns • Penetration • Message memorability • Percentage of sales or sales growth from existing customers	• Sales • Units • Gross margin • Orders • Collections • Sales per rep • Market share • Value perception

Figure 6-3. Components of a typical formal performance management system.

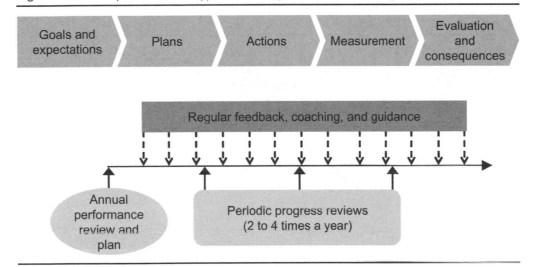

Incentives are most effective when they are based on objectively measurable criteria with short-term impact. If a significant source of income is tied to criteria that cannot be measured accurately, not only is the desired motivational impact of the incentive lost, but the perceived unfairness may demoralize the sales force. Incentives are also most motivating when they are tied to short-term results, rather than to competencies and activities that have long-term impact. Consequently, the measures from the last two columns of Figure 6-2—customer and company results—are typically the most effective measures for incentive plan design. Measures from the second and third columns—salesperson competencies and sales force activities—are typically best controlled using performance management systems rather than incentives. Figure 6-4 illustrates this advice.

High percent incentive pay plans require sound results measurement. If accurate and objective customer and company results measures are not available, then the firm must develop a strong performance management system and should pay the sales force a greater percent salary and a lower percent incentive. In these cases, having a small incentive component of pay tied to activity measures can be motivational to the sales force.

Who Should Take Accountability for the Performance Measures?

Accountability for achieving results across different measures varies by job category within the sales force.

Figure 6-4. Control and impact of different measures.

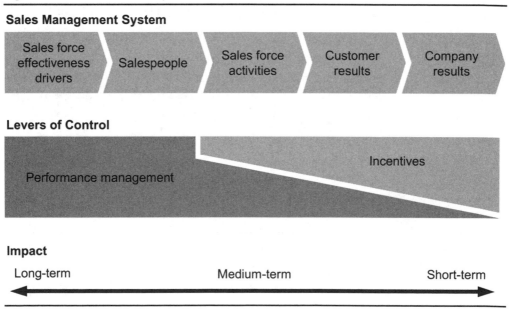

- Sales leadership has primary responsibility for the *sales force effectiveness driver* measures—the measures that reflect the quality of the decisions and programs that define, shape, enlighten, excite, and control the sales force.
- First-line sales managers have primary responsibility for the *salespeople* measures, as they are charged with attracting and retaining high-quality people and developing the knowledge, competency, and skills of the salespeople who report to them.
- Salespeople have primary responsibility for local territory or specific account *activity* measures, such as the quantity and quality of calls.
- Everyone shares responsibility for *customer* and *company results.*
  Figure 6-5 shows which sales team members should be held accountable for the different types of performance measures. The number of stars in each cell signifies the importance of every measurement category for each sales team role.

Measuring the Sales Force Effectiveness Drivers

The sales force effectiveness drivers are the basic decisions that management makes and the processes that are used to influence salespeople. The drivers help to define, shape, enlighten, excite, and control the sales force. Measuring the sales force effectiveness drivers is important because the desired customer and company results will follow if the sales force effectiveness drivers are managed successfully. For example, just how good is the firm's training program? Does the sales force design allow effective execution of the sales strategy? Is the firm attracting and retaining the best salespeople? Measuring these drivers is often difficult and requires a good deal of creativity, yet more and more companies are making progress in this area. Some companies have used a tool called a competency/impact matrix to assess the relative importance of the critical sales force effectiveness drivers and the competency of the firm at executing them. In addition, many firms perform routine assessments and data-driven analyses to determine how well they are executing in key driver areas. Examples of such

Figure 6-5. Measure relevance for different members of the sales team.

	Sales force effectiveness drivers	Salespeople	Sales force activities	Customer results	Company results
Senior sales management	****	**	*	***	****
First-line sales managers	*	****	***	****	****
Salespeople		****	****	****	****

assessments and analyses for measuring the effectiveness of the sales compensation effectiveness driver are discussed in Chapter 2. Sales force effectiveness driver measures should be part of the firm's performance management process for the sales leadership team.

How to Determine the Most Appropriate Sales Incentive Measures: An Advisory

The best incentive plan performance measures share several common characteristics.

- Effective incentive plan performance measures pass the consistency, compatibility, and consequence test (the 3 Cs test).
- They are objectively and accurately measurable.
- They are influenced by sales force capability and activity.
- They do not favor any particular group within the sales force.
- They are adaptive to business strategy change.
- Effective incentive plans use a limited number of performance measures to encourage sales force focus and understanding.

Effective Incentive Plan Performance Measures Pass the 3 Cs Test

The selected incentive plan measures need to be consistent with company marketing and go-to-market strategies as well as with the sales roles that have been defined by the desired selling process. The measures need to be compatible with the other sales force effectiveness drivers, such as performance management systems and sales force culture. In addition, the measures should not produce unwanted behaviors and activities in the field that lead to substandard sales and profit results. A quick qualitative upstream look for consistency, a downstream look for appropriate consequences, and an alignment check for compatibility help sales leaders spot inappropriate measures (see Figure 6-1).

Powerful Incentive Plan Performance Measures Link Business Strategy to Sales Force Activity

Selecting incentive plan metrics is a powerful way to align sales force activities with company goals and strategies. For example, a company with high growth aspirations rewards salespeople for sales growth over the prior year. A company that is attacking the market leader rewards salespeople for competitive wins or market share growth. A sales force that is selling mature, profit-producing products rewards its salespeople for customer retention and contribution.

Effective Incentive Plan Performance Measures Are Objectively and Accurately Measurable

Measurability of the selected performance criteria is critical to the success of any incentive-based plan. If it is not possible to measure performance accurately, then it is impossible to pay fairly on that performance. The less accurate and more subjective the measure, the less desirable it is to reward salespeople with incentive pay based on that measure. When salespeople perceive performance measurement to be unfair, the desired motivational impact of the incentive is lost. Salespeople will spend their time arguing about measures or trying to game the system instead of focusing on customers. The entire incentive plan may backfire, causing low sales force morale and unwanted turnover.

Data Inaccuracies Prevent a Firm From Paying Incentives on Territory Market Share

A firm has a strategic objective of increasing market share in a competitive market, and the sales force plays an important role in achieving this objective. In order to align sales force effort with company strategy, management desires to pay salespeople incentives for increasing market share within their territory. However, market share data is based on a sample and is reliable only at a regional level—in most geographic markets, the sample size is not large enough to provide accurate territory-level results. Consequently, the company continues to pay incentives based on individual territory sales, but also pays a bonus to salespeople in regions that increase market share.

Effective Incentive Plan Performance Measures Should Be Affected by Sales Force Capability and Activity

Causality, or the ability of individual salespeople to affect short-term results, is an important consideration in the selection of the performance measures that will determine incentive pay. Salespeople should be able to affect the measures that will be used to evaluate and reward them. If factors other than current sales force skills, capabilities, and effort have a large impact on a measure, then the motivational impact of that measure is weakened. For example, a sales force without pricing authority has more influence over sales than it does over contribution. Paying salespeople for contribution might create frustration, since the sales force does not influence a significant aspect of the measure. Finding performance measures with high sales force causality can be problematic in team-selling environments, where multiple salespeople often influence results.

Pharmaceutical Company Pays on Units, Not Dollars

The incentive plan for the salespeople who call on physicians for a specialty pharmaceuticals manufacturer pays on unit sales rather than dollar sales. This is because the price that customers pay for drugs is heavily influenced by third-party payers, such as insurance companies or public aid programs (Medicare and Medicaid). Thus, the salespeople who educate physicians about the therapeutic qualities of the firm's drugs have greater control over the units sold in their territory than they do over the dollars.

Effective Incentive Plan Performance Measures Do Not Favor Any Particular Group

The performance measures in an incentive plan should be fair; they should not favor specific territories, accounts, or salespeople with particular characteristics that are outside a salesperson's control. For example:

- An activity metric such as "calls per day" favors salespeople in urban territories with little drive time between calls, while penalizing those in rural territories with significant travel requirements
- A sales volume metric favors salespeople in territories with large market potential and penalizes those with fewer opportunities
- A market share metric favors salespeople in territories with low market potential, who have time to penetrate every account deeply, and penalizes those with too many opportunities to cover effectively.

To compensate for differences across sales territories, companies frequently set territory-specific goals and base incentive pay on goal attainment. For example, a salesperson in a high-potential territory gets a larger sales goal than one in a low-potential territory, so that equal sales skill, salesperson capabilities, and effort in each territory result in the same level of goal attainment and thus the same incentive pay. However, goal-setting processes can also have biases. Figure 6-6 shows data from a sales force with a goal-based plan that was biased toward territories with higher starting market share. Processes for overcoming goal-setting biases are discussed in Chapter 9.

Effective Incentive Plan Performance Measures Are Adaptive to Business Strategy Change

Chapter 1 discussed the need to adapt incentive plans over time as markets and company strategies evolve. Performance measures are an important aspect of this evolution. For example, Figure 6-7 shows how the measures in the firm's com-

Figure 6-6. Example of goal-setting bias: Incentive payout is correlated with starting market share.

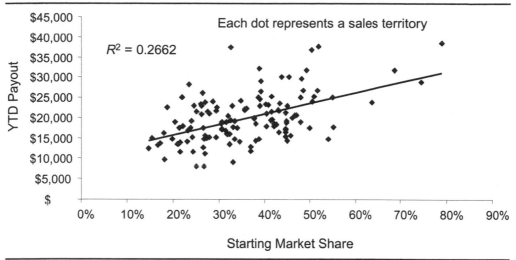

Figure 6-7. Life-cycle effects and sales compensation.

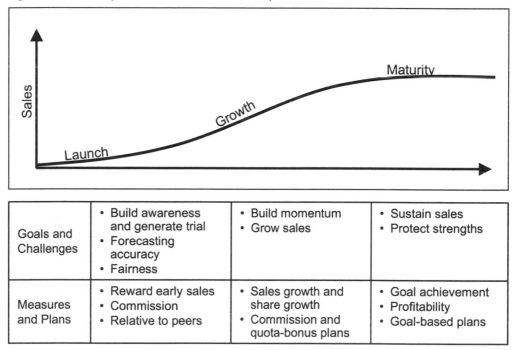

Goals and Challenges	• Build awareness and generate trial • Forecasting accuracy • Fairness	• Build momentum • Grow sales	• Sustain sales • Protect strengths
Measures and Plans	• Reward early sales • Commission • Relative to peers	• Sales growth and share growth • Commission and quota-bonus plans	• Goal achievement • Profitability • Goal-based plans

pensation plan may adapt over time as the firm's sales and marketing strategies change across the product's life cycle.

- During the product launch phase, an incentive plan that pays a commission on sales from the first dollar helps to motivate the sales force to work hard to generate trial among customers without requiring accurate forecasting by the company.

- During the product's growth phase, an incentive compensation plan that rewards growth helps reinforce key company objectives. Tying incentive payout at least in part to the accomplishment of individual sales goals is also effective, since the firm's ability to forecast sales accurately increases significantly as the firm gains experience in the market.

- During a product's maturity phase, effective sales incentive plan measures are often goal-based, rewarding sales retention and profitability.

The Cost of Not Adapting the Incentive Plan Performance Measures Between the Growth and Maturity Stages of a Product's Life Cycle

Recall the diagnostics imaging company from the introduction to this chapter. The company paid its salespeople a commission on sales growth over the prior year, despite the fact that the firm's market share was declining in a stagnant market. The sales force could not grow sales despite its hard work. Salespeople could not make any money, and therefore they started to leave the company. Eventually, the company adjusted the pay plan to pay on sales retention rather than growth.

Keep It Simple: Have No More than Three or Four Total Measures

New measures and features tend to be forced into plans as new objectives and initiatives emerge. For example, new products get launched, business development needs more focus, and product managers ask for unique incentive levers to get the sales force to pay attention to their products. In addition, sometimes companies use multiple measures to increase the objectivity and fairness of a plan. For example, many firms have weighted plans that determine incentive payout by calculating a weighted average of performance across several metrics, including sales of different products, gross margin, market share, customer satisfaction, activity, and salesperson-specific objectives or key performance measures. More information about such plans is included in Chapter 7.

Having too many measures in an incentive plan can be confusing for a sales force, since multiple measures can send mixed signals about company strategy and direction. Salespeople may question which metric is most important or may worry too much about the company's expectations, rather than taking care of customers. Incentives based upon too many measures lose impact. For example, if a sales force that earns 30 percent of its cash compensation as variable pay has a plan with 10 equally weighted measures, each measure contributes just 3 percent to the total pay. Having too many measures can also provide levers that allow salespeople to game some measures at the expense of other measures. For example, if several products have their own payout formulas, salespeople can abandon underperforming products for more lucrative ones, hurting the performance of underperforming products even further. Or they may spend their time on mature products, where goal attainment is easy, and abandon a potential blockbuster product where goal attainment is a stretch. The computation of payouts for complex plans with many different measures can be error-prone and have large administrative costs.

Figure 6-8 shows how one company simplified its incentive plan to improve sales force focus. The old plan (Current Plan) was three pages long and included dozens of different commission rates and multiple bonuses for achievement of various objectives and gates. Management suspected that this plan was not driving the desired behaviors because most of the sales force did not understand it. The new plan (New Plan) fits on a small business card and includes just four possible commission rates, plus a bonus for competitive instrument displacements. The new plan provides salespeople with a clear understanding of what is important to management. Thus, the new plan is a much more effective driver of sales force activities and behaviors.

Effective incentive plans use at most *three* or *four* performance measures. Chapter 7 describes several methods of successfully integrating multiple measures into a single incentive plan. The best incentive plans keep the number of independent measures to a minimum; having too many measures confuses everyone.

Figure 6-8. Example of an incentive plan that was simplified to improve sales force focus.

Current Plan

1. Monthly guarantee: $1,000.00 (no payback required)

2. Instruments payout schedule

    - Model X-1   at 5%
    - Model X-11   at 3.5%
    - Model X-12   at 5.5%
    - Model X-65   at 7.5%
    - Model Z(All)   at 2.5%
    - Model S(All)   at 2.9%
    - Model G(All)   at 1.75%

3. 100% achievement payout

    - Total instruments $1,600
    - 100% XPS target—$1,000

    Gate 1: If at the end of the year,

(This is page 1 of 3 pages)

New Plan

	To Objective	Above Objective
Instruments	5%	11%
Disposables	1%	6%

Competitive displacement: $50 per instrument

Simplifying Sales Incentive Plans at IBM

In 1995, an IBM task force took on the massive project of revamping the company's worldwide sales incentive compensation plan to better align with a new global strategy. One of the major challenges that the task force faced was that the current sales compensation plans in many countries and divisions suffered from what IBM executives called "incentive plan obesity." Sales leaders in many IBM divisions managed the sales force by throwing money at every problem. Corporate provided its own set of incentive measures, such as revenue or market share, and then divisional sales leaders would add their own sales contests onto those measures to focus salespeople on specific regional objectives. IBM salespeople were torn between as many as 20 different performance measurements, and focus was taken away from the customer. In some instances, bonuses were awarded for responsibilities that should have been covered by base salary. The new global plan that resulted from the task force's efforts utilized a relevant collection of worldwide performance metrics. To reduce plan complexity, the total number of measures in any single plan was limited to 10.

How to Determine the Most Appropriate Sales Incentive Measures: Specifics

The wide variety of evaluative criteria or measures that can be used to assess sales force performance and determine incentive payment is illustrated in the two incentive compensation plans summarized in Figure 6-9.

The measures used to determine the incentive payout in these two plans differ in several important ways. First, the plans use different *metrics*. Plan A uses territory sales to determine incentive payout, while Plan B uses territory gross margin. A territory sales metric says to the sales force, "Sell!" while a gross margin metric says, "Sell profitable product lines at the highest possible price." Incentive plans can incorporate many different performance metrics. Most firms use sales as their most important metric. Other common metrics include company results metrics like gross margin and market share, customer-oriented metrics like customer satisfaction and repeat rate, sales force activity metrics such as number of calls and proposals, and salesperson capability metrics such as skills and knowledge.

Plans A and B also differ in their *data view*. Plan A determines payout based on sales, beginning with the first dollar sold; it is the absolute level of sales that is important. With Plan B, payout is determined by comparing territory performance to a territory objective that was established ahead of time; it is the comparison with the expectation that is important. Plan B can motivate a sales force to achieve challenging goals, provided that the firm sets goals that are achievable. Plan A may be more appropriate in environments where accurate goal setting is not possible. In addition to absolute performance and percent of goal attainment, data

Figure 6-9. Examples of two incentive plans that use different performance measures.

Plan A	
Product Group	Commission Rate
Core	2.5% of territory sales
Premium	5.0% of territory sales
Commissions paid monthly	
Year-end bonus opportunity of 0–0.5% of sales based on company performance	

Plan B		
	% of Salary Paid as Quarterly Bonus	
Performance to Gross Margin Objective	New Accounts	Existing Accounts
90%	12%	5%
95%	14%	7%
100%	16%	9%
105%	19%	12%
110%	22%	15%
115%	25%	18%

	Plan A	Plan B
Metrics	Territory sales	Gross margin
Data view	Level of sales	% objective
Focus	Premium and core products	New and existing accounts
Timing	Monthly, with year-end bonus	Quarterly

views can include comparison with last year's performance (growth plans) or a ranking relative to peers (ranking plans).

Plans A and B also differ in their *focus,* the emphasis of the metric or level of aggregation. Plan A focuses sales force attention on products. Premium products pay higher commission rates than core products, and thus the message to the sales force is, "Focus on premium products." Plan B focuses attention on market segments. New accounts generate higher bonuses than existing accounts, and thus the message to the sales force is, "Spend time with new accounts." Incentive plans sometimes focus attention on different selling channels or on different levels within the organization. For example, Plans A and B both pay for territory performance, but Plan A also pays a bonus based on total company performance.

Finally, Plans A and B differ in their *timing.* Plan A pays commissions monthly with an annual bonus opportunity. Plan B is a quarterly plan. Some plans pay incentives as often as weekly or even daily. Others pay a bonus once at the end of the year.

As summarized in Figure 6-10, the four dimensions just described—metrics, data views, focus, and timing—are integrated to define the performance criteria or measures that determine incentive plan payout. Plan design considerations for each of these four dimensions are discussed in the following sections.

Figure 6-10. Four dimensions of performance measures.

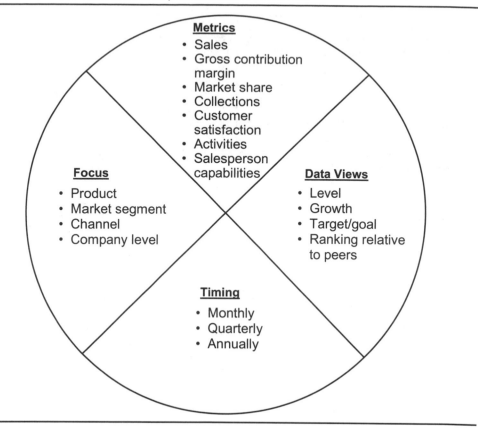

Metrics

Metrics refer to the performance attributes that are measured. Most companies establish several performance metrics from the various components of the sales management system framework (see Figure 6-2). Typically only a few of these metrics are used to determine sales force incentive pay. Company results metrics such as sales are by far the most common measures used in sales force incentive plans; however, in some situations, metrics that reflect other components of the system appear in incentive plans as well. Metrics for each of the four key components of the sales management system are described in more detail here.

Company Results Metrics. Company results can be measured in a number of different ways. Examples of company results metrics used in incentive plans include territory sales, gross margin, and market share. Linking incentives to company results can be a very powerful way to motivate a sales force to achieve short-term corporate financial goals. In addition, incentive plans that are linked to company results are attractive to many firms because they help control sales force costs; the plan does not pay out unless the desired results are achieved. Almost all sales incentive programs tie the majority of sales force incentive compensation to company results metrics. In the Sales Incentive Executive Education Survey (introduced in Chapter 4), for over 95 percent of the sales forces, at least a portion of incentive pay was based on company results metrics; for 55 percent of the sales forces, 100 percent of incentive pay was based on company results metrics.

Company results metrics can apply to all roles within the sales force. A salesperson is rewarded for results at the territory or account level, a district manager for results at the district level, and so on up the sales organization chart. Having consistency of metrics across the various levels can be a very powerful way to focus sales force attention on the metrics that are most important for company success.

Sales force incentives based on company results metrics are most effective in selling environments with most or all of the following characteristics:

- It is possible to measure results accurately at the territory or account level.
- Sales are determined primarily by the skill, motivation, and effort of the individual salesperson.
- Salespeople have a very good understanding of the activities that drive sales success; they are highly qualified and well trained, and they have intimate knowledge of what approach works best with each of their accounts.
- Management has a strong empowerment focus; it feels that salespeople are closest to the customer and should therefore be empowered to determine the appropriate activity and held accountable for company results.
- Management feels that salespeople should assume the risk for the attainment of results and for their own success.
- There is a "pay-for-performance" culture.
- Salespeople value extrinsically based motivators like money and recognition more than they do intrinsically based motivators like job satisfaction and personal growth.

The particular company results metric chosen for an incentive plan usually reflects a firm's strategy. The rationale for choosing three common company results metrics—sales, contribution, and market share—is described here.

Sales Revenue Metrics. Sales is the most commonly used incentive plan metric. Top management promises sales to the shareholders, often specifying the level of sales that can be expected in the next quarter and/or the next year. Delivering on this "sales promise" becomes the responsibility of the sales force. As a result, it is logical that sales metrics should be used to judge sales force performance. Sales is usually also the least complicated of all the company results metrics to measure at the territory or account level, and it is easy for the sales force to understand. In addition, since a salesperson's job is to create sales, it is typically the company results metric that salespeople have the most influence over. In the Sales Incentive Executive Education Survey, for 88 percent of the sales forces, some part of incentive pay was based on sales metrics (revenue or revenue growth).

Contribution Margin and Profit Metrics. Contribution margin can be an effective incentive plan metric for firms focusing on profitability. Paying for contribution margin encourages salespeople to focus on profitable customers and product lines. It also discourages price cutting in sales forces that have pricing authority. In addition, salespeople with such an incentive plan are more likely to exercise expense control. In the Sales Incentive Executive Education Survey, 23 percent of the sales forces had some part of their incentive pay based on profit metrics (profit or profit growth).

Office Equipment Maker Revamps Compensation Plan to Stress Profitability

Recall the office equipment maker from the introduction to this chapter. The sales force was booking almost no sales at list price, despite the fact that the firm's products were widely recognized to be superior to those of its competitors. Since salespeople were paid on sales volume (and not contribution margin), there was little incentive for them to think in terms of profitability. In an effort to discourage discounting, the company restructured its commission plan. A variable commission schedule was developed: a sliding scale that paid $1/2$ of a percent of sales for orders booked at 40 percent off list price, 2.5 percent for those at 20 percent off list, and 6 percent for business sold at list price. This change had a dramatic impact on profitability. In the first year, the average discount dropped from 25 percent to 18 percent. Approximately 40 percent of orders were booked at list price versus virtually none before. Largely because of this, profits increased by $10 million. Successful salespeople earned 12 percent more commission, yet compensation costs as a percent of gross margin declined.

Figure 6-11 shows an incentive plan that bases payout on increase in gross margin over last year. To encourage the sales force to spend time on certain strategic products, gross margin on these products gets double weight in the net gain formula. Since the quarterly payouts are based on year-to-date growth, part of the quarterly commissions are held back and paid out at the end of the year as a fifth-quarter bonus to help ensure that salespeople who start the year strong but finish weak do not owe the firm money at the end of the year.

One of the challenges of paying on territory gross margin is getting the measurement right and gaining sales force understanding and acceptance of the measure.

Understandability of Measures Is Important

In an effort to drive profitability, a lease financing firm changed its revenue-based sales incentive plan to a profit-based plan. The new plan did get salespeople to focus more on the profitability of transactions. However, the territory-level profit calculations were complex and difficult for the sales

Figure 6-11. Example of an incentive plan based on gross margin increase.

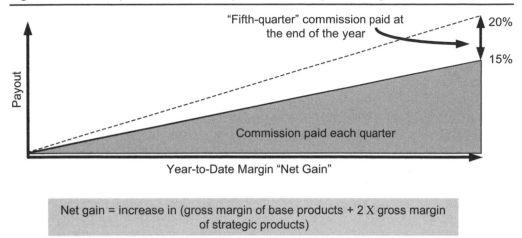

Net gain = increase in (gross margin of base products + 2 X gross margin of strategic products)

force to understand. After a one-year trial period, the company decided to switch back to the revenue-based plan. Management felt that the value of simplicity outweighed the value of having a more strategic measure.

Market Share Metrics. Market share can be a very powerful incentive plan metric for firms in competitive markets. Paying for market share encourages salespeople to focus on winning against the competition. Unfortunately, market share data are not readily available at the territory or account level in many industries. In the Sales Incentive Executive Education Survey, 14 percent of the sales forces had some part of their incentive pay based on market share metrics (market share or market share growth).

Figure 6-12 shows a market share–based incentive plan used at a pharmaceutical company. Payout is determined by a combination of a territory's market share and its market share change from the prior quarter. The payout matrix acknowl-

Figure 6-12. Example of a quarterly incentive plan based on market share and market share change.

Market Share	-2%	-1%	0%	1%	2%	3%	4%	5%
29%	$2,500	$3,500	$4,500	$5,325	$5,575	$5,825	$6,575	$7,500
26%	$1,500	$2,500	$3,500	$4,350	$4,600	$4,850	$5,575	$6,500
23%	$500	$1,500	$2,500	$3,350	$3,600	$3,850	$4,575	$5,500
20%		$750	$1,750	$2,575	$2,825	$3,075	$3,800	$4,750
17%		$250	$1,250	$2,075	$2,325	$2,575	$3,300	$4,250
14%			$750	$1,575	$1,825	$2,075	$2,825	$3,750

Market Share Change from Last Quarter

edges the assumption that for this product, more sales effort is required to grow (or not lose) market share in a high-share territory than in a low-share territory. For example, a salesperson who maintains a 29 percent market share earns more commission than someone who grows market share from 23 percent to 26 percent.

Customer Results Metrics. Common customer results metrics include customer satisfaction, customer retention and repeat rates, and customer returns or complaints. The use of customer results metrics in a sales incentive plan can help reinforce a culture with a strong customer focus. "What gets measured gets done," said William Hewlett, co-founder of Hewlett-Packard Company. If the company wants to "put the customer first" and get competitive advantage from its customer relationships, then it is logical to make the sales compensation plan consistent with this objective by rewarding salespeople for customer results. In addition, customer results measures may be a better reflection of a salesperson's success than company results measures. Company results such as sales, profits, and market share are affected by many factors that are not under the salesperson's direct control, including the economy, market conditions, and competition. Well-designed customer results measures can isolate the true salesperson impact on the customer.

Customer results metrics are particularly relevant in selling environments with some or all of the following characteristics:

- It is necessary to spend a lot of time learning a prospective customer's needs, making it much easier to get new business from existing customers than to sell to new customers.

- Company success depends upon maintaining good relationships with important accounts.

- Management wants to emphasize the development of long-term customer relationships.

- The firm sells in a commodity market, where a strong customer relationship may be the only source of differential competitive advantage.

IT Companies Tie Sales Incentives to Customer Satisfaction

Information technology (IT) companies generally have long selling cycles. To be effective, salespeople must spend a lot of time learning a prospective customer's existing technology, business, and industry. As a result, it is much easier to get new business from existing customers than to court new customers. To encourage the development of long-term customer relationships, some IT companies pay sales incentives based on customer satisfaction. Siebel Systems ties 40 percent of sales force incentive compensation to the results of customer satisfaction surveys.

eBay Improved Customer Satisfaction Through Its Incentive Plan

eBay bases up to 25 percent of a salesperson's compensation on customer service scores. Customer satisfaction scores for the entire sales force are posted, and sales managers are encouraged to have weekly coaching sessions on how to improve the scores. As a result, customer satisfaction scores at eBay improved by 30 percent in one year.

Objective measures of customer results, such as repeat rate or customer returns, can be used effectively at the territory level. More subjective measures like customer satisfaction, however, may lack veracity at the territory level for several reasons. When a salesperson knows that he will be evaluated or possibly paid in part on customer satisfaction survey results, the salesperson has significant incentive to influence the results. For example, car salespeople have been known to "buy a score"—to promise customers free merchandise or a free tank of gas in exchange for positive ratings on a customer satisfaction survey. One customer successfully negotiated $150 off the price of a car by agreeing to fill out a customer satisfaction survey with all "excellent" ratings. Customer satisfaction surveys can also suffer from small sample size problems. Many salespeople do not have enough responding customers for the results of such surveys to be statistically valid, particularly when the data are collected over a short period of time. Selection bias can also be a problem with customer satisfaction surveys. Frequently, the customers who are most likely to fill out such surveys are those who have had a bad experience with the salesperson. Thus the survey may not be a true reflection of the overall customer base.

During the 1990s, many companies tried using territory customer satisfaction metrics as a basis for determining short-term incentive pay for salespeople. The popularity of this practice has declined in recent years. In the Sales Incentive Executive Education Survey (which includes data from 2000 to 2004), under 8 percent of sales forces reported the use of customer satisfaction as an incentive pay determinant.

While survey-based customer satisfaction measures frequently fail at the individual salesperson level, such measures can be used quite successfully to identify general trends and issues with customer relationships across an entire region or for the whole company. Sample size and salesperson "rating chasing" tend to be significantly less problematic when the data are summarized at a more aggregate level. In addition, customer satisfaction always needs to be assessed relative to company sales and profitability. Obviously, customers are very satisfied if they can have the product for free.

Customer Satisfaction Measurement Flawed at Southern California Edison

In 1997, the California Public Utilities Commission (PUC) implemented a new performance measurement system designed to encourage Southern

California Edison to meet several operational goals. Each year, the company could receive monetary bonuses for scoring well on customer satisfaction surveys, reducing the frequency and duration of blackouts, and holding employee injuries below a certain threshold. Edison could also be penalized for poor performance in each category. Unfortunately, the system created an incentive for Edison management to falsify data. The measurement of worker injuries was so flawed that in 2004 the company was unable to document the safety improvements that it had been claiming for seven years. Even more embarrassing for the company was the admission by management that some staff members had manipulated records so that a survey firm could not track down people who might give the utility low marks for customer satisfaction. Instead, they steered the firm toward friends whom they knew would provide top ratings. In November 2004, the company proposed to return $35 million in worker safety bonuses and $14.2 million in customer satisfaction bonuses, while consumer groups pressured the PUC to investigate further.

Activity Metrics. Activity metrics are tracked at many companies in order to drive specific sales force behaviors. Examples of activity metrics include calls per day, customer reach and frequency, and number of demonstrations, proposals, or service calls. In the Sales Incentive Executive Education Survey, only 15 percent of sales forces reported using activity metrics as a measure for determining incentive pay. However, many companies use activity measures to enhance their performance management system.

The rationale behind using activity metrics is that sales force activity drives customer and company results. A high quantity and quality of sales force activity generates incrementally better results. A poor quantity and quality of activity generates incrementally inferior results. The firm benefits when the sales force performs the activities that make up a successful selling process effectively. So why not pay on activity? There are several reasons that most firms choose not to base the majority of their incentive pay on activity:

- The firm's investors reward the company for results, not activity.
- It is very difficult to measure activity accurately:
  - Salespeople report when it is convenient.
  - Salespeople may misstate what they actually do.
- While tracking activity metrics often motivates an increase in the quantity of the desired activity, it may also trigger a decrease in the quality of that activity.

Still, there are situations in which activity measurement is more appropriate than results measurement. These situations are summarized in Figure 6-13. Activity measurement is used primarily as part of performance management (rather than as a determinant of incentive pay). Thus, the salary component of the incentive plan assumes that the sales force engages in the appropriate activity. Activity, performance management, and salary increases are linked at many companies to drive sales success.

Executive Search Firm Uses Activity Measures for New Salespeople

Recall the story from Chapter 1 about a small executive-search firm. Experienced salespeople are paid a straight commission, while new salespeople who are just learning the business earn a salary plus about 20 percent of their compensation based on the achievement of activity goals. The goals are based on activities that lead to sales success, such as daily calls to potential job candidates, company visits, and "balls in the air," or leads that could be converted to sales. A new salesperson who meets all of his or her activity goals earns $400 a month in bonuses on top of her salary. Management has observed that the program gives sales training more focus and new salespeople more confidence. It encourages new salespeople to establish a network that will generate the referrals they will need if they are to succeed down the road. Management understands what steps it takes to be successful in the industry, and thus it rewards new salespeople for following those steps.

Activity Goals Are Common for Retail Merchandisers

It is very difficult to measure the sales contribution of the retail merchandisers who are part of the sales force for many consumer packaged goods firms. These individuals spend their time in retail stores restocking merchandise, rearranging shelves, and setting up displays. Attractive displays sell merchandise—but how much? Nonmerchandising activities, such as consumer advertising, store promotions, and the efforts of salespeople at the retailer's headquarters, clearly play an important part in creating sales as well. As a result, incentives for merchandisers are often based on activity metrics, such as the number of stores visited or the number of displays set up.

Activity-Based Incentives Encourage Systems Selling at Slater

Slater Industrial Supply is a distributor of abrasives used in manufacturing. Slater management realized that in order to fuel sales growth, it was necessary to demonstrate to customers how they could save money through the use of new products and systems improvements. This required a systems selling approach, which was incompatible with the current sales force incentive plan that paid commission on sales volume alone. To encourage the new selling approach, Slater added a new activity-based bonus to its

Figure 6-13. Conditions favoring activity versus results metrics.

Conditions Favoring Activity Metrics	Conditions Favoring Results Metrics
• Company and customer results are not measurable at the territory level. For example, sales disappear in a reseller channel and never get properly attributed to individual salespeople.	• Company and customer results can be measured accurately at the territory level.
• The sales force has low causality. Other marketing influences in addition to the sales force have a significant impact on sales.	• The sales force has high causality. Sales are primarily driven by the skill, motivation, and efforts of the individual salesperson.
• Salespeople work in teams, making it difficult to value each individual's specific contribution; the entire team may be rewarded for results, but each individual's reward is based on her specific activities.	• Salespeople create sales on their own.
• The sales force is expected to perform nonselling activities, such as providing customer service.	• The sales force is expected to sell. Nonselling activities are performed by other channels.
• The firm has the best understanding of the most effective sales force activities.	• The salesperson has the best understanding of the most effective sales force activities.
• The sales force is inexperienced; activity goals double as a training device and help ensure that salespeople engage in the right activities.	• The sales force is experienced; salespeople know which selling activities are most effective.
• The company wants to control sales force activity. The company (and not the sales force) assumes the risk for sales success.	• The company wants to empower the sales force to create results. Salespeople assume the risk for their own success.
• The company wants to encourage a specific sales force behavior for a short period of time in order to drive long-term results (for example, service calls on key customers timed to thwart a competitive launch).	• The company trusts that salespeople will do what it takes to drive results.
• The company wants to build a loyal sales organization that is motivated by intrinsically based factors like job satisfaction, rather than by money.	• Achieving sales targets is the highest priority.

traditional commission plan. Salespeople could receive extra cash for performing activities that demonstrated cost-saving opportunities to customers. For example, a salesperson could earn a bonus for initiating and reporting on a new product test with a customer or for improving a process at the customer's shop. Customers liked the idea that salespeople were paid for finding cost-saving opportunities, not just for selling more.

Salespeople Metrics. Metrics in the "salespeople" category focus on the knowledge, skills, and attitudes of individuals within the sales force. Companies track these metrics because improvement of salespeople ultimately leads to better results. Salespeople metrics can include tests that measure the knowledge, competency, skills, and attitudes of the sales force, as well as measures, such as employee turnover, that provide insight about employee satisfaction. Since salespeople metrics encourage the personal and professional growth of the sales force, they can be used for people at all levels within the selling organization. First-level sales managers often have goals encouraging them not only to develop themselves professionally, but also to develop the salespeople who report to them. Sales leadership needs to maintain high standards across the entire sales force: "You need to have the right people on the bus."

Since metrics in the "salespeople" category have a long-term effect on the firm, the immediate impact of these metrics on company results can be very difficult to measure. Most firms track salesperson metrics through performance management processes, but do not tie these metrics to short-term monetary incentives. Focus on salespeople metrics is more common in sales forces where:

- The culture encourages long-term success rather than short-term results.

- The culture stresses intrinsic rewards such as job satisfaction and professional growth over financial rewards.

- The firm has a philosophy of hiring salespeople with minimal experience and developing them, rather than hiring only experienced salespeople.

Data Views

Metrics can be viewed from different perspectives or data views, either as absolute values or as comparisons. Sales, gross margin contribution, number of calls, and customer satisfaction scales are all examples of absolute-level metrics. Here, the precise level of the metric is important. Level metrics can be evaluated with phrases such as "low, average, or high" or "weak, good, or exceptional." Alternatively, metrics can be stated as comparisons with some standard or level of expectation. Specifying the comparison computation within the measure enhances comparability. For example, metrics can be contrasted with the past (e.g., growth or decline over last year), compared to a goal or target (e.g., percent of goal attainment), or compared to a peer group (e.g., district or region ranking). The circumstances under which different data views are appropriate in an incentive plan are discussed here.

Absolute-Level Metrics. Paying incentives based on the absolute value of a metric (for example, a straight commission on all sales) is a very straightforward incentive approach that is easy for salespeople to understand. A problem with paying incentives on absolute-level metrics is that often these measures are strongly influenced by territory differences. For example, high sales occur in territories with high potential, independent of sales effort. Thus, an incentive plan that pays on total sales favors salespeople with high-potential territories. Similarly, level metrics that pay salespeople on market share favor low-potential territories. Metrics that compare performance in each territory to last year or to a goal are typically fairer across the sales force. Level metrics are often appropriate for new products or when an existing product is entering a new market. In these cases, reliable forecasting is difficult, and there is no historical trend against which to compare.

Comparing to Past Performance. Many incentive plans determine incentive payout by comparing this year's performance with last year's performance. Popular measures used in incentive plans include sales, profit, and market share growth and retention. In the Sales Incentive Executive Education Survey, 42 percent of sales forces reported that growth measures were used as part of the formula for determining incentive pay. Figure 6-14 shows an example of an incentive plan that pays out based on a comparison with last year's sales. The sales force was selling beverage products in a declining market, so payout begins when just 95 percent of last year's sales is achieved.

Growth and retention measures are easy for the sales force to understand and relate to. Data analysis reveals that in most markets, last year's performance is an excellent predictor of likely performance this year. However, incentive plans that pay out solely based on a comparison with last year may ignore differences in the future potential across salespeople. For example, a plan that pays for sales growth penalizes a salesperson who worked especially hard last year to achieve high sales and penetration. To make money this year, he must sell even more than last year, and he may have less territory potential remaining.

Comparing to a Goal. Tying incentive pay to goal attainment can be very powerful for several reasons:

Figure 6-14. Example of an incentive plan for a declining market that is based on comparison with last year's performance.

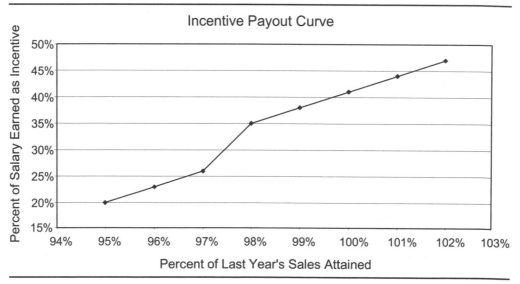

- Effective goals can energize salespeople, driving their behavior and significantly increasing their motivation to succeed.

- Goals help salespeople understand what is important to the company and what is expected of them.

- Goals provide a benchmark against which sales force performance can be measured, controlled, and rewarded.

- If set properly, goals make it possible to recognize personal and territory differences when evaluating and rewarding salespeople. Each person can be given a customized goal that is appropriate for her situation.

Most sales incentive plans are goal-based. In the Sales Incentive Executive Education Survey, 82 percent of sales forces reported the use of goal-based metrics as a basis for determining incentive pay.

Individuals and organizations that set goals generally achieve better results than those that do not. However, setting fair and realistic goals may not always be easy, or even possible. If territory- or account-level data on revenue and market potential are not accurate, salespeople will view their goals as unfair. In these situations, sales managers may spend a great deal of time managing and arbitrating complaints about unfairness in territory-level goals. Figure 6-15 contrasts the conditions that favor a goal-centered compensation approach with those that do not.

Care must be exercised with goal-based incentive plans. An aggressive management team can demoralize a sales force if it asks salespeople to achieve unrealistic sales goals. Companies set sales expectations for stockholders, and these expectations become sales goals for the sales force. The company can actually jeopardize the likelihood of its achieving its Wall Street forecast if the forecast is unrealistically high. The sales force could become disengaged when it discovers that its incentive pay is out of reach.

Figure 6-15. Conditions favoring goals versus no goals.

◄ Conditions Favoring a Goal-Centric Approach	Conditions Favoring No Goals ►
• Sales are predictable.	• Random sales are high; for example, it is difficult to set fair and realistic goals because forecasting is unreliable as a result of new product launches, new market entry, or competitive markets with high volatility.
• Free sales are high; for example, carryover is high.	
• It is critical for the company to hit its sales target.	
• Sales territories are out of balance in terms of market potential and earnings opportunity.	• Sales territories have unlimited potential. "The world is our oyster—go get it all" is the attitude in the sales force.
	• Sales management wants to empower each salesperson to achieve all that he can.

Biotech Start-up Shifts Emphasis on Goals as Market Experience Grows

The sales management team at a new biotech start-up felt that goal-based incentives could provide powerful motivation for the firm's start-up sales force to succeed. Goals would help salespeople understand what was important to the company and what was expected of them, and could provide an important benchmark for measuring, controlling, and rewarding sales force performance. However, with the launch of the firm's first major new product on the horizon, management faced the challenge of setting realistic sales goals in a new and largely unknown market. The team did not have a high degree of confidence that its national sales forecast was accurate. Predicting sales at the local territory level was virtually impossible. Thus, during the first few months after the new product's launch, the sales force incentive pay was based on achievement of individual salesperson objectives that were developed using a management-by-objectives (MBO) approach. Points were awarded to a salesperson for strategically important activities such as completing product training, developing account plans, and making sales calls. A salesperson's incentive payout was determined by the number of points he earned. Several months following the launch, as access to historical data increased and the firm's ability to predict sales improved, the firm changed to a sales incentive plan based 50 percent on MBO attainment and 50 percent on territory sales. Territory sales were tracked against a territory quota, but since management still did not have a high degree of confidence that the quotas were accurate, commissions were based on total territory sales, with an added bonus if the national sales quota was achieved.

In the second full year following launch, the firm's management feels that it has enough experience and data to establish reasonable territory-level quotas that accurately reflect territory differences. The firm plans to move to a true territory quota–based incentive plan. Salespeople will begin to receive incentive payout when 80 percent of quota is attained, and the payout rate will accelerate beyond 100 percent attainment. The 80 percent is reasonable, since there will still be some uncertainty in the sales forecast. The majority of incentive money will be tied to territory sales quota achievement, with a smaller portion linked to individual MBO attainment and national quota achievement.

Figure 6-16 shows an example of a goal-based incentive plan. Each salesperson receives a quarterly territory sales goal for Products A, B, and C, and incentive payout is based on weighted goal attainment across the three products. The weights reflect the strategic value of each product to the company and the potential market for each product. Individual territory product goals are set based on factors such as past territory sales performance, territory growth potential, competitive intensity, and the salesperson's skill and experience.

Figure 6-16. Example of a multiproduct incentive plan that is goal-based.

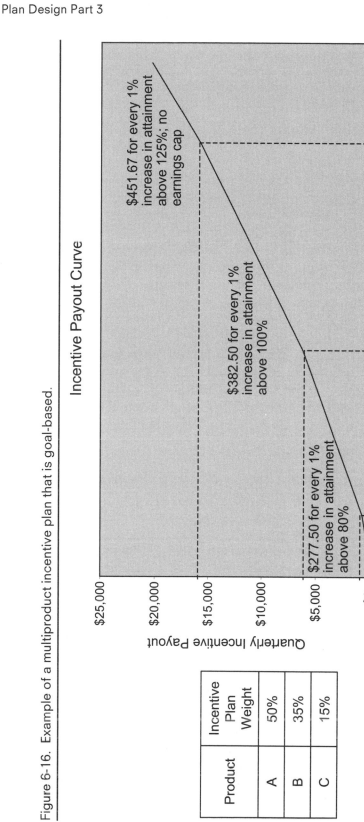

Incentive Payout Curve

$451.67 for every 1% increase in attainment above 125%; no earnings cap

$382.50 for every 1% increase in attainment above 100%

$277.50 for every 1% increase in attainment above 80%

Weighted Goal Attainment

Quarterly Incentive Payout

Product	Incentive Plan Weight
A	50%
B	35%
C	15%

Product attainment = quarterly product sales/quarterly product goal

Weighted goal attainment = Product A attainment X 50% + Product B attainment X 35% + Product C attainment X 15%

Some plans use goals for only a subset of products in the incentive plan. The type of goal can also vary by product. For example, Figure 6-17 shows a plan that includes three products, each with a different goal type.

> ## Point-Based Goals Protect the Sales Force in a Market with Volatile Pricing
>
> Goal-based incentive plans are frequently tied to sales revenue metrics, but they can be tied to other types of metrics as well, such as market share, gross margin, and customer retention. A computer manufacturer used point-based goals in its sales incentive plan, to make sure that salespeople's chance of achieving annual revenue goals was not hurt by the constant lowering of prices in the computer industry. Rather than setting goals based on dollar volume, the company assigned each product a number of points at the beginning of the year, based on the list price of the product at that time. All goals were expressed in terms of points. The company considered the anticipated price reductions when determining the total point goal to assign to the sales force, so that when salespeople hit their point goal, the company would also hit its revenue goal.

All of these approaches require that goals be set appropriately for each salesperson. A detailed presentation of effective goal-setting approaches is provided in Chapter 9.

Figure 6-17. Example of a multiproduct incentive plan using a variety of product goals.

Product	Quarterly Target Incentive	Basis for Determining Payout	Rationale
Inline Product A	$2,000	• Matrix of territory sales goal attainment ranking versus national sales goal attainment.	• Reward individual contribution. • Link total sales force payout to national goal attainment. • Encourage teamwork.
Inline Product B	$500	• National sales goal attainment (if the company makes goal, every salesperson gets $500; if not, every salesperson gets $0).	• Encourage teamwork in a market where accurate territory-level performance measurement is not available.
New Product C	$2,500	• No goals; fixed dollar commission for every unit sold, beginning with the first unit.	• Reward early successes in a market where accurate territory-level goal setting is not possible.

Ranking Relative to Peers. Forced ranking of salespeople relative to one another is an alternative way to determine incentive payout. Figure 6-18 shows an example of an incentive plan based on forced ranking. Salespeople are ranked on three key metrics, and those who fall in the bottom 20 percent of the sales force on a particular metric receive no incentive money for that metric. Payout for those in the top 80 percent is determined by relative position on the ranked list.

Forced ranking plans should be used with caution. Since by definition there will be winners and losers with a forced ranking plan, these plans can generate a lot of internally focused competition. Salespeople may become more concerned with how they compare to their peers than they are with serving customers and beating competitors. In addition, forced ranking plans can tell a sizable fraction of the sales force that they are "losers," since many salespeople will not feel successful unless they are ranked at the top. For these reasons, ranking plans tend to work best in situations where the incentive component is a small portion of total pay (15 percent or less), so that the incentive program is viewed by the sales force as a fun way to earn some extra cash, not as an integral part of take-home pay.

It is important to note that forced ranking should be contemplated only if the sales territories are balanced. Forced rankings will not reflect true performance if territory differences favor some salespeople over others.

Forced Ranking System Breaks Down at a Pharmaceutical Firm

In 2001, sales management at a pharmaceutical firm decided to eliminate its goal-based sales incentive plan and move to a plan based on relative ranking of salespeople. This eliminated the need to set goals in an uncertain environment where forecasting was challenging. The relative ranking plan was simpler and easier to communicate to the sales force, and it eliminated the administrative headache of setting goals and making mid-period goal adjustments. However, by 2004, several serious problems with the relative

Figure 6-18. Example of an incentive plan with forced ranking.

Relative performance in peer group	
Top 10%	3.0 X target pay
Next 20%	2.0 X target pay
Next 50%	1.0 X target pay

Quarterly target pay for the following metrics:	
Goal attainment on total sales	$1,000
Share growth of Product A	$500
New product share	$600

ranking plan had surfaced. Management disliked the fact that not everyone could win with a forced ranking plan. The plan generated a lot of internally focused competition. In addition, the plan was not linked to the national goal, making it possible for the sales force to make a lot of money even when it fell well short of the national goal. Without sales goals, it was difficult for sales managers to convince salespeople that it was necessary for them to reach all their targeted accounts in order to make the national goal. Management also felt that the ranking resulted in forced differentiation between similarly performing salespeople. High-performing salespeople were often uncomfortable disclosing their "winner" status to the rest of the sales force because of the perceived unfairness of the plan. Finally, management felt that the ranking did not adequately account for differences in territory potential. In 2005, management decided to move the sales organization back to a goal-based incentive plan, with a renewed emphasis on realistic and fair goal setting.

Focus

Focus describes the level of aggregation and the emphasis of a measure. For example, companies can evaluate results at the product, market segment, and/or channel level. The focus chosen for the incentive plan helps to communicate to the sales force what is most important. Results can also be evaluated at different levels within the selling organization, such as territory, district, region, and nation.

Market Segment Focus. Incentive plan measures that target market segments can direct sales force attention to strategically important and/or profitable customer types. For example, the incentive plan shown in Figure 6-19 was used by a firm that wanted to encourage the sales force to achieve goal and spend more time developing new accounts.

Product Focus. Product-focused measures can be used to direct the sales force to product lines that are more profitable and/or have greater strategic importance. For example, the incentive plan shown in Figure 6-20 tells the sales force that selling new equipment is more important to the firm than selling refurbished equipment.

Channel Focus. Incentive plan measures can also focus sales force attention on different selling channels. For example, the plan in Figure 6-21 focuses on both market segments and channels. The intent of the plan is to encourage Internet sales, particularly for strategic customers, while discouraging the sales force from spending time with select customers.

Organizational-Level Focus and Team Rewards. Performance measures can also focus on different levels within the selling organization. Some firms base a sales-

Figure 6-19. Example of an incentive plan with market segment–focused performance measures.

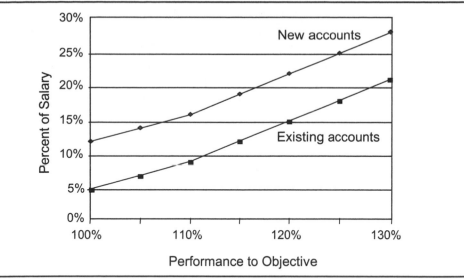

Figure 6-20. Example of an incentive plan with product-focused performance measures.

Institutional Kitchen Equipment Company

Target variable pay = $10,000 (15% of base pay)

Product line	Target at 100% of goal
New equipment	$8,000
Refurbished equipment	$2,000

Figure 6-21. Example of an incentive plan based on measures that are focused on customer type and channel.

Sales Commission Rates

	Direct Sales	Internet Sales
Strategic customers	4%	4%
Key customers	4%	2%
Select customers	0%	0%

Bonus rate on total sales over quarterly objective: 2.4%

person's entire incentive payout on performance within her individual territory, while other firms link components of incentive pay to the performance of a larger area, such as a district, region, or business unit. Figure 6-22 shows a plan that links incentive payout to a combination of territory and business unit performance. With this plan, territory performance has a larger impact on an individual's incentive payout than does business unit performance; the reward for improving territory performance is three times greater than the reward an individual would receive should the entire business unit improve performance by the same percentage.

The proportion of an individual's incentive payout that is linked to group versus individual performance depends upon the company culture and the nature of the expected interactions between group members. Conditions that favor individual rewards versus team rewards are listed in Figure 6-23.

Encouraging Teamwork Among Salespeople Who Work Independently

Salespeople tend to dislike group incentives if the "team" consists of salespeople who work individually with their own customers but who happen to report to the same unit. For example, basing individual incentives on district-level performance may not be very effective in a sales district consisting of salespeople who work independent geographic sales territories. Teamwork and best practice sharing among salespeople in this environment can be encouraged through such means as group training or district meetings, rather than through financial incentives.

Figure 6-22. An incentive plan that links payout to both territory and business unit performance.

		Territory Performance (% Objective)					
		80%	90%	100%	110%	120%	130%
Business Unit Performance	80%	0.2	0.5	0.8	1.1	1.4	1.7
	90%	0.3	0.6	0.9	1.2	1.5	1.8
	100%	0.4	0.7	1.0	1.3	1.6	1.9
	110%	0.5	0.8	1.1	1.4	1.7	2.0
	120%	0.6	0.9	1.2	1.5	1.8	2.1
	130%	0.7	1.0	1.3	1.6	1.9	2.2

Matrix contains multiples of target payout.

Figure 6-23. Conditions favoring individual rewards versus team rewards.

Favors Individual Rewards	Favors Team Rewards
• There is a strong culture of individual achievement.	• There is a strong culture of teamwork.
• Salespeople work individually with their own customers. For example, a sales team consists of salespeople working independent geographic sales territories who report to a common district sales manager.	• Salespeople operate as a true team; they are in a position to influence the same customers, and each individual's sales are affected by the efforts of other team members. For example, a sales team consists of account managers and product and technical specialists who work together to meet each customer's needs.
• Individual contribution to group performance can be measured accurately.	• Individual contribution to group performance cannot be measured accurately.

Measurement Accuracy Influences the Organizational-Level Focus of a Pharmaceutical Incentive Plan

A pharmaceutical sales force sells a drug that is administered via IV infusion. Salespeople call on physicians who prescribe the drug for their patients, but sales are tracked to the patient's infusion site, which is often at a different location from the prescribing physician's office. In metropolitan areas covered by several salespeople, sales sometimes "travel" from one salesperson's territory to another—the physician who writes the prescription is in a different territory from the infusion center to which the sale is tracked. This leads to imperfect measurement of sales at the territory level. To help compensate for these traveling sales, the sales incentive plan has a 20 percent component based on district performance. That way, if a salesperson generates a sale that gets tracked to another part of the district, the salesperson still gets credit for that sale through the district component. Many of the firm's district managers feel that tying incentives for salespeople in part to district performance has additional teamwork benefits as well.

The proportion of incentive payout tied to group versus individual performance often varies across sales roles. For example, Figure 6-24 shows how performance at different levels of the organization contributes to the overall incentive payout for the individuals in three different sales roles.

True team-selling environments often must rely heavily on group incentives. Figure 6-25 shows an example of an incentive plan used by a firm with a team-selling structure. A customer representative, a technical specialist, and a service representative work together to make a sale and share the commission earned on that sale according to a prespecified allocation formula.

Figure 6-24. Measures of performance for determining incentives for different sales roles.

| Title | ← Measure of Performance → | | | |
	Territory	District	Region	Company
Sales representative	75%	25%		
Key account manager	75%			25%
District manager		75%	25%	

Figure 6-25. Example of the distribution of incentives in a team-selling environment.

Account commission earned = 12.5% of gross margin, to be shared as follows among team members:

60%—Customer representative

20%—Technical specialist

20%—Service representative

The firm in Figure 6-26 uses a different approach to crediting team members for sales. Every team member involved in a sale gets credit for the entire sale; as a result, some sales are double- and triple-credited. Sales teams consist of a field account manager, a field systems engineer, and an inside sales representative. The teams sell computer hardware and software to large and medium-sized businesses. The measures used to determine variable pay and the salary–incentive mix vary across the three sales roles.

Other approaches that companies use to allocate team incentives across multiple team members include the following:

- Use results measures to determine total team reward, but allocate incentives among team members based on activity measures (for example, total number of hours worked on the account).

- Allocate incentives among team members according to manager discretion.

- Have team members rate one another. This generally works best when the team has a short life, and members will not need to continue working together in the same way in the future.

Linking incentive compensation to team-level performance has helped many sales forces successfully encourage teamwork, get salespeople to take on nonselling responsibilities (for example, servicing), and achieve long-term goals. However, team rewards do have several disadvantages:

Figure 6-26. Compensating sales teams at a computer hardware and software firm.

Sales Role	Sales Role Description	Compensation Plan Measures and Mix
Field account manager	Build and nurture relationships with accounts in assigned territory. Develop new accounts and protect and grow current accounts.	• Commission on revenues that accelerates with quota achievement. • 75% of total pay is variable.
Field systems engineer	Act as technical lead for accounts in assigned territory. Provide specific solution, technology, and product consulting and other technical sales support.	• Commission on revenues that accelerates with quota achievement but is capped. • Bonus for customer satisfaction and MBO achievement. • 25% of total pay is variable.
Inside sales representative	Provide telephone sales support for accounts in assigned territory. Do cold calling and account profiling of prospective accounts, close deals with smaller accounts, and provide postsales support for larger accounts.	• Commission on revenues that accelerates with quota achievement. • Bonus for customer satisfaction and MBO achievement. • 50% of total pay is variable.

- Team-based incentive plans are usually harder to understand and administer than are plans based on individual performance alone.

- Team-based plans can attract "security-minded" salespeople rather than the go-getters who are likely to become superstars.

- Team-based plans can create a "free-rider" problem, where a few nonperforming members of a team benefit from the actions of the productive members. Star performers may subsidize poor performers. To avoid this problem, the firm's sales managers need to know who the stars are and need to make sure that the stars are recognized and rewarded.

Timing

The timing of incentive payments is another important incentive plan design decision. Timely measurement of results and prompt payment of rewards for performance are critical for incentive plan success. The motivational power of incentives diminishes significantly when there is a long lag in measuring the results and/or when salespeople are not rewarded soon after they complete the work that creates the results.

How Often Should Incentives Be Paid? Incentives can be paid to a sales force annually, semiannually, every trimester, quarterly, monthly, weekly, or even daily.

The most common frequencies of incentive payout are monthly and quarterly. Several factors influence payment frequency:

- *The amount of the incentive.* The larger the incentive amount, the higher the frequency of payout.

- *The type of incentive.* Most commissions are paid monthly or more frequently, while bonuses are more likely to be paid quarterly, semiannually, or annually.

- *The length of the firm's sales process.* The longer the sales process, the less frequent the payout.

Figure 6-27 shows that companies with a larger proportion of variable pay tend to pay incentives more frequently.

Frequent incentive payment has several advantages. Salespeople usually prefer more frequent payouts; they like to feel continually rewarded for their efforts. Also, frequent payouts make it easier to make adjustments to goals as markets and company priorities change.

Figure 6-27. Frequency of incentive payout in the Sales Incentive Executive Education Survey.

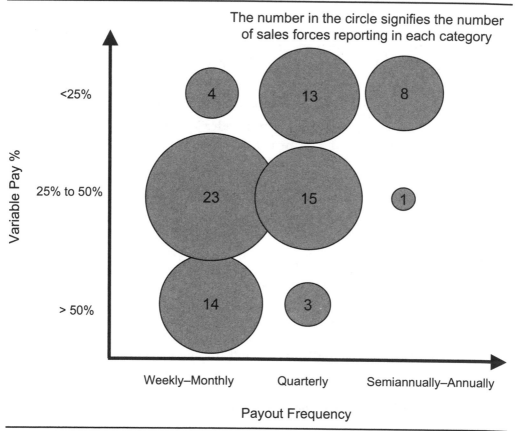

There are also arguments for paying incentives less frequently:

- Less frequent payments mean that each payment will be larger and more impressive to the salesperson.

- With goal-based plans, less frequent payment allows more time for goals to drive behavior, and less time is consumed by the difficult and resource-intensive task of goal setting.

- Longer time lags between payments can encourage the sales force to address the longer-term needs of customers, rather than focusing on maximizing short-term performance.

- It is easier to change from a plan that is less frequent to one that is more frequent—the sales force is likely to resist a change in the other direction.

- Incentive compensation plan administration time is greatly reduced with fewer payments. There will also be fewer computational errors to upset the sales force.

As a general rule, an incentive plan should pay incentives as frequently as is possible without compromising customer focus, generating excessive administrative overhead, or making the award size trivial.

Sales Force Resists Move to Quarterly Incentive Payout at a Health-Care Firm

A health-care firm had historically set monthly sales goals and paid the sales force based on goal attainment every month. Quarterly goals and payments were the norm in the industry, and the firm wanted to move the sales force to a quarterly bonus plan. "If we could get away from a monthly plan, salespeople would think about the bigger picture and long-term strategy," reasoned one of the firm's product managers. In addition, management felt that quarterly payouts would be easier and less costly to administer, would have less variability, and, since the amount of each payment would be larger, would be more appreciated by the sales force. However, the field strongly resisted the move to quarterly payments. "If we move to quarterly payouts, people will leave," threatened a sales district manager. "I have been with the company for a long-time, and I am a monthly person," said one of the firm's regional directors. As a first step in the transition to the quarterly plan, the firm is considering setting quarterly goals, but continuing to pay out monthly based on progress toward the quarterly goal.

Should Incentives Be Paid When the Order Is Taken or When the Company Collects the Funds From the Customer? The salesperson's main job is to get the order or book the sale. Incentives are most motivating when they are granted soon after the selling success. This argues that incentives should be attached to the order. However, often there are time lags between the time the order is placed, when it is shipped, and when money is collected. This creates a dilemma for compensation planners: Should payment occur when orders are taken or when monies are collected? An intermediate strategy is also possible: Pay some fraction of the total incentive at the time of the order and pay the rest at the time of collection. Figure 6-28 describes some of the conditions that favor each approach.

Timing of Incentive Payout Affects Sales Force Motivation

Salespeople at an equipment manufacturer were paid commissions when an order was shipped, rather than when it was booked. Because the firm had a long product delivery cycle, salespeople often wouldn't receive their commission checks until 8 to 15 months after making a sale. This took away from the immediate thrill of success and thus had an adverse effect on sales force motivation. In order to drive sales growth, the company changed its pay plan so that salespeople received 35 percent of their commission up front when the order was booked, with the remaining 65 percent received upon shipping. After the change, revenue grew by 35 percent.

Figure 6-28. Conditions favoring payment of incentives at time of order versus time of collection.

← Conditions Favoring a Larger Incentive Payment at Time of Order	Conditions Favoring a Larger Incentive Payment at Time of Collection →
• Collection is almost certain.	• There is a high risk of cancellation or nonpayment.
• Long selling cycles exist.	• The salesperson participates in postorder activity such as managing the installation.
• The salesperson can become a nuisance for the customer.	• The company desires to accelerate collection, and the salesperson can help achieve this goal.
	• High inflation rates exist in some countries, and it is important to collect money as quickly as possible.

CHAPTER 7

Plan Design Part 4
Determining the Right Performance–Payout Relationship

How This Chapter Is Organized

Introduction	226
Is the Most Appropriate Performance–Payout Relationship Used for Determining the Incentive Plan Payout?	227
Representing Performance–Payout Relationships	228
Decision 1: Bonus Plan or Commission Plan?	231
A Comparison of Plan Structures	231
Which Plan Structure Is Appropriate for the Selling Environment and Management Culture?	235
Decision 2: Progressive or Regressive Plan?	237
Payout Curve Possibilities	238
Payout Curves and the Achievement of Sales Force Objectives	239
Decision 3: Caps or No Caps?	243
Decision 4: Pay from the First Dollar or from Goal or a Fraction of Goal?	245
Paying from the First Dollar	247
Paying from Goal or a Fraction of Goal	248
A Company Perspective	248
A Sales Force Perspective	248
A Marketplace Perspective	250
Decision 5: Single Measure or Multiple Measures?	251

Single-Measure Approach   251
Multiple-Measure Approaches   251
    Single Measure with Multiple Qualifiers   252
    Multiple Independent Measures   253
    Multiple Integrated Measures   253
        Weighted Measures   253
        Matrix   255
    Points   257
    The Impact of Aggregation   259
Concluding Insights   261
Use Commission Plans when Short-Term Sales Force Causality Is
High   261
Use Bonus Plans when Considerable Management Flexibility Is
Needed   261
Tie Payout to Territory Goal Attainment when Sales Territories Have
Unequal Potential   262
Aggregate Plan Measures Whenever Possible   262
Invest in Goal-Setting Methodologies if High Plan Excitement Is
Desired   262
Adapt Performance–Payout Strategies for Volatile Markets   263
Create Simple and Memorable Plans for High Impact   263

Introduction

The performance–payout relationship defines how incentive payments are calculated and how they vary with measured performance. For example:

- Should incentive payments be determined by multiplying a commission rate by a territory performance measure? Or should a fixed bonus amount be paid when a specified performance level, such as a territory goal, is attained?

- Should incentive payments accelerate as performance increases, or should they slow down to ensure that sales force costs are contained in volatile markets?

- Should sales force earnings be capped?

- Should the incentive plan pay out from the first dollar, from goal, or from some fraction of goal?

- Should payout depend on a single performance measure or on multiple measures?

The performance–payout relationship is an important incentive plan design decision.

Is the Most Appropriate Performance–Payout Relationship Used for Determining the Incentive Plan Payout?

The impact of choosing the wrong performance–payout relationship for the incentive plan is significant. Consider the following three examples:

High Commission Rates Create Undeserved Sales Force Earnings at Entrepreneur Group

Advertising revenues at magazine publisher Entrepreneur Group grew substantially during the late 1980s, as the number of advertising pages in *Entrepreneur* magazine increased significantly and ad rates went up. The sales force was paid entirely on commission, with salespeople receiving a 6 percent commission on repeat business and 8 percent on new advertising. The sales force was benefiting considerably from the rapid growth of the magazine and the ad rate increases; sales force earnings had accelerated considerably, even though the sales force was not working any harder than before. Management was concerned that sales force pay was becoming excessive and unwarranted.

Commission Plan That Pays from the First Dollar Creates Unfairness When Sales Territories Have Unequal Potential

A chemical company paid its sales force a commission on sales from the first dollar sold. Analysis revealed that the highest-paid salesperson had a sales territory with four times the sales potential of the average territory. This person was skimming the cream off the best accounts, earning high commission dollars, but leaving tens of thousands of dollars of sales opportunity unrealized. The salesperson's financial success had little to do with his own efforts, but instead was primarily the result of his lucrative sales territory. This person had become very complacent and chose not to develop new business. Salespeople in low-potential territories were frustrated because they were making much less money despite their hard work.

IDC Incentive Plan Encourages Salespeople to Stop Selling When They Achieve Goal

Salespeople at International Data Corporation (IDC), a publisher of market research for the technology industry, earned a percentage commission on every sale, but a very large portion of their incentive pay came in the form of a bonus for hitting a sales quota. Salespeople who achieved their quota before the end of an incentive period often held over subsequent deals until after the start of the next period, so that those deals could count toward the achievement of the next period's quota. This holding over of sales was not in the customer's or the company's best interest. IDC's revenue stream would dry up at the end of each period, leaving the firm with a depleted cash flow and customers waiting for product.

Authors' note: Since many salespeople at IDC were able to achieve quota well before the end of the incentive period, perhaps the quotas were set too low?

These examples illustrate how important it is to use the most appropriate performance–payout relationship in an incentive plan. When Entrepreneur Group pays salespeople a steep commission rate that is too generous for current market conditions, sales force pay may accelerate to a level beyond what the sales job is worth to the company. When the chemical company pays on sales from the first dollar even though sales territories vary widely in terms of potential, salespeople's earnings may not be a reflection of their true performance, and salespeople with low-potential territories are penalized. When IDC ties a large portion of incentive pay to short-term goal attainment, salespeople may influence the timing of sales to maximize their personal earnings, ignoring what is best for the customer and the company.

The diagnosis of performance–payout relationships begins by examining the three views within the sales management system framework:

1. The downstream *consequences* of performance–payout relationship decisions for salespeople, sales force activities, and customer and company results

2. The upstream *consistency* of performance–payout relationship decisions with marketing and go-to-market strategies, sales processes, and sales force roles

3. The *compatibility* of performance–payout relationship decisions with other sales force effectiveness drivers, such as salespeople's skills and capabilities, sales force culture, performance management systems, and nonmonetary sales force motivators.

Figure 7-1 provides a template for diagnosing whether the appropriate performance–payout relationship is being used in the sales incentive plan and suggests some possible signs of trouble.

Representing Performance–Payout Relationships

A plan's performance–payout relationship is commonly represented visually using a graph called a *payout curve*. The graph's horizontal axis represents a performance measure (for example, sales or percentage of goal attained), and the vertical axis represents the payment that the salesperson receives for each level of performance. A payout curve facilitates quick recognition of the details of a performance–payout relationship. Throughout this chapter, payout curves will be used to represent different plan choices.

Figure 7-1. Some signs that the compensation plan *may* have an inappropriate performance–payout relationship.

Consistency with . . .	Compatibility with . . .	Consequences . . .
• Sales and marketing strategies • Sales process • Sales roles	• Performance management systems • Sales force culture • Sales force motivators • Sales force hiring and development processes	• Company results • Customer results • Sales force behaviors and activities • Sales force quality
• The compensation plan has not changed since the product launch and rewards for free sales, which thwarts sales growth. • The sales process requires increased support of the customer, but the compensation plan has not changed to reflect this. • The sales territories are unbalanced in terms of market opportunity, creating unfairness in payout based on sales and/or market share.	• The company is paying out too much undeserved incentive money as a result of poor sales forecasting and goal setting. • Incentive plan decelerators and caps are incompatible with a sales force culture that is sales-centered, competitive, and focused on short-term results. • Management talks about a "pay-for-performance" culture, but the best performers are not always the ones earning the most money. • The hiring profile is not compatible with the degree of leverage in the plan.	• Sales, profit, and/or market share goals are not being achieved because the plan structure and the performance–payout relationship encourages the wrong sales force behaviors. • Salespeople are unmotivated because the incentives do not kick in early enough; engagement is too low. • The salespeople stop working once they reach a sales level where decelerators and earnings caps kick in. • Salespeople manage the timing of sales to maximize personal earnings, rather than doing what is best for the customer and the company.

The basic construction of a payout curve is shown in the two examples in Figure 7-2. The payout curves show the incentive plans of two medical device sales forces that were merging. The products of the two firms were largely complementary, but the two sales force compensation plans were quite different. Company A had a monthly commission plan. Salespeople earned a modest salary plus a 2 percent commission on the first $500,000 in sales, 3 percent on the next $500,000, and 4 percent on sales above $1 million. Company B had a quarterly bonus plan. Salespeople earned a higher salary plus $1,500 at 95 percent of sales objective, an additional $1,500 at 100 percent, and then another $600 per percent of objective over 100 percent. The merger of these two sales forces created several difficult sales force compensation challenges. A merger task force had to determine which performance–payout relationship would be most effective for the newly merged sales organization and how to make the transition to the new plan successfully.

There are numerous possible plan performance–payout relationships. This chapter organizes the performance–payout relationship design choice into five

Figure 7-2. Examples of payout curves for two merging medical device sales forces.

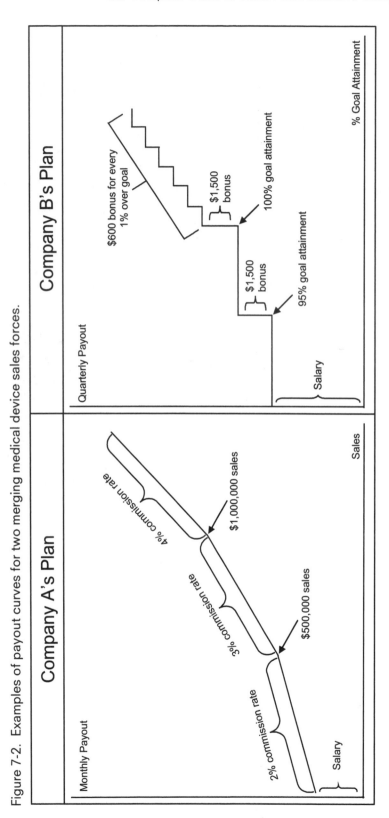

decisions, summarized in Figure 7-3. These performance–payout decisions, along with their drivers and influences, are developed in the remainder of the chapter.

Decision 1: Bonus Plan or Commission Plan?

A Comparison of Plan Structures

Bonus plans and commission plans have fundamentally different structures. With a bonus plan, each salesperson is typically given a goal or quota for his territory, and incentive payments begin when the salesperson performs at some predefined success level relative to that goal or quota. Bonus plans often involve multiple bonus payouts tied to defined goal gates, targets, or thresholds. For example, a salesperson might receive a first bonus payment when she achieves 90 percent of goal, a second payment at 100 percent attainment, and a third at 110 percent. Bonus plans typically include a sizable salary component, so that if a salesperson does not sell enough to earn the bonus, he can still earn a decent living. Two examples of bonus plan payout curves are provided in Figure 7-4.

Commission plans pay continuously for every sale. A commission rate is multiplied by the company-selected performance measure, such as sales or gross profits, to determine payout. Salespeople may earn the same commission rate on every sale, or the commission rate can vary by product or by customer. Commission rates can also vary depending upon the level of performance attained by the salesperson. For example, a salesperson might earn a certain rate on all sales up to a territory goal and then a higher rate on all sales beyond that goal. Many commission plans include a salary component, but usually the salary component is smaller and the variable component is larger than in a typical bonus plan. With most commission plans, the salesperson relies on commission earnings, in addition to salary, to make a decent living. Three examples of commission plan payout curves are included in Figure 7-5.

Figure 7-3. Five performance–payout decisions and their drivers and influences.

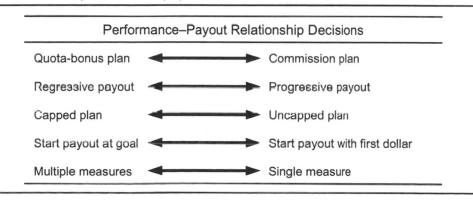

Figure 7-4. Examples of bonus plan payout curves.

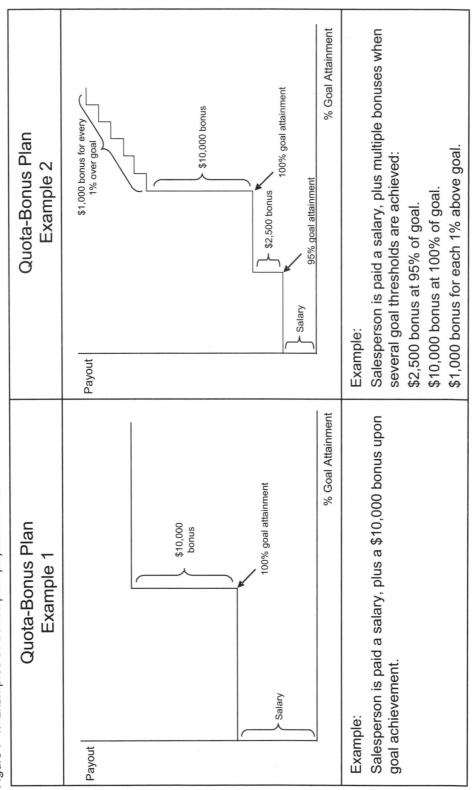

Quota-Bonus Plan Example 1

Payout

$10,000 bonus

100% goal attainment

Salary

% Goal Attainment

Example:
Salesperson is paid a salary, plus a $10,000 bonus upon goal achievement.

Quota-Bonus Plan Example 2

Payout

$1,000 bonus for every 1% over goal

$10,000 bonus

100% goal attainment

$2,500 bonus

95% goal attainment

Salary

% Goal Attainment

Example:
Salesperson is paid a salary, plus multiple bonuses when several goal thresholds are achieved:
$2,500 bonus at 95% of goal.
$10,000 bonus at 100% of goal.
$1,000 bonus for each 1% above goal.

Figure 7-5. Examples of payout curves for commission plans.

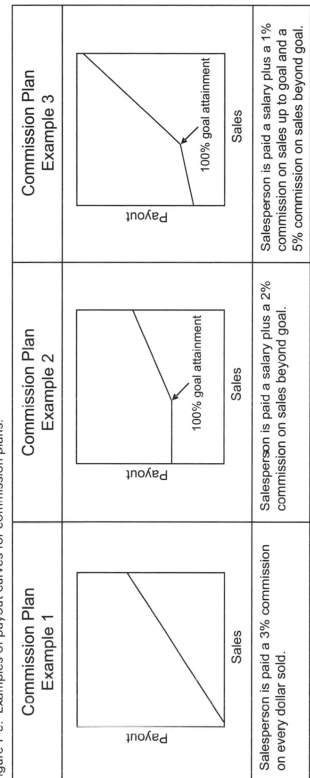

Commission Plan Example 1	Commission Plan Example 2	Commission Plan Example 3
Salesperson is paid a 3% commission on every dollar sold.	Salesperson is paid a salary plus a 2% commission on sales beyond goal.	Salesperson is paid a salary plus a 1% commission on sales up to goal and a 5% commission on sales beyond goal.

Figure 7-6 shows another example of a commission plan. In this plan, the commission rate is tied to goal attainment by product group.

It is possible to mix elements of bonus and commission plans together in a single plan. For example, the plan represented by the payout curve in Figure 7-7 includes both commissions and bonuses tied to goal attainment. The plan summarized in Figure 7-8 pays a mix of bonuses and commissions, depending on the product and the goal attainment level. Additional bonuses can be earned if all product goals are met and if the district and the territory both achieve goal.

Figure 7-6. Example of a commission plan tied to goal attainment by product group.

% Product Group Objective Achieved	Product Group A Commission Rate	Product Group B Commission Rate
0–100%	2.5%	3.5%
101–110%	3.5%	4.5%
Over 110%	4.0%	5.0%

Figure 7-7. Example of a payout curve for a mixed bonus and commission plan.

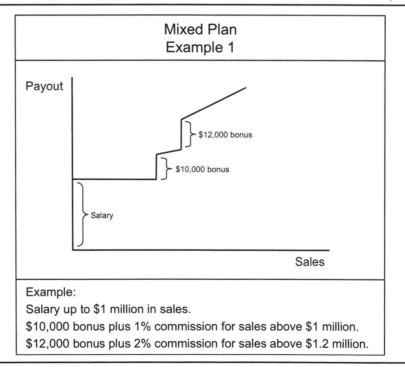

Mixed Plan
Example 1

Payout

$12,000 bonus

$10,000 bonus

Salary

Sales

Example:
Salary up to $1 million in sales.
$10,000 bonus plus 1% commission for sales above $1 million.
$12,000 bonus plus 2% commission for sales above $1.2 million.

Figure 7-8. Example of a quarterly plan combining bonuses and commissions.

	90%–100% of Goal	Commission Rate Above Goal
Product A	$200 per %	2.5%
Product B	$100 per %	2.0%
Product C	None	5.0%

New Product D: Commission rate = 10%; goal = $10,000

All product territory goals met (A, B, C, and D): $500

District >100% of goal and territory >100% of goal: $500

Target incentive for quarter = $5,000
($2,000 + $1,000 + $0 + $1,000 + $500 + $500)

Which Plan Structure Is Appropriate for the Selling Environment and Management Culture?

Several aspects of a firm's selling process and environment influence the type of plan structure—bonus, commission, or mixed—that is appropriate. Key influences on the plan structure decision include the importance of the sales force in creating short-term sales (short-term causality), the firm's ability to predict demand accurately, the degree to which sales territories have equal potential, and the sales management culture and philosophy. Figure 7-9 summarizes several characteristics of the selling process, the sales force culture, and demand predictability that favor a commission plan versus a bonus plan.

The Bonus Versus Commission Decision Influences Employee Attraction and Retention

The decision on whether to have a bonus plan or a commission plan affects the firm's ability to attract and retain salespeople with particular skills and personalities. Commission plans that pay mostly variable pay with little or no salary tend to attract results-oriented salespeople who believe that they can sell anything to anyone. Such plans also encourage poor performers to leave the firm, as they will not make enough money to earn a decent living. However, such plans generate little firm loyalty from salespeople. A salesperson who is paid mostly on commission is very likely to jump ship if a competitor makes a better offer, and may take many of the firm's clients with him. Bonus plans that have a higher salary component, on the other

Figure 7-9. Characteristics of the selling process, the sales force culture, and demand predictability that favor a commission plan versus a bonus plan.

Commission Plan	Bonus Plan
Selling Process Characteristics	
• Sales force causality is high—sales are determined primarily by the skill and effort of salespeople and are not substantially affected by factors outside an individual salesperson's control.	• Sales force causality is moderate—sales are influenced by the skill and effort of salespeople, but are also affected by factors outside an individual salesperson's control.
• Selling success is primarily the result of an individual salesperson's effort (as opposed to a team effort).	• Selling is a team effort, making it difficult to attribute specific results to an individual salesperson.
• Carryover sales—sales that occur as a result of past sales force effort—are low, so that commissions reward recent sales effort. (Commissions paid on carryover sales generate "automatic" income for the salesperson, and thus are actually a "hidden salary.")	• There are high carryover sales that are generated without any extra effort or skill. A bonus plan allows the firm to set performance thresholds above the carryover sales level, inspiring salespeople to work hard to earn their bonus.
• Selling cycles are short and performance measures are straightforward, allowing frequent performance measurement and incentive payout.	• Selling cycles are long and/or performance measures are complex, making it difficult to measure performance and pay incentives frequently.
Sales Force Culture Characteristics	
• Sales management does not feel that it is important to closely control sales force effort; the sales force is managed on the results it achieves.	• Sales management wants to control sales force effort.
• The sales force is expected to sell; nonselling duties (such as service) are assigned to other company employees.	• Salespeople are expected to perform nonselling tasks as part of their job.
• Sales territories are equitable, so that earnings depend on skills and effort and not on the territory.	• Sales territories may not be equitable. A bonus plan allows management to assign each salesperson an appropriate goal based on territory potential, so that earnings are driven by the salesperson's performance and not by territory assignments.
• It is unnecessary to manage salespeople's earnings to a specified level; salespeople who deliver should have unlimited earnings potential, even if they are among the highest-paid people in the company.	• Salespeople's earnings need to be managed to a specified level so that salespeople's income is consistent with that of other company employees in similarly valued jobs.
• The company wants to closely manage the sales force expense to sales ratio.	• The company feels that it is more important to manage sales force expenses to a predetermined budget than as a percentage of sales.
Demand Predictability	
• The market is volatile, making it difficult for the company to predict future demand.	• The market is fairly stable, and the company can predict future demand with a high degree of accuracy.
• Data for setting accurate goals at the territory level are not available.	• Data are available that allow management to set accurate goals at the territory level.

hand, attract salespeople with a longer-term focus who are more likely to stay with the firm. They also attract salespeople who, in addition to selling, are interested in problem solving, consulting, and servicing customers. Thus, the desired firm culture and the sales force skills necessary for implementing an effective selling process are important considerations when making the commission versus bonus plan decision.

Commission Plan Makes Change Difficult at a Chemical Company

Recall the chemical company described in the introductory section of this chapter. The company paid its sales force a commission on sales from the first dollar sold, despite the fact that sales territories varied greatly in terms of market potential. Salespeople in high-potential territories could call on the easy-to-sell accounts and earn high commissions without having to work very hard. They did not need to develop new business. Meanwhile, millions of dollars of sales opportunity companywide were unrealized. In order to improve customer coverage and give everyone in the sales force a more equal chance to earn higher commissions, management considered realigning sales territories. However, it feared that territory changes would be met with considerable resistance by salespeople in lucrative, high-potential territories. These salespeople controlled many of the firm's most important customer relationships, and management did not want to risk losing those relationships. Thus, management was forced to back off from its effort to make sales territory changes.

A solution to this common problem is to change the structure of the sales force compensation plan. A goal-based plan provides greater flexibility to make territory changes than a commission plan that pays from the first dollar does, because territory quotas or goals can change whenever territories are realigned. Thus, if a salesperson with a high-potential territory has accounts taken away, her quota is adjusted downward appropriately. Sales forces that anticipate a need for future territory realignment—such as those that are planning to expand—should consider implementing a quota-based plan rather than a plan that pays from dollar one in order to maintain greater flexibility.

Decision 2: Progressive or Regressive Plan?

An incentive plan can include many possible relationships between performance and payout. The most appropriate relationship—or the shape of the payout curve—is driven by the degree to which the firm can predict demand accurately, as well as by the firm's financial and marketing goals and its management culture and philosophy.

Payout Curve Possibilities

Payout curves and example plans for four possible relationships are shown in Figure 7-10. The possibilities are:

1. A linear plan, or constant plan, pays the same "flat" commission rate for each level of sales.

2. A progressive plan pays at a higher rate as sales increase.

3. A regressive plan pays at a lower rate as sales increase. A plan with a cap (discussed further later in this chapter) is an extreme example of a regressive plan.

4. A mixed plan has a combination of higher and lower rates as sales increase. A mixed plan typically has an S-shaped payout curve, with the steepest part of the payout curve being at goal. Thus, the rate is high around goal to inspire salespeople to stretch to meet and exceed their goal, but it then decreases to protect the firm from paying excessive incentives if the goal is set too low and is too easily achieved.

Figure 7-10. Four possible relationships between performance and payout.

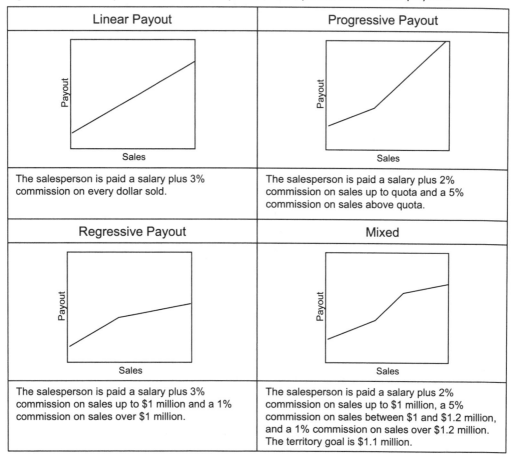

Linear Payout	Progressive Payout
The salesperson is paid a salary plus 3% commission on every dollar sold.	The salesperson is paid a salary plus 2% commission on sales up to quota and a 5% commission on sales above quota.
Regressive Payout	Mixed
The salesperson is paid a salary plus 3% commission on sales up to $1 million and a 1% commission on sales over $1 million.	The salesperson is paid a salary plus 2% commission on sales up to $1 million, a 5% commission on sales between $1 and $1.2 million, and a 1% commission on sales over $1.2 million. The territory goal is $1.1 million.

Payout Curves and the Achievement of Sales Force Objectives

Each performance–payout option—a linear plan, a progressive plan, a regressive plan, and a mixed plan—has advantages and disadvantages. The relative importance of different sales force objectives determines which option is most appropriate. For example:

- If "make the plan easy to administer" and "prevent undeserved sales timing behavior" are primary objectives, then a linear plan is preferred. Linear plans are the easiest to compute, administer, and explain. They also eliminate the incentive for salespeople to try to shift sales forward or backward in time in order to increase their personal earnings.

- If "increase sales force motivation" and "reward top performers" are primary management objectives, then a progressive plan is the best option. When territory goals are fair and accurate and when increasing levels of sales are the result of the effort and skill of the individual salesperson, a progressive plan will inspire hard work by providing unbounded greater rewards for higher levels of achievement.

- If "provide cost protection when there is significant demand uncertainty" or "moderate demand when capacity is tight" are primary objectives, then a regressive plan is preferred. A regressive plan discourages overselling when there is a serious limitation on production or delivery capacity and also protects the firm from paying significant undeserved incentives when product sales are underforecast.

- The S-curve plan combines the advantages of the progressive and regressive plans into a single plan. But salespeople tend to complain frequently about the regressive portion of such payout curves.

Progressive Plans Are Self-Funding

While progressive plans can lead to excessive sales force earnings if initial volume forecasts are too low, such plans are at least self-funding. Commission earnings rise as the company sells more and covers its fixed costs. Hence, salespeople earn more when the company can afford to pay more. Although costs appear to be out of control when compared to the initial budget, at least they can be covered through higher sales. Also, since salespeople are likely to have diminishing utility for money, progressive plans may begin to offer them more money just as their interest in working harder to earn more money wanes.

Progressive Plans Encourage Salespeople to Continue Selling Even After They Have Achieved Goal

Recall the problem at International Data Corporation (IDC) described in the introductory section of the chapter. This publisher of market research data paid its sales force a percentage commission on every sale, plus a large bonus for hitting sales quota. Salespeople who earned the bonus would often hold over subsequent deals until the next incentive period, so that those deals could count toward achievement of the next period's quota. This behavior was not good for customers and created cash flow problems for IDC. To alleviate the problem, the firm implemented a 1.5 percent kicker for all sales beyond quota. Thus, a salesperson who had already achieved quota would earn more commission by making an additional sale in the current incentive period than she would by holding that sale over to the following period.

Progressive Pay Curve Encourages Distributors to Collude

A manufacturer that sold through distributors got into trouble when two of its distributors who sold in different geographic territories began to conspire together to take advantage of the firm's progressive commission payout structure. The firm paid distributors whose quarterly sales exceeded a specified goal an accelerated commission rate. The two distributors felt that they could not achieve this goal alone, so they agreed to work together to game the system. One quarter, Distributor A purchased enough goods from the firm to cover the demand of both its own customers and the customers of Distributor B; Distributor B purchased nothing from the manufacturer, but instead purchased goods from Distributor A. The next quarter, the two distributors reversed roles; Distributor B purchased a large quantity from the manufacturer, and Distributor A purchased only from Distributor B. This arrangement enabled both distributors to earn accelerated commissions every other quarter. Firms in situations where this type of gaming is possible should strongly consider using a linear pay curve to prevent such undesirable behaviors.

Figure 7-11 compares how well the various performance–payout options can help the firm achieve different sales force objectives. The plan rankings shown in the figure will be accurate in a majority of cases, but it is impossible to generalize accurately for every possible environment.

Figure 7-12 summarizes the main advantages and management challenges of each of the four performance–payout relationships.

Salespeople Dislike Regressive Incentive Plans

The sales profession attracts people who are competitive and driven by the promise of financial reward for their achievements. Hence, salespeople generally dislike regressive incentive plans. As part of a recent consulting

Figure 7-11. Criteria for evaluating alternative performance–payout relationships.

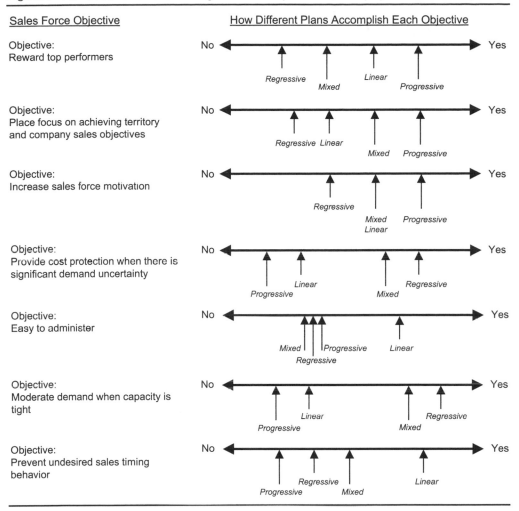

| Sales Force Objective | How Different Plans Accomplish Each Objective |

project with a firm that had a regressive plan, we conducted dozens of field interviews with salespeople and first-line sales managers. Practically every person we spoke with felt that it was unfair that the company reduced its commission rates for beyond 120 percent goal attainment. "You're taking money away from me" was the general sentiment, even though only two out of 200 salespeople had achieved over 120 percent of goal in the past two years. Of course, the company was not taking money away from those two salespeople; it was simply paying out at a slower rate to acknowledge that 120 percent goal attainment was likely to be the result of a goal-setting error, not of superior performance. The low incidence of people exceeding 120 percent of goal probably made the regressive feature an unnecessary public relations problem—the company would have been better off without the slowdown in payouts.

Figure 7-12. Advantages and management challenges of various performance–payout relationships.

Payout Curve	Advantages	Management Challenges
Linear *(graph: Payout vs. Sales, linear rising line)*	• Easy to understand and administer. • Prevents undesired sales timing behavior.	• Providing sufficient incentive and reward for achieving and exceeding objectives.
Progressive *(graph: Payout vs. Sales, upward curving line)*	• Enhances sales force motivation. • Provides incentive and reward for achieving and exceeding objectives. • Rewards top performers.	• Setting accurate goals. • Preventing windfall gains when forecasts are too conservative. • Managing undesired sales timing behavior (e.g., holding sales over to next period when goal is not achievable this period, or bringing sales from next period forward to get windfall gains this period after attaining goal in this period). • Managing disproportionate effort to boost measures (such as specific product sales) that are above goal at the expense of measures that are below goal.
Regressive *(graph: Payout vs. Sales, concave flattening line)*	• Provides cost protection when forecasts are uncertain. • Moderates demand when capacity is tight by discouraging overselling.	• Setting accurate goals. • Motivating top performers. • Providing sufficient incentive to keep selling once objective is achieved. • Managing undesired sales timing behavior (e.g., holding sales for next period after goal attainment this period). • Managing the negative perception of such plans among salespeople.
Mixed *(graph: Payout vs. Sales, S-shaped line)*	• Inspires salespeople to stretch to meet a goal, yet provides cost protection when forecasts are uncertain.	• Setting accurate goals. • Administering a complex plan. • Managing the negative perception of the regressive features of the plan.

The Sales Force Became Unhappy when a Magazine Publisher Flattened Payout Curves

Making the transition to a flatter payout curve for a sales force is always challenging. Recall the predicament of the magazine publisher Entrepreneur Group described in the introductory section of this chapter. The firm paid its advertising sales force entirely on commission with a steep payout curve. Rapid company growth and price increases led to excessive acceleration in sales force earnings. To reverse the trend, management overhauled the sales compensation plan, adding a base salary and slashing commission rates. Under the old plan, salespeople received a 6 percent commission on repeat business and 8 percent on new advertising. Under the new plan, salespeople received a $2,000 monthly salary, and they became qualified for a commission schedule if monthly sales exceeded $45,000. Commission rates varied from 1 percent at $45,000 up to a maximum of 2.85 percent at $105,000 in monthly sales. Many of the company's nine salespeople were upset by the new pay structure, saying that it undermined their earning potential. At current sales levels, the new plan was a considerable pay cut. Management countered that since there was no cap on earnings, salespeople who hustled could earn as much or more than under the old plan. If commission schedules are kept stable for a period of time, salespeople expect future stability and perceive a "loss" if a change is made. However, if commission rates are revised regularly while managing stable target earnings, salespeople get used to such changes.

Decision 3: Caps or No Caps?

A capped incentive plan is a conspicuous example of a regressive plan. An incentive plan with a cap or a ceiling limits the amount of money that a salesperson can earn in a single time period or for a single transaction or account. Caps can be expressed as a certain dollar amount, as a percentage of base salary, or as a multiple of target earnings. Examples of some of the ways in which companies cap earnings are provided in Figure 7-13. In the Sales Incentive Executive Education Survey, 24 percent of companies placed some sort of cap on incentive plan earnings.

The decision as to whether or not to cap an incentive plan is driven by the firm's ability to predict demand accurately, as well as by the firm's financial goals, culture, and philosophy. Caps have some considerable disadvantages. They can dampen the motivation of top performers. Salespeople stop working hard if they know that they will not earn any incremental income from their efforts. Caps often encourage salespeople to hold sales over to the next period, when those sales can help them earn incremental income. At the same time, if caps are reached too easily, the incentive plan becomes a "salary" plan.

Soft Caps

One company has a policy that when calculated incentives exceed 150 percent of a salesperson's base salary, the extra amount is placed on hold, and is payable only if the salesperson makes her goal the following year and is still employed by the firm.

Can the Need for Caps Be Eliminated Through Better Territory Alignment?

Some companies place a cap on earnings to prevent a small number of salespeople from being overpaid. Often in such cases, the high-earning

Figure 7-13. Examples of incentive plan caps described in the Sales Incentive Executive Educational Survey.

Caps expressed as a multiple of target earnings
- Incentive pay cannot exceed 150 percent of target earnings (semiconductors)
- Incentive pay cannot exceed 200 percent of target earnings (high-tech)
- Incentive pay cannot exceed 4 times target earnings (pharmaceuticals)
- Incentive pay cannot exceed 7 times target earnings (transportation)

Caps expressed as a percentage of base salary
- Incentive pay cannot exceed 5 percent of base salary (manufacturing—telesales)
- Incentive pay cannot exceed 20 percent of base salary (hardware)
- Incentive pay cannot exceed 50 percent of base salary (health care)

Caps expressed as dollar limits
- Incentive pay cannot exceed $7,000 per quarter (media)
- Incentive pay cannot exceed $9,000 per quarter (software)
- Incentive pay cannot exceed $15,000 per quarter (medical sales)
- Incentive pay cannot exceed $19,000 per year (pharmaceuticals)
- Incentive pay cannot exceed $36,000 per year (chemicals)
- Incentive pay cannot exceed $500,000 per year (biotechnology)

Caps expressed as dollar limits per transaction or account
- Incentive pay cannot exceed $250,000 per transaction (computer maintenance)
- Incentive pay cannot exceed $10,000 per account per year (security)

Dollar limits with exceptions
- Incentive pay cannot exceed $150,000 per year plus up to $100,000 per year for new contracts (telecommunications)

> salespeople have sales territories with huge potential and more accounts than they can handle effectively. Their territories allow them to skim the cream off the top and earn high incentives without having to work very hard. Instead of capping earnings, consider redesigning the territory of a salesperson who is approaching the earnings cap. Good territory alignment improves customer coverage and allows everyone in the sales force a fair chance to succeed.

Despite the danger of damaging the motivation of hard workers, income caps have an advantage in volatile markets, where it is difficult for management to predict future demand accurately. Using an income cap prevents unearned sales force "windfalls" in the event that target income is set for a sales level that turns out to be easily attainable. This happens with poor forecasting or unanticipated market factors, such as market growth, weak competition, or significant unexpected product demand. When results are not clearly related to effort, rewards appear unfair and arbitrary. Caps smooth income in highly volatile markets. Caps can also be used to moderate sales if product availability is limited or if the firm has capacity constraints that make it unprofitable to accept and deliver additional orders when the annual sales plan has been exceeded by a large amount. Caps can also help to encourage internal pay equity between the sales force and other company departments.

To mitigate the adverse effect of caps on sales force motivation, consider adding a special discretionary bonus such as a "President's Award" to a capped plan. This bonus is awarded to those who management feels have been unfairly hurt by the cap. The magnitude of the bonus can be tied to the degree to which outstanding goal attainment is a true reflection of performance rather than a reflection of low goals.

Salespeople Dislike Caps

A decision to cap an incentive plan is always unpopular with the sales force. Salespeople usually feel that caps are unfair and tend to distrust management's motives for using them. They may feel that caps are a way to keep salespeople from earning enough to be "independent-minded" and quit or to prevent salespeople from making more than executives. Some companies take a calculated risk that the savings from a capped program are not worth the negative impact on sales force morale.

Caps and Guarantees Are Common in Start-up Firms

In start-up firms, where management is unclear as to how much revenue a territory will generate, a salesperson's commission earnings are often capped. This protects the firm from paying out excess, undeserved money to the sales force if company performance significantly exceeds management expectations. More often, however, an optimistic management team at a start-up firm overestimates demand, leaving the sales force hanging if sales fall well short of expectation. A start-up firm that hopes to attract top-notch salespeople should consider offering the sales force protection on the downside. For example, a salesperson might be guaranteed, at least for the first year, a minimum payout of 60 to 75 percent of estimated target commission earnings, regardless of the firm's performance.

Decision 4: Pay from the First Dollar or from Goal or a Fraction of Goal?

The possibilities for when to begin incentive payments are summarized in Figure 7-14. The decision on when to begin payout—from the first dollar, at goal, or at

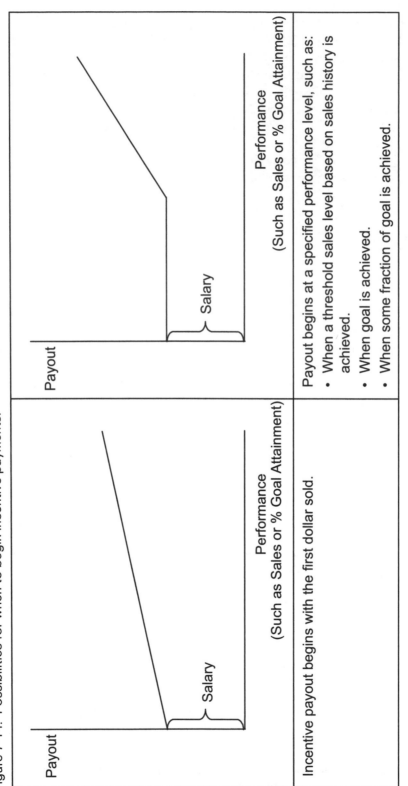

Figure 7-14. Possibilities for when to begin incentive payments.

some fraction of goal—is influenced by the importance of the sales force in creating short-term sales (short-term causality), the firm's ability to predict demand accurately, and the sales management culture and philosophy.

Paying from the First Dollar

Typically, incentive plans that begin with the first dollar are commission-based, with variable pay (as opposed to salary) being a large proportion of total pay. This type of plan ties a monetary incentive to each sales transaction and is most appropriate in certain selling environments and sales management cultures (see Figure 7-9). Commission plans that pay from the first dollar are common in industries such as insurance, stockbrokerage, real estate, and office supplies. These are commodity industries that rely on the skills of salespeople to differentiate a particular company. The millions of salespeople who sell products direct to consumers for companies such as Avon and Amway are also paid on commission from the first dollar sold.

Caution: Paying from the First Dollar Rewards Salespeople for Free Sales

Commission plans that pay salespeople from the first dollar sold reward all sales, including *free sales* (sales that the salesperson did not have to work for). Free sales may be the result of past years' sales efforts (carryover sales) or can be attributed to a strong brand identity or superior products (franchise sales). Commissions on free sales are actually a "hidden salary"—they will be paid regardless of what the salesperson does. In selling environments with high free sales, paying commissions from the first dollar has multiple consequences. Salespeople become very motivated and focused on building a solid book of business. However, experienced salespeople who have built a book of business can earn substantial commissions on free sales, and thus may not be motivated to work hard to develop new customers and drive sales growth. At the same time, new salespeople who have not yet developed strong customer relationships may have trouble earning sufficient money, making it difficult for the firm to attract and retain new sales staff. This problem of sales force complacency combined with high new salesperson turnover is very common at firms that reward salespeople with commissions from the first dollar sold when a substantial portion of sales are free sales. And, with the customer control that salespeople develop in such environments, it can be difficult to change or restructure the incentive model to fix the problem. When initiating a commission plan that pays from the first dollar sold, one has to look ahead several years and anticipate the future needs of the firm and the salespeople. A forward-looking approach helps to ensure that the incentive structure provides the

appropriate balance of flexibility and cost control for the firm, and also provides sufficient motivation for the sales force, both today and in the future.

Paying from Goal or a Fraction of Goal

For goal-centric compensation plans, the decision on whether to begin paying at
goal or at some fraction of goal is complex. Insight can be gained by examining
the following perspectives to reach a decision: a company perspective, a sales force
perspective, and a marketplace perspective.

A Company Perspective. Sometimes we hear senior management in companies
saying, "The goal is the goal—we are not successful unless we make our goal. So,
why should we ever pay incentives if the goal has not been achieved?" This all-or-
nothing view is rarely shared by sales managers and compensation experts. The
company has to realize that the purpose of incentives is to engage and motivate a
large proportion of the sales force, and so payouts should logically begin at a point
such that a large proportion of salespeople can increase their earnings by working
harder. This is the *engagement* concept introduced in Chapter 2.

A Sales Force Perspective. The sales force perspective argues that incentive payouts
should begin at some fraction of goal. Since salespeople usually work alone, there
are few opportunities for management to acknowledge their success. Receiving a
bonus and reaching a higher commission gate are two visible and vital ways in
which salespeople are recognized and rewarded. If the gates are set too high and
only a few people achieve them, the message to the salespeople is that they have
failed. If their failure is the result of unattainable goals, they feel like victims. Even
if the company meets its overall goal, the salespeople who do not make their
individual goal will feel like failures. Figure 7-15 shows a typical distribution of
performance to goal on top, and the percent of salespeople who make goal as a
function of company performance on the bottom. Notice that when the company
achieves exactly 100 percent of goal, only 46 percent of the sales force makes goal.
Company goal attainment needs to be between 115 and 120 percent in order for
80 percent of the sales force to make goal.

  People do not like to fail, and excessive unwarranted failure leads to a morale
crisis. Consider starting incentive payouts at a fraction of goal that ensures that in
moderate-incentive environments (20 to 35 percent of total cash compensation
at risk), at least 70 percent of the sales force receives some sort of incentive payout.
This should help keep the sales force engaged. If 70 percent of the sales force
does not deserve an incentive payout, the problem is larger than the incentive
plan. It is likely that there are problems with hiring, training, or management.
The percentage of salespeople receiving some incentive compensation needs to be
close to 100 percent when incentives are over 50 percent of total cash compensation.

Figure 7-15. Typical performance distribution and link between company performance and goal achievement.

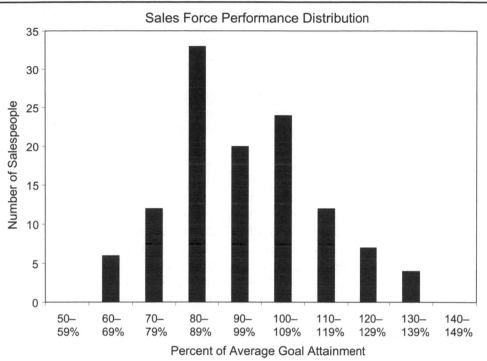

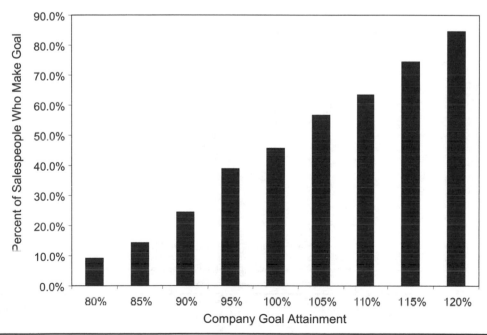

A Marketplace Perspective. The marketplace perspective supports the belief that market volatility affects when incentive payments should begin. Some markets are fairly stable, and sales can be projected with considerable accuracy. Other markets present high levels of uncertainty. An uncertain market is likely to have more salespeople performing below goal than a highly certain market. This is usually a result of the vagaries of the market and the difficulty of setting accurate goals, not of a lack of skill, capabilities, and effort on the part of the salespeople. An intelligent incentive compensation plan acknowledges the statistical uncertainty in markets, allowing incentive pay to begin at a lower level of goal achievement and rise more slowly in a highly volatile market than in a market that has high certainty. For example, for an established product in a stable market, a salesperson might begin to receive incentive pay when she reaches 90 percent of goal. For a product in an environment that is less predictable, the same salesperson might begin to receive incentive pay when she reaches just 75 percent of goal. With this compensation structure, more salespeople will make at least some incentive money if the goals for the product in the uncertain market turn out to be unrealistically high. To guard against goal-setting errors on the low side, some firms use earnings caps or decelerators to prevent the payout of excessive unearned incentive money (decelerators and caps are described elsewhere in this chapter). Figure 7-16 displays the contrast in payout between plans in high- and low-volatility markets.

New York Times Adapts Incentive Payout Start for Market Volatility

Management at the *New York Times* felt that the incentive compensation plan used by the advertising sales department did not fairly reward effort

Figure 7-16. Incentive payout schemes that acknowledge uncertainty in markets.

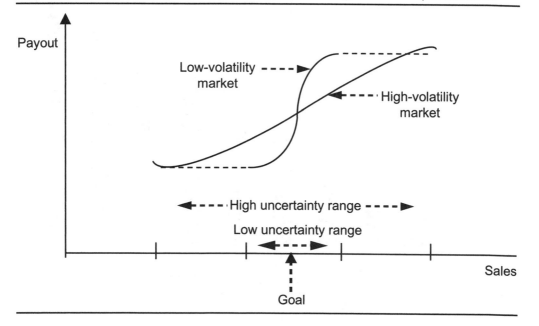

against results. The sales force worked in teams, which were organized by market. Some teams worked in more stable markets, where revenue was easier to predict, but many of the smaller teams worked in volatile markets where accurate prediction was difficult. Thus members of small teams often received windfall gains or losses in incentive pay as a result of serendipitous events external to their selling effort. The firm wanted a new compensation plan that was more fair and would be motivational to all participants. A new plan was developed that explicitly addressed the issue of market volatility. Salespeople working in volatile industries could start receiving incentive pay when they achieved just a portion of their sales goal—for example, 80 percent attainment. Teams in the more stable markets had to come closer to their goal—for example, within 95 percent of attainment—before receiving incentive pay. The sales force embraced the new incentive plan and perceived it to be fair and motivational.

Decision 5: Single Measure or Multiple Measures?

Chapter 6 discussed the wide variety of different performance measures that companies use in their incentive plans. While some plans base payout on a single performance measure, others incorporate several different performance measures. The decision on how many different measures to use and how to combine those measures in the incentive plan is driven by the firm's sales and marketing goals, as well as by data accuracy and availability.

Single-Measure Approach

Plans based on a single performance measure are usually straightforward, easy for the sales force to understand, and easy to administer. Such plans are preferred in situations where management feels that a single measure captures the essence of what it wants salespeople to accomplish. Figure 7-17 shows an example of a plan that is based on a single measure: sales goal attainment.

Multiple-Measure Approaches

Often, a single measure cannot adequately capture everything that management wants the sales force to accomplish. Both sales strategies and the quality and measurability of performance data may vary across products and customer segments. Often, multiple measures are needed to measure sales force performance effectively. There are many different ways to incorporate multiple measures into an incentive plan. Four common approaches are the single measure with multiple qualifiers approach, the multiple independent measures approach, the multiple integrated measures approach, and the points approach.

Figure 7-17. Example of a plan that uses a single measure.

Salary plus:
A $5,000 bonus when each of the following gates is attained: 95%, 100%, 105%, 110%, 115%, and 120% of sales goal.

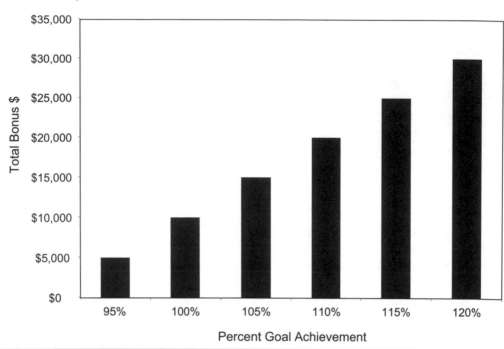

Percent Goal Achievement

Single Measure with Multiple Qualifiers. With this approach, a single measure drives incentive payout. However, the extent of the payout depends upon the simultaneous achievement of subgoals, such as product goals, customer goals, or activity goals. These subgoals are called *qualifiers.* Figure 7-18 shows an example of a plan that determines incentive payout by a single measure with multiple qualifiers.

Beware of Plans That Severely Penalize Salespeople for Failing to Achieve Qualifiers

When a firm was getting ready to launch an exciting new product, management was concerned that salespeople might underpromote highly profitable core products and devote too much time to the new product. To prevent this, the following qualifier was added to the incentive plan: "A salesperson must achieve goal on core products in order to earn bonus money on the new product." This resulted in harsh penalties for several salespeople who were extremely successful in selling the new product, but who came in at just 95 to 99 percent of goal on core products and therefore could earn no new product bonus money.

Figure 7-18. Example of a plan that uses a single measure with multiple qualifiers.

Salary plus:
A $5,000 bonus when each of the following gates is attained: 95%, 100%, 105%, 110%, 115%, and 120% of sales goal. Three qualifier possibilities are:
• 25% increase in payout if the individual sales goals for all three product lines are achieved.
• 15% increase in payout if the qualifier for customer satisfaction is achieved.
• 10% increase in payout if several activity goals are accomplished.

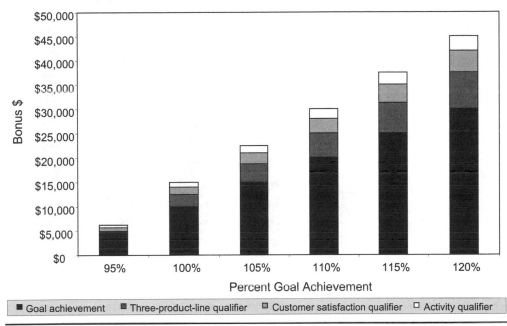

Multiple Independent Measures. With this approach, incentive payouts are calculated independently based on multiple measures. This approach works well when there are multiple goals that management wants the sales force to achieve. The magnitude of the payout associated with each goal helps the sales force set priorities. Figure 7-19 shows an example of a plan that determines incentive payout using multiple independent measures.

Multiple Integrated Measures. With this approach, multiple measures are combined to calculate the incentive payout. Two ways to accomplish this are the weighted-measures approach and the matrix approach.

Weighted Measures. The weighted-measures approach reduces multiple performance measures to a single measure by attaching weights to each independent measure and aggregating the measures. Since the individual metrics may be measured on different scales, computing a straight weighted average is usually not appropriate. For example, averaging sales and market share produces a number that is not meaningful. Individual measures need to be normalized first so that adding the weightings makes sense. Normalizing in terms of goal attainment is a good way to accomplish this when a goal-centric incentive plan is used. The example in

Figure 7-19. Example of a plan that uses multiple independent measures.

Salary plus:
A $5,000 bonus when each of the following gates is attained for Product A sales: 95%, 100%, 105%, 110%, 115%, and 120% of sales goal.
A $3,000 bonus when each of the same gates is attained for Product B sales.

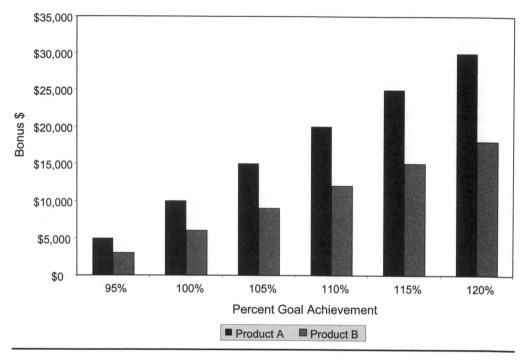

Figure 7-20 shows how to calculate a weighted measure that integrates the sales of three products.

Figure 7-20 uses one measure, goal achievement, across different products. A weighted plan may also use multiple measures, such as sales revenue, profit contribution, market share, and call activity, to replace Products A, B and C in

Figure 7-20. Example of a plan that uses weighted measures.

Product	Weight (weights used in the incentive plan)	Percent Goal Attained (example)	Weighted Goal Attainment (calculation)
A	50%	110%	55%
B	30%	90%	27%
C	20%	105%	21%
	Overall Goal Achievement (calculated by summing the weighted goal attainment of the three products)		103%

the table in Figure 7-20. The approach is the same even when a variety of different measures are used.

Matrix. The matrix approach integrates two measures into an incentive plan, using a matrix to show the various payout possibilities. Matrix plans can help make complex plans tangible and can incorporate a wide variety of different row and column measures, including the following:

- Salesperson performance and company performance (Figure 7-21)
- Territory sales and pricing discount (Figure 7-22)
- The salesperson's sales forecast and territory sales (Figure 7-23)
- Territory share and share gain
- Territory performance and district performance
- Existing product sales and new product sales
- Sales to new customers and sales to repeat customers

Figure 7-21. Example of a plan that uses a matrix.

Company Performance (% objective)	Salesperson Performance (% Objective): 80%	90%	100%	110%	120%
80%	0.2	0.4	0.8	1.2	1.7
90%	0.3	0.5	0.9	1.3	1.8
100%	0.4	0.7	1.0	1.5	2.0
110%	0.6	0.8	1.1	1.6	2.1
120%	0.7	0.9	1.2	1.7	2.2

Multiple of target payout

Target payout = $25,000

Figure 7-22. Example of a plan that uses a matrix.

Pricing Discount (coverage across all business)	Territory Sales ($ Millions): 1.3	1.5	1.7	1.9
19.0%	1.3	1.5	1.7	1.9
22.0%	0.9	1.1	1.3	1.5
25.0%	0.5	0.7	0.9	1.1
28.0%	0.1	0.3	0.5	0.7

Multiple of target payout

Target payout = $25,000

Figure 7-23. Incentive payout matrix that encourages accurate forecasting.

		Gross Margin Achieved ($ Millions)					
		2.50	2.75	3.00	3.25	**3.50**	3.75
Gross Margin Objectives	3.50	10.5	17.8	27.3	40.6	**62.0**	70.6
	3.25	12.3	20.9	32.1	**47.7**	57.2	65.2
	3.00	14.5	24.6	**37.7**	44.0	52.8	60.2
	2.75	17.0	**28.9**	34.8	40.6	48.7	55.5
	2.50	**20.3**	26.6	32.0	37.5	44.9	51.2

Payout Matrix ($100s)
(Salesperson picks the objective)

The matrix in Figure 7-21 shows the payout that a salesperson will receive for different combinations of salesperson performance (matrix columns) and company performance (matrix rows). The matrix entries are multiplied by the target payout to determine the final payout. This plan helps the company protect its downside, since the company pays less when it does not perform well.

The matrix plan in Figure 7-22 is designed to motivate salespeople to hold the line on price concessions to customers.

Payouts in a Matrix Plan Can Be Either Additive or Synergistic

With an additive matrix (for example, Figure 7-22), the entry differentials between columns and between rows are constant throughout the matrix. With a synergistic matrix (for example, Figure 7-21), payouts accelerate as one moves diagonally from one corner of the matrix to the opposite corner; salespeople can earn greater incentives if they simultaneously perform well on both the column and the row dimensions.

One of the most innovative incentive plans is a matrix plan suggested by Jacob Gonik, author of "Tie Salesmen's Bonuses to Their Forecasts" (*Harvard Business Review*, 1978), for IBM in Brazil. It is a plan that motivates salespeople to forecast their territory sales accurately. The plan is shown in Figure 7-23.

The rows represent the salesperson's gross margin forecast at the beginning of the planning period, and the columns represent the actual territory gross margin at the end of the period. The salesperson's payout depends upon both his forecast and his actual gross margin. Having estimated their expected gross margin, salespeople find themselves restricted to one of the rows. Notice that the payout numbers in each row are increasing. Therefore, salespeople receive increasing compensation as they increase margin. They should be motivated to continue profitable selling as much as possible. On the other hand, the columns are developed so that the largest payout appears in the row where the salesperson's forecast matches the actual gross margin. Hence, salespeople will earn the most when they forecast accurately.

With traditional incentive plans, salespeople do not have a financial motivation to forecast accurately. For example, in a sales plan tied to overall territory sales, a salesperson is likely to forecast low so that she can earn more money by exceeding the forecast and appear to be a star performer. With the Gonik plan, the sales force is rewarded for both good performance and a good forecast. This plan is especially useful when the company relies on the sales force forecast to set its production and manufacturing requirements. The plan also encourages the sales force to plan better.

The Gonik plan applies real economic costs to the sales force. Underforecasting results in stock-outs, and overforecasting produces extra inventory. The incentive payout differences down the columns can incorporate some fraction of these costs. As a result, the sales force shares in the real costs of stock-outs and carrying excess inventory.

While this is an innovative and useful type of plan, it suffers from some disadvantages. The plan is somewhat complicated and can be difficult to explain to a sales force and hard to administer. In addition, because each salesperson self-selects his territory forecast, there is no guarantee that the sum of the territory forecasts will equal a national forecast that meets the expectations of top management and shareholders.

Points. Another type of incentive plan that allows companies to integrate diverse measures into a single plan is a point-based plan. Figure 7-24 illustrates such a plan.

In this example, points are assigned to unit sales of different products, and a point multiplier is applied based on the achievement of gross margin goals. Salespeople accumulate points based on their results. The total number of points a salesperson accumulates during the incentive period relative to a predetermined point goal decides her incentive payout. Point-based plans can provide the mechanism for creating a common currency for valuing diverse results measures, such as sales of different product lines, sales to different customer groups, or sales through different channels. Point-based plans allow salespeople considerable flexibility as to how they want to earn their points; this can be both a disadvantage and an advantage to the firm. On the positive side, a points plan gives salespeople freedom to focus on their strengths and earn money in whatever way they choose; this can be very motivational. On the negative side, a salesperson can earn a high number of points by focusing on a single product line or a subset of performance

Figure 7-24. Example of a point-based plan.

Product	Points/Unit		% of Point Goal	Quarterly Payout
5000 series	5		90%	$3,000
7000 series	10			
8000 series	12		$300 per % of point goal over 90%	
			$500 per % of point goal over 100%	

Gross Margin	Point Multiplier
<90% of goal	0.5
Multiplier increases by 0.05 for each % over 90%	
Multiplier further increases by 0.1 for each % over 100%	

Examples of Payout Calculations

		Salesperson 1	Salesperson 2
Units sold	5000 series	47	22
Units sold	7000 series	10	30
Units sold	8000 series	20	24
Margin achieved		104%	98%
Margin multiplier		1.4	0.9
Unit points		575	698
Margin-adjusted points		805	628
Point goal		600	650
% goal achieved		134%	97%
Calculated payout		$23,000	$5,100

measures while ignoring others; this is not likely to be what the company wants. Further, points are intangible, unlike dollars, and the linkage between the original measures and point totals can sometimes be very unintuitive.

Biotech Start-up Uses Points-Based Plan Tied to MBO Achievement

A point-based plan was used by a biotech start-up when it launched its first product. Variable sales force pay was determined through points tied to salesperson MBO achievement while the sales force was involved in pre-launch activities and during the first few months following the product's launch. Points were awarded to each salesperson for achieving strategi-cally important objectives, such as completing product training, developing account plans, and making initial sales calls on prospective customers. Salespeople could earn up to 10 points for achieving five territory-specific objectives: 2 points for each objective that was fully achieved, 1 point for each objective that was partially achieved, and no points for objectives that were not achieved. Salespeople earned $500 per point; if all objectives were fully achieved, the salesperson would receive $5,000 in variable pay. As market experience grew and management's forecasting ability improved, the company phased out the MBO-based incentive plan and eventually replaced it with a more traditional sales quota-based incentive plan.

The Impact of Aggregation. When a plan provides an accelerating payout as performance increases, the choice of whether to aggregate multiple performance measures or to base payout on several independent measures has important implications for salespeople and for the firm. The example shown in Figure 7-25 illustrates this point. Plan 1 separates incentives between two product groups. Plan 2 integrates sales from both product groups and uses total sales to determine the salesperson's payout. In the example, Plan 1 costs the firm $24,000 in payout for $1,050,000 in sales, while Plan 2 costs the firm just $22,500 in payout for the same level of total sales.

Plan 1 is likely to be preferred by the sales force because it gives salespeople greater flexibility. A salesperson can achieve a higher commission level by exceeding objective for either of the two product groups. If sales of both product groups are above objective or both are below objective, the Plan 1 and Plan 2 payouts are identical. However, when one of the two product lines is underperforming, Plan 1 gives the sales force the option of focusing on the other product line that is doing well in order to make more money. The impact of this flexibility multiplies as the number of independent plan components increases. Salespeople have more ways to succeed and can pick and choose the easiest ways to earn money.

From a company perspective, Plan 2 is likely to be preferred. Plan 2 has a cost advantage. Whenever product performance is unbalanced (i.e., one product exceeds objective, but the other does not), the cost of Plan 2 is less than the cost of Plan 1 for the same level of territory sales. Additionally, Plan 1 may encourage the sales force to abandon an underselling product line; salespeople will probably choose to focus their energy on the product line that has already met objective in

Figure 7-25. Comparison of payouts using independent and integrated measures.

Plan 1

Product Group	Goal ($000)	Rate to Goal	Rate Above Goal	Actual Sales	Payout
A	$500,000	2%	5%	$450,000	$9,000
B	$500,000	2%	5%	$600,000	$15,000
Total	$1,000,000			$1,050,000	$24,000

Plan 2

Product Group	Goal ($000)	Rate to Goal	Rate Above Goal	Actual Sales	Payout
All products	$1,000,000	2%	5%	$1,050,000	$22,500

order to make more money. Plan 2 is more likely to encourage the sales force to continue a balanced selling effort, regardless of each product line's performance.

Figures 7-26 and 7-27 show two alternative methods of integrating independent performance measures to encourage a sales force to continue supporting an underperforming product. In Figure 7-26, Plan 1 has independent incentives for two product groups, while Plan 2 has both independent incentives and a combined product incentive that kicks in once a combined product goal is achieved. With Plan 1, salespeople will tend to ignore the underperforming product group (A) and focus on the product group that is exceeding goal (B) in order to make more money. With Plan 2, however, salespeople have greater incentive to continue selling Product Group A because sales of either product help them achieve the combined product goal (all products, A + B), and the individual product line commission rate above goal (3 percent) is not very much larger than the commission rate below goal (2 percent).

Figure 7-26. An indirect method of performance measure integration.

Plan 1

Product Group	Goal ($000)	Rate to Goal	Rate Above Goal	Actual Sales	Payout
A	$500,000	2%	5%	$450,000	$9,000
B	$500,000	2%	5%	$600,000	$15,000
Total	$1,000,000			$1,050,000	$24,000

Plan 2

Product Group	Goal ($000)	Rate to Goal	Rate Above Goal	Actual Sales	Payout
A	$500,000	2%	3%	$450,000	$9,000
B	$500,000	2%	3%	$600,000	$13,000
All products	$1,000,000		2%	$1,050,000	$1,000
Total					$23,000

Figure 7-27 shows another alternative method of integrating independent performance measures to ensure that underperforming products are not ignored by the sales force. Plan X has independent incentives for two product groups with commission rates that accelerate beyond goal. Plan Y has independent incentives with base commission rates and multipliers that kick in once total commission thresholds are achieved. With Plan Y, a salesperson's first $50,000 in commission is earned at a base rate, which varies by product. The next $50,000 in commission is earned at an accelerated rate; base-rate earnings are multiplied by 1.10 to determine payout. Commissions beyond $100,000 are accelerated even further, with base-rate earnings being multiplied by 1.25 to determine payout. With Plan X, salespeople may ignore an underperforming product to focus on the product that is exceeding goal in order to make more money. With Plan Y, however,

Figure 7-27. An indirect method of performance measure integration.

Plan X		
Product Group	Base Rate	Rate Beyond Goal
A	4.5%	7.0%
B	2.5%	6.0%

Plan Y	
Product Group	Rate
A	4.5%
B	2.5%
Base Commission Multipliers	
$0–50K	1.0
$50K–100K	1.10
>$100K	1.25

salespeople have an incentive to continue selling the underperforming product because all sales help them achieve the total commission thresholds that result in accelerated earnings.

Concluding Insights

Here are some concluding insights that can help you determine the most effective performance–payout relationship for your sales incentive plan.

Use Commission Plans when Short-Term Sales Force Causality Is High

Selling environments with high short-term sales force causality usually favor commission plans that pay salespeople for every closed sale. Salespeople like to feel that their work effort will be rewarded. When work effort has a high short-term sales impact, immediate sales increases occur when the sales force puts forth extra effort. A commission plan rewards salespeople immediately for those sales increases. Salespeople see sales rise, they feel a sense of accomplishment, and they receive a commensurate financial reward. The synergistic effect of high causality and a commission plan structure that pays salespeople for every transaction can be very motivating.

Use Bonus Plans when Considerable Management Flexibility Is Needed

Companies that anticipate a need for future territory realignment—such as those planning to expand or redefine sales roles—should consider implementing a bonus plan rather than a commission plan in order to maintain greater flexibility. With a commission plan that pays from the first dollar, salespeople are likely to vehemently fight giving up any of their accounts, since the change directly affects their ability to earn money. With a bonus plan, however, territory quotas can change whenever territories are realigned. If a salesperson with a high-potential territory has accounts taken away, his quota is adjusted downward appropriately. This makes it possible for management to implement territory alignment changes without excessive resistance from the sales force.

Tie Payout to Territory Goal Attainment when Sales Territories Have Unequal Potential

The success of a commission plan that pays from the first dollar hinges on an equitable and balanced sales territory alignment. If territories are not comparable, salespeople can be rewarded for having a good sales territory and not for their performance. A bonus plan allows management to assign each salesperson an appropriate goal based on territory potential, so that earnings are driven by salesperson performance and not territory assignments. Thus, if sales territories have unequal potential, a goal-based incentive plan is preferred.

Aggregate Plan Measures Whenever Possible

When multiple divisions within a company share the same sales force, the sales incentive plan often consists of many disaggregated measures; each division gets a "line item" in the incentive plan. While appealing from an organizational perspective, this type of plan can create disastrous results for the firm. Disaggregated plans give salespeople many ways to succeed. A salesperson is sure to choose the easiest ways to earn money and is likely to ignore some line items that are of strategic importance to the firm. Incentive plans that aggregate across measures are more likely to encourage a balanced selling effort and are usually less costly to the firm as well.

Invest in Goal-Setting Methodologies if High Plan Excitement Is Desired

An effective performance–payout relationship creates considerable sales force excitement in the performance range where capable salespeople operate. For example, increasing the payout rate, and therefore the *Excitement Index* (see Chapter 2), as sales approach a territory goal is likely to inspire salespeople to work harder and stretch to meet that goal. Effective goal setting makes it possible to create considerable excitement; the steepest payouts can be concentrated across a narrow range of likely "stretch" performance. However, when accurate territory-level goal setting is difficult, the range of likely performance for each salesperson becomes greater. Incentive payouts must be spread across that wider performance range in order to ensure sufficient sales force engagement. Accurate territory-level goals allow steeper payout curves and larger payout rates over a tighter range of performance, while inaccurate goals favor flatter payout curves and smaller payout rates over a greater performance range. Improvements in goal-setting processes often allow steeper payout curves that create greater sales force excitement.

Adapt Performance–Payout Strategies for Volatile Markets

In highly volatile settings, accurate forecasting at the territory level can be extremely difficult. Some strategies for creating an effective performance–payout relationship include the following:

- Do not tie payout to territory goal attainment; for example, use a commission plan that pays from the first dollar;
- If a goal-based plan is desired:
    - Set goals with short time frames; that way, if a goal is unrealistic, the sales force is affected for only a limited period of time, and the impact of the error is minimized.
    - Begin incentive payout at a lower level of goal achievement and have the payout rise more slowly than in a market that has high certainty; that way, more salespeople will make at least some incentive money, even if the goals turn out to be unrealistically high.
    - Consider the use of earnings caps or decelerators to ensure that the company will not have to pay out excessive unearned incentive money in the event that goals are set too low.

Create Simple and Memorable Plans for High Impact

Design creep happens frequently in sales incentive compensation plan design. A main incentive plan is laid out, and then everyone wants to add just a little bit here and a little bit there. Pretty soon, the plan is so complex that the sales force doesn't understand it.

- *"Our plans are too hard to understand; there are too many inconsistent variables,"* complains a high-technology salesperson.
- *"Don't worry about the compensation plan—it's so complex that it's nearly impossible to understand it. Just do your job,"* advises a sales manager during new salesperson training.

A plan that is too complex will be either ignored or misinterpreted by the sales force. When designing your incentive plan, keep in mind that:

$$\sum many\ great\ ideas\ =\ one\ terrible\ idea$$

A well-designed plan is simple and memorable; a plan summary should fit on a card small enough to be carried around in the salesperson's wallet. Another good rule of thumb is that whenever a new feature is added to the incentive plan, an existing feature should be taken out.

Evaluating Proposed Sales Incentive Compensation Plan Alternatives and Selecting a New Plan

How This Chapter Is Organized

Introduction 265

An Overview of Candidate Sales Compensation Plan Assessment 267

Quantitative Assessment of a Candidate Sales Compensation Plan 271

Introduction to the MRG Company Case Study 271

A Quantitative Assessment Framework 273

Step A: Create a Performance Database 274

Step B: Superimpose the Candidate Plan 276

Step C: Quantitative Analysis 276

Test 1: Plan Cost, Payout Distribution, and Engagement and Excitement Analytics 276

Test 2: Risk Assessment 281

Test 3: "Who Gets Helped" and "Who Gets Hurt" Analysis 288

Test 4: A "Pay-for-Performance" Check 290

Test 5: Sensitivity Analysis of Plan Features 291

Step D: Test Plan Design Changes 291

Qualitative Assessment of a Candidate Sales Compensation Plan 295

Qualitative Assessment of Consequences 295

Consequences for Salespeople 295

Test 6: Qualitative Questions for Assessing Salespeople Consequences	295
Test 7: Sales Force Input	295
Consequences for Sales Force Activities	301
Test 8: Qualitative Questions for Assessing Sales Force Activity Consequences	301
Test 9: Adverse Sales Force Behaviors Check	301
Consequences for Customer Results	301
Test 10: Qualitative Questions for Assessing Customer Results Consequences	301
Consequences for Company Results	301
Test 11: Qualitative Questions for Assessing Company Results Consequences	301
Qualitative Assessment of Consistency	304
Test 12: Consistency Check with Sales Force Definers	304
Qualitative Assessment of Compatibility	305
Test 13: Compatibility Check with Other Sales Force Effectiveness Drivers	305
Future-Proofing Assessment of a Candidate Sales Compensation Plan	306
Test 14: Compatibility Check with Future Company Needs	308
Conclusion: From Objectives to Reality	308

Introduction

It is important to test a sales incentive plan before it is implemented. Numerous stories illustrate possible consequences of failing to thoroughly evaluate and assess the potential impact of a new compensation plan.

An Untested Incentive Plan Becomes a Runaway

A start-up firm introduced a new computer networking technology in the early 1990s. The company offered its sales force an incentive compensation plan that paid a 3 percent commission on all sales. For the first few years, salespeople had to work hard to earn their pay, as customers had to be educated and convinced to try the new technology and customer relationships needed to be established. But by the mid-1990s, the nature of the sales job was changing. Internet usage was growing at an astounding rate, fueling the demand for networking solutions, and company sales were skyrocketing. The sales force reaped the benefits of the phenomenal market growth. Many salespeople were earning well over $1,000,000 a year, and some did so with minimal effort. Since the company was incredibly profitable, it could afford to pay the sales force generously, and the original 3 percent commission structure remained unchanged. This caused resentment among employees working in internal departments, such as marketing and research and development, who felt that it was unfair for the sales force to be paid so much. In addition, several competitors were entering the market and prices were eroding. Management became concerned that the company could not afford its high sales force costs much longer. Yet changing the compensation plan would be very disruptive and unpopular with the sales force.

Authors' note: Company leadership had expected market growth to help drive future sales and success. Had the firm tested the financial implications of the original incentive plan beyond the first year or two, it is likely that a plan with greater flexibility to adapt to a rapidly growing market would have been adopted.

Failure to Test an Incentive Plan Contributes to Low Sales Force Motivation and Poor Performance

Salespeople at a consumer financing company are paid commissions based on the loan volume they generate. Each salesperson has a territory goal, and commission payouts accelerate once 100 percent of goal is reached. While the sales force plays a very prominent role in creating the demand for loans, interest rates are also an important determinant. Last year, interest rates went up unexpectedly, and as a result, the demand for loans was well below expectation. Less than 10 percent of the sales force made goal, and hence, over 90 percent of salespeople did not earn the accelerated commission rate. The sales force was extremely unhappy; they felt that they were being penalized for circumstances beyond their control. Salespeople became demotivated, which further depressed loan sales, and the company had one of its worst years in terms of sales goal achievement.

Authors' note: If the incentive plan had been tested more thoroughly up front for the effect of possible environmental changes, such as an interest rate increase, it is likely that a plan that was fairer to the sales force would have been adopted.

Undesired Sales Force Behaviors Are Not Anticipated Because of Lack of Testing

Desirous of making the company goal every month, a medical device company instituted a compensation plan in which each salesperson was paid a

> base commission rate on sales up to his goal and an accelerated commis-
> sion rate on sales over the monthly goal. It did not take the poor performers
> long to figure out that rather than be at 90 percent of goal two months in a
> row, they could easily generate a 60 percent goal achievement month fol-
> lowed by a 120 percent goal achievement month by managing the timing of
> customer orders. With no more overall sales, they could earn the acceler-
> ated rate on their sales every other month.
>
> *Authors' note: Selling every other period is a common concern with
> plans that restart every period and have accelerators at goal. This behavior
> needs to be managed if this type of plan is adopted. A plan paying on
> cumulative goal attainment can moderate the sales-timing behavior.*

By evaluating and testing proposed incentive compensation plan alternatives, sales leaders can compare different candidate plans objectively and encourage the selection of a plan that is consistent with company strategy, is compatible with sales effectiveness drivers, and has appropriate consequences for salespeople, sales force activities, customer results, and company results. Testing of candidate sales incentive plans also enhances understanding of the financial risks and the antici- pated sales force behavior associated with each plan. For example, what if the sales forecast turns out to be too high—will sales force engagement decline, and to what extent is sales force motivation likely to suffer? Alternatively, what if the sales forecast turns out to be too low—how much undeserved incentive money will the firm pay out, and what impact will the windfall gain have on the sales force's expectations for future earnings? Plan testing helps sales leaders anticipate possible outcomes, build contingency plans, and ensure that incentive plans can continue to thrive despite an uncertain future.

Plan testing can also help sales leaders foresee and manage any undesired sales force behaviors that a plan may create. No single incentive plan can solve every sales management problem. A compensation plan that has many advantages will, at the same time, encourage some sales force behaviors that may be detrimental to the firm. For example, a plan that pays on units sold may encourage salespeople to cut price in order to build volume, hurting company profitability. A plan that pays for team performance can encourage "free riders" who are content to relax and reap the benefits of their teammates' work. A plan that pays for carryover sales resulting from selling effort applied years ago encourages complacency. Plan testing can help a management team anticipate unwanted side effects of a sales incentive plan prior to implementation so that the undesired sales force behaviors can be managed appropriately.

An Overview of Candidate Sales Compensation Plan Assessment

Candidate plans can be tested for their effectiveness within the categories in the 3 Cs framework.

- *Consistency.* Is the candidate plan *consistent* with the firm's marketing strategy, go-to-market strategy, sales processes, and sales force roles (an upstream view of the sales management system)?

- *Compatibility.* Is the candidate plan *compatible* with other salesperson effectiveness drivers, such as salespeople skills and capabilities, sales force culture, performance management systems, and sales force motivators?

- *Consequences.* Will the candidate plan have the appropriate *consequences* for salespeople, sales force activities, and customer and company results (a downstream view of the sales management system)?

Recall that the incentive plan design process begins with an assessment of the current (or incumbent) plan to identify shortcomings or gaps that need to be remedied in order to adapt to changing conditions and improve the sales organization. This current plan assessment process, which is described in Chapter 2, includes a number of quantitative and qualitative tests that address important questions within the 3 Cs framework. A similar set of tests can be used to assess a candidate plan to determine whether the plan is appropriate for the sales organization and is ready for implementation.

As summarized in Figure 8-1, quantitative and qualitative assessments usually focus on different components within the 3 Cs framework. Quantitative approaches are most useful for understanding company results consequences of the candidate plan, such as incentive plan costs and financial risk, as well as consequences for salespeople, such as income distribution and incentive plan engagement and excitement. These are issues that tend to be of high concern to most sales leaders. Qualitative assessment further enriches the quantitative assessment of company results and salespeople consequences, and is most useful for assessing compatibility with company sales and marketing strategies, consistency with other sales force effectiveness drivers, and consequences for sales force activities.

The remainder of this chapter describes various tests that have been used successfully by firms to evaluate candidate sales compensation plans prior to implementation. Quantitative tests are discussed first, followed by qualitative tests. The tests described represent a comprehensive set of possibilities. Not every test is needed in every situation. The Sales Incentive Compensation Plan Assessment Scorecard in Figure 8-2 can help incentive plan designers:

- Identify those tests that are relevant to their specific needs and concerns.

- Summarize the results of the various tests that make up the assessment.

The scorecard allows easy comparison of the relative strengths and weaknesses of an incumbent plan and alternative candidate plans on important dimensions. Recall from Chapter 2 that these objectives should be set at the start of the plan design process and are the criteria against which all candidate plans should be judged. Depending upon the particular circumstances, some evaluation areas may merit a more detailed breakdown, while other areas may be less relevant. The

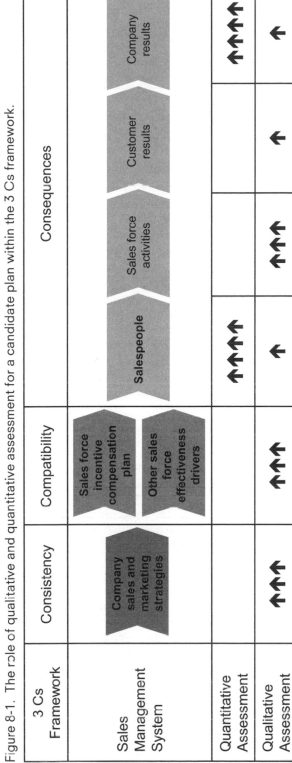

Figure 8-1. The role of qualitative and quantitative assessment for a candidate plan within the 3 Cs framework.

Figure 8-2. An example of a Sales Incentive Compensation Plan Assessment Scorecard.

Use the assessment techniques described in *The Complete Guide to Sales Force Incentive Compensation: How to Design and Implement Plans That Work* to rate incentive compensation plan effectiveness in the following areas using the following rating scale: 5 = Excellent; 4 = Very good; 3 = Good; 2 = Fair; 1 = Poor.

#	Name of Test	Perform This Test If You Want To . . .	Incumbent Plan Rating (1–5)	Candidate Plan Rating (1–5)
Quantitative Tests				
1	Plan cost, payout distribution, and engagement and excitement analytics	• Predict plan costs. • Predict salesperson pay levels and income distribution. • Predict plan impact on sales force motivation.		
2	Risk assessment	• Assess financial and sales force risk with different levels of uncertainty in future sales force performance.		
3	"Who gets helped" and "who gets hurt" analysis	• Compare predicted pay levels with last year's pay for each salesperson. • Make sure that important sales force constituencies are not hurt by the new plan.		
4	A "pay-for-performance" check	• Compare predicted pay levels with performance evaluation results for each salesperson. • Make sure that the plan rewards "winners."		
5	Sensitivity analysis of plan features	• Assess the impact of changing specific plan features to help fine-tune and improve plan elements.		
Qualitative Tests				
6	Qualitative questions for assessing salespeople consequences	• Anticipate possible plan consequences for salespeople.		
7	Sales force input	• Understand the sales force's perception of the plan. • Get a preview of issues that are likely to arise when the plan is communicated to the entire sales force.		
8	Qualitative questions for assessing sales force activity consequences	• Anticipate possible sales force activity consequences resulting from the plan.		
9	Adverse sales force behaviors check	• Anticipate and manage any undesired sales force behaviors that the plan may encourage.		

10	Qualitative questions for assessing customer results consequences	• Anticipate possible plan consequences for customer results.
11	Qualitative questions for assessing company results consequences	• Anticipate possible plan consequences for company results.
12	Consistency check with sales force definers	• Check for consistency with company strategy and sales force definers (sales strategy, go-to-market strategy, and sales force design).
13	Compatibility check with other sales force effectiveness drivers	• Check for compatibility with culture and other sales effectiveness drivers.
14	Compatibility check with future company needs	• Check to ensure that the plan is compatible with future sales force strategies and structures.

Note: This scorecard is an example that highlights some commonly used tests and evaluation criteria for sales compensation plan assessment. The scorecard needs to be tailored to a company's situation. Some areas may not be relevant, while others may need more detail and texture.

scorecard is most effective when the list of evaluation criteria is tailored to specific sales force issues, problems, situations, and objectives.

Quantitative Assessment of a Candidate Sales Compensation Plan

Quantitative assessment helps plan designers understand the financial and sales force impact of a candidate sales compensation plan.

Introduction to the MRG Company Case Study

The discussion of quantitative assessment is enriched through examples from the MRG Company case study that was introduced in Chapter 2. Recall that the current incentive compensation plan at MRG (the MRG incumbent plan) is a bonus–commission plan that begins its incentive payout once territory goal is achieved. The plan is depicted in Figure 8-3 along with the last 12 months' payout distribution. Over 60 percent of the salespeople did not achieve their territory goal and hence did not receive any incentive compensation. The company was very disappointed with the 96 percent achievement of the overall company sales goal. MRG's leadership team realized that the sales force incentive compensation plan had misfired, and was a key cause of the low morale and sales force underperformance.

The MRG sales incentive compensation design team has developed an alternative candidate plan. This plan has a lower salary, begins the incentive pay at 80 percent of goal attainment, and has accelerators at 100 percent and 110 percent

Figure 8-3. The MRG incumbent plan, along with incentive statistics and payout distribution for the last 12 months.

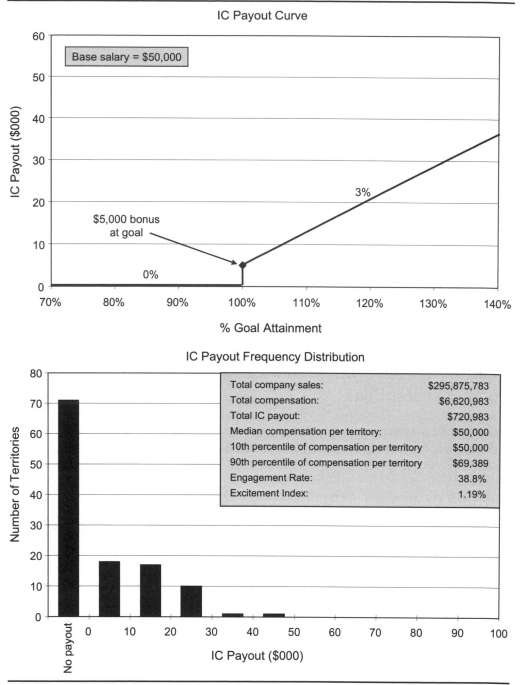

of goal attainment. The design team feels that the candidate plan will improve plan engagement and will also increase the incentive component of total income for salespeople. It is anticipated that these two plan aspects will result in higher sales force motivation and will drive better sales results, since there is high sales force causality and measurability. The MRG candidate plan is shown in Figure 8-4.

MRG management wants to launch the candidate plan immediately, but the vice president of human resources suggests that the plan be tested to make sure that there are no unfavorable surprises upon implementation. The MRG incentive design team organizes an assessment approach that includes a number of quantitative tests to determine whether the MRG candidate plan should be implemented.

A Quantitative Assessment Framework

The framework for quantitative assessment uses historical data to evaluate the potential future consequences of a candidate plan. It requires three inputs:

- Specification of the candidate plan
- Next year's national sales forecast or goal
- Historical data reflecting last year's performance distribution across the sales force

Figure 8-4. The MRG candidate incentive plan for next year.

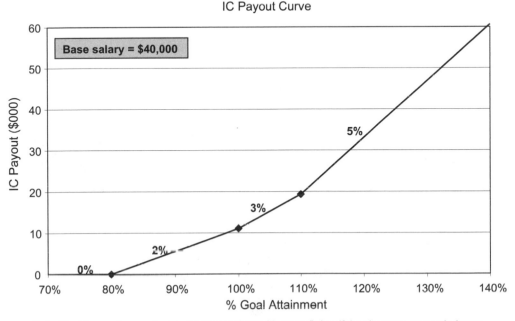

Note: The IC payout curve depicted is for a territory of "average" size. If the plan pays a commission on nominal sales, actual payout at a given level of goal attainment will vary with territory goal size.

These inputs are gathered, and various outputs that address key questions about the likely sales force and financial consequences of the candidate incentive plan are created.

Figure 8-5 suggests a four-step approach for conducting the quantitative assessment. Each of the steps is described in detail in the subsequent discussion, using the MRG analysis as an example.

Step A: Create a Performance Database. Most organizations can produce a performance distribution showing how key incentive plan performance measures vary across the sales force. For example, Figure 8-6 shows how sales and goal attainment were distributed across the MRG salespeople for the last 12 months. Note that the distribution is likely to be built on a rolling 12 months of data, since the analysis may take place before the current year ends.

From the historical performance distribution, a potential performance distribution for next year can be generated. As a starting point, it is reasonable to assume that next year will have the same performance distribution as last year, since performance typically follows a similar pattern year after year. Alternative performance distributions can be used if it is felt that they better represent next year's performance behavior. Analysis that involves shrinking and expanding the

Figure 8-5. A quantitative assessment approach for evaluating the consequences of a candidate plan.

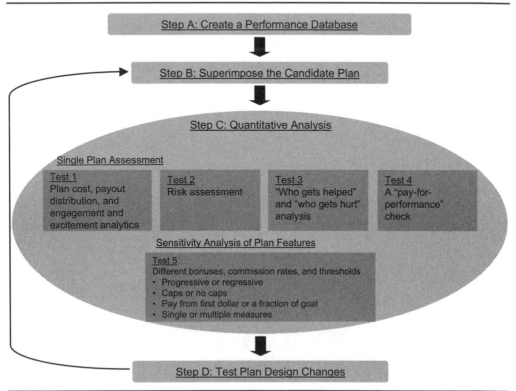

Figure 8-6. MRG sales and goal attainment distribution for the last 12 months.

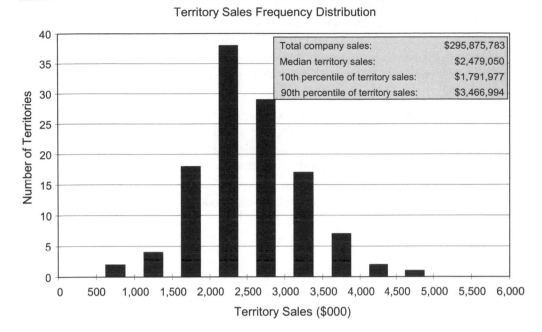

Territory Sales Frequency Distribution

Total company sales:	$295,875,783
Median territory sales:	$2,479,050
10th percentile of territory sales:	$1,791,977
90th percentile of territory sales:	$3,466,994

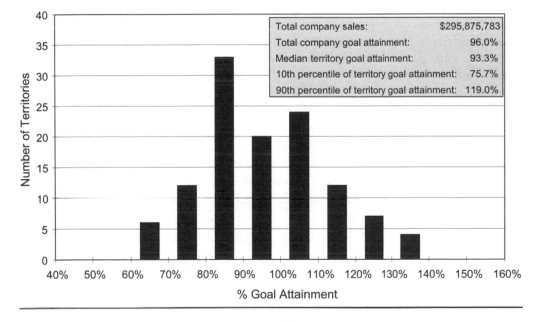

Goal Attainment Frequency Distribution

Total company sales:	$295,875,783
Total company goal attainment:	96.0%
Median territory goal attainment:	93.3%
10th percentile of territory goal attainment:	75.7%
90th percentile of territory goal attainment:	119.0%

distribution is demonstrated later, within the battery of risk assessment analyses in Test 2.

Figure 8-7 shows an estimated distribution for MRG for next year, assuming that the last 12 months of sales and goal attainment are representative of what can be expected for next year. Notice that the sales are shifted up because company management expects a 10 percent sales increase over last year.

Step B: Superimpose the Candidate Plan. Figure 8-8 shows how the payout curves for the MRG incumbent plan and the MRG candidate plan can be superimposed upon the projected performance distribution. The distribution graph shows how many salespeople are expected to be at various performance levels, and the payout curves show what payout those salespeople can expect to receive if either the incumbent plan or the candidate plan is used next year. The payout distribution assumes that next year's company goal of 10 percent growth is attained.

Step C: Quantitative Analysis. The quantitative analysis is made up of five different tests. An incentive design team can conduct some or all of these tests, depending upon its needs and the objectives of the incentive plan. Tests 1, 2, 3, and 4 are an assessment of a single plan design, while Test 5 involves analyzing the sensitivity of the assessment to changes in plan design features.

Test 1: Plan Cost, Payout Distribution, and Engagement and Excitement Analytics. A good place to start a quantitative analysis is by calculating and evaluating the expected plan payout and the distribution of that payout across members of the sales force. By combining the performance distribution, which projects how much each member of the sales force will sell next year, with the payout curves, it is possible to calculate the total cost of each plan and estimate how incentive pay will be distributed across the sales force. Figures 8-9 and 8-10 provide these forecasts for the MRG incumbent and candidate plans. Summary statistics for each distribution are compared side by side in Figure 8-11.

The distributions and statistics help the incentive design team address some important questions about the candidate plan's consequences for salespeople and company results. For example:

- Are plan costs within budget and in line with projected sales?

- Does the plan pay enough? Are individual earnings consistent with historical company norms and competitive with going labor market rates?

- Is the income distribution across the sales force consistent with company and industry norms?

- Is the income distribution well aligned with sales force performance? For example, with the MRG candidate plan, the highest-paid salespeople

Figure 8-7. Projection for sales and goal attainment at MRG based on the last 12 months' performance history and a projected 10 percent growth goal for next year.

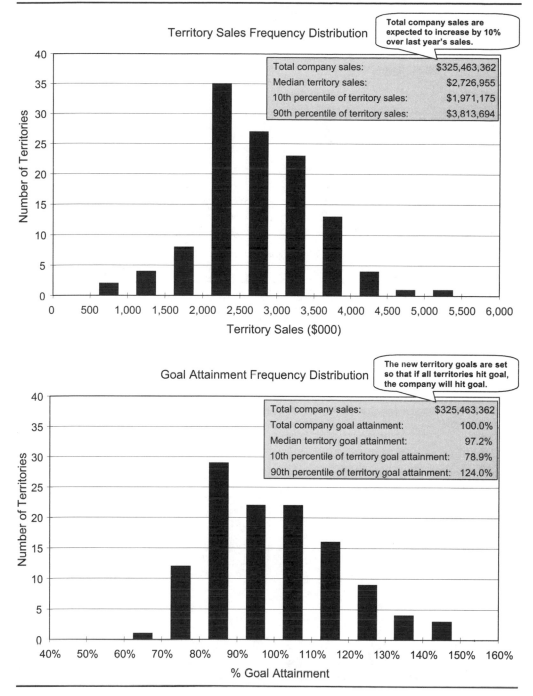

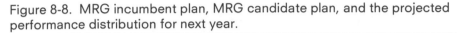

Figure 8-8. MRG incumbent plan, MRG candidate plan, and the projected performance distribution for next year.

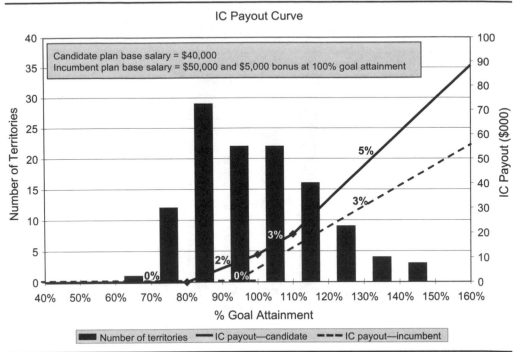

Figure 8-9. MRG incumbent plan cost and payout distribution forecasts for next year.

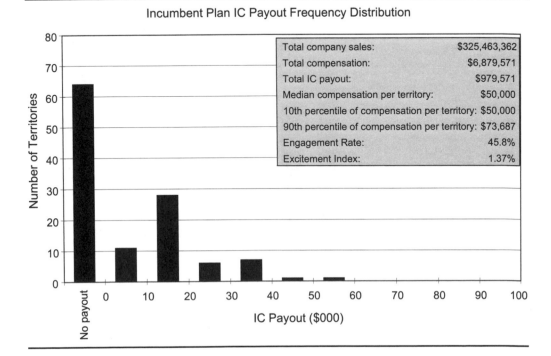

Figure 8-10. MRG candidate plan cost and payout distribution forecasts for next year.

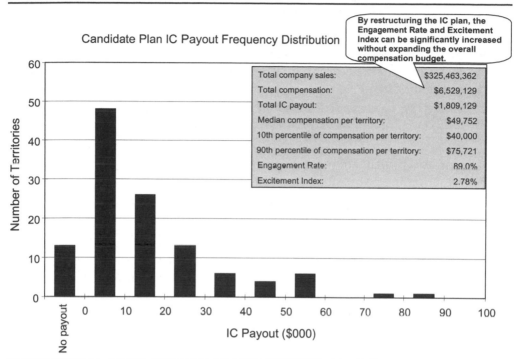

Figure 8-11. Side-by-side statistical comparison of the MRG incumbent and candidate sales incentive plans.

Statistic	Incumbent Plan	Candidate Plan
Total compensation	$6,879,571	$6,529,129
Total IC payout	$979,571	$1,809,129
Total IC payout % of total comp	14%	28%
Median compensation	$50,000	$49,752
10th percentile	$50,000	$40,000
90th percentile	$73,687	$75,721
Engagement Rate	46%	89%
Excitement Rate	1.37%	2.78%

(90th percentile) earn about 52 percent more than the median income, and the lowest-paid salespeople (10th percentile) earn about 80 percent of the median. These pay differences should reflect the value that salespeople contribute to the company.

- Will top performers earn enough money? Every company likes its highest-performing salespeople to be competitive with high performers elsewhere in the industry.

- Is the incentive plan a profit-sharing plan or a performance-rewarding plan? A profit-sharing plan has a tight distribution of incentive payout—everyone earns about the same amount of money. In a performance-rewarding plan, the distribution of payout is usually wider and reflects variation in performance across salespeople.

- Will the incentive plan engagement and excitement have the desired impact on sales force motivation?

Some interesting observations can be made by comparing the payout distribution and summary statistics for the MRG incumbent and candidate plans.

- The median income for both the incumbent and candidate plans is roughly the same, although it is slightly lower for the candidate plan.

- The incentive component of the pay mix has increased from 14 percent in the incumbent plan to 28 percent in the candidate plan. The increased variable component is consistent with what the incentive design team was trying to accomplish.

- The Engagement Rate has increased from 46 percent in the incumbent plan to 89 percent in the candidate plan. This increased engagement is also consistent with what the incentive design team wanted to accomplish.

- The candidate plan has considerably higher engagement and excitement, yet total compensation costs are actually lower with the candidate plan than with the incumbent plan.

- The candidate plan pays high performers more and low performers less than the incumbent plan.

These effects are the result of the combined impact of several features of the candidate plan:

- A reduction in salary
- A lowering of the percent of goal attained at which payout begins
- An acceleration of payout at higher levels of quota achievement

Note that all the calculations in this test assume that the company's sales goals are met. This assumption is changed later in the analyses in Test 2.

Industry Benchmarking

There are many surveys available that allow companies to benchmark their pay levels and pay mix against other companies in their industry or against other industries from which they want to recruit salespeople. See Chapter 4 (Figure 4-6) for a partial listing of organizations that provide pay benchmarking data. Benchmarking information can also be obtained through exit interviews and discussions with candidates who are given job offers. An external benchmark becomes more important if the level or mix of pay in a candidate plan is very different from what the company currently offers its salespeople.

It is interesting to note that when it comes to the sales force, every company we have worked with tries to be at or above the average pay level for its benchmark of peers. How is this possible? We have observed that companies select their peer group of companies to create a benchmark to which their target pay level compares favorably.

The MRG example shows how plan cost, payout distribution, and engagement and excitement can be projected for a plan that uses a single measure as a determinant of incentive pay—in this case, percent of quota achievement. These statistics can also be calculated for more complex incentive plans, including plans in which multiple measures are used. With multiple-measure plans, Engagement Rate and Excitement Index statistics can sometimes be calculated for each measure to further enrich the analysis. For example, Figure 8-12 shows a plan cost, payout distribution, and engagement and excitement analysis for a firm that is comparing two alternative plans with payout curves that vary by product line. The top half of the figure summarizes the two plan alternatives. Alternative 1 ties incentive payout to goal attainment for three independent product lines. Alternative 2 is tied to goal attainment as well, but two of the goals are aggregated—the Series A and X goals are combined, and there is a goal on total sales across all three product lines. The bottom half of the figure shows some predicted plan statistics. The Engagement Rate is projected by product line to help the incentive plan designers assess the extent to which balanced selling across product lines is encouraged by each of the two plans.

Test 2: Risk Assessment. This test involves assessing the financial risk to the company and the sales force associated with an unexpected change in the environment that affects sales force performance. The projections in Test 1 assume that the company goal will be obtained precisely. This is a gallant assumption. It is important to assess the payout risk associated with company performance that is either above or below the company's stated sales goal. In Figure 8-13, sensitivity analysis is used to examine the impact of a change in company sales on the incentive payout for the MRG incumbent and candidate plans.

Some key observations from the analysis include the following:

Figure 8-12. Side-by-side statistical comparison of two plan alternatives with multiple measures.

Alternative 1

	Products		
	Series A	Series X	Supplies
% objective threshold	80%	80%	80%
Pay per % point from threshold to 100%	$50	$100	$125
Pay per % over 100%	$150	$250	$300

Assuming All Products at 100% of Goal

Average incentive	$10,319
80th percentile	$18,900
Median	$7,550
20th percentile	$1,870
Engagement Rate	91%
Series A engagement	64%
Series X engagement	80%
Supplies engagement	85%

Alternative 2

	Products		
	Series A + X	Supplies	Total Sales
% objective threshold	80%	80%	85%
Pay per % point from threshold to 100%	$200	$125	$150
Pay per % over 100%	$200	$200	$200

Assuming All Products at 100% of Goal

Average incentive	$10,731
80th percentile	$18,930
Median	$8,975
20th percentile	$1,870
Engagement Rate	89%
Series A engagement	81%
Series X engagement	81%
Supplies engagement	87%

Figure 8-13. Risk analysis for the MRG incumbent and candidate plans—what if national goal attainment varies from expectation?

Sensitivity Analysis for Incumbent Plan

% of Company Sales Goal Achieved	Total Company Sales	Total Compensation	Total IC Payout	Median Territory Compensation	10th Percentile of Territory Compensation	90th Percentile of Territory Compensation	Engagement Rate	Excitement Index
90%	$292,917,026	$6,321,693	$421,693	$50,000	$50,000	$64,569	24.6%	0.74%
95%	$309,190,194	$6,597,101	$697,101	$50,000	$50,000	$69,321	39.0%	1.17%
100%	$325,463,362	$6,879,571	$979,571	$50,000	$50,000	$73,687	45.8%	1.37%
105%	$341,736,530	$7,226,380	$1,326,380	$56,360	$50,000	$78,053	56.8%	1.70%
110%	$358,009,698	$7,588,110	$1,688,110	$60,660	$50,000	$83,606	63.6%	1.91%

Sensitivity Analysis for Candidate Plan

% of Company Sales Goal Achieved	Total Company Sales	Total Compensation	Total IC Payout	Median Territory Compensation	10th Percentile of Territory Compensation	90th Percentile of Territory Compensation	Engagement Rate	Excitement Index
90%	$292,917,026	$5,674,747	$954,747	$44,203	$40,000	$61,135	67.8%	1.84%
95%	$309,190,194	$6,064,640	$1,344,640	$47,030	$40,000	$68,444	82.2%	2.41%
100%	$325,463,362	$6,529,129	$1,809,129	$49,752	$40,000	$75,721	89.0%	2.78%
105%	$341,736,530	$7,059,530	$2,339,530	$53,088	$41,699	$84,602	94.4%	3.21%
110%	$358,009,698	$7,639,509	$2,919,509	$57,231	$43,760	$94,333	95.8%	3.47%

- The candidate plan pays high performers more than the incumbent plan when the company makes or exceeds goal. However, when company goal attainment is poor, high performers make less with the candidate plan than with the incumbent plan. This is due to the reduction in salary. Low performers make less with the candidate plan and more with the incumbent plan at all levels of company goal attainment.

- The Engagement Rate and Excitement Index of the candidate plan is much higher than those of the incumbent plan at all levels of company performance.

- Both total compensation and total IC payout are more sensitive to changes in total company sales with the candidate plan than with the incumbent plan. Much of the stability of the incumbent plan is due to the high percentage of salary.

- Total compensation is higher with the candidate plan only at high levels of company goal achievement.

Figure 8-14 illustrates an analogous sensitivity analysis for a plan with multiple measures.

The projections in Test 1 also assume that the performance distribution across the sales force will be the same this year as it was last year. This is not always an accurate assumption. It is important to assess the payout risk associated with a sales force performance distribution that is different from last year's distribution. In Figure 8-15, sensitivity analysis is used to examine the impact on the incentive payout for the MRG incumbent and candidate plans if the performance distribution is either tighter or more spread out than last year's distribution. The scenarios vary the standard deviation of performance variability; the 50 and 75 percent scenarios have less variability and therefore a tighter performance distribution than last year, while the 125 and 150 percent scenarios have greater variability and therefore a wider performance distribution than last year.

Some key observations from the analysis include the following:

- The impact of a 25 percent shift in the standard deviation of performance variability (Figure 8-15) is relatively minor compared to the impact of a 10 percent shift in overall company performance (Figure 8-13).

- Increased variability in performance causes the range in payout between high performers and low performers to widen—the low performers get paid even less, and the high performers get paid even more. The gap is greater with the candidate plan than it is with the incumbent plan.

- The Engagement Rate and Excitement Index of the candidate plan are much higher than those of the incumbent plan at all levels of performance variation.

By evaluating different scenarios for sales force performance, the incentive design team gains a better understanding of possible incentive plan consequences

Figure 8-14. Sensitivity analysis of plan alternatives with multiple measures.

Alternative 1

	Products		
	Series A	Series X	Supplies
% objective threshold	80%	80%	80%
Pay/% threshold to 100%	$50	$100	$125
Pay/% over 100%	$150	$250	$300

	Assuming All Products at 100% of Goal
Average incentive	$10,319
80th percentile	$18,900
Median	$7,550
20th percentile	$1,870
Engagement Rate	91%
Series A engagement	64%
Series X engagement	80%
Supplies engagement	85%

Alternative 2

	Products		
	Series A + X	Supplies	Total Sales
% objective threshold	80%	80%	85%
Pay/% threshold to 100%	$200	$125	$150
Pay/% over 100%	$200	$200	$200

Average incentive	$10,731
80th percentile	$18,930
Median	$8,975
20th percentile	$1,870
Engagement Rate	89%
Series A engagement	81%
Series X engagement	81%
Supplies engagement	87%

(continues)

Figure 8-14. Continued.

Assuming All Products at 95% of Goal

Average incentive	$7,962	$8,459
80th percentile	$15,095	$15,550
Median	$5,475	$6,438
20th percentile	$995	$975
Engagement Rate	89%	87%
Series A engagement	60%	74%
Series X engagement	75%	74%
Supplies engagement	81%	83%

Assuming All Products at 105% of Goal

Average incentive	$12,921	$13,195
80th percentile	$22,710	$22,270
Median	$10,150	$11,825
20th percentile	$2,800	$3,520
Engagement Rate	94%	92%
Series A engagement	66%	85%
Series X engagement	86%	85%
Supplies engagement	91%	92%

Figure 8-15. Risk analysis for the MRG incumbent and candidate plans—what if this year's performance distribution varies from last year's?

Sensitivity Analysis for Incumbent Plan

% of Base Case Performance Variability	Total Company Sales	Total Compensation	Total IC Payout	Median Territory Compensation	10th Percentile of Territory Compensation	90th Percentile of Territory Compensation	Engagement Rate	Excitement Index
50%	$325,238,305	$6,521,650	$621,650	$50,000	$50,000	$64,296	45.8%	1.37%
75%	$325,350,833	$6,700,610	$800,610	$50,000	$50,000	$68,992	45.8%	1.37%
100%	$325,463,362	$6,879,571	$979,571	$50,000	$50,000	$73,687	45.8%	1.37%
125%	$325,575,890	$7,058,531	$1,158,531	$50,000	$50,000	$78,383	45.8%	1.37%
150%	$325,688,418	$7,237,492	$1,337,492	$50,000	$50,000	$83,078	45.8%	1.37%

Sensitivity Analysis for Candidate Plan

% of Base Case Performance Variability	Total Company Sales	Total Compensation	Total IC Payout	Median Territory Compensation	10th Percentile of Territory Compensation	90th Percentile of Territory Compensation	Engagement Rate	Excitement Index
50%	$325,238,305	$6,181,820	$1,461,820	$50,462	$44,634	$62,385	100.0%	2.73%
75%	$325,350,833	$6,331,314	$1,611,314	$50,191	$42,278	$67,895	94.9%	2.76%
100%	$325,463,362	$6,529,129	$1,809,129	$49,752	$40,000	$75,721	89.0%	2.78%
125%	$325,575,890	$6,754,029	$2,034,029	$49,419	$40,000	$83,547	83.1%	2.76%
150%	$325,688,418	$6,999,864	$2,279,864	$49,053	$40,000	$91,373	76.3%	2.71%

and can therefore build the needed flexibility into the plan. A thorough risk analysis helps to ensure that a plan will motivate the sales force and reward salespeople fairly under a range of different future performance outcomes.

Test 3: "Who Gets Helped" and "Who Gets Hurt" Analysis. A person-by-person analysis of the impact of a candidate incentive plan shows which salespeople will be helped and which will be hurt by a new plan. This helps the design team assess the attractiveness of the plan to various constituencies within the sales force and the ease of sales force acceptance, as well as the fairness of the plan and the extent to which the plan pays for performance. It is useful to compare the amount of pay that each salesperson received last year with the incumbent plan to the projected amount that that salesperson will receive next year if the candidate plan is implemented. This analysis of "who gets helped" and "who gets hurt" by a candidate plan provides insight about how challenging the new plan will be to implement. Selling organizations like to either keep salespeople "whole" or ensure that the redistribution of income resulting from a plan change matches income to performance. "Salespeople should not lose income because we change our incentive compensation plan," says one national sales manager. The vice president of sales adds, "Certainly, high performers should make as much or more under the new plan."

Figure 8-16 shows how total income might change for individual salespeople if the candidate plan is implemented at MRG. The graph plots last year's income with the incumbent plan versus the projected income for next year if the candidate plan is adopted for each salesperson. There is a cluster of salespeople who earned in the $60,000 range last year with the incumbent plan whose income is likely to be less if the candidate plan is adopted. Even though the salespeople in this group are average or slightly below average performers, it is a sufficiently large group for MRG sales leaders not to want to alienate it. The design team is also concerned that the median income with the candidate plan is somewhat lower than with the incumbent plan.

Figure 8-17 illustrates another way to display who gets helped/who gets hurt information. It shows the projected income difference between next year's income with a candidate plan and last year's income with the incumbent plan for a consumer packaged goods company.

Who gets helped/who gets hurt analysis is particularly important during plan structure changes. For example, when switching from a commission plan that pays from the first dollar sold to a goal-based plan that pays from a threshold percentage of goal attainment, territories with high sales but low goal attainment will lose earnings to territories with low sales but high goal attainment. In such cases, it is useful to identify the individual salespeople who are likely to be affected so that a transition strategy can be developed.

Good candidate compensation plans are not inadvertently biased against important constituencies within the sales force. Whenever there is a significant correlation between incentive payout and an independent territory variable that does not reflect a salesperson's effort or skill, there is a possible incentive plan (or goal-

Figure 8-16. Who gets helped and who gets hurt analysis for MRG.

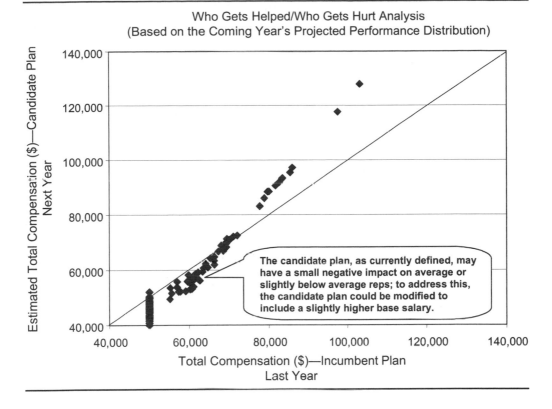

Figure 8-17. An individual impact analysis for a consumer packaged goods company.

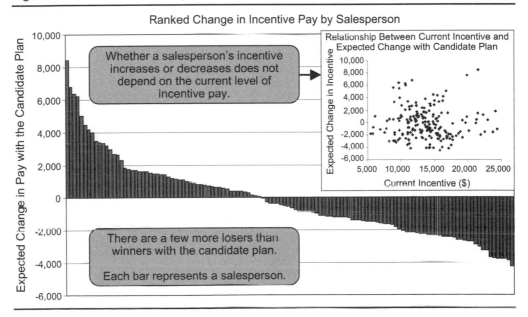

setting) problem. Analyses like this have been used to reveal incentive plan biases based on variables such as territory size, geographic region, served market segments, market potential, past sales level, market share, and quota increase. Examples of some bias tests are provided in Chapter 2.

Test 4: A "Pay-for-Performance" Check. This test checks to see how long-term predictors of salesperson success are aligned with the short-term rewards in the incentive plan. It is particularly important to ensure that a new incentive plan is not biased against salespeople with strong long-term potential. One effective way to identify salespeople who are expected to be long-term high performers is to use performance ratings from the sales force performance evaluation system. Figure 8-18 plots recent performance rank percentiles (based on the performance evaluation system for MRG salespeople) against the projected earnings for each salesperson with the candidate plan. The performance rank percentile considers long-term success measures such as product and market knowledge, selling skills, relationship management, and mentoring, in addition to sales results. By studying the relationship between the performance ratings and the projected payout, the company gains insight into the extent to which the firm's high performers will be rewarded by the candidate compensation plan. Salespeople in the "overpaid" quadrant are projected to receive above-average earnings despite below-average performance ratings. Similarly, salespeople in the "underpaid" quadrant are projected to receive below-average earnings despite above-average performance ratings. Having a large number of salespeople in these quadrants is often an indi-

Figure 8-18. A "pay-for-performance" check for MRG.

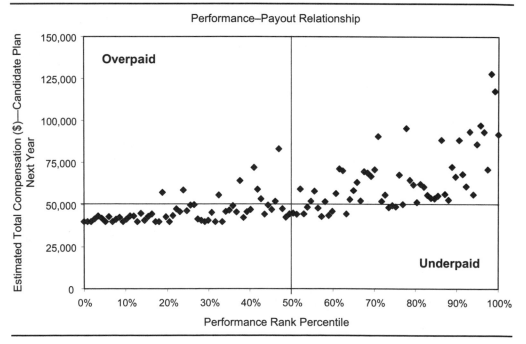

cation that there is a problem with a candidate plan, since the plan is not consistently rewarding the salespeople that the firm hopes to keep.

Test 5: Sensitivity Analysis of Plan Features. Incentive compensation designers usually lock on to a plan structure early in the design process. Through testing, they fine-tune the specific plan elements. By doing a sensitivity analysis of plan features such as the specific measures used, the percent of goal at which payouts begin, bonuses and commission rates, and caps, plan elements can be improved. Sensitivity analysis can be used to examine the impact of specific changes in plan design on expected plan costs, payout distribution, and sales force engagement and excitement.

Figures 8-19 and 8-20 show how sensitive various plan performance statistics are to changes in plan design parameters for MRG.

Step D: Test Plan Design Changes. The quantitative assessment process sometimes reveals problems with a candidate incentive plan that can be addressed by revising the plan design. When this happens, a revised candidate plan is proposed, and the quantitative testing process begins again.

The incentive design team at MRG concludes that 80 percent is a good place to begin the incentive payout and that the steepness of the payout curve in the original candidate plan is appropriate. However, the design team is concerned because the person-by-person analysis of the candidate plan reveals that a large number of average or slightly below average performers will receive less income with the candidate plan. The design team does not want to create a morale crisis by angering this large and important group of salespeople. (In some instances, plan changes are designed to reduce the income of this very group.) Hence, the team develops a revised candidate plan that includes a salary increase from $40,000 to $42,500. Then it repeats several of the quantitative analyses described in Step C for the revised candidate plan. Figure 8-21 shows the results of Test 1 (payout distribution and statistics) for the MRG revised candidate plan. Summary statistics are compared side by side with statistics for the incumbent plan and the original candidate plan in Figure 8-22. Figure 8-23 shows the results of Test 3 (who gets helped and who gets hurt) for the revised candidate plan.

Some key observations from the analysis include the following:

- The revised candidate plan raises the median income above that of the incumbent plan.

- The revised candidate plan protects the large group of average to slightly below average salespeople, thus enhancing the new plan in the eyes of the sales force.

- The total cost of the revised candidate plan is slightly more than that of the original candidate plan, but still less than that of the incumbent plan. The incentive design team feels that this cost increase in the revised plan

Figure 8-19. Sensitivity of plan performance statistics to changes in the goal attainment level at which the payout begins.

| Statistic | Goal Attainment Level at Which Payout Begins | | | | |
	70%	75%	80% (Candidate Plan)	85%	90%
Total compensation	$7,136,202	$6,824,480	$6,529,129	$6,251,680	$6,013,622
Total IC payout	$2,416,202	$2,104,480	$1,809,129	$1,531,680	$1,293,622
Total IC payout % of total comp	34%	31%	28%	25%	22%
Median compensation	$55,734	$52,602	$49,752	$46,953	$43,988
10th percentile	$44,707	$42,182	$40,000	$40,000	$40,000
90th percentile	$81,528	$78,200	$75,721	$73,433	$71,145
Engagement Rate	99.2%	94.1%	89.0%	81.4%	64.4%
Excitement Index	2.98%	2.88%	2.78%	2.63%	2.29%

Figure 8-20. Sensitivity of plan performance statistics to changes in payout curve steepness.

Statistic	Steepness of the Payout Curve*		
	2%–3%–4% (Flatter Curve)	2%–3%–5% (Candidate Plan)	1%–4%–6% (Steeper Curve)
Total compensation	$6,417,292	$6,529,129	$6,327,711
Total IC payout	$1,697,292	$1,809,129	$1,607,711
Total IC payout % of total comp	26%	28%	25%
Median compensation	$49,752	$49,752	$44,912
10th percentile	$40,000	$40,000	$40,000
90th percentile	$72,557	$75,721	$77,375
Engagement Rate	89.0%	89.0%	89.0%
Excitement Index	2.51%	2.78%	2.81%

*The three percentages for each payout curve option are the commission rate for three levels of goal attainment: 80–99% attainment, 100–109% attainment, and 110% or higher attainment.

Figure 8-21. MRG revised candidate plan cost and payout distribution forecasts for next year.

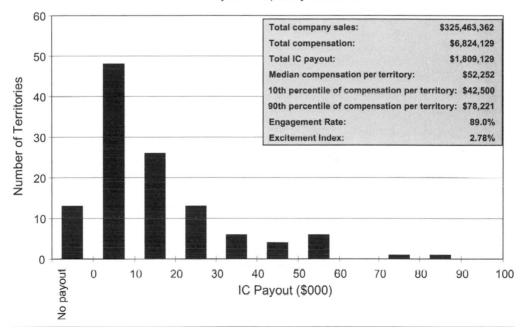

IC Payout Frequency Distribution

Total company sales:	$325,463,362
Total compensation:	$6,824,129
Total IC payout:	$1,809,129
Median compensation per territory:	$52,252
10th percentile of compensation per territory:	$42,500
90th percentile of compensation per territory:	$78,221
Engagement Rate:	89.0%
Excitement Index:	2.78%

Figure 8-22. Side-by-side statistical comparison of the MRG incumbent, candidate, and revised candidate sales incentive plans.

Statistic	Incumbent Plan	Candidate Plan	Revised Candidate Plan
Total compensation	$6,879,571	$6,529,129	$6,824,129
Total IC payout	$979,571	$1,809,129	$1,809,129
Total IC payout % of total comp	14%	28%	27%
Median compensation	$50,000	$49,752	$52,252
10th percentile	$50,000	$40,000	$42,500
90th percentile	$73,687	$75,721	$78,221
Engagement Rate	46%	89%	89%
Excitement Rate	1.37%	2.78%	2.78%

Figure 8-23. A "who gets helped"/"who gets hurt" analysis for the MRG revised candidate plan with a base salary of $42,500.

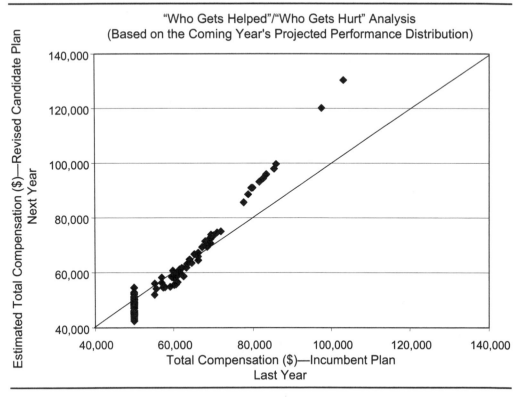

is likely to be self-funding through higher sales force morale and increased motivation.

The incentive design team presents the revised candidate plan to the sales leadership team. The vice president of sales is concerned that the plan involves a salary reduction averaging $7,500 per salesperson and feels that this reduction will be difficult for the sales force to accept. He asks to see what the costs of the new plan would be if the current salary level of $50,000 were maintained. The incentive design team runs some additional scenarios with a $50,000 salary and three different incentive payout curve options. The results of the analysis appear in Figure 8-24. The CFO and the vice president of sales are scheduled to meet the next day to decide on a plan. What do you think they will decide?

Qualitative Assessment of a Candidate Sales Compensation Plan

Qualitative assessment of a candidate compensation plan adds texture to the rigor of quantitative approaches. Qualitative assessment helps plan designers evaluate a candidate plan across all the components of the 3 Cs framework: consequences for salespeople, sales force activities, customer results, and company results; consistency with company sales and marketing strategies; and compatibility with other sales force effectiveness drivers.

Qualitative Assessment of Consequences

Qualitative assessment helps sales leaders understand the consequences of a candidate sales compensation plan for salespeople, sales force activities, customer results, and company results.

Consequences for Salespeople. Test 6: Qualitative Questions for Assessing Salespeople Consequences. By debating a number of qualitative questions, sales leaders can gain perspective on how salespeople will react to a candidate sales compensation plan. Figure 8-25 provides some examples of the types of questions that can be asked.

Test 7: Sales Force Input. It is often useful to engage the sales force in the incentive plan design process. As described in Chapter 2, asking the sales force what it likes and dislikes about the current sales compensation plan can provide valuable input for the design of a new plan. In addition, salespeople's opinion of candidate plans can shed light on issues that may easily be overlooked by an incentive design team, which relies primarily on graphs and numbers in its decision process. Sales force input often helps sales leaders anticipate important issues that may arise when the

Figure 8-24. Side-by-side comparison of the MRG incumbent plan, the revised candidate plan, and three scenarios where the current salary level is maintained.

Statistic	Incumbent Plan	Revised Candidate Plan	Steepness of the Payout Curve ($50,000 Salary)*		
			1%–3%–5%	2%–3%–4%	1%–4%–6%
Total compensation	$6,879,571	$6,824,129	$7,271,187	$7,597,292	$7,507,711
Total IC payout	$979,571	$1,809,129	$1,371,187	$1,697,292	$1,607,711
Total IC payout % of total comp	14%	27%	19%	22%	21%
Median compensation	$50,000	$52,252	$54,880	$59,752	$54,912
10th percentile	$50,000	$42,500	$50,000	$50,000	$50,000
90th percentile	$73,687	$78,221	$81,145	$82,557	$87,375
Engagement Rate	46.0%	89.0%	89.0%	89.0%	89.0%
Excitement Index	1.37%	2.78%	2.35%	2.51%	2.81%

*The three percentages for each payout curve option are the commission rate for three levels of goal attainment: 80–99% attainment, 100–109% attainment, and 110% or higher attainment.

Figure 8-25. Sample questions for evaluating the consequences of a candidate sales incentive plan for salespeople.

- Will the sales force think that the incentive plan is competitive?
- Will the plan be perceived as fair?
- Does the plan provide rewards commensurate with activity and results?
- Will the new plan affect the firm's retention rate of salespeople who are expected to be long-term high performers?
- Will the new plan induce adequate turnover of nonperformers?
- Will the new plan help the firm be successful at attracting top candidates?
- Will the new plan motivate the sales force to accomplish important goals?

new plan is communicated to the entire sales force, allowing time to formulate appropriate responses and to develop an effective communication program. The meaning of sales force input should always be interpreted with caution, since salespeople may selectively share opinions that they believe will benefit them personally. For this reason, sales force qualitative input should be used as a supplement to and not a substitute for input obtained from other, more analytical and unbiased sources.

Companies can use several methods to gather sales force input about candidate incentive plans, including one-on-one interviews and focus groups with selected salespeople and sales managers. Some sample questions to be asked during these sessions are listed in Figure 8-26.

Figure 8-27 summarizes the responses that one company gathered from its sales force through field interviews and focus groups. This field input not only influenced the company's choice of plan, but also helped to demonstrate to the rest of the sales force that salespeople's opinions were important in the plan design process.

Another, more innovative, approach to gathering sales force opinions uses a

Figure 8-26. Sample questions for salespeople.

- Do you think the incentive plan is competitive?
- Do you think the incentive plan is fair?
- Does the plan make sense?
- Which aspects of the plan are difficult to understand or seem too complex?
- What do you see as the positive and negative features of this plan?
- What concerns do you have about the plan?
- Which features do you like or dislike?
- What is the best way to sell this plan to the rest of the sales force?

Figure 8-27. Summary of comments made during field interviews and focus groups to discuss proposed sales incentive plans.

- General
  - "Plans presented are fair."
  - "Thank you for developing what look like fair and reasonable plans."
  - "I do not agree that I will work harder depending upon which plan is in place: I always do my best!"
  - "Money, while an incentive, is not my primary motivation for increased performance."
- Caps
  - "None of the plans should have caps because it lowers the incentive to move from one performance level to the next."
  - "Show me a noncapped plan, and I'll show you what I can do."
  - "Corporations tend to set targets way out of reach, but will always say the carrot is open-ended."
- Goal Setting
  - "Reliance on goals as a basis for all plans is problematic."
  - "It doesn't matter what plan is picked as long as the goals are set fairly for each rep."
  - "Goal needs to be perceived as attainable."
  - "Just make the goal and budget attainable and fair."

survey, such as the IC Choice Survey in Figure 8-28, to assess the sales force's preference for different incentive plan features. The survey presents salespeople with a choice of incentive plans and asks salespeople to rank-order the various options. In the Figure 8-28 survey, the first choice (Plan A) is the current incentive plan, and the seven additional choices (Plans B through H) are candidate plans with varying pay mixes and commission structures. For example, Plan E is entirely variable pay (no salary) and has the highest total compensation opportunity at high levels of sales but the lowest opportunity at low sales levels. Plan H is entirely salary with no variable pay opportunity; pay is the same regardless of how much a salesperson sells. Plans E, F, and G pay a constant commission rate, while Plans A, B, C, and D pay an accelerating rate as the sales level increases. Plan C pays a higher commission rate than Plans A, B, and D, but commissions are paid only on sales beyond goal. The aggregate ranking across the entire sales force reveals the sales force's risk tolerance and preference for the various plan features. These preferences can then be incorporated into the incentive plan design. Plans that have high preference are more likely to be motivational.

Results from surveys like this reveal a fairly universal and important result: *There is a wide range of preferences within every sales force.* No one plan will be preferred by everyone (unless, of course, there is a clearly dominant plan that gives large sums of money to the sales force in return for very little work). Figure 8-29 provides a set of histograms representing the number of first, second, third, and so forth votes that each plan option in Figure 8-28 received from the 37 sales-

Figure 8-28. An example of an IC Choice Survey.

☐ IC Choice Survey

Please rank-order the following 8 alternative plans. (Note that Plan A is your current plan.)

Plan	Base Salary		Sales Level[1] 0–200K	Sales Level[1] 200–400K	Sales Level[1] 400–600K	Sales Level[1] 600–800K	Sales Level[1] 800–1,000K	Sales Level[2] +1,000K	Your Rank
A (Current)	$40,000	Commission rate	3.0%	4.0%	5.0%	6.0%	7.0%	8.0%	
		Total comp	$46,000	$54,000	$64,000	$76,000	$90,000	$106,000	
B	$48,000	Commission rate	3.8%	3.8%	3.8%	4.0%	4.0%	4.0%	
		Total comp	$55,600	$63,200	$70,800	$78,800	$86,800	$94,800	
C	$48,000	Commission rate	0.0%	0.0%	0.0%	7.0%	8.0%	9.0%	
		Total comp	$48,000	$48,000	$48,000	$62,000	$78,000	$96,000	
D	$48,000	Commission rate	3.0%	3.5%	4.0%	5.0%	6.0%	6.0%	
		Total comp	$54,000	$61,000	$69,000	$79,000	$91,000	$103,000	
E	$0	Commission rate	9.0%	9.0%	9.0%	9.0%	9.0%	9.0%	
		Total comp	$18,000	$36,000	$54,000	$72,000	$90,000	$108,000	
F	$30,000	Commission rate	6.3%	6.3%	6.3%	6.3%	6.3%	6.3%	
		Total comp	$42,600	$55,200	$67,800	$80,400	$93,000	$105,600	
G	$40,000	Commission rate	5.0%	5.0%	5.0%	5.0%	5.0%	5.0%	
		Total comp	$50,000	$60,000	$70,000	$80,000	$90,000	$100,000	
H	$74,822	Commission rate	0.0%	0.0%	0.0%	0.0%	0.0%	0.0%	
		Total comp	$74,822	$74,822	$74,822	$74,822	$74,822	$74,822	

[1] Total comp calculation is computed at the maximum sales level for the indicated range.

[2] Total comp calculation for the $1,000K+ level is computed at $1,200,000.

Figure 8-29. Sales force preferences for the eight incentive plan options in Figure 8-28 (bars indicate the number of salespeople out of 37 for each ordinal rank).

Preference Measurement—Individual Plan Preference Rankings

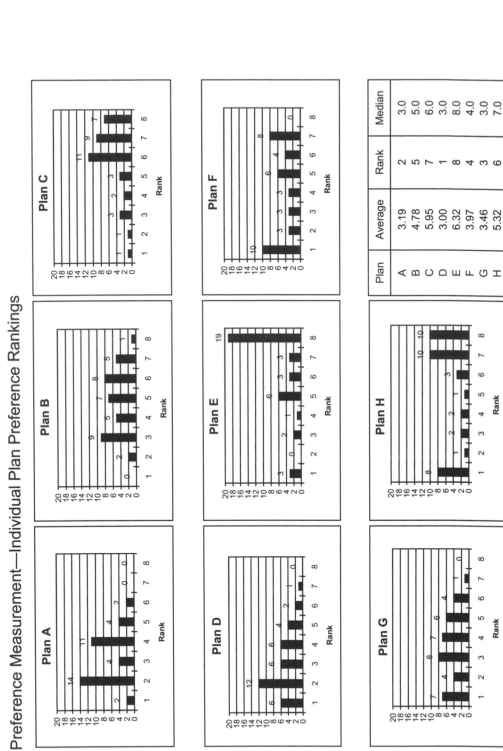

Plan	Average	Rank	Median
A	3.19	2	3.0
B	4.78	5	5.0
C	5.95	7	6.0
D	3.00	1	3.0
E	6.32	8	8.0
F	3.97	4	4.0
G	3.46	3	3.0
H	5.32	6	7.0

people who answered the survey. For example, Plan A (the current plan) received 2 first-place votes, 14 second-place votes, 4 third-place votes, and so forth. Plans that many responders ranked near the top (i.e., those with bars that are highest on the left-hand side of the graph) dominate plans that many responders ranked near the bottom (i.e., those with bars that are highest on the right-hand side of the graph). The table in the bottom right corner provides summary statistics for the eight plans. The sales force has the highest preference for Plan D.

Incentive plan designers must accept the fact that their plan will not be universally liked by everyone. It is especially important to consider the preferences of the better-performing salespeople in the organization. For example, Figure 8-30 shows the preferences of 18 of the 37 salespeople from the Figure 8-28 survey whom management considers to be high performers. Note that the current plan (Plan A) has the highest preference among the high performers, while Plan D has the highest preference among all performers.

Consequences for Sales Force Activities. *Test 8: Qualitative Questions for Assessing Sales Force Activity Consequences.* Answers to several qualitative questions help sales leaders understand the sales force activity consequences of a candidate sales compensation plan. Figure 8-31 provides some examples of the types of questions that can be asked.

Test 9: Adverse Sales Force Behaviors Check. Experienced plan designers have come to the following realization: *A foolproof plan does not exist. Every plan has the potential to elicit some unwanted sales force behaviors.* Figure 8-32 presents a list of plan features and the unwanted behaviors that might result with these features. It is wise to anticipate the unwanted behaviors associated with a candidate plan and to think through how they can be managed. Every candidate plan needs an adverse sales force behavior check.

Consequences for Customer Results. *Test 10: Qualitative Questions for Assessing Customer Results Consequences.* A number of qualitative questions can be asked to help sales leaders anticipate the customer results consequences of a candidate sales compensation plan. Figure 8-33 provides some examples of the types of questions that can be asked.

Unwanted behaviors inspired by an incentive plan are particularly problematic when these behaviors adversely affect customer results. Inappropriate customer-focused activity needs to be managed, as it can seriously compromise long-term success. A quick check for unwanted customer-focused behaviors provides insight into the attractiveness of a candidate plan. Figure 8-34 provides a scorecard for comparing an incumbent plan and a candidate plan on the potential for encouraging adverse sales force behaviors that compromise customer results.

Adverse behaviors need to be managed. *"It is not all about incentives; it is also about management."*

Consequences for Company Results. *Test 11: Qualitative Questions for Assessing Company Results Consequences.* Quantitative analysis is usually the best way to

Figure 8-30. Preferences of the high performers for the eight incentive plan options in Figure 8-28 (bars indicate the number of salespeople out of 18 for each ordinal rank).

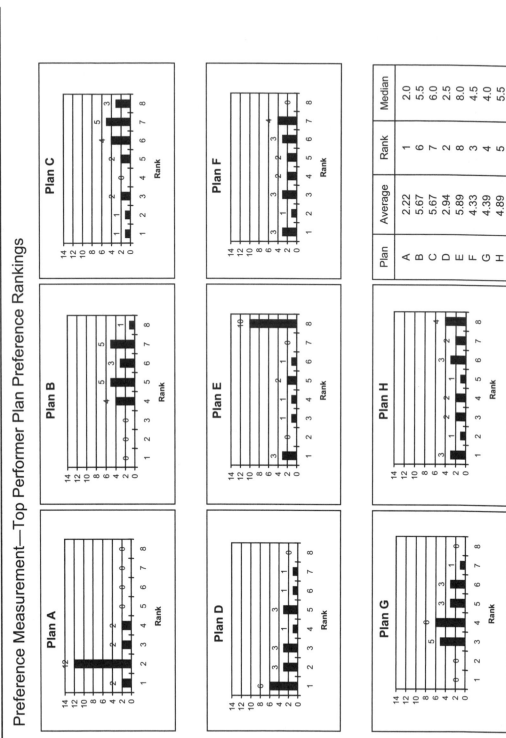

Preference Measurement—Top Performer Plan Preference Rankings

Plan	Average	Rank	Median
A	2.22	1	2.0
B	5.67	6	5.5
C	5.67	7	6.0
D	2.94	2	2.5
E	5.89	8	8.0
F	4.33	3	4.5
G	4.39	4	4.0
H	4.89	5	5.5

Figure 8-31. Sample questions for evaluating the sales force activity consequences of a candidate sales incentive plan.

* Will the plan inspire salespeople to work hard?
* Will salespeople allocate their time to the right products, customer segments, and selling activities?
* Will the sales force be confused by what is expected of them?
* Will too much time be spent with easy-to-sell-to customers (friends and family)?
* Will too much time be spent on nonessential activities?

Figure 8-32. Examples of unwanted sales force behaviors.

Incentive Feature	Unwanted Behavior
• Monthly objective with overachievement bonus	• Sell every other month
• Incentive based on customer satisfaction	• Seek satisfaction at the expense of seeking sales
• Paid on share	• Shrink territory
• Paid on sales	• Enlarge territory
• Team incentive	• Relax
• Caps	• Hoard sales
• Complex plan	• Ignore it
• Manager sets objectives or determines reward	• Work the manager, not the customers
• Very high incentive component	• Sell at all costs, invent applications
• Paid on units	• Discount

Figure 8-33. Sample questions for evaluating customer results consequences of a candidate sales incentive plan.

* How will the new plan affect sales force–customer relationships?
* Will salespeople be encouraged to engage in the activities that meet customer needs?
* Does the plan encourage any undesirable behaviors from the customer's perspective, such as overselling, ignoring customers, overlooking service, creating distrust, skipping steps of the selling process, or selling the wrong products?

Figure 8-34. A scorecard for evaluating incumbent and candidate plans on their potential for encouraging activities that can create unfavorable customer results.

Sales Force Behaviors That Create Undesired Customer Results	Likelihood of Behavior (Rating 1–5) 1 = Highly Unlikely; 5 = Highly Likely	
	Incumbent Plan	Candidate Plan
Overselling		
Ignoring the customer		
Overlooking servicing or other important steps of the sales process		
Creating distrust		
Selling products that do not meet customer needs		
Selling to the wrong customers		

assess company results consequences. However, a number of qualitative questions can also be debated to help sales leaders gain perspective on the company results consequences of a candidate sales compensation plan. Figure 8-35 provides some examples of the types of questions that can be asked.

Qualitative Assessment of Consistency

The candidate incentive compensation plan needs to be consistent with company marketing strategies, as well as being in alignment with the sales force definer decisions of sales strategy, go-to-market strategy, and sales force design. Assessment of consistency tends to be qualitative and judgmental.

Figure 8-36 illustrates just a few of the many demands that a company's marketing strategy may place on an incentive plan. A candidate plan that encourages sales force activities and behaviors that are inconsistent with marketing strategy can undermine the strategy.

Test 12: Consistency Check with Sales Force Definers. A compensation plan that is not aligned well with the firm's sales force effectiveness definer decisions (sales strategy, go-to-market strategy, and sales force design) sends mixed signals to salespeople and may not encourage the right sales force activities. It is important that the sales incentive plan reinforce the definer decisions. Several illustrative

Figure 8-35. Sample questions for evaluating the company results consequences of a candidate sales incentive plan.

- Will the plan help the firm achieve sales, profit, and market share goals simultaneously?
- How risky is the plan?

Figure 8-36. Examples of questions for assessing the consistency of a candidate plan with company marketing strategy and examples of potential inconsistencies.

Questions to Ask	Example of Potential Inconsistency
• Does the incentive plan encourage the sales force to sell the right products?	• The marketing strategy is focused on key products, yet the candidate plan pays for sales of all products. • The marketing strategy calls for cross-selling of products and services across company divisions, but the candidate plan pays salespeople only for sales of their own division's products and services.
• Does the incentive plan encourage the sales force to focus on the right customers?	• The marketing strategy is focused on key customers, yet the candidate plan pays for sales to all customers.
• Does the incentive plan encourage the sales force to engage in appropriate selling activities?	• The marketing strategy calls for significant time to be spent servicing customers, but the candidate plan has a large variable component and pays on sales.

questions for assessing the consistency of the definer decisions with a candidate incentive plan and examples of potential inconsistencies are listed in Figure 8-37.

Qualitative Assessment of Compatibility

The candidate incentive compensation plan needs to be compatible with other sales force effectiveness drivers. A reasonable assessment process evaluates each driver to see if an incompatibility will be created if the new plan is implemented.

Test 13: Compatibility Check with Other Sales Force Effectiveness Drivers. Figure 8-38 provides some examples of the types of questions that can be asked and addressed to qualitatively evaluate the compatibility of a candidate plan with other sales force effectiveness drivers, along with examples of potential incompatibilities.

The Cost of Incentive Compensation Plan Administration

Plan administration costs typically add 2 to 15 percent to total incentive compensation costs. Since the cost of administering a plan can be significant, this is an important consideration in plan selection. Administration costs are influenced by plan complexity, by the quality and compatibility of the administration system, and by the amount of flexibility for making changes that the firm demands. Firms can reduce their administration costs considerably by simplifying their plans, streamlining their administration systems, and restricting the number of plan adjustments that are allowed. The firm's ability to administer a new plan efficiently and effectively should be an important factor in the plan selection process. See Chapter 12 for more information on incentive compensation plan administration.

Figure 8-37. Examples of questions for assessing the consistency of a candidate plan with sales force definers and examples of potential inconsistencies.

Questions to Ask	Examples of Potential Inconsistency
• Is the incentive plan consistent with the go-to-market strategy?	• The go-to-market strategy encourages sales through channel partners, yet the candidate plan penalizes salespeople for indirect channel sales by reducing the salesperson's revenue credit to compensate for the commission paid to the channel partner.
	• The go-to-market strategy encourages Internet sales, but the candidate plan does not reward salespeople when their customers purchase from the company's web site.
• Is the candidate plan appropriate for the various sales roles?	• Hunters and farmers have similar pay plans.
• Does the sales force structure allow accurate performance measurement for the candidate plan?	• The candidate plan rewards individual results, yet the sales force structure is team-based and individual contribution is difficult to ascertain.
• Does the sales territory design allow fair incentive pay with the candidate plan?	• The candidate plan ties a large variable-pay component to total territory sales, but territories vary widely in terms of potential; hence, pay is more closely linked to sales territory opportunity than it is to personal performance.
	• The candidate plan determines incentive pay by rank-ordering salespeople on territory market share, but territories have unequal potential—again paying for the sales territory and not salesperson performance.

Future-Proofing Assessment of a Candidate Sales Compensation Plan

Even though incentive compensation plans focus sales force attention on near-term results, the plans themselves have to be cognizant of the future. An incentive plan that works well in the current environment can fail in tomorrow's context. Incentive plans vary in their flexibility and their ability to adapt to company and market change. Consider the following examples:

- A company launches a new product in a new and largely undeveloped market. Salespeople are paid a commission on sales from the first dollar sold, and this commission rate is not changed for several years. During the first few years, the incentive plan works well, as salespeople are rewarded for their hard work to develop the market and drive sales growth. To support this growth, the company's management decides to hire additional salespeople. Existing salespeople vehemently resist giving up any accounts to new hires because of the adverse impact on their personal

Figure 8-38. Examples of questions for assessing the compatibility of a candidate plan with other sales force effectiveness drivers and examples of potential incompatibilities.

Questions to Ask	Example of Potential Incompatibility
• Will the candidate plan attract and retain the type of salespeople who are compatible with the company's hiring and training profile?	• The company wants to hire risk takers, but pays a large fraction of the mix in salary. • The company has no formal sales training program, yet does not pay enough to attract high-performing experienced salespeople.
• Will the candidate plan encourage salespeople to embrace the company's training philosophy?	• The company is developing an attractive professional development program and wants salespeople to spend at least 40 hours per year in training, yet the compensation plan is entirely commission-based starting with the first dollar.
• Is the candidate plan aligned with the company's coaching and performance management philosophy?	• Sales managers coach behaviors such as emphasizing customer service and developing long-term customer relationships, yet salespeople who "sell at all costs" make the most money.
• Does the company provide adequate targeting data and tools to allow salespeople to be financially successful with the candidate plan?	• The incentive plan pays for new customer development, yet the sales force gets no information on where to find new customers. • The sales force gets monthly commissions, yet sales tracking is inconsistent and is often months late getting to the field.
• Does the incentive plan align well with the sales force culture?	• Income decelerators and caps in the candidate plan are incompatible with a sales force culture that is sales-centered, competitive, and focused on short-term results. • The large variable-pay component of the candidate plan is incompatible with a sales force culture that is customer-centered, team-oriented, and focused on long-term success.
• Can the incentive plan be communicated and administered?	• The plan is too complex for sales managers to understand and explain effectively to the sales force. • Current sales systems cannot handle many plan features efficiently; updating the systems will be prohibitively time-consuming and costly.

earnings. Several salespeople threaten to leave for competitors (and take accounts with them) if management reduces their account base. As a result, the company undersizes its sales force during important growth years.

• Several years later at the same company, the incentive plan begins to cause even more trouble. Successful salespeople are earning high commissions on repeat sales to existing accounts that require only minimal sales effort. The sales force has become complacent, and pay has escalated beyond the value that many salespeople bring to the job. Variation in pay across the sales force is linked less to the quality of the salespeople and their work than to the book of business they have built or inherited. Since the sales force controls many important customer relationships, the company is held hostage by the sales force's power. Sales leadership is concerned that if it reduces sales force earning potential by lowering commission rates, salespeople will leave for competitors.

- Another company pays its salespeople a commission on sales growth. When sales were growing rapidly, the plan successfully focused salespeople on the desired result of growing the business. But as sales have flattened out, and more and more sales force energy is spent on protecting existing accounts, salespeople are no longer earning enough incentive money, and the growth-focused plan has become a demotivator.

- At still another company, salespeople have traditionally worked largely alone. Over time, however, as the portfolio of products and customers has increased, the company has evolved to a team-based structure in which account managers and product specialists work together to meet customer needs. The sales process now requires teamwork, yet the pay plan still rewards individualistic behaviors.

Unfortunately, at all of these companies, the incentive compensation plan was not "future-proofed." Plans that have limited ability to change as markets and company strategies evolve create considerable risk for companies. For example, plans that pay a fixed commission on all sales often severely limit future management flexibility. If commission rates are fixed for a few years, salespeople begin to feel that they are entitled to those rates. Generally, incentive plans that link payout to goal achievement (rather than paying for all sales) have much greater flexibility, as territory goals can be adjusted appropriately as circumstances change.

An important part of any compensation plan review is anticipating likely market and company strategy changes and ensuring that the incentive plan either can continue to thrive or can be changed appropriately as needed. While some degree of stability in the incentive plan is usually desired, periodic plan changes in dynamic environments create an expectation of change among salespeople and allow future plan changes to be accepted more readily by the sales force.

Test 14: Compatibility Check with Future Company Needs. To test whether a plan is compatible with the future, sales leaders and incentive compensation plan designers should ask questions such as the ones in Figure 8-39.

Conclusion: From Objectives to Reality

The various tests described in this chapter help sales leaders select an incentive compensation plan that encourages sales force success. At this point, it is useful to

Figure 8-39. Examples of questions for assessing the compatibility of a candidate plan with future sales force structures, sales roles, and success measures.

Questions to Ask	Examples of Potential Inconsistency
• What will happen to pay levels as sales grow (or decline) in future years? Will pay levels remain consistent with the value the salesperson brings to the job?	• The sales job will be similar, but pay levels will escalate because the commission structure, which pays from the first dollar sold, will reward salespeople for increasingly high levels of carryover sales.
• How is the sales process likely to evolve? Does the incentive plan encourage the sales force behaviors needed for future success?	• The sales job is becoming more consultative, with longer selling cycles and bigger deal sizes. A plan that pays for quarterly sales is effective at encouraging short-term goal attainment in the current environment, but is likely to misdirect sales effort in the future as the sales process evolves.
• Will the incentive plan limit management's flexibility to change sales force structure and size in the future?	• The company's product line and customer base are expected to grow, and future sales force expansion and specialization are planned. The incentive plan pays a commission on sales from the first dollar and thus encourages salespeople to build and protect their book of business. Hence, the sales force is likely to resist the planned sales force structure change because it could reduce their earning power.
• Are there specific plan elements that will become dysfunctional in the future?	• Since sales cycles are short today, goals are set monthly. With the introduction of some new products, the length of the sales cycle is expected to increase, and there will be fewer but larger transactions. Accurate monthly goal setting will become impossible, and payouts will be erratic and not reflective of true performance.
• Are future performance measures likely to be different from what they are now?	• Focus is shifting from growth to retention or from volume to profitability, while the plan focuses on short-term volume growth.
	• Next year, a much larger proportion of revenues is expected to come from renewals of existing contracts, which require minimal sales force effort. The plan pays the same commission rate on renewal sales as on new sales.

summarize the process described so far in this book that leads to an effective plan selection. Chapter 2 provides a framework for assessing a current sales incentive plan and developing objectives for a new plan. Chapters 3 through 7 provide design advice for developing an incentive plan that will meet the objectives of the new plan. This chapter presents a number of tests that can be used to estimate the degree to which a candidate plan is likely to meet the specified design objectives. The plan designer needs to select the appropriate tests for each relevant design objective. Both the design objectives and the plan tests are organized in terms of the 3 Cs framework. A candidate plan is ready for implementation once it has been tested and the test results indicate that the plan is consistent with company strategies, is compatible with sales effectiveness drivers, and has appropriate consequences for salespeople, sales force activities, customer results, and company results.

The remaining chapters of this book focus on designing some of the supplemental details of a sales incentive plan (including goal setting, SPIFFs, sales contests, and recognition programs) and effective compensation plan implementation. In many situations, implementing a new sales incentive compensation plan successfully is even more challenging than designing and selecting the plan.

CHAPTER 9

Setting Effective Goals and Objectives

How This Chapter Is Organized

Introduction	313
Are Your Sales Force Goals Appropriate?	314
Are There Errors in Aggregate Forecasting?	314
Are Company and Territory Goals Too High?	314
Are Company and Territory Goals Too Low?	318
What Percent of the Sales Force Should Make Goal?	320
Are Goals Allocated Appropriately Across Salespeople?	321
Financial Cost of Goal-Allocation Errors	321
Who Is Reaching Goal and Who Is Not?	323
Types of Goals	327
Goals That Are Primarily Controlled by Performance Management: Salesperson and Activities Goals	328
Goals That Are Primarily Controlled by Incentives: Customer and Company Results Goals	330
How to Set Effective Sales Force Goals: A Five-Step Process	330
Step 1: Understand Product and Market Expectations and Set National Goals	331
Step 2: Understand Territory Expectations and Behavior	334
Product Sales in Any Given Year Are Highly Correlated with Product Sales for the Prior Year.	335

Product Sales in Any Given Year Are Positively Correlated with Market Sales in the Prior Year.   336

Product Sales in Any Given Year Are Positively Correlated with Surrogates for Market Potential.   336

Product Sales in Any Given Year Are Positively Correlated with a Competitor's Sales in the Prior Year.   337

The Market Share Change Expected for Any Given Year Is Related to the Starting Market Share in That Year.   337

Measuring Territory Market Potential   338

Step 3: Develop Alternative Territory Goal-Setting Formulas or Processes   343

Formula-Based Territory Goal-Setting Approaches Based on Historical Sales   344

Maintenance Plus Standard Growth Method   344

Territory Forecast Method   346

Formula-Based Territory Goal-Setting Methods Based on Historical Sales and Market Potential   348

Maintenance Plus Adjusted Growth Method   348

Weighted Index Method   351

Regression Method   352

Performance Frontier Method   353

Share Growth Method   355

Percent of Remaining Share Method   356

Formula-Based Territory Goal-Setting Method Based on Historical Sales, Market Potential, and Sales Effort   357

Sales Response Method   357

Sales Force Input–Based Territory Goal-Setting Method   359

Bottom-Up Method   359

Goal-Setting Approaches for New Products   361

Market Potential Method   362

Constant Allocation Method   362

Summary of Methods   362

Step 4: Evaluate the Consequences of Each Alternative and Select the Best Approach   363

Step 5: Review and Finalize Goals with Field Sales Managers   365

Tracking Performance Against Goals   369

Systems for Providing Feedback on Goal Attainment   369

Handling Midyear Goal Corrections   370

Goal-Setting Recommendations   372

In Volatile Business Environments, Goals with Short Time Frames,
Broad Payout Ranges, and Earnings Caps Are Appropriate   372

Stretch Goals Can Be Effective, Provided They Are Attainable   373

Rank Ordering of Salespeople Is an Alternative to Goal Setting, but
Should Be Used with Caution   374

The Number of Goals Should Be Limited to Three   375

Concluding Insights   375

Poor Goal Setting Leads to Increased Costs and Lower Sales   375

The Most Suitable Goals Depend on Business Objectives and the
Business Environment   375

The Process of Setting Goals Can Be as Beneficial as the Goals
Themselves   376

Introduction

A vacationer traveling in Vermont to see the fall colors was surprised to see dozens of targets painted on one of the traditional red barns. He stopped the car and got out to take a closer look. The vacationer was astonished to see a bullet hole in the center of each target. When the farmer came out of his barn holding his rifle, the vacationer asked, "I've never seen shooting this good! How did you do it?" The farmer replied, "I shot first."

Unfortunately, we have to draw the target first when setting goals, objectives, or quotas for salespeople. Goal setting, like much of sales management, is part science and part art. Setting territory-level goals that are fair, realistic, and motivational is a significant sales management challenge. Salespeople want easy goals that allow them to earn a good income. Shareholders want aggressive goals that help the firm achieve and exceed its financial objectives. Customers want goals that encourage the firm to meet their needs. Finding the right balance between these competing objectives when setting goals can be difficult, yet having the right goals is extremely important to sales success.

Motivational research shows that people who are given specific, challenging goals consistently outperform those who are not given any goals or who are given vague goals such as "do your best." As a result, organizations and individuals that are goal-focused are typically more successful in the long run than those that do not set goals. Most sales incentive plans are goal-based. When we surveyed the managers of 110 sales forces of varying sizes and in various industries who attended our sales compensation executive education programs at Northwestern University between 2000 and 2004 (the Sales Incentive Executive Education Survey), 82 percent reported that goals are used as part of their incentive compensation plans.

Effective goals can energize salespeople and organizations. Goals that are sufficiently challenging, yet attainable, drive sales force behavior and increase sales force motivation. Goals also communicate what is important and suggest an allocation of effort that reflects management's priorities and the desired level of customer focus. In addition, goals help management evaluate sales performance. They provide a benchmark against which sales force activity and results can be measured and controlled. Goals provide a convenient way for management to recognize personal and territory differences when evaluating salespeople. Each salesperson can be given a different goal, taking into account such factors as the salesperson's skills and experience along with territory characteristics such as growth potential and competitive intensity.

Are Your Sales Force Goals Appropriate?

Goal setting is a problem area that is often overlooked by sales organizations. The compensation plan structure is frequently blamed for goal-setting inadequacies, and companies often abandon good compensation plans simply because they are not supported by sound goal-setting practices. Poor goal setting can seriously undermine the success of a sales force. The diagnosis of goal-setting problems begins by examining the three views within the sales management system framework:

- The downstream consequences of sales force goals for salespeople, sales force activities, and customer and company results
- The upstream consistency of sales force goals with marketing and go-to-market strategies, sales processes, and sales force roles
- The compatibility of sales force goals with other sales force effectiveness drivers, such as salespeople's skills and capabilities, sales force culture, performance management systems, and nonmonetary sales force motivators

Figure 9-1 provides a template for diagnosing whether appropriate sales force goals are being used in the sales incentive plan and illustrates some possible signs of trouble.

Goals that are too difficult, too easy, or not assigned fairly across the sales force have an adverse impact on sales force motivation and morale, costs, and expectations. Most companies risk two major goal-setting errors: (1) The company forecast is either too high or too low, resulting in territory goals that are either uniformly too high or uniformly too low, and (2) the company goal is not allocated appropriately across the sales force.

Are There Errors in Aggregate Forecasting?

Are Company and Territory Goals Too High?

Goals That Are Too High Discourage a Beverage Sales Force

A beverage bottler in Mexico paid its sales force a base salary plus commissions on all sales over last year's sales. With the economy weakening

Figure 9-1. Some signs that sales force goals may not be appropriate.

Consistency with . . .	Compatibility with . . .	Consequences . . .
• Sales and marketing strategies • Sales process • Sales roles	• Performance management systems • Sales force culture • Sales force motivators • Sales force hiring and development processes	• Company results • Customer results • Sales force behaviors and activities • Sales force quality
• Marketing strategy emphasizes profitable growth in key customer segments, yet sales force goals are based on sales volume by product. • Sales success depends on effective teamwork, yet inappropriate goal allocations across sales team members encourage salespeople to hoard quality leads and withhold good ideas in order to get greater sales credit. • Sales territories have unequal potential, yet every salesperson has the same sales or market share goal. • Salespeople have sales goals, yet sales managers have profit goals.	• The goals set through the performance management system are at odds with the goals used for incentives. • Cultural statements like "our potential is unlimited" and "the world is our oyster" collide with goal-based incentives. • The sales force wants goals that are easy to understand and calculate, yet the sales analysis group uses complex regression models for accuracy. • The compensation plan relies heavily on territory results goals, yet the sales analysis group invests little time and effort in the goal-setting process. • The compensation plan relies heavily on territory results goals, yet no reliable data exist for determining sales potential.	When goals are too high: • Hardly anyone is making goal—even the best performers. • Salespeople give up or leave the firm because they perceive goals to be out of reach. When goals are too low: • Almost everyone is making goal—even poor performers. • Many salespeople achieve their goal early in the incentive period, then stop working hard. • Too many salespeople reach the incentive cap or the point at which decelerators kick in. When goals are not allocated fairly: • Goal attainment seems unrelated to performance. • The sales force is unhappy because of goal-setting biases. • The sales force achieved its goal, but incentive plan costs are higher than expected.

and the market shrinking, the firm's sales were flat or declining in most areas, and it became increasingly difficult for salespeople to beat last year's numbers and earn commissions. As engagement in the commission plan decreased, sales force morale and motivation suffered, and sales force turnover increased significantly. To improve the situation, the company changed the incentive plan to start commission payments at just 90 percent of last year's sales. This revised goal was much more reasonable given the new market conditions, and sales force engagement in the plan increased substantially.

Figure 9-2 shows how sales suffer when motivation falls off for one salesperson as her cumulative goal attainment gets smaller over time.

Figure 9-2. A salesperson's sales trail off when her goal seems unattainable.

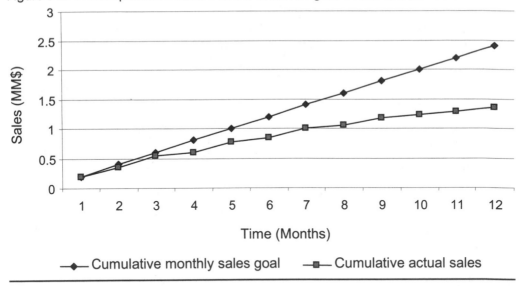

The negative effect on sales force motivation of goals that are too high has considerable sales and profit impact. Figure 9-3 shows an analysis performed at one company to estimate this impact. The firm had an incentive plan that began to pay out at 80 percent of goal attainment, and paid at a higher rate beyond 100 percent attainment. Goals were set too high for one of the firm's products, and over two-thirds of the sales force did not make the product goal—overall achievement of the national goal was only 93 percent. Based on observation and management input, the firm estimated that there was a 30 percent productivity loss among salespeople who did not reach 80 percent of goal (area A on the graph in the figure). This productivity loss was attributed to a lack of motivation to work hard to try to achieve an unrealistic goal. The firm also estimated that there was a 15 percent productivity increase among salespeople who achieved over 100 percent of goal (area C on the graph in the figure). This productivity increase was attributed to increased motivation to work hard to exceed goal and earn the higher payout rate. The table in the figure shows the sales impact of setting more realistic goals. If the goals had been set at a level that resulted in national attainment of 100 percent rather than 93 percent, more salespeople would have been in the high-motivation zone (C), and fewer would have been in the low-motivation zone (A). The company estimated that salespeople could affect 50 percent of territory sales in the current year (with the remaining 50 percent being attributed to carryover from the prior year's sales force effort). Thus, more realistic goals would lead to higher sales force motivation and $13.7 million in incremental sales. Incentive plan cost would also increase by $4 million, but since the firm had profit margins of approximately 95 percent, the overall impact would have been significantly higher firm profits.

Figure 9-3. Sales impact of goals that are too high at one firm.

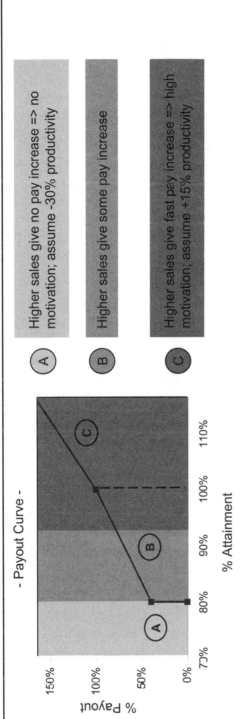

- Payout Curve -

% Payout: 0%, 50%, 100%, 150%

% Attainment: 70%, 80%, 90%, 100%, 110%

A — Higher sales give no pay increase => no motivation; assume -30% productivity

B — Higher sales give some pay increase

C — Higher sales give fast pay increase => high motivation; assume +15% productivity

Attainable goals shift more people into the high-motivation zone (C) and away from the no-motivation zone (A)

	Number of Territories				
Incentive to Increase Sales	Current Goals (93% Attainment)	Attainable Goals (100% Attainment)	Change	Impact on Sales (%)	Impact on Sales* ($ MM)
A—None	102	47	-55	-30%	+ $8.2MM
B—Medium	255	237	-18	—	—
C—High	168	241	73	+ 15%	+ $5.5MM
				Total impact	+ $13.7 MM

*Assumes sales ~$1MM/territory, 50% affectable by reps

Total sales up $13.7MM, or 3%

Total incentive plan costs up $4MM

Unrealistic Sales Goals Lead to Excessive Sales Force Turnover

At a large service firm, systematic padding of sales forecasts from the top down resulted in unrealistic goals for the sales force. The firm would start with a reasonable sales budget, but then behind closed doors the CEO would add 5 percent to the budget before passing it down to the next executive, who tacked on another 5 percent, and so on. By the time the sales force received the budget, the forecast was so inflated that some salespeople had goals that were 200 percent above the previous year's sales—a forecast that the salespeople knew was completely unrealistic. The combination of the out-of-reach goals and a high-pressure atmosphere took its toll on the sales force. Many top performers left the firm to join rival companies. One manager joked that the company had become a training camp for competitors. And as many top performers left, marginal performance became the cultural norm. The sales force received the counterproductive message that failing to make quota was okay.

In response to its troubles, the company set out to transform itself. As a first step, management began providing more realistic, well-defined goals to the sales force. As a result, the caliber of people attracted to the sales organization improved significantly.

Authors' note: When a small percentage of the sales force misses its goals, the problem can be with the salespeople. When the majority of salespeople miss their goal, the problem is with those at the top setting the overall goal in the first place.

Are Company and Territory Goals Too Low?

Goals That Are Too Easy Can Encourage Undesirable Sales Force Behaviors

A large industrial firm found that its best performers were reaching their sales goal by midyear and then basically quit working hard. As the year end approached, the sales force delayed closing additional deals in order to count those deals toward meeting next year's goal.

"We underestimated the success of our products and set territory revenue goals too low. Everyone made their goal easily, and the entire sales force was walking around with smiles on their faces."

CEO at a start-up medical device firm

The financial cost to the firm of a sales goal that is too low can be substantial, especially when plans have accelerators. For example, consider a company using the sales incentive compensation plan illustrated in Figure 9-4. The plan pays a salary plus 2.5 percent commission on every dollar in sales up to a territory goal

Figure 9-4. Example of a growth-oriented sales compensation plan.

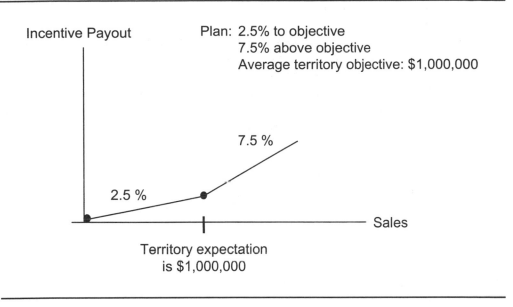

and 7.5 percent commission on every dollar for all sales that exceed this goal. This is a growth-oriented plan because it aggressively rewards extra effort at a point where the company expects that extra effort will be required.

Suppose the company forecasts that if its 10 salespeople all do a reasonable amount of work, they will sell $10 million. Thus, the average salesperson is given a goal of $1 million and is expected to earn $25,000 in incentive pay. However, suppose the company underprojects its sales success and, in reality, the 10 salespeople all do a reasonable amount of work but sell $12 million. The $2 million above the firm's projection is not the result of exceptional sales force effort, but instead is a windfall gain caused by the fact that the goal was not set accurately. The average salesperson sells $1.2 million and earns $40,000 in incentive pay (2.5 percent of $1 million plus 7.5 percent of $200,000). Had the goals been set accurately at $1.2 million per territory from the start, the average salesperson would have earned $30,000 in incentive pay (2.5 percent of $1.2 million). Thus, the goal-setting error results in the average salesperson getting paid $10,000 more than she truly deserves based on her work. Forecasting errors like this can require firms with large sales forces to pay out millions of dollars in undeserved incentive pay.

The Long-Term Impact of Goals That Are Too Low

Goals that are too easily achieved not only cost the firm money in the short term, but also have a significant impact on long-term sales force expectations. A sales force that earns high incentive pay without having to work very hard may expect this situation to continue. This makes it difficult for the firm to set more challenging goals in the future without adversely affecting sales force morale.

What Percent of the Sales Force Should Make Goal? There is much debate about what proportion of a sales force should make goal. Many companies follow the logic that in order to be motivational, goals must be attainable by average performers in the sales force. Goal attainment is an important signal of a salesperson's success, in addition to being a determinant of financial reward. If average performers cannot achieve goals, they may not feel successful, and sales force morale may suffer.

> *"At IBM, there was an aura around 100 percent goal attainment. There was a 100% Club, and everyone in the club got to go on a trip. If you didn't make it into the club, you felt like dog meat."*
>
> A former IBM marketing representative

When we asked members of our Incentive Compensation Advisory Board (ICAB), "What percent of the sales force do you think should make goal?" responses were evenly spread across a range from 50 to 80 percent. The reasons given to justify responses across this range are summarized in Figure 9-5.

The targeted percentage of salespeople expected to make goal should be influenced by the message that management wants to send to the sales force. For example, a new sales force that has just hired a team of superstars may want all salespeople to feel like winners. In this situation, goals should be set at a level such

Figure 9-5. ICAB member rationale for responses to the question, "What percent of the sales force do you think should make goal?"

Response	Rationale
50–60%	"If the national goal is accurate, national attainment will be right around 100 percent. This means that approximately half of the sales force will make goal and half will not. Payout should start at some fraction of goal so that the majority of the sales force is engaged in the incentive plan, but a sufficiently challenging national goal implies that many individuals will not make their individual goal."
60–70%	"When about 2/3 of the sales force achieves goal, the majority of salespeople feel successful, yet those in the bottom 1/3 feel like they'll need to hustle more to make it at the company. Limiting goal attainment to the top 2/3 of the sales force prevents complacency among mediocre performers. In addition, a 2/3 level of goal attainment is consistent with our financial projections; the 1/3 of the sales force that misses goal funds the additional incentive money paid to those who overachieve."
70–80%	"Making goal is your target—the quest to make goal is what makes your business run. Anyone who doesn't make goal will not feel successful. In a strong sales force, the vast majority of salespeople should make goal so that the sales force feels successful."

that almost everyone who does a reasonable amount of work can attain them. On the other hand, if a more mature sales force has become complacent and management wants to shake things up, a more challenging goal that fewer salespeople will achieve is appropriate. For example, management might set goals such that if all salespeople continue to work at their current level, only the top 60 percent of the sales force will achieve them. Those in the bottom 40 percent are challenged to work harder in order to be successful. Those who are unwilling to do this may be asked to leave the company.

When assessing your current goal-setting process, consider what percent of the sales force has achieved goal in the last several incentive periods. Is the attainment level consistent with the message you want the sales force to receive?

Reconciling Financial Goals and Sales Force Motivation

Unfortunately, sales leaders frequently do not have much control over how challenging their sales goals will be. National sales forecasts are often driven by Wall Street expectations and are handed down to the sales force from the executive suite. In the words of one sales director, "We are passive victims in the process." The goal level that the sales leaders feel is realistic and appropriate from a sales force motivation perspective is frequently less than the goal that top management insists is necessary from a financial perspective. Managing the gap between what the sales force feels it can achieve and what top management demands requires considerable management energy and focus. Effective sales leadership involves convincing the sales force that specific programs, activities, and behaviors can enable the sales force to close this gap.

Are Goals Allocated Appropriately Across Salespeople?

Goal-setting problems can also arise when the company goal is set accurately, but the goal is not allocated appropriately across salespeople.

Financial Cost of Goal-Allocation Errors. Errors in goal allocation can be costly. For instance, consider again the company with the growth-oriented sales incentive compensation plan illustrated in Figure 9-4. This time, the company's projection of $1 million average sales per territory turns out to be accurate—if the firm's 10 salespeople all put in a reasonable amount of work, they will end up selling a total of $10 million. The amount of money the company pays out in incentives depends upon how accurately the $10 million goal is allocated to the individual salespeople. For example, suppose that, for simplicity, the company assigns every salesperson the same goal—$1 million. Figure 9-6 compares the firm's total incentive payout for varying degrees of accuracy in this goal allocation. In the "perfect accuracy" scenario, Scenario A, each salesperson performs a reasonable amount of work and achieves his goal of $1 million exactly. Thus, the company pays out a

Figure 9-6. A cost comparison of scenarios with different goal-allocation errors.

Scenario	Sales Results	Company Sales	Individual Incentive Payouts	Company Incentive Payout	% Over the Cost of Scenario A
A Perfect accuracy	10 people sell $1,000,000	$10,000,000	10 @ $25,000	$250,000	0%
B Some error	1 person sells $1,100,000 8 people sell $1,000,000 1 person sells $900,000	$10,000,000	1 @ $32,500 8 @ $25,000 1 @ $22,500	$255,000	2%
C More error	2 people sell $1,200,000 4 people sell $1,000,000 4 people sell $900,000	$10,000,000	2 @ $40,000 4 @ $25,000 4 @ $22,500	$270,000	8%
D Significantly more error	5 people sell $1,250,000 5 people sell $750,000	$10,000,000	5 @ $43,750 5 @ $18,750	$312,500	25%

total of $250,000 in incentives. Scenarios B, C, and D introduce varying degrees of goal-allocation error. In each of these scenarios, some of the 10 salespeople sell more than $1 million and others sell less than $1 million. Of course, these sales variations could be due to differences in the salespeople's performance, but the assumption for this example is that the variation is due to territory differences and that the goals were not set accurately. Because of the goal-allocation error, the firm's total incentive payout is greater than it was with the "perfect accuracy" scenario. For example, Scenario B suggests that the goal of $1 million was not accurate for two of the territories. Since the salesperson in one territory performed a reasonable amount of work and sold $1.1 million, the goal for that territory should have been $1.1 million. The salesperson in the other territory did a reasonable amount of work and sold $900,000; accordingly, that goal should have been $900,000. Eight territories had accurate goals. In this scenario, one person gets a windfall gain and one person is underpaid—all because the goals were not set accurately. The company's total payout is $255,000, or 2 percent above what it would have been if it had set its goals correctly. The additional scenarios demonstrate the extent to which the company's costs accelerate with increasing goal-setting error.

It is often difficult to determine whether a salesperson exceeded goal because the goal was too low, or because the salesperson performed really well. The assumption for this example is that the goals were not set accurately. Inaccurate goals for a sales force with many overperforming and many underperforming salespeople will increase the cost of poor goal setting even further.

Notice that in each scenario in Figure 9-6, the company sold $10 million. Management is pleased because the company made its goal. However, sales force costs swing significantly depending on how accurately the national goal was allocated across individual salespeople.

This example highlights the cost of annual goal-setting errors across territories. Companies that set quarterly goals may experience the same cost run-up when goal-setting errors occur over time. Salespeople receive windfall gains in quarters when the goals are set too low and lose motivation in quarters when the goals are set too high.

Figure 9-7 shows actual quarterly payout data for a sales force selling financial services to motorized vehicle dealerships. The dark line at $7,000 represents the quarterly incentive payout at 100 percent goal attainment. The lumpy payouts correspond to widely varying goal achievement for each salesperson over time. The company revisited its goal-setting approach and obtained smoother performance and payout in subsequent years.

Who Is Reaching Goal and Who Is Not? Errors in goal allocation are a particularly significant problem when some of the salespeople who are overpaid are weak performers and some of the salespeople who are underpaid are strong performers. Often, when sales managers receive a goal that they know will be challenging to achieve, they ask their strongest performers (the people they always rely on) to deliver a disproportionately large proportion of that goal. As a result, the strongest performers may not achieve their goal. They become frustrated because, as a result of unfair goal setting, they are not rewarded enough for their hard work and superior performance. At the same time, the sales force observes that some poor performers who were given easier goals make more money than some of the top performers. This sends the wrong message to salespeople and has a negative impact on morale. One salesperson who worked in a sales organization that did not allocate its national goal appropriately to salespeople told us, "Our comp plan is no more than a lottery!"

Effective goal-setting methods ensure that the right salespeople get rewarded. High performers consistently exceed their targets. Low performers do not. Either they show improvement over time or they leave the firm.

Figure 9-8 shows an example of a "quick check" analysis that sales leaders can use to determine if the company's goal-setting process is rewarding the right salespeople. Recent performance evaluation ratings for each salesperson are plotted against the incentive earnings percentile for that salesperson. The performance rating percentile considers long-term success measures such as development, mentoring, and training, in addition to sales results. (*Author's note: An alternative approach for determining the performance rating percentile would make use of the performance grid introduced in Chapter 4.*)

The other axis, incentive earnings percentile, is based entirely on this year's sales results relative to each territory's goal. In this example, most of the salespeople who achieved their sales goal and therefore have a high earnings percentile have high performance ratings, but there are some that do not (those in the "overpaid" quadrant). Similarly, the majority of salespeople who did not achieve their goal and therefore have a low earnings percentile have low performance ratings, but there are several that do not (those in the "underpaid" quadrant). It is to be expected that a few salespeople will fall into the overpaid and underpaid quadrants temporarily as a result of explainable factors, such as unexpected market dynamics or characteristics of the salespeople themselves. For example, one sales-

Figure 9-7. Payout over time demonstrating that quarterly goal setting can be challenging.

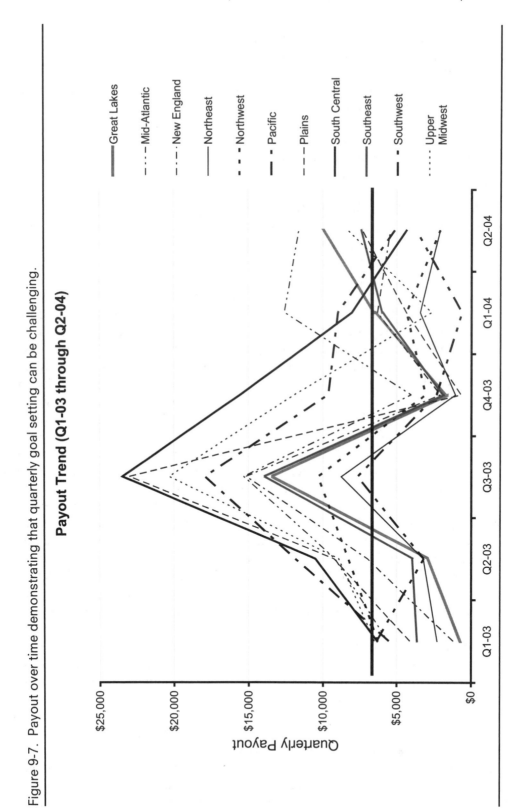

Payout Trend (Q1-03 through Q2-04)

Figure 9-8. Quick check analysis: Does the goal-setting process reward the right salespeople?

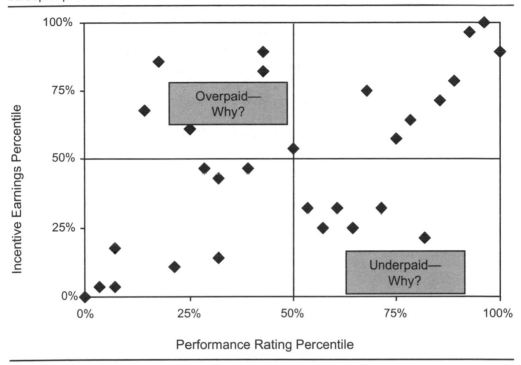

person in the underpaid quadrant had such exceptional selling skills that management had assigned her to all the hardest-to-sell prospects. One salesperson in the overpaid quadrant sold large contracts with long selling cycles, and since a handful of particularly large sales had "hit" recently, his incentive earnings for the year were abnormally high. While there will always be a few exceptions like these, having a large number of salespeople in the overpaid and underpaid quadrants is often an indication that there is a goal-setting problem.

Goals that reward the wrong salespeople are often the result of goal-setting methods that are biased toward salespeople or territories with predictable characteristics.

Is It Fair to Set Goals Based on Last Year's Sales?

Many firms set sales goals that are based heavily on past territory sales. For example, each salesperson is asked to maintain last year's sales, plus grow sales by a specified percentage. Sales managers and salespeople may lament, "I had a great year, and what do they do? They significantly raise my goal for next year." Or, "I am not going to make my goal this year, so the best strategy is to hold back so that I can get a low goal next year."

Goal setting based on prior year's sales tends to work best in selling situations with a high level of *free sales*. Free sales are made up of franchise sales and carryover sales. The term refers to sales that are realized even in the absence of sales force effort as a result of a variety of factors, including customers who purchase the company's products out of habit, long-term contracts, high customer switching costs, or other marketing activities. When free sales are high, it is reasonable to expect salespeople to maintain their past sales level—after all, a large proportion of their sales will be realized regardless of their effort, simply because of carryover.

In selling situations with low levels of free sales (for example, in competitive commodity markets), setting goals based on last year's sales penalizes salespeople who have high sales already, particularly if differences in market potential between territories are not accounted for. A salesperson who worked hard last year to exceed a challenging sales goal gets an even tougher goal for next year. It may be impossible for the salesperson to work hard enough to protect and grow that volume, particularly if he has already captured a high share of his territory's market potential. Such situations often result in goal oscillation, or alternating high and low goals from year to year. By incorporating territory characteristics such as market potential into the goal calculation, firms can smooth the oscillation.

Figure 9-9 shows territory-level data for one company that set goals for a new product that were biased toward territories with low growth goals. Goal attainment is significantly higher among salespeople with low growth goals than it is among salespeople with high growth goals. Statistical analyses like this are a very useful way to reveal goal-setting problems. Whenever there is a significant correlation between goal attainment and an independent territory variable that does not reflect a salesperson's effort or skill, there is a possible goal-setting problem. Anal-

Figure 9-9. Goal-setting bias toward territories with low growth goals for a new product.

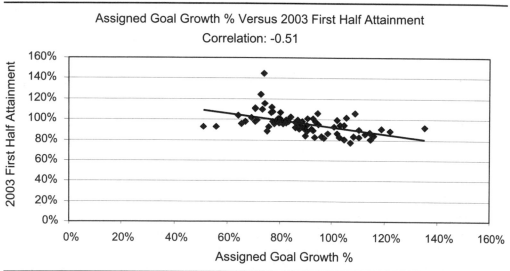

yses like this have been used to reveal goal-setting biases based on variables such as territory size, geographic region, served market segments, market potential, past sales level, market share, and quota increase.

> ### Assigning Equal Growth Goals to Every Territory Can Be Unfair as Well
>
> One firm set quotas by assigning an equal percentage growth over last year to every territory. The field complained loudly that as a result, territories with high past sales were being punished with quotas that were not achievable. Sure enough, an analysis (similar to the one in Figure 9-9) found a high negative correlation (R^2 of $-.39$) between the previous year's territory sales and quota attainment. The goal-setting methodology was biased against territories with high past sales.

Types of Goals

Sales forces have many different types of goals. This chapter focuses on goals that are set by management and disseminated to the sales force, but salespeople and sales teams can also set personal goals for themselves. Figure 9-10 provides some examples of sales force goals. The examples are organized by the four components that make up the sales management system framework. Most firms set goals for all components, but the type of goal that has the most salience depends upon an individual's position within the selling organization, the firm's selling environment, the sales force culture, and the availability and accuracy of performance measures (see Chapter 6 for more information on performance measures).

Goals play an important role as a *controller* within the sales management system. Goals help to define success, set expectations, and encourage sales force behaviors that are aligned with the firm's objectives. Sales leaders employ two important and complementary sales force effectiveness drivers to manage goal achievement: sales incentives and sales performance management. Sales incentives tie goal achievement to a salesperson's pay. Performance management involves managers working with salespeople to develop plans for achieving goals and providing coaching and guidance as each salesperson takes action to carry out those plans. In a performance management system, ongoing performance relative to goals is measured, feedback is provided, and appropriate consequences for achievement or nonachievement are implemented.

As shown in Figure 9-11, the importance of the two control vehicles (incentives and performance management) varies across the different goal types. Achievement of salesperson and sales force activities goals (the two left-hand columns of Figure 9-11) are typically controlled primarily through performance management processes. Achievement of customer and company results goals (the

Figure 9-10. Examples of sales force goals for each component of the sales management system framework.

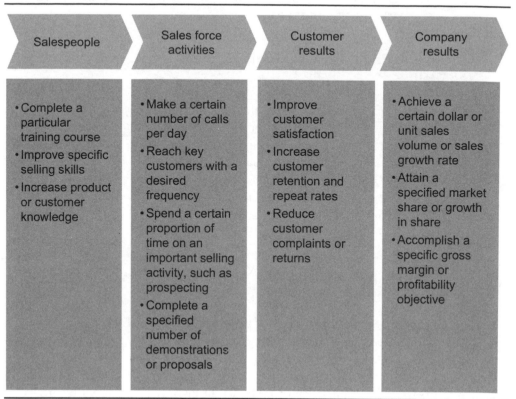

Salespeople	Sales force activities	Customer results	Company results
• Complete a particular training course • Improve specific selling skills • Increase product or customer knowledge	• Make a certain number of calls per day • Reach key customers with a desired frequency • Spend a certain proportion of time on an important selling activity, such as prospecting • Complete a specified number of demonstrations or proposals	• Improve customer satisfaction • Increase customer retention and repeat rates • Reduce customer complaints or returns	• Achieve a certain dollar or unit sales volume or sales growth rate • Attain a specified market share or growth in share • Accomplish a specific gross margin or profitability objective

two right-hand columns of Figure 9-11) are typically managed through incentives, with performance management processes playing a secondary role.

Goals That Are Primarily Controlled by Performance Management: Salesperson and Activity Goals

Goals in the salesperson and activities categories are part of most sales force performance management systems. Many sales forces use a KPI (key performance indicator) or an MBO (management by objectives) approach, in which each salesperson works with her manager to set specific capability and activities objectives for skill development and effective activity focus. Performance management is the preferred lever of control for the achievement of these goals because:

- Achievement of salesperson and activities goals tends to have a long-term impact on results; short-term incentives are most appropriate for rewarding short-term results.

- Measurement of salesperson and activities accomplishment is typically less accurate than results measurement, and frequently depends on some sort

Figure 9-11. Impact and control of goals.

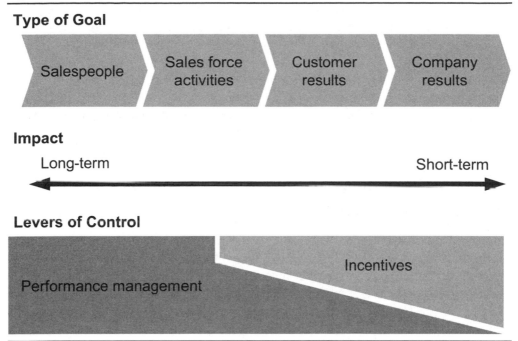

of self-reporting mechanism (for example, self-reported salesperson call data) or on management judgment (for example, a manager's assessment of a salesperson's selling skill improvement).

Occasionally firms use incentives effectively to drive the achievement of activities goals. Activities incentives can work when it is difficult to measure sales results or to attribute sales results to a specific salesperson. For example, in team-selling environments where it is not possible to determine the value of each individual's specific contribution, the entire team may be rewarded based on results, but each individual's reward may be based on her achievement of specific activities goals. In addition, activities incentives can be effective when management wants to encourage specific short-term sales force behaviors that are necessary to drive long-term results. For example, the firm might pay salespeople an incentive for the attainment of a specific number of key customer visits during the launch of a major competitor's new product.

Activities Goals in the Yellow Pages Advertising Industry

A Yellow Pages advertising sales force has promotional campaigns organized around the publication date of various Yellow Pages directories. Several months prior to a directory's publication, salespeople blitz businesses in the geographic area that the directory covers. It is imperative that every local business be contacted during the campaign period, since having 100

> percent coverage makes the Yellow Pages directory significantly more valuable to consumers. Salespeople are given daily routes and are paid an incentive if they contact every business on their assigned route. Salespeople also receive incentives based on the advertising revenues they generate.

There is an important caution for a management team contemplating the use of activities goals in the incentive plan: When activities goals are tied directly to monetary rewards, they often motivate an increase in the quantity of the desired activities but a decrease in the quality of those activities.

Goals That Are Primarily Controlled by Incentives: Customer and Company Results Goals

Almost all goal-based incentive programs tie the majority of sales force incentive money to the accomplishment of results goals. Company results goals (for example, sales, gross margin, and market share goals) are used almost all the time, while customer results goals (for example, repeat rate or customer satisfaction goals) are used by about 10 percent of all companies. Incentives are an effective means of controlling the achievement of results goals because:

- Results goals tend to be short term (for example, a quarterly sales goal). Most sales forces have significant short-term pressure to drive results, and incentives are very good at influencing short-term behavior and activity that drives results.
- Results measures are typically accurately and objectively measurable.
- Results goals encourage incentive plan fiscal responsibility, as incentive costs are incurred only when results are generated to pay for those costs.

Since most companies use company results goals as the primary basis for their incentive programs, the remainder of this chapter focuses on how to effectively set company results–oriented goals that will be used as a basis for determining sales force incentive pay.

How to Set Effective Sales Force Goals: A Five-Step Process

Many companies spend a considerable amount of time, energy, and money on determining goals. Despite this effort, goal-based incentive plans are a frequent source of dissatisfaction for salespeople. The process by which goals are set at a firm significantly influences both the quality of the goals and the degree to which the sales force will be committed to those goals. A goal-setting process that is very centralized and does not incorporate significant input from the sales force may be difficult for salespeople to understand and embrace. Salespeople may become suspicious that they are being treated unfairly and that local conditions have not been taken into account. On the other hand, a goal-setting process that is very decentralized may not be objective. Forecasts that rely solely on estimates provided by salespeople often produce results that are not aggressive enough to meet corporate goals. A salesperson is likely to underreport the true potential of her accounts if she knows that the information will be used to set her goals.

The best goal-setting processes incorporate elements of both centralized and decentralized goal-setting approaches. Centrally created potential-based models provide a benchmark goal for each territory. This benchmark is based on consistent, objective business criteria for every salesperson. The benchmark goals are reviewed and adjusted appropriately by field sales managers, to ensure that local conditions are taken into account. The process of incorporating local input also facilitates acceptance of the goals by the entire sales organization.

The five-step goal-setting process shown in Figure 9-12 has been used successfully by many firms to improve goal setting. Each of the five steps of this process is described further in the following sections. In each section, the relevant step is highlighted within an abbreviated version of the framework picture for reference.

Step 1: Understand Product and Market Expectations and Set National Goals

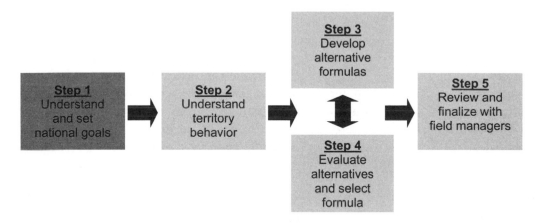

National goals are one significant way in which management communicates to the sales force what is important to the firm. Goals for revenue growth, unit growth, profit growth, share gain, sales retention, customer satisfaction, and market penetration are strong statements of the firm's strategy and intent. Companies can also state goals by product line and customer segment, further refining their objectives.

At most companies, the national goal is set by top management. While sales management may have input into the process, it usually does not decide the final

Figure 9-12. A process for establishing territory-level goals.

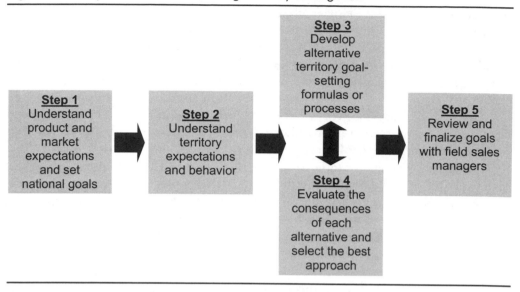

outcome. Determining the right national goal can be quite difficult. Accuracy depends upon management's ability to predict the impact of future influences, events, and trends taking place both inside and outside the company—a complex task. How quickly will customer needs evolve and change? What will happen with competitors? What about the economy? Will the new product be successful? Can the firm's productivity enhancement initiative deliver on its promise to increase sales? All of these unknowns make it quite difficult for management to forecast exactly how well the company is likely to perform in the future.

Most companies rely on input from three major sources when setting national goals. The first of these inputs comes from the top down. Shareholders have expectations, and top management has aspirations. Corporate objectives are often the primary driver of national goals. Yet smart management teams recognize that top-down objectives alone are usually not sufficient for determining the best national goals. Top-down goals may be overly aggressive if success is measured in terms of growth. On the other hand, these goals may be too conservative if success is measured in terms of goal attainment.

A second source of information for national goal setting is the firm's marketing department. Marketing has opinions about product potential. The accuracy of these marketing estimates is enhanced when good forecasting methods are used. Such methods consider historical sales and market trends and the judgment of experienced sales and marketing people. Valuable forecasting techniques have been developed and refined over the last 30 years. Some techniques, such as econometrics and time-series analysis, use historical data. Others, such as Delphi forecasting, summarize judgmental data in an objective way. Systematic use of these techniques improves the accuracy of national goals.

Example of a Structured Approach to National Goal Setting

One firm's marketing department improved its ability to set national goals significantly when it began using a structured analytical approach. First, the historical sales trend for each key product is examined, and sales are projected assuming that the historical trend continues. Next, anticipated events that will affect next year's sales are accounted for. For example, an expected competitive launch may have a negative impact on sales, while development of new markets, a new promotional campaign, and increased sales force effort will have a positive impact. Both quantitative and judgmental inputs are considered in the analysis that estimates the sales impact of these events. Contingencies for events that are not part of the core forecast are also examined. For example, the possibility of price erosion, a price increase, or a second competitive launch is considered, and the likely impact on sales is determined. This structured approach to national goal setting increased product forecasting accuracy, and thus made it possible for the sales force to set more realistic territory-level goals.

Third, input for national goal setting can be obtained from the sales force. Often, this involves summing together forecasts developed for individual sales territories, districts, or regions to derive a total business goal. Some firms have a sales analysis group that examines historical sales, market potential, and/or call data at the territory level to project future performance. Additionally, salespeople and sales managers may be asked for their opinions. Asking the sales force for input for national goal setting allows local conditions to be taken into account and encourages sales force acceptance of the national goal. The sales force is likely to provide the best estimate in environments involving complex, high-priced products, those where there are many participants in the buying process, and those with long selling cycles. However, bottom-up goals based exclusively on sales force input may be understated, since salespeople have an incentive to provide conservative forecasts, so that they will appear successful when they exceed those forecasts. Clever design of the process for gathering bottom-up forecasts from the sales force can discourage underforecasting (see the bottom-up method of goal setting described later in this chapter).

Analytical Approaches Enhance Forecasting Accuracy

Historically, a $40 million software company with a 30-person sales force had set its national sales goals based on guesstimates developed by top management. These guesstimates took into account factors such as what investors wanted the firm to do, the previous year's numbers, and how management thought the firm's competitors were doing. When the firm substantially missed its sales goal two years in a row and had to lay off salespeople, the traditional goal-setting process was replaced by a more rigorous and data-driven approach. National sales goals were determined based on data reflecting existing market demand, regional demand, and sales closing ratios. The new process created a much more reasonable goal, which the sales force was able to meet.

Often, management teams integrate top-down numbers, marketing forecasts, and sales force estimates to derive their final national forecast. Negotiation between sales, marketing, and top management may be required before a final number is agreed upon. Determining the right final number is extremely important for sales force success. If a national sales goal is not realistic or attainable, or if it is too easy, it will be impossible to set good territory-level goals.

Unrealistic Goals Can Lead to Unethical Behavior

Unrealistically high goals can be a significant source of stress for salespeople, particularly in situations where considerable amounts of money are tied to goal attainment. As evidenced by the numerous corporate scandals in the press lately, top executives sometimes resort to desperate measures in order to achieve short-term financial goals. For example, in a desperate attempt to inflate revenues just as the dot-com bubble was bursting in 2000 and 2001, several executives at America Online and its former business partner software company PurchasePro.com engaged in schemes to artificially inflate revenues through secret side deals, back-dated contracts, and revenue swaps. Several executives were charged with numerous violations, including conspiracy, securities fraud, and obstruction of justice. Unrealistic goals that are tied to significant incentive dollars can encourage salespeople to engage in unprofessional and even unethical behaviors.

Step 2: Understand Territory Expectations and Behavior

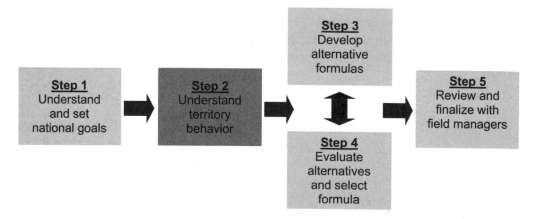

In order to set effective goals for salespeople, it is important to understand territory behavior and dynamics. Thus, the next step of the process for establishing territory-level goals is to analyze historical data in order to enhance this understanding.

Territory results are directly affected by the performance of the salesperson. However, many other factors also influence territory performance. For example, historical territory sales are a good indication of how much territory momentum exists and how high carryover sales are likely to be. Territory market potential or demographics may be a reflection of future territory opportunity. Such factors provide a good baseline for the level of sales the firm can reasonably expect from each territory in the future.

Statistical analysis of data for benchmarking territory goals is easy to perform and usually provides good results. An example of such an analysis is provided in Figures 9-13, 9-14, 9-15, and 9-16. The analysis is for a sales force that sells a medical instrument along with test strips for that instrument. The instrument and strips are purchased at retail stores by consumers, but the consumers' purchase decision is influenced by pharmacists, physicians, and nurses. The analysis reveals a number of factors that correlate well with territory sales, including historical company sales, market potential, population demographics, and competitors' sales. Depending on data availability, different companies will analyze other factors. The goal of the analysis is to identify factors outside of a salesperson's effort that affect territory sales so that these factors can be included in the goal-setting process.

Product Sales in Any Given Year Are Highly Correlated with Product Sales for the Prior Year. The relationship between sales this year and sales last year for the medical instrument company is shown in Figure 9-13. It is evident from the

Figure 9-13. This year's sales versus last year's sales.

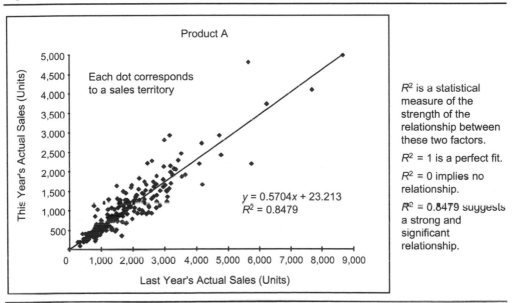

strength of this relationship that a sound goal-setting process for this company should acknowledge the prior year's sales.

Product Sales in Any Given Year Are Positively Correlated with Market Sales in the Prior Year. The relationship between this year's sales and last year's market sales for the medical instrument company is shown in Figure 9-14. Even though this relationship is not as strong as the one with prior year's sales, past market sales is usually a very good predictor of future sales. The market data include sales of key competitive products and were purchased from an outside data supplier to this industry. Analyses like this not only are useful for goal setting, but also provide insights about the performance of individual salespeople. Underperforming territories are usually the ones that fall significantly below the trend line in Figure 9-14. Plots like this can also be used by companies to determine the right total pay variation distribution for a sales force (see the discussion of performance grids in Chapter 4).

Product Sales in Any Given Year Are Positively Correlated with Surrogates for Market Potential. In many industries, precise market sales figures are difficult to obtain at the territory level. However, surrogates such as SIC sales, number of employees, building square footage, population, and consumer buying power

Figure 9-14. This year's sales versus last year's market sales.

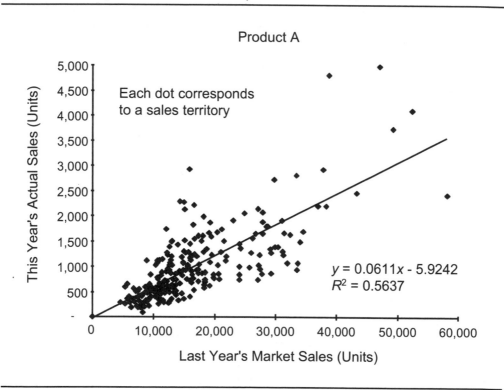

$$y = 0.0611x - 5.9242$$
$$R^2 = 0.5637$$

index are usually available. Territory sales are usually correlated with some of these surrogates. This suggests that companies that want to set high-quality goals at the territory level should strive to obtain a reasonable surrogate for territory-level market potential. The relationship between territory sales and population for the medical instrument company is shown in Figure 9-15.

Product Sales in Any Given Year Are Positively Correlated with a Competitor's Sales in the Prior Year. The sales of a competitor usually give a good indication of what our product sales are likely to be. This is especially useful information when launching a new product into an established market. If data on a competitor's sales are available at the territory level, this information can be used to establish goals for salespeople. The relationship between territory sales and a competitor's sales for the medical instrument company is shown in Figure 9-16.

As in the prior analyses, insights about performance can be gleaned from the graph. Territories that fall significantly below the trend line in Figure 9-16 are underperforming relative to the competitor.

Create a Matrix to View Correlations Across Multiple Factors at a Glance

This matrix summarizes the extent to which several different territory factors correlate with Product A sales for the medical instruments company.

Explanatory Variable	R^2 (Measures Correlation)
Last year's sales	0.8479
Last year's market sales	0.5637
Population	0.5358
Last year's sales of competitor 1	0.3738

The Market Share Change Expected for Any Given Year Is Related to the Starting Market Share in That Year. There is much debate about the relationship between territory market share and market share growth. The traditional view is that low market share (or low penetration) suggests a large opportunity, while high market share suggests significant penetration and little growth opportunity. This intuitive effect has been observed with many well-established products and sales territories. A high growth rate is not sustainable forever. There are only so many customers in each territory, and once they have all been penetrated, sales cannot continue to grow significantly. Data for highly penetrated territories provide an indication of the limits to growth in other territories.

Interestingly, the traditional, intuitive view of this relationship between terri-

Figure 9-15. This year's sales versus population.

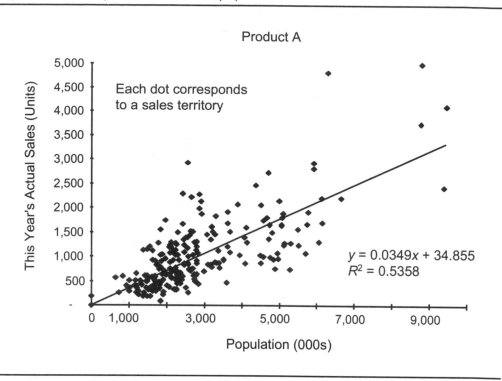

tory market share and sales growth is frequently not supported by data for new products or in very low-share territories. In fact, low-share products and territories often do not grow as quickly as medium-share products and territories. This leads to the conclusion that small market share does not always imply an immediate growth opportunity. Low-share products and territories do not benefit from the power of significant word of mouth among customers and prospects, which can accelerate sales quickly. In addition, low share may signal a problem. A competitor may be very strong, with a large, loyal customer base. There may be low awareness of the firm's product or service. Or the low-share territory may have been serviced by a poor-performing salesperson who weakened customer goodwill. In any case, it takes time to realize the opportunity, and share gains will not be immediate.

Figure 9-17 shows the relationship between territory market share and share growth for three different pharmaceutical products. The relationship varies depending upon the product and the situation. The relationship between these variables tends not to be as strong statistically as the relationships between sales and potential measures (as shown in Figures 9-13 through 9-16). Still, a relationship often exists, and plotting it can be very useful for understanding territory dynamics and setting realistic sales goals.

Measuring Territory Market Potential. Several of the analyses just discussed require data on territory market potential. In many industries, objective and accu-

Figure 9-16. This year's sales versus last year's competitor's sales.

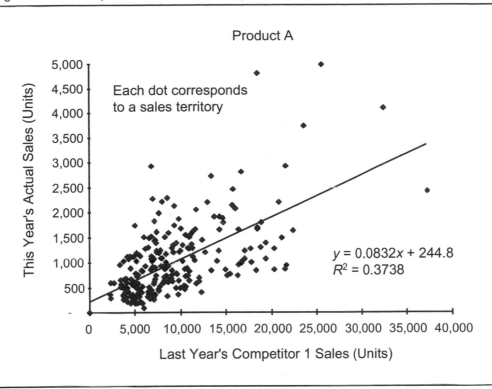

Product A

Each dot corresponds to a sales territory

$y = 0.0832x + 244.8$
$R^2 = 0.3738$

This Year's Actual Sales (Units)

Last Year's Competitor 1 Sales (Units)

rate territory-level market potential data are difficult to obtain. Creative approaches are often required in order to develop surrogate measures of territory potential. Such measures can be found for virtually every industry. Figure 9-18 provides some examples of surrogate market potential measures that various companies have used. Sources of market potential data include the U.S. Census Bureau, industry trade associations, *Sales and Marketing* magazine's Buying Power Index, and data and research companies such as Cahners, Global Insight (formerly DRI-WEFA), and Dun & Bradstreet.

Should Salespeople Provide Estimates of Account Potential?

Often, companies ask their sales force to provide estimates of account potential. Such data can be extremely valuable for account targeting and for territory planning and alignment. However, if input about account potential from salespeople is used for goal setting, salespeople may develop a pessimistic view of account potential!

Salespeople Have Developed Outstanding Customer Databases

A large medical imaging company developed an exceptional database when it collected the type and manufacturer of installed equipment as well as the

Figure 9-17. Market share change versus starting market share.

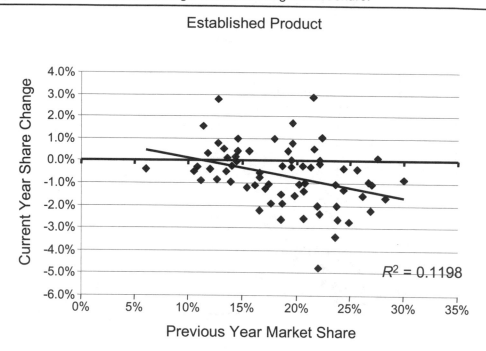

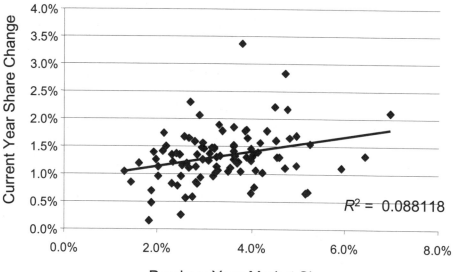

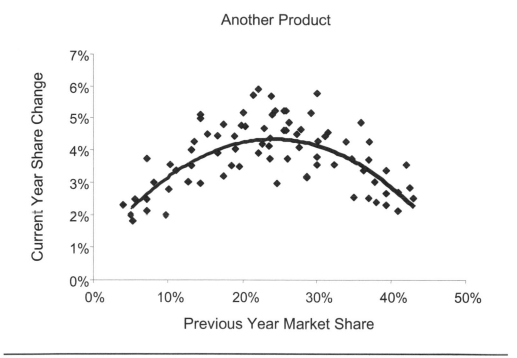

Figure 9-18. Surrogate measures of market potential for different industries.

Industry	Surrogate Measure of Market Potential
Building materials	Number of households earning over $100K, housing starts.
Computer software and peripherals	Installed number of different types of computers, overall company revenue, and number of company locations.
Health and beauty aids sold in retail stores	Type of outlet (mass merchandiser, drugstore, grocery store, etc.), commodity sales volume in each store.
	Buying Power Index—census track data on income, retail sales, and population.
Insurance	Number of employees.
Office equipment	Number of white-collar workers by industry.
Pharmaceuticals	Historical prescriptions written for a particular drug category in countries where pharmacy records are kept electronically.
	Physician office size, physician specialty, size of patient waiting area, and patient demographics in countries where electronic pharmacy records are not available.
Surgical instruments and supplies	Number of surgical procedures.

date of acquisition for each hospital and imaging lab in the country. The sales force provided the input for the database and used it for account planning, visiting prospects when their imaging equipment became dated.

Frequently, companies find it useful to translate surrogate potential measures into potential revenue dollars. This makes the sales potential estimate more meaningful and able to be acted upon. Heuristic approaches accomplish this translation in a systematic and rational way. Two variations of a useful heuristic approach are described here.

Start by segmenting accounts based on surrogate measures such as industry and number of employees. Then study the sales to accounts in each segment and develop a rule for estimating the level of sales that should be possible for each account. For example, consider the frequency distribution of sales at accounts in the market segment shown in Figure 9-19. There are 100 accounts in the segment. The height of each bar shows how many of these accounts produce the sales levels identified on the horizontal axis. One approach to estimating sales potential is as follows:

- Determine a certain percentile—for example, the 80th percentile of sales for the segment (i.e., determine the level of sales such that 80 percent of the accounts in the segment have sales below this level). In the example, 80 percent of the accounts fall below $50,000 in sales.

Figure 9-19. Frequency distribution of sales to accounts in one market segment.

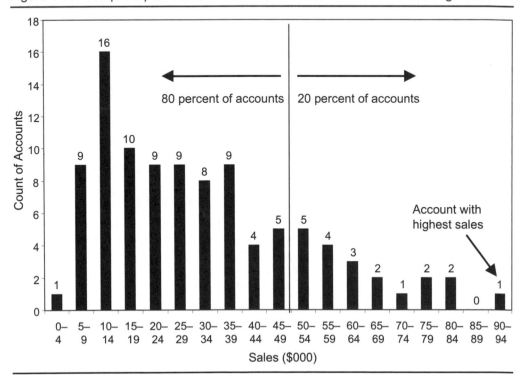

- Use this as a proxy for the sales potential of all accounts in the segment whose sales are lower than this level. In the example, any account with less than $50,000 in sales would have a potential of $50,000.

An alternative heuristic for translating surrogate potential data into revenue dollars is:

- For each segment, calculate the maximum sales that any account in the segment has achieved. In the example, maximum sales are $92,000.
- Define the possible sales increase in the other accounts as the difference between the account's current sales and a certain percentage, such as 50 percent, of the gap to the maximum. In the example, if an account has current sales of $30,000, its potential is estimated as $30,000 + 0.5 * ($92,000 − $30,000) = $61,000.

The appropriate percentile (in the first heuristic) or percentage (in the second heuristic) to use for estimating potential depends on the stage of the product or customer in the life cycle. In the growth stage, a higher percentile or percentage is appropriate. In the mature stage, a lower percentile or percentage is appropriate. Different heuristics may be appropriate for customers and prospects, or for low-penetration and high-penetration accounts. Heuristic approaches are approximate, yet they can be extremely valuable to sales organizations that wish to develop meaningful estimates of account sales potential.

Step 3: Develop Alternative Territory Goal-Setting Formulas or Processes

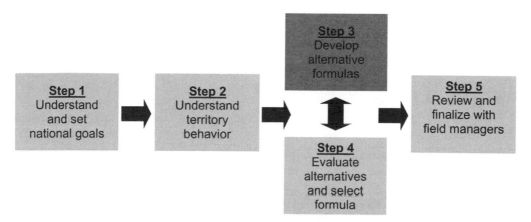

A solid understanding of territory expectations and behaviors forms the basis for determining the best formulas and processes for setting territory goals. Some selling organizations set territory-level goals using the subjective judgment of district and regional sales managers exclusively. Others rely on formulas (sometimes very complex formulas) to set territory goals. The best goal-setting processes typically rely on a combination of both data analysis and sales force input, with the relative importance of each being determined by the firm's selling situation and analytical capabilities, as well as the availability and accuracy of territory-level data.

Goal-setting formulas can be used successfully with most sales forces. Formulas help to make the process objective, explicit, and fair. Salespeople are less likely to feel that their goals are arbitrary. Sales managers are liberated from the hassle of developing and justifying territory goals. Even companies that rely completely on the first-line sales manager's discretion to set territory goals typically provide some guidelines. For example, managers may be told that each territory's goal cannot be less than last year's sales.

Goal-setting formulas are most effective when the sales force has many customers and transactions, and when history has a big impact on future sales. In addition, formulas require the company to have or acquire accurate and reliable territory-level data. Sales forces that do not meet these criteria will need to rely more extensively on sales force input in their goal-setting processes.

Various goal-setting formulas and processes have been developed and are being used by companies. Several recommended approaches are presented here. These approaches are organized into four categories. The first three categories contain formula-based approaches, which are organized according to their data requirements and complexity. The first category includes some basic methods that require only accurate historical territory-level sales data, the second category includes some more sophisticated formulas that also require territory-level potential data, and the third category includes the most complex approach, which also requires territory-level sales force effort or call data. The final category includes a bottom-up method of goal setting that is appropriate for situations where historical data are not a good predictor of future performance. The description of each approach includes an example that shows how to perform the necessary calculations.

The Simplicity Versus Fairness Trade-Off in Goal Setting

With formula-based goal-setting approaches, there is an inherent trade-off between fairness and simplicity. Simpler methods are easier to implement and to explain to salespeople, but they tend to be less fair to the sales force. More complex methods tend to be fairer, but often are data intensive, involve complex calculations, and are hard to explain to salespeople. Each selling organization needs to find its own appropriate balance.

Formula-Based Territory Goal-Setting Approaches Based on Historical Sales. Two methods of territory goal setting require only historical territory sales data: the maintenance plus standard growth method and the territory forecast method.

Maintenance Plus Standard Growth Method. The maintenance plus standard growth method is a commonly used goal-allocation formula. As illustrated in Figure 9-20, maintenance plus growth methods assume that each territory will maintain last year's sales and grow through additional sales.

There are two different ways in which territory growth is estimated using the standard growth method. The first method asks every territory to grow at the projected national growth rate. An example calculation using this method is shown in Figure 9-21. The total goal for every territory includes a maintenance goal and a growth goal. The maintenance goal is last year's sales. The growth goal is determined by multiplying the national growth goal of 10 percent by each territory's maintenance goal.

An alternative way to calculate territory growth goals using the maintenance plus standard growth method is to give each territory the same absolute growth amount, rather than the same percentage growth. In the example in Figure 9-21, the projected national growth of 400 units would be divided equally among the three territories, so that each territory would receive a growth goal of 133 units.

A method analogous to the maintenance plus growth method can be used for declining products. In this case, the formula starts with last year's sales in each territory and then reduces those sales by either a constant percentage or a constant dollar amount. The method might be more accurately called "last year's sales minus decline" when it is used for a declining product.

The maintenance plus standard growth method is simple and easy to explain to the sales force, and requires only data that typically are readily available—historical sales at the territory level. However, the method is not very fair because differences in market potential are not accounted for. If every territory is expected to grow at the projected national growth rate, salespeople who already have high sales are penalized by being given larger growth goals. On the other hand, if every

Figure 9-20. Maintenance plus growth method of goal allocation.

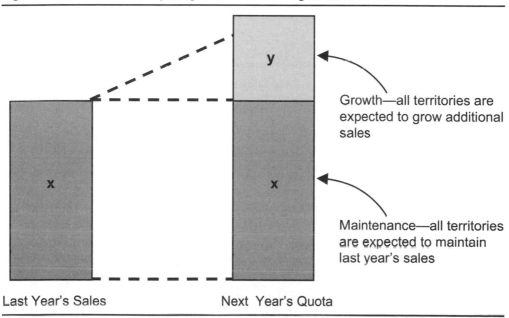

Growth—all territories are expected to grow additional sales

Maintenance—all territories are expected to maintain last year's sales

Last Year's Sales   Next Year's Quota

Figure 9-21. Maintenance plus standard growth method—example calculation.

	Previous Period Sales
	Units
Territory A	1,000
Territory B	1,000
Territory C	2,000
Nation	4,000

	Goal Calculations			Goal
	Maintenance Sales	Sales Growth Goal*	Sales Growth Goal	Maintenance Plus Growth Sales Goal
	Units	Percent	Units	Units
Territory A	1,000	10%	100	1,100
Territory B	1,000	10%	100	1,100
Territory C	2,000	10%	200	2,200
Nation	4,000	10%	400	4,400

*Same percent growth expected of every territory.

territory is expected to grow by the same absolute amount, salespeople with low sales are penalized by being given growth goals that require them to grow sales by a larger percentage.

Territory Forecast Method. The territory forecast method of goal setting uses historical sales patterns to project future sales in a territory. A forecast can be developed either by using the specific territory or by using analogous territories. Figure 9-22 shows an example of the territory forecast method using three specific sales territories. A time-series regression model uses sales data for each of the three territories in the previous eight quarters to project sales for the next quarter. The method assumes that the historical pattern of sales growth in each territory will continue into the future.

The territory forecast method using specific territories is based on a standard regression model that is usually fairly easy to use and is not difficult for salespeople to understand. However, this approach may not be appropriate when significant local changes are expected in a territory, such as when a new salesperson is assigned to the territory. The past territory sales trend was affected by the skills and experiences of the prior salesperson or by the territory's vacancy, and a new salesperson will change that trend. An alternative approach that overcomes this problem uses historical trends in analogous territories to project future growth.

Figure 9-22. Territory forecast method—example calculation.

Data	1999				2000			
	Quarter 1	Quarter 2	Quarter 3	Quarter 4	Quarter 1	Quarter 2	Quarter 3	Quarter 4
	Units	Units	Units	Units	Units	Units	Units	Units
Territory A	100	126	155	172	200	225	258	275
Territory B	130	131	132	134	137	139	142	144
Territory C	75	88	102	113	127	147	167	180
Nation	305	345	389	419	464	511	567	599

Goal	2001 Quarter 1
Territory A	302
Territory B	146
Territory C	193
Nation	641

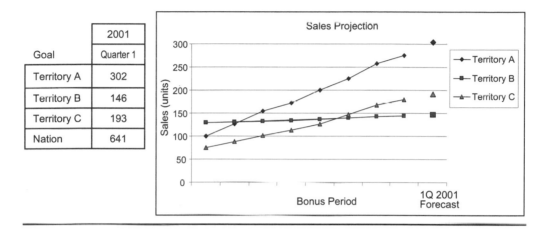

Territories are categorized along relevant dimensions, such as territory demographics (for example, rural versus urban) or region of the country. A forecast for each territory is then developed based on the aggregate trend across all territories with similar characteristics. This approach is slightly more complex, but it helps to avoid the biases that exist when the trend in only a single territory is considered.

The territory forecast method is appropriate in stable markets where no major new events that might disrupt existing sales trends, such as a new competitive launch or a major economic shift, are expected. If a major event is expected, each territory sales trend will need to be adjusted up or down appropriately in order to account for the event. An additional complication of using the territory forecast method is that the territory goals resulting from the calculations will not necessarily sum to equal the national goal. Appropriate adjustments will be needed in order to reconcile territory goals with the national number. The most significant shortcoming of the territory forecast method is that it does not account for market potential differences between territories.

Goals That Ignore Market Potential Differences Demoralize a Medical Device Sales Force

Management at a medical device company set territory goals using the maintenance plus standard growth method. This formula worked well in the firm's early years, when markets were growing and there was limited competition. However, as market growth slowed and competition intensified, salespeople in low-potential territories began to feel that their goals were unfair, since market potential differences across territories were not accounted for. To make things worse, management underestimated the impact of increased competition and set a national goal that was approximately 10 percent too high. About 75 percent of salespeople did not make goal that year, and the sales force was extremely frustrated and demoralized. One salesperson complained, "Management set goals simply according to their desired growth . . . those goals did not reflect the reality of market conditions."

Formula-Based Territory Goal-Setting Methods Based on Historical Sales and Market Potential. Territory goal-setting methods can be improved if data measuring territory market potential are available. Ideas on how to obtain measures of potential to project demand at the individual sales territory level are discussed earlier in this chapter.

Several methods for territory goal setting analyze data on historical sales and market potential to develop more realistic territory goals. These methods include the maintenance plus adjusted growth method, the weighted index method, the regression method, the performance frontier method, the share growth method, and the percent of remaining share method.

Maintenance Plus Adjusted Growth Method. The maintenance plus adjusted growth method is a more sophisticated implementation of the maintenance plus standard growth method illustrated in Figure 9-20. In the standard growth approach described in the prior section, every territory gets the same percentage growth or sales or unit growth goal. With the adjusted growth method, every territory gets a unique growth goal that is based on the amount of market potential in the territory that has not yet been penetrated. Thus, the territories with the lowest market share receive the largest growth goals, while those that have already been highly penetrated receive smaller growth goals. This method improves upon the standard growth method because it accounts for differences in territory opportunity. However, as described earlier in this chapter, empirical data do not always support the assertion that it is easier to grow sales in very-low-share territories.

An example of how goals are calculated using the maintenance plus adjusted growth method is shown in Figure 9-23. In this example, a national growth goal of 10 percent is allocated across the territories. The maintenance goal for each territory replicates last year's sales. The growth goal for each territory is allocated based on each territory's percentage of national unpenetrated market (unpenetrated market equals previous period market sales minus previous period product sales). An alternative and slightly simpler approach to this method allocates the growth goal for each territory based on each territory's percentage of national market potential.

Figure 9-23. Maintenance plus adjusted growth method—example calculation allocating a 10 percent growth rate.

	Previous Period Market Sales	Previous Period Product Sales	Unpenetrated Market	Unpenetrated Market
	Units	Units	Units	Percent of Nation
Territory A	10,000	1,000	9,000	46%
Territory B	7,500	1,000	6,500	33%
Territory C	6,000	2,000	4,000	21%
Nation	23,500	4,000	19,500	100%

	Goal Calculations		Goal
	Maintenance Sales Goal	Sales Growth Goal*	Maintenance Plus Growth
	Units	Units	Units
Territory A	1,000	185	1,185
Territory B	1,000	133	1,133
Territory C	2,000	82	2,082
Nation	4,000	400	4,400

*Sales growth goal = nation growth goal allocated based on unpenetrated market potential in each territory.

An Alternative View of Maintenance Sales

Using last year's sales as the "maintenance" portion of a territory goal may not be appropriate when a new salesperson is assigned to the territory. Last year's sales were affected by the skills and experiences of the prior salesperson, or perhaps by the territory's vacancy.

Some companies use free sales as an alternative to maintenance sales for territory goal setting. Free sales are sales that will occur even in the absence of sales force effort. Free sales happen for a number of reasons: because customers continue to purchase the company's products out of habit, because of long-term contracts, because of high switching costs, and because of marketing inertia. Some products have very high levels of free sales (80 percent or more), while others have very low levels of free sales (20 percent or less). Sales in vacant territories are a good example of free sales.

Free sales can be used as an alternative to maintenance sales when estimating territory goals. Free sales are calculated by multiplying last year's territory sales by an estimated carryover rate. Incremental sales, or *salesperson sales*, are those sales that require sales force effort, and they are allocated to each territory based on potential or other relevant territory and salesperson factors.

Free sales are an especially good estimate of maintenance sales in declining markets. They provide a baseline, and the incremental goal above baseline can be allocated based on territory market potential.

Pharmaceutical Sales Force Uses Carryover Rates to Improve Territory Goal Setting

Management at a pharmaceutical firm recognized that its products had high free sales and that many sales would be realized regardless of current sales force effort. The firm devised a territory goal-setting formula that accounted for this carryover. Through data analysis and management input, product-specific carryover rates were established. Drugs that treat acute conditions and are generally taken by patients for a short period, such as antibiotics and antihistamines, had lower carryover rates. Drugs that treat chronic conditions and are generally taken by patients for a longer period, such as high-blood-pressure medications and treatments for Alzheimer's disease, had higher carryover rates. To set territory goals, first, carryover sales were calculated for each product in each territory by multiplying last year's territory sales times the estimated carryover rate. Next, incremental sales, or those sales that require sales force effort to obtain (equal to this year's forecast minus last year's sales times the carryover rate), were allocated to each territory based on potential or other relevant territory and salesperson factors.

At first, the new goal-setting plan was quite effective. Territory goals were more fair and equitable across the sales force. However, over time, as salespeople began to understand the nuances of the allocation formula, some of the firm's best salespeople devised a way to use the formula to their advantage. The salespeople with the largest-volume territories and high market share recognized that they would benefit if carryover rates were reduced. With a lower carryover rate, each high-volume, high-market-share territory would get a proportionately smaller goal, while historically low-volume territories with low market share would get proportionately higher goals. Thus, salespeople in high-volume territories, who had significant power with management as a result of the large volume of business they controlled, negotiated with management for lower carryover rates. Eventually, they were successful at negotiating carryover rates down to unrealistic levels, which resulted in goals that were too easy for salespeople in high-volume territories and too challenging for salespeople in low-volume territories. After several years, the carryover-based goal-setting scheme was scrapped and replaced.

Authors' note: Rather than scrapping the plan, the firm could have tried

> *harder to manage the negotiation. Powerful and persuasive people can negotiate anything, and some salespeople will find a way to negotiate for their own personal advantage no matter what the incentive plan.*

Weighted Index Method. The weighted index method recognizes that many different territory characteristics can influence territory sales. In the maintenance plus adjusted growth method described in the prior section, two factors determine territory goals: past territory sales and unpenetrated market potential. In the weighted index method, additional factors can be considered as well. For example, a geographically dispersed territory may have lower sales than a highly concentrated urban territory as a result of the greater travel requirements. A territory in an area of high population growth may have greater opportunity than one in an area of declining growth. With the weighted index method, goals are allocated to territories based on a weighted average of multiple factors. Typical factors include unpenetrated market potential, market share, market growth, previous period sales, sales growth, key customer penetration, customer demographics, and land area.

The weighted index method for goal allocation effectively accounts for differences between territories. Since many different factors can be considered, it is likely that the formula contains at least one component desired by each salesperson. Thus, salespeople are more likely to feel that the goal allocation process is fair and unbiased. Additionally, the effect of data errors is reduced, since the allocation is not based on a single measure.

However, determining the best factors and the appropriate weighting for those factors can be difficult. Many firms rely on management judgment for this purpose. The weights assigned to the various factors should be tied to the firm's strategy. For example, the weighted index goal-allocation formula for a high-growth product may be weighted heavily (perhaps 80 percent or more) toward market potential. With a more mature product, a greater proportion of the weight (perhaps 60 percent or more) may be placed on past sales. The weights not only influence goal allocation, but also communicate strategy to the sales force. For example, a goal that is based 50 percent on the performance of a specific competitive product says to the sales force, "Go after that competitor." A goal that is based 75 percent on last year's sales says, "Maintain your current base of business." Determining the right factors and weights for the goal allocation index is very important. If factors and weights are determined arbitrarily or nonobjectively, the resulting allocation may be inappropriate.

An example of how goals are calculated using the weighted index method is shown in Figure 9-24. First, management determines the appropriate factors and weightings for the goal-allocation formula—in this case, 30 percent weight on previous period sales, 60 percent weight on uncaptured market sales, and 10 percent weight on penetration of key customers. Next, the percentage that each territory contributes to the national total for each of the selected factors is calculated. Then a goal-allocation percentage is calculated for every territory based on the weighted sum of the various factor percentages.

Figure 9-24. Weighted index method—example calculation where the national goal is 1,000 units.

	Factor 1		Factor 2		Factor 3	
	Previous Period Sales		Uncaptured Market Sales		Penetration of Key Customers	
	Units	Percent of Nation	Units	Percent of Nation	Relative Concen-tration	Percent of Nation
Territory A	100	14%	900	13%	4	33%
Territory B	200	29%	1,600	23%	3	25%
Territory C	400	57%	4,500	64%	5	42%
Nation	700	100%	7,000	100%	12	100%

Weighting	0.3	0.6	0.1

	Goal Calculations	Goal Allocation Percent	Goal Units
Territory A	14% X 0.3 + 13% X 0.6 + 33% X 0.1 =	15%	150
Territory B	29% X 0.3 + 23% X 0.6 + 25% X 0.1 =	25%	250
Territory C	57% X 0.3 + 64% X 0.6 + 42% X 0.1 =	60%	600
Nation		100%	1,000

Regression Method. Some companies use regression models to derive the factors and weights that should determine territory goals. The regression method is similar to the weighted index method described in the prior section, except that regression techniques, rather than management judgment, are used to determine the appropriate factors and weights. Regression models evaluate the strength of the relationship between territory performance and independent territory factors from a statistical perspective. For example, regression models can show what sales to expect in a territory given the territory's market potential, market share, market growth, previous period sales, sales growth, key customer penetration, customer demographics, and/or land area. An appropriate weight for each factor can be derived based on the relative strength of the correlation between that factor and territory sales.

Regression models are particularly useful in data-rich environments. They can provide an objective and unbiased way to determine the factors and weights that can best account for differences across territories. Regression models can incorporate many different factors, so that sales force acceptance is enhanced and the effect of data errors is reduced. The challenge of using regression models for goal setting is that they involve large amounts of data and complex calculations. They can be difficult to explain and "sell" to the sales force. In addition, regression-based territory forecasts may not sum exactly to the national goal. Thus, goals calculated using a regression model will need to be adjusted appropriately.

An example of how one company calculated goals using dual regression models is shown in Figure 9-25. In the example, two independent simple regressions are used to predict territory market share growth, one based on market size and the other based on market share. The relative strength of the relationship with each of the two predictor variables caused management to decide to use a 40-60 weighting of market size and market share in the goal-setting formula. A more sophisticated regression-based approach uses multivariate regression to analyze numerous predictor variables simultaneously. The actual coefficients derived from the regression model can be used as weights for calculating territory goals.

Performance Frontier Method. The performance frontier approach to territory goal setting requires that salespeople strive to perform as well as the best performers in the selling organization. This approach uses cross-sectional historical data analysis to determine what level of performance is possible for each territory. The analysis uses statistical techniques to control for territory differences. Once territory-specific factors have been accounted for, any variation in the sales data can then be attributed to salesperson performance. Market potential and prior sales history are good territory factors to try to account for. The performance frontier approach is most intuitive when it is viewed in two dimensions. The vertical axis reflects the measure of performance that the goals will be based upon (for example, sales). The horizontal axis reflects an independent territory characteristic that is thought to influence the performance measure (for example, market potential). The relationship between the two selected measures can help reveal what level of performance is possible in each territory.

Figure 9-26 shows an example of the performance frontier method from the pharmaceutical industry. A territory's starting market share is thought to influence the amount of market share growth that is possible. The graph shows the scatter of territories plotted according to their starting market shares and market share growth. The best-performing territories are those that have the highest market share growth, given their starting market share. The line arcing across the top of the graph joins these top-performing territories. This line, called the performance frontier, represents the best share growth that has been attained by members of this sales force for every starting market share. Salespeople in territories that fall below the performance frontier are underperforming, because other salespeople with similar starting market shares have demonstrated that higher share growth is attainable.

Performance frontier analysis can be used to determine territory goals. Those salespeople who are performing below the frontier are given goals that challenge them to move closer to the frontier. For example, the tips of the three vertical arrows in Figure 9-26 show the new goals for three selected territories that challenge these salespeople to move their territory market share 50 percent closer to

Figure 9-25. Regression method—example calculation.

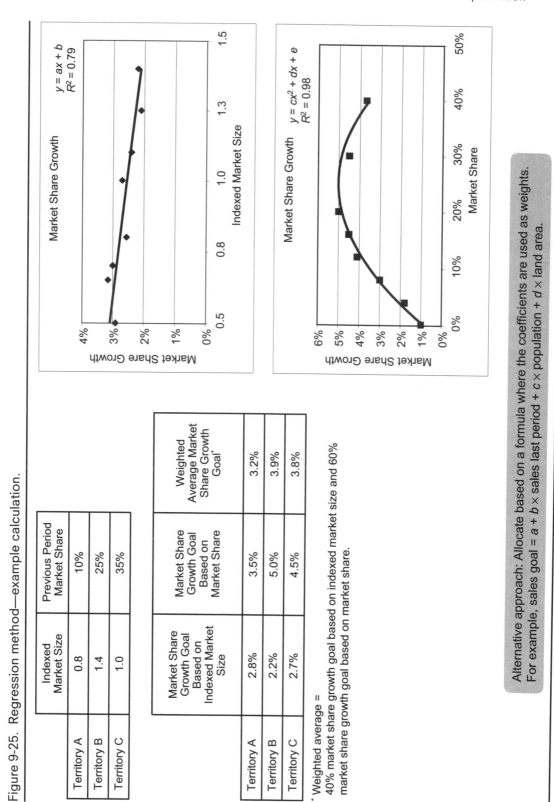

	Indexed Market Size	Previous Period Market Share
Territory A	0.8	10%
Territory B	1.4	25%
Territory C	1.0	35%

	Market Share Growth Goal Based on Indexed Market Size	Market Share Growth Goal Based on Market Share	Weighted Average Market Share Growth Goal*
Territory A	2.8%	3.5%	3.2%
Territory B	2.2%	5.0%	3.9%
Territory C	2.7%	4.5%	3.8%

*Weighted average =
40% market share growth goal based on indexed market size and 60% market share growth goal based on market share.

Alternative approach: Allocate based on a formula where the coefficients are used as weights. For example, sales goal = $a + b \times$ sales last period + $c \times$ population + $d \times$ land area.

Figure 9-26. Performance frontier method—example.

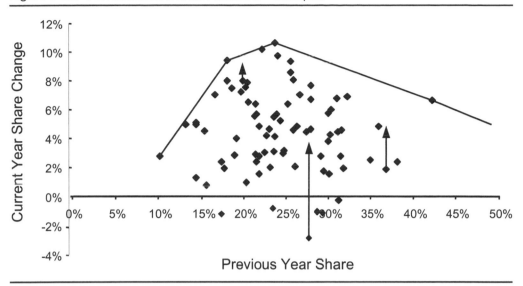

Previous Year Share

the frontier. The appropriate percentile depends not only on the degree to which management desires to challenge low performers, but also on the life cycle of the product. A higher percentile might be appropriate for a product with significant untapped opportunity and growth potential, while a lower percentile might be appropriate for a more mature product with less growth potential.

The challenges of using the performance frontier method are a consequence of the method's complexity. The statistical data analysis can be difficult to perform and communicate to the sales force when two or more territory characteristics are deemed essential to help explain territory sales. Also, the calculated territory goals will not add up to the national goal, so adjustments will be required.

Many companies will take a single measure, such as territory market potential, and develop a two-dimensional plot. The risk with this simple approach is that an important factor that is outside of a salesperson's control can make the performance frontier goal unrealistic for some salespeople.

Share Growth Method. Goals computed by the share growth method ask each salesperson to grow the market share in his territory by the amount by which national market share is expected to grow. Figure 9-27 shows an example of how the method works for two sales territories. Last year's actual market share for each territory is estimated by dividing territory sales by territory market potential. Next, the gain in national share points implied by next year's national sales goal is computed. In this example, next year's national sales goal implies a share gain of two points, so each territory gets a goal reflecting a two-point territory share gain. This method can also be used for products with declining share. In this case, each territory gets a goal reflecting a share loss equal to the projected national share loss.

Figure 9-27. Share growth method—example calculation for two territories.

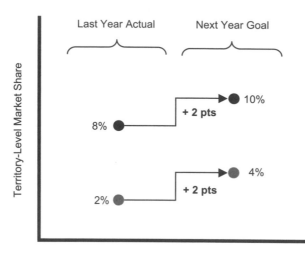

The share growth method is used frequently by companies that track and manage territory market shares. The method is fairly easy to communicate and calculate. However, the method is not always fair because it ignores territory differences.

Percent of Remaining Share Method. A salesperson who has already attained high market share in her territory might argue that the share growth method just described is unfair. The approach expects a salesperson with high share to grow share points by the same amount as a salesperson with low share, even though there is less remaining opportunity in a high-share territory. An adaptation of the share growth approach that acknowledges this unfairness is called the percent of remaining market share approach. Remaining market share is defined as the difference between a territory's market share and the highest market share that it is possible to attain (based on management input and existing market share data). Each territory is asked to get the same percentage of remaining share, rather than the same absolute share growth. Figure 9-28 shows what share increase each of the territories shown in the previous example (Figure 9-27) would be expected to attain using this method. Assume, as in the prior example, that the national market share is expected to grow by 2 points (assume a current national market share of 4 share points and a share implied by next year's national sales goal of 6 share points).

Figure 9-28. Percent of remaining share method—example calculation for two territories.

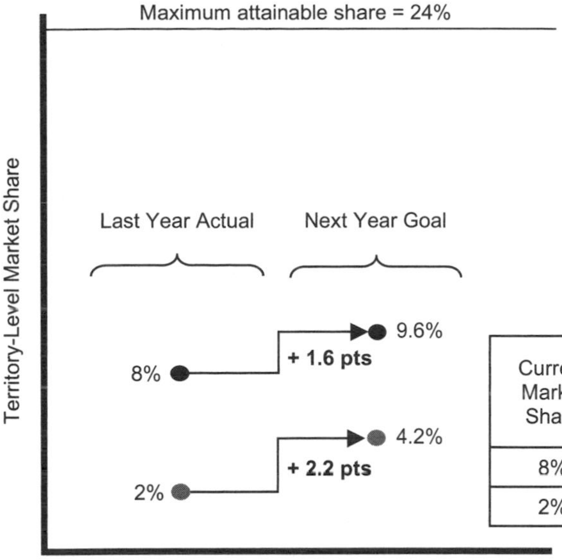

Current Market Share	Remaining Share (Maximum = 24%)	10% of Remaining Share	Goal Next Year
8%	16%	1.6%	9.6%
2%	22%	2.2%	4.2%

Management feels that the highest possible market share that could ever be attained is 24 share points. Thus, the current national available share is 20 points (24 highest possible share points minus 4 current share points), and the company wants to get 10 percent of these 20 points (or 2 share points) next year. Thus, each salesperson is asked to grow share by 10 percent of his available share. Since a territory with lower starting market share has more remaining market share than a territory with higher starting market share, the small-share territory is expected to contribute more share point growth than the large-share territory.

While this method accounts for territory market share differences, it is somewhat difficult to communicate to the sales force. Also, the calculated territory goals may not add up to the national goal, so adjustments may be required.

Formula-Based Territory Goal-Setting Method Based on Historical Sales, Market Potential, and Sales Effort. Territory goal setting can be improved even further in cases where data on historical sales effort are available at the territory level, along with data on sales and market potential. The sales response method described here has the potential to improve goal-setting accuracy significantly; however, since the method is complex and requires detailed data, it has had only limited use by companies.

Sales Response Method. Like the performance frontier method, the sales response method uses the best possible territory performance as a benchmark for goal setting. What makes this method unique is that territory results are tied to sales force effort. Sales response models not only estimate what level of performance is possible in each territory, but also show what effort allocation across customers, market segments, or products can enable a salesperson to attain that level of performance.

A simple sales response relationship for a territory is presented in Figure 9-29. The graph shows what sales a salesperson can expect to achieve if she directs different levels of effort (frequency of calls) toward two different account segments—high-potential and low-potential accounts.

The model shows the salesperson how to spend her time in order to get the greatest return. Additional effort directed toward the high-potential accounts generates incrementally more sales, and consequently more gross margin, than a similar investment of effort in low-potential accounts (assuming similar pricing in each segment). The recommended allocation of time to each account segment depends upon the cost of a sales call. For example, assume that all accounts in a territory are currently covered with low frequency. To decide whether or not to increase the frequency for each account segment, compare the cost of the additional calls with the expected gross margin increase resulting from the higher call frequency. For example, assume that increasing from low to moderate frequency on high-potential accounts generates more in gross margin than the cost of the additional sales calls, but increasing from low to moderate frequency on low-potential accounts does not generate enough gross margin to pay for the cost of the additional calls. In this case, the best call strategy is to increase the call frequency on high-potential accounts but keep a low call frequency on low-potential accounts.

The most sophisticated sales response models consider the gross margin that

Figure 9-29. A simple sales response relationship.

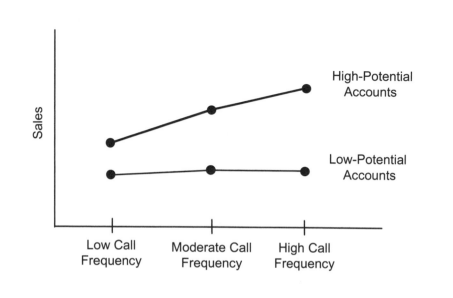

sales calls generate not only this year, but also in future years. Many selling situations have significant carryover—some sales generated this year will be retained in future years, without additional sales force effort. Considering the long-term impact of sales calls makes it attractive to call on more customers with greater frequency than when only the current-year impact is considered.

Sales response models predict what sales are achievable if a salesperson spends his time in the smartest possible way. The goals that result from the analysis are truly stretch goals—they challenge salespeople to make the best use of their time in order to attain the highest possible level of performance.

Despite the theoretical attractiveness of the sales response method of goal setting, this method is rarely used in practice. It requires detailed sales and activity data. These data do not exist at many companies, and investment is required to develop them. Even with good data, this method is usually difficult and expensive to implement, as it requires statistics and complex modeling at the individual territory level. In addition, this method is difficult to explain to the sales force.

While sales response modeling is very difficult to implement successfully at the territory level, many firms have used it effectively as an important input for setting national goals. National models can be built using data at a more aggregate level and thus are more manageable and more likely to produce reliable results than territory-level models. The process of developing the national model can identify high and low performers, insights that can be used in the territory goal-setting process.

Sales Force Input–Based Territory Goal-Setting Method. Formula-based goal-setting methods do not work in situations where historical data are not available or are not good predictors of future performance. In such situations, sales force input can contribute to the goal-setting process. Sales force input can be collected in an organized way using the bottom-up method.

Bottom-Up Method. The bottom-up method of forecasting requires that each salesperson set the goal for her own territory, with management guidance. This encourages sales force commitment to territory goals. The method works especially well in situations where each salesperson has a better understanding of the future potential in her territory than the company does. Situations with complex, high-priced products, many participants in the buying process, many steps in the selling funnel, a limited number of accounts, and long selling cycles provide conditions in which bottom-up forecasting may be appropriate. A good key account manager understands the needs of his customers intimately, and is thus uniquely qualified to provide the best estimate of how much each customer will buy in the future. Others at the company do not have the knowledge, data, or depth of understanding required to make such an estimate accurately.

Forecasting with Sales Force Input Is Sometimes the Only Option

Territory goal setting is particularly challenging in environments with long selling cycles, where salespeople make just a few major sales every year.

> In such situations, sales can be difficult to predict. There are so few trans-actions that the statistical law of large numbers cannot help to balance out prediction errors. In these situations, the account plans developed by individual salespeople often contain the only reliable information about what sales are in the pipeline and how likely they are to close. Thus, reliance on sales force input is the only feasible way for management to determine reasonable goals. In situations like this, where results are difficult to predict, it is common for salespeople to be given other types of objectives, such as customer service or activity objectives, in addition to company results goals.

The biggest problem with the bottom-up method of forecasting is that unless it is managed carefully, salespeople do not have an incentive to forecast accurately. If salespeople know that they will be judged on goal attainment, they may be very conservative in estimating potential. That way, they can easily attain goal, earn more money, and appear to be high performers.

Bottom-Up Goals Contribute to Slow Growth for a Printing Ink Maker

A seller of printing inks asked the sales force to provide estimates of projected sales by account to be included in the annual business plan. With only minor adjustments, this information was also used to establish territory goals. The process resulted in goals that were very conservative and easily reachable within the current customer base. Almost every salesperson made goal three years in a row, despite the fact that company sales growth lagged significantly behind industry growth.

Clever design of the goal-setting process can guard against the problem of underforecasting. For example, Jacob Gonik, author of "Tie Salesmen's Bonuses to Their Forecasts" (*Harvard Business Review,* 1978), developed an innovative goal-setting plan for IBM in Brazil. Each salesperson was asked to select her own territory goal from a territory-specific matrix of choices, as shown in Figure 9-30.

The rows of the matrix represent the salesperson's forecast at the start of the planning period, and the columns represent the actual territory sales at the end of the period. The salesperson's payout depends both on her forecast and on actual sales. Once the salesperson decides upon her forecast, the payout possibilities are restricted to the corresponding row of the matrix. Notice that the numbers in each row are increasing. Therefore, the salesperson receives increasing compensation as she increases sales. Thus, the salesperson is always motivated to continue selling as much as possible. On the other hand, the columns are developed so that the largest payout appears in the row where the salesperson's forecast matches actual sales. Hence, salespeople earn the most money when they forecast accurately.

The Gonik plan rewards the sales force for performance, and also for good forecasting. This plan is especially useful when the company relies on the sales

Figure 9-30. Incentive payout matrix that encourages accurate forecasting by salespeople.

Territory Sales ($ Millions)

		2.50	2.75	3.00	3.25	3.50	3.75
	3.50	10.5	17.8	27.3	40.6	**62.0**	70.6
Objectives ($ Millions)	3.25	12.3	20.9	32.1	**47.7**	57.2	65.2
	3.00	14.5	24.6	**37.7**	44.0	52.8	60.2
	2.75	17.0	**28.9**	34.8	40.6	48.7	55.5
	2.50	**20.3**	26.6	32.0	37.5	44.9	51.2

Payout Matrix
(Salesperson picks the objective)

force to forecast production and manufacturing requirements. Poor forecasting increases manufacturing costs. Underforecasting results in stock-outs, and over-forecasting produces extra inventory. The incentive payout differences down the columns incorporate some fraction of these costs. As a result, the sales force shares in the real costs of stock-outs and excess inventory.

This is an innovative and useful type of plan; however, it also has disadvantages. It is complicated and requires clear communication to the sales force.

Goal-Setting Approaches for New Products. Goal setting for new products is fraught with uncertainty. No historical sales data are available. Firms must rely on data that reflect potential, such as market sales, competitive sales, or demographic information, to forecast likely sales in each territory. Until a new product is launched, the ability of a management team to set accurate territory-level sales goals is always limited. Sometimes, there is so much uncertainty with a new product that it is best not to set territory-level goals at all. Instead, each salesperson might earn a commission percentage on every sale. With time, as knowledge of the market increases and historical sales data become available, goals can be established and added to the incentive plan.

Two goal-setting approaches that can be used with new products are the market potential method and the constant allocation method.

Market Potential Method. With the market potential method, sales are allocated to territories based on market potential. For example, a territory that has 2 percent of national market potential is assigned 2 percent of the national goal. Market potential can be captured in a single measure or in a combination of weighted measures (see the weighted index and regression methods described earlier).

Constant Allocation Method. The constant allocation method for goal setting is also used frequently with new products. This method assumes that each salesperson has to sell a constant amount and that this amount is tied to the quantity of activity that each salesperson has time to perform. For example, suppose the firm estimates that, on average, it will take 10 hours of selling effort to close each $10,000 deal. If each salesperson has 1,500 hours of selling time available in a year, a realistic goal is for each person to sell ($10,000/10 hours per deal) × 1,500 hours available = $1,500,000. The constant allocation method works particularly well for new products with significant potential, where the amount of available sales force time limits how much of that potential can be captured in a given time frame. The constant allocation method can also be combined with other goal-setting methods. For example, each salesperson might be asked to sell a constant allocation amount, plus additional sales to be allocated according to another method, such as the market potential, regression, or weighted index method.

Summary of Methods. As stated earlier, a firm's selling situation and analytical sophistication, along with the availability and accuracy of territory-level data, determine what goal-setting method is most reasonable. In many situations, these factors limit the possible choices. For example, if historical data are not available or are not accurate predictors of what is likely to happen in the future, the bottom-up approach or one of the new product approaches to goal setting makes the most sense. Similarly, if a formula-based approach is desired, but market potential data or reasonable surrogates are not available at the territory level, the firm is limited to using a method that requires only data that are available, such as territory-level sales. Also, firms with limited analytical capabilities will be better off choosing one of the less complex goal-setting methods.

Firms that have territory-level market potential data, along with strong analytical capabilities, have many more goal-setting options. To determine the best approach, management at these firms must assess the trade-off between simplicity and accuracy of the goal-setting process. A complex goal-setting formula or process may create a more accurate result, but it will probably be more difficult and costly to implement and to explain to the sales force. Sometimes a simpler process, though less exact, creates a better result because the goals will be more readily understood and embraced by salespeople and sales managers. Often, companies that are unsure about which goal-setting method is best use several of the methods to set goals. Then, they evaluate and compare the results of each method in order to select the best one. More information about how to evaluate the consequences of alternative goal-setting approaches is described in Step 4.

Pharmaceutical Firm Considers Trade-Offs Between Goal-Setting Accuracy and Sales Force Commitment to Goals

A multinational pharmaceutical company had developed a complex and very accurate goal-setting model. This model had evolved over a number of years and was based on extensive physician-level data on prescriptions written by each physician for both the firm's products and competitive products. Using the model, the company could predict sales at the territory level with a high degree of accuracy. Goals with the appropriate degree of challenge were consistently set: Almost every incentive period, approximately 80 percent of the sales force achieved goal. Yet the sales force did not embrace the goals. The model was developed at headquarters and involved complex data modeling and statistics that the sales force did not understand. Even though the headquarters group had explained the model to the sales force on several occasions and had provided concise summary information, most salespeople felt that their goals were developed in a black box and were arbitrary. Management struggled with what to do. Should it simplify the model so that the sales force could understand it, even if this meant sacrificing accuracy?

Step 4: Evaluate the Consequences of Each Alternative and Select the Best Approach

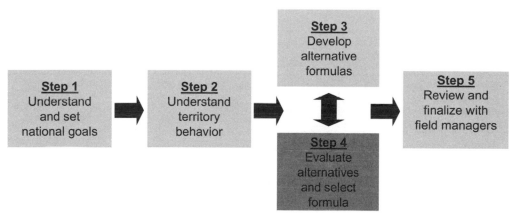

Any new formula or process for goal setting should be tested before it is implemented. This is especially true if a significant portion of the sales force's incentive compensation is tied to goal attainment. One valuable testing approach is to evaluate the consequences of the goals developed from a proposed new formula using historical data. This involves calculating what the goals would have been last year if the proposed goal-setting formula had been implemented a year ago and last year's national sales had hit last year's national goal exactly. Then, the calculated goals are compared to last year's actual sales by territory to see how goal attainment for each salesperson would have been affected. In short, the new goal-setting formula is tested by applying it to data from two years ago (the data that would have been used to set goals for last year) and then comparing the results with how last year actually turned out.

Figures 9-31 and 9-32 show the results of this test for one sales district at a firm that is deciding between two possible goal-setting approaches: the maintenance plus adjusted growth method and the weighted index method. A goal for last year is calculated for each territory by applying the new proposed formula to

Figure 9-31. Testing of goal-setting alternative 1, maintenance plus adjusted growth method.

Salesperson	Sales 2 Years Ago ($000)	Goal for Last Year ($000)	Sales Last Year ($000)	Difference ($000)
Anderson	1,840	1,940	1,920	-20
Brown	1,600	1,698	1,680	-18
Carlson	1,500	1,575	1,720	145
Donahue	1,300	1,333	1,450	117
Everett	1,220	1,315	940	-375
Fink	1,120	1,176	1,140	-36
Good	880	967	1,030	63
Harper	620	716	840	124
Total	10,080	10,720	10,720	0

Figure 9-32. Testing of goal-setting alternative 2, weighted index method.

Salesperson	Sales 2 Years Ago ($000)	Goal for Last Year ($000)	Sales Last Year ($000)	Difference ($000)
Anderson	1,840	1,790	1,920	130
Brown	1,600	1,662	1,680	18
Carlson	1,500	1,490	1,720	230
Donahue	1,300	1,018	1,450	432
Everett	1,220	1,254	940	-314
Fink	1,120	1,051	1,140	89
Good	880	1,233	1,030	-203
Harper	620	1,222	840	-382
Total	10,080	10,720	10,720	0

territory data from two years ago. This goal is then compared to actual sales data from last year, and the difference is computed.

The credibility of the new goal-setting approach is enhanced when the difference between the goal suggested by the new formula and actual sales performance for each salesperson has an intuitive explanation. For example, suppose management knows that Everett has had serious performance problems. Both proposed goal-setting approaches are consistent with this knowledge, since they both show that Everett would have failed to make goal by a substantial margin. In addition, if management feels that Harper is a consistently strong performer whom they want to retain, the maintenance plus adjusted growth method (alternative 1) works well, but the weighted index method (alternative 2) does not because Harper would have missed goal by a lot.

Testing the consequences of alternative goals using historical data provides valuable insights. The test, however, makes a strong assumption. It assumes that the goal itself would not have motivated the salesperson to act any differently, whereas goals are usually motivational. Hence, it is likely that this test understates the level of expected goal achievement. The test errs on the conservative side. For example, the test assumes that Anderson would have missed goal by $20,000 if the maintenance plus adjusted growth method (alternative 1) had been used for goal setting. It is likely, however, that the alternative goal of $1.94 million for Anderson's territory would have motivated him to work harder to sell an additional $20,000 in order to make goal. Still, testing provides valuable information that can be used to determine which salespeople are likely to get hurt and which are likely to be helped by alternative goal-setting processes.

Chapter 8 develops a number of tests for candidate sales incentive plans. Several of the same tests can be used for checking alternative goal-setting formulas. Specifically, the "who gets helped/who gets hurt" analysis, the goal attainment and payout distributions, and the engagement and excitement rates can help provide data for the selection of the best goal-setting formula.

Step 5: Review and Finalize Goals with Field Sales Managers

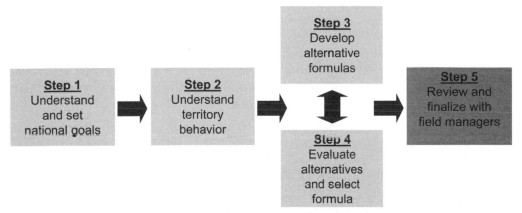

It is critical for field sales managers to be involved in the final territory goal-setting decision for two primary reasons. First, field sales managers may have important local knowledge that should be considered in the goal-setting process. A sales manager may be aware of special circumstances that render a calculated territory goal unfair or unattainable. For example, there may be territory differences caused by local economic conditions or specific competitive situations. New salespeople, vacant territories, sick leave, near retirement, and special relationships are also factors that may need to be considered when finalizing goals. For example, recently filled territories that were vacant for an extended period of time may be less productive than calculated because of lost carryover.

A second reason to involve field sales managers in the goal-setting process is to facilitate their understanding of how the goals were set and to increase the sales force's commitment to the goals. Sales managers will have to live with the goals and be prepared to defend them to their salespeople for the entire incentive period. Managers are more likely to support goals that they understand well and have had input into setting.

The first step in involving the field in the goal-setting process is education. Goals are central to salespeople. They define performance and determine rewards. Salespeople need to know that their goals are not arbitrary. Firms often conduct presentations at national or regional sales meetings to inform the sales force about how goals were developed and what rules and procedures exist for making adjustments. The information shared at the meeting can be supplemented with short handouts or Web-based documents summarizing important details. One advantage of using a more straightforward goal-setting formula, such as maintenance plus growth or weighted index, it that such a formula is easier for the sales force to understand. It is possible to describe the exact goal calculation formula, and each salesperson can confirm that her goal is correct by applying the formula to data for her own territory. This often increases the sales force's comfort level with the goals. With more complex formula methods, such as regression or frontier, it is not necessary and usually not possible for the field to understand all the details of goal calculation. However, it is important to educate salespeople and managers about the logic behind the approach and to get their conceptual buy-in to the factors that have been considered.

Companies with large sales forces and multiple management levels typically use a waterfall approach for allowing field review and adjustment of goals. For example, suppose salespeople report to district managers, who report to regional directors, who report to a vice president of sales. A goal-setting formula suggests goals from the bottom up; goals are estimated for each sales territory, and these goals are then summed together to develop goals for districts and regions. The field management review process, on the other hand, works in the reverse order, with goal review cascading from the top down to the regional directors and then the district managers.

The goal review process just described might proceed in the following way. First, the vice president of sales reviews the formula-determined goals for each region (which are determined by summing the formula-derived goals for all territories within the regions) and makes any adjustments that he feels are appropriate. Usually the sales vice president seeks input from the regional managers before finalizing their goals. If any goal changes are made, then the goals for territories within the affected regions are adjusted appropriately. This is typically done using a formula that redistributes the additional goal (or the reduction in goal) logically across all the territories in the region. Different redistribution formulas can be used, including proportional allocation of the change across territories and allocations based on historical territory sales, untapped potential, or constant growth. Next, the cascade continues as the regional directors review the formula-determined goals for each of the districts within their region (which are the sum of the adjusted goals for all territories within the districts). The regional directors make any adjustments they feel are appropriate, and again, if adjustments are made, the goals for territories within the affected districts are adjusted appropriately. Finally, district managers are given a chance to adjust the territory-level goals within their district. Changes at all levels must sum to zero. For example, if a district manager reduces the goal for one sales territory, she must increase the goal for another territory by the same amount (or alternatively, the amount of the goal reduction can be spread as a goal increase across several territories).

Establishing House Accounts

Some firms allow sales managers to allocate a portion of their goal to a house account at the district, region, or national level. For example, if a district sales manager is responsible for selling to a large key account that influences business throughout the entire district, the goal for that account can be given to a district house account, rather than being allocated to individual salespeople. This allows the district to get credit for sales to the account while protecting salespeople from being evaluated on sales that they do not control.

Web-based systems are used by many companies to facilitate field manager review of territory goals. Using these systems, managers in the field can propose changes to territory goals based on local knowledge. Field sales managers access a secure web site that provides historical performance data about their territories and the proposed goals for each territory. The managers then review these data and submit suggested adjustments to territory goals for approval by headquarters. Once approved, the changes are applied immediately. A Web-based system allows faster turnaround between goal creation and rollout. It also ensures greater accuracy, since the system enforces zero-sum changes and allocates revisions to subordinate territories fairly. The Web-based system also provides an audit trail of changes, so that all adjustments are properly documented and can be tracked easily.

Goal-Setting Adjustments and Legal Issues

One advantage of using formula-based goal-setting processes is that they are more legally defensible than subjective processes. A salesperson who is fired for consistent failure to achieve goals will have difficulty claiming in a lawsuit that her goals were unfair if the same goal-setting formula is used for everyone in the sales force. For this reason, many firms require any management adjustments to formula-derived goals to be documented carefully. Some firms set rules about how much adjustment is allowed—for example, a manager may adjust a goal by no more than 10 percent from the formula-suggested goal. Rules and documentation requirements can be easily enforced through the use of Web-based systems.

By studying the adjustments that field sales managers make during the goal review process, companies sometimes discover ways to improve their goal-setting formulas. Systematic adjustments to goals across the sales force can signal that the goal-setting formula is biased. For example, if goals in territories with high market share are consistently reduced during field review, then perhaps the goal-setting formula needs to change so that territories with high market share get smaller goal allocations. In another example, if the field consistently reduces goals in rural territories and increases them in urban territories, then perhaps travel time needs to be considered explicitly in the goal-setting formula.

Does Allowing Field Sales Managers to Adjust Formula-Based Goals Improve Goal-Setting Accuracy?

One sales force did a study to find out the answer to this question. Accuracy was measured by examining how close actual territory results came to both the formula-derived goals and the field-adjusted goals. This is a simplistic view of goal accuracy, as it assumes that all territory results are the consequence of reasonable workload and not exceptional effort on the part of salespeople. Nevertheless, the analysis provides interesting insight regarding the value of goal adjustment by the field sales managers in this sales force. Sales managers were allowed to adjust formula-based goals by up to 12 percent; adjustments were made to approximately one-quarter of the goals. Field-adjusted goals were found to be more accurate than formula-derived goals in cases where the goals had been adjusted downward, suggesting that managers were good at identifying territory problems. However, the field-adjusted goals were less accurate than the formula-derived goals in cases where the goals had been adjusted upward, suggesting that managers were not as good at identifying territory opportunities. Overall, field adjustments resulted in only a slight improvement in the accuracy of the goals. Despite this fact, the company decided to continue allowing field managers to adjust goals because the process significantly enhanced sales force understanding of and commitment to goals, and the adjustments did not significantly increase the overall incentive budget.

Tracking Performance Against Goals

Effective goals energize a sales force. When implemented well, they are great motivators for salespeople. However, in order for goals to motivate, feedback is necessary. Salespeople need to know how they are doing relative to a goal, if that goal is to affect their behavior.

Systems for Providing Feedback on Goal Attainment

Most sales forces provide performance feedback to salespeople at regular intervals, such as monthly or quarterly. This feedback usually includes reports that track territory performance against goals and can be distributed in many different forms, including Web-based, e-mail, and hard copy. In addition, many sales force automation systems include performance tracking features that allow salespeople to sort, graph, and manipulate performance tracking data on a laptop computer.

Managing all the data for tracking performance relative to goals can be a significant challenge. Many smaller sales forces use internally developed Excel spreadsheets for this purpose. Larger sales forces with multiple incentive plans often use more powerful incentive compensation management systems to facilitate efficient and error-free incentive compensation administration. These systems give sales managers and salespeople the ability to measure their performance against goals in real time. Leading firms in this field include Callidus, Centive, Siebel, Synygy, and ZS Associates. See Chapter 12 for more information about incentive compensation plan administration.

> ### Incentive Compensation Administration System Provides Sales Force with Timely Goal Attainment Feedback
>
> Features of an incentive compensation administration system can be very motivational for a sales force. For example, at one company, salespeople can visit a secure web site that contains the latest "scorecard" of performance for their territory. The scorecard provides immediate access to goal and attainment information, based on the latest available data. On the web site, salespeople can use a "payout calculator" to compute their incentive payout for different goal achievement scenarios. For example, they can calculate how much incentive pay they will receive if they continue selling at the same pace. Alternatively, salespeople can calculate how much more they would need to sell to make a desired higher bonus.

Web-based goal attainment tracking systems have many advantages. First, they allow salespeople access to the latest data as soon as those data are available. Next, they reduce the cost of plan administration, since hard copy reports do not need to be produced and shipped to the field. Third, they provide a single place for salespeople to access performance data provided by different vendors. Fourth, they allow errors to be caught early. Finally, their interactive "what-if" features help focus salespeople on the right activities and motivate them to get results.

Handling Midyear Goal Corrections

Occasionally, it becomes evident partway into an incentive period that a company's initial forecast was inaccurate. If this happens, should the company revise its forecast and reset goals accordingly? Management needs to balance its desire to have commitment to goals and integrity in the goal-setting process with fairness to the sales force.

Theoretically, decisions concerning midyear goal adjustments should be symmetric; if a management team raises goals when overachievement is evident, it should be willing to lower goals when they cannot be achieved. However, the practical answer to handing midyear goal corrections is often asymmetric. Firms are usually more likely to reduce goals that are unachievable than they are to increase goals that are too easy because of circumstances outside the sales force's control. Often, management teams reason that if goals are too easy, it's best to ride it out; the negative impact on morale of increasing a goal is greater than the cost of paying the sales force a windfall gain.

> "Loan volume is driven largely by interest rates. Last year interest rates went down unexpectedly, so we raised our loan volume goals in midstream. The takeoff was not as we expected, and the sales force was irate. 'The company is ripping us off,' was the prevailing sentiment throughout the field."
>
> Sales VP at a consumer finance company

Many sales organizations that allow midyear changes to goals limit the number and scope of changes by having policies and approval processes that limit changes to the most compelling situations. These might include significant events outside the control of the sales force, such as major economic changes, currency and pricing changes, or acts of nature. Having restrictions on goal changes helps to protect the integrity of the goal-setting process and minimizes the number of trivial requests for goal adjustment.

The Goal Adjustment Dilemma of 2001

With the economy booming, many sales organizations set aggressive sales goals for 2001. But when the economy slowed significantly during the first part of the year, it became abundantly clear to many companies that sales goals based on the pattern of the previous year would never be achieved. Management at these companies faced a dilemma: Should they scrap their old sales goals and establish more realistic, reduced goals that would be motivational to the sales force, giving the salespeople a reasonable chance to maintain their income level? Or would it be better to stay committed to the original goals, expecting the sales force to share in the pain of the economic downturn by taking significant reductions in incentive pay?

A management team that is known for trying to set the most realistic, fact-based goals, and that is willing to consider midyear corrections in appropriate situations, will receive the support of the sales force.

Contest Generates Sales Force Excitement When Goal Is Out of Reach

Management at a financial company overestimated national demand for the firm's services and set sales force goals much too high. By the end of August, less than 10 percent of salespeople were on track to make goal. This meant that over 90 percent of the sales force would most likely not earn the accelerated commission rate for sales above goal. Management did not want to establish a precedent of reducing a national goal that was too challenging. However, it feared that many salespeople would "check out" for the rest of the year, saving their efforts for the following year, when goals might be more attainable. Management needed to generate some short-term excitement. So, it established a special contest for the sales force based on the last trimester sales. In addition, the incentive plan was revised for the following year, so that modest commission acceleration kicked in at 80 percent of goal attainment, with additional acceleration once goal was achieved. This helped to protect the sales force in the event that goals were once again set too high. For example, if the new plan had been in place in the current year, over 75 percent of the sales force would have earned some accelerated commissions (versus less than 10 percent with the current plan).

Payout Curve Design Can Compensate for National Goal-Setting Errors

Some sales incentive plans have a mechanism for rescuing the sales force and protecting the company in the event that national goals are unrealistic. Cleverly designed payout curves can help to ensure that sales force motivation stays high in the event that goals are too high and that the company does not pay out too much in undeserved incentive if goals are too low. In these *shifting performance achievement* plans, an individual's incentive payout is a function of two comparisons: his own territory performance relative to goal and his goal attainment relative to the rest of the sales force. A salesperson who achieves 100 percent of goal earns a target incentive amount if the average goal attainment across the sales force is also

100 percent. However, if the average goal attainment across the sales force is only 90 percent, an individual at 100 percent attainment earns more than the target incentive. If the average goal attainment across the sales force is 110 percent, an individual at 100 percent attainment earns less than the target incentive. Such plans help manage sales force motivation in unpredictable environments and also improve forecasting of sales incentive compensation costs.

Authors' note: A plan like this requires management to admit to the sales force that missing goal is a realistic possibility. This may not be acceptable in some sales force cultures or in some selling environments. For example, in very-high-causality environments—where the salesperson's efforts have a very direct impact on short-term results—most sales leaders will be unwilling to state up front that failing to reach goal is acceptable. A plan like this is more likely to succeed in a moderate-causality environment, where random sales are significant or where many factors in addition to the sales force influence short-term results.

Goal-Setting Recommendations

In Volatile Business Environments, Goals with Short Time Frames, Broad Payout Ranges, and Earnings Caps Are Appropriate

The business environment can present high levels of uncertainty. In highly volatile settings, accurate forecasting of national sales goals is difficult enough; the uncertainty is only amplified when territory-level goals need to be established. One goal-setting strategy for unpredictable selling environments is to set goals with short time frames. That way, if a goal is unrealistic, the sales force is affected only for a limited period of time, and the impact of the error is minimized.

Another strategy for goal setting in unpredictable environments is to use goals that define a broader realistic range of performance. For example, suppose a salesperson begins to receive incentive pay when he reaches 90 percent of goal for an established product in a fairly stable market. The salesperson might begin to receive incentive pay when he reaches just 75 percent of goal for a product in an environment that is less predictable. That way, more salespeople will make at least some incentive money, even if the goals turn out to be unrealistically high. To guard against goal-setting errors on the low side, some firms in uncertain environments use earnings caps or decelerators to ensure that they will not have to pay out excessive unearned incentive money. For example, a salesperson's earnings might be limited to a certain dollar amount, to a multiple or fraction of salary, or to a multiple of target earnings. More information on how to adapt an incentive plan for a volatile market is included in Chapter 7.

Goal-Setting Strategies for New Products

There is often considerable forecasting uncertainty with new products. Hence, goal-setting approaches that work in volatile business situations, such as short time frames, broad payout ranges, and earnings caps, are typically also appropriate with new products.

Stretch Goals Can Be Effective, Provided They Are Attainable

Sometimes, companies add stretch to their goals in order to challenge and motivate the sales force. For example, if a firm uses a blend of top-down, data-modeling, and bottom-up inputs to derive a best-guess forecast of $100 million for next year, an aggressive management team may intentionally set the sales force goal at $110 million. Stretch goals can be effective so long as they are attainable. They are more likely to work well in selling environments with high sales force prominence, where increases in sales force effort translate directly into short-term sales. For example, in competitive commodity markets such as office supplies or insurance, sales force effort has a high short-term impact. Stretch goals can be motivational to the sales force, or at least not demotivational, because salespeople know that their increased effort can create higher sales in the current incentive period. On the other hand, in environments that involve a lot of customer service and maintenance, salespeople have less ability to affect short-term sales. Stretch goals in such situations often fail because additional sales force effort may not yield significant results until future incentive periods. Stretch goals that are unrealistic or perceived by the sales force to be unattainable will only frustrate salespeople, reducing sales force motivation and morale.

Companies should be willing to pay out more incentive money for attainment of the stretch goal than they would for attainment of the realistic goal. The payout curve should be steep in the range between the realistic goal and the stretch goal because the realistic goal can be attained through reasonable sales force effort, but attainment of the stretch goal requires exceptional effort.

Example Implementation of Stretch Goals

An Italian company wanted to challenge its sales force to stretch and exceed the company's sales goal. If the company achieved 100 percent of its goal, the sales force earned a trip to a nice resort in Italy. If the sales force achieved 105 percent of goal, the trip would be to an even fancier resort elsewhere in Europe. If the sales force achieved 110 percent of goal, the trip would be to an even more elegant, first-class resort in the United States.

Companies that use stretch goals need to be aware that the practice can be risky, particularly in situations where a significant portion of sales force pay is tied to goal attainment. Goal attainment hinges on the likelihood that the stretch goals can be achieved. If they can, and if a desirable incentive is attached to that achievement, then motivation will rise and the company will sell more. If the stretch goal is unachievable, then a large number of salespeople will not make their stretch goal, engagement will be low, and motivation will suffer significantly. Sales leaders need to assess the likelihood of goal achievement and the two inherent risks before deciding to use stretch goals. (*Authors' note: Unachievable occurs more often than achievable.*)

Rank Ordering of Salespeople Is an Alternative to Goal Setting, but Should Be Used with Caution

Some companies find goal setting inaccurate, contentious, or frustrating. Yet, they need a mechanism for evaluating and rewarding their salespeople. Rank ordering of salespeople on one or more measures is an alternative to goal setting for evaluating and rewarding. Salespeople who are ranked high are viewed as top performers, and those who are ranked low are regarded as low performers. The greatest incentive pay is awarded to the top performers. Systems based on a forced rank ordering can work, but their success hinges on an equitable and balanced sales territory alignment. If territories are not comparable, salespeople can be rewarded for having a good sales territory and not for their performance. Sometimes, in order to improve the fairness of ranking salespeople with dissimilar territories, companies try to incorporate multiple factors into the ranking. For example, they might rank on sales growth within tiers or groups of salespeople based on their territory size. As additional factors are incorporated, the ranking process becomes increasingly complex until it is almost as difficult as the original quota-setting process that it was designed to replace.

Ranking systems have some additional significant disadvantages. Management compromises the power of its leadership by not providing meaningful performance goals. Remember, you can't achieve goals if you don't have them. In addition, salespeople may not have a good idea of how well they are performing until after the ranking is complete. Ranking systems also create internal competition among salespeople, since by design there will be winners and losers. Any organization that decides to abandon goals should have compelling reasons for doing so, and must be prepared to deal with the problems that can arise when ranking salespeople.

Knoll Pharmaceuticals Eliminates Territory Goals

The sales force at Knoll Pharmaceuticals was unhappy with the company's quota-based incentive compensation system. The vast majority of salespeople felt that the quota system was unfair. Sales management spent massive amounts of time setting, managing, and arbitrating complaints about quotas, time it felt could be better spent on more productive endeavors.

In 1996, Knoll eliminated its quota system for all 600 of its field salespeople and replaced it with an incentive plan that compared salespeople's performance to one another. A companywide incentive pool was established, the size of which would shrink and grow with company earnings. Each salesperson's share of the pool was determined by her sales growth ranking on key products. For example, the highest-ranked seller might make three times as much as an average performer, while the lowest-ranked salesperson might earn nothing. To make the plan fairer, salespeople were compared only against those with similar territory potential. In the two years after the quota system was eliminated, turnover of the sales team decreased.

Authors' note: We know of many companies that have made the opposite change as well: They have replaced their ranking system with a quota-based system in order to increase incentive plan fairness, reduce internally focused competition, and create stronger links between sales force and company goals.

The Number of Goals Should Be Limited to Three

Too many goals confuse people and tend to scatter sales force effort and energy.

Concluding Insights

Poor Goal Setting Leads to Increased Costs and Lower Sales

When goals are set unrealistically low, many salespeople receive unearned income. Some may become complacent with their earnings and stop working hard. Similarly, the sales force loses motivation if goals are so high that they are unachievable. Salespeople may give up, thinking, "Management knows that we can't make it; they are just fooling themselves and us." The result in either case is lower profitability, which could have been avoided had the goals been set more realistically. Goals that are challenging, yet realistic and fair to the sales force, are very important to sales success.

The Most Suitable Goals Depend on Business Objectives and the Business Environment

Goals communicate what is important to the firm. As a result, goals will change over a product's life cycle. The following three examples illustrate this point.

1. For products in the high-growth stage of their development, growth in sales or market share is a good measure for goal setting.

2. For companies that are attempting to maintain and penetrate existing customers, goals stated in terms of customer service, customer satisfaction, and revenue growth are appropriate.

3. In mature markets with limited growth opportunity, profitability must be watched carefully. A company sacrifices profits if it generates too many sales at a reduced price. Territory goals focused on profitability work well.

The Process of Setting Goals Can Be as Beneficial as the Goals Themselves

Setting goals allows the company to communicate its strategy in a tangible way. The company tells its salespeople what they can do to help the company make its corporate goal. Also, a well-administered process of quota setting allows the company to show its salespeople that they are being treated fairly. It also enables the management team to see who is performing well and who is performing poorly. Web-based systems can streamline the process of incorporating field input and disseminating key information to salespeople.

Increasing Sales Force Motivation Through Sales Contests, SPIFFs, and Recognition Programs

How This Chapter Is Organized

Introduction   378

   What Are Sales Contests and SPIFFs?   378

   What Are Recognition Programs?   379

   The Role of Add-on Programs in Incentive Compensation   380

Sales Contests and SPIFFs   380

   How to Determine if Sales Contests and SPIFFs Are Effective   384

      Data Analysis Can Help Determine Whether a SPIFF or
Contest Is Effective   385

   Designing Effective Sales Contests and SPIFFs   388

      Sales Contests and SPIFFs: Purpose, Company Factors, and
Decisions   388

      Contest and SPIFF Design Issues   392

         *Should the Contest or SPIFF Be Based on Activity
Measures or Results Measures?*   392

         How Many Winners?   395

         *Cash Awards or Merchandise or Travel or Recognition
Awards?*   396

         How Long Should the Sales Contest or SPIFF Last?   399

         *How Many Contests and SPIFFs Should Be Used, and
with What Frequency?*   399

    Companies That Help Manage Noncash Incentive Programs   402

Recognition Programs   403

Insights   407

    Ensure *Consistency* with Strategy and Sales Roles   407

    Ensure *Compatibility* with Other Sales Force Effectiveness Drivers   408

    Ensure Appropriate *Consequences* for Salespeople and Company
Results   408

Introduction

Sales contests, SPIFFs (Special Performance Incentives for Field Force), and recognition programs are powerful and relatively inexpensive ways to enhance a firm's sales force incentive program. When used appropriately, such add-on incentives can effectively focus sales force attention on specific short-term goals, improve morale and team effort, or recognize the extraordinary efforts of top-performing salespeople. Yet contests, SPIFFs, and recognition programs harbor some dangers. Too many additional incentives can confuse salespeople or divert sales force attention from strategically important products, customers, or activities. This chapter provides advice on how to create and manage effective sales contests, SPIFFs, and recognition programs that are aligned with the firm's strategic goals.

What Are Sales Contests and SPIFFs?

Sales Contest Creates Sales Force Energy at Canvas Systems

Management at Canvas Systems, a provider of IT servers and equipment, wanted to boost quarterly sales of some specific, highly profitable product lines. The company held a Texas Hold 'Em poker tournament in which salespeople were awarded a poker card for every sale of a targeted product line. The player with the winning hand at the end of the contest won a weekend getaway to Las Vegas. Other quarterly contests at Canvas Systems have been inspired by popular reality television shows, such as *Survivor* and *Fear Factor*.

A SPIFF Jump-Starts First-Quarter Sales at Nexaweb Technologies

Management at Internet software company Nexaweb Technologies knew that it was imperative to inspire the sales team in the first quarter of the year in order to drive exceptionally strong annual performance. A SPIFF helped motivate the sales force and set the right tone for the rest of the year. During the first quarter only, the firm offered salespeople $500 for each new account brought in that was worth over $75,000, with a minimum of three acquired accounts.

Sales contests and SPIFFs are nonrecurring sales incentive programs designed to motivate sales force behavior and reward *short-term* results. A typical sales contest or SPIFF lasts not more than a few months and focuses on specific products, customer types, or sales activities. Prizes can include cash, merchandise, and/or travel awards.

The terms *sales contest* and *SPIFF* are sometimes used interchangeably. In this book, we use the term *SPIFF* to refer to programs with a high participation rate, where a considerable proportion (at least 60 percent) of salespeople earn money and/or prizes. We use the term *sales contest* to describe programs with a lower participation rate, where salespeople compete with one another to earn a limited number of prizes or cash awards. Although the actual percentage of salespeople who are winners in a sales contest may be small, a large proportion of salespeople must feel that they have a reasonable chance of winning so that they are motivated to participate.

What Does SPIFF Stand For?

There is little consistency across firms and across the sales literature as to what the acronym SPIFF (or SPIF) stands for. Some possibilities include special program incentive funds, sales promotion incentive fund, salesperson incentive funds, sales performance incentive fund, and special performance incentive for field force. Some firms also use the lowercase spif or spiff when referring to such programs.

What Are Recognition Programs?

Global Recognition Program at NCR Dates Back Almost a Century

In 1907, John Patterson, the founder of National Cash Register (now known as NCR), created the Century Point Club, the firm's first formal sales recognition program. In that year, 50 top sellers of the company's mechanical cash register were taken to the company's first national convention in Chicago, an extravagant trip at a time when very few people (even traveling salesmen) ever traveled more than a few hundred miles from their hometown. Almost a century later, the Century Point Club was still going strong at NCR as part of a larger Global Recognition Program that was highly coveted by employees. In 1999, the sales force's Century Point Club members, along with recognized peers from research and development, consulting, and administration, went to Singapore to celebrate their success.

Recognition programs reaffirm that the company values the consistently effective behaviors and strong results of its best personnel by highlighting their achievement before their peers, management, and/or customers. Recognition programs typically reward performance over a longer period of time than a sales contest or SPIFF—usually one year or more. Winners of recognition programs are often entitled to a trip and/or to membership in a select group, such as the President's Club. Public recognition is an important aspect of recognition programs, as management uses these programs to signal to the rest of the company, "These are our winners and role models."

The Role of Add-on Programs in Incentive Compensation

Figure 10-1 shows the typical participation rate and time frame for sales contests, SPIFFs, and recognition programs. This chart also positions these add-on programs relative to the variable pay and salary components of the main incentive compensation plan.

This chapter focuses first on SPIFFs and sales contests and includes discussion of when to use them, how to determine their effectiveness, and how to design and manage successful programs. Following this is a brief discussion of sales recognition programs.

Sales Contests and SPIFFs

Sales contests and SPIFFs are designed to motivate immediate sales force behavior and reward *short-term* results. Hence, such programs are most effective in sales

Figure 10-1. Participation rate and time frame of performance evaluation for salary and various types of sales incentives.

Participation Rate	Time Frame of Performance Evaluation and Reward		
	Short-Term (A Quarter or Less)	Medium-Term	Long-Term (A Year or More)
High (greater than 60%)	SPIFFs	Variable pay	Salary
Limited (less than 15%)	Contests		Stock options
		Recognition	

environments with high short-term causality—those where sales are driven primarily by the current skills, motivation, and efforts of salespeople. In these environments, the extra effort put forth by salespeople in response to a SPIFF has immediate sales impact. Salespeople see sales rise and feel a sense of accomplishment. The SPIFF provides them with commensurate financial rewards. SPIFFs and sales contests are much less effective in environments that have high free sales—that is, in environments with high carryover sales or long selling cycles, or where other factors besides current sales force effort, such as brand name and non-sales force marketing instruments, have a large impact on sales. In these environments, a good portion of short-term sales may be driven by past sales efforts or by factors outside a salesperson's control. SPIFFs and sales contests are most effective when they reward true accomplishment. They lose their emotional impact when a salesperson feels that her actions do not have a large effect on the outcome.

When used appropriately, sales contests and SPIFFs have many advantages:

- They are generally well liked by salespeople, and they can create considerable sales force excitement.

- They are an effective way to focus sales force attention on specific near-term tactical events that might otherwise get insufficient attention—for example, launching a new product, combating a competitive entry, or providing a midyear boost to lagging sales.

- They are usually relatively low cost and have relatively low risk for the firm.

More advantages of sales contests and SPIFFs from a sales force, customer, and firm perspective are enumerated in the top half of Figure 10-2.

Although SPIFFs and sales contests usually represent less than 10 percent of the total incentive compensation budget, their impact has the potential to do serious harm to a firm if the programs are not centrally coordinated and strategically aligned with company priorities. SPIFFs and sales contests can redirect sales force effort from core products, diluting the impact of the main incentive compensation plan. Some additional challenges when using sales contests and SPIFFs effectively from a sales force, customer, and firm perspective are enumerated in the bottom half of Figure 10-2.

Product Manager–Controlled SPIFFs Can Create Sales Force Effort Allocation Problems

Aligning sales contests and SPIFFs with strategic priorities is particularly difficult in organizations with decentralized marketing departments, where product managers have budgets to spend on sales force SPIFFs without any central marketing or sales force control. In such environments, product managers may compete for sales force time by trying to outdo one another

Figure 10-2. Advantages and challenges of sales contests and SPIFFs.

	Impact on Salespeople	Impact on Customers	Impact on Firm
Advantages	• Liked by salespeople, are motivating and fun, and provide variety and excitement. • Provide extra compensation; "free money." • Often provide more frequent payment than the main IC plan. • Provide recognition among peers and management and pride in the job, particularly for salespeople who work alone and unsupervised and face frequent rejection.	• May introduce customers to products and/or services that are not typically discussed. • Sales force's increased energy, motivation, and focus may improve customer relationship.	• Effective at creating sales at relatively low cost. • Not a significant financial risk; typically only a short-term commitment. • Effective way to focus attention on specific near-term tactical events that might otherwise get insufficient attention (for example, selling overstocks, combating a competitive entry, or providing a midyear boost to lagging sales). • Allow management to continuously reinforce what is important to the company.

	• Often reward with extravagant treats (such as exotic trips or luxury automobiles) that salespeople might not purchase for themselves.	• Effective way to compensate the sales force when goals are too high and the sales force is not making incentive money. • Can build morale, create excitement, and foster teamwork.	
Challenges	• Can confuse the sales force and lose impact if there are too many at once. • Can have a negative impact on morale if the same people win every time or if some have an unfair advantage.	• Can encourage salespeople to sell SPIFFed products instead of what the customer really needs. • Can encourage salespeople to engage in other behaviors (such as moving inventory forward) that hurt customers. • Can create internal competition, diverting sales force focus away from customers.	• Can redirect sales effort away from strategic priorities, if contests focus on secondary priorities. • Create administrative overhead. • Can create internal competition that can prevent sharing of best practices and divert sales force focus away from external competitors. • Can encourage salespeople to engage in behaviors (such as moving inventory forward) that hurt the company.

with more creative and extravagant SPIFFs. The result is a SPIFFs arms race, in which overall sales effort does not increase, but is just redirected to the product with the best current SPIFF. The company ends up spending a lot of money on prizes and awards, but gets very few incremental sales in return. In addition, since sales contests and SPIFFs can focus attention on products and customers that are not part of the main incentive plan, sales in areas with the greatest strategic importance often suffer.

How to Determine if Sales Contests and SPIFFs Are Effective

Was IBM Addicted to Sales Contests?

During the 1980s and 1990s, the IBM sales force was well known for running many sales contests and SPIFFs. Some IBM executives referred to this as "incentive plan obesity," or the tendency to overload the incentive plan by "throwing money at every problem." An ex-director of sales compensation for IBM confessed, "IBM gave bonuses and awards for every imaginable action by the sales force. The more complex it got, the more difficult it was to administer, and the results were not convincing. When we began to ask ourselves why DEC had salespeople, who were tough competitors, on straight salary, we decided perhaps we'd gone overboard a bit."

Too Many SPIFFs Distract a Pharmaceutical Sales Force

Sales leaders at a large pharmaceutical company were concerned that the sales force was being distracted by the large number of sales contests and SPIFFs initiated by the firm's marketing department. Individual product managers had budgets and authority to introduce contests and SPIFFs to the sales force, and there was no coordinated central control to ensure that these programs were aligned with strategic sales force objectives. At one point, there were 48 different contests and SPIFFs running at the same time. When sales management asked salespeople to recall these various programs, most salespeople were not able to even name more than a handful of them, let alone explain their purpose or specific rules. The company was spending a lot of money on SPIFFs and contest prizes and was getting very little extra effort from the sales force in return.

Sales Force Desire to Win a Contest Encourages Unethical Behavior

Several weeks into a three-month contest on sales for a specific product, the vice president of sales began to get unconfirmed reports of behaviors that were not in the company's or customers' interests. Several sales-people who ordinarily operated with considerable integrity were aggres-sively manipulating customer product selection and the timing of orders in an effort to maximize sales during the contest period, at the expense of sales in future periods. It appeared that customers were being asked to order contest products, with the full intention of changing the order once the contest was over. Some salespeople seemed to have the attitude, "It's just a contest, so it's okay to push the rules a little, just like in any game."

Mismatch Between Award Value and Effort Required to Earn Bank Teller SPIFF

Recall from Chapter 1 the story of a bank that established a SPIFF for tellers to encourage them to upsell customers when they came into the bank to deposit money. Tellers were offered $10 for every customer who opened an account with the bank's investment division as a result of teller referral. The SPIFF had almost no impact on teller behavior; the vast major-ity of tellers felt that the prospect of earning a measly $10 reward was simply not worth the effort and the possible humiliation of appearing to be "pushy."

There can be many signs that the current sales contests and SPIFFs are not work-ing well. Figure 10-3 lists some common symptoms of problems with these pro-grams. The symptoms fall into clear categories within the sales management system framework introduced in Chapter 1.

Data Analysis Can Help Determine Whether a SPIFF or Contest Is Effective. A 2005 survey by Inventive Federation, Inc., discovered that 74 percent of respon-dents are placing a strong emphasis on the ROI of sales contests and SPIFFs. Experimentation and time-series analysis are two approaches that can provide an assessment of these incentive programs.

In an experiment, two groups are formed. The experimental group is given the sales contest or SPIFF. The control group operates in a status quo mode. Differences in group performance on a metric such as sales, contribution, or mar-ket share are recorded. These differences enable an ROI calculation. While this ROI calculation is quite reliable, experiments tend not to be used very often. Sales contests and SPIFFs usually have a specific purpose and are time-critical. Establishing and controlling random experimental and control groups is disrup-tive and counter to the company's business purpose.

Time-series analysis provides a noninvasive approach to determining the im-pact of a sales contest or SPIFF. To illustrate, Figure 10-4 provides the monthly sales for a product over a three-year period. There are two interventions during this time frame. The first is a SPIFF for Product A. The second is a sales contest for Product B, another product that the sales force sells. The ROI analysis begins

Figure 10-3. Some signs that sales contests and SPIFFs *may* not be effective.

Consistency with . . .	Compatibility with . . .	Consequences . . .
• Sales and marketing strategies • Sales process • Sales roles	• Performance management systems • Sales force culture • Sales force motivators • Sales force hiring and development processes	• Company results • Customer results • Sales force behaviors and activities • Sales force quality
• There are too many sales contests and SPIFFs focused on noncore business areas. • Individual product managers have the budget and authority to introduce contests and SPIFFs. There is no central control that ensures alignment with strategic objectives, and product managers try to outdo one another in a SPIFFs "arms race." • Contests and SPIFFs are undermining a successful sales process built around long-term customer focus and relationship building. • SPIFFs and contests give salespeople with high-potential territories a natural advantage. • SPIFFs discourage using the most effective channels; for example, moving customers direct when the Internet would be a better way to connect with the company.	• Contests and SPIFFs are used to compensate for an ineffective incentive compensation system. • The performance management system is compromised by continued SPIFFing. • Too many contests and SPIFFs are undermining a culture that is customer-centered, team-oriented, and focused on long-term success. • A lack of contests and SPIFFs is incompatible with a culture that is sales-centered, competitive, and focused on short-term results. • As the sales force becomes more diverse, traditional prizes, such as golf clubs and trips, are no longer appealing to many salespeople. • Contests and SPIFFs are designed to encourage specific activities (like new account development), but salespeople are not trained to do these activities effectively. • Calculating winners for the sales contests and SPIFFs consumes excessive administrative time.	• Contest winners are not making goal on core products. • Contests and SPIFFs are creating too much internal competition, diverting sales force focus away from external competitors and customers. • Contests and SPIFFs are not effective at encouraging the desired sales force behaviors. • Sales force effort is unfocused because there are so many sales contests and SPIFFs with varying objectives. • Salespeople engage in greedy and unprofessional behaviors in order to win sales contests and get SPIFFs rather than doing what is best for the customer and the company. • Salespeople can't remember or explain all the SPIFFs and contests. • The same salespeople win every contest, which negatively affects morale among those who work hard but never win.

by deriving a baseline trend from the monthly sales data for Product A. Using statistical approaches, the baseline trend can incorporate market, economic, and competitive factors in addition to the time trend. The impact of the two incentive programs on Product A sales can be understood by examining actual sales relative to the baseline trend. The impact of the Product A SPIFF on sales is observable and positive; sales during the Product A SPIFF period are well above the baseline. This information can be used to estimate the impact of the SPIFF. An ROI is calculated by dividing the gross margin impact by the SPIFF's cost. The second

Figure 10-4. An illustration of product sales before and after a Product A SPIFF and a Product B contest.

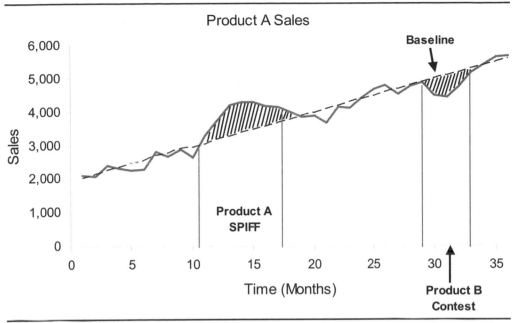

impact on Product A sales is associated with the contest for Product B. The impact of this contest on Product A is also observable in the data and is slightly negative. The sales force diminished its effort on Product A in order to focus on Product B during the contest period. Sales below the baseline trend are an estimate of the impact of the Product B contest on Product A sales. The lost Product A gross margin should be added to the cost of the Product B contest when calculating the ROI for that contest. Using the same logic, the impact of the Product A SPIFF on Product B's sales needs to be estimated in order to compute a more accurate ROI for the Product A SPIFF.

When conducting a time-series analysis, it is important to include the time before and after the contest or SPIFF to account for any unintended consequences that the incentive program produces. For example, if salespeople know that an attractive SPIFF is about to start, they may delay closing sales until the SPIFF is in effect. After the SPIFF has expired, sales may fall off dramatically because the sales force "pushed ahead" as many transactions as possible in order to maximize sales during the SPIFF period. If a company consistently sees sales fall below the baseline before and after a contest or SPIFF, perhaps its contests or SPIFFs are too predictable and susceptible to the timing of sales.

Estimating the ROI of a sales contest or SPIFF can be straightforward or highly complex, depending upon the externalities and accounting for the aforementioned unintended consequences. Time-series analysis can be a powerful way for management to learn which types of short-term incentive programs work and which do not, making it possible to design and implement more effective SPIFFs and contests in the future.

Time-Series Analysis Provides Insights for a Pharmaceutical Firm

A pharmaceutical firm conducted a time-series analysis to determine what impact SPIFFs have on sales force activity, sales, and profits. Data for five SPIFFs on four different products were examined. Each SPIFF lasted between three and six months. The analysis was particularly difficult because the ability of a pharmaceutical salesperson to affect short-term sales is quite low and because numerous external factors (such as negative press about one of the firm's drugs) and other marketing influences in addition to the sales force had a large impact on sales. Despite these difficulties, several interesting conclusions emerged from the analysis in this particular case, including the following:

- The SPIFFs led to an increase in both the quantity and quality of call activity (salespeople made more calls to more high-potential accounts during the SPIFF periods).

- These behavior changes drove small sales improvements.

- Profit outcomes were mixed; one of the SPIFFs had a positive ROI, but the others did not.

- In most cases, the SPIFFs helped the firm achieve the market share outcome it desired.

- Sales force effort on the other products in the portfolio was sustained during the SPIFF periods.

Designing Effective Sales Contests and SPIFFs

Sales Contests and SPIFFs: Purpose, Company Factors, and Decisions. There are a number of SPIFF and contest decisions that need to be made. They are listed in the middle column of Figure 10-5 and described in detail in the subsequent section. These decisions depend upon the purpose of the SPIFF or contest and several company factors.

An Incentive Designed to Encourage Support for Underemphasized Sales Priorities

The vice president of sales at Concerto Software needed a new, creative, and fun way to motivate sales force goal attainment. Traditionally, the company's national sales goals were achieved not because every region consistently met its numbers, but because one region would make up for the slack of another. The vice president challenged the sales force by offering to shave his head if all four worldwide regions of the sales team hit their fourth-quarter quotas. Every sales team made its numbers, and overall rev-

Figure 10-5. Sales contests and SPIFFs: purpose, company factors, and decisions.

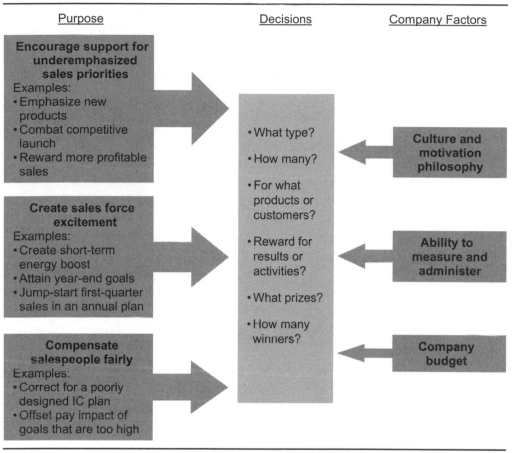

enue increased by 4 percent for the quarter and 8 percent for the year. The stunt also raised $4,000 for charity, as salespeople were allowed to bid for a chance to shear off a strip of the boss's hair with an electric razor on stage at the annual sales kickoff meeting.

A Contest Designed to Create Sales Force Excitement

A leading digital printing manufacturer wanted to create some sales force excitement in anticipation of a large industry conference. The event was expected to generate many potential sales leads, and management felt that a unique sales contest was needed to energize the sales force for this important event. The firm developed an online incentive program that allowed participants to accumulate credits for sales and redeem them through an online catalog of unique gifts. The program allowed participants to select the prizes they valued most (for example, electronics, sports equipment, travel, or luxury items), and also saved sales management the hassle of guessing which prizes people might want and how many to preorder. The program is credited with helping the sales force exceed its sales goals for the conference.

A Contest Designed to Supplement the Main Incentive Plan

Management at a financial company overestimated national demand for the firm's services and set sales force goals much too high. By the end of August, less than 10 percent of the salespeople were on track to make goal. This meant that over 90 percent of the sales force would not earn the accelerated commission rate for sales above goal. Management did not want to establish a precedent of reducing a national goal that proved too challenging. However, it feared that many salespeople would "check out" for the rest of the year, saving their efforts for the following year, when goals might be more attainable. In order to generate some short-term excitement, management established a special contest for the sales force based on the last trimester sales. This also helped to ensure that the sales force, which had worked hard, was compensated fairly and was not unduly penalized for the firm's goal-setting error.

Figure 10-5 lists three primary reasons that a management team might decide to use sales contests and SPIFFs to motivate and reward the sales force. The reasons are:

1. *To encourage support for underemphasized sales priorities.* A new product needs to be launched hard. Market segments that are threatened by competitors need to be defended. Products that are not on track to make goal need an extra boost. The sales force may not exert the requisite energy to accomplish these objectives within the existing incentive compensation scheme. A SPIFF or contest can provide the necessary impetus to focus sales force effort.

2. *To create ongoing sales force excitement.* Sometimes sales forces slow down. SPIFFS and contests can help provide a short-term energy boost when quarterly sales are lagging, when important messages need to be reinforced, or when the efforts of top performers deserve greater recognition.

3. *To compensate salespeople fairly.* Too frequently, the corporate revenue goal is set unrealistically high. Incentive compensation plans are geared to the high goal. When achievement becomes unattainable, the variable-pay component for the sales force dwindles. Sales force motivation and morale begin to suffer, and the sales shortfall can grow. Sales leadership can use SPIFFs and contests to supplement the incentive plan and revitalize the sales force.

Not only does the purpose of the SPIFF or contest drive its design, but company factors such as the following also contribute:

1. *Firm culture and motivation philosophy.* Sales leaders' philosophy about how to best motivate the sales team influences a firm's SPIFF and contest strategy. Some sales leaders like to rely heavily on such programs to enhance short-term sales force motivation. Others prefer to use the firm's main incentive program or performance management processes, such as coaching and feedback, as primary sales force motivators. Contests and SPIFFs are most compatible with a sales force culture that is sales-centered, competitive, and focused on short-term results. Excessive use of SPIFFs and contests can undermine a culture that is customer-centered, team-oriented, and focused on long-term success.

2. *Ability to measure results and administer the program.* Successful contests and SPIFFs require accurate and timely results measurement. If the company is unable to measure attainment correctly and quickly, the program will not have meaning to the sales force. Contests and SPIFFs create administrative overhead. Many firms that run sales contests and SPIFFs regularly report that the cost and complexity of administering such programs is a significant concern.

3. *Firm budget.* Contests and SPIFFs are generally considered to be a fairly inexpensive way to generate extra sales effort. Award values tend to be small, and, in the case of sales contests, there tend to be a limited number of winners. Nevertheless, both the cost of awards and the cost of administration can accumulate. The firm's sales force budget influences how many SPIFFs and contests and how many and what type of awards the firm can offer.

SPIFFs and Contests with a Limited Budget

SPIFFs and sales contests do not have to cost the firm a lot of money to have a large impact. In fact, often the recognition and trophy value associated with a sales contest or SPIFF are more valuable than the tangible prize that a winner receives. Be sure to leverage this value by:

- *Making a big deal out of the award presentation.* Present even inexpensive awards (such as gift cards or sports event tickets) personally and offer sincere congratulations.

- *Making it humorous and symbolic.* For example, top sellers at a commodities firm get the Beaver Award (a stuffed beaver with an engraved plaque), because the beaver is the hardest-working creature in the animal kingdom.

- *Making it fun.* For example, a telemarketing firm gives its telephone sales reps pennies for closing sales, and these are dropped into a gumball machine. Small cash awards are given, depending on the color of the gumball that comes out.

- *Announcing winners to the entire staff.* For example, a bank publishes articles in an employee newsletter highlighting the accomplishments of top performers.

- *Providing a lasting memory.* Cash awards can be used to pay the bills and are soon forgotten. Merchandise awards, even inexpensive ones, are a visible reminder that the salesperson is valued by the company. Abbott Laboratories puts a star on the business cards of its top sales performers.

Contest and SPIFF Design Issues. Some of the most frequently asked questions about how to design effective sales contests and SPIFFs are listed and discussed here.

Should the Contest or SPIFF Be Based on Activity Measures or Results Measures? Sales contests and SPIFFs can be tied to numerous different performance measures. The most commonly used measures are results measures, such as sales, growth, quota attainment, and market share. Since the ultimate purpose of most SPIFFs and contests is to produce sales results, it is logical to tie awards directly to measures that directly reflect those results.

In general, the advice provided in Chapter 6 on how to select performance measures for an incentive plan applies to the selection of measures for sales contests and SPIFFs as well. The best performance measures for sales contests and SPIFFs are:

- *Consistent with business strategy.* Measures are an effective way to tell the sales force what is important and what the company hopes to accomplish through a sales contest or SPIFF. For example, a contest that is designed to energize the sales team to achieve a national goal becomes more powerful if it rewards for territory goal attainment. A SPIFF that is intended to thwart a competitor sends a more potent message if it awards for share gain or competitive wins. On the other hand, a SPIFF on sales gains for a secondary product can distract salespeople from the more important corporate product priorities.

- *Objectively and accurately measurable.* If salespeople perceive performance measurement to be unfair, the desired motivational impact of the contest or SPIFF is lost, and the program may backfire. For this reason, results-based measures (such as sales and market share) are usually preferred over more subjective measures, such as activity measures, which often rely on management judgment or salesperson self-reporting.

- *Directly affected by the sales force.* Salespeople should be able to directly affect the measure that will be used to determine sales contest and SPIFF awards. If other factors besides current sales force skills, capabilities, and effort have a large impact on the measure, then the motivational impact of the program is weakened. For this reason, sales contests and SPIFFs are usually most effective in selling environments with considerable sales force prominence and high short-term sales force causality.

- *Fair.* Measures should not favor territories or salespeople with specific characteristics that are outside of the salesperson's control. For example, when a travel company ran a contest to promote sales of international business travel, many salespeople did not have enough corporate customers with international travel needs to compete effectively. As a result, the majority of the salespeople became disengaged quickly. The short-term nature of a SPIFF or contest sometimes makes fairness less important than the other criteria mentioned here. For example, if there is a contest that rewards the highest sales gain in a month for a new product, there are likely to be biases in opportunity, but most sales forces are able to move on after the apparent unfairness has played out.

Many companies have used activity-based contests and SPIFFs successfully to encourage a specific sales force behavior in order to drive long-term results. Some examples of situations in which activity-based measures can work successfully include the following:

- *Activity awards are useful when territory results cannot be measured.* A seller of hair care products awards gift certificates to the two salespeople each month who "touch the most customers" (including customer classes taught, cold calls, appointments, and visits). The danger in running an activity-based contest like this is that the contest will motivate an increase in the quantity of the desired activity, but it may also trigger a decrease in the quality. Such contests are typically most effective when they are used only for short periods of time to energize the sales team to accomplish a specific short-term goal.

- *Activity awards can energize a service organization.* Mercury Interactive Corp, a software company, had a sales force plus a service group that performed onsite maintenance and troubleshooting for customers' computer systems. The company wanted to encourage the service technicians to look for sales opportunities while working with clients and to pass those leads on to the sales force. At first the company asked the technicians to do this voluntarily, but the program was only moderately successful. To provide greater incentive, the company implemented an online rewards program. Technicians could earn points redeemable for merchandise by providing leads and even more points by providing leads that generated business. The program cost the company just $7,000 and is credited with generating over $600,000 in new business.

- *Activity awards can spark new product sales.* When IBM launched its OS/2 operating system, it encouraged all employees to help generate demand by referring potential customers to an IBM dealership for a demonstration. Employees who made 15 referrals earned bronze medals; those who made more referrals earned silver and goal medals.

- *Sales force assistance in recruiting is a best practice.* Every selling organization tries to attract and retain the best salespeople. It is widely recognized that sales force referrals provide a very good group of candidates. Companies often offer prizes or cash awards to salespeople who provide candidates that join the organization and stay for a predetermined period of time, usually at least six months.

Shell Oil Creates Special Incentives for Wholesalers to Focus on Customers

Only 20 percent of the 14,000 Shell gas stations across the United States are fully serviced and operated by Shell Oil Company; the majority are owned or franchised and supplied by approximately 700 independent gasoline wholesalers. A special Go Further incentive program for the wholesalers helps the firm ensure that customers get a uniformly good experience at every Shell station, regardless of ownership. Wholesalers can win trips to exotic locations, such as Sydney, Venice, and Prague, if their stations are compliant with a 10-point customer value proposition (CVP) that includes standards for competitive pricing, cleanliness, lighting at night, working equipment, landscaping, and other services. The stations are rated twice a year by mystery shoppers. Stations with high CVP scores attract greater brand loyalty and sell 5 percent more gasoline than noncompliant stations.

Should Sales Contests and SPIFFs Reward Individual or Team Performance?

In selling environments where causality at the individual salesperson level is high and results can be measured accurately, individual rewards are generally preferred over team rewards. Individual rewards allow salespeople to feel that they have greater control over the performance outcome and are therefore usually more motivational. However, in selling situations where salespeople must work together as a true team to create results, where team selling is part of the culture, and where measurability at the individual salesperson level is poor, team-based contests can be an effective way to motivate a team to work together to accomplish a goal. Awards in team settings not only reward team members for their efforts, but also can have a side benefit of encouraging socialization among team members to encourage stronger teamwork in the future. Examples of team rewards include closing down the office for an afternoon to attend a group outing, an all-expense-paid trip for the team, a group lunch or dinner, or a victory party to celebrate the achievement of an important goal.

How Many Winners? This question relates more to sales contests than to SPIFFs. A SPIFF (as we define it in this book) has a large Engagement Rate. Almost everyone in the sales force will earn money and/or prizes if it is successful. A successful sales contest, on the other hand, has a limited number of winners and is designed to appeal to the competitive nature of salespeople. Deciding on the right number of winners for a sales contest involves a delicate balance that can be illustrated through an example. Suppose a sales manager has a $10,000 budget to be used as prize money in a quarterly sales contest for 20 salespeople. Which of the following sales contest designs is likely to produce the best results?

- Contest A: The top 10 performers get $1,000 each.
- Contest B: The single top performer gets $10,000.

The answer to this question is not straightforward. A successful sales contest requires high levels of sales force traction. Traction is a function of both the chance of winning and the award desirability. Contest A has a relatively large number of winners, so more salespeople will feel that they have a reasonable chance of winning. This helps traction. On the other hand, some salespeople may decide that a prize of just $1,000 and the distinction of "being in the top half" is not attractive enough to justify the extra effort required to win. The small perceived prize value discourages participation. Contest B, on the other hand, has just one winner. There is a risk that many salespeople will believe that they cannot win and give up too soon. A low chance of winning lowers traction. On the other hand, the award has 10 times the dollar value and the greater prestige associated with being the top seller. High award desirability enhances traction. As a general rule, sales contests with a mid range of winners are most effective, as they achieve the right balance between the chance of winning and award desirability.

Some additional suggestions for managing the number of winners through sales contest design include the following:

- Rather than specifying the number of contest winners up front, consider tying the contest to goal achievement and then managing the number of winners through the difficulty of the goal. For example, a contest that promises a trip to every salesperson who makes 105 percent of a sales goal will have more winners than one that awards the trip only to those who achieve 110 percent. Goal-based contests are appealing because salespeople know up front what they need to do to win, and everyone who is willing to work hard enough can be a winner. There is less internally fo cused competition than is likely when the number of winners is limited and winners are based on a forced ranking of salespeople. However, salespeople are a competitive group, and some level of internal competition can spark greater interest in a contest. In addition, when the number of available prizes is limited (for example, when there are only 10 hotel rooms available), it is impractical to run a contest in which the number of winners is not specified up front.

- Consider balancing the number of winners across sales divisions or regions. For example, specify that winners will include the top 10 percent of the sales force plus any salesperson who comes in first or second in his region (even if he is not in the top 10 percent nationally). This helps to compensate for any regional biases that may exist and ensures that each region or division is engaged.

- When the number of available prizes is limited, consider a lottery format. For example, when a salesperson reaches a contest goal, her name is entered into a lottery for a chance to win a luxury automobile. Salespeople who pass higher performance hurdles get additional entries, thereby increasing their chance of winning. With a lottery format, everyone feels that she has a shot at winning (even historically poor performers), and everyone is likely to be inspired to participate. In addition, there is evidence that some randomness in a sales contest can be very motivating to salespeople, as the element of luck makes the contest more fun and creates additional excitement. A significant risk in such schemes is that the highest performer is unlikely to be the winner, even though he has the highest chance of winning.

Cash Awards or Merchandise or Travel or Recognition Awards? Selecting the right award is important to the success of any sales contest or SPIFF. If an award is very desirable to the sales force, salespeople are more likely to put forth extra effort in hopes of attaining it, and incremental sales will be higher.

A challenge for incentive plan designers is that most sales forces are made up of a diverse set of salespeople with varied award preferences. A cash reward appeals to salespeople who are motivated by money; however, many salespeople are motivated by other factors besides money. Research has identified five universal motivators that explain what drives salespeople: the need for achievement, social affiliation, power, ego gratification, and survival. Of these needs, only three—achievement, ego gratification, and survival—can be satisfied directly with money. Noncash awards will be much more effective for salespeople who are motivated primarily by a desire for power and/or social affiliation. Noncash awards (in addition to money) can fulfill the need for achievement and ego gratification as well. Several examples of noncash awards that appeal to each of these motivators are listed in Figure 10-6. A portfolio of cash and noncash awards should meet the motivation needs for the entire sales force.

Consider Awards That Appeal to Top Performers

When selecting awards for a sales contest or SPIFF, consider what awards are most likely to appeal to the group of salespeople at which the contest

Figure 10-6. Examples of SPIFF or sales contest noncash awards that appeal to each of the five motivators.

Motivator	SPIFF or Sales Contest Awards That Appeal to This Motivator
Achievement	• Recognition at a national sales meeting or banquet or in a company newsletter. • Being listed on a "Sales Leader Board." • Membership in an elite club such as the "President's Club" that gives recognition, status, and special privileges to top performers (read more about recognition programs later in this chapter). • Top performers attend a week-long executive seminar at a prestigious business school.
Social affiliation	• A party to celebrate team success. • An outing for successful team members; for example, the entire sales team from a New York radio station was treated to a day-long yacht cruise around Manhattan. • An extravagant trip for top performers and their spouses.
Power	• Participation on an advisory council to the company's top executives. • An opportunity to act as sales manager for a day.
Ego gratification	• Luxury gifts (for example, Mary Kay Cosmetics awards pink Cadillacs, mink coats, and diamond rings to leading independent sellers). • An engraved plaque or trophy. • An opportunity to present best sales practices at a local sales meeting. • An opportunity to mentor new salespeople.
Survival	• Usually provided for by salary and other cash rewards.

is targeted. For example, if an objective of a sales contest is to motivate and reward top performers, consider awards that will appeal particularly to top performers rather than average performers. Top salespeople are often competitive and hard-working and love challenges. Trips to exotic destinations and extreme activities may be particularly appealing to this group. If the SPIFF's goal is to boost overall sales, then the focus broadens to most of the sales force.

Studies have found that even though most salespeople say that their preferred reward in a sales contest is cash, a sales force will actually work harder for a non-cash award. Several psychological dynamics help to explain this. Noncash awards, particularly luxury items such as a trip to an exotic destination or an extravagant car, are generally perceived by salespeople to be more valuable than their retail cash value. This happens for several reasons:

• Noncash awards are more likely to appeal to a broad range of the basic human motivators identified earlier.

• A trip or car is more separable, unique, and memorable. Cash awards are more likely to be lumped together with salary and other compensation in the mind of a salesperson.

- Salespeople may not be able to justify spending a monetary award on a frivolous trip or a fancy luxury car. Instead, they may spend it on more practical things, like paying bills. But if they earn the trip or car through hard work and must "use it or lose it," there is no need to justify the expense.

- A trip or car is more visible to peers, has trophy value, and provides a visible link between the award and the company.

- Cash awards have a short "half-life": Salespeople who get the award relish it, but forget it quickly, too. A prominent noncash award is remembered for a long time. Long after an award is given, you hear winners reminiscing, "Do you remember the time two years ago when . . . ?"

At the same time, there are some advantages to using cash awards for SPIFFs and contests. Cash can be used by everyone; almost all salespeople say they like getting cash, whereas noncash awards do not suit all winners. Cash awards are usually easier to administer: There is no need to select the awards, plan the trip, or handle the logistics of award distribution.

Gift card credits redeemable through online catalogs are used by many companies as awards for sales contests and SPIFFs. Such awards allow companies to realize many of the benefits of both noncash and cash awards simultaneously. Like cash, gift cards and online catalogs allow salespeople to select items that they truly want. They also free companies from having to select and distribute awards. Yet unlike cash, gift cards and catalog items can be branded, personalized, or customized, and are more targeted and memorable than cash awards.

Clintar's Incentive Program Offers Choice Through an Online Catalog

Prior to 2000, Canadian groundskeeping company Clintar occasionally ran sales incentive programs, although most of them were not very memorable to franchise owners. Owners would compete for a single prize (such as a set of golf clubs or a television set), which someone at the home office would select and distribute to winners. Invariably there were complaints about prizes; winners would want to trade a prize in for something else or would discover product defects. Distributing and replacing prizes became a logistical nightmare for the company. In order to improve this situation, Clintar decided to change its awards. Today, franchise owners who grow monthly sales earn credits redeemable though an online catalog for a variety of products, including electronics, housewares, sports equipment, travel, and luxury items. Franchise owners can select the prizes they really want. Since an outside vendor handles all the data gathering, communications, and prize distribution, the home office is freed of these time-consuming responsibilities. Sales have increased by at least 10 percent each year since the program was introduced, justifying the $25,000 annual cost of the program.

How Long Should the Sales Contest or SPIFF Last? Generally, sales contests and SPIFFs are designed to motivate the sales force for a limited period of time. If a sales contest or SPIFF is put in place for too long, the "winners" begin to become clear, and the rest of the sales force can become disengaged. In most instances, such programs cover a period of one to three months. As the period gets longer, contests and SPIFFs begin to interfere with the role of the primary incentive program.

The time period can also be tied to the purpose of the program. Consider the following examples:

- An auto dealership noticed that its salespeople experienced occasional "down" days and that they worked like "lone wolves." It decided to run periodic one-day sales contests. The first person to sell a car on a given day would get $5. Then that salesperson would get $5 for every other car sold by any member of the sales team that same day. The second person to sell a car would get $5 for the sale plus $5 for every subsequent car sold by the team, and so on. The first person to make a sale could win $100 in a day just for selling one car, and would often earn $200 to $300 if she sold more cars.

- The nine "competitive" salespeople at a video game distributor became very motivated when they were ranked each month on gross profit. The top-ranked salesperson got a $500 bonus and the best office in the department.

- A high-tech company with an annual incentive program puts in place a "FastStart" SPIFF for the first quarter, where salespeople get the following awards:
  - Exceed 22 percent of the quarterly goal: a 32″ plasma TV or equivalent
  - Exceed 27 percent of the quarterly goal: a 42″ plasma TV or equivalent
  - Exceed 32 percent of the quarterly goal: a 50″ plasma TV or equivalent

- The sales force of a medium-sized company selling computer servers was demotivated, since most salespeople were not making the overly aggressive goals for a new server line. The company put in a program where a supplemental bonus of $200 per server was paid for sales of the new product during the last five months of the year.

How Many Contests and SPIFFs Should Be Used, and with What Frequency? Recall that sales contests and SPIFFs are most effective in sales environments with high short-term sales force causality and considerable sales force prominence—where the extra effort put forth by salespeople in response to a SPIFF or contest has immediate sales impact. In environments with very long selling cycles, or where other factors besides current sales force effort have a large impact on sales, sales contests and SPIFFs should be used rarely, if ever, to motivate effort.

The Effectiveness of SPIFFs Changes as a Sales Process Evolves

Computer hardware vendors once used SPIFFs to encourage their distribution partners to sell specific products. This type of SPIFF has lost its effectiveness as the sales approach for these distributors has evolved over the last several years. Partners once engaged in transactional selling of products. Today, successful partners must consultatively sell complex multivendor solutions. Customers look to these partners as trusted advisers that solve complex business and technology problems. SPIFFs on specific products are at odds with the new sales approach, since they enable salesperson behavior to be influenced by an agenda other than doing what is best for the customer. In 2004, Cisco adapted its incentive program for partners to align it more closely with this new reality. Distribution partners receive rebates for sales only when specified levels of customer satisfaction are reached.

Given an appropriate selling environment, several internal factors determine how many and how often sales contests and SPIFFs should be used. These factors include the following:

- *Culture.* Some companies have very "contest-friendly" cultures. They run SPIFFs and sales contests all the time. Salespeople come to expect these programs to be an ordinary occurrence. This happens particularly at companies with many products and those where add-on incentive programs are controlled and paid for by product managers. Some of these companies run dozens of contests simultaneously, many of them lasting only a month or even a week. Salespeople eagerly await the announcement of the latest and greatest program, standing ready to change their sales focus in order to maximize their earnings. Other companies have cultures that are incompatible with this approach. Too many SPIFFs and sales contests run counter to a culture that is focused more on long-term success than on short-term results, emphasizes teamwork, and has a strong customer orientation.

- *Ability and willingness to administer them.* Contests and SPIFFs can be very difficult, time-consuming, and costly to administer effectively. Frequent and accurate tracking and communication of progress to the sales force is needed to keep salespeople focused on their goals and engaged in the program. A common pitfall is to communicate program guidelines only at the beginning of the program and to offer progress reports only at the end; in the meantime, the sales force loses focus, and motivation wanes. Particularly at companies that run multiple SPIFFs and sales contests simultaneously, sales administration departments often report that one of their greatest challenges is administering all the add-on incentive programs. A company that wants to run many sales contests and SPIFFs must be willing to invest in the administration systems and processes required to do so successfully.

MCI Telecommunications Runs First Internet-Based Sales Contest

The Internet provides an ideal mechanism for administering a sales contest or SPIFF because the program can be updated and accessed in real time. MCI Telecommunications ran what may have been the first Internet-administered sales contest in the fall of 1995. Salespeople gained points for revenue increases that could be redeemed for more than three hundred prizes in an online catalog. Since salespeople could connect to the MCI network through their laptop, they could find out at any time where they stood and what prizes were available. A significant side benefit of the contest was that in order to track their progress and obtain prizes, the salespeople had to learn how to use the firm's new Internet product, internetMCI, just as they were getting ready to go out and sell the product to customers.

Online Incentive Administration Enhances Productivity at Citigroup

In 2001, a push to cut costs at Citigroup led the international financial services firm to replace its paper-based employee incentive program. As the company grew, it had become prohibitively expensive to print and distribute prize catalogs to 270,000 employees in more than a hundred countries. In addition, administration of the program had become unmanageable. The company's human resources staff, as well as each manager responsible for department-level awards, could easily dedicate up to one day per week to administering the program. This was a considerable drain on productivity.

Citigroup worked with an incentive company to replace the paper-based program with a branded Citigroup employee intranet site, where participants could log on and convert their award to a gift certificate from one of thousands of worldwide retailers. The "self-service" aspect of the program reduced administration headaches for HR and department managers, and significantly decreased production and lost-time expenses.

- *Goal-setting certainty and degree of stretch in goals.* Firms sometimes run contests and SPIFFs to remedy unfairness in the main compensation plan.

If the sales force is well below targeted incentive earnings because management set goals too high, a SPIFF or sales contest can boost morale and provide additional earnings opportunity for salespeople. For this reason, the degree of reliance on sales contests and SPIFFs is in part a function of the probability that the sales force will miss its sales goal. In volatile environments where it is difficult to set accurate goals, or when management sets very demanding stretch goals to challenge the sales force, a larger budget for SPIFFs and sales contests is advised so that add-on programs can be used as needed.

Expectancy Theory Applied to Sales Contest and SPIFF Design

A framework used in the academic literature on sales incentive compensation provides a convenient way to think about sales contest and SPIFF design. The framework is based on expectancy theory, a theory that attempts to isolate the variables and processes that influence individual motivation. Expectancy theory identifies three psychological processes that drive motivation and therefore effort: expectancy, instrumentality, and valence. The following table explains these processes and provides advice for designing sales contests and SPIFFs that align with the processes.

Psychological Processes That Drive Individual Motivation	Advice for Designing Sales Contests and SPIFFs That Align with These Processes
Expectancy Salespeople must believe that greater effort will lead to greater performance.	• Select measures that the sales force can affect. • Favor individual rewards over team rewards unless team selling is the norm. • Allow enough time (for example, one sales cycle) for salespeople to influence the performance measures. • Do not use sales contests and SPIFFs in environments where sales force causality is low or results measurement is poor.
Instrumentality Salespeople must believe that greater performance will lead to rewards.	• Set realistic performance goals. • Select measures that are accurate and objectively measurable. • Favor results/output measures over activity/input measures. • Have enough winners so that a considerable percentage of the sales force feels that it has a chance.
Valence Salespeople must believe that the reward will make them happy.	• Select prizes that are desirable to all salespeople. • Favor noncash awards such as merchandise and travel over cash awards. • Limit the number of winners to increase the cash and prestige value of awards.

Companies That Help Manage Noncash Incentive Programs. Figure 10-7 provides a list of the larger companies that provide noncash program assistance. These companies can help with program design, program tracking, and reward distribution.

Figure 10-7. A list of some of the larger noncash incentive management companies.

Company Name	Web Site	Description
All Star Incentive Marketing	www.incentiveusa.com	Full-service incentive company; also designs customer loyalty programs.
American Express Incentive Services	www.aeis.com	Numerous rewards options, including Amex Travelers Cheques and Amex Rewards cards.
Carlson Marketing Group	www.carlsonmarketing.com	Marketing communications firm whose incentive offerings include www.salesdriver.com.
Globoforce	www.globoforce.com	Offers global incentive programs in 35 countries with multiple language and currency support.
Incent One	www.incentone.com	Incentive portfolio includes building company-branded sites for award redemption.
Maritz	www.maritz.com	Global firm with over $1B in annual revenue focused on "people and potential."
Marketing Innovators	www.marketinginnovators.com	Exclusive distributor of JCPenney gift cards. Offers a number of incentive programs.
Meridian Enterprises	www.meridianenterprises.com	Offers a variety of reward systems, including www.gorillarewards.com.
O.C. Tanner	www.octanner.com	Providing incentive solutions for over 75 years; crafted Olympic medals for 2002 Winter Olympics.
Universal Certificate Group	www.ucgroupllc.com	Focusing on online rewards, this firm is the parent of GiveAnything.com, CorporateRewards.com, and CorporateLoyalty.com.

Recognition Programs

The President's Club at Checkpoint Systems

At Checkpoint Systems, a multinational manufacturer and marketer of security systems, the top eight salespeople for the year are recognized and invited to join the President's Club. Club members get a five-day group trip to an exotic location. But the greatest honor given to the group is that it gets to act as an advisory council to the company's top executives.

Many firms have formal sales force recognition programs to showcase and reward the medium- and long-term efforts of high-performing salespeople. Recognition is usually based on performance over a longer period than sales contests and SPIFFs—typically one year or more. Salespeople who are selected for recognition programs may receive cash, merchandise, or travel awards, but the most important part of the recognition program is typically the highlighting of their achievements before their peers, management, and/or customers. Often, recognition programs include an invitation to be part of a select group, which might be called the President's Club, the Inner Circle, or Million Dollar Roundtable. Recognition programs not only reward top performers, but are also a way for management to signal to the rest of the sales force what it takes to be successful. In many companies, recognition programs may have greater impact on morale and motivation for a much lower cost than sales contests or SPIFFs.

> "We work for money, but we strive for plaques."
>
> Andy Anderson, former vice president of sales, Searle

Recognition programs are generally well liked by salespeople. Such programs are much respected and considered to be almost sacred by the sales force at many companies. Some observations about successful sales recognition programs are provided here.

- *What should the reward be?* The most important aspect of a recognition program is the publicity for those being recognized. Being called on stage at a national sales meeting, being written up in the company newsletter, or being honored at a banquet in front of peers, management, and/or customers can have considerable impact, not only on those being recognized, but also on the rest of the sales force, which sees those selected as role models of success. Usually, some type of tangible award accompanies the recognition, such as a trip, a plaque, a ring, or other merchandise. Award receivers can also be rewarded with a promotion or a special assignment. Often companies have special provisions for recognizing multiyear participants or salespeople who reach significant career milestones. For example, a payroll services company awards gold rings to salespeople who sign a career total of 300 new clients; salespeople receive additional diamonds when they reach 500, 1,000, and 2,000 new clients.

What About Stock Options?

As an enhancement to a recognition program, some companies give stock options to salespeople who have performed consistently well over a period of time. This practice was especially popular a few years ago (between approximately 1998 and 2001) and was used as a strategy for preventing good salespeople from leaving their jobs to join Internet start-ups. Although the popularity of the practice has declined considerably in recent years, stock options are still used in some sales forces as a retention strategy for top performers. The number of stock options a salesperson receives is usually based on a combination of the salesperson's performance and her tenure. For example, a grid might determine the number of stock options a salesperson receives based on years with over 100 percent goal attainment and total years with the company; more options are offered to those ranking high in both categories.

- *What criteria for selection?* Criteria for selection in a recognition program are usually a combination of annual results metrics and behaviors that the firm considers important for long-term success. Results metrics, such as quota achievement, gross margin growth, or achievement of multiyear sales goals, are typically consistent with those used in the firm's main sales incentive plan. Other criteria can include manager-rated characteristics such as teamwork, leadership, citizenship, and customer service. There are usually some qualifiers designed to ensure that those who are selected are good role models for the rest of the sales force. Qualifiers might include provisions such as, the salesperson must not be on probation, must have achieved certain MBOs, or must have been in his position for at least one year. It is a fine balance to combine objective metrics such as results with subjective criteria that may be biased as a result of management favoritism. Some programs also have provisions to make certain that recognition is given to a cross section of the sales force. For example, a stipulation that the top salespeople in each region are recognized, even if they are not among the highest nationally, helps to ensure that there will be role models that the entire sales force can relate to and that all regions are engaged in the recognition program.

- *How many should be recognized?* In large sales forces, recognition is usually limited to the top 5 to 10 percent of the salespeople. In smaller sales forces, the percentage is slightly higher, usually 15 to 20 percent. The number of salespeople recognized should be consistent with a message that the group is exclusive ("These are our real winners and role models"), yet at the same time the number should be large enough for many salespeople to believe that they have a reasonable shot at being recognized.

Does the Number Recognized Need to Be Limited?

Some recognition programs do not limit the number of salespeople who are recognized; instead, they acknowledge everyone who achieves a specified goal. For example, a "100 Percent Club" in one company recognizes everyone who achieves her sales goal two years in a row. There are some advantages to not limiting participation in a recognition program to a specific number: Salespeople know up front what they need to do to be recognized, and everyone who is willing to work hard enough can be recognized. This eliminates internally focused competition for "spots"; salespeople will be more likely to focus on beating competitors rather than on beating peers. However, since salespeople are generally quite competitive by nature, being recognized based on competition with peers may be considered a greater honor and therefore may be preferred by the sales force. In addition, accurate goal setting is absolutely critical to the success of any program that does not limit the number of salespeople recognized. If the goals are achieved too easily, everyone is recognized, and the group is no longer exclusive. If the goals are too challenging, no one is recognized, and the sales force feels demoralized. There may be practical reasons for limiting the number of salespeople recognized as well. For instance, it is difficult to plan a reward trip (which must be arranged many months in advance) without knowing how large the group will be.

Recognition Programs Can Be Highly Political and Therefore Difficult to Change

At many companies, recognition programs have been around for years, are part of the sales force culture, and are considered to be almost sacred. Anyone who proposes a change in the program faces considerable political challenge. For example, following a major corporate merger, we worked to create a single merged sales force from the two formerly independent sales organizations. The project was very demanding, as we were working with the two merger partners to successfully blend their diverse cultures and retain the best salespeople, all under intense time pressure. Surprisingly, one of the greatest challenges was to create a sales recognition program on which both merger partners could agree. Before the merger, one partner had had a program that recognized the top 6 percent of the sales force and included a cash bonus. The other partner's program had been very similar, except that the top 8 percent of the sales force was recognized and the cash bonus was smaller. In addition, the second partner allowed some internal marketing people who interacted with the sales force to be eligible for the program. Despite the seemingly small differences between the two recognition programs, creating a single merged program proved to be challenging, as each partner had considerable emotional and political history invested in its program.

Recognition Programs for Distribution Partners

Firms that sell to customers indirectly through business partners often have formal recognition programs for top-performing partners. For example, at Microsoft Business Solutions (MBS), a select group of MBS partners that achieve outstanding business performance and customer satisfaction is invited to join the President's Club each year. An even more exclusive recognition for MBS business partners is membership in the MBS Inner Circle, reserved for a very few top partners that achieved exemplary accomplishments during the past sales year and exhibited outstanding commitment to the Microsoft mission. The most prestigious award given to any MBS partner is Microsoft's Global Partner of the Year Award. It honors the MBS partner with the most outstanding business performance, including high levels of sales achievement and superior customer satisfaction. The winner of the award for 2004 was ePartners, a leading MBS provider and information technology services organization. According to a Microsoft spokesperson, ePartners was selected for the esteemed award because of its "deep understanding of technology, proven expertise in the Microsoft Business Solutions industry, and a passion for building solutions that solve its customers' business problems in an innovative way." ePartners accepted the award at Microsoft's Worldwide Partner Conference in July 2004 in Toronto, Canada.

Insights

Sales force incentive plans are designed to motivate and direct the selling organization. Sales contests and SPIFFs accentuate short-term needs. Recognition programs enhance and acknowledge the consistently high-performing salespeople. Some concluding insights and guidelines for running successful add-on incentive programs are provided here. The insights are organized around the 3 C's framework.

Ensure *Consistency* with Strategy and Sales Roles

- Limit the number of contests and SPIFFs, keeping salespeople focused on what is most important. Don't let product marketing teams dilute the sales force's strategic focus.

- Tailor contests and recognition programs to the sales role. Contests and SPIFFs work best for sales roles with high short-term causality. Salespeople who work primarily alone and without day-to-day social interaction with peers and managers may need formal recognition programs to help them feel appreciated and connected to the company. On the other hand, less formal recognition and simple pats on the back may be appropriate for salespeople in roles that involve frequent interaction with managers and team members.

Ensure *Compatibility* with Other Sales Force Effectiveness Drivers

- Measure accurately and provide constant feedback. The best sales contests and SPIFFs are easy to track and quick to reward.

- Make sure that the programs meet the needs of the sales force. If sales force needs and interests are diverse, consider offering different programs and prizes to engage as many people as possible.

- Encourage management involvement. Make sure that awards are public and are given by important people in the organization.

- Set fair and challenging goals.

- Make sure that the programs are consistent with the sales force culture. Invent fun themes, and keep prizes consistent with those themes. Deliver on promises. Spread success around.

Ensure Appropriate *Consequences* for Salespeople and Company Results

- Set a time frame that is long enough that salespeople can influence the results and avoid randomness, yet short enough to keep the sales force focused.

- Give more than money.

- Invest in recognition programs; they may be more effective than contests and SPIFFs.

- When salespeople are not making enough money through the main incentive plan as a result of circumstances beyond their control (for example, when national goals are too challenging), consider using contests and SPIFFs to compensate the sales force fairly and keep salespeople engaged.

CHAPTER 11

Making an Effective Transition with a Major Incentive Compensation Plan Change

How This Chapter Is Organized

Introduction   410
   How Difficult Will Change Be?   412
      Company Culture   412
      Circumstances Surrounding the Change 412
      Sales Force Customer Power   413
      Degree of Income Loss   413

**Sales Incentive Compensation Plan Change and the Sales
Management System**   415
   Consequences for Salespeople   416
   Consequences for Customers   418
   Consistency with Strategy and Compatibility with Other Sales Force
   Effectiveness Drivers   419

Challenging Sales Incentive Compensation Plan Transitions   421
   Reducing Pay Levels   421
   Changing the Salary—Incentive Mix   423
      Strategies when Increasing the Incentive Portion of the Mix   427
      Strategies when Increasing the Salary Portion of the Mix   429
   Implementing New Performance Measures or Changing
   Performance–Payout Relationships   430
   Special Situations   433

Territory Realignment   433

New Salespeople   435

A Sales Force Change Process Framework   435

Guiding Principles   437

Activities: Design–Mobilize–Implement   437

Design Activities   437

Mobilization Activities   438

Implementation Activities   442

Communicating Plan Features and Benefits to the Field   443

Developing the Plan Administration Systems and Processes   449

Setting Goals   450

Timing of Implementation with Design and Mobilization Activities   450

Change Outlook   451

Introduction

Companies have different philosophies regarding how much and how often to change their sales incentive compensation plan. Some firms make changes to their compensation plan every year. Management reasons that as markets and company strategies evolve, the sales incentive compensation plan should also be adjusted or even revamped to ensure that sales force energy stays aligned appropriately. Changes in the sales leadership team or in relationships with different compensation consulting firms can also lead to plan changes. For example, Figure 11-1 shows how one firm changed its sales compensation plan over a five-year period as market conditions and company strategies evolved, management philosophies changed, and the firm developed relationships with different consulting firms. The challenge for this firm was to implement each change with as little disruption to the sales force as possible.

At other firms, the compensation plan has not changed in years. Management feels that compensation plan changes disrupt the sales force and divert salespeople's attention from their primary mission of creating sales through providing customer value. Compensation structures are maintained even as products, markets, and company priorities evolve. The challenge at such firms is to encourage the sales force to successfully adapt to changing customer and company needs using means other than incentives.

Figure 11-1. Evolution of the sales incentive compensation plan at a pharmaceutical firm.

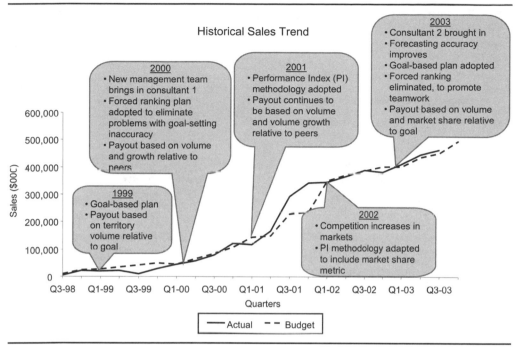

Manufacturer Emphasizes Continuity in Its Sales Compensation Plan

A latching systems manufacturer has maintained the same sales compensation plan for over 30 years. The plan pays 80 percent incentive and 20 percent salary. Incentives are paid as a commission on total revenues, with an accelerated rate for revenues beyond goal. With this plan design, the firm's veteran salespeople earn generous commissions on the book of business they have built over the years. Management has been reluctant to consider any plan changes, for fear of angering the salespeople who control the majority of the business. However, lately recruiting and hiring new salespeople at the low guaranteed salary level the firm offers has become increasingly difficult. In addition, e-commerce has affected the industry and has changed the mix of products sold by the sales force and the role of the salesperson. Management wonders if perhaps the time has come to revamp a sales incentive plan that has served the firm well for so many years.

When we asked managers at 88 companies of varying sizes and in various industries who attended our sales compensation executive education programs at Northwestern University between 2000 and 2003, "How often do you make major changes to your sales force incentive compensation?" the average answer was every two to three years. Minor adjustments occur more frequently.

How Difficult Will Change Be?

The difficulty of implementing a successful incentive plan change is influenced by:

- Company culture
- The circumstances surrounding the change
- Sales force customer power
- The degree of income loss

Company Culture. A company that changes its sales force incentive plan frequently is likely to face less sales force resistance to any change than a company that rarely alters its plan.

Circumstances Surrounding the Change. The circumstances surrounding a sales incentive compensation plan change influence the difficulty of implementing the change. Some incentive plan changes are in response to a major event, such as:

- A merger or acquisition
- A considerable change in the firm's go-to-market strategy
- The creation of a new sales force
- A significant sales force restructuring
- The launch of a new product

Such events require significant and immediate management attention. The sales force is likely to anticipate and expect that changes to the sales incentive compensation plan will be necessary. These events will trigger other sales force changes as well; for example:

- New sales roles may be created.
- Customer assignments may change.
- Management expectations may rise.

Perhaps the biggest sales management challenge when implementing incentive plan changes in conjunction with a major event is to help the sales force understand, integrate, and assimilate in a short period of time all of the various changes that are going to be required.

Not all sales incentive compensation plan changes are event-driven. Often, sales leadership's desire for constant improvement precipitates change. The sales leadership team may feel that there are problems with the current incentive compensation plan, such as:

- Not paying for performance
- Not attracting and retaining the right people
- Costing the firm too much money

In addition, sales leadership may feel that evolutionary changes in the firm's situation and environment are affecting the sales force, such as:

- Maturing product lines
- Intensifying competition
- A consolidating customer base

Adapting the compensation plan is one way to respond to these changes. Implementing significant compensation plan changes in non-event-driven situations can be difficult because the need to change a plan may not be immediately evident to the sales force. The sales management challenge is to sell the sales force on the need for and the benefits of making the change.

Sales Force Customer Power. Sales force customer power reflects the degree of influence or control each salesperson has over his accounts. Salespeople with high customer power have the ability to leave the firm and take their accounts with them. This happens frequently in industries such as financial services, insurance, and office supplies, where products are mostly nondifferentiated commodities, the salesperson is the major link between the firm and each customer, and sales are strongly relationship-driven. The more customer power a sales force has, the more difficult it will be to implement incentive plan change successfully.

Degree of Income Loss. Plan changes that produce a risk of income loss for a significant number of salespeople can be difficult to implement. Income loss will occur when the total compensation payout is reduced across the entire sales force or when the total variable pay gets redistributed among salespeople. The "who gets helped" and "who gets hurt" analysis from Chapter 8 provides insight into the extent to which income loss will occur. Figure 11-2 provides an example of this type of analysis for a consumer packaged goods company. Bars above the horizontal line represent salespeople who are expected to gain income when the new plan is implemented, while those below the line represent salespeople who are expected to lose income. Plan designers should look at the extent of income loss when assessing a candidate plan to determine whether the plan can be implemented successfully.

Income loss resulting from a plan change can occur in various ways. A considerable change in the salary–incentive mix, a change from paying on all sales to a goal-based plan, or adding incentive caps can trigger income loss. A successful transition to a new incentive plan may not be possible in a situation where there is income loss for a significant number of salespeople and the sales force has considerable customer power. A noticeable negative change in income may anger too

Figure 11-2. "Who is helped" and "who is hurt" by a new compensation plan for a consumer packaged goods sales force.

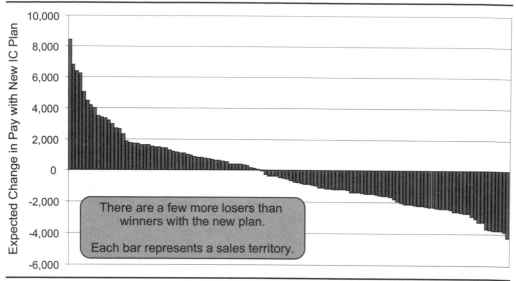

There are a few more losers than winners with the new plan.

Each bar represents a sales territory.

many salespeople, causing them to leave the firm and take their customers with them.

Significant Sales Force Customer Power Makes Incentive Plan Change Difficult

A financial services firm selling investment products to high-net-worth individuals paid its salespeople a commission on the investments they sold. Veteran salespeople who had established relationships and built their book of business earned a lot of money; many made well over $1 million a year while working only 30 hours a week. A new management team at the company felt that the sales force was overpaid. Without asking the sales force for input, it designed a new team-based incentive compensation plan that was designed to reduce the customer power of salespeople. It also cut commission rates in half. The sales force was extremely angry. Over half of the salespeople quit, taking business representing more than 60 percent of the firm's assets with them.

An Ounce of Prevention

There are some situations in which it is virtually impossible to change a sales compensation plan successfully. A non-event-driven compensation plan change that significantly redistributes income among salespeople who have considerable customer power and who have been paid the same way for years is almost guaranteed to fail. If the change causes the majority of

> salespeople to leave the firm and take customers with them, it may take years for the firm to recover financially. In competitive markets, the firm may not even survive. A management team facing this delicate situation must tread carefully. Although a sudden, drastic change in the way the sales force is paid may not be possible, successful evolutionary change can usually be implemented. Management must think in terms of prevention, asking, "What steps can we take today to ensure that we are not in this predicament five years from now?" An ounce of prevention goes a long way toward ensuring long-term sales force success.

This chapter focuses on the successful implementation of major sales incentive compensation plan changes. Insights are provided on the various challenges associated with making different types of incentive compensation plan modifications. The chapter concludes with a framework for understanding and implementing sales force change, along with specific suggestions for successfully implementing a new incentive compensation plan.

Sales Incentive Compensation Plan Change and the Sales Management System

The decision to change the sales incentive compensation plan significantly should never be taken lightly. Sales compensation decisions affect the salespeople who drive sales force activities. These activities influence customer results, and customer results have an impact on company results. Recall the 3 Cs approach to diagnosing sales incentive compensation plan effectiveness, summarized in Figure 11-3. Effective sales incentive compensation plan change has appropriate *consequences* for company and customer results, sales force behaviors and activities, and sales force quality. Effective compensation plan change is also *consistent* with sales and marketing strategies and sales processes and roles, and is *compatible* with other sales force effectiveness drivers, such as performance management systems and sales force culture, motivators, and hiring and development processes.

Companies that thoroughly assess their candidate plans before selecting the final plan will experience a smoother implementation than those that implement

Figure 11-3. The 3 Cs approach to diagnosing sales incentive compensation plan effectiveness.

Consistency with . . .	Compatibility with . . .	Consequences . . .
• Sales and marketing strategies • Sales process • Sales roles	• Performance management systems • Sales force culture • Sales force motivators • Sales force hiring and development processes	• Company results • Customer results • Sales force behaviors and activities • Sales force quality

a plan without first testing it. Chapter 8 provides a framework for evaluating candidate plans in terms of the 3 Cs before selecting the final plan.

Consequences for Salespeople

It is essential to focus on the needs of salespeople when the sales incentive compensation plan changes. A major change creates uncertainty for the sales force, which leads to stress for salespeople. Even if the company is able to demonstrate to the sales force that the new plan will be fairer and more equitable, salespeople will still be anxious and concerned about the change. An incentive plan change means that the company wants salespeople to behave differently from the way they have behaved in the past. Salespeople may have to work harder, learn something new, or interact with customers in a different way. They will wonder whether or not they will be successful in the new environment. How will their income be affected? How will their performance under the new plan compare with that of their peers? Will they still make the President's Club? They may even fear that the change threatens their job security. Other companies may take advantage of this anxiety by attempting to hire away the firm's top salespeople. Sales force recruiters often target people at firms that are going through transitions. Ambitious sales personnel may reason that given the uncertainty, perhaps the time is right to consider a job change.

Salespeople will want to know, "How does the change affect me?" It is important to let salespeople know how they would have done last year if the new plan had been in place. Hopefully, top performers would have made more money.

Salespeople who are opposed to a sales incentive compensation change can react in several ways:

- Openly oppose the change by complaining or even slowing down work.
- Quietly oppose the change through diminished loyalty and decreased motivation.
- Leave the company (and possibly take accounts to a competitor).

Firms must pay special attention to their top-producing salespeople during times of incentive compensation plan transition. These are the salespeople that the firm cannot afford to lose—and the ones that other sales forces will pursue most aggressively.

Medical Device Firm Adopts a "Follow the Stars" Strategy for Incentive Plan Change

Sales leadership at a medical device firm was evaluating some possible major sales incentive compensation plan changes. There was significant concern that any plan change might upset many of the firm's salespeople and cause significant sales force turnover. To address this issue, sales leaders identified 20 "star" performers—the top-producing salespeople that the firm could not afford to lose. As changes to the compensation plan were evaluated, the analysis focused on the impact of the proposed change on each of these 20 stars. If a change hurt many of the stars, it was immediately scrapped or redesigned. This "follow the stars" strategy helped ensure that the firm retained its best salespeople after the transition.

Effective strategies for dealing with sales force resistance to incentive compensation plan change vary with the degree of income loss expected, as shown in Figure 11-4. When the expected degree of income loss is small, communication and involvement of the sales force in the change process are often enough to facilitate a smooth transition. Moving quickly also helps to minimize the impact of sales force anxiety. However, as the degree of income redistribution increases, there is a need for more formal transition strategies. Leveraging "winner" power is especially important, meaning that salespeople who benefit from the change (which hopefully includes many of the firm's most respected salespeople) should

Figure 11-4. Effective strategies for dealing with sales force resistance to incentive compensation plan change.

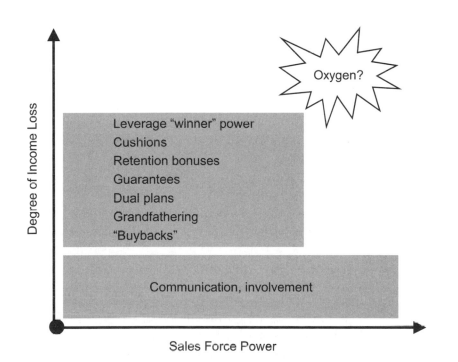

be vocal supporters of the change. In addition, intermediate or transition compensation plans can facilitate implementation. Transition plans include:

- *Cushions and retention bonuses.* Give people a bonus for staying with the firm for a period following implementation. This should be used with caution; paying salespeople to stay with the company conflicts with a "loyal" sales force culture.

- *Guarantees.* Guarantee that salespeople will make at least a certain amount with the new plan (for example, at least as much as last year). The guaranteed amount declines over time and eventually is phased out.

- *Dual plans.* Calculate incentive payouts with both the old and new plans and pay the higher of the two for a period following implementation.

- *Grandfathering.* Exempt veteran salespeople from following all the rules of the new plan. This should be used with caution; if too many salespeople are grandfathered, the ability of the new plan to change sales force behavior and meet company objectives is significantly reduced.

- *Buyback arrangements.* Continue to pay salespeople for performance at accounts that were reassigned to another salesperson (for example, as the result of realignment) for a period following implementation.

A successful conversion to a new incentive plan may not be possible in a situation where the degree of income loss is significant and the sales force has considerable customer power. As Figure 11-4 shows, there may be no "oxygen" in the northeast corner. A drastic change to the incentive plan may anger too many salespeople, causing them to leave the firm and take their customers with them. Thus, a firm where the sales force has significant customer power has limited opportunity to change its sales incentive compensation plan without considerable sales force disruption.

Consequences for Customers

It is also important to examine the impact of any sales force incentive compensation plan change from a customer perspective. A change in the incentive plan will influence salespeople and their activities and behaviors. This has the potential to affect customers, both positively and negatively.

Some incentive plan changes are designed specifically to enhance customer relationships. For example, a firm might reduce the variable portion of its compensation plan and increase the salary portion, in order to reduce sales force focus on short-term results and increase its focus on long-term customer needs. In addition, a firm might add measures such as repeat business rate or a customer satisfaction score to the incentive plan in an effort to encourage sales force behaviors that make customers happy and improve customer retention.

Best Buy Eliminates Commissioned Salespeople Based on Customer Feedback

In 1989, consumer electronics retail chain Best Buy eliminated its commissioned sales force based on feedback from customers. The chain adopted a straight salary plan after conducting customer focus groups and discovering that customers just didn't trust commissioned salespeople. The chain established "answer centers" in each store where customers could come with questions if they needed help. Customers liked the new no-hassle approach and felt much more comfortable shopping in the no-commission environment. The sales force liked the changes as well because Best Buy became a friendlier place to work and salespeople made a good salary every day, regardless of how busy the store was. Three years after the change, salesperson turnover had decline by 50 percent.

Sometimes sales incentive compensation plan changes encourage unintended sales force behaviors that make customers unhappy. Consider the following situations:

- More aggressive commission accelerators encourage salespeople to over-sell and disregard customer needs.
- An increase in performance-based incentive opportunity coupled with a cut in salary encourages salespeople to spend all their time selling, ignoring important customer service needs.
- An increase in commission rates on high-margin products encourages the sales force to sell these products, even when a low-margin product is better for the customer.
- Monthly objectives with an overachievement bonus encourage salespeople to delay placement of customer orders at the end of every other month.

Whenever the sales incentive compensation plan changes, undesirable behaviors such as these must be anticipated and addressed up front. Management must rely on sales force effectiveness drivers other than the incentive compensation plan to minimize these undesirable behaviors. For example, coaching by sales managers and the firm's performance management systems might help to create a more customer-focused culture and reduce greedy sales force behaviors. However, it is important that the messages sent are reasonably consistent across all of the sales force effectiveness drivers. A manager who tells her salespeople, "Do whatever it takes to make the customer happy," will lack credibility if the compensation plan sends the message "sell at all costs."

Consistency with Strategy and Compatibility with Other Sales Force Effectiveness Drivers

Sales leaders must also pay close attention to the impact of a new sales compensation plan on all of the other sales force effectiveness drivers. The upstream driver decisions (such as sales and marketing strategies and sales processes and roles) should be consistent with the overall corporate strategies and should always precede decisions about the sales compensation plan. An effective sales compensation plan reinforces company strategies and is aligned with the sales force role. The consistency check of candidate incentive plans described in Chapter 8 screens for plans that will be consistent with sales and marketing strategies and sales processes and roles when implemented.

Compatibility with other sales force effectiveness drivers is also important. Whenever the sales compensation plan changes, many additional sales force effectiveness drivers typically require adjustment as well. For example, suppose a sales organization changes its incentive compensation plan from a plan that pays mostly variable pay to a plan that pays mostly salary. Required adjustments to various sales force effectiveness drivers may include the following:

- Hiring profiles for sales and sales management positions may need to change, as the job will require salespeople who are less focused on short-term sales and more oriented toward problem solving and the development of long-term customer relationships.

- Performance management systems may need to be revised, as management will need to oversee sales force activities more closely, since compensation is no longer tied as directly to results.

- Sales information and support systems will certainly be affected as well, since the sales organization may need different information and resources to do the job effectively.

The compatibility check described in Chapter 8 tests candidate plans and eliminates those that do not align with sales force effectiveness drivers such as performance management systems and sales force culture, motivators, and hiring and development processes.

Redesigning sales force systems, processes, and programs can be a major undertaking, and significant time and resources may be required to align these systems effectively. Yet achieving complete alignment is critical to delivering a consistent message to the sales force that reinforces company goals and culture.

Making Cross-Selling Work at Brenton Banks

Recall from Chapter 1 the story about Iowa-based Brenton Banks. Management wanted to facilitate the cross-selling of banking and brokerage products. The two departments operated as "silos," and bankers and brokers rarely referred customers to one another. Brenton's management recognized that incentives alone would not be enough to change this culture. To encourage sharing of leads, management redrew the organization chart, creating a single Brenton sales force. Bankers and brokers were given a single net income goal that was not broken down according to the old banking and brokerage divisions. Bankers and brokers met twice a week to discuss plans and share client names. Joint sales calls crossing the traditional banking and brokerage boundaries were encouraged. The entire sales force was trained on the full range of product offerings. The incentive plan was revamped so that bankers could receive commissions for broker product sales, and brokers could receive commissions for bank product sales. The new approach encouraged all bankers and brokers to be much more proactive cross-sellers.

Challenging Sales Incentive Compensation Plan Transitions

This section of the chapter focuses on some particularly challenging incentive compensation plan transition situations, some success strategies for dealing with these situations, and some cautions about what to avoid. Much of the discussion is organized around the four key incentive plan design choices introduced earlier in this book: pay level, mix, performance measures, and performance–payout relationship. In addition, implementation challenges that arise in several special transition circumstances—incentive plan adjustments following a territory realignment and initial plans for new salespeople—are discussed.

Reducing Pay Levels

Increases in sales force pay levels are easy to implement, but decreases are not. Factors that might lead a firm to cut sales force pay can originate either outside of the sales force or within the sales force. Several examples are:

- The sales force is paid well above the industry norm; turnover (particularly of mediocre performers) is almost nonexistent because people cannot make this much money anywhere else.

- There is an abundant supply of qualified salespeople; good salespeople are willing to come to work for the firm for substantially less money than the existing sales force is paid.

- The company is under severe pressure to cut costs; across-the-board pay cuts are necessary to ensure long-term viability.

- The sales force is overpaid relative to people in comparable positions in other departments, and the extreme envy of the sales force is hurting overall company productivity.

- The role of the salesperson is changing from one that adds significant customer value to one that adds only modest value as product lines and selling processes evolve.

Communication with the sales force during a sales force pay cut is critical. Salespeople need to understand why the change is being made. Salespeople are typically more willing to accept pay cuts that are event-driven—for example, when the firm has missed its numbers several years in a row, when a competitive launch has eroded the firm's market share, or when a major sales force restructuring has diminished the role of the salesperson. Pay cuts that are driven solely by the need to "trim fat" or to bring costs in line with industry norms are very difficult to implement without a significant negative impact on sales force morale.

When cutting sales force pay, be prepared to lose some salespeople, particularly if the pay cut makes the firm's sales force pay scale less favorable than that of other firms in the industry. If there are salespeople that the firm cannot afford to lose, consider the following strategies:

- Give top performers additional responsibilities that allow them to enhance or at least maintain their current pay level.

- Freeze pay levels rather than cutting them, and phase in the pay cut over time.

- Instead of cutting pay levels, cut sales force size and eliminate the jobs of poor performers.

- Offer a severance package that encourages the highest-paid veteran salespeople to take early retirement.

- Make improvements to other sales force effectiveness drivers to compensate for the lower pay. For example, eliminate some sales force paperwork or improve nonmonetary motivational programs. Salespeople may be willing to work for less pay if the sales force culture is more favorable.

- Most importantly, sales leadership should be prepared to take a pay cut as well. News of the pay cut will be more readily accepted by salespeople if they know that management, too, is sacrificing.

Telecommunications Firms Pay Big Executive Bonuses while Laying Off Workers

When the telecommunications industry took a dramatic downturn beginning in mid-2000, firms in the industry were forced to implement massive downsizing and cost-cutting measures. Yet despite the substantial cuts, several firms paid top executives generous retention bonuses. For example, at WorldCom, the CFO and CEO received $10 million each in 2000 to stay with the firm for two years, while thousands of other workers were being shown the door. Similarly, in 2002, Lucent Technologies paid $16.2 million to entice four senior executives to stay with the firm for a year, with additional bonuses promised in the future. At the same time, Lucent's chairman was urging workers to "share in the pain." Salaries had been frozen since December of 2000, performance bonuses for nonexecutive managers were suspended indefinitely, and more than half of the firm's employees had been let go.

When a company is going through a merger or a difficult time, retention bonuses for top executives often make good economic sense, since the cost of replacing a top executive is typically much greater than the cost of a retention bonus. However, employees will undoubtedly challenge generous payments to top executives during tough times, and the negative impact on employee morale cannot be ignored. In the case of Lucent and WorldCom, experts outside the two firms questioned whether the awards were necessary, given the scarcity of jobs at all levels, including the most senior levels, within the industry.

There are also some effective long-term strategies that a firm can use to avoid the need to implement a drastic sales force pay cut. Prudent use of resources during good times reduces the likelihood that sales force pay must be cut during bad times. Strategies include the following:

- Save money during successful years rather than spending extravagantly; this puts the firm in a strong position to survive lean years without making drastic cuts.

- Evaluate the long-term consequences of any candidate incentive plan (see Chapter 8). For example, check to see if sales force pay will get out of hand if company sales grow precipitously.

- When structuring the sales force pay plan, keep in mind that some elements of compensation are easier to reduce than others. For example, it is easier to cut incentive pay than it is to cut salary. A company that pays its sales force 100 percent salary will have a more difficult time implementing a pay cut than one that has the option of reducing costs by cutting incentives while maintaining salaries.

- Include special short-term features in the incentive plan during good years, such as special sales contents, SPIFFs, or incentive trips. Make it clear to the sales force that these "perks" will not be offered in the less successful years.

Changing the Salary–Incentive Mix

Significant changes in the salary–incentive mix are particularly challenging to implement, since mix decisions have considerable impact on sales force culture and values. Salary oriented sales forces tend to be customer-centered. They emphasize the achievement of long-term results through cooperation of sales team members, control of sales force activity, and professional development of the sales staff. Incentive-oriented sales forces, on the other hand, tend to have many of the opposite characteristics. They emphasize the achievement of short-term results through competition between salespeople, empowerment of the sales force, and a sales-focused culture. Because of these considerable differences, a significant change in the salary–incentive mix can lead to substantial sales force turnover. It is not uncommon for more than 50 percent of salespeople to leave a company within three years after a significant mix change is implemented.

Significant mix changes are usually driven by changes in sales force causality, or the ability of the firm to attribute results to an individual salesperson's efforts. Increases in sales force causality frequently lead companies to shift to greater incentives and less salary. This happens in a number of situations, including:

- When a company that formerly used distributors begins to sell direct
- When a company's offerings become commodities and the selling process changes from selling solutions to selling products
- When the sales force focus shifts from retaining and servicing customers to driving new sales and growth
- When industry deregulation creates a need for the firm to compete for customers for the first time

Decreases in sales force causality frequently lead to shifts toward more salary and less incentive. Examples of situations where this occurs include:

- When the focus of the sales force shifts from pressure and relationship selling of products to partnering and consultative selling of solutions
- When sales roles change from individual "lone rangers" to team selling with more specialized and loosely defined roles
- When a new product is launched and sales are very difficult to forecast
- When market volatility increases, creating an increase in sales force windfall gains or losses

Mix changes are also driven occasionally by a sales leadership change. A new sales management team may feel that an existing culture is either too aggressive or too passive. In either of these cases, a move to modify the culture can coincide with a mix change. An aggressive sales force may be moderated by moving toward a plan with a higher salary component, and a passive sales culture may be moved toward a more aggressive posture by increasing the variable-pay component.

A Newspaper Changes Its Incentive Plan Based on a Better Understanding of the Market's Response to Its Selling Effort

A number of years ago, a small newspaper company in Indiana began a sales force incentive design project for its advertising sales force. Like most newspapers across the United States, this firm was using a mostly salary plan. Small bonuses were awarded to the sales force if the newspaper had a banner year. The newspaper was managed by editorial people who placed little credence in the sales function. "Newspapers are sold because of content, and advertisers have little choice as to how they can reach the local audience," was their point of view. However, after some reflection, management realized that advertising sales is an environment with strong sales force causality and the ability to easily measure sales force results—implying that sales force incentives can have considerable impact on sales results. The newspaper designed and implemented a new plan with a significant variable-pay component. The sales force responded with a 35 percent growth in advertising sales in the year after rolling out the new program.

Since a significant change in the salary–incentive mix influences sales force culture and values, it is critical to understand how individual salespeople are likely to feel about a mix change. Salespeople who prefer salary-oriented compensation plans typically have a very different personality profile and tolerance for risk from salespeople who like incentive-oriented plans, and usually a person's profile and risk tolerance cannot be changed. It is useful to segment salespeople based on relevant personality traits and risk-taking tolerance to anticipate their reaction to the proposed mix change. Figure 11-5 shows some typical characteristics of salespeople who prefer salary-oriented plans and incentive-oriented plans. By profiling each person in the sales force on these and other relevant characteristics, management can learn whom the new plan is likely to appeal to and who will dislike it. Management can then begin to develop strategies for dealing with the individuals in each group.

If the proposed mix change is significant, it is likely that a large proportion of the sales force will have a personality profile that is incompatible with the new compensation plan, and significant sales force turnover should be expected. Figure

Figure 11-5. Characteristics of salespeople who prefer salary and those who prefer incentives.

Salespeople Who Prefer Salary . . .	Salespeople Who Prefer Incentives . . .
Are customer-centered; they like to focus on problem solving and meeting customer needs.	Are sales-centered; they like to focus on short term results.
Are motivated by security, belonging, and opportunities for professional development.	Are competitive and highly motivated by money.
Like being part of the team.	Seek personal recognition.
Want direction from management.	Want to be empowered to make their own decisions.
Have low tolerance for risk; they like the security of a guaranteed income and are willing to accept lower pay in exchange.	Have high tolerance for risk; they are willing to forgo income guarantees in exchange for the possibility of higher pay.

11-6 illustrates a framework for analyzing the situation. The northeast and southwest quadrants of the framework illustrate compatibility between the profile of the existing salespeople and the company's pay plan. However, the northwest and southeast quadrants of the framework are problematic. If a firm with a sales force made up of salespeople who prefer salary wants to implement a compensation plan with high variable pay (northwest quadrant), the firm should expect significant turnover of salespeople. This new pay plan will create considerable stress for a work force that is customer-centered, is security- and belonging-focused, and likes to minimize risk.

Government Deregulation Affects the Profile of Utility Industry Salespeople

Deregulation of the utility industry in the late 1990s brought about dramatic changes in how utility companies sell. Prior to deregulation, utility companies were monopolists. Their customers were captive, so there was no real need for them to sell. In many cases, utility sales forces were made up of salaried engineers on a two-year rotation before their next promotion. With deregulation came competition, and utility companies had to adopt a much more proactive selling approach. The traditional, salaried sales forces were eliminated, and new, sales-oriented sales forces were established. Salespeople at some companies were offered significant financial incentives to establish important customer relationships quickly, before competitors became entrenched. In many cases, utility companies had to hire entirely new sales forces, made up of people who were aggressive, risk

Figure 11-6. Framework for understanding mix decisions and the sales force personality profile.

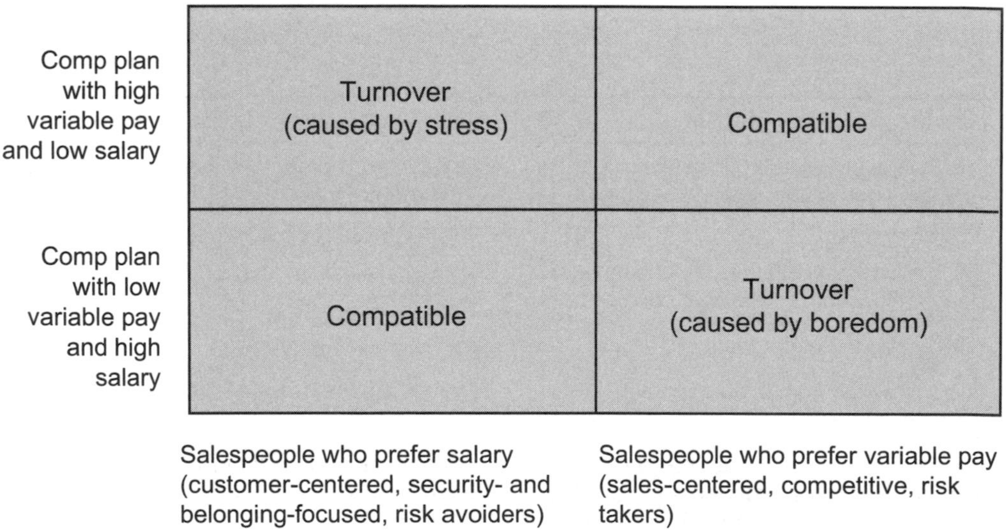

	Salespeople who prefer salary (customer-centered, security- and belonging-focused, risk avoiders)	Salespeople who prefer variable pay (sales-centered, competitive, risk takers)
Comp plan with high variable pay and low salary	Turnover (caused by stress)	Compatible
Comp plan with low variable pay and high salary	Compatible	Turnover (caused by boredom)

taking, and flexible—a completely different profile from that of their prede-regulation salespeople.

Similarly, if a sales force made up of salespeople who prefer variable pay wants to implement a compensation plan with high salary (southeast quadrant), the firm should expect considerable turnover of salespeople. Salespeople will miss the excitement of competition, the drive for short-term results, and the opportunity for significant incentive pay tied to performance, and may leave the firm out of boredom and frustration.

Personality Traits Linked to Sales Success in Automobile Sales

A study revealed that successful automobile salespeople are of two different personality profiles:

- *Profile 1.* Assertive and aggressive self-starters who are ego-driven, outgoing, and confident. Profile 1 types are usually successful in the short term, but are unlikely to stay in the job for very long.

- *Profile 2.* Thorough, cautious, accommodating, and sociable veterans who start out slowly, but who blossom into excellent salespeople over the years as they build a substantial clientele and win repeat and referral business.

Unfortunately, the highly commission-based sales pay plans offered by most automobile dealerships are attractive primarily to Profile 1 salespeople, who tend to view the job as short term. Profile 2 salespeople are apt to get discouraged in their early years, because they have not yet established enough customer relationships to make sufficient money and to feel successful. As a result, turnover of salespeople at many dealerships is very high. Some dealers have successfully reduced this turnover by offering newcomers a different compensation plan from veterans. Rookies receive more salary and less commission during a training period. Over time, as they learn the job and establish a customer base, their compensation plan switches to the traditional commission-based plan.

Strategies when Increasing the Incentive Portion of the Mix. There are two situations in which an increase to the incentive portion of the mix is particularly challenging.

1. When a straight salary sales force receives incentives for the first time, even if the incentive portion of pay is not large (15 percent or less), the move is an important signal that things are changing, which may be disturbing to many salespeople.

2. When a sales force with low to moderate incentives (25 percent or less) receives a substantial increase in the incentive component of compensation, so that the majority of sales force earnings now come through

variable pay, salespeople must adjust to a mindset change, as incentives become a "must have" part of their earnings rather than "nice to have" spending money.

Increases in the incentive portion of the mix tend to be easier to implement than decreases. Plans with a larger incentive component tend to have greater variation in earnings across salespeople than plans with a larger salary component. Thus, top performers typically make relatively more money when the incentive component is large, while poor performers will make relatively more when the salary component is large. A move to a larger incentive component of compensation is likely to be viewed positively by top-performing salespeople. At the same time, the change may encourage low performers to leave the firm.

A challenge in implementing a shift to a greater incentive portion of the mix is cutting a salesperson's salary. Salespeople often view salary as an entitlement. If possible, instead of cutting salaries, consider eliminating raises and using the money saved to fund incentive pay. The downside of this approach is that it may take several years to make the transition to the desired salary–incentive mix. If the firm cannot afford to wait, it is possible to successfully cut salary and use the savings to fund a larger incentive component. If salespeople can see that they can earn more money under the new plan, as long as they make their sales goal, it will be easier to reduce salary. For example, the plan shown in Figure 11-7 gives back the lost salary plus some, as long as the territory goal is achieved.

> ## Best Practice: Sell the New Plan to the Sales Force
>
> When compensation shifts from salary to incentives, show salespeople how much they would have earned last year had the new plan been in place. Typically, the above-average salespeople would have made more money. In addition, show salespeople the upside earnings potential for increasing sales over last year's levels to encourage them to work even harder.

A change from a salary plan to a plan with significant variable pay can also affect cash flow for salespeople. Salespeople who are used to receiving a fixed amount of money every pay period will now experience income swings from pay period to pay period. Some firms help ease this transition for salespeople by allowing draws against incentive payments equal to some portion of the difference

Figure 11-7. Example of a plan that eases the transition from a salaried to a variable plan.

	Year 1	Year 2
Salary adjustment	($5,000)	($5,000)
Bonus attainable at territory goal	$6,250	$12,500

between the new and old base salaries. There are some downsides to offering draws:

- A salesperson may end up owing the company money if her performance does not meet expectations.
- Draws can be costly and difficult to administer.
- Draws can dilute the motivational power of incentives.

Strategies when Increasing the Salary Portion of the Mix. Increases in the salary proportion of the mix tend to be more difficult to implement than increases in the incentive proportion, because such changes often have a negative impact on the earnings of top-performing salespeople. Plans with a large salary component tend to have smaller variation in earnings across salespeople than plans with a large incentive component. Thus, top performers typically make relatively less money when the salary component is large and relatively more when the incentive component is large. As a result, a move to a larger salary component runs the risk of disappointing top-performing salespeople and causing undesired sales force turnover. For this reason, sudden and drastic reductions in the incentive portion of sales force pay are very hard to implement successfully.

> ### Sudden Change to All-Salary Sales Compensation Plan Hurts Short-Term Results
>
> Recall from Chapter 1 the story about a maker of preprinted business forms. The firm was in an intensely competitive and fragmented industry that had been driven historically by an aggressive sales culture. During the late 1990s, the industry changed dramatically as electronic forms that customers could design and modify themselves began to dominate the market. A new, more customer-focused sales approach was needed to be successful in the new environment. As a first step toward implementing this new approach, the company eliminated its highly leveraged sales force incentive plan and began to pay salespeople salary exclusively. The sales force was not happy about this change. Most of the firm's salespeople were aggressive risk takers who had thrived in the high-risk, high-return environment. The firm's entire culture was incompatible with a salaried sales environment. While the move to a salaried sales force was right in the long term, the dramatic change in pay structure was too sudden, and its incompatibility with the firm's people and culture hurt short-term financial results.

Many companies have been successful in reducing the incentive portion of pay (while increasing the salary portion) by phasing in the change over time. A fraction of incentive pay is moved into salary each year, and after several years the firm attains the desired salary–incentive mix. When a more rapid change is desired, transition compensation strategies can help keep top performers "whole" after a move to a plan with more salary and less incentive. For example, the firm might consider guaranteeing that top-performing salespeople will make at least a certain amount with the new plan (for example, at least as much as last year).

Increasing the salary component of the mix is easier if there is already low variation in incentive payout across the sales force. Incentive payout variation comes from two sources: performance differences and territory differences. For example, in a sales force that earns a commission on sales, if salespeople have comparable performance and have territories with roughly equal potential, incentive earnings across the sales force will be fairly equal. On the other hand, if there is significant performance variation across salespeople and/or if sales territories vary greatly in potential, there may be substantial differences in incentive earnings across salespeople. In such a case, implementing a move to more salary will lead to significant income redistribution, making the change more difficult to implement successfully.

Implementing New Performance Measures or Changing Performance–Payout Relationships

A change in the performance measures that drive the sales incentive compensation plan or in the plan performance–payout relationship can be fairly easy or very challenging to implement, depending upon the degree of income loss that results from the change. Changes in performance measures include:

- New metrics (for example, paying on territory market share instead of sales)
- Different data views (for example, paying on performance relative to a goal rather than on absolute performance)
- New focuses (for example, paying for team results rather than individual results)
- Different timing of payments (for example, paying for quarterly results instead of monthly results)

Changes in the plan performance–payout relationship include:

- Changing from a bonus plan to a commission plan or vice versa
- Changing rates, accelerators, or decelerators in a commission plan
- Tying the point at which payout begins to a more or less challenging result (for example, raising or lowering the threshold where incentives kick in)
- Placing a cap on a plan

Incentive plan measures and plan performance–payout relationships sometimes change in response to new company marketing strategies. For example:

- A product line matures, and marketing strategy shifts from a growth focus (measured by territory sales growth) to a sales maintenance focus (measured in terms of territory sales goal attainment percentage) to a profitability focus (measured by territory gross margin goal attainment percentage).

- A competitor becomes more aggressive, and a market share change metric is added to the incentive program.

- A new product is introduced, and commission rates are adjusted to reflect new product priorities.

- The sales force structure becomes more team-oriented, and a portion of incentives is tied to team performance in addition to individual performance.

- Market volatility increases, weakening the firm's ability to predict future sales. The incentive plan is capped to prevent the payment of undeserved incentives because of poor forecasting.

Other times, incentive plan measures or plan performance–payout relationships change simply because new and better data become available. For example:

- A distributor starts to provide the firm with data detailing sales to end users, making it possible to evaluate results for salespeople who focus on the end-user market.

- The firm's accounting systems are updated, so that results can be tracked more immediately at the territory level.

- The firm acquires market potential data, making it possible to set more accurate territory goals. The commission plan is replaced with a bonus plan tied to goal attainment.

At some firms, changes in incentive plan measures and plan performance–payout relationships occur quite frequently. Over time, salespeople become accustomed to these changes; they expect change with some regularity, and they accept change with little resistance. This culture of flexibility allows the firm to adapt the incentive plan easily as company priorities, markets, and performance data evolve.

When incentive plan measures or performance–payout relationships change, some salespeople will be helped by the change, and others will be hurt by it. The "who is helped" and "who is hurt" analysis described in Chapter 8 (also see the example in Figure 11-2) shows how last year's data can be used to assess how each salesperson is affected by the plan change and to make sure that top performers will not be hurt. Formal transition plans such as cushions, guarantees, and dual plans can help strong performers who are hurt by plan changes maintain their income level in the short term. Sales leadership needs to develop ways to ensure that positive banter about the change dominates negative banter. Salespeople who benefit from the change (which hopefully include many of the firm's most respected salespeople) are likely to be vocal supporters of it.

When changing the performance measures in an incentive plan, incorporate the new measures into sales reports and performance management systems three to twelve months before the measures are incorporated into the incentive compensation plan. This provides the sales force with time to get used to the new measures and the sales support group time to adjust. Inevitably, some exceptions and needed clarifications to new measures will not be discovered until the measures are rolled out to the field. For example, an added incentive on sales to new accounts may create controversy about exactly which accounts qualify as "new." These issues can typically be resolved much more easily when an individual's incentive pay is not at stake.

Changes in performance measures and performance–payout relationships sometimes affect the timing of incentive payouts and thus the cash flow for salespeople. For example, a change from a monthly commission plan to a quarterly bonus plan might be met with resistance by salespeople who like receiving more frequent incentive payments. Some firms in this situation allow salespeople to make draws against future incentive payments for a period of time following the transition, while the sales force is adjusting to the new plan.

Firm Makes the Transition from Dollar-Based to Goal-Based Performance Measurement and Incentive Payment

A start-up medical device firm paid salespeople a commission on sales, with commission rates accelerating as sales increased beyond established thresholds. This plan worked well when the firm's product line was relatively new, as it motivated salespeople to work hard to generate product trial and rewarded their early success. Over time, as management gained market knowledge and improved its ability to accurately predict future sales, interest in developing a goal-based plan for the sales force grew. Management felt that goals would motivate salespeople to continue to work hard to grow the business and would help to tie individual achievement to the attainment of corporate goals. In addition, as the products matured and competition intensified, management felt that differences in potential across sales territories were becoming more apparent. Having the same commission thresholds for every salesperson was no longer fair because territories varied considerably in potential.

As a first step, a unique territory goal was established for each salesperson, based on territory and salesperson characteristics. These goals were disseminated to the sales force. Performance against goal was tracked for each salesperson and became an important element in the sales force performance management system. Salespeople adjusted to the new goal-based performance tracking method and worked with management to improve the accuracy of the goals and to address specific exception conditions.

After a year of experience using the goals with the sales force, management felt that the majority of the kinks had been ironed out of the system, and that sales force acceptance of the goals was high. At that point, the goals were incorporated into the incentive plan. Commission rates were tied to goal attainment, with payout accelerating as salespeople met and exceeded territory goals.

Despite the sales force's positive experience with territory goals in the performance management system, the change to a goal-based incentive plan was a major adjustment. The new plan resulted in a considerable redistribution of income among salespeople. The former plan had favored salespeople in territories with large potential, who were able to achieve the standard sales thresholds more easily than those with less territory opportunity. With the new plan, salespeople in high-potential territories were given higher goals, and achieving the new goal-based thresholds was much more challenging. To ease the transition for the sales force, the firm guaranteed each salesperson that his earnings would be at least as much as last year's during the first year following implementation of the new plan. The guarantee declined and eventually was phased out after three years.

Special Situations

Territory Realignment. Changes in sales force size and structure often require territory realignment, with many accounts being reassigned from one salesperson to another. In industries where salespeople need in-depth customer knowledge to be effective, this disruption in salesperson–customer relationships can be costly. Customer knowledge and relationships may be lost in the transition, causing customers to consider competitive offerings or to just take their business elsewhere. Sales incentive compensation can play an important role in easing this transition following realignment.

There is significant evidence suggesting that a well-thought-out, comprehensive relationship transition program reduces lost sales resulting from account disruption during realignment. An industrial products distribution sales force found that following realignment, sales to disrupted major accounts were maintained when a formal relationship transition program was implemented, but fell by 20 percent when no such program was put in place. The transition program involved having the exiting salesperson introduce each customer being transferred to the new salesperson. Together, the two salespeople coordinated the transition.

Monetary incentives can play an important role in encouraging effective account transitions. Incentives that encourage teamwork between the new and the exiting salespeople can help maintain important customer–company relationships. For example, the plan shown in Figure 11-8 pays a salesperson based on sales performance at both her old accounts and her new accounts for a period following realignment.

Transition compensation programs are particularly important at companies

Figure 11-8. Transition incentive plan following major territory realignment.

Salesperson Assigned to the Account	% of Account Incentive Pay in Each Quarter After the Transition		
	Q1	Q2	Q3 onwards
Current salesperson	50%	75%	100%
Prior salesperson	50%	25%	0%

with long selling cycles, because they protect salespeople who have major prospects in the pipeline. For example, a transition compensation program can be implemented that encourages a salesperson to stay involved with a sales process that she has started, even if she will no longer be responsible for the customer after the reorganization. This also encourages an effective transition from a customer standpoint. The customer has confidence that the knowledge gained by the exiting salesperson during the sales process is not lost. The new salesperson is fully informed about the customer's needs and has gained the customer's confidence by the time the transition is complete.

Transition incentive compensation plans also help the sales force accept an account realignment. Often, the existing sales incentive compensation plan is a major obstacle to making sales territory changes. Salespeople do not want to give up income. A salesperson whose territory is targeted to be realigned may fight to keep it with the following argument: "I have done a good job for you. I built this territory. It is unfair that my 'reward' is to have my territory split." Or: "I have established these relationships, and they will be lost if you assign the accounts to anybody else." If management receives too many of these complaints, it may relent in its realignment effort. We have observed that many sales forces that have compensation plans with large variable components have significant opportunity imbalances in their territory alignments. Many of them are also undersized because their salespeople fight giving up accounts so vehemently.

The resistance to realigning sales territories increases as the proportion of pay represented by incentives (as opposed to salary) increases. This is because the higher the incentive component of compensation, the more likely it is that a change in territory boundaries will affect a salesperson's income. The type of incentive plan also influences the degree to which a sales force is likely to resist realignment. Resistance in sales forces that have a bonus plan is typically low to moderate because territory quotas can be adjusted when the territory alignment changes, leading salespeople to feel that their income potential will be similar before and after realignment. However, with a commission plan that pays for total sales, a change in a salesperson's territory directly affects his ability to earn money, and resistance to realignment is typically much higher. Firms that expect to grow or realign their sales organizations regularly should consider having an expansion-friendly incentive plan (such as a bonus plan tied to quota attainment) that allows territory realignment without significant sales force resistance. Transition incentive compensation plans can also encourage sales force acceptance of a territory realignment.

> ### Transition Compensation Plan Encourages Sales Force Acceptance of Realignment
>
> A firm that paid its sales force a commission on sales from the first dollar implemented a transitional compensation plan to reduce the sales force's resistance to realignment. The company estimated that the business each salesperson would lose when her territory was split would be replaced in three years. During that three-year period, the company agreed to pay the salesperson a portion of what he had earned before the split, as long as the salesperson met or exceeded a performance standard. For example, in the first year with a new territory, the salesperson was guaranteed 100 percent of last year's pay, then 75 percent the second year, and 50 percent the third. Making the guarantee contingent upon meeting a performance standard was important, as it prevented the sales force from becoming complacent.

New Salespeople. New salespeople need time to learn the products and customers before they can be fully effective. The compensation plan for a new salesperson often provides a salary supplement in place of a portion of the incentive component until a salesperson is fully effective. Figure 11-9 shows an example of such a plan.

A Sales Force Change Process Framework

Any major modification in the sales incentive compensation plan can be challenging to implement, as any direct effect on sales force income is guaranteed to elicit emotion and controversy. Figure 11-10 shows a sales force change process framework that was developed to help firms implement many different types of sales force change, including both transitions to new sales and go-to-market strategies and changes in sales force size, structure, and territory alignment, in addition to

Figure 11-9. Example of a sales compensation plan for new salespeople.

Year	Base Annual Salary	12-Month Salary Supplement	Target 12-Month Incentive	Payout Rate at 100%
First year	$45,000	$10,000	$5,000	$60,000
Second year	$47,000	$5,000	$13,000	$65,000
Third year	$50,000	0	$25,000	$75,000

Figure 11-10. Sales force change process framework.

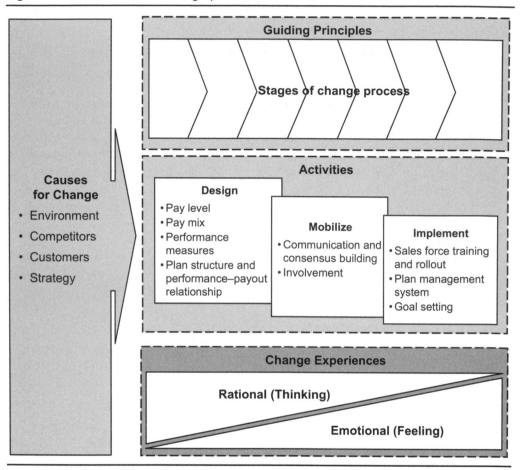

the implementation of new incentive compensation programs. Here, we focus specifically on the application of the framework in a sales incentive compensation plan transition. Examples of project work plans and implementation best practices follow the description of the general framework.

The impetus for sales force incentive compensation plan change can come from outside or inside the company. The need to change can be motivated by the firm's customers, its competitors, or the environment, and also by company strategy changes and initiatives to continuously improve. The change process involves three major activities: design the new plan, mobilize the resources to make it happen, and implement it. Guiding principles define the firm's goals and specify important rules for decision making throughout the various stages of the change process. In addition, the process acknowledges the viewpoint of the people who are affected by the change. This includes appealing to both the rational (why are we doing this?) and the emotional (how does this affect me?) needs of the sales force and other stakeholders involved.

Guiding Principles

Guiding principles (also called incentive plan objectives) answer the question, "Why are we doing this?" These principles define the rules of the game and provide an objective way to resolve any dilemmas that arise during the change process. Guiding principles are tied to company goals and are typically statements of strategy—for example, "We want to pay for performance," "We want to get closer to our customers," or "We want to increase sales and reduce costs."

Guiding principles become rules for decision making throughout the incentive plan change process. For example, suppose a company is deciding whether to cap its incentive plan. The plan pays a commission on sales, with an accelerated rate for sales beyond goal. The marketing department does not have a high degree of confidence in some of the product forecasts, and the finance department is concerned that if the forecasts are too low, sales force goals will be too easy, and salespeople will earn accelerated commissions without having to work very hard. This will result in excessive sales force incentive plan costs. Yet the firm's high-performing salespeople have made it clear that they dislike caps and find them demotivating. The firm looks to the guiding principles to make a decision about whether to cap the plan. If a primary guiding principle is "contain incentive plan costs," then the plan is capped. On the other hand, if a primary guiding principle is "retain good salespeople," then the plan is not capped. More examples of guiding principles for incentive plans are provided in the last section of Chapter 2.

Activities: Design–Mobilize–Implement

The sales force change process involves three major activities: design, mobilize, and implement. These activities facilitate the discovery of a good sales force compensation plan design and, at the same time, ensure successful implementation.

Design Activities. Design activities include making all of the sales incentive compensation plan design decisions that have been discussed throughout this book. An overview of the design process, along with appropriate chapter references, is provided in Figure 11-11.

> ### Who Should Be on the Sales Incentive Compensation Plan Design Committee?
>
> A typical incentive compensation plan design group consists of a project leader and team from the sales compensation group (usually part of Sales Operations, but sometimes part of Finance, Marketing or HR), along with:
>
> - The vice president of sales (or an equivalent leader of the sales force).
> - The regional directors or one or two representative regional directors.
> - A field advisory board (including a selection of salespeople and first-line sales managers) that helps to shape the plan by providing input

Figure 11-11. Sales incentive compensation plan design process.

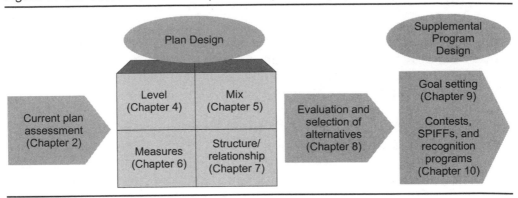

from a field perspective. This can be done through one-on-one interviews, small focus groups, or a larger group meeting with strong facilitation.

- Representation from Marketing for input regarding product/market issues and strategies and the behavior/activity that Marketing would like from the field.

- Representation from Finance for input regarding budgets and financial modeling.

- Representation from HR for input regarding corporate pay philosophies and available market surveys.

- Representation from IT to ensure that the new plan design can be implemented from a systems perspective in a reasonable time frame without excessive cost or support risk.

Mobilization Activities. Mobilization activities focus on providing the organization with the understanding, motivation, and resources to make the change when the time comes. These activities build consensus and create confidence that a new compensation plan can really work. Sales leadership needs to get behind the initiative. It needs to participate in the decision making and should be kept continuously informed about the project's progress. Key members of the sales force also need to be informed so that they can provide suggestions and help roll out the changes as they are announced. Involvement creates more support for the change effort because when people have input into defining changes that affect their work, they are more likely to take ownership of the results.

IBM Relies on Sales Force Input When Redesigning Its Worldwide Incentive Plan

When IBM took on the massive project of revamping its worldwide sales incentive compensation plan in 1995, sales force input was critical to the project's success. The project leader and four sales managers spent a full year collecting over four thousand pieces of anecdotal information about the existing incentive plan from the sales force. Electronic messages were sent to IBM salespeople all over the world, asking for descriptions of specific incentive plan problems they had encountered. The team also met with IBM incentive managers from North America, Latin America, Europe, and Asia Pacific to discuss the various challenges faced in each region and to identify similarities and differences across the various countries. The final plan design was developed during a week of intensive all-day meetings attended by 10 IBM compensation managers from all over the world.

In addition to the sales force, there are many other people and departments within the company that should be involved in the planning of a major sales compensation plan redesign. Figure 11-12 summarizes the different viewpoints and varying objectives for the sales compensation plan that different company stakeholders have. Sales management needs to work together with representatives from top management, Finance, Human Resources, Marketing, Systems, and any other relevant departments to ensure that all these varying and sometimes competing objectives are balanced appropriately.

Who Owns the Sales Compensation Plan?

At the majority of companies, ultimate authority for sales compensation resides within the sales department, often within the Sales Operations group. However, it is also common for groups within HR, Finance, or Marketing to own the sales compensation plan. There is frequent debate among professionals from these departments as to who should be the rightful owner of the sales compensation plan.

- HR argues, "We are experts on pay, and we have a broad perspective on corporate pay philosophies. HR should own sales compensation because we are experienced in designing incentive plans, good at interpreting market survey data, and in the best position to ensure that sales force pay is consistent with pay in other departments."

- Finance argues, "Sales compensation is one of the firm's largest budget items. Finance should own sales compensation because we will ensure fiscal responsibility and the financial viability of this very significant cost item."

- Marketing argues, "Sales is a critical component of the firm's marketing strategy. Marketing should own sales compensation because we will ensure that the sales pay plan drives behavior that is consistent with product and customer marketing strategies."

- Sales argues, "Sales compensation is one of many key sales force effectiveness drivers that influence salespeople, their activities, and cus-

Figure 11-12. Multiple stakeholders and their objectives for sales compensation plan design.

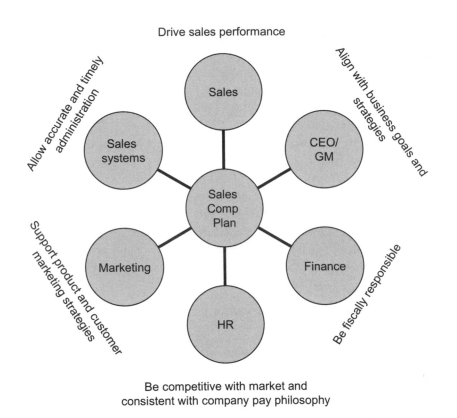

tomer and company results. Sales should own sales compensation because we are in the best position to ensure compatibility and consistency of the compensation plan with all the other sales force effectiveness drivers."

Regardless of who the ultimate owner of the sales compensation plan is, it is clear that professionals from many different departments must work together to ensure that the sales compensation plan meets many competing objectives.

Change leaders within the company must assess how the various stakeholders need to be engaged in the change process, how they influence others within the organization, and how they are likely to view the changes that are taking place.

The allies map shown in Figure 11-13 provides a good framework for thinking through this assessment. Within the firm, there will be stakeholders that support the change effort and those that oppose it. Some will be very active in expressing their views and getting involved, while others will be more passive. Where each stakeholder falls on the allies map determines how that person should be approached about and involved in the change effort. Strong, visible, and effective sponsorship is a major factor in any project's success. The more active supporters a project has (top right "engaged" corner of the allies map), the easier the change will be to implement. Change leaders within the company need to recruit as many active supporters as possible, and to expand the group by energizing the "aligned" and "constructive" segments. To do this, they must generate excitement among passive supporters by communicating a compelling vision and strategy. Time spent with those who are actively opposed to the change effort (bottom right

Figure 11-13. Allies map.

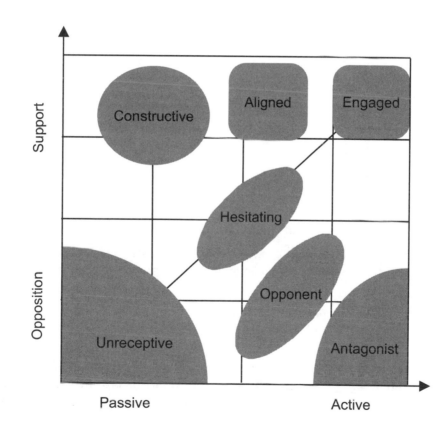

"antagonist" corner of the allies map) is usually time wasted. The goal with this segment is to diminish the negative impact that its active opposition to the changes might have on the rest of the group.

The "who gets helped" and "who gets hurt" analysis developed in Chapter 8 provides a means to classify the salespeople who might fall into the "support" and "opposition" groupings. Managerial judgment can reflect on who would take a passive and who would take an active stance on the proposed incentive compensation change.

Fifth Third Bank Focuses on Implementation During Incentive Plan Redesign

In the early 2000s, Cincinnati's Fifth Third Bank was a recognized industry leader, with consistently strong financial performance and a reputation for having excellent salespeople. Yet management felt that the bank's short-term sales incentive plan was not driving sales force behaviors and results as effectively as possible. In 2001, new incentive plans for more than 30 different sales roles were designed and implemented. A strong mobilization focus throughout the entire project contributed significantly to the new plan's acceptance and success. Multiple cross-functional teams were formed—a steering committee (leadership), a technology team, a design team, and multiple implementation teams. Having these multiple teams allowed input from many experts within the company to be heard, and also facilitated buy-in and consensus of key stakeholders. A "change process owner" was appointed to lead the implementation effort on several fronts, including the following:

- *Leadership.* Stay informed about company leaders' wishes and keep them up-to-date on project progress.

- *Involvement.* Talk with employee stakeholders "offline" to learn what they are afraid of and what they are thinking is good.

- *Communication.* Write rollout documentation, Q&A documents, and executive presentations; develop earnings calculators; facilitate road shows.

The bank estimated that incremental profits from the new incentive plan were more than 10 times the incremental investment in incentive pay.

Implementation Activities. Implementation activities focus on making the new incentive compensation plan a reality. A transition plan is put into action. A sales force communication plan is developed and executed, including compensation plan materials such as overview brochures, pocket cards, and commission calculators. "Road show" presentations are orchestrated for rolling these materials out to the sales force. If the plan is goal-based, new territory goals are developed and disseminated. Meanwhile, the company's sales systems and processes must be realigned to allow ongoing performance reports to be produced and goals to be set and refined as needed.

Figure 11-14 shows two examples of project work plans for managing the implementation of a new sales incentive compensation plan. These work plans show summarized views; a more detailed breakdown of the activities, responsibilities, and deadlines within each of the major work steps is also needed. The first company had a six-month time frame for implementation, and the second had a three-month time frame, plus three additional months of administrative support from a consultant. The amount of time required for implementation varies depending upon the size, complexity, and capabilities of the organization as well as the extent of the changes being implemented.

Some best practices for key implementation activities are described here.

Communicating Plan Features and Benefits to the Field. A well-thought-out and effectively executed plan for communicating the benefits and features of a new incentive plan to the sales force is absolutely critical. If the field does not accept and understand the plan, the plan will fail, no matter how clever its design. Good plans usually fail when there is poor communication and when there is too little training of the sales force.

The communication plan for a new sales incentive plan includes two major activities:

1. Developing the plan documentation, communication materials, presentations, and training aids

2. Executing the field rollout

Documentation and training materials for the new plan include several items for each salesperson.

- A plan overview document explains why the change is happening, along with details about the new plan objectives, structure, and features. The typical length of this document is 20 to 30 presentation slides for a complex plan and less for a more straightforward plan. A sample table of contents for the plan overview document is provided in Figure 11-15.

- A list of frequently asked questions and answers (FAQs) addresses the majority of anticipated field concerns. A sample list of FAQs is provided in Figure 11-16.

- A pocket card summarizes key plan details. Salespeople should be encouraged to keep the card in their wallet as a quick, handy reference. An example of a pocket card for a complex plan is shown in Figure 11-17.

- A customized monthly payout table or personal incentive calculator helps salespeople understand how much incentive money they can make at dif-

Figure 11-14. Examples of work plans for implementing a new sales incentive compensation plan.

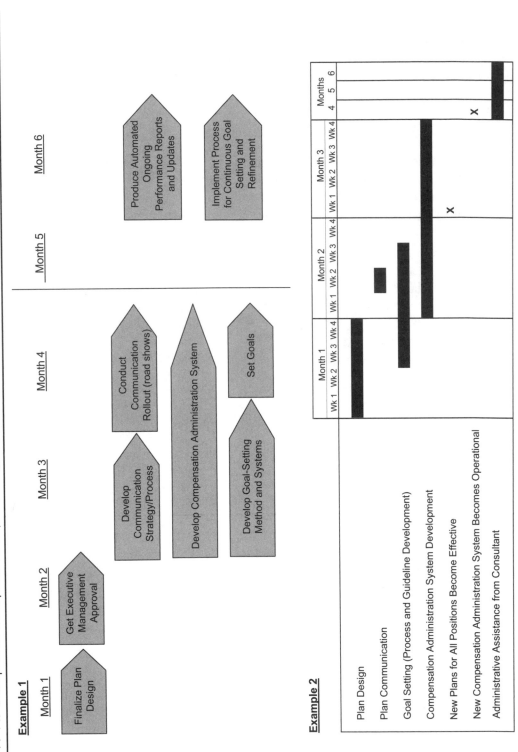

Example 1

| Month 1 | Month 2 | Month 3 | Month 4 | Month 5 | Month 6 |

- Finalize Plan Design
- Get Executive Management Approval
- Develop Communication Strategy/Process
- Conduct Communication Rollout (road shows)
- Develop Compensation Administration System
- Develop Goal-Setting Method and Systems
- Set Goals
- Produce Automated Ongoing Performance Reports and Updates
- Implement Process for Continuous Goal Setting and Refinement

Example 2

| | Month 1 | | | | Month 2 | | | | Month 3 | | | | Months | | |
| | Wk 1 | Wk 2 | Wk 3 | Wk 4 | Wk 1 | Wk 2 | Wk 3 | Wk 4 | Wk 1 | Wk 2 | Wk 3 | Wk 4 | 4 | 5 | 6 |

- Plan Design
- Plan Communication
- Goal Setting (Process and Guideline Development)
- Compensation Administration System Development
- New Plans for All Positions Become Effective
- New Compensation Administration System Becomes Operational
- Administrative Assistance from Consultant

Figure 11-15. Sample table of contents for a plan overview document.

New Incentive Plan Overview Document
Table of Contents

- Message from Sales Leadership
- Plan Design Overview
    - Design process
    - Who was on the design team
    - Key guiding principles and strategic rationale behind the changes
- Plan Features
    - Summary of basic plan features and what is different from the current plan
    - Monthly scorecards
    - How to calculate payouts
    - How goals are determined
    - Additional plan features
        - New salesperson plan
        - President's Club
- Frequently Asked Questions (FAQs)

ferent performance levels. These materials can be provided in hard copy as part of the plan overview document or as an electronic spreadsheet that allows salespeople to run "what if" scenarios linking different sales results with how much they will be paid. Spreadsheets can be updated on an ongoing basis with actual sales results, and can thus be a very effective motivational tool. More information and an example of a spreadsheet personal incentive calculator are provided in Chapter 12.

- A detailed document outlining all the rules and exceptions in the plan provides a useful reference for first-line sales managers as specific questions and situations arise after the new plan is implemented.

- Sales manager plan support materials should also be provided if sales managers have their own incentive plan.

Should You Pilot-Test the Incentive Plan Communication Materials?

Consider testing your communication materials and training process with a pilot group of salespeople and/or first-line sales managers prior to finalizing the content. This will allow time to adjust for unanticipated or confusing issues that arise during the pilot. While pilot tests can provide valuable feedback, there are two reasons that management teams frequently choose not to run a pilot. First, there is often not enough time to complete

Figure 11-16. Sample list of FAQs.

New Incentive Plan
Frequently Asked Questions

Plan Design
- Why was there a need for a new plan?
- Who designed the new plan?
- What was senior management's involvement in the design of the new plan?
- What were some top field issues with the former plan?
- What were the objectives for the design of the new plan?

General Plan
- How does this plan meet the stated objectives?
- Why will this plan be an improvement over the previous plan?
- Will I make more or less money now, compared to the previous plan?
- Does this plan treat reps in different types of territories fairly?
- How does this plan pay in comparison with competitors' plans?

Plan Features: Goals and Payout Curves
- How will the goals be set?
- Is the national product forecast fair?
- How will history be used in setting goals?
- How will (untapped) potential be used in setting goals?
- How is (untapped) potential determined?
- Will a good quarter/semester hurt me in the next quarter/semester?
- What is included in my goals and sales?
- What are the target products and customer types?
- What is the unit of measurement for goals and sales?
- Are there any other details I should know?
- Is the payout table fair?
- The payout table shows payouts in portfolio attainment increments of 5 percentage points. How do I compute the payout for a portfolio attainment in between those increments?
- Will there be controls to prevent regional managers from showing favoritism?

Plan Implementation
- When will the new plan be effective?
- How will territory realignments affect this plan?
- Will including or deleting accounts affect goals and sales performance?
- What happens if product launches are delayed?

Plan Communication
- What communication documents will I receive?
- What will the monthly performance reports contain?
- Will there be any comparisons to others in the region?
- Whom should I ask if I have a question?

---

a pilot without compromising the new plan's implementation date. Second, there can be concern that if some salespeople learn of the new plan's design prior to the national rollout, misinformation and rumors will spread in the field. Some management teams prefer that the entire sales force receive a consistent communication about the new plan simultaneously, just prior to the new plan's start date.

Figure 11-17. Example of a pocket card.

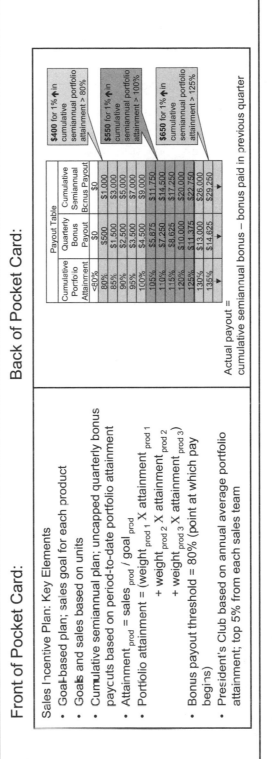

Once all the communication materials have been developed, the new incentive plan can be announced to the sales force, and the communication and training process begins. This effort involves:

- Selling the benefits of the new plan to the sales force
- Educating salespeople about how the new plan is different from the existing plan
- Ensuring that the sales force understands how payouts will be determined
- Answering questions and providing resources for future help

The logistical difficulty of this effort varies greatly, depending upon the size and geographic dispersion of the sales force. With a large national or multinational sales force, "road show" presentations at multiple locations are usually required. First-line sales managers typically play a key role in these presentations and act as trainers for the salespeople who report to them. Some success strategies for executing a successful field rollout include the following:

- Announce the new plan to the sales force shortly after a payout period in the old incentive plan has ended; avoid distracting the sales force during the final weeks of the previous incentive period.

- Ask sales leadership to make the initial announcement. A carefully crafted message articulates the objectives of the new plan and inspires commitment from the sales force. A national sales meeting is an ideal forum for accomplishing this, but if timing is tight, a live videoconference or Webcast can also work.

- Train the entire sales management team on the new plan before training the rest of the sales force. First-line sales managers who thoroughly understand and are sold on a plan significantly enhance acceptance of the plan at the salesperson level; salespeople are much more likely to embrace a plan that they perceive as coming from their manager, rather than from the home office.

- Ask first-line sales managers to conduct the new plan training sessions for their salespeople. If some managers are reluctant to lead this session because they feel that the new plan is complex or hard to explain, alleviate their discomfort by having easy-to-understand and well-organized training materials. In addition, a conference call for all first-line sales managers just prior to the national rollout can be an effective way to increase sales managers' comfort level and get last-minute questions answered quickly.

- Plan a series of communications with the field over the first few months after the plan is implemented. Include reminders and other plan reinforcements via the company's intranet or sales force newsletter.

JCPenney Focuses on Implementation During a Major Compensation Plan Redesign

The compensation team at JCPenney faced a major challenge when top management asked it to completely overhaul the company's 20-year-old pay program in less than a year. The new compensation plan would support a transformation of the company's business model and work culture that management felt was necessary to restore profitable growth and help the firm succeed in the highly competitive retail industry. The compensation team worked with an outside consultant to determine market prices for the firm's various jobs, to group jobs according to their relative impact on the company, and to link jobs to established career paths. Successful implementation of the changes required significant and meaningful communication throughout the firm. With the support of top management, the compensation team led all of the following implementation activities:

- Posted frequent project updates on the company HR home page.

- Distributed a newsletter to all sales managers outlining the changes.

- Held department meetings one week before the changes were implemented.

- Prepared meeting leader scripts to ensure message consistency.

- Created a video discussing the benefits of the new program.

- Developed and distributed Q&A materials.

- Wrote personal letters communicating associates' job band and market pay range.

Developing the Plan Administration Systems and Processes. Developing or adapting the administrative systems and processes to support a new incentive plan can be a significant undertaking. The difficulty of this effort depends upon the size and complexity of the sales force, the intricacy of the incentive plan or plans, and the amount and types of changes being implemented. Implementation may be fairly straightforward for a small sales force whose incentive compensation systems and processes are administered by one individual using spreadsheet software. On the other hand, implementation may require considerable time, planning, and resources for a large sales force that is implementing considerable change in many complex incentive plans for multiple sales roles.

In large, complex sales forces, often the information technology (IT) group is involved in implementation. Strong communication between IT and the incentive compensation (IC) group is critical. IT managers are technology experts; they may not understand all the issues and intricacies of incentive compensation. IC managers know the needs of the sales force and the incentive program, but may not understand all the technology implications of proposed changes. Tension between the IC and IT groups is common, and is often the result of gaps between the business rules that the IC team provides to the IT group and the level of specificity that IT requires. Some common areas of ambiguity include:

- Eligibility for the incentive plan
- Handling of employment changes (for example, new salespeople, transfers or promotions, and terminations)
- Handling of account changes and reassignments
- Policy on sales crediting, order returns or cancellations, and sharing credit among multiple salespeople
- Goal adjustment policies and procedures

A successful implementation of new incentive plan systems and processes can be encouraged by:

- Keeping rules across multiple sales teams and plans as consistent as possible
- Documenting all business rules and exceptions
- Building the necessary flexibility into the system for managing exceptions and changes
- Avoiding the resetting of objectives in the middle of the compensation period
- Having a process to deal with payout issues or errors

Because of the complexity and amount of detail in compensation plan administration, expect errors to occur. Be proactive in communicating and fixing errors, and document all changes. Chapter 12 describes the various information processing and logistical elements required to support an effective incentive compensation plan.

Setting Goals. For an incentive plan that is goal-based, setting territory-level goals is the third main component of plan implementation. A goal-based plan will fail if territory goals are not both sufficiently challenging and perceived as realistic and fair by the sales force. Many companies spend a lot of time and money on sales incentive plan design, but treat the goal-setting process as an afterthought. This is a serious mistake. Successful goal setting requires a considerable investment of time and effort. Effective processes for goal setting are discussed in detail in Chapter 9.

Timing of Implementation with Design and Mobilization Activities. Figure 11-18 illustrates the timing of organizational energy across the three sales force change activities: design, mobilize, and implement. Companies that implement incentive compensation plan change successfully typically do not wait until the design is

Figure 11-18. Organizational energy throughout the sales force change process.

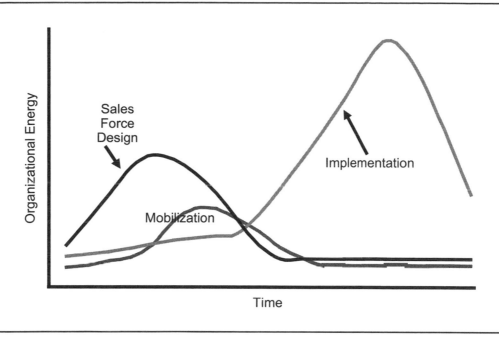

complete to begin mobilizing and planning for implementation. In fact, when teams that have been responsible for implementing organizational change are asked what they would have done differently, most say that they would have begun their mobilization and implementation planning activities earlier, instead of viewing them as add-ons. For example, if key stakeholders are consulted during the design stage, the design will be better, and there will be greater organizational support. In addition, if implementation issues are anticipated up front, downstream problems will be anticipated early, while there is plenty of time to avoid or solve them, and implementation will be easier.

Change Outlook

When an incentive compensation plan changes, it is essential that the thoughts and feelings of the people who are affected by the change are acknowledged and dealt with on both rational and emotional levels. When a new incentive plan is first announced by top management, most salespeople will react to news of the change rationally. They focus on broad issues of strategy and customer and product impact. As the news of the change begins to sink in, however, people begin to focus on specific personal issues. Often, emotions take over. People wonder, "How much is my life going to change?" They worry about whether the new incentive plan will affect them negatively. They speculate, "How much less money will I make with the new plan?" "How much harder am I going to have to work to make the same amount of money?'' Companies that deal with these emotions directly can avoid trouble down the road.

Effective communication both from management and with peers can help people understand and accept change. Often, communications from the leadership team are most appropriate for helping people comprehend change on a rational level, while discussions with peers have the biggest impact on an emotional level. Both levels of communication are essential to symbiotically cover people's rational and emotional needs.

CHAPTER 12

Incentive Compensation Plan Administration

How This Chapter Is Organized

Introduction   454

    What Is Incentive Compensation Plan Administration?   454

    Why IC Plan Administration Is Important but Difficult   456

Is the Incentive Compensation Plan Administered Well?   458

    Characteristics of Well-Administered Incentive Compensation Systems   459

    Symptoms of Poorly Administered Incentive Compensation Systems:
A 3 Cs Framework   460

IC Plan Administration Systems and Processes   461

    Systems of Varied Complexity   461

        A Simple System   462

        A Moderately Complex System   462

        A Highly Complex System   462

    An IC Plan Administration Flowchart   463

        Inputs   463

            Sales Transactions and Account Assignments   463

            Sales Roster and Eligibility   464

            Other Data and Metrics   464

            IC Plan   464

        Outputs   464

        Payroll Outputs   465

        Scorecards and Field Management Reports   465

        Plan Health Reports   465

        Compliance Reporting and Other Stakeholder Outputs   466

    IC Administration System Requirements   469

        Data Management   469

        Reporting   470

        Quality Assurance and Control   475

How to Design an Effective IC Plan Administration System   476

    Design Elements   476

        People   476

        Processes   477

        Tools   481

    Design Influences   482

        Business Goals   482

        Situation Complexity   484

    What Should Be the Role of External Partners in IC Administration?   485

        Should the Firm Make or Buy the IC Administration System Tools?   486

        Should the Firm Outsource Ongoing IC Administration or Do It In-House?   486

Summary   489

Introduction

A sales compensation program cannot succeed without a well-defined and effectively executed incentive plan administration system. Developing and maintaining this system can be challenging, particularly when unplanned measurement and payout adjustments are made, introducing opportunities for error and delay.

What Is Incentive Compensation Plan Administration?

Incentive compensation (IC) plan administration systems consist of the people, processes, and tools that enable an incentive plan to operate and adapt over time. Figure 12-1 shows the role of an IC plan administration system within the larger scope of sales incentive compensation program management. The activities shown in the top rectangle of the figure, incentive plan design and implementation, are discussed in previous chapters of this book. The activities shown in the bottom

Figure 12-1.Components of sales incentive compensation program management.

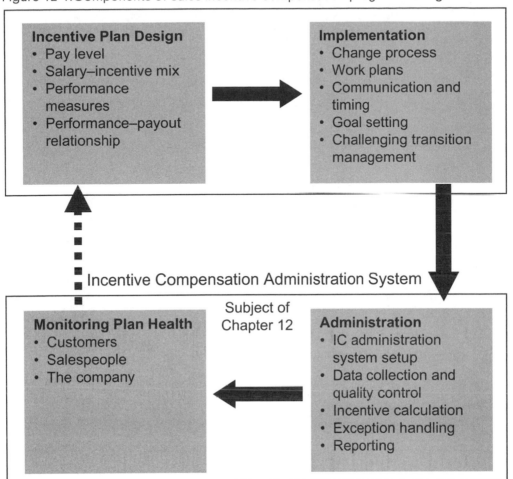

rectangle of the figure make up the incentive compensation administration system and are the subject of this chapter. The IC administration system includes traditional IC administration activities such as developing the IC administration system, collecting data, calculating incentives, handling exceptions, and distributing reports and payouts. It also includes monitoring the health of the plan by evaluating the plan's impact on customers, salespeople, and the company so that adjustments can be made as needed.

The major outputs of an effective IC plan administration system are shown in Figure 12-2. At a minimum, the IC administration system must produce accurate and timely *payroll outputs,* shown at the base of the triangle. By moving from the base toward the top of the triangle, companies can gain powerful additional benefits. *Scorecards* produced on a regular basis provide feedback so that salespeople and sales managers can see how they are doing and identify ways to improve. *Plan health reports* show sales leaders and incentive plan designers how effectively the plan is working. These health reports can be a very powerful management tool,

Figure 12-2. IC plan administration system outputs.

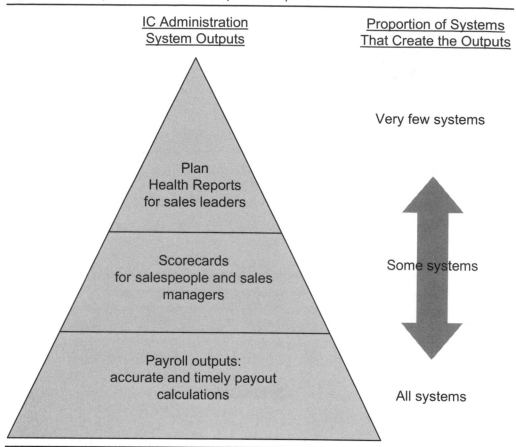

allowing timely course corrections to be made by adjusting the plan as needed. Effective scorecards and plan health reports can increase the power of an incentive program significantly, yet many companies lack IC administration systems that create effective scorecards, and even fewer have systems that produce plan health reports. Examples of scorecards and plan health reports are provided later in this chapter.

Why IC Plan Administration Is Important but Difficult

IC plan administration costs typically add 2 to 15 percent to total incentive compensation costs. The percentage is usually at the lower end of the range for large sales forces and at the higher end for smaller sales forces. The IC plan administration system has considerable influence on the success of a sales compensation plan. When a well-designed plan is administered effectively, it energizes the sales force and motivates salespeople to engage in activities and behaviors that drive sales success. An ineffective IC plan administration system significantly undermines the incentive plan's power as a sales effectiveness driver. Since incentive money is highly visible and personal for sales forces, errors in sales crediting or payment are discovered quickly. As one vice president of sales put it, "The calculations are simultaneously under 3,500 microscopes." A sales force will quickly become frustrated with an IC plan administration system that routinely produces inaccurate or late payments. As sales force distrust of the system grows, sales force motivation declines, and salespeople spend more and more time on "shadow accounting" (chasing invoices, verifying pay calculations, and lobbying management for payout corrections) rather than spending time with customers.

Unfortunately, IC plan administration can be highly complex and error-prone. Complexity increases with sales force size, diversity of sales roles, the use of multiple performance metrics, the number of data sources, and the intricacy of business rules for eligibility and exception handling. In addition, sales leaders are acutely aware of the motivational power of incentives, and therefore they tend to want to adapt and make course corrections as new information emerges or as the business situation changes, even within a single incentive cycle. Midstream adjustments, such as changes in sales crediting, territory alignment, or plan eligibility, introduce new opportunities to make errors. This makes IC plan administration particularly challenging for companies in complex situations that want both accuracy and flexibility in their systems. It has been our experience that managers of complex IC plan administration systems that also demand considerable flexibility can expect small errors to occur frequently and big errors to occur as much as 10 to 20 percent of the time.

How to Handle an Incentive Overpayment?

A company made a change to one of the business rules in its incentive plan, but unfortunately that change was not implemented correctly in the plan administration system. As a result, five thousand people received overpayments of incentives totaling almost $5 million. The company was faced with a dilemma: Do we require employees to pay back the money that they received but did not earn, or do we let them keep it in order to avoid sales force dissonance? Incentive overpayments, including both those that are never discovered and those that are caught but not corrected, can add significantly to incentive plan costs.

Complexity and Frequent Change

"Fairness" is a primary guiding principle of one firm's sales incentive plan. As a result, the firm's sales leaders make many incentive plan decisions based on equity for the sales force, even when these decisions introduce considerable complexity into the IC plan administration system. For example, at a national district sales managers' meeting, the vice president of sales announced a sales force hiring freeze for the last quarter of the year. Several district managers who had current territory vacancies strongly objected, stating that this was unfair because a substantial portion of their bonus was tied to total district performance. The vice president agreed, and promised that districts with territory vacancies would have their goal adjusted so that managers would not be held accountable for fourth-quarter performance in vacant territories. This change appeared simple to the vice president, but it turned out to be an administrative nightmare. The change was impossible within the architecture of the current IC plan administration system. A completely new and separate computer program had to be written just to handle this special situation.

Authors' note: Tracking and accounting for exception conditions in order to be fair to everyone is usually costly; it not only takes time and resources but also introduces considerable possibility for error. Sometimes, it is best to just acknowledge that the system cannot be completely fair and that inequities will even out across the sales force over time; this acceptance can cut plan administration costs considerably. It is often advisable to make desired managerial adjustments outside the formal IC administration systems rather than burdening the systems with nuances that threaten accuracy and timeliness.

Is the Incentive Compensation Plan Administered Well?

Sales Force Grows Beyond an IC Plan Administration System's Capabilities

Over the last three years, the sales force has grown from 50 to 150 salespeople. There are now two full-time people doing IC plan administration, handling 150 separate spreadsheets. Every month, they allocate the sales, update the eligibility, adjust for new hires and departures, deal with transfers and promotions, and produce the reports for each salesperson and manager. This is not working very well, as it is very expensive and there are many mistakes. The IC plan administration team is looking to move to a more systematic and stable solution.

IC Plan Administration System Can't Deal with an Expanding Product Line

The software for a company's IC plan administration system was developed 12 years ago. At that time, the company had a narrow and relatively stable product line, and hence the products and product weights for the incentive plan were hard-coded into the system. As the company's product line has grown through a combination of new product development and acquisition, sales leaders need to change products and product weights within the incentive plan to align with continuously evolving company strategies. The current IC plan administration system has to be reprogrammed every time a change is made. A recent and relatively minor adjustment in product prioritization and weights required 73 different computer code changes. The changes introduced several errors into the system and delayed incentive payments. This angered and frustrated the sales force.

IC Plan Administration Can't Handle All the Sales Contests and SPIFFs

To spark sales, a sportswear manufacturer gave product managers budgets to spend on sales force contests and SPIFFs. As a result, the product managers are fiercely competing for the sales force's time by trying to outdo one another with more creative and extravagant programs. Last week, a one-month sales contest on ladies' running shoes was launched. This week, a SPIFF on certain high-margin soccer apparel items went into effect. On average, a new SPIFF or sales contest is launched every two weeks. The sales administration group is going crazy. Its automated system is not built to handle a large number of ad hoc programs efficiently. Each program is being tracked separately on a spreadsheet, but the process involves many manual steps and is highly error-prone. Some temporary people have been hired to help compute payouts for all of these incentives, but there is considerable concern that adequate quality control procedures cannot be maintained much longer.

Characteristics of Well-Administered Incentive Compensation Systems

An effective IC plan administration system:

- Produces results that are accurate and timely.
- Provides insights to the sales force and to sales leaders about ways to improve.
- Maintains an appropriate balance between flexibility and cost effectiveness.

An effective IC plan administration system produces consistently accurate results. Incentive payment errors frustrate salespeople, damage management's credibility, and contribute to sales force turnover. If salespeople distrust the system, they spend their time on "shadow accounting" rather than on high-value-added selling activities. One firm estimated that shadow accounting costs were approximately $1,500 per salesperson per year. Timeliness of results is also very important. If reports are late, the value of prompt feedback is lost, and the motivational impact of the incentive plan is diminished. Late payments cause the sales force to get upset, and morale suffers. Error-prone administration systems are frustrating and demotivating for IC administrators, who have to respond to the field's often angry inquiries. A poor system can lead to high turnover among IC administrators.

An effective IC plan administration system provides insights to the sales force and to sales leaders. If salespeople receive accurate and timely feedback on their performance, they will be motivated to continue what they are doing and work hard to reach a goal, or they will discover how to make suitable adjustments in order to improve their performance. If sales managers receive appropriate feedback on how their people are doing, they can coach them effectively to help them improve their performance. If sales leaders receive accurate and timely feedback on how the incentive plan is working, they can make needed changes quickly and keep the organization on track to achieve important goals.

Finally, an effective IC plan administration system maintains an appropriate balance between flexibility and cost. An inflexible system may be very cost-efficient, but if the system is unable to adapt effectively to business changes, then the incentive plan, and consequently sales force activity, soon becomes disconnected from company needs and strategies. On the other hand, with a system that allows unlimited changes, costs can quickly get out of control, and accuracy and timeliness are compromised. Firms often maintain a balance between cost and flexibility by having documented guidelines for how to execute plan changes, including who is responsible for such changes and how often changes can occur.

Symptoms of Poorly Administered Incentive Compensation Systems: A 3 Cs Framework

An effective incentive compensation administration system operates harmoniously with the 3 Cs framework introduced in Chapter 1. The system:

- Is *consistent* with sales and marketing strategies, sales processes, and sales roles.

- Is *compatible* with other sales force effectiveness drivers, such as performance management systems, culture, sales force motivators, and hiring and development processes.

- Acknowledges the *consequences* for company and customer results, sales force activities, and sales force quality.

There can be many signs that the sales incentive compensation plan administration system is not working well. Figure 12-3 lists some common symptoms of problems.

Figure 12-3. Examples of indications that the incentive compensation plan administration system is not working well.

Consistency with . . .	**Compatibility with . . .**	**Consequences . . .**
• Sales and marketing strategies • Sales process • Sales roles	• Performance management systems • Sales force culture • Sales force motivators • Sales force hiring and development processes	• Company results • Customer results • Sales force behaviors and activities • Sales force quality
• Marketing strategies and product emphasis change every quarter, but the system is unable to deal with the changes. • The system is not flexible enough to implement course corrections within an incentive period. • The system melts down every time the sales force reorganizes. • The system uses ad hoc worksheets that worked well in the past, but as the sales force has grown and become more diverse and complex, the system is unable to keep up. • The system cannot handle routine territory alignment changes.	• The system cannot accommodate the most appropriate performance measures. For example, the system is unable to calculate sales growth at the account level because account-level history is not stored in the system. • The flexibility of the system does not match the rapidly changing sales environment and culture. For example, the system cannot handle the frequent ad hoc sales contests that marketing wants to run. • The system produces complex scorecards and feedback reports that the sales force does not understand. • The system is not compatible with the IC plan design. For example, the monthly plan has a high variable-pay component and therefore requires frequent sales force feedback, yet the system cannot deliver quick, accurate payout information.	• Senior management does not know in a timely way if incentive payouts are consistent with performance and if the plan is working as desired. • Salespeople do not understand how their payout is calculated. • Calculations are frequently wrong. Salespeople spend a lot of time correcting measures or checking and challenging calculations, time that could be spent with customers. • Calculation errors result in some people being overpaid and others being underpaid; this adversely affects sales force motivation and defeats the whole purpose of the IC plan. • Reports are frequently late, weakening the feedback loop for the IC plan and hurting sales force motivation. • There are no salesperson scorecards; the lack of feedback significantly reduces the power of the incentive plan to motivate the sales force.

IC Plan Administration Systems and Processes

Systems of Varied Complexity

IC plan administration systems and processes vary greatly in their complexity. Here are several company examples.

A Simple System. A firm is getting ready to launch its first product and plans to pay the sales force incentives based on sales growth. No money has been budgeted for incentive plan administration, so management wants a system that can be developed quickly and cheaply and that will "get us through the first year without any errors." The firm hires a sales analyst, who spends three months developing a spreadsheet-based tool that can accommodate the firm's territory sales and eligibility data, calculate quarterly incentive payouts, and create monthly sales reports for the firm's 80 salespeople and sales managers. The analyst spends approximately one week per month maintaining the data in the system, handling a small number of adjustments, generating the necessary outputs, and e-mailing the information to the sales force. The analyst's work involves following a series of detailed steps. Meticulousness is critically important to ensure that no errors are made. The company expects to expand the sales force and launch a second product next year, and since this will complicate the incentive plan considerably, management is concerned that a more robust IC plan administration system may be needed to ensure continued high-quality output.

A Moderately Complex System. A sales force has 1,200 salespeople, organized into four different selling teams. The incentive plans are quite similar across the four teams, and all are goal-based. There are a few special situations: A small number of salespeople are paid incentives on MBO achievement, and a few products have special kicker bonuses. The firm has been managing its incentive plan in-house, but as the number of salespeople and plan complexity have grown, the in-house system has become overly cumbersome with the addition of new steps that apply temporary fixes to work around inherent system deficiencies. Thus, the firm's enterprise technology (ET) group has enlisted the help of a consulting firm to administer the incentive compensation program. Every month, the ET group processes the sales and account assignment data. The consulting firm manages the eligibility data, determines payouts, and creates monthly sales reports for the field force. A suite of tools developed by the consulting firm is used to manage the process and ensure that no errors are made. The process takes approximately two weeks to complete. The IC plan administration team consists of two employees plus two full-time people at the consulting firm. The firm spends about $1 million a year, or about 5 percent of sales incentive costs, to administer the sales force incentive program.

A Highly Complex System. A sales force has 3,500 salespeople organized into 15 different selling teams. The teams are divided into four regional business units, each with different customers, data, and incentive plans. Some of the plans are goal-based, some are ranking-based, others are commission-based, and still others are tied to MBO achievement. The firm's IT group worked with a sales incentive compensation management software provider to develop the systems required to handle all of the firm's diverse needs. Every month, the system processes millions of data records, and, on average, hundreds of adjustments are required. The IC plan administration team consists of eleven employees plus two full-time outside consultants. The firm spends over $3 million a year administering the sales force incentive program.

An IC Plan Administration Flowchart

The flowchart in Figure 12-4 shows the inputs, outputs, and system requirements of a typical IC plan administration system. Each part of the system is described further in the following sections.

Inputs. The inputs to the IC plan administration system include data sources capturing performance, sales force responsibilities, and incentive plan specifics. The inputs include the following elements.

Sales Transactions and Account Assignments. Since almost all incentive plans are tied at least in part to sales metrics, sales transactions and account assignments are important inputs into the IC plan administration system. By linking sales transactions to salespeople using the appropriate table of account-to-salesperson assignments, sales can be attributed to the correct salesperson. Keeping data at the account level, rather than at the salesperson level, is advantageous because as account assignments change, historical performance can be determined for any new territory configuration. This is important for calculating metrics such as territory sales growth. Sometimes, in order to simplify the system and limit data volume

Figure 12-4. An IC plan administration system flowchart.

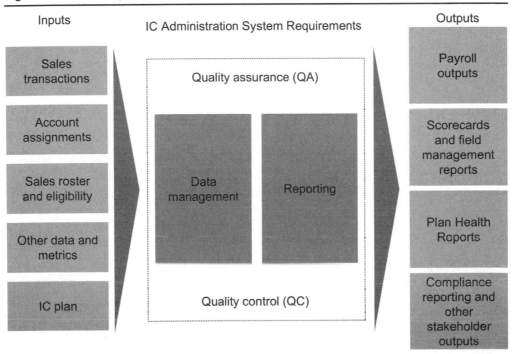

and complexity, companies use worksheet-based systems and keep sales history summarized to the salesperson level rather than at the account or transaction level. This helps to minimize system complexity; however, if the company needs to implement plan features that require account-level sales or historical sales for a new territory configuration, one has to go back to the original source of the sales data.

A common incentive plan administration mistake is using the wrong table of account assignments when processing the data. Checks and balances should be established to ensure that the appropriate alignment is used so that salespeople get credit for the correct sales.

Sales Roster and Eligibility. The sales roster and eligibility information keeps track of who is eligible for different plan elements. For example, participation in a quarterly bonus program may require that a salesperson have worked the entire quarter in a particular territory. Eligibility for a recognition program may require that a salesperson has worked in a territory for the entire year. Companies usually have special rules for dealing with midplan changes in employment (for example, new hires, terminations, deaths, or retirements) and midplan changes in job responsibilities (for example, transfers or promotions, temporary assignments, leaves of absence, sickness or disability, or sales territory changes). A salesperson who switches jobs within the firm midplan might be treated differently for incentive purposes from one who leaves to work for another company midplan. Eligibility issues can be quite complex and are a frequent cause of plan administration errors. A well-defined process can assure quality by using verification steps to minimize problems.

Other Data and Metrics. The other data and metrics required as inputs to the IC plan administration system depend on the incentive plan design. Territory- or account-level goals are needed if the plan is goal-based. Relevant performance metrics such as market share, customer satisfaction scores, or activity data are needed if the plan is tied to these metrics.

IC Plan. The specific plan design parameters need to be input into the system. This includes payout curve data such as commission rates, bonus amounts, thresholds for accelerators or decelerators, appropriate groupings of product or customer types for incentive purposes, and eligibility, as well as other business rules that determine payouts. The best IC plan administration systems use tables or parameter files that are external to the software to keep track of the various payout curves, groupings, and business rules. If such data are hard-coded into the software, the system becomes highly inflexible and difficult to change.

Outputs. The outputs of the IC plan administration system include payroll outputs, scorecards and reports for salespeople and sales managers, and plan health reports for sales leaders.

Payroll Outputs. The most basic, and frequently the only, focus of IC plan administration systems is to produce the information necessary to pay salespeople their incentive earnings. Needless to say, these outputs will be subject to intense sales force scrutiny.

Could There Be Errors in the Three Thousand E-Mailed Reports Each Month?

"One of the scariest things I do is to hit the 'send' key that triggers over three thousand e-mails sending customized reports to the entire sales force with performance and earning summaries. You wait with apprehension for hundreds of e-mails back the next morning, and what a relief it is when most of the 20 or 30 e-mails back are seeking clarification and not pointing out errors. A spelling error in three thousand e-mails is embarrassing; a calculation error is disastrous."

Stephen Redden, Manager, ZS Associates

Scorecards and Field Management Reports. Scorecards are the regular reports provided to salespeople tracking their performance and payouts. In addition to tracking historical performance, the most effective scorecards focus attention on how the salesperson can enhance her performance and what the positive consequences of a performance increase are likely to be. Scorecards share critical information that can motivate salespeople to improve. They can provide direction to salespeople on how they can best spend their time. On effective scorecards, information is presented clearly, so that sales force understanding of performance is enhanced. Figure 12-5 summarizes some key characteristics of effective scorecards.

Figures 12-6 through 12-9 show specific examples of scorecard features that enhance understanding, clarity, direction, and motivation.

In addition to scorecards for individual salespeople, field management reports provide region and district sales managers with valuable information for coaching their salespeople to improve their performance. Figure 12-10 provides an example of a field management report generated by an IC plan administration system.

Plan Health Reports. The focus of plan health reports is to provide sales leaders and incentive plan designers with timely information for assessing whether the plan is doing what it was designed to do, and at the same time not producing undesirable side effects such as unfair payouts. Many of the analyses described in Chapter 2 for assessing a current incentive compensation plan can be created routinely as outputs of the IC plan administration system. For example, the IC plan administration system has all the information necessary to create the analysis shown in Figure 12-11. The graph depicts the incentive plan structure and the distribution of goal attainment across the sales force based on performance to date. The table shows some summary statistics (projected for the year based on

Figure 12-5. Key characteristics of effective scorecards for salespeople.

Understanding	• Help salespeople understand their territory performance and track improvement over time.
Clarity	• Make the payout immediately obvious. • Make all steps in the calculation of the payout easy to follow. • Exclude extraneous information.
Direction	• Communicate to salespeople what behavior is requested of them. • Link to other performance improvement tools to help salespeople see how to improve.
Motivation	• Show salespeople the positive consequences of better performance, thus motivating them to work harder.

performance to date) and provides a comparison to what the firm had targeted for the year. Notice that many of the key statistics, such as company goal attainment, median and 90th percentile compensation, and the Engagement Rate, are running well behind what the firm had targeted. If sales leaders get this information quickly through a strong IC plan administration system, they can analyze the situation and determine if adjustments need to be made to help put the company back on track.

Figure 12-12 shows another example of a plan health report. This report includes graphics that alert the sales management team to potential incentive plan problems. For example, the report shows management whether the pay distribution across salespeople is appropriate, whether the incentive costs are allocated strategically across products, and whether the plan pays for performance.

Compliance Reporting and Other Stakeholder Outputs. While the primary recipients of IC plan administration outputs are members of the sales force, there are other stakeholders who may need information from this system, and their needs should not be overlooked. Often, analysts in Sales, Marketing, or Finance need reports or files for tracking specific performance measures or for conducting ad hoc analyses. In addition, compliance reporting requirements for auditors can be quite significant, particularly for publicly held companies. The Sarbanes-Oxley Act (2002), which was enacted largely in response to a number of major corporate accounting scandals, resulted in major changes in compliance practices for pub-

Figure 12-6. Scorecard example: enhancing understanding through graphics and peer comparisons.

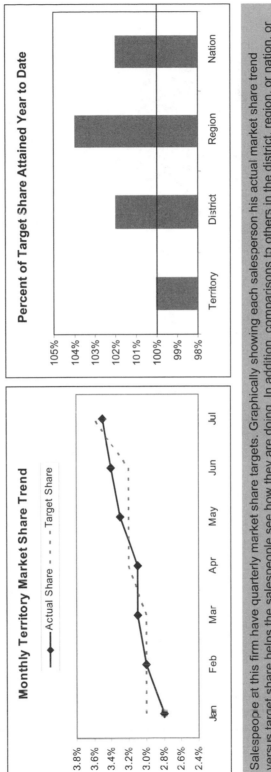

Salespeople at this firm have quarterly market share targets. Graphically showing each salesperson his actual market share trend versus target share helps the salespeople see how they are doing. In addition, comparisons to others in the district, region, or nation, or comparisons to territories with similar characteristics, help salespeople compare their performance against others and see what levels of performance are possible.

Figure 12-7. Scorecard example: providing clarity.

June Payout Scorecard
Sales Specialist: John Doe

Individual Annual Sales Target Bonus = $15,000	Team Contribution Target Bonus = $6,000	Total Annual Target Bonus = $21,000
Latest Pay Period YTD Achievement		
YTD target payout: $7,500	YTD target payout: $3,000	YTD target payout: $10,500
YTD achievement: 108.0%	YTD achievement: 119.7%	YTD achievement: 113.8%
YTD payout earned: $8,693	YTD payout earned: $5,962	YTD payout earned: $14,655

Payout Curve

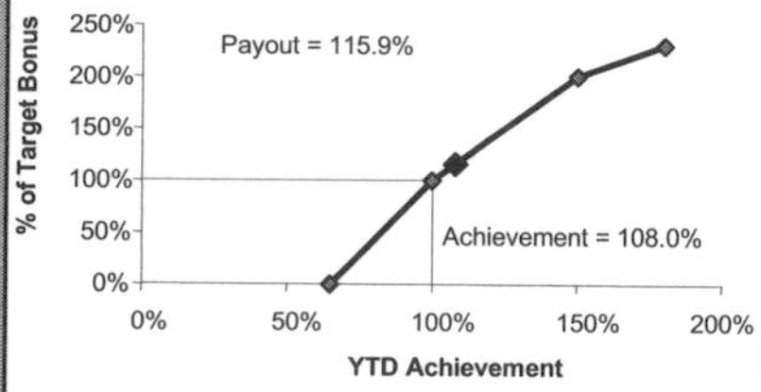

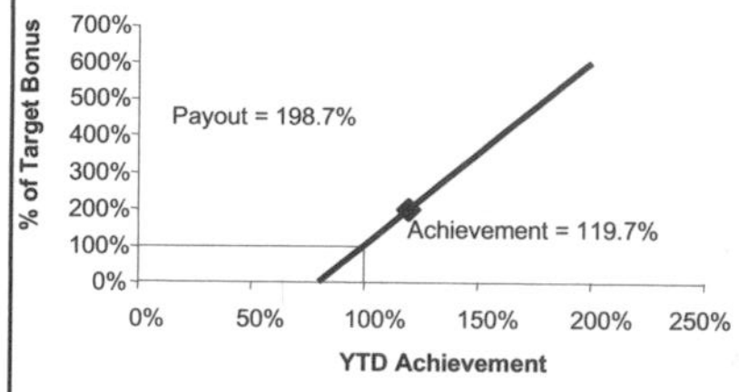

Payout = 115.9%
Achievement = 108.0%

Payout = 198.7%
Achievement = 119.7%

YTD Earnings and Payout Summary

YTD payout earned:	$14,655
Adjustment:	$0
YTD earnings payable:	$14,655
Prior month's payments to date:	$13,194
Overpayment:	$0
Current month's payout:	$1,461

Clutter is reduced by producing scorecards that include only the most essential elements, showing a view of the data that is customized for each salesperson, and by presenting data graphically. The graphs on this scorecard show the salesperson exactly where he stands on each payout curve.

Figure 12-8. Scorecard example: providing direction.

Location: Street (Zip Code)	Tires, Batteries, and Accessories (TBA) Sales Index	Relative Store Volume—All Products	Relative Penetration Index
Five High-Potential Accounts with Low Penetration			
Crawford (60712)	34	261	13
Green Bay (60201)	54	292	18
N. Clark (60626)	59	252	23
Quentin (60067)	123	223	55
Algonquin (60195)	172	311	55

Listing high-potential accounts with low performance suggests to salespeople how they might spend their time to enhance performance. Effective scorecards highlight the products and customer segments that are of greatest strategic importance to the company.

licly held companies in the United States. If incentive payouts are material to a firm's financial statements (which they often are), the act requires that specific controls be put into the IC plan administration system to increase corporate accountability and transparency. This includes process controls (such as input and output validations and audit trails) as well as systems controls (such as security features that track who logs into the system and who makes changes). An auditor can provide advice as to what specific controls are necessary in order to meet the necessary compliance requirements.

IC Administration System Requirements. The IC plan administration system requirements include all the software and processes for managing the IC database, generating reports, and assuring and controlling system quality.

Data Management. Data management refers to the processes and tools that enable incentive plan data to be stored in, verified, modified, and extracted from a database. The sophistication of data management capabilities depends on data volume and complexity of needs, and can range from a simple PC-based spreadsheet or database program to a complex database management and decision support system. From a technical standpoint, the way in which data are organized affects how quickly and flexibly information can be extracted. Most IC administration systems require a high degree of data management flexibility, because data-handling needs (such as payout curve logic and business rules for assigning sales credit, aggregating data, and determining eligibility) tend to be complex and highly specific to the IC administration problem. For this reason, general data management programs are often an awkward solution, and programs designed specifically for IC administration may be more appropriate. An IC plan administrator, working together with a database expert, can assess which data manage-

Figure 12-9. Scorecard example: enhancing motivation through interactive features.

Name:	Rep 1		Date Ending: 31 March
	Incentive Compensation Payout Calculator		
	Product A Component Calculator		
Quarterly quota	$1,434,088		
Current QTD attainment	125%		
Estimated deal	$50,000	← *Enter Estimated deal size*	
New attainment	129%		
Incremental payout	$2,125.00		
New QTD payout	$15,672.68		
	Product B Component Calculator		
Annual quota	$1,058,823		
Current YTD attainment	11%		
Estimated deal	$100,000	← *Enter Estimated deal size*	
New attainment	20%		
Incremental payout	$1,029.80		
New YTD payout	$2,184.91		
	Total Payout Calculator		
Based on your above entries, your total estimated incremental payout would be:			$3,154.80

Calculator payouts are approximate and may not exactly match the payouts as per your performance.
Incentive Calculator values are based on Prorated Target Payout.
Excludes bonus attainment payouts.

This Web-based scorecard has an interactive payout calculator. The salesperson enters an estimated deal size that includes two different product lines to see what would happen to his payout if the deal were realized. Seeing the potential earnings helps motivate the salesperson to work hard to close the deal.

ment tools will work best, given the IC plan administration complexity and input and output needs.

Reporting. Reporting is an important component of a sales IC administration system. Effective reports seek to inform and direct salespeople, assist incentive administrators with quality assurance and control, provide managers with insights regarding the performance of salespeople, and provide executive summaries and plan diagnostics for incentive designers and sales leaders. Reporting processes and tools:

- Enable performance and incentive data to be extracted, manipulated, and formatted in a way that is useful to the sales force.

Figure 12-10. Example of a field management report.

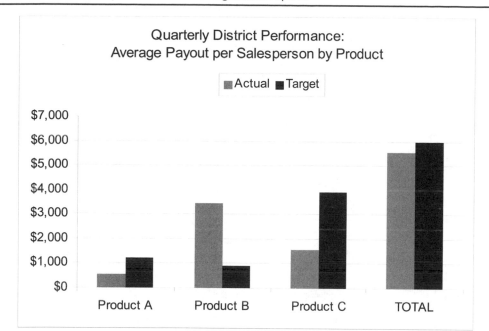

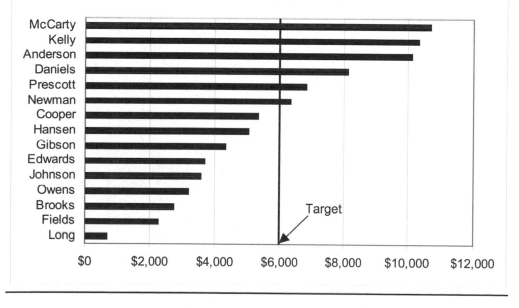

Figure 12-10. Continued.

| Name | Total Payout | % of Target Payout | Product A | | | Product B | | | Product C | |
			% of Target Payout	Share Payout	Growth Payout	% of Target Payout	Share Payout	Growth Payout	% of Target Payout	Growth Payout
Long	$700	12%	25%	$300	$0	44%	$400	$0	0%	$0
Fields	$2,300	38%	75%	$300	$600	44%	$400	$0	26%	$1,000
Brooks	$2,750	46%	21%	$250	$0	0%	$0	$0	64%	$2,500
Owens	$3,200	53%	25%	$300	$0	44%	$400	$0	64%	$2,500
Johnson	$3,600	60%	21%	$250	$0	94%	$400	$450	64%	$2,500
Edwards	$3,700	62%	29%	$350	$0	261%	$400	$1,950	26%	$1,000
Gibson	$4,350	73%	29%	$350	$0	444%	$400	$3,600	0%	$0
Hansen	$5,050	84%	0%	$0	$0	561%	$400	$4,650	0%	$0
Cooper	$5,350	89%	33%	$400	$0	106%	$400	$550	103%	$4,000
Newman	$6,350	106%	21%	$250	$0	567%	$400	$4,700	26%	$1,000
Prescott	$6,850	114%	17%	$200	$0	628%	$400	$5,250	26%	$1,000
Daniels	$8,150	136%	158%	$400	$1,500	694%	$400	$5,850	0%	$0
Anderson	$10,150	169%	171%	$250	$1,800	900%	$400	$7,700	0%	$0
Kelly	$10,350	173%	25%	$300	$0	506%	$400	$4,150	141%	$5,500
McCarty	$10,700	178%	29%	$350	$0	872%	$400	$7,450	64%	$2,500
District Avg.	$5,570	93%	45%	$283	$260	384%	$373	$3,087	40%	$1,567

This report shows a first-line sales manager a summary of how well the district performed on the incentive plan and provides a breakdown by salesperson. The table at the bottom of the report provides details that a manager can use to coach salespeople on areas that need improvement.

Figure 12-11. Example of a plan health report.

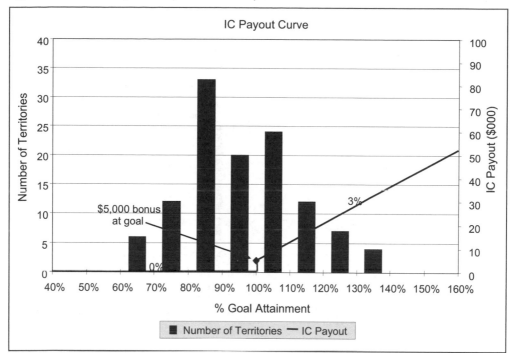

Statistic	Annual Projection Based on Performance to Date	Target
Sales	$295,875,783	$308,204,000
Company goal attainment	96%	100%
Total IC payout	$720,983	$814,000
Median compensation	$50,000	$55,000
10th percentile compensation	$50,000	$50,000
90th percentile compensation	$69,389	$75,000
Engagement Rate	38.8%	50%

- Allow reports to be delivered in a timely and cost-effective manner.
- Allow reports to be archived and stored for future viewing.

Like that of data management, the sophistication of reporting capabilities depends on data volume and complexity of needs. For complex situations, companies use software packages such as Crystal Reports (Business Objects), Cognos, and Siebel Sales Analytics. MS-Access (Microsoft's database and reporting tool) and spreadsheet software are used in simpler situations. Reports take two possible forms:

Figure 12-12. Another plan health report.

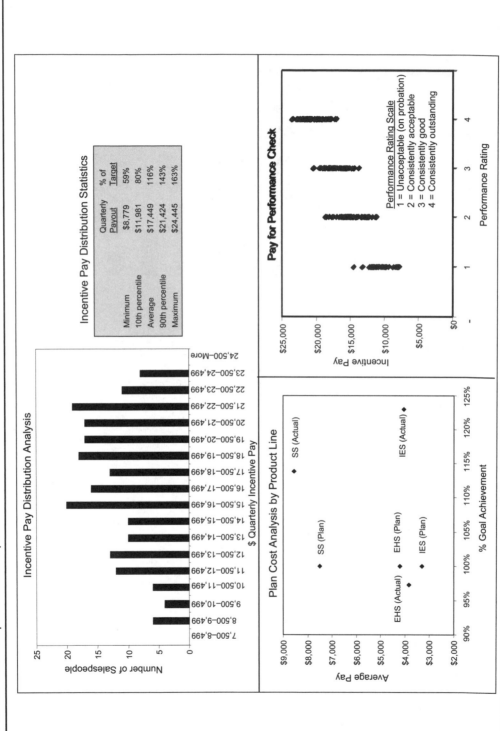

- *Static.* Static reports are created to be viewed on a computer screen or in hard copy.

- *Dynamic.* Dynamic reports are created in real time from a database that is accessible to the user through a computer program that allows data manipulation, including graphing, sorting, or "what if" capabilities. For example, a salesperson can enter a desired performance level, and the software will calculate the resulting incentive payout. Although dynamic reports have more inherent power, this power has to be compared with the cost of dynamic reports. Dynamic reports require more time from salespeople, can fall into disuse if too complex, and can become cumbersome to maintain.

It is worthwhile to integrate incentive information into other reports, such as performance reports, that are delivered to salespeople and their managers on a regular basis. This is easy to do, since frequently these other reports and the incentive reports rely on the same information and data sources. This integration avoids information clutter for the salesperson. It also enhances impact. For example, when sales data are tied to their impact on pay, the data become more meaningful to salespeople.

Report delivery is either pushed or pulled:

- *Push.* Reports are sent, or "pushed," to their users in electronic form via e-mail or in hard copy.

- *Pull.* Users have to ask for, or "pull," a particular report on a company's intranet or other secure company web site.

The push approach has the advantage that all salespeople are assured of getting the report. With e-mail, current reports are immediately accessible on each salesperson's computer, and recipients can print or save reports that they want to view again in the future. Web-based and intranet-based pull approaches can provide easy, menu-driven access to both current and historical reports and can be more powerful, more flexible, and easier to control and archive. Pull approaches do not guarantee that all salespeople will access their reports; however, since the reports involve money, salespeople will be drawn to the site. Software tools are available to help manage Web and e-mail delivery of reports.

The IC administration designer has to consider cost, complexity, capabilities, ease of use, training needs, support needs, flexibility, and scalability in deciding what tools to use for reporting. Internal or external experts are usually available to help assess which report generation and delivery tools are appropriate in light of the IC plan administration situation and needs.

Quality Assurance and Control. Managing quality in the IC plan administration system is critically important. Quality assurance (QA) and quality control (QC) are closely related but different procedures that are integral and vital components of any IC plan administration system. Quality assurance is *process-oriented*; it focuses on ensuring that the steps required to execute the IC plan administration system are well defined, appropriate, and performed correctly in order to produce accurate outputs. Quality control is *output-oriented*; it focuses on discovering errors at key steps of the IC plan administration system and correcting them before they affect future steps. Effective QC procedures ensure that the outputs of the IC plan administration system are complete and error-free. Specific QA and QC processes are discussed in more detail in the next section of the chapter.

How to Design an Effective IC Plan Administration System

A sales incentive compensation plan administration system uses people, processes, and tools to administer a sales compensation program effectively on an ongoing basis. The design of the system varies considerably, depending upon the complexity of the situation and business goals.

Design Elements

People. An effective IC plan administration team consists of people with a mix of different skills. Three broad roles are typically required, as shown in Figure 12-13. These roles can be filled by different people, or one person can perform multiple roles. The size of the team can be anywhere from one to several dozen people, depending upon the complexity of the situation and the extent of outsourcing.

Figure 12-14 adds additional texture to the description of these three roles. Sample activities for each role are described for four typical IC business scenarios.

IC administration systems tend to be customized to the situation, involve large amounts of data and many process steps, combine both technical and business aspects, and evolve continuously. As a result, people working in IC administration positions develop expertise over time. Once a person becomes good at the task, it can be very disruptive if he leaves. It is therefore critical to plan for personnel progression and transitions. It is much easier to manage team changes at predictable times than it is to deal with sudden personnel departures.

An IC System at Risk

A firm has been using a contractor, Bob, for over nine years to handle all the eligibility and reporting requirements for the sales incentive compensation program. Bob's work is very complex and detailed, and he is the only person who completely understands how the whole system fits together. None of his work is documented.

Another part of the firm's IC plan administration system is tied to a computer program written 15 years ago by a long-time company employee,

Figure 12-13. Roles required on the IC plan administration team.

Business Interface Role

Sample activities:
- Understand product and sales force needs
- Prepare field communications
- Train field (or trainers) on incentive plan
- Participate in plan design discussions
- Resolve field queries
- QC final field deliverables

Required skills:
- Communications
- Analytical

Incentive Administrator Role

Sample activities:
- Gather and validate inputs
- Create reports
- QC reports and data—communicate with data sources to resolve issues
- Translate business requirements into well-defined process steps
- Update tools as business rules change

Required skills:
- Quality focus
- Detail orientation
- Data management
- Analytical

Incentive Analyst Role

Sample activities:
- Track incentive plan performance
- Understand results (and reasons for results)
- Analyze impact of potential incentive plan changes
- Analyze impact of potential quota-design changes
- Ad hoc analysis

Required skills:
- Analytical
- Communications

Linda. The program was written in a programming language that is no longer used, and Linda is the only person in the company who still knows how to program in this language. Hence, Linda must personally make all of the programming changes required to keep the system current.

Management has become very concerned . . . what will happen if Bob or Linda leaves the company?

Processes. A company should have a structured process and timeline for running the IC administration system each incentive period. Structure helps to ensure that sufficient time is allowed for quality control, that errors are squeezed out of the system through repeated use, and that the process improves over time. Processes should be well defined, vigilantly documented, and rigorously followed. Effective QC procedures include checks and balances that encourage errors to be caught as far upstream in the plan administration system as possible, thus minimizing processing time and costs and increasing the chances that an error will be caught before it reaches the field. Figure 12-15 shows an example of a structured process and timeline used at one company. The process takes seven working days each

Figure 12-14. Examples of activities performed by the IC administration team under several IC business scenarios.

IC Scenario	Business Interface Activity	Analyst Activity	Administrator Activity
The IC plan changes	• Participate in discussions with sales force on plan changes • Create communication material • Train field • Work with admin. team to design new scorecard and other reports • Provide follow-up training and communications during plan period	• Provide analysis to support decision to change plan • Model impact of plan changes • Analyze impact of plan change after implementation	• Discuss difficulty of implementing plan changes before they are finalized • Work with business interface to design new scorecard and other reports • Implement changes to the system
Sales leadership concludes that sales force activity needs to change	• Discuss findings and brainstorm solutions	• Perform additional analysis as required	• Provide reports showing sales force activity • Work with rest of IC team to review and interpret reports
New software tools become available	• Determine likely requirements (e.g., plan changes, business changes, flexibility, scalability)	• Review new software versus current software and expected needs (especially as it relates to analysis support)	• Review new software versus current software and expected needs (especially as it relates to production administration)
An IC error occurs and the field is overpaid	• Discuss issue and possible resolution with sales force	• Analyze impact (e.g., how much overpayment? how much could be withheld from next payouts?)	• Determine exact extent of issue • Determine cause of issue • Determine other deliverables at risk because of this or similar issues • Implement processes to ensure that this or similar issues are not repeated

Note: The business interface and analyst role are combined in many organizations.

month. Adhering to this process enables the company to routinely produce IC administration outputs on time and with very few errors.

Quality assurance (QA) includes step-by-step procedures for handling the various situations that can occur. Figure 12-16 provides a representative (though incomplete) list of situations that should be anticipated. A strong QA approach requires documentation that outlines the work steps, accountabilities, and timing for handling such situations. Even in small sales forces with a simple IC plan

Figure 12-15. Example of a structured process and timeline for IC administration.

IC Administration Activities	Day 1	Day 2	Day 3	Day 4	Day 5	Day 6	Day 7
All input data received	■						
All input files prepared and loaded		■					
System run and validations reviewed			■				
Input and output validation reports generated and reviewed				■			
Scorecards and management reports generated						■	
Scorecards and management reports approved						■	
Reports published							■

Figure 12-16. Situations that require detailed documentation as part of QA.

What will we do if . . .

- There are territory alignment changes?
- There is a territory vacancy?
- A salesperson goes on temporary leave?
- One salesperson assists with another territory temporarily?
- A distributor has a temporary glitch in data feeds?
- A salesperson gets promoted in the middle of an incentive period?
- A person joins the firm in the middle of an incentive period?
- A salesperson requests a quota adjustment because of circumstances beyond her control?
- A new product launch is delayed and the sales forecast is built into the quotas?

administration system, such documents are needed to provide clarity to the sales force and to prevent both errors and unwarranted lawsuits.

Good IC Plan Managers Anticipate Future Scenarios

Even with a comprehensive list of detailed business rules that are rigorously followed, errors in IC plan administration occur. Errors are very common when more than one exception condition applies to a single salesperson within the same incentive period. For example, system logic that works flawlessly for one salesperson whose territory alignment changes and for a second salesperson who gets promoted before the end of the incentive period may break down completely for a third salesperson for whom both exception conditions (an alignment change and a promotion) occur together within the same incentive period. Effective IC plan managers anticipate possible combinations of circumstances so that their systems can handle such scenarios correctly. Even though situations such as these "double-exception" cases may be rare, they are almost guaranteed to happen at some point in time. IC plan managers of very large sales forces should expect them to occur in virtually every incentive period.

The list of situations and exception rules should be dynamic: It needs to be updated whenever new situations arise and new rules are created so that today's unanticipated situations become anticipated in the future.

In addition, effective IC plan administration processes include rigorous QC procedures and checks for common problems, including those listed in Figure 12-17.

Creative QC Approaches

If a report is to be distributed to two thousand salespeople, consider sending the report to a small number of salespeople (say 20) first, then waiting a day or two before sending the rest. That way, if there is an error affecting a large number of salespeople, it is likely to be caught and can be corrected before the entire sales force is involved. This approach is particularly useful when significant plan or process changes are made. A variation on this approach is to send reports to managers first.

The importance of structured processes for IC administration is becoming even greater as more and more companies share work processes across borders.

Figure 12-17. Common problems that need to be checked for as part of QC.

Check the inputs to be sure that . . .

• The sales data (or other data and metrics) have no errors and are complete.

• The assignment of salespeople to sales transactions (the alignment) is correct and is accurately applied.

• The eligibility information is correct and up-to-date.

• The correct IC plan is used.

Check the outputs to be sure that . . .

• There are no calculation errors.

• All the expected reports are generated.

• Numbers are consistent within a single report and across reports.

• Any "special cases" are handled properly.

Already today, many firms have outsourced the IC administration function to operations in other countries, such as India, and the prevalence of this practice is expected to increase dramatically over the next decade. Clear communication and documentation of processes will be critical to the success of this transition.

Tools. Companies have a choice of two major categories of tools for managing their IC plan administration system:

- General-purpose tools, such as spreadsheet software.
- Software tools designed specifically for IC plan administration. These tools may be developed internally by a firm's IT group or can be purchased from a variety of software and service vendors.

General-purpose tools usually work best for small to medium-sized sales forces (typically less than 100 salespeople) with low to moderately complex IC plan administration needs. IC-specific tools are most appropriate for larger sales forces and for sales forces with complex and frequently changing needs. When evaluating and comparing different tools choices, look for tools that:

- Support a fully repeatable process with very few or no manual steps.
- Are transparent (easily understood).
- Match established business processes.
- Have QC procedures integrated at each step.
- Are flexible so that they will support plan changes.
- Are scalable to support company growth.

Sales Incentive Management Software and Service Is a Growing Industry

Because of the importance and difficulty of IC plan administration, sales incentive compensation management software is a rapidly growing industry. There are several specialized software and service vendors that provide IC-specific applications, either as stand-alone systems or as part of a larger enterprise incentive management (EIM) system. Companies in this business include Callidus Software, Centive, Oracle, PeopleSoft, SAP, Siebel, Synygy, and ZS Associates.

Despite the rapid growth of this industry, the vast majority of companies still use general-purpose software tools, such as spreadsheets, to administer their incentive programs. Some larger companies have their own homegrown systems.

As the IC-specific technologies offered by software and service vendors advance, these solutions are becoming increasingly scalable and effective across a wider range of complexity. The solutions offered by some vendors allow smaller companies to purchase scaled-down versions of a larger system, creating a solution that is cost-effective and appropriate in the short term and at the same time allows the firm to seamlessly increase solution sophistication as the company's needs grow.

Design Influences

As shown in Figure 12-18, business goals and situation complexity are the two primary influences on the design of the IC plan administration system.

Figure 12-19 shows how different business goals and situation complexities combine to suggest different IC plan administration system solutions.

Business Goals. Figure 12-20 lists several important business goals for an incentive compensation administration system and suggests how accomplishment of these goals can be encouraged through system design. While all of these goals are important to most sales forces, the relative importance of each goal influences plan administration system design choices. For example, accuracy and timeliness are encouraged by enforcing strict processes and limiting ad hoc requests; however, this limits flexibility. Having both flexibility and high accuracy may be possible with a larger IC plan administration team; but this adds to costs. When designing the plan administration system, business goal priorities influence important design choices.

Figure 12-18. The IC plan administration drivers.

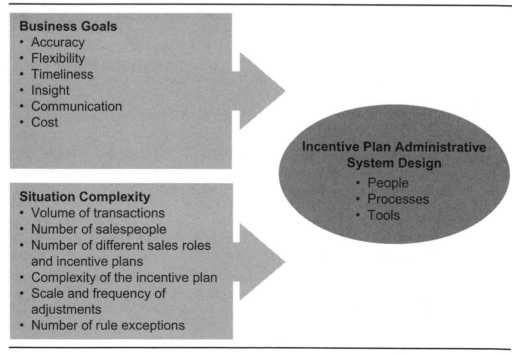

Figure 12-19. Examples of IC administration solutions in complex and simple situations.

	Complex Situation	Simple Situation
Situation complexity	Large sales force, varied sales roles and metrics, multiple incentive plans, complex plans, several data sources, large volume of data, many business rules with numerous exceptions.	Small sales force, simple sales force structure, single data source, moderate volume of data, manageable number of business rules and exceptions.
Business goals	Accuracy is most important (situation is highly error-prone).	Adaptability and accuracy are equally important (situation is likely to change frequently).
People	Team, including experts from IT, Sales Operations, and HR.	One IC manager, a generalist with broad skills (versatility is important).
Processes	Well-defined processes, highly standardized and repeatable. QC checks at every step. Ad hoc requests are closely controlled. Very limited midperiod changes are allowed.	Simple, stepwise processes for maintaining the system. Many manual checklists for ensuring quality. Midperiod changes and ad hoc requests are allowed within established guidelines.
Tools	Standardized IC-specific tools, customized to meet the firm's needs by a third-party software and service vendor.	General-purpose spreadsheet software; spreadsheet is developed and maintained by the IC plan manager.

The IC Plan Flexibility–Cost Trade-Off

There is a clear trade-off between allowing IC plan flexibility and minimizing plan administration costs and the number of errors. For example, a large multinational company with over three thousand salespeople and over a dozen sales roles had an incentive plan administration system that was extremely complex. Plan administration costs were more than 7 percent of total incentive costs. Much of the cost was attributed to the large number of queries and case-by-case adjustments that the firm allowed. Sales management would adjust territory goals at almost any time during an incentive period, in response to changes in expected sales or changes in contract status with buying groups. Handling all of these adjustments correctly was very difficult, making the plan administration process highly inefficient and error-prone. To reduce costs, the company simplified the plan and considerably restricted the number of midyear goal corrections that would be allowed. This drastically reduced IC plan administration complexity, decreased the number of errors, and cut plan administration costs to just 2 percent of total incentive costs. It did, however, create an incentive plan that was more rigid and less responsive to changes in the environment.

Figure 12-20. How business goals can be accomplished through plan administration process design.

Business Goals	How to Accomplish the Goal Through IC Plan Administration System Design
Accuracy	• Apply stringent input validations • Document business rules in detail • Leverage a repeatable process • Understand and answer the right questions • Utilize strict quality and process control checklists • Measure error significance and quantity for ongoing enhancement of quality assurance procedures

Flexibility	• Anticipate and accommodate change in
	    – Input content and layout
	    – Business rules
	    – Plan specifics
	    – Adjustments and exceptions
	    – Contests
	    – Reports
	• But . . . keep the plan simple

Timeliness	• Establish a production process • Anticipate issues • Plan ahead for changes • Defer ad hoc requests
Insight	• Review plan performance regularly • Ensure that plan evolves as business evolves, and continues to appropriately motivate the field • Provide clear, frequent diagnostic reports to sales management • Conduct "what if" analyses to assess impact of plan changes
Communication	• Ensure that field reports are simple, correct, and on time • Ensure field understanding and buy-in of compensation program • Provide management with timely information (preview and actual)
Reasonable cost	• Build a system that is appropriate for the level of complexity • Track costs and response times to continuously improve processes • Evaluate the costs and benefits of proposed system enhancements

Situation Complexity. Situation complexity also influences the IC plan administration process. As shown in Figure 12-21, there are several dimensions of complexity in an IC plan administration system.

It is important to match the IC plan administration solution to the complexity of the situation. Generally, for a small to medium-sized sales force (typically less than 100 salespeople) with low to moderately complex IC plan administration needs, an appropriate solution includes:

- *People.* A generalist who possesses business, analytical, and IT skills.
- *Tools.* Spreadsheet-based.
- *Processes.* Structured but flexible.

For a larger sales force with complex and frequently changing needs, an appropriate solution includes:

Figure 12-21. Dimensions of complexity in an IC plan administration system.

Simple Situation	Complex Situation
Small sales force	Large sales force
Few transactions	Many transactions
Single sales role	Many sales roles
One incentive plan	Multiple incentive plans
Single performance metric	Many performance metrics
Simple plan design	Complex plan design
Single data source	Multiple data sources
Few business rules	Many business rules
Few exceptions to rules	Many exceptions to rules
Limited compliance needs (private firm)	Extensive compliance needs (public firm)

- *People*. A team of specialists that includes people with business skills, analytical skills, and IT skills.
- *Tools*. IC-specific tools.
- *Processes*. Well documented and rigorously followed.

As Figure 12-22 shows, an inappropriate solution creates a gap between firm needs and system capabilities. The left-hand side of the figure shows that in situations of low to moderate complexity, an appropriate solution includes an IC administration generalist, spreadsheet tools, and flexible processes. If this simple solution is applied to a situation with moderate to high complexity, system limitations are likely to create inefficiencies and make IC plan administration highly error-prone. On the other hand, the right-hand side of the figure shows that in situations of moderate to high complexity, an appropriate solution includes an IC administration team, IC-specific tools, and rigorous processes. If this highly sophisticated solution is applied in a situation of low to moderate complexity, the "heaviness" of the solution introduces its own inefficiencies and creates unnecessary plan costs.

What Should Be the Role of External Partners in IC Administration?

Some firms manage their IC administration exclusively with in-house staff, while others use partners extensively. There are two key decisions to be made regarding the role of partners in IC administration.

Figure 12-22. Matching solutions to situations.

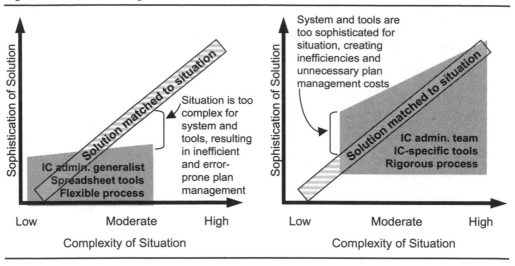

1. *The "make or buy" decision.* Should the initial system tools be created by internal staff, or should they be purchased or leased from an external partner?

2. *The "outsource or in-house" decision.* Should the ongoing administration of the system be performed internally, or should it be outsourced to an external partner?

The range of possible choices is illustrated in Figure 12-23. A system with internally developed tools will typically be administered by internal staff. With externally created tools, the firm can usually either purchase the software tools and administer and maintain the system internally, or lease the software tools and outsource the ongoing administration function to the partner.

Should the Firm Make or Buy the IC Administration System Tools?

In-House IC Plan Administration System Development Is Challenging

A team of seven people spent a year and $1.5 million in direct costs developing the software tools for an in-house IC plan administration system. In addition to the direct costs, substantial time was dedicated to the project by many salespeople and sales managers, as well as numerous marketing and finance personnel. The system has never worked, and there has been a lot of finger-pointing. IT says, "The sales managers don't know what they want and keep changing their minds." The sales managers say, "IT is too rigid and is not focusing on our issues." Marketing says, "I told you this

Figure 12-23. IC administration and the role of partners.

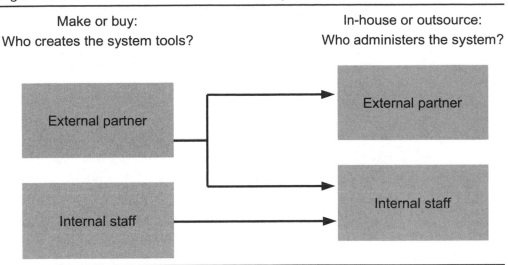

would never work." The finance person who is the project leader leaves the company, disheartened and frustrated.

Authors' note: Bad experiences with developing software tools for IC administration are not limited to in-house development teams. Companies can experience frustrations when working with outside partners as well. With outside partners, the sources of frustration tend to involve responsiveness, flexibility, and cost.

Developing IC administration tools can be a considerable challenge. Figure 12-24 shows the potential benefits and risks of buying or leasing system tools from an outside vendor versus developing them in-house.

The decision to make or buy IC administration system tools should be driven by an assessment of the extent to which internal versus external solutions meet the firm's needs. The time, effort, cost, and risk associated with each potential solution are important considerations. Often, internal solutions work well in simple situations where the tools will have a very finite life (one to two years). Complex situations and situations with rapidly evolving needs are often best handled with IC administration tools developed by a partner with specialized expertise. The ongoing operation of a system built with externally developed tools can usually be either outsourced to the partner or kept in-house.

Should the Firm Outsource Ongoing IC Administration or Do It In-House?
Some firms manage their ongoing IC plan administration entirely in-house, while others outsource the function. Figure 12-25 summarizes several potential benefits and risks of each of these options.

In-house IC plan administration is likely to be the best choice in situations where:

Figure 12-24. Should the firm make or buy the IC administration system tools?

	Make	Buy
Potential Benefits	• Firm has more control over the solution. • The solution can be more tailored to the firm's needs. • Integration into current environment is easier.	• Software has greater development and support resources and a wider user base; quality may be better. • May be easier and cheaper to migrate to newer options in the future. • Can usually be implemented in a shorter time frame.
Potential Risks	• It is always more difficult than it seems (IT often wants to build, but seldom really can in complex situations). • It is hard to anticipate tomorrow's needs. • There is not enough knowledge and skill with the technology platform. • System maintenance can become very expensive.	• The vendor may be financially unsound or the product may be immature. • Expensive customization may be required to meet needs. • May limit plan design. • May require changes in existing business practices.

- Needs are simple.

- Needs are complex, but there is substantial expertise and coordination across sales management, sales operations, and IT.

- There is strong team sustainability and evolution (it is possible to manage knowledge walking out the door).

Outsourcing is the best option when:

- Needs are complex, and an external solution exists that fits the need.

- Team strength or sustainability is low.

Financial analysis can be used to compare the total costs and productivity benefits of in-house versus outsourced IC administration. Costs attributed to the IC administration system can include:

- Consulting fees

- The cost of internal IC and IT support staff

- Incentive overpayments (resulting from inaccuracies in the system)

- Report production and distribution costs

- The cost to change the system to reflect incentive plan adjustments

Figure 12-25. Should ongoing IC plan administration be done in-house, or should it be outsourced?

	In-House	Outsource
Potential Benefits	• Control: *"IC is very central to how I run my sales force; I want the plan administration to be under my control as well."* • Responsiveness: *"I can walk down the hall with my question and don't have to wait for our IC plan administration vendor to provide the answer."* • People development: *"I want to provide my team the opportunity to learn and grow."*	• Expertise: *"These people do it all the time. They will always be better than we can ever be at this. They will anticipate things that we can learn only after we have made a mistake."* • Focus: *"I want my team to focus on sales; this plan administration stuff is a distraction."* • Accuracy: *"The low error rate makes my job easier."* • Risk: *"We don't have the luxury of getting it wrong a few times before we get it right."*
Potential Risks	• Turnover: *"I lost two people, and all the learning has walked out the door. We are in a jam."* • Career path: *"The better the team gets at doing this, the more I want to keep them in this job. What if they tire of it?"* • Evolution: *"We are changing so fast that our team just can't anticipate our future needs and keep up."*	• Dependence: *"We are too dependent on our vendor. Every time we make a new request, a larger bill follows."* • Flexibility: *"Whenever we want a midstream change, they fight it on 'quality control' grounds—but this is hampering our business."*

Productivity benefits attributed to the IC administration system can include:

- Improvements in system accuracy that lead to higher sales force morale, reduced sales force turnover, and increased selling time (since less time is spent on shadow accounting)
- Timely and insightful scorecards and tools that lead to enhanced sales force understanding and motivation
- Reductions in internal IC and IT support needs that free up time for internal staff to work on creative, higher-impact productivity enhancement programs

A careful examination of all of these costs and benefits will help a firm determine which IC administration solution—in-house or outsourced—is likely to have the most favorable profit impact.

Summary

IC plan administration goes beyond calculating payouts. It involves communicating timely information to the sales force through reports and dashboards so that salespeople know how they are doing and where and how they can improve. With this vital information, salespeople can "work the IC plan" and accomplish important company objectives. In addition, IC plan administration involves creating plan health checks that allow sales leaders to assess the quality of the plan and take mid-course corrective steps if needed.

IC plan administration is a very important job. The job can be frustrating at times, since IC plan administrators often hear complaints when things go wrong, yet rarely get accolades when things go right. The most effective IC plan administrators automate the routine aspects of IC administration so that they have considerable time to spend on higher-value-added activities, such as improving business processes, evaluating new technologies, and designing creative reports that provide sales leaders with strategic business insights. With a well-designed and efficient IC administration process, the job of an IC plan administrator can be both challenging and rewarding.

IC plan administration needs to be done well to make an incentive plan successful. IC plan administration that is both effective and efficient is very difficult to achieve, particularly in complex situations where constant unanticipated course corrections are needed. Ineffective plan administration can be detrimental to a firm. Having the right people, systems, and processes in place, along with a strong quality focus, enables the firm to minimize errors and optimize cost-effectiveness. Successful incentive plan administration significantly enhances the power of an incentive program as a key sales force effectiveness driver.

Index

absolute-level metrics, 209–210
accountability, 12, 190–191
account assignment, 463–464
acquisitions, *see* mergers
actual pay mix, 94–95
adaptation
    need for, 12–15, 40–41
    of performance measures to business strategy change, 195–196
additive matrix, 255, 256
add-on programs, *see* recognition programs; sales contests; SPIFFs (Special Performance Incentives for Field Force)
administration, *see* incentive plan administration
aggregation of plan measures, 259–261, 262
Alexander Group, Inc., 122
Allen-Bradley, 75
All Star Incentive Marketing, 403
American Express Incentive Services, 403
America Online, 334
Anderson, Andy, 404
assessment process, 34, 36
    for candidate incentive plan, 264–310
    for incumbent incentive plan, 38–92
at-risk pay, 97, 147–148, *see also* salary-incentive mix
attraction of sales force
    consequences of incentive compensation for, 47, 50–52
    pay levels in, 111, 130
    performance-payout relationships and, 235–237
awards, *see* recognition programs; sales contests; SPIFFs (Special Performance Incentives for Field Force)

base salary, 94
benchmarking
    consequences for salespeople, 47, 52–53
    industry norms in, 52–53, 120–125, 173–174, 281
    of salary-incentive mix, 173–174
    of sales force pay levels, 120–125
    of sales goals, 11–12, 331
    of sales territory goals, 335
Best Buy, 13, 419
bias check, 59–62, 126, 194
bluebirds, 101–103, 169–170, 319–320
Blue Cross Blue Shield (BCBS) of Massachusetts, 173–174
bonuses
    commissions versus, 231–237, 261–262
    executive, 422–423
    problems with goal-setting and, 64–65, 227–228, 239–240, 242–243
    retention, 118
bottom-up method of goal setting, 359–361
brand name, sales force causality and, 166
Brenton Banks, 5, 420–421
business development activities, 29–30
buyback arrangements, 418

Callidus Software, 369, 481
Canvas Systems, 378
capped incentive plans, 231, 243–245, 250
career stage, pay levels in, 111–112
Carlson Marketing Group, 403
carryover sales, 100–101, 236, 349–351
causality, sales force, *see* sales force causality/prominence
Centive, 369, 481

changes in sales force compensation, 423–430
    communication of, 416–419, 443–449
    company culture and, 177–178
    compatibility with other effectiveness drivers, 419–421
    consequences of incentive compensation, 415, 416–419
    consistency and, 419–421
    impact of, 13, 25, 31, 242–243, 429
    need for, 6–7, 13, 237, 412–413, 419, 426–427
    plan administration and, 449–450
    plan design and, 25, 291–295, 419, 437–438
    problems with, 43, 412–415
    sales management system and, 415–421
    start-up firms and, 432–433
    testing, 291–295
    timing of, 451
    see also implementation process
channel strategy
    consistency with incentive compensation, 81
    as focus of performance measurement, 216, 217
Checkpoint Systems, 403–404
Circuit City, 13
Cisco, 81, 400
Citigroup, 401
Clark/Bardes Consulting, 122
Clintar, 398–399
coaching, 21–23
Cognos, 473
commissions
    bias check for, 62
    bonuses versus, 231–237, 261–262
    customer results and, 71–72
    ethics and, 71–72
    in high percent incentive pay plans, 142, 144, 155–157, 227
    on new product sales, 5–7, 9, 329, 393–394
    payment from first dollar, 231, 247–248
    payment from goal or fraction of goal, 231, 248–251
    problems of, 9
    product life cycle and, 5–7, 9, 78–79, 164–165
communication
    of changes in sales force compensation, 416–419, 443–449
    as Controller in sales force effectiveness, 21, 22
company budget, 127–129, 391–392
company culture, 129–132, 235–237, 400, 412
company history, salary-incentive mix in, 175–178
company influences
    on pay levels, 125–132, 138–139
    on pay variation, 132–137, 139
company results
    consequences of incentive compensation for, 23, 28–29, 47, 72–76, 108–109, 143–149, 301–304
    cost analysis in, 47, 72–74, 81
    evaluating measurability of, 170–173
    goal setting for, 328, 330
    improving gross margins, 15–16
    metrics for performance measurement, 188, 200–204, 208
    problems of, 45
    qualitative diagnosis in, 47, 74–76
    salary-incentive mix in, 170–173, 175–176
    sales contests and SPIFFs and, 392–395
    in sales management system, 19, 20, 23
Compaq, 13–14, 153
Compass Bank, 31–32

compatibility with other effectiveness drivers, 23, 24–25, 81–83
  of add-on incentive programs, 386, 408
  changes in sales force compensation and, 415, 419–421
  in incentive plan administration, 460, 461
  in incentive plan redesign, 85, 89, 92
  pay level and, 110–112, 113, 114
  performance measures and, 187, 192
  performance-payout relationship and, 228, 229
  plan assessment scorecards, 48, 89, 268–271
  problems of, 45
  qualitative tests of, 46, 48, 82–83, 305, 307, 308, 309
  quantitative tests of, 46, 48, 268–271
  salary-incentive mix, 143, 144, 145, 150–151
  sales force culture in, 48, 81–83, 150–151
  sales force goals and, 315
compensation, see also incentive compensation
  in sales force effectiveness, 21, 22
complexity of incentive plan, 7, 10, 484–485
  administrative costs and, 74
  minimizing, 263
  plan traction and, 47, 56–57
  sales force activities and, 47, 69–70
  tests of, 69
complexity of sales process
  salary-incentive mix and, 159–160
  sales force causality and, 97–101, 117–119, 159–160, 165–170
  see also sales force causality/prominence
compliance reporting, 466–469
consequences of incentive compensation
  add-on incentive programs, 386, 408
  assessment of incentive plan, 45–76, 268–271, 274, 295–304
  changes in sales force compensation and, 415, 416–419
  for company results, 23, 28–29, 47, 72–76, 108–109, 143–149, 301–304
  for customer results, 23, 27–28, 47, 70–72, 108–109, 143–149, 301, 303, 418–419
  effectiveness drivers and, 22–23, 25–29
  in incentive plan administration, 460, 461
  in incentive plan redesign, 85, 88, 92
  pay level and, 108–109, 113, 114
  performance measures and, 187, 192
  performance-payout relationship and, 228, 229
  plan assessment scorecards, 47–48, 88–89, 268–271
  problems of, 45
  qualitative tests of, 46, 47, 48, 65, 69–72, 74–76, 295–304
  quantitative tests of, 46, 47, 50–65, 66–68, 72–74, 268–271
  salary-incentive mix, 143–149
  for sales force activities, 23, 26–27, 47, 65–70, 108–109, 143–149, 301, 303
  sales force goals and, 315
  for salespeople, 26, 47, 48–65, 108–109, 143–149, 295–301, 416–418
consistency, 23–24
  of add-on incentive programs, 386, 407
  changes in sales force compensation and, 415, 419–421
  in incentive plan administration, 460, 461
  in incentive plan redesign, 85, 89, 92, 110
  of pay level, 110, 113, 114, 124–125
  of performance measures, 187, 192
  performance-payout relationship and, 228, 229
  plan assessment scorecards, 48, 89, 268–271
  problems of, 45
  qualitative tests of, 46, 48, 77–81, 304–305, 306
  quantitative tests of, 46, 48, 268–271
  of salary-incentive mix, 143, 144, 145, 149–150

with sales and marketing strategy, 10–11, 23, 48, 77–81
  of sales force goals, 315
constant allocation method of goal setting, 362
consultants, compensation surveys of, 122
contribution margin, metrics for performance measurement, 201–203
Controllers, 21, 22, 83, 148–149, 150–151
coordination systems, as Controller in sales force effectiveness, 21, 22
cost analysis, see plan cost analysis
cost-to-sales ratio, 128–129
cross-selling, 4–5, 385, 420–421
Crystal Reports, 473
Culpepper and Associates, 122
culture, see also sales force culture
  company, 129–132, 235–237, 400, 412
cushions, 418
customer results
  consequences of incentive compensation for, 23, 27–28, 47, 70–72, 108–109, 143–149, 301, 303, 418–419
  customer input and, 70–72
  evaluating measurability of, 170–173
  goal setting for, 328, 330
  metrics for performance measurement, 188, 204–206, 208
  problems of, 45
  salary-incentive mix in, 170–173
  sales contests and SPIFFs and, 392–395
  in sales management system, 19, 20, 23
customer satisfaction, metrics for performance measurement, 205–206
Cutler-Hammer division, Eaton Corporation, 74–76

data management, 469–470
data views
  nature of, 199, 209
  in performance measurement, 199, 200, 209–216
  types of, 209–216
Definers, 20–22, 77–81, 304–305
degree of income loss, 413–415
Delphi forecasting, 332
demand
  for labor, 119–120
  predictability of, in commission versus bonus plans, 236
  sales force role in creating, 115–119, 136
Digital Equipment Corporation (DEC), 13–14, 145–146, 152–153, 384
Disney Attractions, 178
documentation, for changes in sales incentive compensation plan, 443–449
Dodson, John D., 162–163
drivers of sales force compensation, 12–17
  desire for improvement, 15–17
  market drivers, 138, 139
  need to adapt, 12–15
  pay mix, 160–170
  reasons for reassessing incentive plan, 14–15, 16–17
  sales role drivers, 138, 139, 153–157, 160–170
  see also effectiveness drivers, of sales force; sales force activities
dual plans, 418
Dun & Bradstreet, 174
dynamic reports, 475

Eaton Corporation, 74–76
eBay, 205
econometrics, 332
effectiveness drivers, of sales force, 19, 20–23, 42
  assessment of, see assessment process

compatibility with compensation plan, 23, 24–25, 48, 81–83, 110–112, 305, 307
consequences for downstream components, *see* consequences of incentive compensation
Controllers, 21, 22, 83, 148–149, 150–151
Definers, 20–22, 77–81, 304–305
Enlighteners, 21, 22, 83
Exciters, 21, 22, 146–148, 150–151, 262–263
goals and, 327, *see also* goal setting
metrics for performance measurement, 188, 198–209
need to adapt all of, 40–41
Shapers, 21, 22, 83, 143–146
effective pay mix, 147–148
employment opportunities, 119–120
Engagement Rate
    described, 55
    incentive payment from goal or fraction of goal, 248–251
    in MRG Company case study, 55–56, 276–281, 284
    plan traction and, 47, 53–57
    sales contests and SPIFFs and, 395–396
    sales force activities and, 47, 67–68
Enlighteners, 21, 22, 83
enterprise incentive management (EIM) system, 149–150, 481–482
enterprise technology (ET) group, 462
Entrepreneur Group, 227, 228, 242–243
ethics
    commissions and, 71–72
    sales contests and, 384–385
    unrealistic goals and, 334
excellence incentive, 95
Excitement Index
    described, 55
    motivation and, 151
    in MRG Company case study, 55–56, 276–281, 284
    plan traction and, 53–57
    sales force activities and, 47, 67–68
    see also Exciters
Exciters, 21, 22, 146–149, 150–151, 262–263, *see also* Excitement Index
exit interviews, as information source, 51–52, 123
expectancy theory, 402
external events, sales force compensation change and, 13, 412–413, 419, 426–427

FedEx, 3–4
feedback, on goal attainment, 367–368, 369–370
field sales managers
    communication of changes in sales force compensation and, 448
    field management reports, 465, 471–472
    in goal setting process, 365–368
Fifth Third Bank, 442
fixed pay/compensation, 141–142, *see also* salary-incentive mix
focus, 199, 200, 216–221
focused sales objectives (FSOs), 14
forced ranking systems, 215–216
Ford Motor Company, 10
forecasting, for goal setting, 314–321
    goals too high, 314–318
    goals too low, 318–321
    national goals, 333–334, 371–372
    territory forecast method, 346–348
formula-based goal setting, 344–359
    historical sales, marketing potential, and sales effort, 357–359
    historical sales and market potential, 348–357, 364
    historical standards, 344–348
franchise sales, 99–101
free-rider problem, 221, 267

free sales, 97–101, 117–119, 147–148, 165–170, 247–248, 325–326, 349–351
Fusion Sales Partners, 144–145

General Electric, 75, 110, 144–145
geographic bias, 60, 61
global strategy, 10–11, 168–169
Globoforce, 403
goals, *see* goal setting; sales goals
goal setting, 43, 314–376
    adjusting goals in, 366–368, 370–372
    appropriate sales force goals, 314–327
    benchmarking in, *see* benchmarking
    for changes in sales incentive compensation, 450
    goal allocation across salespeople, 321–327
    impact of, 313–314
    importance of, 313–314
    for incentive plan administration systems, 482–484
    midyear goal corrections, 370–372
    national, 331–334, 371–372
    for new products, 5–6, 7, 361–362, 373
    number of goals, 375
    phases of, 330–368
    problems of, 64–65, 227–228, 239–240, 242–243, 314–327, 334, 371–372, 375
    process of, 376
    recommendations for, 372–374
    for sales territories, 314–318, 326–327, 334–363
    stretch goals and, 373–374, 401–402
    tracking performance against goals, 369–372
    types of goals, 327–330
    Web-based tracking systems, 367–370
Gonik, Jacob, 256–257, 360–361
go-to-market strategy, 20, 21, 23, 77–81, 412
grandfathering, 418
gross margins, 15–16, 201–203
guarantees, 245, 418

Hay Group, 122, 125
Hewitt Associates, 122
Hewlett, William, 204
Hewlett-Packard Company, 153, 204
high-leverage plans, 96, 135, 142, 144, 155–157, 158, 164
hiring profiles, 24–25, 420
horizontal communication, as Controller in sales force effectiveness, 21, 22
house accounts, 367

IBM, 10–11, 94, 144–145, 152–153, 197–198, 256–257, 320, 360–361, 384, 393–394, 438–439
implementation process, 36–37, 409–452
    change outlook and, 451–452
    for changing performance-payout relationships, 430–435
    for changing salary-incentive mix, 13, 423–430
    for cross-selling initiatives, 4–5, 385, 420–421
    difficulty of change, 412–415
    evolution of, 411
    framework for, 435–452
    for new performance measures, 430–435
    for new salespeople, 435
    for pay reductions, 8–9, 421–423
    sales management system and, 415–421
    for territory realignment, 433–435
    timing of, 450–451
incentive compensation
    administration of, *see* incentive plan administration
    assessment of, *see* assessment process; consequences of incentive compensation
    changes in, *see* changes in sales force compensation
    compatibility with other sales force effectiveness drivers, *see* compatibility with other effectiveness drivers

incentive compensation (*continued*)
   complexity of, *see* complexity of incentive plan
   consequences on sales force effectiveness drivers, *see*
      consequences of incentive compensation
   consistency of, *see* consistency
   costs of, *see* plan cost analysis
   design of, *see* plan design; sales force design
   desired results from, 7–8
   feedback on goal attainment, 367–368, 369–370
   impact of, 2–3, 9
   implementation of, *see* implementation process
   performance measures for, *see* performance measures
   reasons for using, 11–12
   role in sales management system, 23–29
   sales force pay reduction and, 8–9, 421–423
   successes and failures of, 3–11
   target pay in, 94–95, 112–114
Incentive Compensation Advisory Board (ICAB),
   320–321
incentive pay/compensation, *see* incentive compensation; salary-incentive mix
incentive plan administration, 453–490
   challenges of, 458–459
   of changes in sales incentive compensation, 449–450
   characteristics of poorly-administered systems,
      460–461
   characteristics of well-administered systems, 459–460
   components of, 455–456
   contractors of, 122, 369, 473, 476–477, 481,
      485–489
   cost of, 74, 305
   difficulty of, 456–458, 461–463
   effectiveness of sales force and, 43
   errors in, 457–458, 465, 478–480
   external partners in, 122, 369, 473, 476–477, 481–
      482, 485–489
   flowchart for, 463–476
   importance of, 456–458
   nature of, 454–456
   payout curves and, 239
   plan complexity and, *see* complexity of incentive plan
   plan design and, 464, 476–485
   of sales contests and SPIFFs, 400–401, 402–403, 459
   scorecards in, 455–456, 465–470
   system requirements for, 469–476
incentive plan obesity, 7, 10, 384, *see also* complexity of
   incentive plan
Incent One, 403
income range, 113–114
industry norms
   for benchmarking pay statistics, 52–53, 120–125,
      173–174, 281
   comparing salary-incentive mix, 173–174
   information sources for pay levels, 120–125, 281
   for sales force pay level, 52–53, 120–122
   surrogate measures of market potential, 341, 342–343
information sources
   exit interviews, 51–52, 123
   on pay levels, 120–125, 281
inputs
   in assessing candidate incentive plan, 273–274
   customer results and, 70–72
   defined, 125
   in goal setting process, 359–361
   for incentive plan administration, 463–464
   in job value assessment, 125–126
inside sales roles, defining, 24
internal events, sales force compensation change and, 13,
   412–413, 419
International Data Corporation (IDC), 227–228,
   239–240
Internet
   incentive plan administration via, 401

Web-based tracking systems, 367–370
Inventive Federation, Inc., 385

JCPenney, 449
job value assessment, 125–126
Johnson & Johnson, 110

Knoll Pharmaceuticals, 374–375
KPI (key performance indicator), 328–330

labor market value, 119–125
   industry norms in, 120
   information sources for determining pay levels, 120–
      125, 281
   labor supply and demand in, 119–120
leadership
   changes in salary-incentive mix and, 424–425
   as Exciter in sales force effectiveness, 21, 22
leverage multiple, 95–96, 135
low-leverage plans, 96, 135, 142–143, 145, 154–155,
   156, 158, 164
Lucent Technologies, 422–423

maintenance plus adjusted growth method of goal setting, 348–351, 364
maintenance plus standard growth method of goal setting, 344–346
management by objectives (MBO), 212, 258–259, 328–
   330, 462–463
management philosophy
   performance-payout relationships and, 235–237
   salary-incentive mix in, 178–179
Maritz, 403
Marketing Innovators, 403
marketing strategy, *see* sales and marketing strategy
market potential, *see* sales territories
market potential method of goal setting, 362
market segment, as focus of performance measurement,
   216, 217
market share
   bias based on, 60, 61
   change related to starting market share, 337–338
   metrics for performance measurement, 203–204
   of sales territories, 25
market size bias, 60, 61
market volatility, sales force causality and, 101–103,
   169–170
Marsh Inc., 71
Marsh & McLennan Cos., 71
MathWorks, 24
matrix approach, 255–257
MCI Telecommunications, 401
McLagen Partners, Inc., 122
meaningful work, as Exciter in sales force effectiveness,
   21, 22
Merck, 151
Mercury Interactive Corp., 393
mergers
   changes in incentive compensation and, 412
   consistency of pay levels and, 13, 110
   executive bonuses and, 422–423
Meridian Enterprises, 403
metrics
   absolute-level, 209–210
   nature of, 198–199
   in performance measurement, 188, 198–209
   types of, 200–209
Microsoft Business Solutions (MBS), 406–407
mixed bonus and commission plans
   advantages and challenges of, 242
   nature of, 234–235
   payout curves for, 238
MNP Inc., 84–92

motivation
    compatibility with incentive compensation, 12, 23,
        243–245
    as Exciter in sales force effectiveness, 21, 22, 151
    expectancy theory and, 402
    payout curves and, 239
    pay variation in, 132–135
    plan traction in measuring, 47, 53–57
    problems of, 45
    in quantitative tests of consequences of incentive com-
        pensation, 53–57, 66–68
    recognition programs and, *see* recognition programs
    research on, 313
    sales contests and, *see* sales contests
    sales force activities and, 66–68
    sales force causality and, 166–167
    sales force goals and, 315–318, 321
    sales force performance and, 266
    SPIFFs and, *see* SPIFFs (Special Performance Incen-
        tives for Field Force)
MRA-The Management Associates, Inc., 122
MRG Company case study
    assessment of candidate incentive plan, 268–306
    assessment of incumbent incentive plan, 49, 55–57,
        72–73, 272, 276–281
    introduction, 48
MS-Access, 473
multiple performance measures, 196–198, 231, 251,
        253–261, 262–263
    impact of aggregation, 259–261, 262
    matrix approach, 255–257
    points approach, 257–259
    weighted-measures approach, 253–255

national accounts
    goal setting and, 331–334
    team selling and, 168–169
National Cash Register (NCR), 379–380
national goal setting, 371–372
NCR, 379–380
new account development, problems of, 43
new businesses, *see* start-up firms
new products
    changes in incentive compensation and, 7
    future-proofing incentive plans for, 306–307
    incentive compensation and, 5–7, 9, 78–79, 329,
        393–394
    performance measures for, 195
    sales goals for, 5–6, 7, 361–362, 373
new salespeople, sales incentive compensation plan for,
        435
New York Times, 250–251
Nexaweb Technologies, 378–379
non-capped incentive plans, 231, 243–245, 250
non-sales force marketing instruments, sales force causal-
        ity and, 166
Northwestern University, 14–15, 16–17
    Incentive Compensation Advisory Board (ICAB),
        320–321
    Sales Incentive Executive Education Survey, 151–152,
        203, 206–208, 210, 211, 222, 243, 244

objectives of firm
    incentive compensation versus, 3
    sales goals and, 375–376
objectives of incentive plan
    nature of, 84
    setting new, 84–92
O.C. Tanner, 403
Olsen, Ken, 145–146, 152–153
Oracle, 481
output orientation, 476

outputs
    defined, 125
    for incentive plan administration, 464–469
    in job value assessment, 125–126
outside sales roles, defining, 24

Patterson, John, 379–380
pay-for-performance, 135, 136, 290–291
pay level, 106, 107–139
    company influences on, 125–132, 138–139
    compatibility of, 110–112, 113, 114
    consequences of, 108–109, 113, 114
    consistency of, 110, 113, 114, 124–125
    determining correct, 108–112, 115–137
    historical, 126–127
    information sources for determining pay levels, 120–
        125, 281
    labor market value for position, 117, 119–125
    nature of, 103–104, 108
    overpaid salespeople, 108, 109, 113, 227, 228, 242–
        243, 323–327
    range of sales force, 112–115
    sales force role in demand creation, 115–119, 136
    underpaid salespeople, 108, 109, 114, 323–327
pay mix, *see* salary-incentive mix
payout distribution
    achievement of sales force objectives and, 239–243
    in MRG Company case study, 49, 55–57, 272,
        276–281
    in progressive versus regressive plans, 237–243
pay reductions, implementation process for, 8–9
payroll outputs, in incentive plan administration,
        455–456
pay variation
    company influences on, 132–137, 139
    individual performance and, 132–135, 139
    nature of, 114–115
    number of job levels in, 135–137
    sales force culture and, 137
    salesperson tenure in, 135–137, 165
PeopleSoft, 481
percent of remaining share method of goal setting,
        356–357
performance database, 274–276
performance distribution analysis, 47, 57–59, 89
performance evaluation ratings, 62–65, 90, 323
performance frontier method of goal setting, 353–355
performance grids, 132–135, 323
performance management
    compatibility with incentive compensation, 23, 420
    as Controller in sales force effectiveness, 21, 22
    goals controlled by, 328–330, *see also* sales force activi-
        ties; salespeople
    pay levels in, 112
    problems of, 45
performance measures, 106, 183–224
    appropriate, determining, 184–187, 191–224
    bias avoidance with, 194
    comparing to a goal, 210–214
    comparing to past performance, 210
    compatibility with other effectiveness drivers, 187,
        192
    consequences of incentive compensation for, 187, 192
    consistency of, 187, 192
    data views in, 199, 200, 209–216
    focus of, 199, 200, 216–221
    implementation process for, 430–435
    measurability of, 192–193
    metrics in, 188, 198–209
    multiple types of, 196–198
    nature of, 104–105
    sales force activities and, 192, 193
    simplicity of, 196–198

performance measures (*continued*)
  timing of, 199, 200, 221–224
  types of, 187–191
performance pay, 97–101, 117–119, 147–148, 165–170
performance-payout relationships, 105, 106, 225–263
  advantages and challenges of, 242
  appropriate, determining, 227–228, 239–240
  changing, 430–435
  criteria for evaluating, 241
  decision 1: bonus versus commission plans, 231–237, 261–262
  decision 3: capped versus non-capped plans, 231, 243–245, 250
  decision 4: pay from first dollar versus from goal or fraction of goal, 231, 245–251
  decision 2: progressive versus regressive plans, 231, 237–243, 262
  decision 5: single versus multiple measures, 196–198, 231, 251–261, 262–263
  diagnosis of, 228, 229
  in mixed plans, 234–235
  representing, 228–231
  role of, 226–227
Phoenix Technologies, 69–70
plan cost analysis
  administrative costs of incentive plan, 74, 305
  breakdowns by product, 73–74, 91
  for candidate incentive plan, 276–281
  company results and, 47, 72–74, 81
  pay level in, 127–129
plan design, 34–36, 225–263
  add-on programs in, *see* recognition programs; sales contests; SPIFFs (Special Performance Incentives for Field Force)
  assessment in, *see* assessment process
  challenge of, 17–19
  for change implementation, 437–438
  compatibility of, *see* compatibility with other effectiveness drivers
  consequences of, *see* consequences of incentive compensation
  consistency of, *see* consistency
  framework for, 18
  fundamentals of, 93–106
  goal setting in, *see* goal setting
  holistic view of, 106
  incentive plan administration and, 122, 369, 464, 473, 476–489
  input of sales force in, 295–301
  key decisions in, 103–106
  leverage in, 95–96, 135
  new plan objectives and, 83–92
  pay level in, *see* pay level
  performance measures in, *see* performance measures
  performance-payout relationships in, *see* performance-payout relationships
  recognition programs in, *see* recognition programs
  redesign principles, 84
  risk in, 96–97
  salary-incentive mix in, *see* salary-incentive mix
  sales contests in, *see* sales contests
  SPIFFS in, *see* SPIFFs (Special Performance Incentives for Field Force)
  terminology of, 93–106
  testing candidate plans, 291–295
  total pay components in, 94–96
  total sales components in, 97–103
plan health reports, 455–456, 465, 473, 474
plan traction, 47, 53–57
PNCBank, 131–132
pocket cards, 447
pods, 75–76
point-based goals, 214

points approach, 257–259
PPG, 122
process orientation, 476
Procter & Gamble, 111
product, as focus of performance measurement, 216, 217
product assignment, fairness of, 59
product life cycle
  growth phase, 195, 196
  incentive pay plan and, 5–7, 9, 78–79, 164–165
  launch phase, 5–7, 9, 195, *see also* new products
  maturity phase, 195, 196
  performance measures and, 195–196
  salary-incentive mix and, 164–165
product sales
  correlation with competitor's sales, 337
  correlation with market sales for prior year, 336
  correlation with product sales for prior year, 335–336
  correlation with surrogate for market potential, 336–337
profitability, pay levels and, 127–129
profit metrics, for performance measurement, 201–203
progressive plans, 231, 237–243, 262
  advantages and challenges of, 242
  payout curves for, 238, 239–240
prominence, sales force, *see* sales force causality/prominence
Prosoft, 126
pull reports, 475
PurchasePro.com, 334
push reports, 475

qualitative tests
  of candidate incentive plan, 268, 270–271, 295–306
  of incumbent incentive plan, 46–48, 65, 69–72, 74–76, 82–83, 295–305, 307–309
quality
  of incentive plan administration, 475–476, 478–480
  of sales force, problems of, 45
quality assurance (QA), 475–476, 478–480
quality control (QC), 475–476, 480–481
quantitative tests
  of candidate incentive plan, 268–295
  of incumbent incentive plan, 46–48, 50–68, 72–74, 268–271
quick check analysis, 323, 325
quotas, bias check for, 60–62

Radford Division, Aon Consulting, 122
random sales, 101–103, 169–170
ranking relative to peers, 215–216
recognition programs, 403–407
  design of, 404–407
  nature of, 379–380, 403–404
recruiting
  compatibility with incentive compensation, 23
  pay levels in, 111, 112, 132
  problems of, 45
  sales contests and SPIFFs and, 394
  as Shaper of sales force effectiveness, 21, 22
recruiting interviews, as information source, 123
Redden, Stephen, 465
referrals, in cross-selling, 4–5, 385, 421–421
regression method of goal setting, 352–353, 354
regressive plans, 231, 237–243, 262
  advantages and challenges of, 242
  payout curves for, 238, 240–243
reports
  compliance, 466–469
  field management, 465, 471–472
  incentive plan administration, 465, 470–475
  plan health, 455–456, 465, 473–474

push versus pull, 475
static versus dynamic, 475
results, *see* company results; customer results
retention bonuses, 418
retention of sales force
    consequences of incentive compensation for, 43, 47,
        50–52
    performance-payout relationships and, 235–237
return on investment (ROI) analysis, 385–388
rewards
    as focus of performance measurement, 216–221
    individual versus team, 219
risk assessment
    for the company, 281–288
    for the salesperson, 96–97
RR Donnelley, 174

salary-incentive mix, 140–182
    actual pay mix, 94–95
    changes in, 424
    compatibility of, 143, 144, 145, 150–151
    consequences of, 143–149
    consistency of, 143, 144, 145, 149–150
    determining correct, 143–151, 160–170
    as driver of sales force compensation, 160–170
    effective pay mix, 147–148
    high percent incentive pay plans, 96, 135, 142, 144,
        155–157, 158, 164
    implementation process for, 43, 423–430
    industry norms for, 173–174
    low percent incentive pay plans, 96, 135, 142–143,
        145, 154–155, 156, 158, 164
    moderate percent incentive pay plans, 157, 158
    nature of, 104, 141–143
    pay for performance and, 135, 136, 290–291
    pros and cons of, 141
    range of, 151–160
    sales force causality and, 159–160, 165–170, 171–173
    sales force roles and, 153–157, 160–170
    scorecard for, 179–182
    70/30, 142–143, 159–160
    target pay mix, 94–95, 106
sales and marketing strategy
    consistency of incentive compensation with, 10–11,
        23, 48, 77–81
    as Definer of sales force effectiveness, 20, 21, 77–81
    problems of, 45
    salary-incentive mix and, 152–153
sales contests
    ad hoc, 43
    administration of, 400–401, 402–403, 459
    advantages and challenges of, 381–384
    design of, 380–384, 388–403
    determining effectiveness of, 384–388
    motivation and, 397
    nature of, 378–379
    sales goals and, 6, 43, 371
sales force activities
    business development, 29–30
    consequences of incentive compensation for, 23, 26–
        27, 47, 65–70, 108–109, 143–149, 301, 303
    engagement and excitement decomposition, 47,
        67–68
    goal setting for, 328–330
    metrics for performance measurement, 188, 192, 193,
        206–208
    motivation and, 66–68
    plan complexity and, 47, 69–70
    problems of, 45
    sales contests and SPIFFs and, 392–395
    in sales management system, 19, 20
    sales tracking analysis, 47, 66
    time allocation analysis, 47, 67

sales force causality/prominence
    changes in salary-incentive mix and, 424
    complexity of sales process and, 97–101, 117–119,
        159–160, 165–170
    as driver of pay level and variation, 117–119
    nature of, 97–101
    performance measures and, 192, 193
    salary-incentive mix and, 159–160, 165–170,
        171–173
sales force culture
    change in, 31–32
    in commission versus bonus plans, 236
    compatibility with incentive compensation, 23
    compatibility with other effectiveness drivers, 48, 81–
        83, 150–151
    pay variation and, 137
    problems of, 45
    retention problems and, 43, 47, 50–52
    salary-incentive mix and, 144–146, 150–151, 152–
        153, 158–160, 175–178
    sales contests and SPIFFs in, 400
    as Shaper of sales force effectiveness, 21, 22, 143–146
sales force customer power, 413
sales force design
    consistency of incentive compensation with, 23,
        77–81
    defined, 22
    as Definer of sales force effectiveness, 21, 22, 77–81
    sales force compensation change and, 13, 25, 419
sales force hiring profile, 24–25, 420
sales force prominence, *see* sales force causality/
        prominence
sales force roles
    outside versus inside, 24
    pay alignment with, 118–119, 138, 139
    problems of, 45
    salary-incentive mix and, 153–157, 160–170
    Yerkes-Dodson law and, 162–163
sales goals
    benchmarking, 11–12, 331
    comparing performance to, 210–214
    consequences of incentive compensation for sales-
        people and, 51, 227–228, 239–240, 242–243
    fairness of, 60
    incentive payment relative to, 231, 245–251
    multiproduct incentive plans and, 212–214
    for new products, 5–6, 7, 361–362, 373
    payment from first dollar, 231, 247–248
    sales contests and, 6, 43, 371
    setting, *see* goal setting
    SPIFFs and, 6
    for volatile markets, 263, 372–373
sales information and support systems, 420
sales management system, 19–32
    changes in incentive compensation and, 415–421
    company results, 19, 20, 23, *see also* company results
    components of, overview, 19–23
    customer results, 19, 20, 23, *see also* customer results
    diagnosing sales force issues in, 29–32
    role of incentive compensation in, 23–29
    sales force activities, 19, 20, *see also* sales force activities
    sales force effectiveness drivers, 19, 20–23, 42, *see also*
        effectiveness drivers, of sales force
    salespeople, 19, 20, *see also* salespeople
salespeople
    attitudes toward compensation plan, 65, 245, 295–
        301, 425
    attraction and retention of, 50–52
    bias check for, 47, 59–62
    changes in sales force compensation and, 416–418
    consequences of incentive compensation for, 26, 47,
        48–65, 108–109, 143–149, 295–301, 416–418
    goal allocation across, 321–327

salespeople (*continued*)
  goal setting for, 328–330, *see also* goal setting
  incentive plan problems and, 265–267
  metrics for performance measurement, 188, 208–209
  motivation of, *see* motivation
  new, implementation process for, 435
  overpaid, 108, 109, 113, 227, 228, 242–243, 323–327
  performance distribution analysis and, 47, 57–59, 89
  performance evaluation ratings, 62–65, 90, 323
  personality traits in automobile sales, 427
  rank ordering of, 374–375
  risks of incentive plan for, 96–97
  in sales management system, 19, 20
  underpaid, 108, 109, 114, 323–327
  see also effectiveness drivers, of sales force; sales force activities; sales force causality/prominence
salesperson sales, 97–101, 117–119, 147–148, 165–170
sales response method of goal setting, 357–359
sales roster, 464
sales territories
  bias check for, 59–62
  goal setting for, 314–318, 326–327, 334–363
  in incentive plan administration, 464
  market potential of, 25, 30–31, 59, 227, 237, 262, 336–337, 338–343, 348–359, 362
  market share of, 25
  pay alignment with, 30–31, 41–43, 59, 149–150, 243–244
  realignment of, 433–435
sales tracking analysis, 47, 66
SAP, 481
scorecards
  in incentive plan administration, 455–456, 465–470
  plan assessment, 47–48, 88–89, 268–271
  salary-incentive mix, 179–182
Searle, 404
Sears Auto Center, 71–72
selling process, in commission versus bonus plans, 236
sensitivity analysis, of candidate incentive plan, 284–288, 291, 292, 293
severance packages, 422
shadow accounting, 459–460
Shapers, 21, 22, 83, 143–146
share growth method of goal setting, 355–356
Shell Oil Company, 394
Siebel Sales Analytics, 369, 473, 481
single performance measures, 196–198, 231, 251, 252–253, 262–263
Slater Industrial Supply, 207–208
Southern California Edison, 205–206
SPIFFs (Special Performance Incentives for Field Force)
  ad hoc, 43
  administration of, 400–401, 402–403, 459
  advantages and challenges of, 381–384
  design of, 380–384, 388–403
  determining effectiveness of, 384–388
  motivation and, 397
  nature of, 378–379
  sales goals and, 6, 43
Square D, 75
start-up firms
  changes in salary-incentive mix, 432–433
  incentive plan problems of, 265–266
  sales goals of, 212
static reports, 475
stock options, in recognition programs, 404–405
stretch goals, 373–374, 401–402
synergistic matrix, 255, 256

Synygy, 369, 481

Tandem Computers, 13–14
target pay/incentive, 94–95, 112–114, *see also* incentive compensation; salary-incentive mix
target pay mix, 94–95, 106
team selling
  company results and, 75–76
  as focus of performance measurement, 216–221
  incentive plan administration and, 462
  salary-incentive mix and, 149–150, 174
  sales contests and SPIFFs and, 394
  sales force causality and, 166, 167–169
territory forecast method of goal setting, 346–348
throughputs, 125–126
time allocation analysis, 47, 67
time-series analysis, 332, 385–388
timing
  of changes in sales incentive compensation, 450–451
  frequency of incentive payment, 221–223
  of incentive payment relative to order, 223–224
  nature of, 199
  in performance measurement, 199, 200, 221–224
Top Five Data Services, Inc., 122
total pay, 94–96
total sales, 97–103
Towers Perrin, 122
training
  for changes in sales incentive compensation plan, 443–449
  compatibility with incentive compensation, 23
  misdirection problems and, 43
  pay levels in, 112, 132
  as Shaper of sales force effectiveness, 21, 22
TruStar Solutions, 151
turnover of sales force
  changes in compensation plan and, 13, 25, 31, 429
  consequences of incentive compensation for, 50–52
  exit interviews in analyzing, 51–52, 123
  pay level and, 108, 131
  pay variation and, 137
  sales force culture and, 43
  sales goals and, 318

Universal Certificate Group, 403
US West, 19

variable pay/compensation, 141–142, 144, *see also* incentive compensation; salary-incentive mix
vertical communication, as Controller in sales force effectiveness, 21, 22

W. L. Gore, 82–83
Wal-Mart, 169
Watson Wyatt Data Services, 122
weighted index method of goal setting, 351–352, 364
weighted-measures approach, 253–255
Western Management Group, Inc., 122
Westinghouse, 75–76
who gets helped/who gets hurt analysis, 288–290, 294, 414, 431
windfalls, 101–103, 169–170, 319–320
Wm. H. Mercer Inc., 122
WorldCom, 422–423

Yellow Pages advertising, activities goals for, 329–330
Yerkes, Robert M., 162–163
Yerkes-Dodson law, 162–163

ZS Associates, 369, 465, 481